Bach Studies

This volume draws together a collection of Robin A. Leaver's essays on Bach's sacred music, exploring the religious aspects of this repertoire through consideration of three core themes: liturgy, hymnology, and theology. Rooted in a rich understanding of the historical sources, the book illuminates the varied ways in which Bach's sacred music was informed and shaped by the religious, ritual, and intellectual contexts of his time, placing these works in the wider history of Protestant church music during the baroque era.

Including research from across a span of forty years, the chapters in this volume have been significantly revised and expanded for this publication, with several pieces appearing in English for the first time. Together, they offer an essential compendium of the work of a leading scholar of theological Bach studies.

Robin A. Leaver is professor emeritus of sacred music, Westminster Choir College, Princeton; and has previously been visiting professor at the Juilliard School, New York, Yale Institute of Sacred Music, and Queen's University, Belfast, Northern Ireland. Between 1984 and 2018 he wrote the program notes for the Bach Choir of Bethlehem, Pennsylvania, and from time to time contributes similar writings for the Bach Collegium Japan. Professor Leaver is a past president of both the Internationale Arbeitsgemeinschaft für Hymnologie and the American Bach Society, and is an honorary member of the American Bach Society and the Riemenschneider Bach Institute. He is the author of many Bach articles that have appeared in such journals as the *Bach Jahrbuch*, the *Journal of the Riemenscheider Bach Institute*, and *Early Music*, and has contributed to standard reference works and volumes of essays on Bach and his world. As an editor he oversees monographs in the series Contextual Bach Studies, and his most recently edited Bach publications include the *Routledge Research Companion to Johann Sebastian Bach* (2016), *Exploring Bach's B-Minor Mass* (2020), with Yo Tomita and Jan Smaczny, and *Bach and the Counterpoint of Religion* (2018).

Bach Studies
Liturgy, Hymnology, and Theology

Robin A. Leaver

LONDON AND NEW YORK

First published 2021
by Routledge
2 Park Square, Milton Park, Abingdon, Oxon OX14 4RN

and by Routledge
52 Vanderbilt Avenue, New York, NY 10017

Routledge is an imprint of the Taylor & Francis Group, an informa business

© 2021 Robin A. Leaver.

The right of Robin A. Leaver to be identified as author of this work has been
asserted by him in accordance with sections 77 and 78 of the Copyright,
Designs and Patents Act 1988.

All rights reserved. No part of this book may be reprinted or reproduced or utilised
in any form or by any electronic, mechanical, or other means, now known or
hereafter invented, including photocopying and recording, or in any information
storage or retrieval system, without permission in writing from the publishers.

Trademark notice: Product or corporate names may be trademarks or registered trademarks,
and are used only for identification and explanation without intent to infringe.

British Library Cataloguing-in-Publication Data
A catalogue record for this book is available from the British Library

Library of Congress Cataloging-in-Publication Data
A catalog record has been requested for this book

ISBN: 978-0-367-24271-8 (hbk)
ISBN: 978-0-367-70186-4 (pbk)
ISBN: 978-0-429-28147-1 (ebk)

Typeset in Times New Roman
by Newgen Publishing UK

Contents

List of examples	vii
List of figures	viii
List of tables	ix
Preface	xi
List of abbreviations	xv

PART I
Liturgy   1

1 Bach's cantatas and the liturgical year   3

2 Bach's music and the Leipzig liturgy   22

3 Bach's Agnus Dei compositions   49

4 Bach's parody process: from cantata to *Missa*   67

5 Bach and the cantata controversy of the early
   eighteenth century   83

PART II
Hymnology   119

6 Bach and Johann Christoph Olearius   121

7 Bach's *Christ lag in Todesbanden* (BWV 4): hymnology
   and chronology   137

8 Bach's *Orgelbüchlein*   150

vi *Contents*

9 Bach and the hymnic aria   183

10 Bach and the letter codes of the Schemelli *Gesangbuch*   203

PART III
Theology   217

11 Bach and Pietism   219

12 Bach, Gesner, and Johann August Ernesti   248

13 Bach and Erdmann Neumeister   274

14 Bach's *Clavierübung III*   308

15 Bach and anniversaries of the Reformation   328

Bibliography   352
Index   380

Examples

3.1	Tone I Kyries and Agnus Dei	52
3.2	Transition from Recitative to Chorus (BWV 23/2–3)	57
3.3	Fugal subjects of BWV 233a/233	60
4.1	Comparison of "Friede" (BWV 67/6) with "et in terra pax" (BWV 234/2)	78
4.2	Similarities among BWV 67, BWV 158, and BWV 234	78
4.3	The discarded "Corno" part of BWV 67/6 with the later four-part homophonic chorus BWV 234/10	80
4.4	Comparison of "Friede" (BWV 67/6) with "glorificamus te" (BWV 234/2)	81
9.1	Communion hymns for Easter	201
9.2	Communion hymns for Pentecost	202
15.1	BWV 50: fugue subject and its inversion	349

Figures

2.1	Outline of the *Hauptgottesdienst*	28
2.2	Outline of the *Vespergottesdienst*	43
7.1	Christ lag in Todesbanden (Luther, 1524)	140
7.2	Comparisons of different metrical stress patterns	144
15.1	Michael Praetorius's title page block	348
15.2	Diagrammatic representation of BWV 50	350

Tables

1.1	Epistles and Gospels for the Church Year	7
2.1	Hymns at the beginning of the Leipzig Hauptgottesdienst	31
3.1	Textual and musical structure of the Agnus Dei in the B-minor Mass	65
5.1	Cantata libretti (1725–1727) from two printed sources	108
5.2	Single cantata libretti (1725–1727) from three printed sources	108
5.3	Anonymous cantata libretti (1726–1727)	109
6.1	J. C. Olearius's *Dispositionen* preached in Arnstadt, 1698–1704	129
8.1	Chorales in the early cantatas	154
8.2	*Graduallieder* in J. C. Olearius, *Evangelischer Lieder-Schatz* (1705–1707)	158
8.3	Projected contents of the *Orgelbüchlein*	160
9.1	Bach's use of Gerhardt's hymns in the vocal works	185
9.2	Freylinghausen melodies edited by Bach in the Schemelli *Gesangbuch*	193
9.3	Eighteenth-century texts Bach set in the Schemelli *Gesangbuch*	196

Preface

The chapters of this book are based on articles and chapters I have published over the years. However, none is a straight reprint: all have been revised, many substantially, and all contain a significant amount of new material; a few make their debut in print. The following paragraphs explain the background of the printed sources on which each chapter is based, and describe the extent of the new material. The observant reader will notice that the original studies in the chapters that appear in this book were either published before the mid-1990s or after 2011. The explanation of this apparent twenty-year hiatus is twofold. On the one hand, I did publish individual Bach studies during this period, but they either did not fit into the overall structure of this book, or they have already been reissued in other publications. On the other hand, during this period I was researching, writing, and publishing on other matters relating to sacred music, liturgy, and hymnology.

The starting point for Chapter 1 is to be found in two articles: "Bach's Understanding and Use of the Epistles and Gospels of the Church Year," *BACH* 6/4 (October 1975), 4–13; and "The Liturgical Place and Homiletic Purpose of Bach's Cantatas," *Worship* 59 (1985): 194–202. Information from these two studies has been conflated and substantially reworked, with significant omissions, revisions, and new material.

Chapter 2 began as a paper given at the 2008 EROI [Eastman Rochester Organ Initiative] conference at Eastman School of Music. It was later revised and published as "Bach's Organ Music in the Context of the Liturgy," *Keyboard Perspectives III: The Yearbook of the Westfield Center for Historical Keyboard Studies 2010*, edited by Annette Richards (The Westfield Center, 2011), 147–60. It has been substantially further revised to embrace all of Bach's liturgical music instead of being narrowly focused on the organ music.

Chapter 3 brings together the substance of two chapters: "Bach and the German Agnus Dei," in *A Bach Tribute: Essays in Honor of William H. Scheide*, edited by Paul Brainard and Ray Robinson (Kassel: Bärenreiter, 1993), 163–71; and "Agnus Dei Compositions of J. S. Bach: Some Liturgical and Theological Perspectives," in *Das Blut Jesu und die Lehre von der Versöhnung im Werk Johann Sebastian Bachs*, edited by Albert A. Clement (Amsterdam: The Royal xii *Preface*

Netherlands Academy of Arts and Sciences, 1995), 233–49. The two chapters have been substantially revised to form a coherent whole.

Chapter 4 is a conflation and revision of two articles that grew out of a paper originally given at the Internationale Bachakademie, Stuttgart, Germany, in 1988: "Bach's Reworking of BWV 67/6 as the First Movement of the *Gloria in excelsis Deo* in the *Missa* in A, BWV 234," in *Internationale Bachakademie Stuttgart: Parodie und Vorlage. Zum Bachschen Parodieverfahren und seiner Bedeutung für die Hermeneutik, 17–20 März 1988. Referate. Protokolle. Materialen*, edited by Renate Steiger (Heidelberg: Arbeitsgemeinschaft für theologische Bachforschung, 1988), 50–71; and "Parody and Theological Consistency: Notes on Bach's A-Major Mass," *BACH* 21/3 (1990): 30–43.

Chapter 5 appeared originally in German: "Oper in der Kirche: Bach und der Kantatenstreit im frühen 18. Jahrhundert," *Bach-Jahrbuch* 99 (2013): 171–203. It appears here for the first time in English, slightly revised and with English translations of cited German sources.

The original manifestation of Chapter 6 was as a paper given at the Baroque Music conference, Southampton University, United Kingdom, July 2012, later published as: "The Organist Encounters the Hymnologist: J. S. Bach and J. C. Olearius in Arnstadt," *Understanding Bach* 7 (2012): 21–28." It is here reworked and significantly expanded with further research.

Chapter 7 was given as a paper at the conference and exhibition hosted by the Newberry Library, Chicago, September 1997: "The Music and Mind of Bach." It was later revised and expanded and appears here for the first time.

Chapter 8 began as a commissioned article for the Bach year 1985: "Bach and Hymnody: The Evidence of the *Orgelbüchlein*" that appeared in *Early Music* 13 (1985): 227–36. It has been substantially rewritten and expanded. I am particularly grateful to William A. Wojnar and Lynn Edwards Butler for their assistance in clarifying details relating to the new research.

Chapter 9, in its original form, was published as "Congregational Hymn and Soloistic Aria in the Music of Johann Sebastian Bach," in *The Hymnology Annual: An International Forum on the Hymn and Worship*, edited by Vernon Wicker, vol. 3. (Berrien Springs, MI: Vande Vere, 1993), 109–19. It has been substantially revised and expanded.

Chapter 10 was originally published as "Letter Codes Relating to Pitch and Key for Chorale Melodies and Bach's Contributions to the Schemelli *Gesangbuch*," BACH 45/1 (2014): 15–33. Here it appears in a lightly revised form.

Chapter 11 was originally a paper given at the First Annual Symposium on the Lutheran Liturgy and Hymnody, at Concordia Theological Seminary, Fort Wayne, IN, January 1990, and later published as: "Bach and Pietism: Similarities Today," *Concordia Theological Quarterly* 55 (1991): 5–22. It has been substantially revised, with a third or more of the original being replaced by new material from other unpublished research.

Chapter 12 is a revision and expansion of the article "*Bachii, Musici Lips. laus*: Bach in a Philological Footnote," that appeared in *Musicology Australia*

Preface   xiii

41:2 (2019): 121–34, the Festheft marking Janice (Jan) B. Stockigt's 80th birthday. It also adapts and expands some paragraphs that appear toward the end of my chapter "Churches" in *The Routledge Research Companion to Johann Sebastian Bach*, edited by Robin A. Leaver (London: Routledge, 2017), 185–88.

Chapter 13 is a much expanded revision of part of the article that appeared as: "The Libretto of Bach's Cantata No. 79: A Conjecture," *BACH* 6/1 (January 1975), 3–11; a revised German version, "Der Text von Bachs Kantate Nr. 79: Eine Mutmassung," appeared in *Theologische Bach-Studien I* (Beiträge zur theologischen Bachforschung 4), edited by Walter Blankenburg and Renate Steiger (Stuttgart: Hänssler, 1987), 109–16. I am grateful to Steven Zohn and Ellen Exner for guidance on Telemann sources.

Chapter 14 was commissioned by the late Peter Williams and published as "Bach's *Clavierübung III*: Some Historical and Theological Considerations," in *The Organ Yearbook* 5 (1975): 17–32; it appears here in a revised form.

Chapter 15 in its earliest manifestation was prepared as a paper for the Bach Colloquium that met at Harvard University in May 2007: "Bach and Celebrations of the Reformation." An abbreviated version was published as "Bach and the Bicentenary of the Reformation, 1717," in *Im Klang der Wirklichkeit: Musik und Theologie*, edited by Norbert Bolin and Markus Franz (Leipzig: Evangelische Verlagsanstalt, 2011), 49–62; presented here is a revision of the complete paper.

I am indebted to many people whose expertise I have benefitted from over the years. First among them, of course, is my wife, Sherry Vellucci, whose personal support and encouragement have been, as always, invaluable, as are her professional skills as a music librarian. I have special thanks for Jacob Fuhrman who prepared the musical examples. Others from whom I have recently benefitted from their knowledge and insight are thanked in the appropriate places. Over the course of the decades during which many of these studies were first explored, there were others to whom I am not only sincerely grateful for their answers to my specific questions but also for the informal conversations about many things that were both stimulating and insightful. To name them would create a long list, but I sincerely thank them all.

However, there is one name that I cannot omit, and that is Daniel Zager, colleague and friend, who for nearly thirty years has been a scholarly sounding board for practically everything I have written during this time. He has had a distinguished career as a leading music librarian, heading the libraries at Oberlin Conservatory of Music, the University of North Carolina at Chapel Hill, and, for the past twenty years, Sibley Library at Eastman School of Music. There he is associate dean and teaches in the musicology, organ, sacred music, and historical keyboards departments. He is also an experienced and superb editor, with an enviable track record, for example editor of *Music Library Association Notes*, between 1992 and 1997; and editor of *Cross Accent: Journal of the Association of Lutheran Church Musicians*, between 2000 and 2002. He also has experience of editing collections of

xiv *Preface*

essays, such as the one that came as a complete surprise to me, *Music and Theology: Essays in Honor of Robin A. Leaver* (Scarecrow, 2007). Much of his influence on my work has been behind the scenes, but more recently our collaboration has produced two volumes in the series published by Wayne Leupold Editions: *Organ Accompaniment of Congregational Song: Historical Documents and Settings* (2017). As I have taught my musicology students for years, success in musicology will only be possible with the assistance of a music librarian, who will point you to the sources, reveal what has recently been published, guide you through the labyrinth of databases and catalogues, and at the same time question your logic, conclusions, and style. I am privileged to have such a colleague in Dan Zager, who, as it were, is at my elbow as I research and write.

Robin A. Leaver

Abbreviations

Agenda	*Agenda: Das ist, Kirchen-Ordnung, Wie sich die Pfarrherren und Seelsorger in ihren Ämtern und Diensten verhalten sollen.* Leipzig: Lanckisch, 1712. Originally published at the beginning of the Reformation in Leipzig in 1539, slightly revised the following year, after which it was continuously reprinted without alteration, apart from the year at the end of the preface which, sometime during the seventeenth century, was misprinted as "1536" and repeated in many subsequent reprints.
Anh.	Anhang/Appendix
BACH	Bach: Journal of the Riemenschneider Bach Institute. 1970– .
BC	*Bach Compendium. Analytisch-bibliographisch Repertorium der Werke Johann Sebastian Bach*, 4 vols. Edited by Hans-Joachim Schulze and Christoph Wolff. Leipzig: Peters, 1985–1989.
BC-K/W	*The Book of Concord: The Confessions of the Evangelical Lutheran Church.* Edited by Robert Kolb and Timothy J. Wengert. Minneapolis: Fortress, 2000.
BDok	*Bach Dokumente.* Edited by Andreas Glöckner, Anselm Hartinger, Karen Lehmann, Michael Maul, Werner Neumann, Hans-Joachim Schulze, Christoph Wolff. 7 vols. Kassel: Bärenreiter; Leipzig: Deutscher Verlag für Musik, 1953–2008.
BG	*Johann Sebastian Bach's Werke.* Complete edition of the Bach Gesellschaft. 46 vols. Leipzig: Breitkopf & Härtel, 1851–1900. Reprint, Ann Arbor: Edwards, 1947.
BJ	*Bach-Jahrbuch.* 1904– .
BWV	*Bach-Werke-Verzeichnis. Kleine Ausgabe.* Edited by Wolfgang Schmieder, revised by Alfred Dürr and Yoshitake Kobayashi. Wiesbaden: Breitkopf & Härtel, 1998.
D-B	Staatsbibliothek zu Berlin/Preußischer Kulturbesitz, and its predecessor institutions.
ET	English translation.

xvi *List of abbreviations*

Jahrbuch KMBM	*Jahrbuch. Ständige Konferenz Mitteldeutsche Barockmusik in Sachsen, Sachsen-Anhalt und Thüringen.* Eisenach: Wagner, 1999–.
KB	*Kritischer Bericht* (critical report) of the NBA.
LKA	*Leipziger Kirchen-Andachten/ Darinnen Der Erste Theil Das Gebetbuch/ Oder Die Ordnung des gantzen öffentlichen Gottes-Dienstes durchs gantze Jahr/ ... Der Ander Theil Das Gesangbuch/ ...* Leipzig: Würdig, 1694.
LKS	*Leipziger Kirchen-Staat/ Das ist Deutliche Unterricht vom Gottes-Dienst in Leipzig/ ...* Leipzig: Groschuff, 1710.
LW	*Luther's Works: American Edition*, 1–55 vols. Edited by Jaroslav Pelikan and Helmut T. Lehmann, St. Louis and Philadelphia: Concordia and Fortress, 1955–1986; vols. 56–82, edited by Christopher Boyd Brown and Benjamin T. G. Mayes. St. Louis: Concordia, 2009– .
MGG2	*Die Musik in Geschichte und Gegenwart*. 2. vollständig neu bearbeitete Ausgabe. *Der Sachteil*, 10 vols. and *Personenteil*, 17 vols. Edited by Friedrich Blume and Ludwig Finscher. Kassel: Bärenreiter, 1994–2007.
NBA	[Neue Bach-Ausgabe.] *Johann Sebastian Bach: Neue Ausgabe sämtlicher Werke*, 110 vols. Edited by Johann-Sebastian-Bach-Institut, Göttingen, and the Bach-Archiv, Leipzig. Kassel: Bärenreiter and Leipzig: Deutscher Verlag für Musik, 1954–2010.
NBR	*The New Bach Reader: A Life of Johann Sebastian Bach in Letters and Documents.* Edited by Hans T. David and Arthur Mendel. Revised and enlarged by Christoph Wolff. New York: Norton, 1998.
NG2	*The New Grove Dictionary of Music and Musicians*, 29 vols. Second edition. Edited by Stanley Sadie. New York: Grove, 2001.
RISM	Répertoíre International des Sources Musícales
Rost	*Nachricht, Wie es, in der Kirchen zu St: Thom: alhier, mit dem Gottesdienst, jährlichen sowohl an Hohen Festen, als andern Tagen, pfleget gehalten zu werden auffgezeichnet von Johann Christoph Rosten, Custode ad D. Thomae, Anno 1716.* Manuscript, continued by later hands, in the archive of the Thomaskirche; no shelfmark.
SiculNAL	Christoph Ernst Sicul, *Neo-annalium Lipsiensium Continuatio II: Oder des mit dem 1715ten Jahre Neuangefangenen Leipziger Jahr-Buchs Dritte Probe.* Leipzig: Autore, 1717.
Spitta	Philipp Spitta, *Johann Sebastian Bach*, 2 vols., Leipzig: Breitkopf & Härtel, 1873–1880; reprint, Wiesbaden: Breitkopf & Härtel, 1964.

List of abbreviations xvii

Spitta ET	Philipp Spitta, *Johann Sebastian Bach, His Work and Influence on the Music of Germany, 1685–1750*, 3 vols., trans. Clara Bell and John Alexander Fuller-Maitland, London: Novello, 1884; reprint, New York: Dover, 1951.
TVWV	Werner Menke, *Thematische Verzeichnis der Vocalwerke von Georg Philipp Telemann*, 2nd ed., 2 vols. Frankfurt: Klostermann, 1988–1995.
ThomDok	*Dokumente zur Geschichte des Leipziger Thomaskantorats. Band 1: Von der Reformation bis zum Amtsantritt Johann Sebastian Bachs*, ed. Michael Maul. Band 2: *Vom Amtsantritt Johann Sebastian Bachs bis zum Beginn des 19. Jahrhunderts*, ed. Andreas Glöckner. Leipzig: Evangelische Verlagsanstalt, 2018–.
UN	*Unschuldige Nachrichten*, with varying titles and publishers, Leipzig, 1701–1761.
Vopelius	Gottfried Vopelius, *Neu Leipziger Gesangbuch/ von den schönsten besten Lieder verfasset/ ... Mit 4. 5. bis 6. Stimmen/ deren Melodeyen ...* Leipzig: Klinger, 1682.
WA	*Luthers Werke: Kritische Gesamtausgabe*, 65 vols. Weimar: Böhlau, 1883–1993.
Wolff BLM	Christoph Wolff, *Johann Sebastian Bach: The Learned Musician*, "Updated Edition." New York: Norton, 2013.
Zahn	Johannes Zahn, *Die Melodien der deutschen evangelischen Kirchenlieder, aus den Quellen.* 6 vols. Gütersloh: Bertelsmann, 1889–1893; reprint, Hildesheim: Olms, 1997.

Part I
Liturgy

1   Bach's cantatas and the liturgical year

There are many studies of the musical form and content of the German church cantata,[1] but not so many discussions of its liturgical context and purpose. However, without an appreciation of the liturgies within which the cantata was performed, together with its close connections with the Lutheran tradition of preaching, its musical form is likely to be misunderstood. The cantata was heard within two primary liturgical environments: the seasons and Sundays of the liturgical year, explored here in this chapter; and the specific liturgical forms of weekly worship that are discussed in Chapter 2.

The liturgical year

Lutheran liturgical worship, derived from earlier Catholic tradition, was an annual cycle of Sundays and specific celebrations. Its twofold structure, each covering approximately six months, dealt first with the life and work of Christ—birth, ministry, death, resurrection, ascension—and, in the second half-year, explored in detail the life and work of the Christian:

Sundays before Christmas

    Advent 1–4

Christmas (Weihnacht)

    Christmas Day (Weihnachtstag—25 December and the two days following)
    Sunday after Christmas
    New Year's Day (Neujahr)/Circumcision (Beschneidung Christi)
    Sunday after New Year

---

1 See, for example, the entries under "Cantata" in such reference works as NG2 and MGG2.

4   *Liturgy*

Epiphany (Epiphanius) = 6 January

Sundays after Epiphany (The length of the Epiphany season in any year is variable, depending on the date of Easter).

Pre-Lent

Septuagesima—third Sunday before Lent
Sexagesima—second Sunday before Lent
Estomihi[2]—Sunday before Lent

Lent

Invocavit—first Sunday in Lent
Reminiscere—second Sunday in Lent
Oculi—third Sunday in Lent
Laetare—fourth Sunday in Lent
Judica—fifth Sunday in Lent

Holy Week

Palm Sunday (Palmarum)
Maundy Thursday (Gründonnerstag)
Good Friday (Karfreitag)

Easter

Easter Day (Ostertag) and the two days following
Quasimodogeniti—first Sunday after Easter
Misericordias Domini—second Sunday after Easter
Jubilate—third Sunday after Easter
Cantate—fourth Sunday after Easter
Rogate—fifth Sunday after Easter

Ascension

Ascension (Himmelfahrt)
Sunday after Ascension (Exaudi)

Pentecost

Pentecost (Pfingsttag) and the two days following

---

2 The Latin name, with those of the Sundays in Lent and post-Easter, is derived from the incipit of the traditional Latin Introit for the day.

Trinity Season

Trinity Sunday (Trinitatis)
Sundays after Trinity—variable in number, to a maximum of 27, depending on the date of Easter.

Festival and Apostle Days[3]

Purification (Fest Mariae Reinigung or Lichtmesse)—2 February
Annunciation (Fest Mariae Verkundigung)—25 March
Visitation (Fest Mariae Heimsuchung)—2 July
St. John the Baptist's Day (Fest Johannes des Taufers)—24 June
St. Michael's Day (Fest Michaelis)—29 September
St. Stephen's Day (St. Stephani)—26 December
St. John's Day (St. Johannis)—27 December

Other Days

Inauguration of the town council (Ratswahl)—last Monday in August
Reformation (Reformationsfest)—31 October

For each of these Sundays and celebrations specific biblical readings—Epistles and Gospels—were prescribed, readings that established the content of the day within one of the seasons of the church year.

Epistles and Gospels in Lutheran worship

The Roman lectionary, the list of passages mostly from the New Testament to be read in the Mass on all the Sundays and festivals of the church year, was an early development.[4] Luther grew up with this one-year cycle of readings that became very familiar to him after he was ordained a priest and regularly celebrated Mass. In the *Formula missae* of 1523 he entertained the possibility that at some time in the future they might be revised,[5] but three years later, in the *Deutsche Messe*, he endorsed their continued use.[6] Thereafter the preexisting

---

3 There were other Apostle days recorded in Saxon liturgical sources, but they were not universally observed.

4 See Adrien Nocent, "The Roman Lectionary for Mass," in *Handbook for Liturgical Studies, III: The Eucharist*, ed. Anscar J. Chupungco (Collegeville, MN: Liturgical Press, 1999), 177–83.

5 LW 53: 23: "the Epistle is read. Certainly the time has not yet come to attempt revision here, as nothing unevangelical is read"; WA 12: 209: "lectio Epistolae. Verum nondum tempus est et hic novandi, quando nulla impia legitur."

6 LW 53: 68: "For the Epistles and Gospels we have retained the customary division according to the church year, because we do not find anything especially reprehensible in this use"; WA 19: 79: "Das wyr aber die Episteln und Euangelia nach der zeyt des jars geteylet, wie bis her gewonet, halten, Ist die ursach: Wir wissen nichts sonderlichs ynn solcher weyse zu taddeln."

6   *Liturgy*

lectionary, with very few minor modifications, was universally adopted in the churches of Lutheran Germany. Since these readings, listed according to the Sundays and celebrations of the church year, are readily available in various sources, they are given here in biblical order (see Table 1.1). The reason is twofold. First, it enables the extent of the biblical material to be seen more clearly. Second, it facilitates the comparative study of Bach's settings of the same or similar texts. The information has been established from contemporary sources, such as Bibles, New Testaments, and supplements containing the complete texts of the readings commonly appended to hymnals.[7] The listings can also be found in various studies of Bach's cantatas.[8] But the primary source for the usage in Leipzig is the seventeenth-century Saxon *Vollständiges Kirchen-Buch*, an anthology of fundamental liturgical and theological documents, reprinted and reissued in every subsequent generation.[9]

Like his contemporaries, Bach had a lifelong association with these passages of scripture. He would have encountered them in his earliest years when attending worship with his family in the Georgenkirche, Eisenach, and then around his eighth birthday, when he entered the *Quinta* of the Latin school, his reading exercises included the study of the Epistles and Gospels of the church year in both Latin and German.[10] Later, as organist in Arnstadt and Mühlhausen, and especially as Konzertmeister in Weimar and Cantor in Leipzig, he was involved in providing specific music for the weekly services that centered on the Epistles and Gospels throughout the church year.

A significant difference between the Roman Mass and Luther's reformed liturgical orders was his insistence that they should always include preaching.

---

7 *Biblia, Das ist: Die gantze Heilige Schrifft Altes und Neues Testaments/Teutsch/Herrn D. Martin Luthers ...* (Ulm: Kühn, 1688); *Das Neue Testament unsers Herrn und Heylandes Jesu Christi/ Verteutschet D. Mart. Luthern* (Hamburg: Holle, 1707); *Die Heilige Schrift/Neuen Testaments unsers Herrn Jesu Christi: Nach der Teutschen Übersetzung D. Martin Luthers* (Lemgo: Meyer, 1734); *Episteln und Evangelia, Mit Nutzbaren und erbaulichen Summarien auf alle Sonntage und fürnehmste Feste durchs gantze Jahr ...* (Dresden & Leipzig: Hekel, 1732); *Die in der Evangelischen Kirche gewöhnlichen Sonn- und Festtäglichen Episteln und Evangelia Mit kurtzen summarischen Betrachtungen ... von Carl Gottlob Hofmann* (Leipzig: Barnbeck, 1743).

8 For example, Charles Sanford Terry, *Joh. Seb. Bach Cantata Texts Sacred and Secular; with a Reconstruction of the Leipzig Liturgy of his Period* (London: Constable, 1926; reprint, London: Holland, 1964); Werner Neumann, *Sämtliche von Johann Sebastian Bach vertonte Texte* (Leipzig: VEB Deutscher Verlag für Musik, 1974); Alfred Dürr, *The Cantatas of J. S. Bach with their Librettos in German-English Parallel Text*, rev. and trans. Richard D. P. Jones (Oxford: Oxford University Press, 2005).

9 *Vollständiges Kirchen-Buch, darinnen die Evangelia und Episteln auf alle Fest-, Sonn- und Apostel-Tage durchs gantze Jahr, die Historien von dem schmertzlichen Leiden, und der fröhlichen Auferstehung des Herrn Christi: samt der erbärmlichen Zerstörung der Stadt Jerusalem, die drey Haupt-Symbola und Augspurgische Confeßion ...* (Leipzig: Lanckisch, 1743). The texts of the Epistles and Gospels of the church year form the first section of this anthology of documents, which have separate pagination.

10 Martin Petzoldt, "'Ut probus & doctus reddar.' Zum Anteil der Theologie bei der Schulausbildung Johann Sebastian Bachs in Eisenach, Ohrdruf und Lüneburg," BJ 71 (1985): 11.

Bach's cantatas and the liturgical year 7

Table 1.1 Epistles and Gospels for the Church Year

Text	Use	Day	Bach's Vocal Works (BWV)
		OLD TESTAMENT	
Exodus			
12:1–13	E	Maundy Thursday	—
Psalms			
22:1–31	alt. E	Good Friday	244, 245, 247
46:1–11	alt. E	Reformation Festival	79, 80
Isaiah			
7:10–15	E	Annunciation	1, 182, Anh. I:199
9:2–7	E	Christmas Day	63, 91, 110, 191, 197a, 248^{I}
11:1–5	E	Visitation	10, 147
40:1–5	E	St. John the Baptist	7, 30, 167
52:13–53:12	E	Good Friday	244, 245, 247
60:1–6	E	Epiphany	65, 123, 248^{VI}
Malachi			
3:1–4	E	Presentation/Purification	82, 83, 125, 157, 158, 161, 200
		APOCHRYPHA	
Ecclesiasticus			
15:1–8	alt. E	3rd Day of Christmas/ St. John	64, 133, 151, 248^{III}
		NEW TESTAMENT	
Matthew			
2:1–12	G	Epiphany	65, 123, 248^{VI}
2:13–23	G	Sunday after New Year	58, 153, 248^{V}
3:13–17	alt. G	Sunday after New Year	58, 153, 248^{V}
4:1–11	G	Invocavit/Lent 1	—
5:20–26	G	Trinity 6	9, 170
6:24–34	G	Trinity 15	51, 99, 138
7:15–23	G	Trinity 8	45, 136, 178
8:1–13	G	Epiphany 3	72, 73, 111, 156
8:23–27	G	Epiphany 4	14, 81
9:1–8	G	Trinity 19	5, 48, 56, Anh. I:2
9:18–26	G	Trinity 24	26, 60
11:2–10	G	Advent 3	186a
12:34–40	G	Trinity 18	96, 169
13:24–30	G	Epiphany 5	—
15:21–28	G	Reminiscere/Lent 2	—
17:1–9	G	Epiphany 6	—
18:1–11	G	St. Michael	19, 50, 130, 149
18:23–35	G	Trinity 22	55, 89, 115
20:1–16	G	Septuagesima	84, 92, 144
21:1–9	G	Advent 1	36, 61, 62
21:1–9	alt. G	Palm Sunday/Lent 6	182
22:1–14	G	Trinity 20	49, 162, 180
22:15–22	G	Trinity 23	52, 139, 163
22:34–46	G	Trinity 18	96, 169
23:34–39	G	2nd Day of Christmas/ St. Stephen	40, 57, 121, 248^{II}

(continued)

8 Liturgy

Table 1.1 Cont.

Text	Use	Day	Bach's Vocal Works (BWV)
24:15–28	G	Trinity 25	90, 116
24:37–51	alt. G	Trinity 27	140
25:1–13	G	Trinity 27	140
25:31–46	G	Trinity 26	70
26:1–27:66	G	Palm Sunday	182
Mark			
7:31–37	G	Trinity 12	35, 69a, 137
8:1–9	G	Trinity 7	107, 186, 187, Anh. I:1 & I:209
16:1–8	G	Easter Day	4, 31, 249
16:14–20	G	Ascension	11, 37, 43, 128
Luke			
1:26–38	G	Annunciation	1, 182, Anh. I:199
1:39–56	G	Visitation	10, 147
1:57–80	G	St. John the Baptist	7, 30, 167
2:1–14	G	Christmas Day	63, 91, 110, 191, 197a, 248^{I}
2:15–20	alt. G	2nd Day of Christmas/ St. Stephen	40, 57, 121, 248^{II}
2:21	G	New Year's Day	16, 41, 143, 171, 190, 248^{IV}
2:22–32	G	Presentation/Purification	82, 83, 125, 157, 158, 161, 200
2:33–40	G	Christmas 1	28, 122, 152
2:41–52	G	Epiphany 1	32, 124, 154
5:1–11	G	Trinity 5	88, 93
6:36–42	G	Trinity 4	24, 177, 185
7:11–17	G	Trinity 16	8, 27, 95, 161
8:4–15	G	Sexagesima	18, 126, 181
10:23–36	G	Trinity 13	33, 77, 164
11:14–28	G	Oculi/Lent 3	54, 80a
13:1–15	G	Maundy Thursday	—
14:1–11	G	Trinity 17	47, 114, 148
14:16–24	G	Trinity 2	2, 76
15:1–10	G	Trinity 3	21, 135
16:1–9	G	Trinity 9	94, 105, 168
16:19–31	G	Trinity 1	20, 39, 75
17:11–19	G	Trinity 14	17, 25, 78
18:9–14	G	Trinity 11	113, 179, 199
18:31–43	G	Estomihi/ Quinquagesima	22, 23, 127, 159
19:41–48	G	Trinity 10	46, 101, 102
21:25–36	G	Advent 2	70a
24:13–35	G	2nd Day of Easter	6, 66, Anh. I:190
24:36–47	G	3rd Day of Easter	134, 145, 158
John			
1:1–14	alt. G	3rd Day of Christmas/ St. John	64, 133, 151, 248^{III}
1:19–28	G	Advent 4	132, 147a
2:1–11	G	Epiphany 2	3, 13, 155
3:1–15	G	Trinity Sunday	129, 165, 176, 194
3:16–21	G	2nd Day of Pentecost	68, 173, 174
4:47–54	G	Trinity 21	38, 98, 109, 188

Bach's cantatas and the liturgical year 9

Table 1.1 Cont.

Text	Use	Day	Bach's Vocal Works (BWV)
6:1–15	G	Laetare/Lent 4	—
8:46–59	G	Judica/Lent 5	—
10:1–11	G	3rd Day of Pentecost	175, 184
10:12–16	G	Misericordiae Domini/ Easter 2	85, 104, 112
14:23–31	G	Pentecost	34, 59, 74, 172
15:26–16:4	G	Exaudi/Ascension 1	44, 183
16:5–15	G	Cantate/Easter 4	108, 166, Anh. I:191
16:16–23	G	Jubilate/Easter 3	12, 103, 146
16:23–30	G	Rogate/Easter 5	86, 87
18:1–19:42	G	Good Friday	245
20:19–31	G	Quasimodogeniti/ Easter 1	42, 67
21:20–24	G	3rd Day of Christmas/ St. John	64, 133, 151, 248^{III}

Acts

1:1–11	E	Ascension	11, 37, 43, 128
2:1–13	E	Pentecost	34, 59, 74, 172
2:29–36	alt. E	3rd Day of Pentecost	175, 184
6:8–15 & 7:55–60	alt. E	2nd Day of Christmas/ St. Stephen	40, 57, 121, 248^{II}
8:14–17	E	3rd Day of Pentecost	175, 184
10:42–48	E	2nd Day of Easter	6, 66, Anh, I:190
13:26–33	E	3rd Day of Easter	134, 145, 158

Romans

3:21–28	alt. E	Trinity 27	140
6:3–11	E	Trinity 6	9, 170
6:19–23	E	Trinity 7	107, 186, 187, Anh.I:1 & I:191
8:12–17	E	Trinity 8	45, 136, 178
8:18–23	E	Trinity 4	24, 177, 185
11:33–36	E	Trinity Sunday	129, 165, 176, 194
12:1–6	E	Epiphany 1	32, 124, 154
12:7–16	E	Epiphany 2	3, 13, 155
12:17–21	E	Epiphany 3	72, 73, 111, 156
13:8–10	E	Epiphany 4	14, 81
13:11–14	E	Advent 1	36, 61, 62
15:4–13	E	Advent 2	70a

1 Corinthians

1:4–9	E	Trinity 18	96, 169
4:1–5	E	Advent 3	186a
5:7–8	E	Easter Day	4, 31, 249
9:24–10:5	E	Septuagesima	84, 92, 144
10:6–13	E	Trinity 9	94, 105, 168
11:23–32	E	Maundy Thursday	—
12:1–11	E	Trinity 10	46, 101, 102
13:1–13	E	Estomihi/ Quinquagesima	22, 23, 127, 159
15:1–10	E	Trinity 11	113, 179, 199

(*continued*)

10 *Liturgy*

Table 1.1 Cont.

Text	Use	Day	Bach's Vocal Works (BWV)
2 Corinthians			
3:4–11	E	Trinity 12	35, 69a, 137
5:1–10	E	Trinity 27	140
6:1–10	E	Invocavit/Lent 1	—
11:19–12:9	E	Sexagesima	18, 126, 181
Galatians			
3:15–22	E	Trinity 13	33, 77, 164
3:23–29	E	New Year's Day/ Circumcision	16, 41, 143, 171, 190, 248^{IV}
4:1–7	E	Christmas 1	28, 122, 152
4:21–31	E	Laetare/Lent 4	—
5:15–21	E	Trinity 20	49, 162, 180
5:16–24	E	Trinity 14	17, 25, 78
5:25–6:10	E	Trinity 15	51, 99, 138
Ephesians			
3:13–21	E	Trinity 16	8, 27, 95, 161
4:1–6	E	Trinity 17	47, 114, 148
4:22–28	E	Trinity 19	5, 48, 56, Anh. I:2
5:1–9	E	Oculi/Lent 3	54, 80a
5:15–21	E	Trinity 20	49, 162, 180
6:10–17	E	Trinity 21	38, 98, 109, 188
Philippians			
1:3–11	E	Trinity 22	55, 89, 115
2:5–11	E	Palm Sunday/Lent 6	182
3:17–21	E	Trinity 23	52, 139, 163
4:4–7	E	Advent 4	132, 147a
Colossians			
1:9–14	E	Trinity 24	26, 60
3:12–17	E	Epiphany 5	—
1 Thessalonians			
4:1–7	E	Reminiscere/Lent 2	—
4:13–18	E	Trinity 25	90, 116
5:1–11	alt. E	Trinity 27	140
2 Thessalonians			
1:3–20	alt. E	Trinity 26	70
2:3–8	E	Reformation Festival	79, 80
Titus			
2:11–14	alt. E	New Year's Day/ Circumcision	16, 41, 143, 171, 190, 248^{IV}
3:4–7	alt. E	2nd Day of Christmas/ St. Stephen	40, 57, 121, 248^{II}
Hebrews			
1:1–14	E	3rd Day of Christmas/ St. John	64, 133, 151, 248^{III}
9:11–15	E	Judica/Lent 5	—

Bach's cantatas and the liturgical year   11

Table 1.1 Cont.

Text	Use	Day	Bach's Vocal Works (BWV)
James			
1:17–21	E	Cantate/Easter 4	108, 166, Anh. I:191
1:22–27	E	Rogate/Easter 5	86, 87
1 Peter			
2:11–17	E	Jubilate/Easter 3	12, 103, 146
2:21–25	E	Misericordias Domini/ Easter 2	85, 104, 112
3:8–15	E	Trinity 5	88, 93
3:30–22	alt. E	Sunday after New Year	58, 153, 248^V
4:8–11	E	Exaudi/Ascension 1	44, 183
4:12–19	E	Sunday after New Year	58, 153, 248^V
5:6–11	E	Trinity 3	21, 135
2 Peter			
1:16–21	E	Epiphany 6	—
3:3–13	E	Trinity 26	70
1 John			
3:13–18	E	Trinity 2	2, 76
4:16–21	E	Trinity 1	20, 39, 75
5:4–10	E	Quasimodogeniti/ Easter1	42, 67
Jude			
14–19	alt. E	Trinity 27	140
Revelation			
12:7–12	E	St. Michael	19, 50, 130, 149
14:6–8[–13]	G	Reformation Festival	79, 80

E = Epistle; G = Gospel; alt. = alternative

In the evangelical Mass he directed that the sermon should always be on the Gospel of the day, and although at first he advocated preaching consecutively through books of the Old Testament at Sunday Vespers,[11] it became customary for the preaching at this afternoon service to be on the Epistle of the day. Thereafter, the pattern was set for Lutheran Germany that on Sundays and primary celebrations of the church year the sermon in the morning evangelical Mass, the Hauptgottesdienst, would be an exposition of the Gospel of the day, and in the afternoon Vespers the preaching would be on the Epistle of the day. Over the next two hundred years or so, pastors would preach annual cycles of sermons on these biblical lections of the church year. Then sometime later many of them would edit and rework one of these annual cycles of sermons for publication as devotional reading. Over the years some preachers published more than one collection of their church-year sermons.

11 LW 53: 68; WA 19: 79.

12 *Liturgy*

At the time of his death in 1750 Bach owned a significant library of devotional/theological books, a significant proportion of them being anthologies of church-year sermons on the annual cycle of the Epistles and Gospels. Bach never made a will and therefore an inventory of his estate had to be drawn up in order that his effects could be fairly distributed among his family: "Specificatio der Verlaßenschafft des 28. July. 1750 seelig verstorbenen Herrn Johann Sebastian Bachs" (Specification of the Estate Left by the Late Herr Johann Sebastian Bach Blessedly Departed 28 July 1750). Chapter 12 of the Specificatio lists "An geistlichen Büchern" (religious books).[12]

Books by Luther form the greater part of Bach's library,[13] among them two different editions of Luther's *Hauspostille*, sermons on the Gospels of the church year, one in folio and the other in quarto (Nos. 7 and 28). These were preached by Luther in Wittenberg between 1531 and 1535, when two of his colleagues, Veit Dietrich and Georg Rörer, made independent shorthand notes of them. These were later edited, published, and continuously reprinted in subsequent generations, each version slightly different from the other: *Haußpostil D. Martin Luther, uber die Sontags, und der fürnembsten Fest Evangelia, durch das gantze Jar. Mit fleyß von newem ubersehen, gebessert und gemehret* [von Veit Dietrich] (House Sermons by Dr. Martin Luther on the Gospels for the Sundays and High Festivals of the Church Year, Diligently Newly Edited, Improved and Enlarged) (Nuremberg: Berg and Neuber, 1544); *Haußpostill uber die Sontags und der fürnemesten Feste Euangelien / durch das gantze Jar / von D. Martino Luthero seligen gepredigt / aus M. Georgen Rörers seligen geschriebenen Büchern ... auffgefasst und zusamen bracht ... u. in Druck geben* (House Sermons on the Gospels for the Sundays and High Festivals of the Church Year, Preached by Martin Luther, Prepared, Assembled and Printed from Georg Rörer's Manuscript Books) (Jena: Rödinger, 1559). While it is possible that Bach owned two different editions of the same version of the *Hauspostille*, it seems more likely that one was the edition of Dietrich and the other was that of Rörer. With these church-year sermons by Luther, the significant Lutheran tradition of published sermons was begun. Sometimes

---

12 BDok 2: 494–96 (No. 627). For the background, see Robin A. Leaver, *Bachs theologische Bibliothek: eine kritische Bibliographie/Bach's Theological Library: A Critical Bibliography* (Stuttgart: Hänssler, 1983). The document is a handwritten copy of the inventory of Bach's estate. There are transcription errors, and the books are listed by abbreviated short-titles, which means that there is some ambiguity with regard to the exact identity of some of the listed titles. Since it is a short-title catalogue, in most cases there is no way of knowing which edition of a particular work Bach owned; see also: Thomas Wilhelmi, "Bachs Bibliothek: Eine Weiterführung der Arbeit von Hans Preuss," *BJ* 65 (1979): 107–29; Johannes Wallmann, "Johann Sebastian Bach und die 'Geistlicher Bücher' seiner Bibliothek," *Pietismus und Neuzeit* 12 (1986): 162–81. Books in Bach's library are cited here by the common numbers used in the studies of Wilhelmi, Wallmann, and Leaver.

13 They include two editions of Luther's collected works, the Jena and Altenburg editions (Nos. 3 and 2, respectively), the *Tischreden* (No. 4), and the Bible commentary edited by Abraham Calov (No. 1), which is in effect another edition of Luther's works arranged in biblical order.

Bach's cantatas and the liturgical year   13

the anthologies were of sermons on either the Epistles or the Gospels of the church year, at other times on both, but always with the complete respective biblical text appearing at the beginning of every sermon.

In addition to the two copies of Luther's *Hauspostille*, Bach also owned a further eight volumes of such church-year sermons, written mostly by well-known pastors whose collected sermons went through many reprints and editions. Three were written by Heinrich Müller (1631–1675), pastor and professor in Rostock—two complementary volumes, one on the Epistles and the other on the Gospels, and another on just the Gospels: *Apostolische Schluß-Kette, Und Krafft-Kern / Oder Gründliche Außlegung der gewöhnlichen Sonn- und Fest-Tags-Episteln* (Apostolic Key-Chain and Strong Marrow, or Thorough Exposition of the Customary Sunday and Festival Epistles) (Frankfurt: Wust, 1663); *Evangelische Schluß-Kette / Und Krafft-Kern / Oder Gründliche Außlegung der gewöhnlichen Sonn- und Fest-Tags-Evangelien* (Evangelical Key-Chain and Strong Marrow, or Thorough Exposition of the Customary Sunday and Festival Gospels) (Frankfurt: Wust, 1671) (Nos. 8 and 20); and *Evangelisches Präservativ wider den Schaden Josephs / in allen dreyen Ständen / Heraußgezogen aus den Sonn- und Fest-Tags Evangelien* (Evangelical Preservative against the Sorrow of Joseph in All Three Estates ... Developed from the Sunday and Festival Gospels) (Frankfurt: Wilde, 1681). (No. 19).[14]

Another three volumes of sermons owned by Bach were written by the prolific August Pfeiffer (1640–1698), archdeacon of the Thomaskirche and professor of Hebrew in Leipzig before becoming superintendent in Lübeck: *Gazophylacion Evangelicum: Evangelische Schatz-Kammer / Allwo bey denen Sonntäglichen / wie auch Haupt-Fest-Evangelien* (Gospel Treasury from the Sunday and Festival Gospels) (Nuremberg: Hofmann, 1686) (No. 15); *Evangelische Christen-Schule ... aus denen Evangelischen Sonn- und Fest-Tags-Texten deutlich gewiesen* (Evangelical Christian School ... Clarified from the Gospel texts for Sundays and Festivals (Leipzig: Frommann, 1688) (No. 36); and *Apostolische Christen-Schule, Darinnen Die ordentlichen Sonntags- und vornehmste Fest-Episteln Durchs gantze Jahr / richtig disponiret und abgetheilet ...* (Apostolic Christian School, in which the Epistles of the Usual Sundays and High Festivals throughout the Whole Year are Correctly Interpreted and Explained) (Lübeck and Rostock: Krüger, 1695) (No. 14). Two other similar anthologies of church-year sermons, both on the Gospels, were also in Bach's library. One was by Nicolaus Stenger (1609–1680), successively cantor, pastor, and professor in Erfurt, *Credendorum & faciendorum Postilla, da aus jeglichem evangelio gezeiget wird ein glaubensschild und ein lebensbild* (Sermons on Believing and Acting, Demonstrated from Each Gospel in Defense of Faith and as a Model for Life (Erfurt: Dedekind, 1661–1662)

---

14 This volume has an appendix of Passion sermons that Picander drew on in creating the libretto of the St. Matthew Passion (BWV 244); see Elke Axmacher, *"Aus Liebe will mein Heyland Sterben": Untersuchungen zum Wandel des Passionsverständnisses im frühen 18. Jahrhundert* (Stuttgart: Hänssler, 1984).

14   *Liturgy*

(No. 23); and the other was by Martin Geier (1614–1680), superintendent in Leipzig at the time he preached these sermons in the Thomaskirche in 1664, *Zeit und Ewigkeit: nach gelegenheit der ordentlichen Sontags Evangelien …* (Time and Eternity: According to the Content of the Customary Sunday Gospels) (Leipzig: Lanckisch, 1670) (No. 25).

Bach also owned other devotional books that were homiletic in nature while not being sermons on the Epistles and/or Gospels, but which were structured according to some other topical ground plan. Nevertheless, such books customarily included a special index that located where the reader could find discussions relevant to the content of the Epistles and Gospels of the Sundays and festivals as they would be encountered throughout the year. Bach had at least two such examples in his library, both written by favorite authors, Müller and Pfeiffer: Heinrich Müller, *Geistliche Erquickstunden, oder Dreyhundert Haus- und Tisch-Andachten* (Rostock: Keyl, 1666) (Spiritual Refreshment Hours: or Three Hundred House and Table Devotions) (No. 42); August Pfeiffer, *Der wohlbewährte Evangelische Aug-Apffel. Oder Schrifftmäßige Erklärung aller Articul Der Augspurgischen Confession …* (The Well-Proven Evangelical Apple of the Eye, or Scriptural Explanation of All the Articles of the Augsburg Confession) (Leipzig: Kloß, 1685) (No. 17). These books—and perhaps others like them—formed the theological and devotional background to Bach's composition and performance of his cantatas.

Epistles and Gospels, and the dissemination of Bach's cantatas

The nineteenth century had its difficulties with the cantatas of Bach, a musical form that had virtually disappeared from the regular worship of Lutheran Germany—a tradition, when discovered, that seemed quite foreign to people of other denominational persuasions and linguistic areas. Moritz Hauptmann, one of Bach's successors as cantor in Leipzig, and the first editor of the cantatas for the Bach-Gesellschaft edition that began to appear in 1851, did not find the form and style of Bach's cantatas particularly accessible. Donald Francis Tovey characterized Hauptmann's understanding of the cantatas in colorful language:

> The first editor of the Bachgesellschaft. Moritz Hauptmann, writing with such insight as could be expected of a man first discovering the existence of this choral music a century after Bach's death, commented on the strange phenomenon of an art-form that usually begins with a fine chorus, follows it with "a luggage train" of wiggy arias and crabbed recitatives, and then concludes with one verse of a plain hymn-tune. Hauptmann obviously did not understand Bach.[15]

---

15 Donald Francis Tovey, *Essays in Musical Analysis* (London: Oxford University Press, 1935–1939), 5:61. Tovey, who does not cite a source, may have been paraphrasing Hauptmann's sentences found towards the end of the second page of his preface to the first BG

Bach's cantatas and the liturgical year 15

Bach's cantatas as a whole were introduced to the world at large in instalments consisting of ten cantatas at a time, as they were ready for publication, though sometimes cantatas for the same occasion did appear together, such as the Advent cantatas 61 and 62, or the Reformation Day cantatas 79 and 80. The cantatas in each instalment were numbered successively, the first from 1–10, the next from 11–20, and so forth until the total of 199 was reached towards the end of the nineteenth century.[16] The numbers therefore had no specific significance other than the sequence in which the cantatas were published in the Bach-Gesellschaft volumes. Although the prefaces to the cantata volumes usually made reference to the occasion for which each cantata was composed, the impression given was that they were independent mini-oratorios. Even though they were without a particular narrative, small in scale, and dependent on a liturgical context, Bach's cantatas were constantly compared to the oratorios of Handel. Thus, Hauptmann, in a letter to Hauser dated 11 April 1859, wrote:

> A large orchestra and chorus do not enhance the beauty of Bach, as a general rule, unless your one aim is material effect ... You can never overdo the thing with Handel; he wrote in London, and knowing he was sure of any amount of resources, wrote accordingly. His composition is transparent; it can be supplemented by any number of voices and instruments.[17]

Awareness of Bach's cantatas following their appearance from the middle of the nineteenth century in the Bach-Gesellschaft volumes has been conditioned by their isolation from both their original liturgical context and their location within the church year. Thus, relationships between cantatas composed for the same day, as well as the connections between the cantatas for the preceding and succeeding Sundays, have not always been recognized—especially as modern performances mostly take place in a concert setting, with programing decisions being made primarily with regard to what particular instruments and/or solo voices are required. The largely meaningless numbering of the cantatas has remained constant in the Bach world. When Wolfgang Schmieder created his thematic catalog *Bach-Werke-Verzeichnis* (BWV) in 1950, he retained the Bach-Gesellschaft numbering for the cantatas, which has not been changed in subsequent revisions of the BWV catalog, and still continues to be used extensively. To give just two examples of collections of cantatas being assembled in their familiar numerical sequence: the historically informed recordings of the complete cantatas,

---

volume: *Johann Sebastian Bachs Werke. Erster Band* (Leipzig: Bach-Gesellschaft, 1851), xvi. Hauptmann, somewhat surprisingly, was frequently critical of Bach's music in letters he wrote to Franz Hauser, director of the Munich conservatory, between 1843 and 1859; *The Letters of a Leipzig Cantor, Being the Letters of Moritz Hauptmann to Franz Hauser, Ludwig Spohr, and Other Musicians*, ed. Alfred Schöne and Ferdinand Hiller, translated and arranged, A. D. Coleridge (London: Novello, 1892), 2: 6, 14–15, 113.

16 Cantata 200 was not published until 1935.

17 Hauptman, *The Letters of a Leipzig Cantor*, 2: 119.

16 *Liturgy*

directed by Nikolaus Harnoncourt and Gustav Leonhardt, issued by *Teldec Das Alte Werk* beginning in 1971; and the recently published Carus complete edition of the vocal works.[18]

The Bach-Gesellschaft, on reaching its goal of publishing the complete works of Bach, was disbanded in 1900, but was immediately replaced by the Neue-Bachgesellschaft. In the early years of the existence of the new society its leaders understood that liturgical issues needed to be addressed. One of the first things the members of the Direktorium did was to sponsor an annual Bachfest in which Bach's cantatas could be heard within a liturgical context, a practice that continues to this day. A few years later the new society issued an edition of all the cantata libretti, edited by Rudolf Wustmann, which were arranged according to the sequence of the church year rather than by the Bach-Gesellschaft numbers.[19] Since then it has become customary for editions of the cantata libretti, as well as commentaries on all of Bach's church cantatas, to follow the sequence of the Sundays and celebrations of the church year.[20] Thus, as connections between the content of the Epistles and Gospels—especially the Gospels—are revealed, the libretti become less opaque, and the ingenuity of Bach's musical genius—in setting both the concepts that lie behind the biblical texts as well as the way they are verbally expressed in the libretti—becomes clearer.

But there is still a disconnect between now and then, between, on the one hand, our reception of the knowledge of the weekly and annual liturgical contexts and, on the other hand, the perception of those who first heard Bach's cantatas within these contexts.

Epistles and Gospels in Lutheran culture

From the perspective of the twenty-first century the Epistles and Gospels of the church year used in Bach's day appear to be a restricted ecclesiastical phenomenon, significant only for a few hours on Sundays and other days. But

18 *Johann Sebastian Bach. Das geistliche Vokalwerk/The Sacred Vocal Music*, ed. Ulrich Leisinger & Uwe Wolf (Stuttgart: Carus, 2017).

19 Rudolf Wustmann, *Joh. Seb. Bachs Kantatentexte*, Veröffentlichungen der Neuen Bachgesellschaft, Jahrgang 14, Heft 1) (Leipzig: Breitkopf & Härtel, 1913); new edition, Werner Neumann, ed., *Johann Sebastian Bach: Sämtliche Kantatentexte; unter Mitbenutzung von Rudolf Wustmanns Ausg. der Bachschen Kirchenkantatentexte* (Leipzig: Breitkopf & Härtel, 1967).

20 For example: Alfred Dürr, *Die Kantaten von Johann Sebastian Bach* (Kassel: Bärenreiter, 1971; 10th ed., 2010); English edition: *The Cantatas of J. S. Bach with their Librettos in German-English Parallel Text*, rev. & trans. Richard D. P. Jones (Oxford: Oxford University Press, 2005); *Bach Compendium. Analytisch-bibliographisches Repertorium der Werke Johann Sebastian Bachs (BC)*, eds. Hans-Joachim Schulze and Christoph Wolff (Leipzig: Peters, 1985–1989); Martin Petzoldt, *Bach-Kommentar: theologisch-musikwissenschaftliche Kommentierung der geistlichen Vokalwerke Johann Sebastian Bachs* (Stuttgart: Internationale Bachakademie, 2004–2019); Hans-Joachim Schulze, *Die Bach-Kantaten : Einführungen zu sämtlichen Kantaten Johann Sebastian Bachs* (Leipzig : Evangelische Verlagsanstalt, 2006).

Bach's cantatas and the liturgical year 17

such an assessment is far too superficial and does not take into account the fact that the church year and its biblical readings permeated virtually every aspect of contemporary life at that time. The Epistles and Gospels, of course, enshrined the teaching on particular days of the weekly services of worship, but they were not confined to such church use. Devotional handbooks, such as the *Leipziger Kirchen-Andachten* (Leipzig: Würdig, 1694) and the *Leipziger Kirchen-Staat* (Leipzig: Groschuff, 1710), supplied personal prayers to be used before, during, and after attending public worship on the Sundays and other days in the church year. Hymnals, such as *Das Privilegirte Ordentliche und Vermehrte Dreßdnische Gesang-Buch* (Dresden and Leipzig: Hekel, 1724, and later reprints) and *Das privilegirte Vollständige und vermehrte Leipziger Gesang-Buch* (Leipzig: Barnbeck, 1734, and later reprints), each included an index of specific hymns that expressed the themes of the Epistles and Gospels that could be sung on each of these days, hymns which, of course, could be sung in the home as well as in church.

According to Luther's *Small Catechism*—which in Bach's day was frequently appended to Bibles and hymnals—it was the responsibility of the head of the household to teach the catechism and lead daily prayers, morning and evening, with the singing of hymns, which customarily would have reflected the time or season in the church year. There was also communal and individual Bible reading in the home. For example, Johann Mattheson (1681–1764) recorded that he had begun reading through the whole Bible, beginning with Genesis, for the 22nd time in 1759.[21] When reading consecutively through the books of the New Testament the reader would often be reminded of the specific Epistles and Gospels, since in a good many New Testaments and Bibles it was customary to mark where the texts of each of the Epistles and Gospels began and ended. For example, in a Bible published in Eisenach in 1704, at the beginning of John's Gospel, chapter 2—the wedding at Cana—, the following appears before the first verse: "(Evangelium am 2. Sonntage nach Epiphaniä)" (Gospel for the Second Sunday after Epiphany).[22] Sermons were also read aloud as part of daily devotions in the home, and many such books were either annual cycles of church year sermons based on Epistles and/or Gospels, or their content was indexed for passages that were illustrative of these weekly biblical lections. In schools attached to churches it was customary for the pupils to study the Epistles and Gospels of the church year in Latin as well as German. Therefore, in church, school, and home, the cycle of Epistles and Gospels was encountered almost daily, one way or another, and even in the wider civic world their presence was fundamental.

During the eighteenth century various Leipzig publishers produced annual almanacs that recorded the departments in government, and the people within them, in both Saxony in general and Leipzig in particular, and also the

21 Beekman C. Cannon, *Johann Mattheson: Spectator in Music* (New Haven: Yale, 1947), 219.
22 *Biblia, Das ist: Die gantze Heil. Schrifft Alten und Neuen Testaments/Verdeutscht durch D. Martin Luthern* (Eisenach: Urban, 1704), [*Neuen Testaments*], 73ᵛ.

18   *Liturgy*

military, the university, the churches, the many different businesses, such as guest houses, coffee houses, book dealers and publishers, art galleries, etc., and especially the detailed postal services. In 1749 a new directory/almanac was published for the first time and thereafter appeared annually for the next sixty-five years: *Leipziger Adreß-, Post- und Reise-Kalender, Auf das Jahr Christi M.DCC. L. worinnen nicht nur Die bey dem Königl. Poln. und Churfl. Sächs. Gouvernement, sämtlichen Collegiis und Expeditionen, E. Lobl. Universität, E. E. Hochw. Raths-Collegio, dem geistl. Ministerio, der Kauffmannschafft und Innungen stehenden Personen; sondern auch der Leipziger Post-Bericht ...* (Leipzig: Büschel, [1749]). The first main section of the almanac/directory was a calendar, from January to December of the respective year, which also recorded such things as the phases of the moon and the expected weather for that time of year. The days of each month were listed vertically and each week began on Sunday. Taking a year beyond Bach's death, the Sundays in the calendar for January 1758 are listed thus:

> S. n. N. J. [Sonntag nach Neue Jahr = Sunday after New Year] Flucht Chr. In Eg. Matth.2. [Christ's flight into Egypt. Matthew 2] ...
>> 1. n. Epiph. [First Sunday after Epiphany] Jes[.] lehret im Temp. Luc.2. [Jesus teaches in the Temple. Luke 2] ...
>> 2. n. Epiph. [Second Sunday after Epiphany] Hochzeit zu Cana, Jon. 2. [Wedding at Cana, John 2] ...
>> 3. n. Epiph. [Third Sunday after Epiphany] Hauptm. z. Capern. Mat. 8. [The Centurion in Capernaum, Matthew 8] ...
> Septuages. [Septuagesima Sunday] Arbeit. im Weinb. Mat.20 [Workers in the vineyard, Matthew 20] ...[23]

Here is the demonstration of just how deeply imbedded these passages of scripture were within Lutheran culture, secular as well as religious. The Sunday-by-Sunday readings had far more significance than simply the scriptural content of public worship; they were foundational for Lutheran identity—for individuals, families, schools, churches, businesses and commercial agencies, as well as both local and regional governments. Thus, when librettists came to write their cantata texts based on these Epistles and Gospels, especially the Gospels, they were able to draw on this shared experience and common consciousness. Similarly, when composers, Bach among others, came to set these libretti—expositions of aspects of the scriptural lections—they were aware of the deep-seated cognition and experience of their congregations. The cantatas were, therefore, heard with a level of sophistication, perception, awareness, and understanding that is lost to us today.

---

23 *Leipziger Adreß-, Post- und Reise-Kalender, Auf das Jahr Christi M.DCC. LXVIII* (Leipzig: Löper [1757]), sig. A2ʳ.

The development of the cantata from the chanted lections

Although the biblical lections in the liturgy were read in order to convey the church's teaching, that "reading" was given in a musical form that would ultimately lead to the creation of the cantata. In the *Formula missae* (1523) Luther directed that the practice of chanting (intoning) the Epistle and Gospel in Latin should be continued,[24] and then in the *Deutsche Messe* (1526) he not only directed that the Epistle and Gospel should also be chanted in German, but even included the musical notation for the singing of these biblical lections.[25] In Bach's day, in university cities such as Jena, Halle, Rostock, and Leipzig, Luther's two liturgical forms were generally conflated. On the one hand, the Epistle and Gospel could be chanted in Latin and then repeated afterward in German, or alternatively, the lections on most Sundays throughout the year would be chanted in German, but on major feasts they would be intoned in Latin. Right from the very beginning of Lutheran liturgical reforms these biblical lections were proclaimed in monodic chant. By the end of the sixteenth century a related musical form developed out of the sung word in the liturgy: the *Evangelienmotette*, Gospel motet, or *Spruchmotette*, Bible-text motet. These were polyphonic settings of the *Kernsprüche*, key verse(s), of the Gospel for the day. How they were used liturgically is not entirely clear. Carlos Messerli makes the following conjecture:

> the fragmentary nature of most of the motet texts and the presence of gospel chant formulas included in some of the collections suggest a ... placement of the motet *within* the chanted gospel itself.[26]

Messerli suggested that the pastor would chant the Gospel of the day until he reached the words that were set in the Gospel motet. The choir would then take over for these consecutive words, and when they were concluded, the pastor chanted the remainder of the biblical lection. But there is no objective evidence that would confirm this conjecture, which seems somewhat tenuous, since by the same logic one could conclude that polyphonic settings of the *Verba Testamenti* replaced the pastor's chanting of these words in the liturgy, a practice that would have raised a number of contentious theological issues. One is on much safer historical and liturgical grounds if one considers that the Gospel motet was most likely to have been sung after the chanted Gospel as an introduction to the sermon. The Gospel

---

24 WA 12: 205–20; LW 53: 19–40.
25 WA 19: 72–113; LW 53: 61–90; see also Leaver, *Luther's Liturgical Music: Principles and Implications* (Grand Rapids, MI: Eerdmans, 2017), 180–88.
26 Carlos Messerli, "Gospel Motet," in *Key Words in Church Music*, rev. ed., ed. Carl Schalk (St. Louis: Concordia, 2004), 274; see also Carlos R. Messerli, "The 'Corona harmonica' (1610) of Christoph Demantius and the Gospel Motet" (PhD diss., University of Iowa, 1974).

20 *Liturgy*

motet would then have been the bridge between the *chanting* of the word and the *preaching* of the word:[27]

> Gospel of the day—intoned
> Gospel motet—on the key verse(s) of the Gospel
> Sermon—on the Gospel of the day

No doubt there were other practical variations, such as: the Latin Nicene Creed being sung from time to time between the Gospel and the Gospel motet; Luther's creedal hymn *Wir glauben all an einen Gott* being sung after the Gospel motet; or, at other times, the German version of the Gospel of the day not immediately following the chanting of the Latin version, but being held over and read at the beginning of the sermon. Whatever the variations, the Gospel motet was an integral part of the ministry of the word. Its function was to make emphatic the key words of the Gospel lection of the day, and also to prepare for the preaching that was about to follow.

The Gospel motet was, therefore, in embryo, the church cantata. What began as a polyphonic motet in the sixteenth century became enriched in the seventeenth century with the provision of independent instrumental parts in a concerted style. Furthermore, in the third quarter of the seventeenth century there was a move away from simply providing a musical setting of the key words of the Gospel of the day. Non-biblical verse was added to the musical exposition of the biblical text. For example, Wolfgang Carl Briegel (1626–1712), Kapellmeister in Darmstadt, issued a collection of Gospel motets between 1660 and 1669 under the title *Evangelischer Blümengarten* (Gospel Flower-garden). Like the traditional Gospel motet, these are choral settings, mostly in a simple chordal style, of the key verse(s) of the respective Gospel lection. But each one ends with what Briegel calls an "aria," a chorale-like setting of strophic verse. Here is the developing cantata growing out of the Gospel of the day, but which, little by little, takes on a more varied type of text and expands its musical form. By the end of the seventeenth century the cantata libretti were usually made up of biblical verses and hymn texts, a form that Bach knew and emulated early in his career, such as in Cantata 106, *Gottes Zeit ist die allerbeste Zeit* ("Actus tragicus"). But the cantata form was expanding both in terms of its use of freely written poetry and of its extended musical content. The pioneer of this "reform" cantata was Erdmann Neumeister (1671–1756), the staunchly orthodox pastor in Hamburg who knew and admired Bach.[28] Neumeister cast his cantata libretti into sections of recitatives and *da capo* arias, following the model of opera, mixed in with

---

27 See Chester L. Alwes, "Georg Otto's 'Opus musicum novum' (1604) and Valentin Geuck's 'Novum et Insigne Opus' (1604): a Musico-Liturgical Analysis of Two Collections of Gospel Music from the Court of Hesse-Kassel" (PhD diss., University of Illinois, 1982).

28 The connections between Bach and Neumeister are explored in Chapter 13.

biblical verses and stanzas of hymns, thus creating the form of the late baroque church cantata that is epitomized in the Leipzig cantatas of Bach.[29]

The function of the cantata, however elaborate its form had become, was exactly the same as that of the more simple Gospel motet, that is, an integral part of the liturgy. Its purpose was to make emphatic and draw out the essential meaning of the Gospel reading of the day or celebration. In doing so, it reinforced what had been heard in the Gospel lection and prepared the way for the sermon that followed, which, like the cantata, applied the message of the Gospel to the faith, life, and witness of the congregation. The church cantata, in contrast to the independent non-liturgical oratorio, was, therefore, strictly liturgical music, in the sense that it was specifically composed for the worship of the gathered congregation and was an integral part of the ministry of the word. It was devotional music in the truest sense; not merely "mood" music but rather "word" music: like preaching, it was the word applied, but in musical form.[30]

---

29 The controversy occasioned by the eighteenth-century reform cantata is the subject of Chapter 5,

30 On what Bach and his contemporaries understood by the phrase "Andächtige Musique" (devotional music), see Robin A. Leaver, "J. S. Bach's Parodies of Vocal Music: Conservation or Intensification?" in *Compositional Choices and Meaning in the Vocal Music of J. S. Bach*, ed. Mark A. Peters and Reginald L. Sanders (Lanham, MD: Lexington, 2018), 187–92.

2 Bach's music and the Leipzig liturgy

The previous chapter explored the cycle for the church year that dominated both secular and religious life. This chapter investigates the weekly pattern of worship within which Bach's music was heard. The concentration is on Leipzig, where his earlier cantatas were reperformed, along with his newly composed vocal works, especially during his early years in the city. We begin with a review of the Leipzig churches, which, in the decades before Bach's arrival in 1723, had experienced a significant period of renewal and expansion.[1]

Churches and choirs

From the end of the seventeenth century, with the increasing population, the two principal churches, St. Nikolaus and St. Thomas, were full to overflowing. As a partial solution a weekday celebration of Communion, in addition to the regular Sunday celebration, was introduced in both churches in 1694, but this did not resolve the issue. The following year, 1695, the Johanniskirche outside the Grimma gate was completely rebuilt and refurbished, and three years later, in 1698, restoration work began on the old Franciscan church, which had not functioned for worship since the Reformation. It was consecrated on 24 September 1699 as the Neukirche. Even though the restoration was undertaken to relieve overcrowding in the two parish churches, the "new" church quickly established its particular identity in the city, especially during the period when Georg Philipp Telemann (1681–1767) directed the church's music between 1702 and 1704, much to the disdain of Bach's predecessor, Cantor Johann Kuhnau (1660–1722).[2] In 1701 work began on rebuilding the hospital church of St. George, physically part of "a house of correction" and an orphanage. It was consecrated for worship early in 1705, the same year

---

1 The following is largely based on Anton Weiz, *Verbessertes Leipzig, oder Die vornehmsten Dingel so von Anno 1698. an biß hieher bey der Stadt Leipzig verbessert worden, mit Inscriptionibus erlautert* (Leipzig: Lanckisch, 1728), 1–30.
2 See the discussion in Chapter 5 on the connections between the Neukirche and the Leipzig opera during Telemann's time in Leipzig.

that new galleries were constructed in the Thomaskirche. The Paulinerkirche was the university's aula, where public lectures, doctoral defenses, and other academic exercises were held. Worship took place in St. Paul's only on the major festivals of the church year. However, in 1710 the university began holding weekly worship in the church in addition to observing the major festivals throughout the year. The same year that the university church began weekly worship, work started on rebuilding the Petrikirche, which since the Reformation had been used for a variety of non-religious purposes. It was consecrated for worship on 29 May 1712. The following year, 1713, work began on the complete restoration of the Lazarethkirche, just outside the city wall by the Ranstädt gate, in which worship was renewed on Easter Day 1714.

There were, therefore, eight Leipzig churches, each with services throughout the week as well as on Sundays, festivals, and other special days, and each staffed by their own complement of clergy, lay assistants, organists, and other musicians.[3] However, as cantor, Bach had no direct involvement in two of the churches, namely the Georgenkirche (or Weisenhauskirche) and Lazarethkirche, and only minimally with the Johanniskirche on major festivals when Choir IV led the singing of chorales (as discussed below).

The Thomasschule had been created in order to provide choirs for the churches in Leipzig, especially the Thomaskirche and Nikolaikirche. As the school regulations of 1634 state:

> That the school's progress and prosperity in previous years were manifestly furthered because the boys who were selected and admitted had a greater aptitude for music than those of the St. Nicholas school and performed in both churches, at funerals and weddings, and, finally, in the rounds of street singing, is beyond any doubt. For many people, sacred music, when sung in the churches and elsewhere, gives rise to an especially intense state of devotion, which is not the least of the reasons why in former times various legacies stipulated the better provisioning of the boys in the said school, and also some people, while still living, generously made weekly or monthly donations to be used for that purpose. For that reason, it is only proper to ensure, when auditioning and admitting boys who are over twelve years of age and desire to board at the school, that they are not untutored in the art of music but are sufficiently experienced, and can perform a piece of music in an accomplished and appropriately artful manner.[4]

---

3 Names of the personnel with their responsibilities in each of the churches, together with the daily pattern of services, for the year that Bach began his career in Leipzig are given in the annual directory: *Das jetzt lebende und florirende Leipzig, Welches die Nahmen, Characteren, Chargen, Professionen und Wohnungen derer Persone ...* (Leipzig: Boetius, 1723), 31–32, 78–84. Six churches had organs with named organists; the Lazarethkirche and the Weisenhauskirche were each served by a "Praecentor."

4 *Des Raths zu Leipzig, Vornewerte Schul-Ordnung* (Leipzig: Köler, 1634); facsimile in Hans-Joachim Schulze, *Die Thomasschule Leipzig zur Zeit Johann Sebastian Bachs: Ordnungen und*

24 *Liturgy*

In the eighteenth century there were attempts to diminish the role of music in the Thomasschule and to expand the intellectual content of its curriculum,[5] but the tradition and history of the school had long been set and Bach upheld what he had inherited.

Up until the end of the seventeenth century the Thomasschule organized four choirs to provide church music for the two principal churches in Leipzig, the Thomaskirche and the Nikolaikirche, to sing at weddings, funerals, and other special occasions, and to raise money for the school by street-singing—the so-called Currende tradition[6]—especially at New Year.[7] With the reopening of the Neukirche and the Petrikirche, there were then four churches to be served. The four choirs together formed an effective graded-choir program, from entry-level Choir IV to the most accomplished Choir I. Choir IV led the singing of German hymns in the Petrikirche on Sundays and also in the Johanniskirche on festival days. This was the least accomplished choir, characterized by Bach in 1730 as "the residue [Ausschuss], namely those who do not understand music and can only just barely sing a chorale."[8] Choir III sang motets and occasionally cantatas, as well as leading the singing of chorales in the Neukirche, but, as Bach explained in 1736, this had "nothing to do with other *Concert Musique*, since the latter is taken care of by the [Neukirche] organist."[9] Choir I and Choir II alternated between the two principal churches Sunday by Sunday. If Choir I was in the Nikolaikirche this Sunday, Choir II would be in the Thomaskirche; the following Sunday the choirs would swap churches. Choir II sang motets and figural works that were less complex than the repertoire of Choir I, and then only on major festivals. Choir I was the most accomplished of the four choirs, as Bach explained in 1736: "the concerted pieces [mostly cantatas] that are performed by the First Choir, which are mostly of my own composition, are incomparably harder and more intricate than those sung by the Second Choir."[10]

Most boys on entering the school were assigned to either Choir IV or Choir III and then progressed to the next level of competence as they gained skill and experience. Only on the rare occasion would a boy, such as Gottlob Friedrich Rothe in 1744, enter immediately into Choir I.[11] The figural music of Choir I was accompanied by the Stadtpfeiffer und Kunstgeiger,[12] and was

---

Gesetze 1634. 1723. 1733 (Leipzig: Zentralantiquariat, 1985); sig. Ciii^v Civ^r; cited in Michael Maul, *Bach's Famous Choir: The Saint Thomas School in Leipzig, 1212–1804*, trans. Richard Howe (Woodbridge: Boydell, 2018), 27.

5 See the discussion in Chapter 12.

6 Wolff BLM 246–47.

7 See Maul, *Bach's Famous Choir*, 76–87.

8 BDok 1: 60 (No. 22); NBR 146 (No.151).

9 BDok 1: 87–88 (No. 34); NBR 175 (No. 183). Between 1720 and 1729 the Neukirche organist was Georg Balthasar Schott; between 1730 and 1761 it was Carl Gotthelf Gerlach.

10 BDok 1: 88 (No. 34); NBR 176 (No. 183).

11 See Chapter 12.

12 Weiz, *Verbessertes Leipzig*, 8: "Die Figural- und Choral-Music wird von dem Cantore and Schülern zu St. Thomae, nebst denen Stadt-Pfeiffern und Kunstgeigern bestellet."

Bach's music and the Leipzig Liturgy   25

directed by Bach. Since the worship of the four churches occurred at the same time on the mornings of Sundays and special days, Choirs II–IV were directed by prefects specially chosen by Bach, a system that ran into difficulties in 1736.[13]

Bach also had responsibilities in the university's Paulinerkirche, which were a matter of dispute during his early years in Leipzig. Bach's predecessor, Johann Kuhnau, was the *Chori Musici Director* for the university and was responsible for the music on the major festivals of the church year in the university church, worship referred to as the "Old Service." When in 1710 the university introduced weekly worship into the church, thereafter known as the "New Service," Kuhnau took over responsibility for directing the music of these additional services. However, when Kuhnau died in June 1722 one of his students, Johann Gottlieb Görner, organist of the Nikolaikirche, took over directing the music for the weekly worship. By the time Bach was appointed as Kuhnau's successor as cantor and director of music in Leipzig in May 1723, the university had confirmed the permanence of Görner as the university's *Chori Musici Director*. Thus, the annual Leipzig directory in 1723 included the following:

> Worship in the university church begins at 9 o'clock on Sundays and on feast days, and at 4 o'clock in the afternoon ... and on high festivals and other days, under the direction of Herr Johann Gottlieb Görner, students and other musicians present solemn church music.[14]

Bach felt that he had been slighted and that a source of income had been denied to him, since his predecessor, Kuhnau, had been responsible for the music of both the "Old Service" and the "New Service." He therefore argued that he should oversee both. The dispute ran on for some years, with Bach sending several letters of appeal to the King Elector stating his case. He was only partially successful, since Görner remained the university's *Chori Musici Director* and continued to oversee the "New Service," as well as providing music for various university occasions. Bach retained the direction of the "Old Service" with Choir I on the major festivals of the church year,[15] but the entry relating to music of the Paulinerkirche in the Leipzig annual directory continued to mention only Görner and not Bach.[16]

---

13 The so-called "Praefektenstreit" is discussed in Chapter 12.
14 *Das jetzt lebende und florirende Leipzig* (1723), 32: "Der Gottesdienst wird in der Universitäts-Kirche Sonn- und Fest-Tages früh um 9 Uhr, nachmittags aber um 4 Uhr angefangen ... an hohen Fest- und andern gewissen Tagen, unter dem Directorio Herrn John. Gottl. Görners, von Studiosis und andern Musicis solenne Kirchen Musicen gemacht."
15 The relevant documents are: BDok 1: 30–45 (Nos. 10–12); NBR 118–25 (Nos. 119a–c); see also the discussion in Wolff BLM, 311–16.
16 For example, *Das jetzt lebende und florirende Leipzig* (1736), 32; see also Weiz, *Verbessertes Leipzig*, 12.

26 *Liturgy*

Liturgical sources and studies

Details of the Leipzig liturgy are not as straightforward as might be assumed. If we were dealing with Roman Catholic worship at this time, it would be a relatively simple matter of consulting the Tridentine Missal with the particular propers for specific German saint's days. Similarly, if we were investigating eighteenth-century Anglican church music, details of the liturgical contexts are clearly set out in the 1662 Book of Common Prayer. But the Lutheran liturgy in Leipzig at the time of Bach was much more fluid than these other liturgical traditions. Instead of one main liturgical source there are a variety of sources to be consulted, even though they are sometimes unclear, ambiguous, and occasionally even contradictory.

The Reformation had been introduced into Albertine Saxony by Luther, who preached in the Thomaskirche, Leipzig, at Pentecost 1539, uniting it confessionally with Ernestine Saxony, which had espoused the Reformation between 1517 and 1523. Later in 1539 an *Agenda*, or *Kirchen-Ordnung*, was drawn up by Wittenberg theologians under Luther, to be used throughout Saxony, both Ernestine and Albertine. It was published in Leipzig, slightly revised in 1540, and thereafter was continuously reprinted in every subsequent generation. This provided basic forms of worship, but it was more of a directory than a fully worked-out sequence of liturgies. It recognized that the needs of churches in villages and small towns were not the same as those in large towns and cities, and therefore there was some flexibility with regard to liturgical detail. For example, in villages and small towns worship was almost exclusively in German, but in larger towns and cities where there were Latin schools and universities, such as Leipzig, both Latin and German were used side by side.[17]

Around the end of the seventeenth and beginning of the eighteenth century individual devotional handbooks were published in Leipzig that give prayers to be said privately at various junctions of the liturgy, which incidentally reveal much liturgical detail, especially with regard to musical content, not readily available elsewhere.[18] Then there are the incidental sources compiled by individuals who describe and comment on details of liturgical practice in the city's churches. They include the manuscript notebook begun in 1716 by the Thomaskirche custos (sexton), Johann Christoph Rost,[19] the descriptions by historian Christoph Ernst Sicul published in 1717,[20] and those by the city

---

17 For example, the *Agenda* gives separate sections for churches in towns and villages, as well as Latin proper prefaces, with chant notation, for major festivals in larger towns and cities.
18 Examples include LKA and LKS.
19 Rost; see also Martin Petzoldt, "Thomasküster Rost, seine Familie und der Leipziger Gottesdienst zur Zeit Johann Sebastian Bachs," in *800 Jahre Thomana: Glauben, Singen, Lernen: Festschrift zum Jubiläum von Thomaskirche, Thomanerchor und Thomasschule*, ed. Stefan Altner and Martin Petzoldt (Wettin-Löbejün: Stekovics, 2012), 163–81.
20 SiculNAL 565–89.

librarian Anton Weiz, published in 1728.[21] Among the attempts to conflate the information from the variety of such sources, the more important are the studies of Charles Sanford Terry,[22] Günther Stiller,[23] and Martin Petzoldt.[24]

Hauptgottesdienst

The principal worship on Sundays, major festivals, and saint's days was the Hauptgottesdienst (main service), the eucharistic rite held in the early morning, thus sometimes referred to as the "early" (*frühe*) service. The Saxon *Agenda* directed that it should be preceded by Matins:

> Early at Matins let the students chant one, two, or three psalms with the antiphon proper to the Sunday or festival, then a reading from the Old Testament, followed by the Benedictus [the Matins canticle] with an antiphon proper for the Sunday or festival, ending with a collect.[25]

By the eighteenth century there was only one church in Leipzig where the office of Matins was sung, unaccompanied in Latin, and that was the Nikolaikirche, beginning at 5:00 am on festivals and 5:30 am on Sundays,[26] led by the Nikolaicantor.[27] Matins was attended only by the St. Nicholas schoolboys – "except for them no one is in church."[28]

Figure 2.1 gives in outline the main content of the Hauptgottesdienst. However, the details changed from season to season, from festival to festival, from day to day, as different items specific to the celebration or observance

21 Weiz, *Verbessertes Leipzig*.
22 Charles Sanford Terry, *Joh. Seb. Bach Cantata Texts, Sacred and Secular: With a Reconstruction of the Leipzig Liturgy of his Period* (London: Constable, 1926; reprint, London: Holland, 1964).
23 Günther Stiller, *Johann Sebastian Bach und das Leipziger gottesdienstliche Leben seiner Zeit* (Berlin: Evangelische Verlaganstalt, 1970); *Johann Sebastian Bach and Liturgical Life in Leipzig*, trans. Herbert J. A. Bouman, et al., ed. Robin A. Leaver (St. Louis: Concordia, 1984).
24 Martin Petzoldt, "Liturgie und Musik in den Leipziger Hauptkirchen," in *Die Welt der Bach-Kantaten*, ed. Christoph Wolff (Stuttgart: Metzler, 1998) 3: 69–93.
25 Agenda 78: "Mag man frühe in der Metten auch einen, zwey oder drey Psalmen die Schüler singen lassen, mit der Antiphon von der Dominica oder Festo, darauf eine Lection aus dem Alten Testament lese, folgends das Benedictus mit einer Antiphon von der Dominica oder Festo und einer Collecte beschliessen."
26 See SiculNAL 567, and the diagram opposite p. 566; see also the diagram based on Sicul's in Arnold Schering, *Johann Sebastian Bachs Leipziger Kirchenmusik* (Leipzig: Breitkopf & Härtel, 1936), 24–25.
27 Weiz, *Verbessertes Leipzig*, 8: "Die Horae Canonicae aber zu St. Nicolai von dem Cantore zu St. Nicolai, als Directore, und einigen Studiosis verrichtet." Johann Hieronymus Homilius (1671–1750) was the Nikolaicantor during Bach's time; Arnold Schering, *Johann Sebastian Bach und das Musikleben Leipzigs im 18. Jahrhundert, Der Musikgeschichte Leipzig Dritter Band, Das Zeitalter Johann Sebastian Bachs und Johann Adam Hillers (von 1723 bis 1800]* (Leipzig: Siegel, 1941), 57–58.
28 LKS 4: "aber ausser diesen niemand in die Kirche."

28   *Liturgy*

	PREPARATION
1	Organ prelude
2	Latin motet, or Introit, or hymn
3	*Missa: Kyrie* and *Gloria*
4	Salutation (intoned)
5	Verse and collect
	MINISTRY OF THE WORD
6	Epistle
7	Graduallied/De tempore Lied/Hymn of the Day
8	Gospel (intoned in German on Sundays; in Latin on festivals)
9	Nicene Creed
10	Cantata
11	Creedal Hymn: *Wir glauben all an einen Gott*
12	Sermon
13	Hymn appropriate to the day or season
	MINISTRY OF THE SACRAMENT
14	Lord's Prayer
15	Verba Testamenti (intoned in German)
16	Communion and *Musica sub Communione*
17	Post-communion collects (intoned in German)
	DISMISSAL
18	Benediction and Benediction response
19	Hymn
20	Organ postlude

Figure 2.1 Outline of the *Hauptgottesdienst*

were added and subtracted. Therefore, the discussion will follow the basic order given in Figure 2.1, but will take account of such changes that were made for the various celebrations and observances that occurred throughout the church year.

Preparation

Organ Prelude. Tower bells were rung from 6:00 am, at 7:00 am candles were lit on the altar,[29] and "the beginning of the Gottesdienst is made with the organ."[30] The organ was employed throughout the liturgy almost every Sunday and every season with the exception of Lent, when the organ was silenced. Apart from the First Sunday in Advent, which celebrated the beginning of the new church year, the other three Advent Sundays were penitential in content and therefore included no concerted music.[31] But organ preludes

---

29 Rost fol. 44ʳ: "Umb 6. Uhr wird wie an einem Fest geläutet. Umb 7 Uhr die Kertzen ausgesteckt."
30 LKS 5: "Der Anfang des Gottesdienstes wird mit der Orgel gemacht;" Rost passim.
31 Parish churches observed this discipline, but court chapels, such as the one that Bach had served in Weimar, provided concerted music in Advent and Lent if their dukes or princes requested such music.

and congregational accompaniments continued during this pre-Christmas penitential period.

The service began with "Praeludieret," as Bach indicated in the liturgical outline he inscribed on the reverse of the title pages of the scores for his two Advent cantatas *Nun komm, der Heiden Heiland* (BWV 61 and 62).[32] The function was developed from the medieval practice of the organ establishing pitch and mode for the plainsong Introit that began the Mass. In Leipzig in Bach's day, it was an improvised prelude that had a similar function, except that it introduced different liturgical music depending on the season of the church year.

Motet, Hymn, or Introit. On most Sundays the organ prelude preceded a motet, sung by Choir I in one of the two main churches, and Choir II in the other church; the same motet would not necessarily have been sung in both churches. The motets were mainly taken from the two sets of part-books edited by Erhard Bodenschatz, *Florilegium Portense* (Leipzig: Lamberg, 1618 and 1621).[33] Together they comprise 271 *stile antico* motets composed during the last quarter of the sixteenth and the early years of the seventeenth century. Most (around two-thirds) are in eight parts divided into two choirs, the remainder being for between four and seven voices, with a significant number of motets for five voices.[34] The range of named composers is remarkably broad, many being represented by a single work. A high proportion of the composers are Italian, such as Balbi, Capilupus, the two Gabrielis, Pallavicino, Valcampi, and Viadana, among many others. But most of the composers having the highest number of motets in the collections are German (or North European), such as Jakob Handl (Gallus) with 19, Martin Roth with 16, Hieronymous Praetorius with 12, and Orlandus Lassus with 9.[35] About 10 percent of the total (26) appear in the Bodenschatz collections as "Anonymous." But as Werner Braun has shown, half of them

---

32 BDok 1: 248 (No. 178); NBR 113–14 (No. 113); and BDok 1: 251 (No. 181). It is difficult to assign a date when they were penned, but this must have been sometime between 1723 and the mid-1730s. Also it is not clear exactly why it was necessary for him to pen the liturgical order almost identically on both cantatas, apart from the addition of the Litany (see further below). Bach's source was most likely Rost, whose liturgical notebook has similar liturgical outlines for the different festivals and observances.

33 Some were to be found in the collections of Melchior Vulpius, *Pars prima Cantionum sacrarum* (Jena: Richtzenhan, 1602) and *Pars secunda selectissimarum Cantionum sacrarum* (Jena: Richtzenhan, 1603). LKA indicates that the Thomasschule also had manuscripts of a further fifteen motets, but these are no longer locatable.

34 Part one comprises eight part-books; Part two, nine part-books, one of which was for *basso continuo*, which implies an accompanied rather than *a cappella* performance practice.

35 The detailed contents of the two *Florilegium* collections can be found in the following: Otto Riemer, *Erhard Bodenschatz und sein Florilegium Portense* (Leipzig: Kistner & Siegel, 1928), 107–17; Holger Eichhorn, "Ein Sammeldruck vom Beginn des Dreißigjährigen Krieges: Das Florilegium Portense," in *Musik zwischen Leipzig und Dresden: Zur Geschichte der Kantoreigesellschaft Mügeln 1571–1996*, ed. Michael Heinemann and Peter Wollny (Oschersleben: Zeithen, 1996), 60–84.

30   *Liturgy*

are motets composed by Adam Gumpelzhaimer,[36] which brings his total number of motets in the two collections to 14.

Along with other Latin propers throughout the church year, the *Leipziger Kirchen-Andachten* lists the appropriate motets for each Sunday or celebration.[37] Only the first line of the text of each motet is given, together with a reference to where it can be found in the anthologies of Bodenschatz and Vulpius; the composers, however, are not identified.[38] References in the *Leipziger Kirchen-Andachten* suggest that the Bodenschatz anthologies were the principal source for the motets sung in the Leipzig churches. The records of the Thomasschule confirm that the Bodenschatz collections were used more commonly than those of Vulpius. For example, in 1729 either the first or second part of Bodenschatz's *Florilegium Portense* was purchased, and was described as an important source "which the scholars use for the music in the churches, as ordered by the honorable and sagacious Council."[39]

The editor of the *Leipziger Kirchen-Andachten* was Johann Friedrich Leibnitz (1632–1696), son of the Leipzig professor of ethics, and brother of the philosopher Gottfried Wilhelm (1646–1716). Johann Friedrich was a teacher (Terzius) in the Thomasschule,[40] and therefore the colleague of Cantor Johann Schelle (1648–1701). It seems unlikely that Leibnitz selected the motets himself, rather that he simply recorded the established practice. The original choice of motets was probably made in the early seventeenth century by one of the senior clergy of the Leipzig churches, or perhaps a group of clergy worked together with the cantor of the time. Whoever was responsible for the choices clearly exercised great care. Both the first and second collections of the *Florilegium* include a church year index, which served as a guide for the choice of motets for particular days, such as Advent Sunday, Christmas Day, Easter Day, Visitation, the days of St. John and St. Michael, and so forth. But these indexes classified the motets mainly by season rather than by Sunday or festival. Therefore, the majority of the choices found in the *Leipziger Kirchen-Andachten* reflect specific Leipzig usage.

What is particularly significant is that, in many cases, these choices of motets could only have been made after a close reading of the traditional propers of each day or celebration. Quite a few of the motets for specific Sundays are on the same biblical text (usually a Psalm) as the traditional Latin Introit; in at least one case (Trinity 12) the motet is on the same text as the monophonic Gradual, which is surprising since Latin Graduals had long

---

36 Werner Braun, "Kompositionen von Adam Gumpelzhaimer im Florilegium Portense," *Die Musikforschung* 33 (1980): 131–35.

37 LKA 1: 248–306.

38 The composers are identified in the literature cited in note 35 above.

39 "welches die Schüler in den Kirchen und zur Music brauchen, laut E. E. Hochweisen Raths Verordnung"; BDok 2: 133 and 199 (Nos. 170 and 271); it is possible that another set was purchased in 1737; see BDok 2: 294 (No. 407).

40 Maul, *Bach's Famous Choir*, 146.

Bach's music and the Leipzig Liturgy   31

since been abandoned in general Lutheran liturgies. In the *Leipziger Kirchen-Andachten* some of the motet titles are given with such annotations as "Ex. Intr.," "Ex Epist.", or "Ex Evang.," that is, with a text taken from the Introit, Epistle, or Gospel of the day or celebration. But some are marked with "Ex Antiph." or "Ex Respons.," that is, from an Antiphon or Responsory, indicating that the motet was perhaps more appropriate for Vespers than the Hauptgottesdienst.

For the Second, Third, and Fourth Sundays in Advent, the Hauptgottesdienst did not continue with a motet after the initial organ prelude. Instead, the respective traditional Latin Introit was chanted, unaccompanied, to its ancient melody. Similarly, during the penitential season of Lent the respective Latin Introits were sung unaccompanied,[41] but without the usual organ prelude at the beginning of the service.

In Advent, Introits were sung at the beginning of the Hauptgottesdienst, but the Christmas season represented a change in practice: in contrast to the Sundays in Advent, no Gregorian Introit or motet was sung in the Christmas season, being replaced by the Latin hymn *Puer natus in Bethlehem*. Christmas established the pattern for the other major festivals of the church year that followed, that the verbal worship began with an appropriate Latin hymn (see Table 2.1).[42] But there remains some ambiguity regarding other major celebrations, such as Christmas Day, as to whether the hymn replaced the Introit, or whether on these special occasions both might have been sung, or whether there might have been a different practice in each of the two principal churches. Although there are a number of unresolved ambiguities as to

Table 2.1 Hymns at the beginning of the Leipzig Hauptgottesdienst

Sundays and/or Celebration	Hymn	Sources
Christmas to Purification	*Puer natus in Bethlehem* Anon. (14/15th cent)	LKA 1:53, 2:253, 2:258; LKS 16; Rost fol. 47ʳ
Purification	*Ex legis observantia* Nicolaus Selneccer (Leipzig, 1587)	LKA 1:56, 293; LKS 21; Rost fol. 7ʳ
Easter Day	*Salve festa dies* Fortunatus (6th cent.)	LKA 2:274
Easter to Ascension	*Heut triumphiret Gottes Sohn* Kaspar Stolzhagen (1591)	LKA 1:63; LKS 16, 26, Rost fol. 26ʳ
Pentecost & Trinity	*Spiritus sancti gratia* Anon. (15th cent.)	LKA 2:281; LKS 16, 27; Rost fol. 30ʳ, fol. 32ʳ

41 Terry, *Bach Cantata Texts*, 21, doubted that Gregorian Introits were being sung in the Leipzig churches during Bach's time, but the manuscript "Manualen der Gottesdienste der Nikolaikirche," for the years 1724–1729, 1730–1742, and 1750–1762, in the Nikolaikirche archive indicate that they continued to be sung.
42 Four-part settings of all these hymns are included in Vopelius.

32 *Liturgy*

what the actual practice was at the beginning of the Hauptgottesdienst, the following pattern seems to be clear:

> Latin Introits: Chanted throughout the seasons of Advent, Lent, and Easter, with the possibility that they were also sung on the three pre-Lent Sundays, as well as on Exaudi (Sunday after Ascension).
>
> Latin Hymns: Sung throughout the seasons of Christmas/Epiphany (until the Purification), Easter to Ascension, on the three days of Pentecost, and the Feast of the Trinity.
>
> Latin Motets: Sung on the other Sundays and celebrations, primarily the Sundays after Trinity.

Kyrie and Gloria. Following the Introit, hymn, or motet, the *Missa* was sung, but this could be done in a variety of ways, though the established pattern of alternation from week to week in the two churches was followed. For example, on ordinary Sundays Choir I might sing a threefold Kyrie Gregorian chant,[43] after which the pastor would chant the intonation "Gloria in excelsis Deo," and Choir I would continue with the remainder of the Gregorian Latin Gloria, "et in terra pax."[44] Then in the other church Choir II might lead the congregation in singing the German hymnic Kyrie, *Kyrie Gott Vater in Ewigkeit*,[45] followed by the pastor singing the chant intonation "Gloria in excelsis Deo,"[46] and Choir II responding to lead the congregation in singing the Gloria hymn: *Allein Gott in der Höh sei Ehr*.[47] Both hymns would normally be introduced with chorale preludes, as is implied by the first part of Bach's *Clavierübung III*:

[*Kyrie*][48]

> *Kyrie, Gott Vater in Ewigkeit* (BWV 669)
> *Christe, aller Welt Trost* (BWV 670)
> *Kyrie, Gott heiliger Geist* (BWV 671)
>
> *Kyrie, Gott Vater in Ewigkeit* (BWV 672)
> *Christe, aller Welt Trost* (BWV 673)
> *Kyrie, Gott heiliger Geist* (BWV 674)

---

43 Vopelius 421; Agenda 99 includes Luther's simple threefold Kyrie chant.

44 Vopelius 421–23.

45 LKA 1: 11: "In der Kirchen aber/ wo der andere Chor ist ... wird das Kyrie deutsch gesungen: Kyrie/ Gott Vater in Ewigkeit" ("In the church where Choir II is, the German Kyrie is sung.") Vopelius 423–25 gives both the German and the Latin original, *Kyrie fons bonitatis*, which implies that this Latin version could be sung by the choir alone.

46 Agenda 99 includes the notation for four different Gloria intonations.

47 LKS 1: 12: "In der Kirchen aber/ wo der andere Chor ist ... wird das deutsch Gloria gesungen ... Allein Gott in der Höh sey Ehr" ("In the church where Choir II is ... the German Gloria is sung").

48 The implication is that the singing of each stanza of the hymn was preceded by a prelude.

[Gloria]

Allein Gott in der Höh sei Ehr (BWV 675)
Allein Gott in der Höh sei Ehr (BWV 676)
Allein Gott in der Höh sei Ehr (BWV 677)[49]

The following Sunday the patterns in the two churches were exchanged.

On major festivals, such as Christmas, Easter, and Pentecost, Choir I might sing a concerted Missa,[50] which would be preceded by an organ prelude in order to cover instrumental tuning,[51] but the pastor would chant the "Gloria in excelsis Deo" intonation between the Kyrie and Gloria. Presumably Choir II either sang the chant Missa in Vopelius, or perhaps a through-composed setting of the Kyrie and Gloria that was less demanding than the Missa sung by Choir I.

The introductory part of the service concluded with the salutation "Dominus vobiscum," sung by the pastor, with the choir's response "Et cum spiritu tuo" in either monodic chant or four-part polyphony.[52] The "Discantisten auf den Chor" (the boys of the choir) then chanted, in German, a biblical verse appropriate for the day. Then the pastor intoned the collect of the day in Latin.[53]

Ministry of the Word

Epistle. The Ministry of the Word began with one of the clergy chanting the Epistle of the day or celebration from the lectern.[54] At its conclusion, there was an organ interlude,[55] presumably providing time for reflection on what had been heard. On most Sundays and celebrations throughout the year the service continued with a hymn that focused on the lections of the day, but during the penitential seasons of Advent and Lent the hymn was preceded

---

49 On the background, see Chapter 14.
50 In addition to his own five settings of the *Missa* (BWV 232–236), Bach had access to, or knew of, settings of the *Missa* by other composers; see Kirsten Beißwenger, *Johann Sebastian Bachs Notenbibliothek* (Kassel: Bärenreiter, 1992); see also Beißwenger, "Other Composers," in *The Routledge Research Companion to Johann Sebastian Bach*, ed. Robin A. Leaver (London: Routledge, 2017), 237–64.
51 Bach: "Praeludieret auf das Kyrie, so ganz musiciret wird" ("Prelude before the Kyrie when music is full"); BDok 1: 248 (No. 178); NBR 113–14 (No. 113).
52 Vopelius 1077–83.
53 LKS 19: "Den Discantisten auf den Chor intoniret." LKS 6: "Ferner singet der Priester eine Lateinische Collecte." The Latin collects are given in LKA 2: 248–304; see also LKA 1: 12; SiculNAL 570; Rost passim. Agenda, 145–257 has German collects, intended for use in small towns and villages.
54 The Epistle chant formulae from Luther's *Deutsche Messe* (1526) are given in the Agenda, 100–4.
55 LKS 6: "Nach Absinget der Collecte gehet ein andrer Priester vor das Pult und singet die Epistel. Nach dieser wird georgelt." The significance of the Epistles and Gospels of the church year is discussed in Chapter 1.

34   *Liturgy*

by the antiphonal singing of the Litany—a small group of boys singing the petitions, and the four-part choir leading the responses of the congregation.[56]

Graduallied. The hymn sung between the Epistle and Gospel was in many ways the most important hymn of the service, since it was chosen for the way it related to the substance of the biblical pericopes of the day, primarily the Gospel.[57] Therefore, the organ prelude on the associated chorale melody had a particular significance.[58]

Gospel. Following the hymn, the pastor at the altar initiated a liturgical dialogue sung between himself and the choir, which responded either in monodic chant, four-part harmony, or, on high festivals, six-part polyphony:

PASTOR: "Dominus vobiscum"
CHOIR: "Et cum spiritu tuo"
Announcement of the Gospel reading by the pastor
CHOIR: "Gloria tibi, Domini"
The intonation of the Gospel by the pastor
CHOIR "Amen."[59]

After the Gospel an organ interlude was played, as was done after the Epistle.[60]

Nicene Creed. Generally on Sundays and celebrations the Nicene Creed was sung to monodic chant. The pastor began "Credo in unum Deum," the choir continuing with "Patrem omnipotentem."[61] However, Rost indicates that the Latin Creed was omitted on the following days: Christmas, New Year, Holy Week, Easter, Ascension, Pentecost, Trinity Sunday, Purification, Annunciation, Visitation, St. John the Baptist, and St. Michael.[62] Since Advent Sunday is not included among these days, the impression is that the Creed must, therefore, have been sung on that day, which is what the *Leipziger Kirchen-Andachten* appears to state on Advent Sunday: "After the Gospel the Latin Symbolum Nicenum is sung."[63] Bach was certainly somewhat confused over the issue, since in his outline of the Hauptgottesdienst for Advent Sunday,

---

56 Vopelius 1018–23; Rost fol. 44^r.

57 Many of the chorale preludes of Bach's *Orgelbüchlein* are settings of these primary church-year hymns; see Chapter 8.

58 Bach: "(6) Wird die Litaney gesungen. (7) Prael: auf den Choral"; BDok 1: 248 (No. 178); NBR 113–14 (No. 113); and BDok 1: 251 (No. 181).

59 Vopelius 1079–83. The Gospel chant formulae from Luther's *Deutsche Messe* (1526) are given in the Agenda, 105–14. Specific voices are not only designated by different melodic formulae but also by different pitches: *Vox Evangelista* (a), *Vox Personarum* (c), *Vox Christi* (f).

60 LKS 6: "Nach dem Lied singet der Priester vor dem Altar das Evangelium. Wenn darauff georgelt wird."

61 Vopelius 497–500.

62 Rost fols. 1^v, 3^r, 17^r, 23^r, 27^r, and 32^r.

63 LKA 1: 52: "Von der Advent ... Sonntag ... Nach dem Evangelio wird das lateinisches Symbolum Nicenum gesungen."

Bach's music and the Leipzig Liturgy   35

which he jotted down on the reverse of the title page of his manuscript score of Cantata 61, he first wrote "(8) Evangelium verlesen, Credo intoniret," but then crossed out "Credo intoniret."[64]

The solution to the apparent conflict is that the two churches did not always follow each other in liturgical detail. Rost makes the following illuminating note: "Wherever the [concerted] music is on Advent Sunday"—that is, the church with Choir I—"the Credo is not intoned."[65] Therefore, in the other church, with Choir II, the Credo was intoned. However, Rost records one occasion when there was a deviation from this pattern:

> Anno 1730. On the first Sunday of Advent Choir II was here at St. Thomas: The *Credo* was intoned, but the *Patrem* was not sung, but rather a piece of music was performed [a cantata] as is customary with Choir I, and thereafter the Glaube [that is, *Wir glauben* (see further below)].[66]

Somewhat later a comment was added to the note indicating that this innovation on the First Sunday in Advent was not to be continued in the future.

While there were through-composed settings of the Nicene Creed, such as Bach's *Symbolum Nicenum* (BWV 232[II]), 1748–1749, and the *Credo in unum Deum* by Giovanni Battista Bassani, for which Bach composed an intonation (BWV 1081) around the same time, there was no regular liturgical necessity that required such settings. These must have been prepared for special occasions.

Cantata. Choir I, under Bach's direction, performed the cantata composed for the particular day or celebration, with a libretto usually closely related to the Gospel of the day. As always with concerted pieces, the cantata was preceded by an improvised organ prelude so that the instrumentalists could tune, as Bach reminded himself in his liturgical outline on the score of BWV 61.[67] On Advent Sunday, when the Nicene Creed was not intoned in the church where Choir I and its instrumentalists were performing, the cantata followed almost directly from the Gospel: "After the Gospel a figural piece or a concerto is performed."[68]

The *Leipziger Kirchen-Staat* refers to Choirs I and II on ordinary Sundays: "Further there either follows concerted music or a hymn in keeping with the Gospel is sung."[69] In other words, the cantata was performed by Choir I in

---

64 BDok 1:248 No. 178).
65 Rost fol. 44r: "NB Wo den 1. Advents Sonntag die Music ist, da wird Credo nicht intoniret."
66 Rost fol. 45r: "Anno 1730. 1. adv. war der andere Chor hier zu St. Thom: Da wurde Credo intoniret, aber Patrem nicht gesung sondern es ward eine Music wie ein ander Chor pfleget gemacht, als denn d. glaube."
67 "(9) Praelud. auf die Haupt Music" (Prelude to the main music); BDok 1: 248 (No. 178); NBR 113–14 (No. 113).
68 LKA 1: 17: "Nach dem Evangelio ein Stück Figuraliter oder ein Concerto musiciret."
69 LKS 6: "Ferner wird entweder musiciret oder ein Lied nach Beschaffenheit des Evangelii [gesungen]."

36 *Liturgy*

one church while at this juncture in the other church an appropriate hymn (*Lied*) was sung by Choir II. Sicul is equally clear:

> in the two main churches, where both concerted and chorale music depend on the direction of the cantor of St. Thomas, there is on ordinary Sundays alternately contrapuntal music in one church, while in the other only German hymns are sung and the organ is played.[70]

At major festivals Choir II would sing a cantata at the same time as Choir I was performing a cantata in the other church, as Johann August Ernesti stated in a memorandum he wrote against Bach during the prefect dispute: "the Second Prefect conducts the concerted music of the Second Choir on Feast Days."[71] The custom of both Choirs I and II singing cantatas in both churches at the same time on major festivals continued until the early years of the cantorate of Johann Friedrich Doles (1715–1797), probably sometime around 1760. A later contributor to Rost's notebook, probably his successor, Christian Köpping, Thomascuster between 1739 and 1763, recorded the following under the heading "Kirchen-Music":

> In the year 17 [the actual year was never filled in] the duplicate church music hitherto customary on high festivals and other feasts at St. Thomas and St. Nicholas was abolished. Before this time there was music in both churches on the first and second days of Easter, Pentecost, and Christmas, and likewise on every other festival day. However, on a presentation of Cantor Doles ... the worshipful consistory resolved to abolish the music of Choir II.[72]

The reason for this was the difficulty of supplying instrumentalists for Choir II. Less clear is what exactly was the repertory of these concerted pieces performed by Choir II.

There is also good reason to believe that on some Sundays Choir II may well have sung one of the Bodenschatz motets at this juncture. After all, many of the motets assigned for each Sunday and celebration were selected for their affinity with the biblical pericopes, especially the Gospel, on a given day.

---

70 SiculNAL 568: "in den beyde Haupt-Kirchen/ beydes die Figural- als Choral-Music von dem Directorio des Cantoris Thomani dependiret/ wird an gemeinen Sonntagen wechselweise in der einen Kirche figuraliter musiciret/ in der andern aber nur Deutsche Lieder gesungen und die Orgel darein gespielet."

71 NBR 184 (No. 186); BDok 2: 274–75 (No. 383): "der andere Praefectus aber, die Music im andern Chor an Festtagen dirigirt." The prefect dispute is discussed in Chapter 12.

72 Rost 154ʳ:

> "Ao 17 wurde die seither gewöhnlicher doppelte Kirchen Music an den hohen und anderen Festtag zu St. Thomas und St. Nicolai abgeschafft. Bis hierher war am 1. Undanderen Feiertag zu Ostern, /Pfingsten und Weihnachten, desgleichen an jeden andern Festtage in beiden Kirchen Music ... Auf geschehenen Vorstellung des Herrn Camtoris Doles aber ... wurde vom hochlöb. Consistorio resolviret, die Music des anderen Chores abzuschaffen."

Bach's music and the Leipzig Liturgy 37

Creedal Hymn. At the conclusion of the cantata (or hymn, or motet), Luther's hymnic version of the Apostles' Creed, *Wir glauben all an einen Gott*, was sung, preceded by an organ chorale prelude.[73] While it was customary for the Nicene Creed to be omitted on some occasions, *Wir glauben* was always sung. For example, on Easter Day Rost states "the Credo is not intoned but the German Glaube is sung."[74] On many Sundays and celebrations, therefore, the cantata was effectively framed by the two creeds: before it the Latin prose of the Nicene Creed and after it the German poetry of Luther's version of the Apostles' Creed.

Sermon. The preacher entered the pulpit during the last stanza of *Wir glauben*, but the sermon was much more than preaching, having a liturgical sequence of its own, being referred to as the "Kanzeldienst" (pulpit service): (1) *Exordium* (or *Praeloquium*, or Antritts-Rede), originally a call to silent prayer, but which by this time had expanded into an introductory discourse that lasted about twenty minutes; (2) one stanza of the pulpit hymn sung by the congregation;[75] (3) silent praying of the Lord's Prayer; (4) the Gospel of the day read in German; (5) exposition of the Gospel that lasted around forty minutes, so that the *Exordium* and exposition together lasted an hour and was timed to begin at 8:00 am and end around 9:00 am.[76]

Rost noted the pulpit hymns on the various Sundays and celebrations as they occurred throughout the year, but toward the end of his notebook there is the following summary:

Pulpit Hymns that are sung through the year

Sung throughout the year on Sundays
Herr Jesu Christ, dich zu uns wend
except for:
Sung inclusive from Christmas to Purification:
Ein Kindelein so löblich.
From Easter to Ascension:
Christ ist erstanden
Ascension:
Christ fuhr gen Himmel
Pentecost:
Nun bitten wir den Heiligen Geist
Lutherfest [Reformation]:
Erhalt uns, Herr, bei deinem Wort

When the sermon had come to an end, the preacher did not leave the pulpit: he had to lead prayers of confession and absolution; the general church prayer;

---

73 LKA 1: 18; LKS 6.
74 Rost fol. 26ʳ: "Credo wird nicht intoniret & sondern der Glaube deutsche gesungen."
75 When sung with organ accompaniment, preceded by a chorale prelude.
76 LKA 1: 18; LKS 7.

38   *Liturgy*

particular intercessions; make announcements of births, marriages and deaths; exhort to almsgiving; and eventually pronounce the Pauline benediction (Philippians 4:7).[77]

The Ministry of the Word was brought to an end by the singing of an appropriate hymn, preceded by an organ chorale, except during Lent when the organ was silenced.[78]

Ministry of the Sacrament

Lord's Prayer. On most Sundays and celebrations the ministry of the Sacrament began with the Lord's Prayer chanted by the pastor standing at the altar: "Vater unser im Himmel."[79] During the penitential seasons of Advent and Lent, the Lord's Prayer was replaced by the pastor reading the paraphrase of the Lord's Prayer and admonition from Luther's *Deutsche Messe* (1526).[80] Immediately following either the chanted Lord's Prayer or the spoken paraphrase and admonition, the pastor continued by chanting the Words of Institution of the Supper, beginning "Unser Herr Jesus Christ, in der Nacht da er verraten ward,"[81] which was then followed by the distribution of Communion.

What is revealing is that on most Sundays and celebrations there was neither the liturgical dialogue—beginning *Sursum corda*—nor *Preface* and *Sanctus*; these were reserved for the major festivals of Christmas, Epiphany, Easter, Ascension, and Pentecost, as well as for some other important days, such as Trinity Sunday and the Feast of St. Michael.[82] The chants for the *Sursum corda* and *Preface* for the celebrant are given in the Saxon *Agenda*,[83] and Vopelius includes the choral responses to the *Sursum corda* in unison chant, four- and six-part settings, together with two chant settings of the *Sanctus*, and a six-part *Sanctus* by Christoph Demantius.[84] Bach composed at least three *Sanctus* settings (BWV 232[III], 237–238), while also using settings by other composers (BWV 239–241).

The texts of Vopelius's settings of the *Sanctus* reveal two forms. On the one hand, the two monophonic chant settings include both the *Osanna* and *Benedictus*.[85] On the other hand, the six-voice setting by Demantius omits

---

77 LKA 1: 18–32; LKS 7–10; see also Terry, *Bach Cantata Texts*, 38–46.

78 LKA 1: 33; LKS 10.

79 Notation given in Agenda 135.

80 Agenda 129–31.

81 Agenda 131–34 gives two different chant forms.

82 LKA 2: 236–[240]; LKA 1: 33: "An den hohen Festen aber wird eine lateinische Präfation vor der Communion von dem Priester am Altar gesungen" (On high festivals a Latin Preface is sung by the pastor at the altar before Communion).

83 Agenda 114–28.

84 Vopelius 1084–97. The six-part *Sanctus*, anonymous in Vopelius, is by Christoph Demantius, published in his part-books *Triades sioniae introitum, missarum et prosarum, quinq., sex, septem & octo vocibus* ... (Freiberg: Hoffmann, 1619).

85 Vopelius 1084–85.

Bach's music and the Leipzig Liturgy   39

these texts and ends with "pleni sunt coeli et terra gloria tua," as do other Leipzig liturgical sources,[86] as well as all three of Bach's known *Sanctus* settings (BWV 237, 238, 232[III]).[87] It is clear that both versions, with and without the *Osanna* and *Benedictus*, were sometimes used in the Leipzig churches, but what remains unclear is what were the criteria for including or omitting the *Osanna* and *Benedictus*.

On major festivals and other special days, after the *Sanctus*, as on other celebrations, the pastor chanted the Words of Institution of the Supper and then began the distribution of Communion. "After the Prayer of Consecration [Words of Institution] such as are truly penitent and have sought absolution may communicate in both kinds."[88]

At the beginning of the distribution of Communion, in the church in which Choir I was officiating, there would be concerted music: either a complete cantata, or the second part of a two-part cantata, or perhaps an aria from another cantata.[89] In a two-part cantata by Bach the second part is sometimes headed "Nach der Predigt" (After the Sermon); but this does not mean "immediately after the preaching stops," rather "after the preacher leaves the pulpit," that is, when he goes to the altar and chants the Words of Institution, after which there is the distribution, when the second part of the cantata would be heard.

When the concerted music had come to an end, it was followed by the alternation of chorale preludes and hymn-singing, as Bach noted in his outline of the liturgy on the scores of his two Advent cantatas: "(14) Preluding on [and performance of] the music [a cantata]. After the same, alternate preluding and singing of chorales until the end of the Communion, *et sic porrò* [and so on]."[90] Appropriate hymns are listed in the *Leipziger Kirchen-Staat*:

During Communion the following hymns may be sung:
1. *Jesus Christus unser Heiland*
2. *Gott sei gelobet und gebenedeiet*[91]
3. *Es wollt uns Gott genädig sein*
4. *Nun lob, mein Seel, den Herren*

---

86 LKA 2:238; *Das Privilegirte Ordentliche und Vermehrte Dreßdnische Gesang-Buch* (1724) (Dresden & Leipzig: Hekel, 1732), 466; *Das privilegirte Vollständige und vermehrte Leipziger Gesangbuch* (1734) (Leipzig: Barnbeck, 1758), 1226. This is also the implication of Rost's note for Easter Day regarding the ringing of a bell after the words "gloria tua"; Rost fol. 26ᵛ.

87 When the 1725 *Sanctus* (BWV 232[III]) was incorporated into the B-minor Mass in 1748–1749, Bach composed settings of the *Osanna* and *Benedictus*.

88 LKA 1: 35: "Nach verrichtetem Gebet und Consecration werden diejenigen, so sich durch wahre Busse und erlangte Absolution hierzu bereitet, *sub utraque specie* communiciret."

89 See Stiller, *Bach und das Leipziger gottesdienstliche Leben*, 83–84.

90 BDok 1: 248 (No. 178): "(14) Praelud. auf die Music. Und nach selbiger wechselweise praelud. v Choräle gesungen, biß die Communion zu Ende & sic porrò"; NBR 113–14 (No. 113).

91 These first two hymns are those that Luther indicated should be sung during the distribution in his *Deutsche Messe* (1526).

40   Liturgy

5. *Der Herr ist mein getreuer Hirt*
6. *Nun freuet euch, lieben Christen gmein*
7. *Wo soll ich fliehen hin*[92]

Note that Bach reminds himself that on Advent Sunday, during the distribution, congregational hymns were to be introduced by chorale preludes. Compared with the briefer chorale preludes necessary elsewhere in the service, of similar length to those of the *Orgelbüchlein* (BWV 599–644), there was more time available, and therefore the organ chorale preludes could be significantly longer during the distribution. Thus, lengthy chorale preludes, like the so-called Leipzig Chorales (BWV 651–668), or the chorale partitas and variations (BWV 766–770), were appropriate for introducing hymns sung during the distribution.

During Lent, of course, the hymn-singing would be unaccompanied, since the organ was suppressed during this penitential season. Without the organ, the task of beginning such unaccompanied singing had its difficulties, as the prefect of either Choir I or Choir II discovered in Lent 1737. A complaint to the consistory, dated 10 April 1737, stated that in the Nikolaikirche the hymn during communion, *Jesu Leiden, Pein und Tod*, was pitched too low by the *"Prae-Centor* auf dem Chor"[93] for the congregation to join in the singing.[94]

In addition to concerted music, organ chorale preludes, and congregational singing (according to the season or celebration), there was also the possibility of other music during the distribution. Thus the *Leipziger Kirchen-Staat* directed: "Depending on whether the number of communicants is large, a Latin motet may also be sung."[95] This suggests, for example, that while Choir I was performing part two of a cantata in one of the churches during the distribution, Choir II could have been singing an appropriate Latin motet at the same liturgical juncture in the other church. But if Choir I's cantata was not a two-part work, then it is possible that Choir I and Choir II could both be singing motets as *musica sub comunione*. This underlines just how important these Latin motets were in the worship of the two principal Leipzig churches during Bach's time: they could be heard at the beginning of the Hauptgottesdienst, as a musical exposition of the Gospel of the day, or as *musica sub communione*.

---

92 LKS 10. LKS 24: "Unter Communion, werden die Lieder meistens gesungen" (During Communion mostly hymns are sung).

93 BDok 2: 285–86 (No. 399). The *Prae-Centor* (prefect) at the time was Christian David Seyferth, a Thomaner between 1731 and 1739 (see B. F. Richter, "Stadtpfeifer und Alumnen der Thomasschule in Leipzig zu Bachs Zeit," BJ 4 (1907): 70 (No. 127)).

94 BDok 2: 285–86 (No. 399).

95 LKS 10: "Doch richtet man sich nach der Zahl der Communicanten, zu vorhero aber wird eine Lateinische Motete gesungen." Rost fol. 17ʳ indicates that on Palm Sunday, following "die verba coenae" (Words of Institution), that is, during the distribution, a motet is sometimes sung. LKA 1: 36: "Unter der Communion ... wird ein Stück musikiret oder eine Motete gesungen" (During Communion a [concerted] piece is performed or a motet is sung).

Bach's music and the Leipzig Liturgy   41

There were, however, still more possibilities for music during the distribution. The Saxon *Agenda* directs (following Luther):

> If at festivals the communicants are many, one may also sing the Latin Agnus Dei, &c. or German hymns (such as *Jesus Christus unser Heiland.* Item, the German Sanctus, *Jesaja dem Propheten das geschah.* Item, the [prose] Psalm [111]: *Ich dancke dem Herrn von gantzem [Herzen]* [I will thank the Lord with my whole heart]). One or more of these can be sung, and one may conclude with the following German *Agnus Dei: Christe, du Lamm Gottes.*[96]

While the prose Psalm 111 had apparently dropped out of Leipzig use,[97] Luther's German Sanctus, *Jesaja dem Propheten das geschah*, continued to be one of the hymns appropriate to be sung during the distribution of Communion.[98] That a German version of the *Sanctus* was prescribed to be sung during the distribution implies that, from time to time, a setting of the Latin *Sanctus* could be sung after the Words of Institution on a Sunday, or a celebration on which there had been no Preface leading to the *Sanctus* before the consecration. One such Sunday appears to have been the First Sunday in Advent, which, while not being a major festival, was a festival nonetheless. In his notes on the Advent season, Rost records that "When it is a feast [that is, the First Sunday in Advent] no preface [with Sanctus] is sung [at the beginning of the ministry of the Sacrament] but only the Lord's Prayer as on another Sunday."[99] Given the significance of Advent Sunday as the beginning of the new church year, a chant or choral setting of the *Sanctus* during the distribution may well have been a way to mark the special nature of the day.

Note the way in which the Saxon *Agenda* frames the music of the distribution by the choir singing the Latin *Agnus Dei* at the beginning and the congregation singing the German version, *Christe, du Lamm Gottes*, at the end. There is something of an anomaly concerning the German *Agnus Dei/Christe, du Lamm Gottes* in that while the text and melody are given in the Saxon *Agenda*, it is not found in the Leipzig *Gesangbücher*. But it is a simple repetitive text and melody that the congregations had clearly memorized, since Bach made significant use of it in his compositions.[100]

---

96 Agenda 138: "Auff die Festa, und so der Commuunicanten viel sind, mag man auch singen das lateinische Agnus Dei, &c. oder, so man der Deutschen Gesange (als Jesus Christus unser Heyland. &c. Item, das deutsch Sanctus, Esaia dem Propheten das geschah. Item, den Psalm: Ich dancke dem Herrn von gantzem etc.) eins oder mehr gesungen hat, mag man mit dem folgenden deutschem Agnus Dei beschliessen."

97 It is included in Vopelius but not in eighteenth-century Leipzig hymnals: *Dreßdnische Gesang-Buch* (1724) and *Leipziger Gesangbuch* (1734) (Leipzig: Barnbeck, 1758).

98 Vopelius, 524; *Leipziger Gesangbuch* (1734), 400.

99 Rost fol. 44ᵛ: "Wenn es gleich ein Fest ist, wird doch keine Praefation gesungen, sondern nur Vater unser wie an einem andern Sontage."

100 Bach's use of the *Agnus Dei* is discussed in Chapter 3.

42   *Liturgy*

Post-communion collects. The Communion is concluded by the pastor intoning one or more collect.[101]

Dismissal

Benediction and Benediction Response. The pastor intoned the Aaronic Benediction (Numbers 6: 24–26) from the altar[102] and the congregation responded with *Gott sei uns genädig und barmhertzig* ... (Psalm 67),[103] sung to the *Tonus peregrinus* with organ accompaniment.

Hymn. A hymn appropriate to the day or season was sung at the end of the service. On special days this final hymn linked with the beginning of the service (see Table 2.1). On the three days of Christmas (25–27 December), the Latin hymn, *Puer natus in Bethlehem*, was sung at the beginning of the Hauptgottesdienst, and its German translation, *Ein Kind geborn zu Bethlehem*, was sung at the end.[104] At the Purification, the *Leipziger Kirchen-Andachten* records that *Ex legis observantia* was sung at the beginning and the end of the morning service.[105] Similarly, the *Leipziger Kirchen-Staat* indicates that the hymn *Spiritus sancti gratia* was sung at the beginning and end of the Hauptgottesdienst on both Pentecost and Trinity.[106] As the German versions of both of these hymns—*Heut hat Marien Kindelein* and *Des Heilgen Geistes reiches gnad* respectively—were in the Vopelius *Neu Leipziger Gesangbuch*,[107] one might conclude that on these days the respective Latin hymn was sung at the beginning of the Hauptgottesdienst and its German version at the end, in the same way that *Puer natus in Bethlehem* and *Ein Kind geborn zu Bethlehem* were sung at Christmas. This raises the possibility that on Advent Sunday in some years, perhaps later in Bach's cantorate, the Latin hymn *Veni redemptor*

---

101 LKS 11; Agenda 139.

102 LKA 1: 38; LKS 11.

103 *Dreßdnische Gesang-Buch* (1724), 258; *Leipziger Gesangbuch* (1734), 89–90.

104 LKA 1:53: "An diesem Feste [Weihnachten] wird der Gottesdienst all 3 Tage (wie auch am Neuen Jahr und Heiligen drey Königen) Vor und Nachmittage mit dem lateinischen Lied angefangen, Puer natus in Bethlehem, und mit dem teutschen Ein Kind gebohrn zu Bethlehem beschlossen" (On this festival [Christmas] the worship on all three days (as well as New Year and Epiphany) before and after midday begins with the Latin hymn *Puer natus in Bethlehem* and ends with the German *Ein Kind geborn zu Bethlehem*).

105 LKA 2: 56: "Wird der Anfang und Ende des Gottesdiensts gemacht mit dem alten Hymno: Ex legis observantia" (The beginning and end of the service is made with the old hymn *Ex legis observantia*);

106 LKS 18: "Das Amt ... wird mit denen Liedern, welche zu Anfang gesungen worden, auch geschlossen" (The service [at Pentecost] that was begun with the singing of a hymn is also closed by it). LKS 27: "Der Anfang und Schluss [Trinitatisfest] ... geschiehet wie am Pfingsten mit dem Hymno: Spiritus Sancti gratia" (The beginning and end [of the Feast of the Trinity] is the same as at Pentecost with the hymn *Spiritus Sancti gratia*).

107 Vopelius 118 and 396. Vopelius also includes both *Salve festa dies* and its German translation *Willkommen sei die fröhlich Zeit*: Vopelius 287 and 288.

1	Organ prelude
2	Motet
3	Psalm(s), Prayer, Lord's Prayer, or cantata on special days
4	Hymn
5	Sermon
6	Intercessions
7	Magnificat
8	Verse and collect
9	Benediction and Benediction response
10	Hymn
11	Catechismus Examen
12	Hymn

Figure 2.2 Outline of the *Vespergottesdienst*

gentium may have been sung at the beginning of the Hauptgottesdienst and *Nun komm, der Heiden Heiland* at its conclusion.

Organ Postlude. The presumption is that because there are constant references to the role of the organ in the sources, the worship must have ended with some kind of organ postlude; however, there is no categorical statement that this was the case.

Vespergottesdienst

The afternoon Vespergottesdienst was much simpler than the morning Hauptgottesdienst and closely followed the structure of the pre-Reformation office (see Figure 2.2). Sunday Vespers was held in both the Nikolaikirche and Thomaskirche.[108]

Organ prelude. The use of the organ at the afternoon Vespergottesdienst was very much the same as at the morning Hauptgottesdienst: "The beginning is made for this purpose with the organ."[109]

Motet. The motet would be chosen from the list for each Sunday, festival, or other occasion, found in the *Leipziger Kirchen-Andachten*.[110] As in the morning service, the motet would most likely have been accompanied by the organ.[111] During the penitential seasons of Advent, Lent, and times of official mourning, the motet was replaced by the singing of Psalm 111 in Latin.[112] On major festivals, in place of the motet an appropriate Latin hymn was sung. The two choirs that had sung in each church in the morning service would attend the other church for Vespers, because Choir I would be required to repeat the cantata it had performed in the other church that morning.

108 LKA 1: 43.
109 LKA 1: 43: "Der Anfang wird hierzu abermahl gemacht mit der Orgel."
110 LKA 1: 248–306.
111 See note 34 above.
112 LKA 1: 43.

44   *Liturgy*

Psalm(s), Prayer, Lord's Prayer, or Cantata. On regular Sundays the pastor read one or two Psalms together with a long devotional prayer, and the Lord's Prayer,[113] which would be omitted on major feasts when a cantata replaced them. As described above, the weekly cantata was presented in alternation in the Hauptgottesdienst in the two churches Sunday by Sunday: Nikolaikirche this week, Thomaskirche next week, and so on. Cantatas were only included in Vespers on the major festivals and were reperformances of the cantata that had been heard in the other church that morning. On the two primary days of the three-day major festivals each cantata was presented twice on the same day. On the third day of the major festivals the cantata was only heard in the morning Hauptgottesdienst in the church where the pastor was also the Superintendent. Therefore, during Bach's cantorate these "third-day" cantatas were only usually heard in the Nikolaikirche, where Superintendent Deyling was the pastor. Here are two examples of how Bach's cantatas were presented in the two Leipzig parish churches. The first is the sequence of cantatas between the Second Sunday after Epiphany and the Annunciation in 1724:[114]

16 Jan.   Epiphany 2. *Mein Gott, wie lang, ach lange* (BWV 155)
          Thomaskirche, Hauptgottesdienst
23 Jan.   Epiphany 3. *Herr, wie du willt* (BWV 73)
          Nikolaikirche, Hauptgottesdienst
30 Jan.   Epiphany 4. *Jesu schläft, was soll ich hoffen* (BWV 81)
          Thomaskirche, Hauptgottesdienst
2 Feb.   Purification. *Erfreute Zeit im neuen Bunde* (BWV 83)
          Nikolaikirche, Hauptgottesdienst
          Thomaskirche, Vespers
6 Feb.   Septuagesima. *Nimm, was dein ist, und gehe hin* (BWV 144)
          Thomaskirche, Hauptgottesdienst
13 Feb.   Sexagesima. *Leichtgesinnte Flattergeister* (BWV 181)
          Nikolaikirche, Hauptgottesdienst
20 Feb.   Estomihi. *Jesu nahm zu sich die Zwölfe* (BWV 22)
          Thomaskirche, Hauptgottesdienst
25 Mar.   Annunciation. *Siehe, eine Jungfrau* (BWV –)
          Thomaskirche, Hauptgottesdienst[115]
          Nikolaikirche, Vespers

---

113 Psalms were assigned for each Sunday, feast day, and observance throughout the church year; see LKA 1: 44–45.

114 *Texte Zur Leipziger Kirchen-Music, Auf den Andern, dritten vierdten Sonntage nach der Erscheinung Christi, Das Fest Maria Reinigung, Und die Sonntage Septuagesimae, Sexagesimae, esto mihi, Ingleichen Auf das Fest der Verkündigung Maria, 1724.* Leipzig: Tietzen [1724]; facsimile, Stuttgart: Carus, [2000].

115 One would have expected the morning performance to have been in the Nikolaikirche, since it was the Superintendent's church. But it seems that there was another pattern of

The second example is of the six cantatas that comprise the Christmas Oratorio (BWV 248), first performed on their respective days December–January 1734–1735:[116]

25 Dec. Christmas Day. *Jauchzet, frohlocket* (BWV 248[I])
Nikolaikirche, Hauptgottesdienst
Thomaskirche, Vespers
26 Dec. St. Stephen. *Und es waren Hirten* (BWV 248[II])
Thomaskirche, Hauptgottesdienst
Nikolaikirche, Vespers
27 Dec. St. John. *Herrscher des Himmels* (BWV 248[III])
Nikolaikirche, Hauptgottesdienst
1 Jan. Circumcision/New Year. *Fallt mir Danken* (BWV 248[IV])
Thomaskirche, Hauptgottesdienst
Nikolaikirche, Vespers
2 Jan. Sunday after New Year. *Ehre sei dir, Gott* (BWV 248[V])
Nikolaikirche, Hauptgottesdienst
6 Jan. Epiphany. *Herr, wenn die stoltzen* (BWV 248[VI])
Thomaskirche, Hauptgottesdienst
Nikolaikirche, Vespers

Hymn. After the Psalms and prayers or cantata, a hymn was sung, usually the same one that had been sung as the Graduallied between the Epistle and Gospel at the morning Hauptgottesdienst.[117]

Sermon. The same "Kanzeldienst" . (pulpit service) structure of the morning Hauptgottesdienst was followed, with some minor modifications: (1) *Exordium*; (2) the same stanza of the pulpit hymn sung by the congregation; (3) silent praying of the Lord's Prayer; (4) the Epistle of the day read in German; and (5) exposition of the Epistle. Like the morning sermon, this lasted about an hour. Similarly, the morning intercessions followed, but without the notices and announcements.

Magnificat. On most Sundays the German *Magnificat, Meine Seele erhebt den Herren*, was sung by the whole congregation to the *Tonus peregrinus* melody.[118] Although strictly speaking a chant rather than a strophic chorale, it

---

alternation: since the cantata was first heard in the Nikolaikirche on the celebration of the Purification (2 February), it was then the turn of the Thomaskirche for the celebration of the Annunciation (25 March). The concerted passion at Good Friday Vespers alternated between the two churches each year in the same way.

116 *Oratorium, Welches Die heilige Weynacht über In beyden Haupt-Kirchen zu Leipzig musiciret wurde, Anno 1734*. Leipzig: Tietzen [1734]; facsimile, Stuttgart: Carus, (2000).

117 As was common elsewhere, both congregational hymnals in use in Leipzig, *Dreßdnische Gesang-Buch* (1724) and *Leipziger Gesangbuch* (1734), included an index (Zweytes Register) that listed the hymns appropriate for each Sunday, festival, and celebration of the church year. LKS 18 lists appropriate hymns to be sung at this juncture on the major festivals.

118 LKA 1: 48–49.

46 *Liturgy*

was nevertheless considered to be a chorale, and therefore was preceded by an organ chorale prelude.[119] Bach's massive organ setting of the melody "Fuga über das Magnificat" (BWV 733) perhaps suggests some special occasion. On major festivals the Latin Magnificat was sung either to unaccompanied chant,[120] or in a concerted setting, such as Bach's E-flat *Magnificat* (BWV 243a), which was composed without the Christmas chorale interpolations that were added for Christmas Day 1723, and its later manifestation, the *Magnificat* in D (BWV 243), dating sometime between 1732 and 1735.[121]

Collect. "When the music is ended the boys of the choir sing" an appropriate biblical verse of the season in German.[122] Then from the altar the pastor intoned the collect of the day, that had been used in the morning Hauptgottesdienst.

Benediction and Benediction Response. As at the morning Hauptgottesdienst, the pastor intoned the Aaronic Benediction from the altar, and the congregation responded with *Gott sei uns genädig und barmhertzig ...*, sung to the *Tonus peregrinus* melody with organ accompaniment.[123] Some have noted that toward the end of his setting of the Latin *Magnificat*, movement 10, *Suscepit Israel*—when the *Tonus peregrinus* melody is heard above the soprano, played by unison oboes—that Bach was reminding the congregation of the beginning of their German *Magnificat, Meine Seele erhebt den Herren*. That may be so, but for the Leipzig congregations in Bach's day the melody had a double significance: it was both the melody of the German *Magnificat*, sung at most services of Vespers, and also the melody of the congregational response to the Benediction that was sung at every service, morning and afternoon.

Hymn. "After the Blessing the following hymn is sung ... *Nun danket alle Gott.*"[124] This hymn was always sung at the end of Vespers, even on Good Friday after a concerted setting of the Passion, when Part 1 had been heard before the sermon, in the place of a cantata, and Part 2 after the sermon, where on other occasions the *Magnificat* would have been heard.

Catechismus Examen. On most Sundays, but not on major festivals and other celebrations and observances, Vespers was immediately followed by an exposition of part of Luther's *Small Catechism*, a copy of which was usually

---

119 Bach's Schübler chorale prelude (BWV 648) was a reworking of the fifth movement of his chorale cantata (BWV 10) composed for the Visitation, 1724.

120 Vopelius 440–43 gives a four-part faburden setting by Johann Hermann Schein, and chants in all eight tones.

121 For the background, see Robert Cammarota, "The Repertoire of Magnificats in Leipzig at the Time of J. S. Bach: A Study of the Manuscript Sources" (PhD diss., New York University, 1986).

122 LKS 19: "Wenn die zu Ende/ so wird von den Discantisten auf den Chor intoniret." Then follow the Biblical verses in German for the major festivals of the church year.

123 LKA 1: 38–39.

124 LKA 1: 50: "Nach dem Segen wird nachfolgend Lied gesungen ... Nun dancket alle Gott/&c."

bound into most hymnals. The "Examen" followed a simple structure: prayers, the reading of a section of the *Small Catechism*, an exposition of the specific section (that should not be longer than half an hour), and the singing of hymns. It appears that the hymn singing was without organ accompaniment since it was led by "der Präcentor auf dem Chor" (precentor of the choir),[125] a phrase that elsewhere designates a prefect from the Thomasschule.

Even though apparently a precentor rather than the organ led the singing of the hymns of the Catechismus Examen, Bach nevertheless put into musical form the teaching of the weekly exercise by composing organ chorale preludes on Luther's hymns on the six main sections of the *Small Catechism* in the second part of his *Clavierübung III*:

Commandments	*Dies sind die heilgen zehn Gebot* (BWV 678, 679)
Creed	*Wir glauben all an einen Gott* (BWV 680, 681)
Lord's Prayer	*Vater unser im Himmelreich* (BWV 682, 683)
Baptism	*Christ, unser Herr, zum Jordan kam* (BWV 684, 685)
Confession	*Aus tiefer Not schrei ich zu dir* (BWV 686, 687)
Lord's Supper	*Jesus Christus unser Heiland, der von uns* (BWV 688, 689)

Bach as the leader of liturgical music

As cantor, Bach was directly responsible for the music of the two Leipzig parish churches, the Thomaskirche und Nikolaikirche, as well as for the music on major festivals in the university's Paulinerkirche. This was primarily through his direction of Choir I, which sang the weekly cantata alternately in the two parish churches, but secondarily with Choir II, directed by a leading prefect appointed by him, which sang motets and occasional cantatas, again alternately, in the other parish church to the one in which Bach was directing Choir I. But he also had oversight of Choir III, which sang motets and chorales in the Neukirche, and Choir IV, which sang only chorales in the Petrikirche and Johanniskirche, each under the direction of other prefects appointed by Bach. Such a finely balanced complexity was dependent on Bach being able to rely on prefects with the necessary musicianship, something that was fraught with uncertainty after 1736.[126]

An important feature of the worship services of the Leipzig churches is the extensive use of motets in the part-books of Bodenschatz. These part-books contain almost three hundred motets by around seventy-six named composers, all composed before 1621, many of them thirty or forty years earlier. Bach rehearsed and performed many of these *stile antico* motets with Choir I alongside his cantatas, and he may also have rehearsed motets with Choir II that would be directed by a prefect in the other principal church.

---

125 LKA 1: 50–51.
126 The "Praefektenstreit" is discussed in Chapter 12.

48   *Liturgy*

And perhaps he also rehearsed motets with Choirs III and IV as part of the process of developing the singers so that they would be ready to be promoted to the next highest choir. Thus, while there have been discussions of Bach's knowledge and performance of earlier music by *stile antico* composers, these motets, fundamental in the worship of the Leipzig churches, have yet to receive the attention they deserve.

These basic liturgical services held in the Leipzig churches each week had, in addition to congregational hymns introduced by organ chorale preludes, an extraordinarily rich variety of music—from the austere unaccompanied chant sung by the single voice of the pastor or the united voices of the choir, through motets composed in the *stile antico*, many of them for double chorus, to the contrapuntal elegance of voices and instruments in Bach's concerted style.

3 Bach's Agnus Dei compositions

Historically, both Catholics and Lutherans sang the Agnus Dei approximately at the same juncture in their respective eucharistic liturgies: Catholics at the end of the Canon of the Mass, Lutherans after the prayer of consecration (*Verba Coena*). However, each of the two liturgical traditions had different theological understandings of the ancient text.

Historical background

The Agnus Dei was the last acclamation to find an established place within the early Catholic Mass, being added to the Kyrie, Gloria, Credo, and Sanctus, to form the Ordinary. Its first appearance in the Mass was probably sometime during the late seventh century, but the connection between the sacrificial Lamb, the sacrifice of Christ, and the sacrament of the altar appears to have been a characteristic of the Syrian rite of earlier centuries. Behind the Syrian rite lies the proclamation of John the Baptist: "Behold, the Lamb of God, who takes away the sin of the world" (John 1:29), which itself echoes the suffering Servant image of Isaiah 53.

In the Roman rite, when leavened bread was still being used, the fraction—the breaking of bread—could occupy some considerable time. The Agnus Dei was, therefore, introduced as a kind of fraction anthem. Unlike later usage, the basic petition, "Agnus Dei, qui tollis peccata mundi: miserere nobis," was repeated continuously until the fraction was completed. With the use of unleavened bread the fraction was terminated in a much shorter space of time and, by the twelfth century, the repetition of the basic Agnus Dei petition was reduced to three times, with "dona nobis pacem" replacing the third "miserere nobis." Although still associated with the fraction, the Agnus Dei in the medieval Mass was sung during the Pax Domini, the exchange of peace between the celebrant and other clergy, immediately following the fraction. If it was sung polyphonically, the Agnus Dei could extend into the following action of distribution. But whether or not the Agnus Dei did so, it was essentially the acclamation that accompanied the fraction, the action of the consecrating priest.

50   *Liturgy*

Lutheran eucharistic theology

In Luther's liturgical provisions, the Agnus Dei, though appearing in a position analogous to that in the Roman Mass, is isolated from the priestly action of fraction and instead is associated with the action of distribution. Indeed, Luther directs that the fraction, and everything that went along with it, should be specifically eliminated from the evangelical Mass. In the *Formula missae* of 1523, after the *Verba Coena*—the Words of Institution, all that remains of the Canon of the Mass in Luther's liturgy—Luther gives the following directions:

> After the Benedictus let the choir sing the Sanctus ... After this, the Lord's Prayer is to be said ... the prayer which follows, *Libera nos quaesumus* ... [the prayer before the fraction] is to be omitted together with all signs [of the cross] they are accustomed to make over the host and with the host over the chalice. Nor shall the host be broken or mixed into the chalice. But immediately after the Lord's Prayer shall be said, Pax Domini, which is, so to speak, a public absolution of the sins of the communicants, the true voice of the gospel announcing remission of sins ... Then let him [the celebrant] communicate, first himself and then the people, while the Agnus Dei is being sung.[1]

Since the fraction is eliminated, the Agnus Dei is therefore unambiguously associated with the distribution of Communion.

Similar instructions are found in Luther's *Deutsche Messe* of 1526. Immediately following the *Verba Coena* Luther indicates that:

> the German Sanctus [*Jesaja dem Propheten*] or the hymn *Gott sei gelobet*, or the hymn of Jan Hus, *Jesus Christus unser Heiland*, could be sung. Then ... the remainder of these hymns are sung, or the German Agnus Dei.[2]

Actually, in the *Deutsche Messe* Luther envisions that the *Verba Coena* would be divided into two parts with a two-stage distribution: first the bread, after the words "this is my body ... do this in remembrance of me," then the wine, after the words "this is my blood ... do this in remembrance of me." He therefore assigns the singing of the Agnus Dei specifically to the distribution of

---

1 Based on LW 53: 28–29; WA 12: 212–13: "Finita benedictione Chorus cantet Sanctus ... Post haec legatur oratio dominica ... omissa oratione sequenti: 'Libera nos quesumus,' ... quae fieri solent super hostiam et cum hostia super calicem, nec frangatur hostia nec in calicem misceatur. Sed statim post orationem dominicam dicatur: 'Pax domini etce.' quae est publica quaedam absolutio a peccatis communicantium, vox plane Euangelica, annuncians remissionem peccatorum ... Deinde communicet, tum sese, tum populum, interim cantetur Agnus dei."

2 Based on LW 53: 81–82; WA 19: 99: "Und die weyl singe das deudsche sanctus odder das lied: Gott sey globet oder Johans Hussen lied: Jhesus Christus unser heyland. Darnach ... singe, was ubrig ist von obgenanten liedern oder das deudsch Agnus dei."

Bach's Agnus Dei compositions 51

the words of administration, "das Blut Jesu Christi." However, the practice proved to be impractical, and while the Braunschweig *Kirchenordnung* of 1528 followed Luther's *Deutsche Messe*,[3] later Lutheran liturgical forms reverted to a single distribution after the uninterrupted *Verba Coena*. Nevertheless, the Agnus Dei remained connected with the distribution of Communion, and especially associated with the words "Das ist das Blut Jesu Christi."

Luther's reference to the German Agnus Dei in the *Deutsche Messe* is somewhat problematic, since, unlike the German Sanctus, it was not actually included within the document. However, the scholarly consensus is that Luther was referring to *Christe, du Lamm Gottes*, which must have existed in 1526, although it did not appear in print until the Braunschweig *Kirchenordnung* of 1528.[4] Since it closely parallels the Tone 1 Kyrie of the *Deutsche Messe* (see Example 3.1), it is highly likely that Luther was responsible for this German translation and its associated melody. Another factor pointing to Luther's work is that this German Agnus Dei is a further example of a principle that the reformer had enunciated in the *Deutsche Messe*, that is, of providing hymnic versions of the different parts of the Ordinary for the congregation to sing. In the course of time particular chorales came into almost universal use throughout Lutheran Germany:

Kyrie	*Kyrie, Gott Vater in Ewigkeit* (anon., Naumburg, 1537)
Gloria	*Allein Gott in der Höh sei Ehr* (Nikolaus Decius, 1522)
Credo	*Wir glauben all an einen Gott* (Luther, 1524)
Sanctus	*Jesaja dem Propheten das geschah* (Luther, 1526)
Agnus Dei	*Christe, du Lamm Gottes* (Luther, 1528), or *O Lamm Gottes, unschuldig* (Decius/Johann Spangenberg, 1522/1545)

Traditionally, the Lutheran understanding of eucharistic theology, as expressed in its confessional writings,[5] stressed the following main points: that the Lord's Supper is dependent on the community of faith not on the offering of a single priest; that individually one attends as a participant rather than an observer; that both consecrated elements (bread and wine), not just one of them, are received; that with the elements forgiveness comes as a gift and not as a reward; and all this is made effective by the presence of Christ.

---

3 *Johannes Bugenhagens Braunschweiger Kirchenordnung 1528*, ed. Hans Lietzmann (Bonn: Marcus & Webber, 1912), 130–31; Johannes Bugenhagen, *Selected Writings*, ed. Kurt K. Hendel (Minneapolis: Fortress, 2015), 1: 1370–71.

4 See *Luthers geistliche Lieder und Kirchengesänge* (Archiv zur Weimarer Ausgabe der Werke Martin Luthers, 4), ed. Markus Jenny (Cologne: Böhlau, 1985), 99.

5 Latin schools, such as the one that Bach attended in Eisenach, and the Thomasschule in Leipzig where he taught for twenty-seven years, used the same basic theological textbook, originally published in Wittenberg in 1610: Leonhard Hutter, *Compendium theologicorum* (Wittenberg: Zimmermann, 1728), text in both Latin and German. The compendium is a digest of Scripture and Lutheran confessional writings. Locus XXI deals with "De Coena Domini/Heil. Abendmahl des Herren."

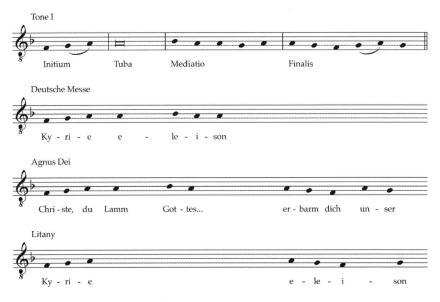

Example 3.1 Tone I Kyries and Agnus Dei

What is important to note here is that, in his liturgies, Luther did not simply alter the liturgical sequence of the Agnus Dei in the Mass, by changing it from the fraction "anthem" into a distribution hymn, but made a more radical change. What was once sung as the accompaniment to the individual act of fraction on the part of the celebrant now becomes the corporate, sung prayer of the whole congregation as it appropriated the visible signs and seals of forgiveness. The Agnus Dei that was once associated with the particular priesthood of Catholicism becomes the expression of the royal priesthood of all believers within Lutheranism. The Agnus Dei in Lutheran usage, therefore, is essentially *musica sub communione* and articulates the congregational response to the "for you" aspect of Luther's, and Lutheran, eucharistic theology. Consequently, it was sung while the words of administration were being spoken. In Leipzig, according to the *Leipziger Kirchen-Andachten* of 1694, these were:

> Take and eat this, the body of Jesus Christ, given unto death for your sins, strengthen and preserve you in true faith unto eternal live. Amen.
> Take and drink this, the blood of Jesus Christ, poured out for your sins, strengthen and preserve you in true faith unto eternal life. Amen.[6]

---

6 LKA 1: 35–36: "Nehmet hin und esset/ das ist der Leib Jesu Christi, für eure Sünde in den Tod gegeben/ der stärcke und erhalte euch im wahren Glauben zum ewigen Leben. Amen ...

But there is a further difference when the Lutheran Mass is compared with the Roman Mass from which it was developed. Unlike the Roman Mass, in which the Agnus Dei was always present as an invariable part of the Ordinary, in Lutheran usage it was one of a number of possible corporate responses to the Eucharist that could be sung at this point. The others were, of course, various eucharistic hymns. For example, the Saxon *Agenda* includes the following prescription:

> If at festivals the communicants are many, one may also sing the Latin *Agnus Dei*, &c. or German hymns (such as *Jesus Christus unser Heiland*. Item, the German *Sanctus, Jesaja dem Propheten das geschah*. Item, the [prose] Psalm [111]: *Ich dancke dem Herrn von gantzem [Hertzen]*. One or more of these can be sung, and one may conclude with the following German *Agnus Dei: Christe, du Lamm Gottes*.[7]

The Agnus Dei in Lutheran usage—whether sung in Latin or in either of the two German hymnic versions, *Christe, du Lamm Gottes*, or *O Lamm Gottes, unschuldig*—is closely associated with the personal appropriation of forgiveness, the fruit of the Passion of Jesus, "in, with, and under"[8] the eucharistic bread and wine, elements that are individually received within the corporate liturgical context, as is signified in the words "Miserare nobis," "Erbarm dich unser" (have mercy upon us).

Bach's *Estomihi* cantatas

It is against this liturgical and theological background that Bach's settings of the Agnus Dei, either Latin or German, need to be considered. It is of the greatest significance that all of them (with one possible exception) are connected with the Passion of Jesus, either in cantatas written for *Estomihi*, the Sunday before Lent, or the Passions composed for Good Friday Vespers:

Estomihi cantatas

Cantata 23	*Christe, du Lamm Gottes*
Cantata 127	*Christe, du Lamm Gottes*

Passions

Johannespassion (second version BWV 245b)	*Christe, du Lamm Gottes*
Matthäuspassion (BWV 244)	*O Lamm Gottes, unschuldig*

Nehmet hin und trincket/ das ist das Blut Jesu Christi/ für eure Sünde vergossen/ das stärcke und erhalte euch im wahren Glauben zum ewigen Leben. Amen."

7 Agenda 138, the German is given in Chapter 2, note 96.

8 Hutter, *Compendium theologicorum*, 357: "in, cum &t sub pane ac vino … In/ Mit/ und Unter Brodt und Wein."

54 *Liturgy*

In addition to specific movements in these works, there is also the *Kyrie* (BWV 233a), which later became the first movement of the Missa in F (BWV 233) that also incorporates the German Agnus Dei: *Christe, du Lamm Gottes*.

As with most of Bach's church cantatas, these two cantatas (BWV 23 and 127) were primarily composed for the eucharistic Hauptgottesdienst for a specific Sunday—in this case *Estomihi*, the Sunday before Lent—and were closely connected to the Gospel of the day. As with Bach's other cantatas, these cantatas were heard within a general eucharistic context, which was intensified if the cantata had two parts. As discussed in the previous chapter, the second part of the cantata would be performed as *musica sub communione*.[9] These general and specific eucharistic contexts frequently gave rise to numerous references and allusions to the "Abendmahl" (literally "evening meal," signifying the Lord's Supper) in the libretti of Bach's cantatas. In the *Estomihi* cantatas an intensification of such eucharistic overtones was bound to have occurred since the day was observed as a kind of Passion Sunday. The Gospel for the day, Luke 18:31–43, includes the predictive words of Jesus regarding his approaching Passion. It begins (vv. 31–33):

> Jesus took the twelve aside and said to them, "See, we are going up to Jerusalem, and everything that is written about the Son of Man by the prophets will be accomplished. For he will be handed over to the Gentiles; and he will be mocked and insulted and spat upon. After they have flogged him, they will kill him, and on the third day he will rise again."

Estomihi was the last Sunday before the season of Lent, the Gospel of the day offering a summary of the events through which the worshipers would be taken during the liturgies of Lent, until the climax was reached in the Good Friday–Easter event. What was celebrated at every Eucharist increased in significance during this period of the church's year. At every Hauptgottesdienst, the fruit of the Passion of Jesus—the forgiveness of sin—was extended to the communicants. The meaning of the Eucharist was therefore intensified by the concentration on the details of the Passion throughout Lent and Holy Week and especially on Good Friday, but it was significantly anticipated on *Estomihi*, immediately before this liturgical and spiritual pilgrimage began. The German Agnus Dei, *Christe, du Lamm Gottes*, with its identification of Jesus as the Passover Lamb sacrificed for the sins of the world, assumed a particular significance on *Estomihi*.

The four cantatas that Bach is known to have composed for *Estomihi* (BWV 22, 23, 127, and 159) are among his most profound compositions. As Renate and Lothar Steiger have shown,[10] Bach explores in each of these cantatas different aspects of this Passion Sunday in many ingenious ways. The concern

9 See Chapter 2, page 39.
10 Lothar Steiger & Renate Steiger, *Sehet! Wir gehn hinauf gen Jerusalem. Johann Sebastian Bachs Kantaten auf den Sonntag Estomihi* (Göttingen: Vandenhoeck & Ruprecht, 1992).

Bach's Agnus Dei compositions 55

here is with just two of these cantatas and the way in which Bach employs the German Agnus Dei, *Christe, du Lamm Gottes*, in them.

Estomihi was an important day for Bach personally, since it was on this Sunday in February 1723 that he performed two cantatas (BWV 22 and 23) in Leipzig as part of his bid to become the Thomaskantor. If he had not done so on this Sunday, he would have had to wait almost two months for the next opportunity to perform concerted music, since *Estomihi* was the last Sunday before the penitential season of Lent, during which time there would be no instrumental music in Leipzig.[11] The next time concerted music would have been heard in the *De tempore* cycle of the church year would have been at Vespers on Good Friday with a performance of a Passion. Thus, there was an important connection between *Estomihi* and Good Friday: the one anticipated the Passion and the other presented the events of the Passion in detail. In between was the period of meditation on the sufferings and death of Jesus for which only simpler forms of music were employed in public worship.

Each of the two cantatas performed at the Hauptgottesdienst in the Thomaskirche on 7 February 1723 expounded one of the two main themes in the *Estomihi* Gospel pericope. Before the sermon, Cantata 22 was performed, *Jesus nahm zu sich die Zwölfe* (the opening words of the Gospel), a musical meditation on the words of Jesus about his impending Passion, Crucifixion, and Resurrection. During the distribution of Communion, Cantata 23, *Du wahrer Gott und Davids Sohn*, was heard. Here the focus is on the blind man who hears the noise of the crowd around Jesus passing by, on its way to Jerusalem, who calls out: "Jesus, Son of David, have mercy on me."

It is in this second cantata (BWV 23) that Bach made use of *Christe, du Lamm Gottes*. As can be found elsewhere in Bach's vocal music, there are several layers of meaning in this use of the German Agnus Dei. First, there is the connection with the blind man in the Gospel pericope who cries out "Have mercy on me." By his use of *Christe, du Lamm Gottes*, with its repeated prayer for mercy, "Erbarm dich unser," Bach was involving each member of the worshiping congregation in the petition of the blind man. Second, by his use of the German Agnus Dei at this juncture, Bach was drawing specific attention to the Eucharist. He does so by encouraging a comparison: on the one hand, there was the blind man who received mercy—the healing of his blindness—from Jesus, who was standing before him; on the other hand, there were the worshipers who were about to receive mercy—forgiveness of sins— from Christ, who was present in the eucharistic action.

Cantata 23 begins with a duet that is a long and poignant prayer for mercy and is linked both to the blind man's cry for mercy in the Gospel for the day and to the liturgical prayer for mercy, the Agnus Dei. Although there is no direct reference, either textually or musically, in the movement, the eucharistic connection is nevertheless implied. In the following recitative the connection

---

11 The one exception was the Feast of the Annunciation on 25 March, which was part of the *Sanctorale* cycle rather than *De tempore*.

56 Liturgy

becomes obvious in the profound conjunction of parallel ideas, one verbal and the other nonverbal. The text is based on the words of wrestling Jacob in Genesis 32:26: "I will not let you go until you bless me." Here the tenor sings on behalf of the attending congregation: a request to the Savior not to leave without imparting his blessing. The nonverbal parallel thought is expressed by the unison oboes and first violins, who together play, in augmentation, the first melodic line of the German Agnus Dei, "Christe, du Lamm Gottes, der trägst die Sünd der Welt, erbarm dich unser," though the words are not heard, only the melody. With this use of the German Agnus Dei Bach particularizes the desire for health and salvation expressed in the recitative.

The third movement, a chorus in rondo form, begins with the words of Psalm 145:15: "The eyes of all look to you, O Lord, and you give them their meat in due season." This is a text that was frequently interpreted eucharistically in homiletic and devotional literature: God feeds the faithful with the body and blood of Jesus Christ. But here it is also an allusion to the blind man, who can now see. What is significant is that the recurring refrain is built upon a bass line that is constructed from the opening phrase of *Christe, du Lamm Gottes*. In another context one might be somewhat skeptical about such a connection, since the bass line appears to be a simple rising figure. But the movement follows on from the preceding recitative in which the *Christe, du Lamm Gottes* melody is clearly heard, played by unison violins and oboes. The two movements are in the same key; therefore, there is an aural connection between them in that the same melodic sequence is heard first at regular pitch in the recitative, and then an octave lower in the following chorus. The expectation for this melodic sequence in the continuo was set up in the preceding recitative. *Christe, du Lamm Gottes* comprises a threefold repetition of a simple melodic phrase (see Example 3.1). In the recitative this phrase is heard only once, played by violins and oboes. The worshipers, having heard this melodic phrase in the recitative, therefore would be expecting to hear its repetition. Bach capitalizes on this expectation, but instead of a simple repeat uses the opening figure as the foundation on which to build this reflective chorus with its markedly distinct eucharistic overtones (see Example 3.2). The text of Psalm 145:15 was interpreted as God's offer of mercy in the eucharistic meal, and this is intensified by the use of the first occurrence of the threefold repeated *Christe, du Lamm Gottes* melody. It also confirms that Bach knew that this second audition cantata was to be heard during the distribution of Communion, as *musica sub communione*, when the German Agnus Dei was frequently sung. The recitative and aria, taken together, thus exhibit an intertwining of theological, liturgical, and musical concerns in a creative tension.

In the original autograph score[12] the words "Il-Fine" are entered at the end of the third movement. This is a sign that these three movements had been composed in Cöthen for the trial audition in Leipzig. The fourth movement,

---

12 D-B Mus.ms. Bach P 69.

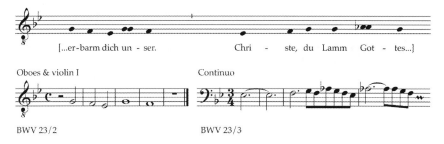

Example 3.2 Transition from Recitative to Chorus (BWV 23/2–3)

Christe, du Lamm Gottes, was, therefore, added as an afterthought—whether it was Bach's own decision, or whether it was brought to his attention that a concluding chorale would be expected, remains unknown. What is clear is that Bach prepared the movement after his arrival in Leipzig for the audition. What is not so clear is whether the movement was newly composed in Leipzig[13] or was a reworking of an earlier composition.[14] I am inclined to the latter: that he brought with him a score of the movement, which most likely had been composed during his Weimar years, from which he personally prepared most of the vocal and instrumental parts in Leipzig.[15]

Bach's use of this *Christe, du Lamm Gottes* chorale movement is quite brilliant in that it makes explicit what is implicit in the three preceding movements. In the first three movements only the melody has been heard from within the polyphonic texture; now the complete German Agnus Dei, both text and melody, is heard. Each time the melodic line of the liturgical prayer is heard, it is given a different musical treatment. The first is a slow Adagio in which the voices are treated mostly homophonically. The orchestral interludes that divide the phrases of the melody employ a falling chromaticism that is akin to the ground bass of the Crucifixus in the B-minor Mass.

The second time the melody is heard, the tempo changes from Adagio to Andante, and the mood becomes more confident. It is a basic cantus firmus setting in which the melody appears in a three-voice canon: soprano, oboes, and violin 1.[16] In some of Bach's organ works, such as the Canonic Variations

---

13 Ulrich Leisinger, "Die zweite Fassung der Johannes-Passion von 1725," in *Bach in Leipzig—Bach und Leipzig*, ed. Ulrich Leisinger, Leipziger Beiträge zur Bach-Forschung 5 (Hildesheim: Olms, 2002), 35–40.
14 Martin Geck, "Bachs Probestück," in *Quellenstudien zur Musik: Wolfgang Schmieder zum 70. Geburtstag*, ed., Kurt Dorfmüller (Frankfurt: Peters, 1972), 55–68; Christoph Wolff, "Bach's Audition for the St. Thomas Cantorate: The Cantata 'Du wahrer Gott und Davids Sohn,'" in Christoph Wolff, *Bach: Essays on His Life and Music* (Cambridge, MA: Harvard University Press, 1991), 128–40.
15 D-B Mus.ms. Bach St. 16; see Wolff, "Bach's Audition for the St. Thomas Cantorate," 132.
16 Here Bach follows in an earlier tradition of Mass composition, that includes composers such as Josquin and Palestrina, in which the middle section of the Agnus Dei is set as a three-voice

58 *Liturgy*

on *Vom Himmel hoch* (BWV 769), and some of the chorale preludes of the *Orgelbüchlein* and *Clavierübung III*, the composer used a canon, the strictest form of counterpoint, to symbolize the Law (in the theological sense). When a canon appears in a Christological context, as here, it alludes to Christ's fulfillment of the Law. In this chorale movement the three-voice canon appears to be a reference to the Lamb who fulfilled the demands of the Law by dying on the cross in the place of sinners.

The setting of the final petition of the Agnus Dei is constructed around the melody in the soprano, which is given out phrase by phrase, with some imitative counterpoint in the lower voice parts and an independent part for oboes. The lack of tension at the end of the German Agnus Dei underlines the prayer for peace: "Gib uns deinen Frieden."

There is, therefore, a theological sequence expounded in each of the three settings of the basic melody: in the first Adagio setting, mercy—forgiveness—is requested; in the second Andante setting, mercy is accomplished in the suffering and death of Jesus; and in the third, the peace of forgiveness is received. The eucharistic connections are obvious, since in the Leipzig liturgy this cantata was heard during the distribution of Communion, *musica sub communione*.

The following year, 1724, Bach used both of these cantatas again for *Estomihi*,[17] but in 1725 he composed a new cantata for that Sunday: *Herr Jesu Christ, wahr Mensch und Gott* (BWV 127), a chorale cantata based on Paul Eber's hymn dating from the middle of the sixteenth century. The opening choral movement is a masterpiece of contrapuntal architecture, interweaving no less than three different chorale melodies within its texture. The cantus firmus, the primary chorale melody, heard in augmentation in the soprano,[18] is a modified form of the 1551 French-Genevan tune for Psalm 127.[19] The opening line of a second chorale melody is heard, slightly modified, several times in the continuo throughout the movement: *Herzlich tut mich verlangen*,[20] associated with Paul Gerhardt's *O Haupt voll Blut und Wunden*, otherwise known as the Passion Chorale. This was certainly appropriate here since *Estomihi* was observed as a Passion Sunday. The third chorale melody is the German Agnus Dei: *Christe, du Lamm Gottes*. Its use in this opening chorus is similar to that of the second movement of Cantata 23, the recitative above which oboes and violins play the first strophe of the chorale melody. Here in the first movement of Cantata 127, beginning in the first measure, segments

---

canon; see, for example, Zoe Saunders, "Hidden Meaning in Agnus Dei Canons: Two Cases from the Alamire Manuscripts," *Early Music* 44 (2017): 593–606.

17 See Alfred Dürr, *The Cantatas of J. S. Bach with their Librettos in German-English Parallel Text*, rev. and trans. Richard D. P. Jones (Oxford: Oxford University Press, 2005), 242.

18 And in diminution in almost every measure as it is passed from voice to voice and instrument to instrument.

19 Zahn 127a.

20 Zahn 5385a.

of the *Christe, du Lamm Gottes* melody are heard successively at different pitches in the orchestral accompaniment: violins first, then oboes, then flutes, then back to violins. This is another example of Bach employing various levels of meaning. By his use of the German Agnus Dei, with its petition for mercy, "Erbarm dich unser," he simultaneously draws attention to the prayer for mercy of the blind man in the Gospel pericope, and also to the Passion of Jesus, which lies at the heart of the Eucharist.

Agnus Dei combined with Kyrie

In the late 1730s Bach created four settings of the Missa (Kyrie and Gloria) in which the movements were adapted from a number of his cantatas. The Kyrie of the Missa in F (BWV 233) is an interesting intertwining of the first and last texts of the Ordinary of the Mass: Kyrie and Agnus Dei (combined with the Kyrie of the Litany)—liturgical prayers with similar petitions: "Kyrie/Christe eleison," "Christe ... erbarm dich unser" (Lord/Christ have mercy upon us). In the five-part texture the three-voice fugal Kyrie is framed by the melody of the German Agnus Dei, *Christe, du Lamm Gottes*, assigned to horns and oboes, and by the Kyrie from the Litany in the vocal bass and continuo. Only the text "Kyrie–Christe–Kyrie eleison" from Luther's *Deutsche Messe* (1526) and Luther's *Deutsche Litanie* (1529) are heard.

Since both Catholic and Lutheran theologians interpreted the liturgical Kyrie (ninefold or threefold) as a statement of Trinitarian theology,[21] the Trinity is here formally symbolized in the three-sectioned, three-voiced fugal counterpoint (SAT). The fugal theme of Christe eleison is an almost exact inversion of the theme of Kyrie I, and Kyrie II combines both themes (Kyrie I and Christe) in a double fugue. This is as much a theological statement as it is a musical one. According to the Nicene Creed, the Son is "begotten from the Father" and the Holy Spirit proceeds "from the Father and the Son." Thus, the fugal theme of Christe eleison is an inversion of the first Kyrie, and in the final Kyrie the "Father" and "Son" fugal themes are intertwined, thus creating a remarkable movement in which the theological statement is created by the musical form (see Example 3.3).

Among later manuscript sources of the movement there is a score,[22] once owned by a successor of Bach in Leipzig, Johann Friedrich Doles (1715–1797), and a set of parts[23] in the hand of Johann Adam Hiller (1728–1804), Doles's successor as Thomascantor, indicating that the movement was in the

---

21 For example, along with other contemporary hymnals, Vopelius includes the texts of the Missa, Kyrie, and Gloria, under the rubric "Von der Heiligen Dreyfaltigkeit"; Vopelius 416. The choraliter Kyrie and Gloria are headed: "Missa, Oder: Das Kyrie Eleison/ neben dem was die alte Kirche zu Lob der Heiligen Drey-Einigkeit weiter hinzu gethan hat" (Missa, or: Kyrie eleison, or what the early church added in praise of the Holy Trinity); Vopelius 421.

22 D-B Mus.ms. Bach P 70.

23 D-B Mus.ms. Bach St 647.

60 *Liturgy*

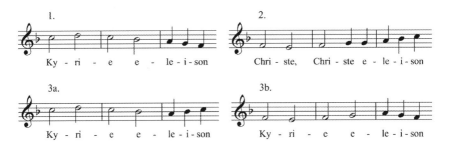

Example 3.3 Fugal subjects of BWV 233a/233

repertory of the Thomanerchor during the second half of the eighteenth century. But they were not copied from Bach's manuscript score of the Missa in F dating from the late 1730s,[24] because of contrapuntal infelicities not found in the Kyrie of the Missa. For example, between the tenor and bass of the score, in measures 16–17, there are hidden parallel octaves that are absent from the Kyrie of the Missa. Hiller saw the error and wrote in the manuscript score "Ey! Ey! Vater Bach!"[25] (which might be translated "Tut! Tut! Father Bach!"). These later sources, therefore, bear witness to an earlier manifestation of the movement, which was later corrected by Bach, perhaps when he incorporated it into the Missa in F. The contrapuntal insecurity points to an original composition sometime early in Bach's career, most likely during his early Weimar years.[26]

In the Missa the three-sectioned, three-voiced fugal Kyrie–Christe–Kyrie is heard against the complete *Christe, du Lamm Gottes* melody assigned to two horns and two oboes, with *colla parte* strings and continuo. But the earlier version is entirely vocal (S^{I}S^{II}ATB), with continuo, in which soprano I sings both the text and melody of *Christe, du Lamm Gottes*. This suggests that the independent movement was originally composed as a complex setting of the German Agnus Dei, intended as *musica sub communione*, rather than as an isolated setting of the Kyrie. If so, this means that in Bach's oeuvre there are two settings of *Christe, du Lamm Gottes* (BWV 23/4 and BWV 233a) that appear to have been composed during Bach's Weimar period and intended as *musica sub communione*.

---

24 D-B Mus.ms. Bach P 15.
25 BDok 3: 623 (Anhang No. 4).
26 Because of similarities between BWV 233a with BWV 106 and BWV 150, together with the penitential nature of the three liturgical items that are combined in the movement (Kyrie, Litany, and the German Agnus Dei), Markus Rathey suggests that it was originally composed for Good Friday 1708; Markus Rathey, "Zur Datierung einiger Vokalwerke Bachs in den Jahren 1707 und 1708," BJ 92 (2006): 73–78, 92.

Estomihi and Good Friday

As discussed above, there were strong connections between *Estomihi* and Good Friday. On the Sunday before Lent the Gospel of the day contained the prediction of the Passion. On Good Friday the focus was on the Passion itself. In between was the season of Lent, which was marked by simple music and penitential prayers, notably the Litany. In 1725 Bach emphasized the season of Lent in a significant way by connecting *Estomihi* with Good Friday, and did so with the German Agnus Dei: *Christe, du Lamm Gottes*.[27]

At Good Friday Vespers in 1725 the second version of the *Johannespassion* (BWV 245) was performed. This was the year when Bach was composing primarily chorale cantatas, and some of the most significant changes made to the work, which had been first performed the previous year, 1724, were the use of extended chorale movements at the beginning and end. Instead of the opening chorus "Herr, unser Herrscher," this second, 1725, version of the *Johannespassion* began with the chorale fantasia *O Mensch, bewein dein Sünde gross*, and at the end the extended chorale *Christe, du Lamm Gottes*, both most likely originally composed in Weimar. The final chorale was, of course, the one that had concluded the cantata *Du wahrer Gott und Davids Sohn* (BWV 23) when it was performed in Leipzig on *Estomihi* in 1723 and again on the same Sunday the following year. By using this movement at the end of the *Johannespassion* in 1725, Bach ensured that the whole of the Lenten season in Leipzig that year was musically framed by the familiar melody *Christe, du Lamm Gottes* and its prayer for mercy. At the beginning of this season of discipline and simplicity, the melody of this German Agnus Dei was heard from within the texture of the first movement of Cantata 127. When Lent had come to a close, at the end of the Good Friday Vespers performance of the second version of the *Johannespassion*, the same chorale was heard. Thus, in 1725 Bach used the familiar *Christe, du Lamm Gottes* melody to bridge the whole season of Lent, with its focus on prayer for mercy and peace, which is also the substance of the Agnus Dei.

Whenever the Agnus Dei was heard by the Leipzig congregations, it must have brought to mind both its liturgical function (the sung prayer during the distribution of Communion), and its eucharistic meaning (the mercy of forgiveness received "in, with, and under" the bread and wine). This was known to Bach and appears to lie behind his use of the other Agnus Dei, *O Lamm Gottes, unschuldig*, in the opening chorus of the *Matthäuspassion*. In Vopelius's *Neu Leipziger Gesangbuch*, *O Lamm Gottes, unschuldig* is included under the rubric "Von Leiden und Sterben Jesu Christi" (On the Passion and Death of

---

27 For an expansive study of this connection, see Eric Chafe, *J. S. Bach's Johannine Theology: The St. John Passion and the Cantatas for Spring 1725* (New York: Oxford University Press, 2014).

62 *Liturgy*

Jesus Christ), where it appears under the heading "Das Agnus Dei."[28] The *Leipziger Kirchen-Staat* indicates that it is the prescribed hymn to be sung "nach der Predigt" ("after the sermon"), that is, immediately before the beginning of the ministry of the Sacrament at the eucharistic Hauptgottesdienst on Good Friday.[29] *O Lamm Gottes, unschuldig* therefore shared the same eucharistic associations as *Christe, du Lamm Gottes*, and perhaps more intensively so because of this use on Good Friday, the day of the Passion.

O Lamm Gottes, unschuldig is not a direct translation of the Agnus Dei but rather a troped version; the simple petitions of the liturgical Agnus Dei are expanded to include reference to the Crucifixion in terms of the imagery of Isaiah 53. The libretto of the first movement of the *Matthäuspassion* is, in a sense, a troped version of the first stanza of *O Lamm Gottes, unschuldig*. The additional material that the librettist Picander introduces is developed from the parable of the wedding feast of Matthew 25:1–13: "Kommt, ihr Töchter, helft mir klagen, Sehet ... den Bräutigam ... als wie ein Lamm!" ("Come, you Daughters [of Zion], help me lament, look ... at the Bridegroom ... just like a lamb!"). When the mixed metaphor of the Bridegroom as the Lamb has been acknowledged, the chorale begins: *O Lamm Gottes, unschuldig* (BWV 244/1 m. 30).

The reference to the imagery of the familiar parable has very strong eucharistic overtones, since it was customary to interpret the wedding feast as symbolic of the eucharist. For example, Philipp Nicolai's (1556–1608) hymn *Wachet auf* is based on the parable, and in the last three lines of the second stanza there is a direct eucharistic statement:

Wir folgen all	We follow all
zum Freudensaal	to the joyful hall
und halten mit das Abendmahl.[30]	and share the Sacrament.

The biblical images from Matthew 25, together with the use of the German version of the Agnus Dei, *O Lamm Gottes, unschuldig*, create a strong eucharistic hermeneutic in this opening movement. It presents the whole of the Passion, in its unfolding details, from the perspective of the Eucharist, the means by which communicants receive the fruit of the Passion.

Bach's superlative music for this opening movement gives this eucharistic hermeneutic an audible form. The emphatic way in which the chorale melody of this German Agnus Dei rings out from the ripieno choir, with organ

---

28 Vopelius 173–75. Both *Christe, du Lamm Gottes* and *O Lamm Gottes, unschuldig* are included under this rubric in Georg Christian Schemelli's *Musicalische Gesang-Buch* (Leipzig, 1736) for which Bach was musical editor.

29 LKS 25; Rost 23ᵛ.

30 There is a striking similarity between the opening melodic lines of the two hymns *Wachet auf* and *O Lamm Gottes, unschuldig*; compare the melodies as given in BWV 140/7 and BWV 244/1.

Bach's *Agnus Dei compositions* 63

support, against the double chorus and double orchestra, is breathtaking and unmistakable. By repeating the opening questions and answers of the libretto at the end of the movement, Bach reinforces the view that the Bridegroom is the Lamb, to whom the prayer of the Agnus Dei is addressed. In the final three measures of this opening movement the words "als wie ein Lamm" are repeated twice in the voice parts of the first chorus (the tenors actually repeat the words three times), and they are joined by the voices of the second chorus for the final cadence to make the emphatic statement: "als wie ein Lamm!" It is only after this powerful statement has been made that the biblical narrative of the Passion can begin.

This magnificent movement is the aural equivalent of a visual image found in the altarpieces of the Wittenberg artist Lucas Cranach and his school. These altarpieces provided the visual background to the celebration of the Lutheran Eucharist. One of the finest examples is in the Stadtkirche in Weimar, a painting that Bach must have known. In this altarpiece, begun by Lucas Cranach the Elder (1472–1553) and completed by his son, the center panel is of the Crucifixion. At the foot of the cross on which Christ hangs is a lamb holding a banner of victory. To the right of the cross stand three people: on the outside is Martin Luther, who points to the verse "The blood of Jesus Christ cleanses us from all sin" (1 John 1:8); in the middle is Lucas Cranach the Elder on whose head falls the blood that arches from the side of the crucified Christ; nearest the cross is John the Baptist, who with one hand points to the Savior on the cross, and with the other points to the lamb at the foot of the cross—a visual representation of the words of the Baptist, "Behold, the Lamb of God, who takes away the sin of the world" (John 1:29). Thus, this visual Agnus Dei interprets both the cross that stands behind it and the Eucharist that is celebrated at the altar standing in front of Cranach's altarpiece. Similarly, Bach's massive opening chorus of the *Matthäuspassion*, which also depicts the Agnus Dei, provides the hermeneutic by which the Passion that is about to unfold is to be understood, that is, as unmistakably linked to the Eucharist.

The Agnus Dei in the B-minor Mass

The last two movements of the B-minor Mass (BWV 232^{IV}) together form a setting of the Latin Agnus Dei. Although Bach was working on these movements during the last months of his life, sometime between August 1748 and October 1749,[31] both are parodies of music he had composed earlier. The first is a recomposition of the alto aria, "Ach, bleibe doch," from the *Ascension*

---

31 See Yoshitake Kobayashi, "Zur Chronologie der Spätwerke Johann Sebastian Bachs, Kompositions- und Aufführungstätigkeit von 1736 bis 1750," BJ 74 (1988): 66; see also Gerhard Herz, "Yoshitake Kobayashi's Article, 'On the Chronology of the Last Phase of Bach's Work, Compositions and Performances: 1736 to 1750': An Analysis with Translated Portions of the Original Text," *BACH* 21/1 (1990): 3–25.

64   *Liturgy*

Oratorio (BWV 11/4), although it is highly likely that Bach worked from his original composition, the aria "Entfernet euch, ihr kalten Herzen" from a lost wedding cantata composed in 1725.[32] There appear to be at least two reasons for Bach's choice of this music for the Agnus Dei. First, the chromaticism of its basic theme has similarities with the fugal subject of the Kyrie with which the whole Mass begins. Second, in the *Ascension Oratorio* the text of the aria is a prayer that the risen Christ will remain present with the worshiper:

Ach, bleibe doch, mein liebstes Leben,	Ah do stay, my dearest Life,
Ach, fliehe nicht so bald von mir!	Ah, do not flee so soon from me![33]

Given the specific eucharistic context of the Agnus Dei, and given also particular Lutheran eucharistic theology in which the presence of Christ in the sacrament is fundamental, it is understandable that Bach was drawn to this poignant aria for his setting of the Latin Agnus Dei. Although the movement is a parody, Bach nevertheless lavished an extraordinary amount of care in recomposing the original *da capo* movement of 79 measures into a through-composed movement of just 49 measures.[34] But it is not a simple reworking of the earlier form; almost a quarter of this movement was newly composed music. Table 3.1 indicates some of the complexities of this short but profound movement.

In the table the complete text is given in a vertical arrangement, rather than in a consecutive horizontal sequence, in order to demonstrate the text repetitions. The text set to parodied music appears in italic; the text set to newly composed music appears in bold. This reveals that the new material was created for the threefold statement of the invocation, "Agnus Dei," with its relative clause "qui tollis peccata (mundi)," of the liturgical prayer. There are various symmetrical paradigms in this compressed counterpoint, such as the ritornelli that occur at the beginning, middle, and end, but the basic symmetry of the newly composed measures is perhaps the most significant. In measures 9–12, and again in measures 31–33, the first and third statements of "Agnus Dei, qui tollis peccata (mundi)" by the alto, are answered each time by violins in canon at the fifth below. These two-part canons effectively frame the second statement, "Agnus Dei, qui tollis peccata mundi," which is echoed by the violins in imitative counterpoint. This two-part texture recalls the central movement of the *Gloria*: Domine Deus ... Agnus Dei (BWV 232[1]/8), a duet that simultaneously sets two related texts: the tenor sings, "Domine Deus, Rex coelestis, Deus Pater omnipotens," against which the soprano sings, "Domine Fili unigeniti Jesu Christe altissime."

---

32 See Alfred Dürr, "'Entfernet euch, ihr kalten Herzen': Möglichkeiten und Grenzen der Rekonstruktion einer Bach-Arie," *Die Musikforschung* 39 (1986): 32–36.

33 Dürr, *The Cantatas of J. S. Bach*, 337.

34 See Christoph Wolff, "The Agnus Dei of the B Minor Mass: Parody and New Composition Reconciled," Wolff, *Bach: Essays*, 332–39.

Bach's Agnus Dei compositions 65

Table 3.1 Textual and musical structure of the Agnus Dei in the B-minor Mass

Ritornello (A+B)	*mm. 1–8*	
Agnus Dei qui tollis peccata mundi	mm. 9–12	Canon
qui tollis peccata	mm. 13–22	
peccata mundi, miserere nobis		
miserere nobis		
miserere nobis		
qui tollis peccata		
peccata mundi, miserere nobis.		
Ritornello (A)	*mm. 23–26*	
Agnus Dei qui tollis peccata mundi	mm. 27–30	Imitation
Agnus Dei qui tollis peccata	mm. 31–33	Canon
qui tollis peccata	mm. 34–44	
peccata mundi		
qui tollis peccata *miserere*		
qui tollis peccata *miserere nobis*		
miserere nobis		
miserere nobis		
miserere nobis		
Ritornello (B)	*mm. 45–49*	

The two-part writing of the duet is obviously symbolic of the relationship of the Second Person of the Godhead to the First. Since the Domine Deus and Agnus Dei movements (BWV 232^I/8 and ^{IV}/4) are linked in their references to the Second Person of the Godhead as the Agnus Dei, the Lamb of God, the two-part canons and imitative counterpoint, newly composed for the penultimate movement of the B-minor Mass, share the same symbolism, that is, the identification of the Lamb of God as the Son of God, who is present in the sacrament of the altar.

Table 3.1 also reveals the unmistakable stress of the verbal repetitions, especially of the words "peccata" and "miserere nobis." Here there are links with the Confiteor of the Credo (BWV 232^{II}/8): "Confiteor unum baptisma in remissionem peccatorum" ("I confess one baptism for the remission of sins"). As Christoph Wolff has pointed out,[35] these are the only two movements in the whole B-minor Mass that employ flattened keys. The Agnus Dei is the only complete movement in a flat key (G minor). Toward the end of the F-minor Confiteor there is not only a change of tempo to Adagio but also an abrupt transposition from sharps to flats that occurs significantly on the word "peccatorum" (mm. 120–22). As explored in Chapter 2, the liturgical Agnus Dei in Lutheran usage accompanied the distribution of Communion,

35 Wolff, "The Agnus Dei of the B Minor Mass," 339.

66 *Liturgy*

the action by which the individual worshiper received forgiveness in the consecrated bread and wine. Baptism is the other sacrament of forgiveness. Therefore, the two sacraments that share a theological unity are also musically linked by Bach in the flattened key relationships of these two movements.

For the final movement, Dona nobis pacem, the final petition of the Agnus Dei, Bach reused music that he had included in an earlier section of the B-minor Mass, the Gratias agimus tibi of the Gloria in excelsis Deo (BWV 232^1/7). This movement was itself a parody of the second movement of Cantata 29, *Wir danken dir*. There is a significant connection between the two movements in the cantata and the Mass, since "Gratias agimus tibi" ("We give thanks to you") is the Latin equivalent of the German "Wir danken dir." In his *Deutsche Messe* Luther directed that at the end of the Eucharist, before the Benediction, there should be a thanksgiving collect. This collect was taken over into many Lutheran liturgies, including the Saxon *Agenda*. It began with the words "Wir danken dir, allmächtiger Herr Gott, daß du uns durch diese heilsame Gabe erquicket hast" ("We give thanks to you, Almighty Lord God, that through these salutary gifts you have refreshed us"). The second movement of Cantata 29 began: "Wir danken dir, Gott, wir danken dir und verkündigen deine Wunder" (Psalm 75:2: "We thank you, O God, we thank you and declare your wonders"). Thus, it may have been this association of similar expressions of thanksgiving in Luther's post-Communion collect, in constant use in Leipzig, and Psalm 75:2, which Bach had set as the second movement of Cantata 29, that gave him the idea of repeating this "thanksgiving" music for the Dona nobis pacem, music he had used earlier in the Gloria. In these two final movements of the Mass, Bach therefore echoes both the Kyrie, in the chromaticism of the Agnus Dei, and the Gloria, in the reuse of the Gratias agimus of the first part of the Mass for Dona nobis pacem.

4 Bach's parody process

From cantata to *Missa*

For a long time the small group of Lutheran Masses (BWV 233–236) were generally dismissed as works that Bach hastily put together from earlier cantata movements. But Christoph Wolff's seminal doctoral dissertation on the *stile antico* in Bach's late works in large measure was responsible for the reassessment of these works in the context of the other Latin compositions of Bach's later years.[1] These Lutheran Masses were closely connected to Bach's growing interest in the Mass compositions of Italian composers. The parodies he used to create them were by no means cursory cut-and-paste substitutions, but were thoughtful and sophisticated adaptations of earlier compositions.[2] Bach evidently wished to preserve what he considered to be some of his finest music—not only in the four Masses but also other works, such as the Christmas Oratorio and the B-minor Mass, which are also made up of parodied movements[3]—and the resulting design shows the composer's very deliberate decisions.

A detailed investigation of the four Lutheran Masses will usually reveal one of two circumstances: on the one hand, if the individual movements are

---

1 Christoph Wolff, *Der Stile Antico in der Musik Johann Sebastian Bachs: Studien zu Bachs Spätwerk* (Wiesbaden: Steiner, 1968).

2 Concerning the general question of parody in Bach's music, see especially Hans-Joachim Schulze, "The Parody Process in Bach's Music: An Old Problem Reconsidered," BACH 20 (Spring 1989): 7–21, reprinted in *Bach*, ed. Yo Tomita (Farnham: Ashgate, 2010), 369–83; and Robin A. Leaver, "J. S. Bach's Parodies of Vocal Music: Conservation or Intensification?" in *Compositional Choices and Meaning in the Vocal Music of J. S. Bach*, ed. Mark A. Peters and Reginald L. Sanders (Lanham: Lexington Books, 2018), 177–203. For a discussion of Bach's cantata parodies, see Hans-Joachim Schulze, "Parody and Text Quality in the Vocal Works of J. S. Bach," in Peters and Sanders, *Compositional Choices*, 167–76; for parody in connection with the work discussed later in this chapter, see Alfred Mann "Missa Brevis and Historia: Bach's A Major Mass," BACH 16 (January 1985): 6–11.

3 Joshua Rifkin has argued that most, if not all, of the movements of the B-minor Mass are parodies of earlier works: see the accompanying text for his groundbreaking 1982 recording (Nonesuch 79036-2); his review of the facsimiles of the 1733 Dresden manuscript score and parts, in *Notes: Quarterly Journal of the Music Library Association* 44 (June 1988): 788–89; and his edition, *Johann Sebastian Bach: Mass in B Minor* (Wiesbaden: Breitkopf & Härtel, 2006), xviii.

68 *Liturgy*

adaptations from earlier cantatas, with a minimum of alteration to accommodate the Latin text in place of the German, then the music will often be found to be remarkable in some way or other; or, on the other hand, if the original cantata movements have undergone some recomposition for the new work, the parody process usually reveals profound changes, which imply a great deal of thought and creativity rather than a simple compilation of existing music with a minimum of adjustment to suit the different texts.[4] In both cases there is the implication that Bach apparently wished to gather together music that pleased him by incorporating these compositions into the later forms. This is suggested by the common structure of the Gloria of these Masses. If these works were simply random compilations of earlier music, pulled together in haste, then one would expect to find the liturgical text treated differently in each *Missa*, with alternative patterns of arias and choruses. All four of these Masses, however, share the same basic chiastic five-movement structure: a central aria framed by two arias and two choruses. Two of the Masses (BWV 233 and BWV 234) not only share the same structure but also the equivalent movements are assigned to the same solo voices or to the chorus:

> *Gloria in excelsis Deo...* (SATB)
>   *Domine Deus...* (B)
>   *Qui tollis peccata mundi...* (S)
>   *Quoniam tu solus sanctus...* (A)
> *Cum sancto Spiritu...* (SATB)

The other two Masses (BWV 235 and BWV 236) have a similar structure though with some variation with regard to the assignment of text and voices:

> *Gloria in excelsis Deo...* (SATB)
>   *Gratias agimus...* (B)
>   *Domine Fili...* (A) or *Domine Deus...* (SA)
>   *Quoniam tu solus sanctus...* (S) or *Qui tollis peccata...* (S)
> *Cum sancto Spiritu...* (SATB)

The central movements of two of the settings of the Gloria are either of "Domini Fili unigeniti" ("O Lord, the only begotten Son") (BWV 235) or "Domine Deus, Agnus Dei" ("O Lord God, Lamb of God") (BWV 236), and the central movements in both of the other two Masses (BWV 233 and BWV 234) are settings of the relative clause "Qui tollis peccata mundi" ("who takes away the sin of the world"). The same focal point is found in the structure of the Gloria of the B-minor Mass, although here the symmetry takes on a more complex form:

---

4 A supreme example is the Agnus Dei in the B-minor Mass, discussed in Chapter 3.

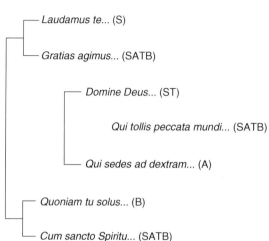

At the center of the *Gloria* of these Masses is the acknowledgment of the redemption of Christ and the prayer for mercy and forgiveness: "Qui tollis peccata mundi, miserere nobis, suscipe deprecationem nostram" ("who takes away the sin of the world, have mercy on us, receive our prayer"), settings that are parodies of earlier cantata movements:

BWV 232/8 = BWV 46/1
BWV 233/4 = BWV 102/3
BWV 234/4 = BWV 179/5[5]

The argument that asserts that Bach's Lutheran *Missae* are works of lesser significance because they are made up of reworkings of earlier cantata movements, while at the same time the B-minor Mass is extolled for its greatness, is therefore untenable. The four Lutheran *Missae*, while not reaching the grandeur of the B-minor Mass, nevertheless represent, in the main, careful and eloquent reworkings of earlier music, and therefore demand the close attention of Bach scholars and performers.

As well as preserving some of his finest vocal music in these four *Missae*, Bach was also making the music available in a more accessible form. A cantata

---

5 The setting of "Qui tollis peccata" in the Gloria of BWV 235, though not the central movement, is a parody of BWV 187/5.

for a particular Sunday or feast day could usually be performed only once a year, since it was closely linked with the Propers for that day, notably the Gospel and/or Epistle. However, if some of the movements were recast into settings of the Kyrie and Gloria—that is in liturgical terms, being changed from Proper to Ordinary—then the music could be performed several times during the church year: at Christmas, Easter, Pentecost, Trinity, and on other special feast days when a concerted Missa was required.

A fundamental question regarding these parodied movements relates to Bach's criteria for selecting movements to be reused. Was his concern merely to preserve music he was particularly pleased at having composed, or was he as much concerned with the theological and liturgical connections between the original cantata movement and the music's new placement within the *Missa*? The evidence would suggest that Bach was indeed aware of these interconnections, and theological and liturgical parallels were as important to him as were purely musical criteria.

A notable example is the Crucifixus of the B-minor Mass. For this central movement of the *Symbolum Nicenum*—indeed, the central movement of the whole Mass—Bach reuses the A section of the *da capo* first chorus of Cantata 12, *Weinen, Klagen, Sorgen, Zagen* (Weeping, lamenting, grieving, trembling). The libretto of Cantata 12 deals with the significance of the cross for Christian life, but does so in a rather oblique, somewhat hidden way. The B section of the second movement speaks of "das Zeichen Jesu" (the sign of Jesus) implying the "sign of the cross," but it is never actually stated

Weinen, Klagen,	Weeping, lamenting,
Sorgen, Zagen,	Grieving, trembling,
Angst und Not	Anguish and distress
Sind der Christen Tränenbrot.	Are the Christian's bread of tears:
Die das Zeichen Jesu tragen.	Those who carry the sign of Jesus.[6]

Thus, at the opening of the cantata movement, after the sequential entry of the voices in descending order, Bach makes a disguised sign of the cross on the score with the successive entries of the tenor, soprano, bass, and alto voices (BWV 12/1 mm. 1–7):

[6] It is the same imagery that begins Cantata 56: "Ich will den Kreuzstab gerne tragen" ("I will willingly carry the beam of the cross"); see Matthew 16:24, Mark 8:34 and 10:21, and Luke 9:23: "take up the cross and follow me."

In the first chorus of Cantata 12, therefore, the theme of the cross was already expounded musically, and consequently was theologically, as well as musically, suitable for later incorporation into the Credo of the B-minor Mass: the text was changed but the underlying motif remained the same (BWV 232/17, mm.5–13):

Another very different example is the movement composed in Weimar (BWV 233a) that in Leipzig became the Kyrie of the *Missa in F* (BWV 233).[7] This extraordinary movement combines the three liturgical prayers for mercy: (1) the threefold Kyrie, set as a three-part, three-section fugue (S^{II}AT), (2) an expansion of the Kyrie from the Litany (B), and against these different Kyries, in the early version (BWV 233a), (3) the complete threefold German Agnus Dei—*Christe, du Lamm Gottes*—sung to its familiar melody (S^I). In the later Leipzig version the movement appears as the Kyrie of the *Missa in F* (BWV 233), but was it originally composed as a setting of the eucharistic Kyrie? Although isolated settings are not unknown—Kyrie without the Gloria—they are rare. As I have argued in Chapter 3, since the complete *Christe, du Lamm Gottes* is heard, both text and melody, the movement is a kind of chorale fantasia in which the melody of the German Agnus Dei is accompanied by settings of the two liturgical Kyries. Thus, given that the common Lutheran liturgical usage was for the Agnus Dei, in either Latin or German, to be sung during communion, *musica sub communione*, it therefore seems most likely that the movement was originally composed to be sung at this liturgical juncture, during the distribution of Communion. When the movement was reworked for the Kyrie of the *Missa in F*, the *Christe, du Lamm Gottes* melody was transferred from the first soprano to unison horns and oboes. Without the associated text, Bach creates a marvelous ambiguity and shifts the stress more toward the Kyrie rather than the Agnus Dei. What was originally intended as *musica sub communione*, near the end of the Hauptgottesdienst, a setting of the German Agnus Dei, is thus adapted to become a setting of the Kyrie, near the beginning of the Hauptgottesdienst. It is a small but significant change that demonstrates Bach's sensitivity and skill in reusing his liturgical music.

A third example, remarkable in its detail, is the opening *Gloria* movement of the *Missa in A* (BWV 234), a reworking of a cantata movement. Cantata 67, *Halt im Gedächtnis Jesum Christ*, first performed on *Quasimodogeniti*

---

7 See the discussion in Chapter 3.

72 Liturgy

(the First Sunday after Easter), 16 April 1724. It has a symmetrical structure revolving around a central chorale:

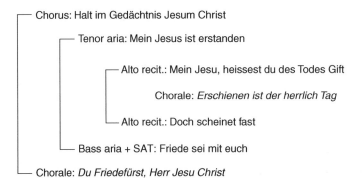

The cantata is thus framed by the opening chorus and closing chorale. It begins with the statement "Halt im Gedächtnis Jesum Christ, der auferstanden ist von den Toten" ("Keep in remembrance Jesus Christ, who is arisen from the dead" [2 Timothy 2:8]), and ends with the following text:

Du Friedefürst, Herr Jesu Christ,	You Prince of Peace, Lord Jesus Christ,
Wahr'r Mensch und wahrer Gott,	True Man and true God,
Ein starker Nothelfer du bist	A strong Helper you are
Im Leben und im Tod:	In life and in death:

The main theme of the cantata is, therefore, Jesus Christ, the resurrected Savior, the "Prince of Peace" (*Friedefürst*), who holds the keys of life and death for believers. At the center, surrounded by the two alto recitatives—in which the "Prince of Peace" theme is enunciated—is the chorale celebrating Christ's Easter victory:

Erschienen ist der herrlich Tag,	Dawned is the glorious day
Dran sich niemand gnug freuen mag:	When no one may rejoice enough:
Christ, unser Herr, heut triumphiert,	Christ, our Lord, today triumphs;
All sein Feind er gefangen führt.	All His enemies He captive leads
Alleluja![8]	Alleluja!

Movement 2, the tenor aria, and movement 6, the bass arioso with soprano, alto, tenor trio, are similarly linked in the symmetrical structure of the

---

[8] There are also parallels here with the central movement of the *Johannespassion* (No. 22): "Durch dein Gefängnis, Gottes Sohn, | Muß uns die Freiheit kommen ... | Denn gingst du nicht die Knechtschaft ein, | Müsst unsere Knechtschaft ewig sein" ("Through your imprisonment, Son of God, | freedom has come to us ... | for had you not entered into servitude, | our servitude would have been eternal").

Bach's parody process: from cantata to Missa   73

cantata. The first speaks of warfare and the second of the victory the Savior has won. The tenor, representing the individual Christian, sings:

Mein Glaube kennt des Heilands Sieg,   My faith knows the Savior's victory,
Doch fühlt mein Herze Streit und Krieg,   yet my heart feels strife and war,
Mein Heil, erscheine doch!   My savior, now appear!

In movement 6 the bass, following the long-standing tradition in Passion music, represents the risen Christ, and sings the greeting: "Friede sei mit euch" (Peace be with you). These words are from the Gospel for *Quasimodogeniti*, John 20:19–31, the greeting of the risen Christ to his disciples, spoken twice to the whole group, and once to doubting Thomas. The implication of the passage is that, since the disciples were meeting on the first day of the week, they were joining in worship: as they are praying together, the risen Christ comes among them and bids them peace.

The cantata libretto, prepared for the contemporaneous congregation assembled for worship, is written from the perspective of the disciples, who, like Thomas, have their doubts and fears. In movement 6 a contrast is drawn between the agitation of the disciples and the peace Christ brings to them. In his AB AB AB AB structure, Bach provides the following: A, a ritornello, an agitated sixteenth-note configuration in 4/4 for strings and continuo (*stile concitato*); B, a contrasting pastoral section in 3/4 (*stile affettuoso*)—scored for the bass who sings the Savior's greeting, "Friede sei mit euch"—is accompanied by flute, oboes d'amore, and continuo. The dualism is emphasized as the movement swings back and forth between the two sections.[9]

Bach is here reflecting in musical terms the dynamic aspect of the atonement as understood by such early Greek fathers of the church as Gregory of Nyssa and Irenaeus, among others, but also enunciated by Luther and some of the later Lutheran theologians. Since the 1930s this classic exposition has been referred to as the *Christus Victor* concept of the atonement, the term derived from the seminal study by the Swedish bishop Gustaf Aulén.[10] It is a dualist and dramatic concept in which Christ engages in warfare with death, hell, the devil, and all evil. Since, it is argued, the Incarnation means that he is true God and true man and, therefore, invincible, the struggle, though real, can have only one outcome: the victory of Christ. Although the cross on Good Friday has the appearance of defeat, Easter Day announces that the apparent defeat is in reality triumph: *Christus Victor*. It is a theme that can be found in Luther's writings again and again, from the earliest to the latest.[11] For

9 For the alphabetically labeled sections of movement 6 in Cantata 67 see the diagram on page 79.
10 Gustaf Aulén, *Christus Victor: An Historical Study of the Three Main Types of the Idea of Atonement*, trans. Arthur Gabriel Hebert (London: SPCK, 1931).
11 A classic example of Luther's exposition of the concept can be found in his 1535 Commentary on the Epistle to the Galatians (on Galatians 3:1); WA 40^1: 440–41; LW 26: 281–82. See also Aulén, *Christus Victor*, 119–27.

74 *Liturgy*

example, in his 1520 treatise *Von der Freiheit eines Christenmenschen* (On the Freedom of a Christian) there is the following classic passage:

> Christ is God and man in one person. He has neither sinned nor died, and is not condemned, and he cannot sin, die, or be condemned; his righteousness, life, and salvation are unconquerable, eternal, omnipotent. By the wedding ring of faith he shares in the sins, death, and pains of hell which are his bride's. As a matter of fact, he makes them his own and acts as if they were his own and as if he himself had sinned; he suffered, died, and descended into hell that he might overcome them all. Now since it was such a one who did all this, and death and hell could not swallow him up, these were necessarily swallowed up by him in a mighty duel (*stupendo duello*); for his righteousness is greater than the sins of all men, his life stronger than death, his salvation more invincible than hell.[12]

This reference to *stupendo duello* is an echo of the great Easter sequence *Victimae paschali laudes*:

Mors et vita duello	Life and death have engaged
conflixere mirando:[13]	in miraculous conflict;
dux vitae mortuus,	the Lord of life is slain
regnat vivus.	but living reigns.

This bold imagery is also found in the fourth stanza of Luther's Easter hymn *Christ lag in Todesbanden*, which Bach early in his career gave dramatic musical form in BWV 4:[14]

Es war ein wunderlicher Krieg,	It was a marvelous conflict,
da Tod und Leben rungen;	when Life and Death contended;
das Leben da behielt den Sieg,	Life won the victory,
es hat den Tod verschlungen.	It has swallowed up Death.
Die Schrift hat verkündiget das,	Scripture has proclaimed this:
wie ein Tod den andern frass,	How one Death the other ate;
ein Spott aus dem Tod ist worden.	Death is made a mockery.
Alleluja!	Alleluja!

In various cantatas by Bach this *Christus Victor* theme is frequently found, and the composer often includes an obbligato trumpet in the musical exposition,

---

12 WA 7:25–26 (German); WA 7: 55 (Latin); LW 31: 351–52.

13 Luther's commentary on Galatians 3:1 in the 1535 commentary quotes these lines of the Latin sequence: "De hoc mirabili duello Ecclesia pulchre canit: Mors et Vita duello conflixere mirando" ("About this wondrous duel the church beautifully sings 'Mors et Vita duello conflixere mirando'"); WA 40^{I}: 439; LW 26: 281.

14 See Chapter 7.

Bach's parody process: from cantata to Missa   75

an audible reference to St. Paul's resurrection trumpet in 1 Corinthians 15:52. Obvious examples are the bass aria, "Er ists, der ganz allein," in the second part of the Ascension cantata (BWV 43/7), and the bass aria, "Grosser Herr, o starker König" in the first part of the Christmas Oratorio (BWV 248/8). A further example is the alto aria, "Es ist vollbracht," in the *Johannespassion* (BWV 245/30). Although the sound of a trumpet is not actually heard in this movement, the vocal line is given a trumpet-like fanfare at the words: "Der Held aus Juda siegt mit Macht. Und schliesst den Kampf" ("The hero from Judah triumphs with power and brings the battle to an end").

It is significant that Bach originally planned to include a trumpet obbligato part for movement 6 of Cantata 67. In the first pages of the manuscript score,[15] measures 1–36, he has provided a separate "Corno" staff—although the individual part implies that a "Zugtrompete" was intended[16]—and composed an obbligato part above the strings for the opening ritornello. But he changed his mind before the movement was completed and crossed out these first nine measures on the "Corno" staff, entering rests for the following B-section ritornello.[17] One can only speculate on the reasons why Bach abandoned this obbligato. Perhaps he realized that the trumpet would sound as a militaristic gloss on the oppression felt by the disciples, rather than sounding a resurrection fanfare. Whatever his reasons for changing his mind, it was clearly his original intention to include the trumpet. The drama of the contrast between the two sections would certainly have been heightened, but even without the trumpet, the contrast between the peace of Christ and the warfare that accomplished that peace can be heard in this musical exposition. The word-painting is obvious and direct. In contrast to the unmoving, static "Friede," "Kämpfen" is angular and energetic. It is a musical portrayal of the *stupendo duello* of the *Christus Victor* understanding of the Resurrection as the victory over death, the devil, and all evil, that Christ imparts to his disciples. Peace is brought about by the warfare of Christ on the cross that was followed by the Resurrection, the demonstration of the indestructibility of the Savior and the invincibility of the promise of grace. It is this cantata movement that Bach reworked for the opening movement of the Gloria in A (BWV 234).

With this in mind we return to three of Bach's settings of the Gloria in excelsis Deo (BWV 232–234). The common focal point of Qui tollis peccata mundi is not only the center of gravity of the three settings (see the diagrams

---

15 D-B Mus.ms. Bach P 95, fols. 7ʳ 8ᵛ.

16 D-B Mus.ms. Bach St 40. The copyist Kuhnau added to the heading of the part the words "da Tirasi" after "Corno," probably signifying "Zugtrompete," although the designation is somewhat problematic; see the discussion in Alfred Dürr, "Zur Bach-Kantate *Halt im Gedächtnis Jesum Christ*, BWV 67," *Musik und Kirche* 53 (1983): 74–77, esp. 76–77. See also Ulrich Prinz, *Johann Sebastian Bachs Instumentarium: Originalquellen, Besetzung, Verwendung* (Stuttgart: Internationale Bachakademie, 2005), 73–77.

17 The remaining measures of this staff are simply left blank; see Robert L. Marshall, *The Compositional Process of J. S. Bach: A Study of the Autograph Scores of the Vocal Works* (Princeton: Princeton University Press, 1972), 1: 220–21.

76 Liturgy

above), it is also the heart of the Lord's Supper itself: the consecrated bread and wine given and received as tokens of the forgiveness that Christ has obtained, and which is now offered and received. Since Bach made theological and liturgical links between the original cantata movements and their adaptations within these later Mass settings, it is possible that they already had eucharistic associations for the composer before he reworked them for the new context.

The practice in Leipzig, as elsewhere in Lutheran Germany, was for concerted music to be heard during the distribution of communion, *musica sub communione*.[18] In his outline of the liturgy for the First Sunday in Advent, found on the covers of the manuscript scores of both BWV 61 and BWV 62, Bach indicates that following the Words of Institution there is to be an organ prelude that leads into concerted music.[19] The origin of this practice is to be found in Luther's *Deutsche Messe* (1526), where he states that the Agnus Dei can be sung after the Words of Institution.[20] Three years earlier, in the *Formula missae* (1523), he had indicated that the message of peace should immediately precede the distribution of communion:

> But immediately after the Lord's Prayer shall be said, "the peace of the Lord," etc, which is, so to speak, a public absolution of the sins of the communicants, the true voice of the gospel announcing remission of sins, and therefore the one and most worthy preparation for the Lord's Table, if faith holds to these words as coming from the mouth of Christ.[21]

There were, therefore, two liturgical expressions of peace associated with the distribution of Communion: the third petition of the Agnus Dei: "Dona nobis pacem" ("Verleih uns deinen Frieden"—"Grant us thy peace"), and the greeting "Pax Domini sit semper vobiscum" ("Der Friede des Herren sei mit euch allen"—"The Peace of the Lord be with you all"). When this connection is recognized, the Agnus Dei with its "Dona nobis pacem" of the B-minor Mass will be understood as *musica sub communione* for special occasions in Leipzig. If it was the practice on ordinary Sundays to employ appropriate sections of cantatas as *musica sub communione*, then it is within the bounds of possibility that Bach may well have used not only Movement 6 of Cantata 67 but also the first movement of Cantata 158 for this purpose. Cantata 158, *Friede sei mit dir*, although originally written for the Feast of Purification, was rewritten for the Third Day of Easter. The structure of the text is similar to that of movement 6 in Cantata 67; indeed, in both works the words of the risen Christ are repeated a number of times. In Cantata 158, "Friede sei mit

---

18 See the discussion in Chapter 2.

19 BDok 1: 248–49, 251.

20 WA 19: 99; LW 53:82.

21 LW 53: 28–29; WA 12: 213: "Sed statim post orationem dominicam dicatur: 'Pax domini etce.' quae est publica quaedam absolutio a peccatis communicantium, vox plane Euangelica, annuncians remissionem peccatorum, unica illa et dignissima ad mensam domini preparatio, si fide apprehendatur, non secus atque ex ore Christi prolata."

Bach's parody process: from cantata to Missa   77

dir" is heard three times; in Cantata 67, "Friede sei mit euch" is heard six times. The suitability of these movements as *musica sub communione* is obvious since their texts are restatements of the liturgical greeting made immediately before the distribution of Communion: "The peace of the Lord be with you all." Movement 6 of Cantata 67 very likely already had such eucharistic associations for Bach, even if he never used it as *musica sub communione*, since the message of peace appears to have been axiomatic for the composer when he adapted it for the first movement of the Gloria in the A-major *Missa.*

Movement 6 of Cantata 67 is a celebration of the victory of Christ over death and evil by a contrasted dualism between the warfare of the Savior, on the one hand, and the resultant peace for the disciples, on the other. It is a joyful celebration of the triumph of the Resurrection over the tragedy of the Crucifixion, and centers on the presence of the risen Christ with his disciples. In these general terms, therefore, the movement was immediately suitable for the opening section of the Gloria in excelsis Deo in the A-major *Missa*: the text of the Gloria swings alternately between the themes of Crucifixion and Resurrection, and centers on the presence of Christ, who offers the peace of forgiveness. The general suitability of the movement in this new liturgical context is readily apparent, but Bach appears to have made an even more significant association. For him the post-Resurrection proclamation of peace by Christ is the fulfillment of the post-Incarnation prophecy of peace by the angelic host, and there is, therefore, a significant connection between "Friede sei mit euch" and "Et in terra pax."[22]

It seems that this Friede/Pax association was probably Bach's starting point in his adaptation of the cantata movement for the Gloria of the *Missa.*[23] The B-section ritornello was rewritten; the instrumentation was changed from flute and two oboes d'amore to two flutes, and the bass "Friede sei mit euch" became the alto "et in terra pax" (Example 4.1). The melodic phrase, which is very similar to that found in Cantata 158, remains basically the same, except for a very significant octave fall at the word "terra" (Example 4.2)— an incarnational pictorialism depicting the descent of the Savior to earth in order to bring peace, a small change in detail but one that reveals how carefully Bach adapted his music.

22 The association can be found in Lutheran sermons; for example, a sermon for this Sunday, *Quasimodogeniti* [Easter 1] by a Nördlingen pastor includes the following: "Christus hat alle Geschenck und Gaben seiner Verheissung mit dem Wörtlein Friede verheissen/ dann er ist der Friedefürst Esa. 9. v. 7. der in seinem gantzen Leben und Verdienst/ lauter Frieden gebracht hat: Da er gebohren ward/ haben die Engel gesungen: Friede auff Erden Luc. 2. v. 14." (With the word "Peace" Christ promises all the presents and gifts of his promise, for he is the Prince of Peace [Isa. 9:7], who in his whole life and ministry brought true peace. When he was born the angels sang: Peace on earth [Luke 2:14]); Georg Albrecht, *Geistreicher Evangelischer Schatz-Kammer ... Darinnen über ein jedes Sonn- und Festtägliches Evangelium durchs gantze Jahr* (Ulm: Görlin, 1662–1663), 2: 209.

23 For the background of the parody process in the A-major Mass, see Emil Platen and Mariane Helms, NBA KB II/2, esp. 61–62.

78 *Liturgy*

Example 4.1 Comparison of "Friede" (BWV 67/6) with "et in terra pax" (BWV 234/2)

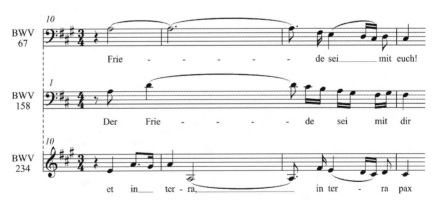

Example 4.2 Similarities among BWV 67, BWV 158, and BWV 234

Bach's parody process: from cantata to Missa   79

Having made this Friede/Pax connection Bach then had to set the text "Gloria in excelsis Deo" within the opening A-section ritornello, which in the cantata was purely instrumental. But this does not seem to have created any particular difficulty for Bach, who simply writes a homophonic setting of the words within the harmonic structure of the existing strings and continuo.

At this point one might have expected Bach to return to his original intention for the cantata—including the obbligato trumpet for the A ritornello in the cantata movement. It would have been appropriate for the Gloria since, for example, he used trumpets for the equivalent movement in the B-minor Mass. However, when the rejected obbligato part for the cantata movement is superimposed on the homophonic chorus (see Example 4.3) it becomes clear that there would have been significant doubling of the voices by the trumpet. In the first and second measures the trumpet would have doubled the tenor, in the third the alto, in the fourth and fifth the soprano, in the sixth the tenor, in the seventh largely the soprano, and in the eighth the tenor. In the cantata movement, if Bach had followed his first intentions, the trumpet would have stood out against the animated strings, but in the Gloria, with the addition of the homophonic four voices, the texture would have been thickened. Thus, it is understandable that Bach did not pursue his original intentions for the obbligato trumpet.

With the first two sections of the cantata movement rearranged for the opening (biblical) text of the Gloria, Bach then had to adapt the remaining sections of the Gloria from the Laudamus te through to the end of Gratias agimus. In order to do this he had to indulge in some text repetition:

Cantata BWV 67		*Missa* **BWV 234**	
A^1	— —	A^1	Gloria in excelsis Deo (SATB)
B^1	Friede sei mit euch (B)	B^1	et in terra pax hominibus bonae voluntatis (SATB)
A^2	Wohl uns! wohl uns,	A^2	Laudamus te, benedicimus te (SATB)
	Jesus hilft uns kämpfen, und die Wut der Feinde dämpfen. Hölle, Satan, weich! (SAT)		
B^2	Friede sei mit euch (B)	B^2	adoramus te (B)
A^3	Jesus holet uns zum Frieden und erquicket in uns Müden Geist und Leib zugleich (SAT)	A^3	glorificamus te, laudamus te, benedicimus te (SATB)
B^3	Friede sei mit euch (B)	B^3	adoramus te (T)
A^4	O Herr! (SAT) Friede sei mit euch (B):1 O Herr, hilf uns und lass gelingen durch den Tod hindurch zu dringen in dein Ehrenreich!	A^4	glorificamus te, laudamus te, benedicimus te, adoramus te, glorificamus te (SATB)
B^4	Friede sei mit euch (B)	B^4	Gratias agimus tibi propter magnam gloriam tuam (SATB)

80 *Liturgy*

Example 4.3 The discarded "Corno" part of BWV 67/6 with the later four-part homophonic chorus BWV 234/10

Example 4.4 Comparison of "Friede" (BWV 67/6) with "glorificamus te" (BWV 234/2)

There are indications that Bach carefully recomposed the voice parts in each section, some more than others, in order to accommodate the new text. Sections A² and A³ are expanded from three to four voices, since the separation of the bass voice from the upper three voices, as maintained in Cantata 67, no longer applied. Sometimes the changes are minimal: for example, at B² the notation of the cantata is extended rather than changed (Example 4.1).

In the repetition of the text Adoramus te, the vocal parts B² and B³ are virtually identical, except that the solo voice in B² is scored for tenor and in B³ for bass.

In the A⁴ section of the cantata the SAT group remains the same as in A² and A³, except for the fact that the bass interjects "Friede sei mit euch" twice. In the four-voice texture of the *Missa* it is still possible to detect—in the vocal bass at mm. 82–83—melodic echoes of the earlier version (Example 4.4).

In the B⁴ section there is a marvelous piece of recomposition where the single bass voice is replaced by four-part chorus, and "Friede sei mit euch" becomes "Gratias agimus tibi propter magnam gloriam tuam" ("We give thanks to thee for thy great glory"). This response of thanksgiving has grown out of Christ's greeting of peace, and the glory of Christ, here celebrated in the *Missa*, is therefore the glory of the triumph over sin and death, signaled in the Resurrection and heralded at the Incarnation.

The subtle changes that Bach made when adapting this movement for its use in the *Missa* in A major indicate that it was the work of a composer who was as much concerned with liturgical and theological interconnections as with musical adaptability. Therefore, in its later form in the *Missa*, Bach's music has a musical and theological integrity equal to that of its original form in the cantata. The secret of the parody is to be found not only in the skill of the composer but also in his theological perception that the underlying celebration of Christ's victory and presence pertain both to the

82   *Liturgy*

original cantata movement as well as to the liturgical Gloria in excelsis Deo. It is Bach's theological equation of Christ's Resurrection peace and the Incarnation peace proclaimed by the Christmas angels that led him to see this particular connection between the cantata movement and the liturgical hymn of praise. Having made this basic theological connection, it was relatively easy—easy for Bach, that is—to rework the earlier cantata movement in a masterly way.

5 Bach and the cantata controversy of the early eighteenth century

Paradoxically, Bach's cantatas are often considered to be too religious for the present day, and yet they are mostly heard in a secular setting; but in Bach's day they were frequently considered to be too secular, and yet they were a regular feature of Sunday worship. Our problem is not with the music, which we love to hear and perform, but with the texts that express a theology and piety that often seems out-of-date in our contemporary world. Their problem was not with the texts but with the music, which sounded out of place, more appropriate for the opera house than for the church. In explanations of how the cantata form was received and understood in the eighteenth century, a simple dichotomy is often presented: those who were Orthodox in their theology promoted the use of cantatas in the liturgy; those who were Pietist in their beliefs and practice spoke out against the use of cantatas within worship. While there are elements of truth in this point of view, the situation was much more complicated than this black-and-white explanation. Thus, it is necessary to appreciate the different nuances in Bach's day, because understanding how the cantata was regarded at that time will help us in our time to appreciate this form of church music that was once widespread in Germany—the musical form that reached its high point in the cantatas of Bach.

The exquisite lullaby "Schlummert ein," in which the termination of life is beautifully expressed in the metaphor of sleep, is one of the best-loved of all Bach's arias. It also seems to have been somewhat special to the composer and his wife, in that the cantata within which it is found, *Ich habe genung* (BWV 82), was performed in four different manifestations between 1727 and 1747, as well as being copied by Anna Magdalena into her second manuscript *Clavierbüchlein* (begun in 1725). An aria has been discovered in an annual cycle of cantata libretti, published a few years before Bach composed his cantata, that has verbal correspondences with this aria by Bach. What is presented here is an investigation of the two libretti, an outline of the identity and activity of the author of the earlier libretto, especially his part in the controversy concerning the introduction of the so-called reform cantata, and a consideration of how much the writings of this author may have been known within Bach's circle in Leipzig.

84 *Liturgy*

Cantata 82

Cantata 82, *Ich habe genung*, was composed for the feast of the Purification (Maria Reinigung), 2 February 1727, and is based on the Gospel of the day, Luke 2: 22–32, the presentation of the infant Christ in the temple and the old man Simeon's reaction to holding the child in his arms and singing his *Nunc dimittis*. The first version was in C minor for bass solo with oboe obbligato, strings, and continuo. In the early 1730s, probably 1731, it was transposed up a third to E minor for soprano with flute obbligato. Around the same time, 1732–1733, Anna Magdalena entered movements 2 and 3 into her second *Clavierbüchlein*—actually, the aria was entered twice.[1] In February 1735 the E-minor version was repeated, and then sometime in the following years it was transposed back to C minor for mezzo-soprano, with oboe obbligato, and around 1746–1747 the cantata was reassigned to the bass voice. The cantata comprises five movements without a concluding chorale: three arias, separated by two recitatives, "Schlummert ein" being the central movement. The author of the libretto is uncertain (see the Excursus at the end of this chapter).

Cantata libretti

In 1725 a former theological student at Leipzig University issued an annual cycle of cantata libretti: Gottfried Ephraim Scheibel, *Poetische Andachten Über alle gewöhnliche Sonn- und Fest-Tage, durch das gantze Jahr/ Allen Herren Componisten und Liebhabern der Kirchen-Music zum Ergötzen, Nebst einer Vorrede von der Hindernüssen derselben* (Leipzig and Breslau: Rohrlach, 1725).[2] The libretto for the Purification includes an aria that begins with significant verbal correspondences with Bach's later aria in the cantata libretto written for the same occasion:

Scheibel, *Am Fest Maria Reinigung*[3]	BWV 82/3
Schlummert ein, ihr **Augen**lieder **Fallet sanft** in Frieden nieder, Schlafft aus. Ich sterbe wie der Simeon,	**Schlummert ein**, ihr matten **Augen**, **Fallet sanft** und selig zu! Welt, ich bleibe nicht mehr hier,

---

1 Johann Sebastian Bach, *Klavierbüchlein für Anna Magdalena Bach 1725*, facsimile ed. Georg von Dadelsen (Kassel: Bärenreiter, 1988), 105–10, 111d–14. NBA V/4: 122–24.

2 Christoph Gottlieb Schröter (1699–1782), who had studied theology in Leipzig with Scheibel, composed settings of the complete Jahrgang of Scheibel's libretti, probably in Minden, where he was organist between 1726 and 1732, but these settings are no longer extant; see Friedrich Wilhelm Marpurg, *Kritische Briefe über die Tonkunst* (Berlin: Birnstiel, 1760–1764), 2: 456–60; NG2, 22: 650–52.

3 Gottfried Ephraim Scheibel, *Poetische Andachten Über alle gewöhnliche Sonn- und Fest-tage, durch das gantze Jahr/ Allen Herren Componisten und Liebhabern der Kirchen-Music zum Ergötzen, Nebst einer Vorrede von der Hindernüssen derselben* (Leipzig and Breslau: Rohrlach, 1725), 47.

Bach and the cantata controversy 85

Und eile nun davon,	Hab ich doch kein Teil an dir,
Weil Jesus mir von ferne	Das der Seele könnte taugen.
Winckt in das Reich der Sterne	Hier muss ich das Elend bauen,
Und in des Himmels Haus.	Aber dort, dort werd ich schauen
Da Capo	Süßen Friede, stille Ruh.
	Da Capo

Slumber, you eyelids,[4]	**Slumber, you heavy eyes,**
Fall softly in peace, relax now.	**Fall softly** and blessedly close!
I die like Simeon	World, I remain here no longer,
And haste now therefrom,	I have surely no part in you,
Since Jesus from far	That my soul might benefit
Beckons me to the kingdom of the stars	I must cultivate misery here,
And to heavens dwelling.	But there, there shall I see
	Sweet peace, quiet rest.

There are differences between the two libretti, notably their metrical structures. Bach's is perhaps better balanced with a brief A section (8.7.) and a much longer B section (7.7.8.8.8.7.), whereas Scheibel's A section is longer (8.10.8.6.) with a much briefer B section (7.7.6.).

It is possible, of course, that the correspondences between the two are purely coincidental, brought about by a similar approach to the same biblical narrative. Elsewhere in Scheibel's cycle of cantata texts there are pre-echoes of other Bach libretti. For example, Scheibel's libretto for the First Sunday in Advent begins with "Jauchzet, frohlocket,"[5] as does the first cantata of Bach's Christmas Oratorio (BWV 248[I]/1), and the first movement of Scheibel's libretto for Easter Day speaks of "Trompeten," "Pauken," and "Saiten,"[6] as does the first movement of *Tönet, ihr Pauken!* (BWV 214/1), the cantata Bach parodied for the opening movement of the Christmas Oratorio. But these are clearly the reflections of the common vocabulary of celebration. However, the concordances between the two "Schlummert ein" aria libretti seem to be more than coincidence and imply that the librettist of the later text knew of the earlier libretto. Consider the following.

Both libretti were written for the Feast of the Purification and are, therefore, meditations on the Gospel for the day: the old man Simeon who can face death now that he has seen the young Christ child. Both arias make use of the same imagery of death as sleep and the closing of the eyes, and the contemporaneous worshiper in both is metaphorically placed alongside Simeon to contemplate the personal transition from earth to heaven.

The first two lines of both arias begin with identical words. This is a phenomenon—phrases from libretti of previous poets being repeated by

---

4 Reading "Augenlider" rather than "Augenlieder"—eye-songs!
5 Scheibel, *Poetische Andachten*, 1.
6 Scheibel, *Poetische Andachten*, 76.

86 *Liturgy*

other poets—that is traceable in other cantata libretti that Bach set. For example, the third movement of the libretto of Cantata 27, *Wer weiß nahe mir mein Ende?*, by an unknown librettist, which Bach composed for the Sixteenth Sunday after Trinity, 6 October 1726, begins with nearly all of the first two lines of the final movement of the libretto for the First Sunday after Trinity that Erdmann Neumeister wrote for the cantata Johann Philipp Krieger composed for the Weißenfels court chapel around 1700:

Neumeister (Trinity 1)[7]	BWV 27/3 (Trinity 16)
Willkommen! will ich sagen,	**Willkommen! will ich sagen**,
So bald **der Tod ans Bette tritt**.	Wenn **der Tod ans Bette tritt**.

A few weeks later, on 27 October 1726, Bach produced another cantata with a libretto (also by an unknown poet) for the Nineteenth Sunday after Trinity. Cantata 51 begins with a close verbal connection to the opening lines of Neumeister's libretto for the Twenty-First Sunday after Trinity, from the same cycle written around 1700:

Neumeister (Trinity 21)[8]	**BWV 56/1 (Trinity 19)**
Ich will den Creuz-Weg **gerne** gehen	**Ich will den Kreuz**stab **gerne** tragen,
Ich weiß da führt mit **Gottes Hand**	Er kömmt von **Gottes** lieber **Hand**,

These are not isolated cases. As Helmut Krausse has demonstrated, there are many examples where lines and phrases of poetry have been taken over and developed by other poets for their libretti, some of which were used by Bach: Neumeister stimulating Salomo Franck and Georg Christian Lehms; and Franck influencing an anonymous poet (or poets).[9] The correspondences between Scheibel's libretto and Bach's aria are of the same kind as these other examples.

The arias in the two libretti form the central movement in each respective cantata. Scheibel's libretto begins with three movements: aria, recitative, and chorale, and similarly ends with three movements: recitative, arioso, and chorale. In the middle is the aria "Schlummert ein," preceded by a brief, introductory two-line recitative:[10]

---

7 Erdmann Neumeister, *Fünfffache Kirchen-Andachten bestehend In theils eintzeln, theils niemahls gedruckten Arien, Cantaten und Oden Auf alle Sonn- und Fest-Tage des gantzen Jahres*, ed. Gottfried Tilgner (Leipzig: Groß, 1716), 294.

8 Neumeister, *Fünfffache Kirchen-Andachten*, 514.

9 Helmut K. Krausse, "Erdmann Neumeister und die Kantatentexte Johann Sebastian Bachs," BJ 72 (1986): 7–31. The practice of using the opening line of an existing poem and then continuing differently (Initialkontrafaktur) has a long history; see Friedrich Gennrich, *Die Kontrafaktur im Liedschaffen des Mittelalters* (Frankfurt: Gennrich, 1965). Neumeister used the technique not only in cantata libretti but also in parodies of hymn texts; see Chapter 13.

10 Scheibel, *Poetische Andachten*, 45–47.

1. *Aria*. Licht des Lebens, leuchte mir. *Da capo*.
2. *Accomp.* [*recit.*] Ich denck meinen Tod.
3. *Choral*. Herr, nun laß in Friede.[11]

4. [*Recit.*] So wollt ich gleichfalls, eh die Augen brechen,
   Eh meine Zunge starrt, noch sprechen:
5. *Aria*. Schlummert ein, ihr Augenlieder. *Da capo*.

6. [*Recit.*] Christus ist mein Leben
7. *Arioso*. Ich will gar gerne sterben.
8. *Choral*. Komm, O Christ, komm uns auszuspannen.[12]

Gottfried Ephraim Scheibel

Gottfried Ephraim Scheibel (1696–1758)[13] is often referred to as a theologian, though he was never ordained. The son of the cantor of the Elisabethkirche, Breslau (now Wrocław), Scheibel studied theology at Leipzig University between 1715 and 1719 but otherwise seems to have spent his life in Silesia, in and around Breslau. The dedication of his treatise *Zufällige Gedancken von der Kirchen-Music* (1721) is signed from Oels (now Oleśnica; about ten miles from Wrocław) but his profession is not recorded, though most likely he was a teacher there. The title page of his *Poetische Andachten* (1725) describes him as "Rev. Min. Cand. Wr. Sil.," that is, "candidate for the holy ministry, Breslau, Silesia." In the mid-1730s he became a teacher in the Elisabeth gymnasium,

---

11 St. 1 of anonymous paraphrase of the Song of Simeon (Nunc dimittis) that first appeared in the fifth edition of *Vollständigen Kirchen- und Haus-Music* (Breslau: Baumann, 1663), and appeared mostly in local Silesian hymnals. This is somewhat ironic since Scheibel criticized Johann Jacob Rambach's cantata Jahrgang for using chorales from Freylinghausen's Halle *Gesangbuch* that were not commonly sung elsewhere; see Gottfried Ephraim Scheibel, *Zufällige Gedancken von der Kirchen-Music* (Frankfurt and Leipzig: "Authore," 1721, facsimile, Stuttgart: Cornetto, 2002), 75–76; an abbreviated translation by Joyce Irwin, "Random Thoughts about Church Music in Our Day (1721)," appears in *Bach's Changing World: Voices in the Community*, ed. Carol K. Baron (Rochester: University of Rochester Press, 2006), 227–49, but does not include this passage. The chorale is designated "*a 1. voix*," and thus represents the single voice of Simeon.

12 Stanza 6 of *O wie selig seid ihr doch ihr Frommen* by Simon Dach (1639).

13 On Scheibel, see: Johann Gottfried Walther, *Musicalisches Lexicon oder Musicalische Bibliothec* (Leipzig: Deer, 1732; facsimile, Kassel: Bärenreiter, 1967), 547; Johann Heinrich Zedler, *Grosses vollständiges Universal-Lexicon aller Wissenschafften und Künste* 34 (Leipzig & Halle: Zedler, 1742), col. 1097; Carl Julius Adolph Hoffmann, *Die Tonkünstler Schlesiens: Ein Beitrag zur Kunstgeschichte Schlesiens, vom 960 bis 1830* (Breslau: Aderholz, 1830), 382–84; Salomon Kümmerle, *Encyklopädie der evangelischen Kirchenmusik* (Gütersloh: Bertelsmann, 1888–1895; reprint, Hildesheim: Olms, 1974), 3: 173–74; NG2, 22: 446–47; Joyce Irwin, "Bach in the Midst of Religious Transition," in Baron, *Bach's Changing World*, 108–26, esp. 115–22. Lexica generally give the year of his death as 1759, but this is an error; see Herbert Lölkes, "Gottfried Ephraim Scheibel als Autor kirchenmusikalischer Schriften," *Jahrbuch für Schlesische Kirchengeschichte* 74 (1996): 257–81.

88   *Liturgy*

Breslau, where his father had been cantor, a position he apparently retained for the rest of his life.

As a student in Leipzig, Scheibel must have heard from time to time the church music of Johann Kuhnau in the Nikolaikirche, Thomaskirche, or Paulinerkirche (the university church), but he appears to have regularly worshiped in the Neukirche where Johann Gottfried Vogler was the director of music. The Neukirche was noted for its operatic style of church music, and Vogler was active in the Leipzig opera house as both violinist and composer.[14] It seems more than likely that Scheibel heard the first concerted Passion performed in Leipzig, on Good Friday 1717 in the Neukirche, and again, either in 1718 or 1719: Telemann's *Brockes Passion* (TVWV 5:1).[15] Presumably it was one of these performances that Scheibel had in mind a few years later:

> I remember that in a certain place on Good Friday there was supposed to be a musical Passion before and after the sermon. The people certainly would not have come to church so promptly and in such a great crowd because of the preacher but probably rather because of the music.[16]

This appears to run counter to the findings of Tanya Kevorkian, whose research reveals that in Leipzig sermons were taken very seriously and that congregants, who might arrive late and leave the service early, made sure that they did not miss any of the sermon.[17] However, these Good Friday Passions in the Neukirche represented a significant new development in Holy Week music that must have aroused significant curiosity, since the music heard throughout the church year in the Neukirche was known to be noticeably different from the other Leipzig churches. In a memorandum on the need to improve church music in Leipzig (29 May 1720), Kuhnau complained that he could not find suitable musicians for his church music in the two principal churches because the most able were involved in the attractive, operatic church music being performed in the Neukirche. His view was that the Neukirche

---

14 Scheibel specifically mentions hearing a German Magnificat, *Meine Seele erhebt den Herrn*, by Vogler; see Scheibel, *Zufällige Gedancken*, 65. Scheibel may have heard the music of Melchior Hoffmann, Telemann's successor at the Neukirche, but Hoffmann died soon after Scheibel's arrival in Leipzig.

15 The Brockes libretto is specifically mentioned; see Scheibel, *Zufällige Gedancken*, 73; see also Andreas Glöckner, *Die Musikpflege an der Leipziger Neukirche zur Zeit Johann Sebastian Bachs*, Beiträge zur Bach-Forschung 8 (Leipzig: Nationale Forschungs- und Gedenkstätten Johann Sebastian Bach, 1990), 79.

16 Gottfried Ephraim Scheibel, "Random Thoughts about Church Music in Our Day (1721)," introduced and translated (with some abbreviation) by Joyce Irwin, in Baron, *Bach's Changing World*, 237 (slightly modified); Scheibel, *Zufällige Gedancken*, 30: "Ich weiß mich zu erinnern/ daß in einem gewissen Orte am Charfreytage vor und nach der Predigt eine Passion solte gemusiciret werden. Des Predigers wegen waren die Leute gewißlich nicht so zeitig/ und mit so grossem Gedräng in die Kirche kommen/ sondern/ wie vermuthlich/ der Music wegen."

17 Tanya Kevorkian, *Baroque Piety: Religion, Society, and Music in Leipzig, 1650–1750* (Aldershot: Ashgate, 2007), 33.

Gottesdienst was being profaned by these young "Operisten," who did not understand the true church style, preferring instead the "lusty music of the opera and coffee houses."[18] As a student in Leipzig, Scheibel must have been one of the "Operisten" that Kuhnau had in mind. In his *Zufällige Gedancken* Scheibel cites the libretto of Telemann's opera *Jupiter und Semele, oder Der unglückliche Alcmeon* (TVWV 21:7; music lost),[19] performed in Leipzig's opera house (number 463 Brühlstraße) in 1716 and/or 1718, and Vogler's *Die über Haß und Liebe triumphitende Tugend, oder Artaxerxes*,[20] performed in 1718.[21] The references to these operas implies at least that he had heard them. However, since the Leipzig opera was to some extent dependent on student performers,[22] it is not beyond the bounds of possibility that Scheibel performed in Leipzig operas during his student years, or was in some way involved in these performances. No doubt Scheibel continued his interest in opera on returning to Breslau, especially after 1725, when Italian opera flourished under the direction of the Venetian impresario Antonio Peruzzi.[23] Scheibel also seems to have maintained links with, or at least an interest in, the Hamburg opera, a conclusion that can be drawn from his book dedications to Telemann, Mattheson, and Brockes.

Opera in church

One of the distinctive features of *Zufällige Gedancken* is Scheibel's advocacy of operatic elements for church music, such as the expression of emotion and even the use of mature female singers in place of indifferent boy sopranos. For example, he wrote:

> I do not know why operas alone should have the privilege of squeezing tears from us; why is that not true in the church? ... if a composer can move (*moviren*) within me the affections in theatrical and secular music, he will be able to do this in spiritual matters, as witness the examples of Messieurs Keiser, Mattheson and Telemann.[24]

---

18 Philipp Spitta, *Johann Sebastian Bach*, 4th ed (Leipzig: Breitkopf & Härtel, 1930), 2: 866; Glöckner, *Die Musikpflege an der Leipziger Neukirche*, 82. See also the discussion of the connections between the Leipzig opera and the Neukirche in Michael Maul, *Barockoper in Leipzig (1693–1720)* (Freiburg: Rombach, 2009), 1: 535–38.

19 Specifically, the first two arias of Scene II, Act I. See Maul, *Barockoper in Leipzig*, 2: 1040–43 (No. 70).

20 Maul, *Barockoper in Leipzig*, 2: 1033–34 (No. 66).

21 Scheibel, *Zufällige Gedancken*, 35–38; Scheibel, "Random Thoughts about Church Music," 239–40. On the Leipzig opera during the years Scheibel was a student (1715–1719), see Maul, *Barockoper in Leipzig*, esp. 1: 107–8, and 2: 862–63.

22 See Maul, *Barockoper in Leipzig*, 1: 250–51; Reinhard Strohm, *Dramma per Musica: Italian Opera Seria of the Eighteenth Century* (New Haven: Yale University Press, 1997), 92.

23 See Strohm, *Dramma per Musica*, 93, 95.

24 Scheibel, "Random Thoughts about Church Music," 240–41 (slightly modified); Scheibel, *Zufällige Gedancken*, 40–41: "Und ich weiß nicht woher die Opern allein das Privilegium

90 *Liturgy*

Scheibel's advocacy of operatic techniques was part of a larger debate concerning musical style in church music that was then being hotly disputed. It would continue for a further twenty years and beyond.[25] Bach scholars, from Spitta on, have tended to underestimate the significance of the new developments in cantata composition, arguing that they represent an ongoing continuity in which the long-standing practical outworking of the Orthodox Lutheran theology of music was given new dimensions, and implying that it was only the Pietists who had any problems with the newly imported style. But as Joyce Irwin points out, that conclusion is at variance with the evidence, and these developments were much more radical and revolutionary—both theologically as well as practically—than has often been understood.[26]

In many respects the debate begins with Erdmann Neumeister,[27] who wrote a complete cycle of cantata libretti for Johann Philipp Krieger at the Weissenfels court[28] in the early 1700s. These texts are characterized by their use of forms, such as recitatives and arias, that until then were usually heard only in an opera house. When the cycle was published anonymously in 1702,[29] the libretti were introduced with a preface[30] by Neumeister that included the following:

> haben/ daß sie uns die Thränen auspressen sollen/ warum geht das nicht in der Kirchen an? … Kan mir ein Componiste in *Theatra*lischen und weltlichen Musicken die Affecten *mo*viren/ so wird er solches in geistlichen Dingen thun können/ wie solches das Exempel *Mons.* Käysers/ Mathesons und Telemanns bezeuget."

25 See the discussion in Joyce Irwin, *Neither Voice nor Heart Alone: German Lutheran Theology of Music in the Age of the Baroque* (New York: Lang, 1993), 127–39; the summary in Joseph Herl, *Worship Wars in Early Lutheranism: Choir, Congregation, and Three Centuries of Conflict* (New York: Oxford University Press, 2004), 122–23; and especially Christian Bunners, "Musiktheologische Aspekte im Streit um den Neumeisterschen Kantatentyp," in *Erdmann Neumeister (1671–1756): Wegbereiter der evangelischen Kirchenkantate*, ed. Henrike Rucker (Rudolstadt: Hain, 2000), 39–50.

26 Irwin, *Neither Voice nor Heart Alone*, 127–28.

27 On Neumeister, see Chapter 13. Of course, Neumeister was not the first to incorporate operatic elements into the cantata form, but he was the most influential proponent.

28 For the background, see Arno Werner, *Städtische und fürstliche Musikpflege in Weissenfels bis zum Ende des 18. Jahrhunderts* (Leipzig: Breitkopf & Härtel, 1911).

29 *Geistliche Cantaten Uber alle Sonn- Fest- und Apostel-Tage/ Zu einer/ denen Herren Musicis sehr bequemen Kirchen-Music In ungezwungenen Teutschen Versen ausgefertiget* ([s.l.]: [s.n.], 1702); see Wolf Hobohm, "Ein unbekannter, früher Textdruck der *Geistliche Cantaten* von Erdmann Neumeister," *Jahrbuch KMBM*, 2000 (2001): 182–86. A second edition appeared two years later: Erdmann Neumeister, *Geistliche Cantaten statt einer Kirchen-Music. Die zweyte Auflage Nebst einer neuen Vorrede* ([Hamburg]: [s.n.], 1704). Further editions were also published, see: Irmgard Scheitler, "Zwei weitere frühe Drucke von Neumeisters *Geistlichen Cantaten*," *Jahrbuch KMBM,* 2003 (2005): 365–67; Ute Poetzsch-Seban, "Weitere Aspekte zu den Geistlichen Kantaten von Erdmann Neumeister," *Jahrbuch KMBM, 2000* (2001): 182–86.

30 See Wolfgang Miersemann, "Erdmann Neumeisters 'Vorbericht' zu seinen 'Geistliche Cantaten' von 1704: ein literatur- und musikprogrammatische 'Meister-Stück,'" Rucker, *Erdmann Neumeister*, 51–74.

Bach and the cantata controversy   91

To express myself briefly, a cantata seems to be nothing else than a portion of an opera composed of *stylo recitativo* and *arien* together ...[31] I have already said that a *cantata* has the appearance of a piece taken out of an opera, and it might almost be supposed that many would be offended in spirit and ask how sacred music and opera can be reconciled, any more than Christ and Belial, or light and darkness. And therefore it might be said I should have done better to choose another form. But I will not strive to justify myself in this matter till first I am answered: Why certain other spiritual songs are not done away with which are the same *genus versuum* as worldly, nay, often scandalous songs? Why the *instrumenta musica* are not destroyed which we hear in churches today, and which only yesterday were performed upon for the luxury of worldly pleasure? And hence, whether this kind of poetry, though it has borrowed its model from theatrical verse, may not be sanctified by being dedicated to the honor of God? Whether the apostle's words may not be applied to this case, as it is written in 1 Cor. 7:14; 1 Tim. 4:5; Phil. 1:18, and whether such an application is not a sufficient answer on my part?[32]

Neumeister had developed his reform cantata libretti in connection with specific courts that were often noted for their performances of opera. His first cantata cycle, as has been observed, was produced for Johann Philipp Krieger,

31 Here Neumeister is echoing the lectures on poetry he gave at Leipzig University in 1695. These lectures were plagiarized, edited, and published by Christian Friedrich Hunold, under the pseudonym Menantes, as *Die Allerneueste Art/ Zur Reinen und galanten Poesie zu gelangen* (Hamburg: Liebernickel, 1707). The section on cantata includes the following: "Also werden nun kürtzlich die *Cantate* auf dieser Art gemacht/ daß man *Stylum recitativum* und *Arien* mit einander abwechselt. Mit einem Wort: Eine *Cantata* siehet aus/ wie ein Stück aus einer *Opera*". (Thus one can briefly state that a cantata is made up in this way: recitatives and arias alternating with each other. In a word: a cantata is to be seen as a piece of an opera). Menantes, *Die Allerneueste Art*, 284–85.
32 Spitta ET I: 473, 478–79. Erdmann Neumeister, *Geistliche Cantaten Uber alle Sonn- Fest- und Apostel-Tage/ Zu beförderung Gott geheiligter Hauß- Und Kirchen-Andacht: In ungezwungenen Teutschen Versen ausgefertigt* (Halle: Renger, 1705), sig. (2ᵛ)–(3ʳ); sig. (7ᵛ– 8ʳ): "Soll ichs kurtzlich aussprechen/ so siehet eine Cantata nicht anders aus/ als ein Stück aus einer *Opera*, von *Stylo Recitativo* und *Arien* zusammen gesetzt ... Doch hatte ich oben gesagt: Eine *Cantata* sahe aus/ wie ein Stück einer Opera; so dürffte fast muthmassen/ daß sich mancher ärgern möchte/ und dencken: Wie eine Kirchen-Music und Opera zusammen stimmeten? Vielleicht/ wie Christus und Belial? Etwan/ wie Licht und Finsternis? Und demnach hätte man lieber/ werden sie sprechen/ eine andere Arth erwehlen sollen. Wiewohl darüber will ich mich rechtfertigen lassen/ wenn man mir erst beantworter hat: Warumb man nicht andere Geistliche Lieder abschaffet/ welche mit Weltlichen und manchmal schändlichen Liedern eben einerley genus versuum haben? Warumb man nicht die instrumenta Musica zerschlägt/ welche heute sich in der Kirche hören lassen/ und doch wohl gestern bey einer üppigen Weltlust aufwarten müssen? Sodann: Ob diese Arth Gedichte/ wenn sie gleich ihr Modell von Theatralischen Versen erborget/ nicht dadurch geheiliget/ indem/ daß sie zur Ehre Gottes gewiedmet wird? Und ob nicht dißfals die Apostolischen Sprüche 1. Cor. VII.14. 1 Tim. IV.5. Phil. 1. 18. in applicatione justa mir zu einer gnugsamen Verantwortung dienen können?"

92 Liturgy

Capellmeister at the court of Weissenfels (1700–1701, published Hamburg 1704, reprinted Halle 1705, and Querfurth, 1727); the second cycle for Philipp Heinrich Erlebach, Capellmeister at the court of Rudolstadt (1707, published Augsburg 1708); and the third and fourth cycles for Georg Philipp Telemann, Capellmeister at the court of Eisenach[33] (the third published in Gotha, 1711, and the fourth in Frankfurt 1714, reprinted in Eisenach 1717). Thus, the new cantata form was first introduced into court chapels, served by musicians who were also actively involved in opera, rather than in parish churches.[34] It was in parish churches where resistance was primarily registered. Thus, Kuhnau complained of the operatic music of the Neukirche, Leipzig, and when Bach succeeded him a few years later as the Thomascantor, he had to sign a similar document to the one Kuhnau had endorsed in 1701. Bach vowed that "In order to preserve the good order in the churches, [I shall] so arrange the music that it shall not last too long, and shall be of such a nature as not to make an operatic impression, but rather incite the listeners to devotion."[35]

Where the new cantata form was encountered as text, then it was received as devotional poetry. In 1715 Johann David Schieferdecker, teacher in the Weissenfels gymnasium, wrote a cycle of cantata libretti, clearly influenced by Neumeister, that was published the following year.[36] The same year Neumeister's four cycles were republished together with a fifth: *Fünfffache Kirchen-Andachten … Cantaten und Oden Auf alle Sonn- und Fest-Tage des gantzen Jahres* (Leipzig: Groß, 1716). Both publications were given brief

33 There was no opera in Eisenach but Telemann continued to compose for the Leipzig opera while in Eisenach, where he wrote four or five complete annual cycles of cantatas, an activity he continued when he moved to Frankfurt in 1712. Four or five of Telemann's operas were performed in Leipzig between 1712 and 1719; see Maul, *Barockoper in Leipzig*, 2: 861–63.

34 For the background, see Konrad Küster, "'Theatralisch vorgestellet': zur Aufführungspraxis höfischer Vokalwerke in Thüringen um 1710/20," in *Barockes Musiktheater im mitteldeutschen Raum im 17. und 18. Jahrhundert*, ed. Friedhelm Brusniak (Cologne: Studio, 1994), 118–41.

35 NBR 105, No. 100; BDok 1: 177 (No. 92): "7). Zu Beybehaltung guter Ordnung in denen Kirchen [soll er] die *Music* dergestalt einrichten, daß sie nicht zulang währen, auch also beschaffen seyn möge, damit sie nicht *opern*hafftig herauskommen, sondern die Zuhörer vielmehr zur Andacht aufmuntere." The document is dated 5 May 1723. Bach's election as Cantor had taken place two weeks earlier, on 22 April, when the minute recording Dr. Steger's vote for Bach included the following directive: "he should make compositions that were not theatrical." NBR 103 (No. 98); BDok 2: 94 (No. 129): "und hätte er solche *Compositiones* zu machen, die nicht *theatralis*ch wären."

36 Johann David Schieferdecker, *Auserlesene aus Fürstlichen Gedancken … Nach Ordnung der Sonn- und Festtäglichen Evangelien, in Geistliche Cantaten verfasset* (Eisleben: [s. n.], [1716]. The libretti were composed and performed in the Schloß-Kirche, Weissenfels, and the Schloss-Capelle, Sangerhausen, in 1715 and 1716, by the two Capellmeistern, Johann Philipp Krieger, and Johann Augustin Kobelius, respectively. Kobelius composed and directed more than twenty operas at the Weissenfels court between 1715 and 1729; see Werner, *Städtische und fürstliche musikpflege in Weissenfels*, 119–20. In 1702 the seventeen-year-old Sebastian Bach was considered for the position of organist in Sangerhausen but was overruled by Duke Johann Georg of Saxe-Weissenfels, who insisted on Kobelius being appointed, who thus also became part of the Weissenfels court establishment; see Chapter 13.

reviews in the Orthodox theological journal, *Unschuldige Nachrichten*,[37] published in Leipzig in 1717.[38] Here it is noted that Neumeister's libretti make possible a new and artistic form of music for public worship, and that Schiefferdecker's poetry is thought to be very well done. But the stress in these reviews is on the textual content; it was when these libretti were set to music that significant reservation or opposition arose. For example, Christian Gerber, writing somewhat later, said: "It is indeed true that there will remain a place for moderate music in the church ... it is at the same time a well-known fact that very often the performances are excessive ... .The reason is that this music often sounds so very worldly and jolly that it is more befitting a dance floor or an opera than the divine service."[39] Friedrich Smend dismisses Gerber's criticism as being typical of a Pietist.[40] But the matter was not that simple: there were protagonists and antagonists on both sides of the Orthodox–Pietist divide, as among both clergy and musicians there were those who argued for and against the operatic texts and their musical settings. Those in favor tended to be connected in some way with music at court, especially where opera was performed, and those against tended to be connected with the music of civic churches.

Neumeister was called to become the primary pastor of the Jacobikirche, Hamburg, in 1715, and the anthology of his five cycles of cantata libretti was published in that city the following year. Significantly, Neumeister's "Vorbericht" to the first cycle, in which he stated that a cantata is essentially a portion of an opera, was not included in the 1716 collection. Instead, a new preface by the editor Gottfried Tilgner, which was much more circumspect and defensive than Neumeister's earlier preface had been, introduced the libretti. After referring to critics of the new cantata form, Tilgner continued:

> Since these clever opponents earnestly protest that they do not intend to censure church music generally but only its degenerating misuse, it freely has the appropriate appearance of being in the right when they zealously

---

37 *Unschuldige Nachrichten*, the first German theological journal, issued between 1701 and 1761 under a number of slightly different titles. The first volume was published by Ludwieg in Wittenberg; thereafter in Leipzig, by Grosse 1702–1719 and by Braun 1720–1761 (hereafter cited as UN).

38 Neumeister, UN (1717): 264–65; Schiefferdecker, UN (1717): 654.

39 Christian Gerber, *Historie der Kirchen-Ceremonien in Sachsen* (Dresden and Leipzig, 1732), cited by Friedrich Smend, *Bach in Köthen*, trans. John Page, ed. Stephen Daw (St. Louis: Concordia, 1985), 155; Friedrich Smend, *Bach in Köthen* (Berlin: Christlicher Zeitschriftenverlag, 1951), 135: "Ob nun wohl eine mäßige Music in der Kirche bleiben kann ... so ist doch bekannt, daß sehr offt damit exediret wird ... Denn es klinget offt so gar weltlich und lustig, dass sich solche Music besser auff einem Tantzboden oder in eine Opera schickte, als zum Gottesdienste." The passage continues with an anecdote of a Passion performance in an unnamed town—once thought to have been a performance of a Bach Passion—when an elderly dowager exclaimed: "It is like being at a comic opera" ("Ist es doch, als ob man in einer Opera-Comödie wäre").

40 Smend, *Bach in Köthen*, 137; ET, 156–57.

94   *Liturgy*

contend that the temple of the Lord should not become an opera house, nor his sanctuary be made into a theater of ear-tickling voluptuousness ... In truth, whoever sings of the painful suffering of our Savior according to the melody of a *folie d'Espagne*[41] or wishes to celebrate his joyous resurrection and ascension with the rhythm of a *courant* or *gigue*,[42] would fairly be considered a very simple-minded worshiper of divine mysteries if not a godless scoffer, and I have no wish to excuse such folly.[43]

The division concerning the new cantata form was to some extent generational, with the older generation being characterized by the younger as being backward-looking, while they saw themselves as forward-looking. Among musicians there perhaps can also be seen an added friction between organists and other musicians. Organists, whose main sphere was the church, were immersed in the old modalism of the chorale melodies with which they were constantly involved,[44] whereas other musicians, who performed in the orchestras and *collegia musica* of opera and coffee houses, generally favored the newer major–minor tonality.[45] This is the friction that burst into flames in the Buttstett–Mattheson dispute of the second decade of the eighteenth century. Johann Mattheson published *Das Neu-Eröffnete Orchestre* (Hamburg: Schiller, 1713) in which he criticized the older practices of Lutheran composers and promoted secular styles. Johann Heinrich Buttstett, organist of the Predigerkirche, Erfurt—and certainly no Pietist—responded with *Ut, Mi, Sol, Re, Fa, La, tota Musica et Harmonia Aeterna* (Erfurt: ca.

---

41 *La Folia*, the theme most commonly used by baroque composers for sequences of variations.
42 "I gladly grant that minuets, jigs, gavottes, passepieds, and so on are not appropriate in church because they induce idle thoughts in the listeners": Scheibel, "Random Thoughts about Church Music," 241; "Ich gebe gerne zu/ daß *Menuet*en/ *Gigu*en/ *Gavott*en/ *Passpieds* &c. sich in die Kirchen nicht schicken/ weil dadurch den Zuhöhrern eitele *Ideen* beygebracht werden": Scheibel, *Zufällige Gedancken*, 41.
43 Neumeister, *Fünfffache Kirchen-Andachten*, sig. (5v–6v): "Denn weil diese viel klügern Gegner ernstlich darwider protestiren, daß sie nicht gesonnen waren die Kirchen-Musick überhaupt, sondern den eingerissenen Mißbrauch derselben anzufechten: so hat es freylich einen ziemlichen Schein des Rechten, wenn sie eifern, daß man den Tempel des Herrn nicht zu einem Opern-Hause, noch sein Heiligthum zu einem Schau-Platze Ohren-kützelnder Uppigkeiten machen solle ... In Wahrheit, wer das schmertzliche Leiden unsers Heylandes nach der Melodie einer 'folie d'Espagne' besingen, oder desselben frölche Auferstehung und Himmelfarth mit Couranten- und Giquen- Tackte bejauchzen wolte, würde billig wo nicht vor einen gottlosen Spötter." Translation based on Irwin, *Neither Voice nor Heart Alone*, 136.
44 Scheibel's comment is revealing: "As far as figured music is concerned, I think that it is greatly to be preferred over chorales, for in this each word expressing feeling is paid its due, which in chorales is just passed over quickly": Scheibel, "Random Thoughts about Church Music," 235; Scheibel, *Zufällige Gedancken*, 23: "Was die *Figural-Music* anbelangt/ so halt ich davor/ daß diese vor der *Choral-Music* einen grossen Vorzug haben müsse. Denn da wird jedem *affectueusen* Worte ein Genügen gethan/ da man in den *Chora*len nur drüber weg geht."
45 On the background, see Joel Lester, "Major-Minor Concepts and Modal Theory in Germany, 1592–1680," *Journal of the American Musicological Society* 30 (1977): 208–53.

Bach and the cantata controversy   95

1715), a point-by-point polemical refutation of Mattheson.[46] In particular, Buttstett bemoans the blurring of the traditional distinction between ecclesiastical and secular styles:

> What difference is there today between church, theater, and chamber music? One is pretty much the same as the other. Nearly every kind of songful stuff is presently brought into the church along with the *stylus recitativus theatralis*, and the more merrily and dancingly it goes, the better it pleases most people (but not all).[47]

Scheibel agreed with Buttstett's assessment that there was little or no distinction between the new music of the church and the music of contemporary opera, but he viewed this as a positive asset, whereas Buttstett saw it only as a negative liability. Scheibel wrote:

> The tone that gives me pleasure in an opera can also do the same in church, except that it has a different object ... If our church music today were a little livelier and freer, that is to say, more theatrical, it would be more beneficial than the stilted compositions that are ordinarily used in churches. When, for example, there is supposed to be pleasant music, a serious, slow air is offered, where the 6/8 beat is played yet more slowly than its nature requires, and thereby the movement of the affections is notably constrained. And this is also the reason why our church music today must suffer along. People are so accustomed to the old humdrum[48] and hammersmith's[49] compositions which contain neither charm nor gracefulness, and most think that whatever sounds nice and old-fashioned and simple fits best in church.[50]

46 On the background, see Beekman C. Cannon, *Johann Mattheson: Spectator in Music* (New Haven: Yale University Press, 1947), 83–84, 134–38.
47 Johann Heinrich Buttstett *Ut, Mi, Sol, Re, Fa, La, tota Musica et Harmonia Aeterna* (Erfurt: Werther, ca. 1715), 64: "Und was ist heut zu tage zwischen Kirchen- *Theatral* und Cammer *Musique* für ein Unterschied? es ist ja fast eine wie die andere. Bringet man doch jetzo nebst dem *Stylo recitativo Theatrali* fasst allen liederlichen Krahm in die Kirche/ und je lustiger und tantzlicher es gehet/ je besser gefället es theils Personen/ (aber nicht allen)." Trans. based on Claude V. Palisca, "The Genesis of Mattheson's Style Classification," *New Mattheson Studies*, ed. George J. Buelow and Hans Joachim Marx (Cambridge: Cambridge University Press, 1983), 410. See also the similar statement that occurs a little later: Buttstett, *Ut, Mi, Sol, Re,*, 81.
48 "Alten Schlendrians." Note that "Schlendrian" is the name of the father in Bach's Coffee Cantata (BWV 211).
49 Pun on the name of Andreas Hammerschmidt (1612–1675), whose church music was widely circulated and performed during the second half of the seventeenth century and the beginning of the eighteenth century.
50 Scheibel, "Random Thoughts about Church Music," 238, 240. Scheibel, *Zufällige Gedancken*, 35, 39–40: "Der Thon/ der mich in einer *Opern* vergnügt/ der kan auch solches in der Kirchen thun/ nur daß er ein anders *Objectum* hat ... wenn unsre Kirchen-Music heut zu Tage ein

96   *Liturgy*

For many, what Scheibel was advocating—along with Neumeister, Mattheson, and others—was a radical agenda. Not surprisingly, Scheibel's treatise was warmly received by Mattheson in Hamburg, who wrote in his *Critica Musica* (1722), "I have never read anything like this that accords so well with my sentiments."[51] Over the years Mattheson made it clear again and again that an operatic style should form the basis for "modern" church music, with such statements as, "Operas are the academies of music, as concerts are its grammar schools, but in the church is found its true calling."[52]

The debate was epitomized by the printed polemics that flowed back and forth between Joachim Meyer in Göttingen, who opposed the intervention of the operatic style, and Mattheson in Hamburg, who promoted it.[53] The first salvo was fired by Meyer, lawyer, professor of music and cantor of the Göttingen gymnasium: *Unvorgreiffliche Gedancken über die neulich eingerissene theatralische Kirchen-Music* (Lemgo, 1726),[54] a title that might have been suggested by Scheibel's *Zufällige Gedancken*, perhaps hinting that Scheibel's thoughts may have been random, but they were biased, whereas in contrast his, Meyer's, were impartial, or at least so he claimed. Mattheson responded to this

---

wenig lebhafftiger und freyer/ *c'est a dire*, mehr *theatra*lisch wäre/ sie würde mehr Nutzen schaffen/ als die gezwungne *Composition*, der man sich in der Kirchen *ordinair* bedienet. Soll zum Exempel etwas erfreuliches gemusiciret werden/ so giebt man ihm ein ernsthafftes langsames *Air*, da der Sechs achtel *Tact* noch einmahl so langsam gemusiciret wird/ als seine Natur mit sich bringt/ wodurch auch die *Motion* der *Affecten* um ein merckliches gehemmet wird; Und dieses ist auch die Ursache/ warum unsre heutige Kirchen-Music so herleiden muß. Die Leute sind des Alten Schlendrians und der Hammer-Schmiedischen *Composition* gewohnt/ da weder Anmuth noch Zierligkeit drinnen stecket/ und die meisten dencken/ alles was fein altväterisch und einfaltig klinget/ schicke sich am besten in die Kirche."

51 Johann Mattheson, *Critica Musica*, I/2 (Hamburg: [Mattheson], 1722), 96: "ich niemahls etwas dergleichen gelesen/ das mit meinen sentimens so wohl übereingekommen wäre"; see also the whole section, I/2: 96–104.

52 Johann Mattheson, *Die neueste untersuchung der Singspiele, nebst beygefügter musikalischen Geschmachsprobe* (Hamburg: Herold, 1744), 103–4: "Die Opern sind der Musik Academien: so wie die Concerte ihre Gymnasien; in der Kirche aber findet sie den rechten Beruf." See also Johann Mattheson, *Der Musicalische Patriot* (Hamburg: [Mattheson], 1728), 9. While advocating operatic elements in church music, Mattheson nevertheless continued to maintain a distinction between Kirchstil, Theatralischenstil, and Kammerstil.

53 Literature includes, Jürgen Heidrich, *Der Meier-Mattheson-Disput: Eine Polemik zur deutschen protestantischen Kirchenkantate in der ersten Hälfte des 18. Jahrhunderts* (Göttingen: Vandenhoeck & Ruprecht, 1995 [= *Nachrichten der Akademie der Wissenschaften in Göttingen. I. Philologisch-Historische Klasse*, Jg. 1995, Nr. 3, 55–107]; Arno Forchert, "Polemik als Erkenntnisform: Bemerkung zu den Schriften Matthesons," in *New Mattheson Studies*, ed. George J. Buelow and Hans-Joachim Marx, 199–212, esp. 209–11; Cannon, *Mattheson: Spectator in Music*, 58, 185–86. Opera itself was not without its critics, and supporters of opera were divided between conservatives, who wanted to continue older traditions, and radicals, who wanted significant reforms; see chapter 4, "The Crisis of Baroque Opera in Germany," in Strohm, *Dramma per Musica*, 81–96.

54 Joachim Meyer, *Unvorgreiffliche Gedancken über die neulich eingerissene theatralische Kirchen-Music und denen darinnen bishero üblich gewordenen Cantaten mit Vergleichung der Music voriger Zeiten Verbesserung der Unsrigen vorgestellet von J. M. D.* ([Lemgo]: [s.n.], 1726).

Bach and the cantata controversy 97

attack on the theatrical style of church music with *Der neue Göttingische aber viel schlechter/ als die alten Lacedämonischen/ urtheilende Ephorus* (Hamburg, 1727), which was dedicated to Scheibel.[55] To reinforce his position, Mattheson brought out a weekly newspaper *Der Musicalische Patriot* (1728), modeled on the general Hamburg newspaper *Der Patriot*, which by installments brought together a comprehensive discussion of the fundamental biblical, theological, philosophical, moral, and artistic principles that undergirded theatrical church music. In so doing, Mattheson again makes approving reference to Scheibel's *Zufällige Gedancken.*[56] While *Der Musicalische Patriot* was still gradually appearing in print, Meyer issued another, longer salvo against Mattheson: *Der anmaßliche Hamburgische Criticus* (Lemgo, 1728).[57] Reviewing the debate, Beekman Cannon characterizes Meyer's literary style as "careless" and his reasoning "somewhat inadequate," and Mattheson's as overwhelming and expressed in his "customary violent, not to say rude, manner."[58]

Musicians continued to be divided over the issue, but among the clergy, not surprisingly, many were generally negative or at least extremely cautious with regard to the new reform style of cantata and its use of operatic forms. Thus, the theological journal, *Unschuldige Nachrichten*, gave space to reviews of both Meyer's negative titles,[59] but not to Mattheson's positive publications.[60] The journal also gave a brief notice to the somewhat inflammatory diatribe against the influence of opera on church music by Martin Heinrich Fuhrmann (1669–1745): *Die an der Kirchen Gottes gebauete Satans-Capelle Darin dem Jehova Zebaoth zu Leid und Verdruß, Und dem Baal-Zebub zur Freud und Genuß ...* (Berlin, 1729).[61] However, while generally supporting Meyer's two attacks on Mattheson, Fuhrmann did not condemn the cantata form as such: "I desire not that one should drive out of the church all cantatas along with the dogs, but only those that are fat and bloated with the spirit of opera."[62]

---

55 Johann Mattheson, *Der neue Göttingische aber viel schlechter, als die alten Lacedämonischen, urtheilende Ephorus, wegen der Kirchen-Music eines andern belehret* (Hamburg: [Mattheson], 1727): "Dem Wol-Edlen, Wolgelahrten Herrn, Gottfried Ephraim Scheibel, Rever. Minist. Candid. Wratisl. Sil. hat, durch freund-willige Zueignung dieses Wercks, seine Danckbarkeit, theils für öffentlich-erwiesene Ehre; am meisten aber für öffentliche Vertheidigung der guten Sache, auch öffentlich bezeugen wollen der Verfasser."

56 Mattheson, *Der Musicalische Patriot*, 105–20.

57 Joachim Meyer, *Der anmaßliche Hamburgische Criticus sine crisi entgegen gesetzet dem so genannten Göttingischen Ephoro Joh. Matthesons, und dessen vermeyntlicher Belehrungs-Ungrund der Verthädigung der Theatralischen Kirchen-Music* (Lemgo: [s.n.], 1728).

58 Cannon, *Mattheson: Spectator in Music*, 186.

59 Meyer's *Unvorgreiffliche Gedancken* (1726) was reviewed in UN (1726), 857, and his *Der anmaßliche Hamburgische Criticus* (1728) in UN (1730), 283–285.

60 The review of Meyer's *Der anmaßliche Hamburgische Criticus* in UN (1730), 283, has a passing reference to a review of Mattheson's *Der neue Göttingische Aber viel Schlechter* (1727) that can be found in "Leipziger Gelehrte Zeitungen 1727. p. 613."

61 UN (1729), 1044–1045.

62 Marco Hilario Frischmuth [Martin Heinrich Fuhrmann], *Die an der Kirchen Gottes gebauete Satans-Capelle Darin dem Jehova Zebaoth zu Leid und Verdruß, Und dem Baal-Zebub zur*

98   *Liturgy*

For Scheibel, much of the problem with the older church music was "the lack of apt texts."[63] He refers to the many annual cycles of cantata texts that were commonly produced and comments "but very few stand the test and are worthy to have a composition made of them."[64] Only three cantata librettists receive his approval: Neumeister (whom he likens to the Psalmists Asaph or David), Johann Jacob Rambach (with some reservations), and Salomo Franck.[65] Presumably because of this perceived general lack, four years after he had published his *Zufällige Gedancken*, Scheibel issued his own annual cycle of cantata libretti, *Poetische Andachten* (1725).[66] Dedicated to Mattheson[67] and Telemann, the volume had a twofold purpose. On the one hand, it contained models of what was required for the modern church cantata, and on the other hand, it furthered the argument for the newer style in the extended preface, running to some forty-eight unnumbered pages, a continuation of what he had begun in his *Zufällige Gedancken*, published four years earlier.

One-affect-theory

Scheibel's primary theme, to which he returns again and again in both the earlier treatise and in the extended preface to his collected cantata libretti,

---

Freud und Genuß... ([Berlin]: ["Heil. drey Könige Erben" (Heirs of the Holy Three Kings)], 45: "Ich will nicht, daß man alle *Cantaten* aus den Kirchen soll peitschen wie die Hunde, sondern nur diejenigen, so fett und feist am *Opern* Geist."

63 Scheibel, "Random Thoughts about Church Music," 241; Scheibel, *Zufällige Gedancken*, 41: "Wiewohl auch der Mangel geschickter Texte hieran schuld/ doch hiervon zuletzte."

64 Scheibel, "Random Thoughts about Church Music," 244–45; Scheibel, *Zufällige Gedancken*, 73: "die wenigsten aber halten den Stich/ und sind nicht wehrt."

65 Scheibel, "Random Thoughts about Church Music," 245; Scheibel, *Zufällige Gedancken*, 74–76, 78. In his later short history of church music, which devotes barely two pages to the contemporary situation, Scheibel adds a few more names of worthy librettists, notably Benjamin Schmolcke; Gottfried Ephraim Scheibel, *Die Geschichte der Kirchen-Music alter und neuer Zeiten* (Breslau: Korn, 1738; facsimile [with *Zufällige Gedancken*], Stuttgart: Cornetto, 2002), 47.

66 In 1734 Scheibel published a book on the improvement of poetry and in 1738 issued a second cycle of cantata libretti: Gottfried Ephraim Scheibel, *Die Unerkannte Sünden der Poeten Welche man Sowohl in ihren Schrifften als in ihrem Leben wahrnimmt. Nach den Regeln des Christenthums und vernünftiger Sittenlehre geprüfet* (Leipzig: Teubner, 1734; facsimile, Munich: Kraus, 1981), dedicated to Barthold Heinrich Brockes; Gottfried Ephraim Scheibel, *Musicalisch-Poetische Andächtige Betrachtungen über alle Sonn- und Fest-Tags Evangelien Durchs gantze Jahre Andächtigen Seelen zur Erbauung ans Licht gestellt* (Breslau: Korn, 1738). He also produced an anthology of versifications for each Sunday, celebration, and observation throughout the church year: Gottfried Ephraim Scheibel, *Andachts-Blumen Der zu Ehren Gottes Blühenden Jugend Oder Gedenck-Reime Uber alle Son[n]- und Festtags-Evangelien ...* (Breslau: Korn, [1750]).

67 In the manuscript catalogue of his library that Mattheson compiled around 1764, Scheibel's *Poetische Andachten* is listed as number 122; Bibliotheksarchiv der Staats- und Universitätsbibliothek Hamburg (Sig. VI, 4): "Verzeichnis der Bücher und Schriften," fol. 4ᵛ; see Hans Joachim Marx, "Johann Matthesons Nachlaß zum Schicksal der Musiksammlung der alten Stadtbibliothek Hamburg," *Acta Musicologica* 55 (1983): 120.

is the need for music—in both theater and church—to express and evoke emotion: "religious and secular music have no distinctions, as far as the movement of the affections is concerned, and therefore a composer must make use of the same kinds of modes-of-operation for these."[68] In order to demonstrate this "Ein-Affekt-Theorie" (one-affect-theory),[69] in which the same affect is effective in both secular and sacred contexts, he quotes the texts of arias from operas by Telemann and Vogler and then parodies each in turn to make them suitable for inclusion in church cantatas,[70] and thus, with the parodied text, to "express precisely the affection the composition brings with it."[71]

The whole of the second chapter of *Zufällige Gedancken* is devoted to "the goal of music or the movement of the affections."[72] The recurring word and concept in his preface to the *Poetische Andachten* is "affect." One of Scheibel's most significant statements comes near the beginning of *Zufällige Gedancken*:

> If someone asks, "What is music?" I answer thus: *quod sit Ars, quae docet per Mutationem Tonorem Affectus movere*,[73] or in the vernacular, that it is an art which shows us how one can move the affections through the changing of the notes.[74]

Mattheson, of course, had written about the possibility of expressing a wide variety of emotions in opera in *Das Neu-Eröffnete Orchestre* (1713),[75] where,

---

68 Scheibel, "Random Thoughts about Church Music," 238 (slightly modified); Scheibel, *Zufällige Gedancken*, 34: "daß die Kirchen- und die Welt-Music/ was die *Motion* der Affecten anbetrifft nicht eignes habe/ und also ein *Componiste* hierzu sich einerley *Modi* bedienen müsse."

69 Maul, *Barockoper in Leipzig*, 1: 536.

70 Scheibel, "Random Thoughts about Church Music," 239–40; Scheibel, *Zufällige Gedancken*, 35–39; see also Maul, *Barockoper in Leipzig*, 1: 532–34. Maul's discussion of Scheibel occurs in his extended study of Melchior Hoffmann's use of Scheibel's church cantatas as sources for his operas. For example, Hoffmann's cantata for Mariae Verkündigung (Annunciation), *Entfernet euch, ihr schmeichelnden Gedanken*, which had been performed in the Neukirche, Leipzig (see Glöckner, *Die Musikpflege an der Leipziger Neukirche*, 52–53 [No. 34]), was parodied in the opera *Ismenie und Montaldo*, staged in the Leipzig opera house in 1713; Maul, *Barockoper in Leipzig*, 1: 529–57, esp. 538–44.

71 Scheibel, "Random Thoughts about Church Music," 239; Scheibel, *Zufällige Gedancken*, 35: "und *exprimire* eben den *affect* den die *Composition* mit sich bringt."

72 Scheibel, "Random Thoughts about Church Music," 232–34; Scheibel, *Zufällige Gedancken*, 10–18.

73 This has the appearance of a citation, but I have been unable to discover a saying remotely similar. The term "movere" is discussed below.

74 Scheibel, "Random Thoughts about Church Music," 230 (slightly modified); Scheibel, *Zufällige Gedancken*, 3–4: "Wenn jemand fragt: Was ist denn die Music? so antwort ich/ *quod sit Ars, quae docet per Mutationem Tonorum Affectus movere*; oder auf gutt deutsch: Die Music ist eine Kunst die uns weiset wie man durch die Abwechßlung der Thone die Affecten bewegen kan."

75 Mattheson, *Das Neu-Eröffnete Orchestre* (Hamburg: Schiller, 1713; repr., Hildeheim: Olms, 1993), 160–61.

100 *Liturgy*

through the skill of composer and singer each and every *Affectus* can be expressed beautifully and naturally better than in oratory,[76] better than in a painting or sculpture, for not only are operas expressed in words, but they are helped along by appropriate actions and above all interpreted by heart-moving music.[77]

But Mattheson had not yet developed his systematic expositions of various aspects of *Affektenlehre*; they came later in his *Vollkommene Capellmeister*, published in 1739.[78] Thus, Scheibel's writings of 1721 and 1725 complement and develop what Mattheson had published in 1713, and do so by referring to rhetorical categories:

> When I regard music and its effects without consideration of temperament, it already has such a connection with our passions, as for instance, sorrow, joy, contentment, anger, and so on, that it must necessarily move (*moviren*) us. If the mere words of an orator are capable of making our hearts cheerful or depressed, how much more is this true of music, which can depict an affection in an even more lively and penetrating manner.[79] ... For music is to be regarded as nothing other than a preparation for devotion, just like the *exordium* in an oration,[80] which is

76 Cannon mistranscribed "oratorie" as "oratorio."

77 Mattheson, *Das Neu-Eröffnete Orchestre*, 167–68: "da durch des *Componisten* und der Sänger Geschicklichkeit alle und jede *Affectus*, besser als in der *Oratorie*, besser als in der Mahlerey, besser als in der *Sculpture*, nicht allein *vivâ voce* schlecht weg, sondern mit Zuthun einer *convenablen Action*, und hauptsächlich vermittelst Herz-bewegender *Music*, gar schön und natürlich mögen *exprimiret* werden." Trans, Cannon, *Mattheson: Spectator in Music*, 129.

78 Johann Mattheson, *Der Vollkommene Capellmeister, Das ist Gründliche Anzeige aller derjenigen Sachen, die einer wissen, können, und vollkommen inne haben muß, der einer Capelle mit Ehren und Nutzen vorstehen will* (Hamburg: Herold, 1739; facsimile, Kassel: Bärenreiter, 1954).

79 Scheibel, "Random Thoughts about Church Music," 233; Scheibel, *Zufällige Gedancken*, 15–16: "Wiewohl wenn ich auch die Music und ihren *Effect* ohne Absicht der *Temperamente* ansehe/ so hat Sie schon mit unsern *Passion*en als da ist Traurigkeit/ Freude/ Zufriedenheit/ Zorn/ etc. so eine *Connexion* daß sie nothwendig *movir*en muß. Sind blosse Worte eines Redners fähig unser Gemuthe frölich oder betrübt zu machen/ wie vielmehr die Music/ die einen Affect noch lebhaffter und *penetrant*er vorstellen kan."

80 The *exordium*, or introduction, is a vital section of an oration, since it sets up the content of the oration itself, and conditions and prepares the auditors for what is to follow; see Quintillian, *Institutio rhetorica*, lib. 4, cap. 1. Scheibel's reference to music at the beginning of worship may well be an allusion to Quintillian's explanation of the Greek *prooimion*, the equivalent of the Latin *exordium*: "Nam sive propterea quod οἴμη cantus est et citharoedi pauca illa quae antequam legitimum certamen inchoent emerendi favoris gratia canunt prohoemium cognominaverunt" (Now *oimē* means song, and lyre-players gave the name *prooimion* to the short pieces they perform to win favour before they begin the formal competition); Quintillian, *The Orator's Education*, ed. and trans. Donald A. Russell [Loeb Classical Library] (Cambridge, MA: Harvard University Press, 2001), 2: 180, 181.

also the reason why the worship service in our churches usually begins with music.[81]

Of course, the connections between rhetoric and music were not new. From the sixteenth century the education offered in Lutheran Latin schools and universities continued to be based essentially on the seven liberal arts (grammar, logic, rhetoric, geometry, arithmetic, astronomy, and music), developed from the curricular provisions of Philipp Melanchthon, who was strongly influenced by classical authors such as Cicero and Quintillian. Cantors who taught music in the schools and directed the music of the churches were very often also required to teach Latin grammar and logic. A significant number of seventeenth-century cantors were also the authors of basic textbooks of music theory, which used rhetorical categories to explain and expound the nature, logic, and meaning of music:[82] they include Joachim Burmeister (1564–1629), Sethus Calvisius (1556–1615), and Johannes Lippius (1585–1612), among others.[83] As inheritors of medieval modal theory in which each mode was seen to reflect a specific emotion, these theorists draw attention to the expressive nature of music to reflect and convey emotional content. But the musical expression of these emotions was conditioned by the text being set. As Quintillian had declared: "Music ... uses all its skill to accord with the emotions required by the words it accompanies."[84] Gioseffo Zarlino (1517–1590), the most widely read music theorist in the seventeenth century, developed the understanding further:

For if the poet is not permitted to write a comedy in tragic verse, the musician will also not be permitted to combine unsuitably these two things, namely, harmony and words. Thus it will be inappropriate if in a joyful matter he uses a mournful harmony and a grave rhythm, neither where funereal and tearful matters are treated is he permitted to use a joyful harmony and a rhythm that is light or rapid, call it as we will. On

---

81 Scheibel, "Random Thoughts about Church Music," 235; Scheibel, *Zufällige Gedancken*, 22 "Denn sie [music] nichts anders als vor eine *Praeparation* zur Andacht anzusehen/ und eben das was das *Exordium* bey einer *Oration*; deßwegen auch meistens mit ihr der Gottes-Dienst in unsern Kirchen angefangen wird."

82 For the background, see for example, Hans-Heinrich Unger, *Die Beziehung zwischen Musik und Rhetorik im 16.-18. Jahrhundert* (Würzburg: Triltsch, 1941; reprint, Hildesheim: Olms, 2000); Brian Vickers, "Figures of Rhetoric/Figures of Music?" *Rhetorica: A Journal of the History of Rhetoric*, 2 (1984): 1–44; Dietrich Bartel, *Musica Poetica: Musical-Rhetorical Figures in German Baroque Music* (Lincoln: University of Nebraska Press, 1997).

83 Joachim Burmeister, *Musica Poetica* (Rostock: Myliander, 1606; facsimile, Kassel: Bärenreiter, 1955); Seth Calvisius, *Exercitatio musica tertia* (Leipzig: Schürerus, 1611; facsimile, Hildesheim: Olms, 1973); Johannes Lippius, *Synopsis musicæ novæ* (Strassburg: Ledertz, 1612; facsimile, Hildesheim: Olms, 2004).

84 Quintillian, *Institutio rhetorica*, lib. 1, cap. 10; Quintillian, *The Orator's Education*, 1: 225 and 224: "[Musice] moderata leniter canit totaque arte consentit cum eorum quae dicuntur adfectibus."

102   *Liturgy*

the contrary, he must use joyful harmonies and rapid rhythms in joyful matters, and in mournful ones, mournful harmonies and grave rhythms, so that everything may be done with proportion.[85]

As the seventeenth century progressed, there was a growing expressiveness in much of the church music, as there was an increase of emotional intensity in the devotional literature of the period.[86] But the aim was to mirror rather than to stimulate emotion; it was an *affectus exprimere*, the reflection or representation of emotion. What was seen as radical and new in the agenda of Mattheson, Scheibel, and others, and in the libretti of Neumeister and those who followed him, was the promotion of an *affectus movere*, the active evocation and stimulation of emotion. There was a radical shift away from the text as the object of composition and instead the listener became the focus of the music, where the aim was to evoke a subjective response to the music as it was being heard.[87]

In a sense it was the recovery of an understanding of rhetoric that was commonly expounded in the sixteenth century but which appears to have been generally overlooked from the early seventeenth century onwards.[88] Renaissance textbooks taught that a primary goal of rhetoric was "to move"

---

85 Oliver Strunk, *Source Readings in Music History.* Revised Edition, ed. Leo Treitler (New York: Norton, 1998), 458; Gioseffo Zarlino, *Le Istitutioni Harmoniche* [1558] (Venice: Senese, 1562), 339: "Percioche si come non è lecito tra i Poeti comporre una Comedia con versi Tragici; cosi non sarà lecito al Musico di accompagnare queste due cose, cioè l'Harmonia, & le Parole insieme, fuori di proposito. Non sarà adunque conveniente, che in una materia allegra usiamo l'Harmonia mesta, & i Numeri gravi; ne dove si tratta materie funebri, & piene di lagrime, è lecito usare un'Harmonie allegra, & li numeri veloci nelle materie allegre; & nelle materie meste le harmonie meste, & li numeri gravi; accioche ogni cosa sia fatta con proportione."

86 See Isabella van Elferen, *Mystical Love in the German Baroque: Theology, Poetry, Music* (Lanham, MD: Scarecrow, 2009); see also John Butt, "Emotion in the German Lutheran Baroque and the Development of Subjective Time Consciousness," *Musical Analysis* 29 (2010): 19–36.

87 Herl suggests that a significant marker of this shift in focus is the replacement of the old term for "congregation" (Gemeine, or Gemeinde) by "listeners," or "audience" (Zuhörer) in the writings that support the new style; see Herl, *Worship Wars in Early Lutheranism*, 123. However, the use of the term was broader; for example, "Zuhörer" was used in this way in the minutes of Bach's election as Thomascantor; BDok 1: 177 (No. 92; item 7). Speaking of supporters of the new style, Herl writes: "They saw the assembly more as passive spectators to be moved than as active participants in the liturgy, at least insofar as the Kirchenmusik was concerned" (ibid.). But it may well be that the opposite was the case—that they saw the hearers of the older church music as impassive spectators and regarded the aroused hearers of the new style as being actively engaged in the emotive music: hearing is passive; listening is active.

88 The decrease in the emphasis on rhetoric as *movere* coincides with the appearance of Aristotelian metaphysics in Lutheran universities in the early seventeenth century; see Jānis Krēsliņš, *Dominus narrabit in scriptura populorum: A Study of Early Seventeenth-Century Lutheran Teaching on Preaching and the* Lettische lang-gewünschte Postill *of Georgius Mancelius*, Wolfenbütteler Forschungen 54 (Wiesbaden: Harrassowitz, 1992), 17, 21–74.

Bach and the cantata controversy 103

the hearer by the content of what was heard, a concept expressed by cognates and synonyms of the Latin *movere*.[89] In this regard the influence of Philip Melanchthon was critical, not only for his specific writings on rhetoric but also in the rhetorical nature of his other writings.[90] His *Elementorum rhetorices* (Wittenberg, 1531), was widely disseminated, with more than fifty editions published by the end of the century,[91] together with various adaptations and translations. Here Melanchthon addresses the distinction between dialectics and rhetoric:

> The distinction, to put it perhaps more properly, is that the end or purpose of dialectics is to teach, but the function of rhetoric is to move (*permovere*) and stimulate minds and thus affect a person.[92]

The same year that Melanchthon's handbook was published (1531), Luther is recorded as making a similar statement: "Dialectic instructs, rhetoric moves (*movet*). The former belongs to the intellect, the latter to the will."[93] The Latin version circulated among academics, but the German version was more widely known from its inclusion in Luther's *Tischreden*, first published in 1566, with numerous later reprints and editions: "Dialectica lehret/ Rhetorica moviret und beweget/ Diese gehört zum Willen/ Jene zum Verstande" (Dialectic teaches, rhetoric moves and provokes; this [rhetoric] belongs to the will, that

---

89 See Klaus Dockhorn, "*Rhetorica movet*: Protestantische Humanismus und karolingische Renaissance," in *Rhetorik: Beiträge zu ihrer Geschichte in Deutschland vom 16.-20. Jahrhundert*, ed. Helmut Schanze (Frankfurt: Athenäion, 1974), 17–42; Fritz Reckow, "Zwischen Ontologie und Rhetorik: Die Idee des *movere animos* und der Übergang vom Spätmittelalter zur frühen Neuzeit in der Musikgeschichte," in *Traditionswandel und Traditionsverhalten*, ed. Walter Haug (Tübingen: Niemeyer, 1991): 145–78.

90 See Karl Bullemer, *Quellenkritische Untersuchungen zum I. Buche der Rhetorik Melanchthons* (Würzburg: Becker, 1902); Michael B. Aune, *To Move the Heart: Philip Melanchthon's Rhetorical View of Rite and Its Implications for Contemporary Ritual Theory* (San Francisco: Christian Universities Press, 1994); Michael Aune, "'A Heart Moved': Philip Melanchthon's Forgotten Truth about Worship," *Lutheran Quarterly* 12 (1998): 393–416.

91 Twenty-two editions were published in Wittenberg between 1531 and 1606; 36 editions were published in other cities between 1532 and 1578.

92 Mary Joan La Fontaine, "A Critical Translation of Philip Melanchthon's *Elementorum rhetorices libri duo*," PhD diss. (University of Michigan, 1968), 85; Philipp Melanchthon, *Elementorum rhetorices libri duo* (Wittenberg: Schleich, 1582), 14: "Iuxta hoc discrimen proprius Dialecticae finis est docere: Rhetoricae autem permovere, at[que] impellere animos, et ad affectum aliquem traducere." This is similar to what Melanchthon had written some years before in the prolegomena of *De rhetorica libri tres* (Basel: Froben, 1519), 6; see Aune, *To Move the Heart*, 14.

93 "Dialectica docet, rhetorica movet. Illa ad intellectum pertinent, haec ad voluntatem." WA *Tischreden*, 2: 359 (No. 2199). See Andrea Grün-Oesterreich and Peter L. Oesterreich, "*Dialectica docet, rhetorica movet*: Luthers Reformation der Rhetorik," in *Rhetorica Movet: Studies in Historical and Modern Rhetoric in Honor of Heinrich F. Plett*, ed. Peter L. Oesterreich and Thomas O. Sloane (Leiden: Brill, 1999), 25–41; see also Birgit Stolt, *Martin Luthers Rhetorik des Herzens* (Tübingen: Mohr Siebeck, 2000).

104   *Liturgy*

[dialectic] to the mind).[94] This may have been a source that influenced Scheibel and others in formulating their thinking with regard to *movere* and music, since Luther's statement in Aurifaber's compilation of the *Tischreden* occurs towards the end of chapter 68, "Von Schulen und Universiteten" (On Schools and Universities), under the subsection "Von gute Künsten" (On Fine Arts; fols. 574^r–577^r), that is, just two page turns from the beginning of chapter 69, "Von der Musica" (On Music; fols. 577^v–578).[95] Whether or not Scheibel was aware of this statement by Luther (or the statements of Melanchthon), it is somewhat remarkable that it was librettists and writers on music, rather than academics in the disciplines that taught and employed rhetoric (notably theology, philosophy, and law), who should revive this primary understanding of rhetoric that had been fundamental to education in the sixteenth century.[96]

Bach and the "theatralische Stil"

It is unlikely that Bach knew Scheibel personally, since the latter had left Leipzig four years before Bach moved to the city, and Scheibel spent the rest of his life in and around Breslau. The fact that Scheibel's *Zufällige Gedancken* (1721) and his *Poetische Andachten* (1725) were both copublished in Leipzig might indicate that the author made an occasional visit to the city where he had attended university, and if so, in later years could have encountered Bach. But this, of course, is mere speculation.

Bach must have been aware of the Leipzig opera and the music performed in the Neukirche long before he moved to the city. From his early Weimar years he had had personal connections with Telemann (his son Carl Philipp Emanuel's godfather in 1714), who in large measure was responsible for introducing the operatic style into the Neukirche while a student in Leipzig, and whose operas continued to be performed in later years in the Leipzig opera house.[97] During his time as Capellmeister in Cöthen Bach had opportunities to be aware of what was then happening in the city. In the account book of the court of Anhalt-Cöthen there is an entry, under the date of 16 December 1718,

---

94 *Tischreden Oder Colloquia Doct. Mart: Luthers*, ed. Johann Aurifaber (Eisleben: Gaubisch, 1566), fol. 576^r; WA *Tischreden* 2: 360.

95 This takes on a particular significance when it is recalled that there was a copy of Luther's *Tischreden* in Bach's personal library; see Robin A. Leaver, *Bachs theologische Bibliothek: Eine kritische Bibliographie* (Stuttgart: Hänssler, 1983), 59–60 (No. 4).

96 Seventeenth- and early eighteenth-century handbooks that deal with rhetoric are mostly concerned with the minutiae of structures, categories, and terminology of rhetoric. Just to take one example: *Hodegeticum Brevibus Aphorismis Olim pro Collegio Concionatorio* (Leipzig: Riese, 1652, later editions 1656 and 1675) by Johann Benedict Carpzov [I] (1607–1657), professor of theology and archdeacon of the Thomaskirche in Leipzig. Designed as an introduction to homiletics for theological students at Leipzig University, it remained in use well into the early decades of the eighteenth century, reissued as *Hodegetici Ad Artem Concionatoriam* (Leipzig: [s.n.], 1689), edited by Tilemann Andreas Rivinus, a later archdeacon of the Thomaskirche.

97 See Malcolm Boyd, ed,, *Oxford Composer Companions: J. S. Bach* (Oxford: Oxford University Press, 1990), 475; Maul, *Barockoper in Leipzig*, 2: 859–63.

Bach and the cantata controversy 105

that records that "Vogler aus Leipzig" had been paid 16 thaler as a guest musician.[98] This is a reference to Johann Gottfried Vogler, organist and director of the Neukirche, Leipzig, who was also violinist and composer for the Leipzig opera. The occasion for Vogler's presence in Cöthen was the celebration of Prince Leopold's birthday on 10 December 1718, for which Bach composed two cantatas: *Lobet den Herrn, alle seine Heerscharen* (BWV Anh. 5) and *Der Himmel dacht auf Anhalts Ruhm und Glück* (BWV 66a). The libretto for each cantata was written by Menantes (Christian Friedrich Hunold). It was Menantes who had edited and published Neumeister's lectures on poetry, and he was recognized as an important poet and librettist in his own right with several substantial volumes of published poetry to his credit. Between 1718 and 1720 Bach collaborated with Menantes for five cantatas composed for the Cöthen court, in addition to the two cantatas mentioned above: *Die Zeit, die Tag und Jahre macht* (BWV 134a) (New Year 1719); *Dich loben die lieblichen Strahlen der Sonne* (BWV Anh. 6) (New Year 1720); *Heut ist gewiss ein guter Tag* (BWV Anh. 7) (Prince Leopold's birthday, December 1720).

His involvement with Menantes at the Cöthen court implies that Bach knew of the author's published poetic writings, and he may well have obtained one or more of them for himself.[99] He must also have had other anthologies of poetry intended for public worship, such as Georg Christian Lehms, *Gottgefälliges Kirchen-Opffer, In einem gantzen Jahr-Gange* (Darmstadt: Bachmann, 1711), which had to have been obtained soon after it was published, since it supplied the libretti for two cantatas Bach composed in Weimar in 1713 and 1714 (BWV 157 and BWV 54 respectively). In addition, since he would also use them at various times as sources for cantata libretti, he is likely to have owned the following volumes, presumably among others: Erdmann Neumeister, *Geistliches Singen und Spielen* (Gotha: Reyher, 1711); Salomo Franck, *Evangelisches Andachts-Opffer* (Weimar: Rumbach, [1715]); Erdmann Neumeister, *Fünffache Kirchen-Andachten* (Leipzig: Groß,1716); Salomo Franck, *Geist- und Weltliche Poesien Zweiter Theil* (Jena: Bielcke, 1717); Erdmann Neumeister, *Geistliche Poesien mit untermischten Biblischen Sprüchen und Choralen auf alle Sonn- und Fest-Tage* (Eisenach: Boetius, 1717); Johann Friedrich Helbig, *Poetische Auffmunterung zur Sonn- und Fest-Täglichen Andacht durchs gantze Jahr* (Eisenach: Boëtius, 1720); and Johann Oswald Knauer, *Gott-geheiligtes Singen und Spielen* (Gotha: Reyher, 1721). It is a matter of great regret that there is no record of the printed anthologies of cantata libretti that Bach owned. The impression is that his collection of such literature must have been fairly extensive, but there is no way of knowing whether Scheibel's *Poetische Andachten* was one of the volumes on his bookshelves.

---

98 BDok 2: 72 (No. 93); NBR 87 (No. 76b).

99 Menantes, *Academische Neben-Stunden allerhand neuer Gedichte* (Halle & Leipzig: Zeitler, 1713) would seem to be a possible volume for Bach to have owned, since the libretto of *Ich bin in mir vergnügt* (BWV 204) includes movements from this source; see the discussion below.

106 *Liturgy*

Some of the things that Scheibel writes about have resonances in what is known about Bach. It is clear that Bach was in favor of the new reform style in cantata composition, which stood in close relationship to the "theatralische stil," since he was foremost in developing it.[100] Scheibel's criticism of most of the published annual cycles of cantata libretti resonate with the fact that unlike other contemporary composers Bach never composed a complete annual sequence of cantata libretti written by a single poet. Instead, he preferred to pick and choose, often just one text, sometimes two or three for successive Sundays or celebrations, rarely more than three for consecutive occasions. Similarly, Scheibel's approval of the cantata libretti of Neumeister, Franck, and Rambach accords with Bach's selection of texts by these poets: all but two libretti of his Weimar cantatas are by Franck,[101] plus one or two of the Leipzig cantatas; five are by Neumeister (BVW 18 and 61 in Weimar; BWV 24, 28, and 59 in Leipzig); and one is based on a libretto by Rambach (BWV 25).

Some of Scheibel's other opinions, however, could not have been shared by Bach, in particular his harsh criticism of older church music. His punning condemnation of Hammerschmidt as representative of old-fashioned church music in *Zufällige Gedancken* has already been noted.[102] In his extended preface to his *Poetische Andachten* Scheibel again condemns such music—with yet another pun—especially its counterpoint:

> When the question is asked: What pleasure is there in the old church music? The answer comes back: It sounds right devout (Es klang fein andächtig). I would have rather expressed it: It glugs right silly (Es klung fein einfältig). To the present time the arsenal of music is overfull of difficult canons, the *Utremifasolitten* (barbarous name! barbarous music!) continues to practice its tyranny from a pharisaic sanctity.[103]

Bach, with his fascination with canonic techniques,[104] his respect for the music of earlier composers,[105] and his knowledge of and expertise in the *stile*

---

100 See Hans Joachim Marx, "Bach und der 'theatralische Stil,'" in *Johann Sebastian Bachs Spätwerk und dessen Umfeld. Bericht über das wissenschaftliche Symposion des 61. Bachfestes der Neuen Bachgesellschaft, Duisburg, 28.–30. Mai 1986*, ed. Christoph Wolff (Kassel: Bärenreiter, 1988), 148–54; trans., by Andrew Talle, as "Bach and the 'theatralische Stil,'" *Bach Notes. The Newsletter of the American Bach Society* 5 (Spring 2006): 1–6.

101 Since Franck was the court poet at Weimar, the question is whether Bach's use of his libretti was by personal choice or ducal decree. The fact that Bach also used libretti by Neumeister and Lehms during his time in Weimar suggests the former.

102 See note 50 above.

103 Scheibel, *Poetische Andachten*, sig. b2 ͬ: "Wenn man sie fragt, was gefiel denn an der alten Kirchen *Music*? So erfolgt die Antwort: Es klang fein andächtig. Ich hätte lieber setzen wollen: Es klung fein einfältig. Zur selbigen Zeit war das Rüsthaus der *Music* hoch voller schweren *Canonen*, die *Utremifasolitten* (*barbara Nomina! Barbara Musica!*) übten noch ihre Tyranney unter einer Pharisäischen Heiligkeit aus."

104 See, for example, David Yearsley, *Bach and the Meanings of Counterpoint* (Cambridge: Cambridge University Press, 2002).

105 See Kirsten Beißwenger, *Johann Sebastian Bachs Notenbibliothek* (Kassel: Bärenreiter, 1992).

Bach and the cantata controversy 107

antico,[106] was clearly out of sympathy with such sentiments. Yet the negatives expressed by Scheibel were part of the significant background to Johann Adolph Scheibe's attack on Bach and others in 1737,[107] and formed part of the articulation and promotion of the emerging galant style. But in Bach's case, much of Scheibel's prose would have been less interesting to him than Scheibel's poetry.

Bach's poets

With regard to cantata libretti, Bach's preference appears to have been to work directly with a poet rather than with preexisting published collections of such poetry. The notable examples are Salomo Franck in Weimar, Menantes in Cöthen, Christiana Mariana von Ziegler and Picander (Christian Friedrich Henrici) in Leipzig, whose texts written for Bach were subsequently published after the compositions were completed. However, this preference was not always a possibility, and in those circumstances Bach turned to printed sources. The period before the intensification of his collaboration with Picander, approximately from the end of 1725 to the middle of 1727,[108] is characterized by the lack of a regular poetic partner in the composition of cantatas. During this period seventeen libretti came from just two sources: Lehms, *Gottgefälliges Kirchen-Opffer* (Darmstadt, 1711) and the anonymous *Sonn- und Fest-Tags-Andachten* (Rudolstadt, 1726) (see Table 5.1). Bach also made use of single libretti from printed anthologies by Neumeister, Franck, and Helbig during these months (see Table 5.2), and during the same period seven libretti have unknown authors (see Table 5.3). A further five, while also being anonymous, are connected in some way with previously published sources.[109] These five libretti are discussed here in chronological sequence.

The libretto of the cantata *Ich bin in mir vergnügt* (BWV 204), composed in 1726 (or possibly 1727) for an unknown occasion, is an ingenious compilation and modification of poetry from two different sources by Menantes, together with additional stanzas by an unknown author. The Menantes sources are

---

106 See Christoph Wolff, *Der stile antico in der Musik Johann Sebastian Bachs: Studien zu Bachs Spätwerk* (Wiesbaden: Steiner, 1968).

107 Michael Maul, "Neues zum Kontext einer musikalischen Debatte: Johann Adolph Scheibes Bach-Kritik," *Bach Magazin* 17 (2011): 9–11.

108 Picander provided two libretti for non-liturgical celebratory cantatas in 1725: *Entfliehet, verschwindet* (BWV 249a) (February) and *Zerreißet, zersprenget* (BWV 205) (August). The earlier cantata *Bringet dem Herrn Ehre* (BWV 148), composed for Trinity 17, 1723, was based on a Picander poem, but someone else may have been responsible for the final form of the cantata libretto.

109 This is not to suggest that such libretti are only to be found in the cantatas of this period. For example, BWV 25, composed in 1723, has a libretto that is a skillful reworking of a cantata libretto by Johann Jacob Rambach; for the details, see Martin Petzoldt, *Bach-Kommentar: theologisch-musikwissenschaftliche Kommentierung der geistlichen Vokalwerke Johann Sebastian Bachs* (Kassel: Bärenreiter, 2004–2019), 1: 388–93.

108   *Liturgy*

Table 5.1 Cantata libretti (1725–1727) from two printed sources

Date	Cantata	BWV	Occasion
	From: Georg Christian Lehms, *Gottgefälliges Kirchen-Opffer, In einem gantzen Jahr-Gange* (Darmstadt: Bachmann, 1711).		
25 Dec 1725	*Unser Mund sei voll Lachens*	110	Christmas Day
26 Dec 1725	*Selig ist der Mann*	57	Second Day of Christmas
27 Dec 1725	*Süßer Trost, mein Jesu kömmt*	151	Third Day of Christmas
30 Dec 1725	*Gottlob! nun geht das Jahr zu Ende*	28	Sunday after Christmas
1 Jan 1726	*Herr Gott, dich loben wir*	16	New Year
13 Jan 1726	*Liebster Jesu, mein Verlangen*	32	Epiphany 1
20 Jan 1726	*Meine Seufzer, meine Tränen*	13	Epiphany 2
28 Jul 1726	*Vergnügte Ruh, beliebte Seelenlust*	170	Trinity 6
8 Sept 1726	*Geist und Seele wird verwirret*	35	Trinity 12
6 Feb 1727	*Ich lasse dich nicht, du segnest mich denn*	157	Funeral
	From: [Anonymous,] Rudolstadt. *Sonn- und Fest-Tags-Andachten über die ordentlichen Evangelia* (Rudolstadt: Löw, 1726).		
30 May 1726	*Gott fähret auf mit Jauchzen*	43	Ascension
23 June 1726	*Brich dem Hungrigen Brot*	39	Trinity 1
21 July 1726	*Siehe, ich will viel Fischer aussenden*	88	Trinity 5
4 Aug 1726	*Es wartet alles auf dich*	187	Trinity 7
11 Aug 1726	*Es ist dir gesagt, Mensch, was gut ist*	45	Trinity 8
25 Aug 1726	*Herr, deine Augen sehen nach dem Glauben*	102	Trinity 10
22 Sept 1726	*Wer Dank opfert, der preiset mich*	17	Trinity 14

Table 5.2 Single cantata libretti (1725–1727) from three printed sources

Date	Cantata	BWV	Occasion
	From: Erdmann Neumeister, *Fünfffache Kirchen-Andachten* (Leipzig, Groß, 1716)		
30 Dec 1725	*Gottlob! Nun geht das Jahr zu Ende*	28	Christmas 1
	From: Salomo Franck, *Evangelisches Andachtsopffer … in Geistlichen Cantaten* (Weimar: Rumbach, [1715].		
27 Jan 1726	*Alles nur nach Gottes Willen*	72	Epiphany 3
	From: Johann Friedrich Helbig, *Poetische Auffmunterung zur Sonn- und Fest-Täglichen Andacht durchs gantze Jahr* (Eisenach: Boëtius, 1720).		
13 Oct 1726	*Wer sich selbst erhöhet*	47	Trinity 17

Bach and the cantata controversy   109

Table 5.3 Anonymous cantata libretti (1726–1727)

Date	Cantata	BWV	Occasion
April 1726	*O ewiges Feuer, O Ursprung der Liebe*	34a	Wedding
20 Oct 1726	*Gott soll allein mein Herze haben*	169	Trinity 18
27 Oct 1726	*Ich will den Kreutzstab gerne tragen*	56	Trinity 19
3 Nov 1726	*Ich geh und suche mit Verlangen*	49	Trinity 20
10 Nov 1726	*Was Gott tut, das ist wohlgetan*	98	Trinity 21
24 Nov 1726	*Falsche Welt, dir trau ich nicht*	52	Trinity 23
5 Jan 1727	*Ach, Gott, wie manches Herzeleid*	58	Sunday after New Year

found in his *Academische Neben-Stunden allerhand neuer Gedichte* (Halle and Leipzig: Zeitler, 1713), a composite work of several sections, each with its own pagination. The two sources of the libretto of Cantata 204 appear in the same section: "Lob- und Glückwünschungs-Schrifften." The first movement, a recitative, is a 24-line poem headed, "Der vergnügte Mensch" (The Contented Person) in Menantes's volume;[110] the manuscript score of Bach's cantata is headed "Cantata von der Vergnügsamkeit" (Cantata on Contentedness).[111] Bach's libretto generally follows Menantes's poetry, apart from some minor matters such as the substitution of "erwünschte" for "gewünschte." But in lines 19 and 20 the concept of fearlessness is substituted for humility:

Menantes	BWV 204/1
Ich bin in mir vergnügt	**Ich bin in mir vergnügt**
…	…
Was meine Wollust ist/	**Was meine Wollust ist,**
ist, meine Lust zu zwingen.	**Ist, meine Lust zu zwingen;**
Die Demuth liebt mich selbst;	Ich fürchte keine Not,
wer es so weit kan bringen,	Frag nichts nach eitlen Dingen.
Der gehet nach dem Fall	**Der gehet nach dem Fall**
…	…
I am content in myself,	**I am content in myself,**
…	…
What my delight is	**What my delight is**
is my desire to restrain.	**is my desire to restrain.**
Humility I myself love	I fear no distress,
Whoever can spread it far and wide.	ask not after vain things.
For after the Fall . . .	**For after the Fall** . . .

---

110 Menantes, *Academische Neben-Stunden*: "Lob- und Glückwünschungs-Schrifften," 40; facsimile, Werner Neumann, *Sämtliche von Johann Sebastian Bach vertonte Texte* (Leipzig: Deutscher Verlag für Musik, 1974), 263.

111 NBA I/40: 81.

110 *Liturgy*

The next five movements (BWV 204/2–6) were taken from a cantata libretto in the same section of Menantes's *Academische Neben-Stunden*: "Cantata Von der Zufriedenheit" (Cantata on Happiness).[112] Again, the text mainly follows Menantes's original but there are some significant alterations, particularly in movement 5. Again, there is a straightforward substitution in line 5, "Ergetzen" (pleasure) being replaced by "Vergnügen" (contentment). Menantes's original movement comprises 20 lines but the movement in BWV 204 has 22 lines. The additional couplet is therefore linked to the alteration of line 5, since it again introduces "Vergnügen," the primary theme of the cantata:

Menantes	BWV 204/5
Und sonder des Gewissens Brand	**Und sonder des Gewissens Brand**
Gen Himmel sein Gesicht gewandt.	**Gen Himmel sein Gesicht gewandt,**
	Da ist mein ganz Vergnügen,
	Der Himmel wird es fügen.
Die Muscheln öffnen sich/ wenn	**Die Muscheln öffnen sich, wenn**
Strahlen darauf schiessen,	**Strahlen darauf schießen,**
Und zeugen **dann in sich die Perlen**	**Und** zeigen **dann in sich die**
Frucht	**Perlenfrucht**
…	…
and without the conscience's	**and without the conscience's**
brandmark	**brandmark**
having its face turned towards heaven.	**having its face turned towards heaven.**
	that is my full contentment –
	heaven will decree it.
Mussels open up when lightning-bolts	**Mussels open up when lightning-bolts**
shoot about them,	**shoot about them,**
revealing **then the crop of pearls**	displaying **then the crop of pearls**
within	**within**

The first two lines of movement 7 of Bach's cantata are the opening movement of Menantes's "Cantata von der Vergnügsamkeit." The remainder of movement 7 and the whole of movement 8 were written by an unknown author, who was most likely responsible for the libretto of the cantata in its present form.

For the Michaelisfest, 29 September 1726, which coincided with the Fifteenth Sunday after Trinity, Bach composed *Es erhub sich ein Streit* (BWV 19). The libretto is another compilation of revised preexisting poetry with newly written verse. This is a reworking of a hymn for the Michaelisfest by

---

112 Menantes, *Academische Neben-Stunden*, 62–64; facsimile, Neumann, *Bach vertonte Texte*, 263.

Bach and the cantata controversy 111

Picander, intended to be sung to the melody *Allein Gott in der Höh sei Ehr*, published in his *Sammlung Erbaulicher Gedancken* (Leipzig, 1724/25).[113] Four of the seven stanzas form the basis of three movements of the seven-movement libretto. The first two movements are closely linked to the Epistle of the day (Revelation 12: the triumph of Archangel Michael and his angels against the minions of the devil) and are by an unknown poet. The third movement comprises the third stanza of Picander's hymn virtually unaltered. In movement 4 the first stanza of the original is modified and expanded and given a different metrical structure:

Picander	BWV 19/4
1. **Was ist der Mensch, das Erden-Kind,**	**Was ist der** schnöde **Mensch, das Erdenkind?**
Der Staub, der **Wurm,** der **Sünder?**	Ein **Wurm,** ein armer **Sünder.**
Daß ihn **der Herr so lieb gewinnt,**	Schaut, wie ihn selbst **der Herr so lieb gewinnt,**
	Daß er ihn nicht zu niedrig schätzet
Und ihm die Gottes **Kinder,**	**Und ihm die** Himmels**kinder,**
Das große Himmels-**Heer,**	Der Seraphinen **Heer,**
Zu einer **Wacht und Gegenwehr,**	**Zu** seiner **Wacht und Gegenwehr,**
Zu seinem Schutz gesetzet.	**Zu seinem Schutze setzet.**
What is humanity, this child of earth,	**What is** this vile **humanity, this child of earth?**
The Dust, **a worm,** a **sinner?**	**A worm,** a poor **sinner.**
That **the Lord loves him so**	See how **the Lord** himself **loves him so**
	That he does not value him too lowly
To make him a child of God,	**To make him a child of** heaven,
And set the great host of heaven	**And set** the Seraphic **host**
For a **watch and defense,**	**For** his **watch and defense,**
For his protection.	**For his protection**.

Movement 5 is loosely connected to the basic concept of three lines of Picander's stanza 6, which speak of joining with the angels to sing of the holiness of God, but in the process Picander's specific allusion to the liturgical Sanctus is lost:

Picander	BWV 19/5
	Bleibt, ihr **Engel**, bleibt bei mir!
	Führet mich auf beiden Seiten,
...	Daß mein Fuß nicht möge gleiten!
Erhebt mit Loben Gottes Reich,	Aber lernt mich auch allhier
Und lasset uns den **Engeln** gleich	

---

113 Picander, *Sammlung Erbaulicher Gedancken über und auf die gewöhnlichen Sonn- und Fest-Tage* (Leipzig: Boetius, [ca.1725]), 434–35; facsimile, Neumann, *Bach vertonte Texte*, 309.

112   *Liturgy*

Sein dreymahl **Heilig! singen.**

...
Exhalt with praise God's kingdom
And let us join with the **angels**
To sing their threefold **Holy!**

Euer großes **Heilig singen**
Und dem Höchsten Dank zu singen!

Stay, you **angels**, stay with me!
Guide me on both sides,
So that my foot may not slip!
But also teach me here
Thy great **holiness to sing**
The Highest to thank with singing!

The sixth movement of the cantata is created from the final two stanzas (6 and 7) of Picander's hymn:

Picander

6. Drum **lasset uns das Angesicht**
Der frommen Engel lieben
Und sie mit unsern Sünden nicht
Vertreiben und **betrüben.**
Erhebt mit Loben Gottes Reich,
Und lasset uns den Engeln gleich
Sein dreymahl Heilig! singen.

7. Befiehlt uns, **Herr**, ein sanffter Tod
Der Welt Valet zu sagen,
So laß uns aus der Sterbens-Noth
Die Engel zu dir tragen.
Verleihe, daß wir nach der Zeit
In deiner sussen **Seligkeit**
Den Engeln ähnlich gläntzen.

BWV 19/6

Laßt uns das Angesicht
Der frommen Engel lieben
Und sie mit unsern Sünden nicht
Vertreiben oder auch **betrüben.**

So sein sie, wenn der **Herr** gebeut,
Der Welt Valet zu sagen,

Zu unsrer **Seligkeit**
Auch unser Himmelswagen.

6. Therefore **let us love the countenance**
Of the godly angels
And with our sins not
Expel and **grieve them.**
Exhalt with praise God's kingdom
And let us join with the angels
To sing their threefold Holy!

7. Command for us, **Lord**, a tender
   death,
To bid the world farewell,
Thus for us from the pains of death
Be borne to thee by angels.
Grant that at the end of time
in thy sweet **blessedness**
The angels will similarly shine.

Let us love the countenance
Of the godly angels
And with our sins not
Expel or also **grieve them.**

So may they be there, when the
   Lord decrees
To bid the world farewell,

To go to our **blessedness**
And also our heavenly chariot.

Bach and the cantata controversy   113

The concluding movement of Cantata 19 (movt. 7) is a chorale, the ninth stanza of *Freu dich sehr, o meine Seele* (first published in Freiburg, 1620).

The remaining three cantatas with anonymous libretti that make use of earlier poetry are discussed at the beginning of this chapter:

6 Oct 1726	Trinity 16	*Wer weiß, wie nahe mir mein Ende!* (BWV 27)
17 Nov 1726	Trinity 22	*Ich armer Mensch, ich Sündenknecht* (BWV 55)
2 Feb 1727	Purification	*Ich habe genung* (BWV 82)

Cantatas BWV 27 and BWV 55 make use of lines from Neumeister's libretti, and the aria *Schlummert ein* in BWV 82 echos lines from Scheibel.

Bach's aria *Schlummert ein* appears to have had some resonance beyond the immediate Bach family.[114] Some years after the composition of Cantata 82, Picander published a libretto for a *Cantate bey der Communion* in which the central aria is based on the same imagery used in the central aria of Bach's cantata, with close verbal correspondences:

Schlaffet ein!	Sleep now!
Schlafft ihr müden Augen-Lieder,	Sleep your tired eyelids,
Und ihr abgezehrten Glieder	And your wearied limbs
Schlaffet ein!	Sleep now!
Laßt die Erde, Erde seyn,	Let the earth remain the earth,
Denn der Himmel ist nun mein,	Because Heaven is now mine,
Schlaffet ein![115]	Sleep now!

Bach employed Johann Elias Bach (1705–1755), second son of his cousin Johann Valentin, as his secretary and teacher of his children between 1737 and 1742. After his time in Leipzig, Johann Elias eventually returned to Schweinfurt, where he became cantor of the Johanniskirche. In a printed Jahrgang of cantata texts, *Texte zu der Schweinfurther Kirchen Musik/ welche in der Kirche zu St. Johannes von dem Choro Musico daselbst abgesungen werden Anno 1744. und 45*, the central movement of the libretto for the Purification is the same as *Schlummert ein*, the central movement of Bach's Cantata 82, composed for the same occasion.[116]

Bach in collaboration with his poets

Bach's composition of church cantatas during the period from the end of 1725 to the middle of 1727 is characterized by two related phenomena. On

---

114 See the first paragraphs of this chapter.

115 *Picanders Ernst-Schertzhaffte und Satyrische Gedichte. Dritter Theil* (Leipzig: Boetius, 1732), 47.

116 See Peter Wollny, "Dokumente und Erläuterungen zum Wirken Johann Elias Bachs in Schweinfurt (1743–1755)," in *Die Briefentwürfe des Johann Elias Bach (1705–1755)*, eds. Evelin Odrich and Peter Wollny, 2nd ed. (Hildesheim: Olms, 2005), 55.

114   *Liturgy*

the one hand, Bach made more use of printed libretti than was his usual custom, and on the other hand, there is a group of cantata texts[117] for which an unknown poet (or poets) made use of the published poetry of others in order to create new cantata libretti. The impression is that during this time Bach was working with one or two of his closest colleagues, actively reviewing published anthologies of cantata texts to find usable libretti, or to discover phrases, lines, rhymes, and concepts that could be refashioned and developed into new libretti. One of those sources appears to have been Scheibel's *Poetische Andachten.* The unanswered question is, of course, how closely was Bach involved in the process of creating these new texts? The implication of his preference for working with poets, rather than published sources, would suggest that it was an active involvement. But the degree of such collaboration cannot be determined. Similarly, what Bach might have thought about Scheibel's libretti as whole cannot be known, but a tentative argument could be made to the effect that since he did not use a complete libretto from the Silesian poet, this might suggest that none completely met his requirements.

Where Bach is likely to have disagreed, and disagreed strongly, is with Scheibel's trenchant criticism of older church music. In his dismissal of solmisation as "barbarous music,"[118] Scheibel was echoing Mattheson's *Das Beschützte Orchestre* (Hamburg, 1717), a substantial part of which is devoted to demolishing Buttstett's *Ut, Mi, Sol, Re, Fa, La, tota Musica et Harmonia Aeterna.*[119] Mattheson described this section of his book on its title page with a pun on the Buttstett title:

> And lastly the long accursed Ut Mi Sol Re Fa La, dead (not total) [Todte nicht tota] music, splendidly accompanied by the twelve Greek modes, are laid to rest with reputable relatives and mourners, and given a monument as an eternal memory.[120]

---

117 Five have been located, but there may be more.

118 See note 103 above.

119 Mattheson's attack on Buttstett was indirectly also an attack on Bach's extended family, since Buttstett was married to Martha Lämmerhirt, a distant cousin of Bach's mother. Further, in *Das Beschützte Orchestre* Mattheson includes a dismissive and demeaning reference to Johann Michael Bach as composer; Johann Mattheson, *Das Beschützte Orchestre* (Hamburg: [Mattheson], 1717), 221–22. Then in a footnote Mattheson makes a rather put-down observation that he does not know whether Johann Sebastian Bach is related to this Johann Michael Bach, but requests that he should nevertheless contribute an autobiography to be included in his projected *Musicalische Ehren Pforte* (BDok 2: 65 [No. 83]). Johann Michael Bach (1648–1694) was, of course, Bach's first father-in-law, whose music he admired, along with that of Johann Michael's brother, Johann Christoph Bach (1642–1703). No doubt these were factors that contributed to Bach's decision to ignore Mattheson's request.

120 "So dann endlich des lange verbannet gewesenen *Ut Mi Sol Re Fa La* Todte (nicht tota) Musica Unter ansehnlicher Begleitung der zwölff Griechischen *Modorum,* als ehrbahrer Verwandten und Trauer-Leute/ zu Grabe gebracht und mit einem *Monument,* zum ewigen Andencken."

Bach and the cantata controversy 115

For Mattheson and Scheibel there was only one way forward, and that was a complete break with the past, but for Bach musical progress had to be made in continuity with the past. It is more than significant that the 1722 title page of *Das Wohltemperirte Clavier* includes a reference to solmisation: "*Praeludia, und Fugen durch alle Tone und Semitonia, So wohl tertiam majorem oder Ut Re Mi an langend, als auch tertiam minorem oder Re Mi Fa betreffend*"[121] (Preludes and Fugues through all the tones and semitones, with the major third, or *Ut Re Mi*, and also the minor third, or *Re Mi Fa*). This use of the Guidonian solmisation syllables puts him at variance with both Mattheson and Scheibel and suggests that he was more in sympathy, though not necessarily in complete agreement, with Buttstett.[122]

Where Bach's views are likely to have coincided with those of Scheibel concern the aims and objectives in creating cantatas: their purpose is liturgical and devotional, expressed in language and music that is up to date, direct, without obfuscation, and with persuasive emotional content. Scheibel writes:

> What should be set to music? ... On the whole one should set something that is contemporary, but its distinctive creativity must be: I. edifying; II. its affect well expressed; III. without obscure rhetoric.[123]

A few pages further on Scheibel returns to his primary theme:

> In the main we should observe that [an appropriate text] should be written by a good master who has well understood the teaching about the affects. If the text is thus so good, and the composition simple, and whether the harmony is similarly appointed, then fine devotion will follow. As I have recorded in a previous chapter, where I demonstrated that the essential natures of church and theatrical composition do not possess different stirrings of the affects, I will not again repeat here. Enough that a composer should so move the hearers in the church as in the theater.[124]

---

121 BDok 1: 219 (No. 152).
122 Walter Blankenburg, "Die innere Einheit von Bachs Werk," PhD diss. unpublished typescript (Georg-August-Universität, 1942), 74–75; David Ledbetter, *Bach's Well-tempered Clavier: The 48 Preludes and Fugues* (New Haven: Yale University Press, 2002), 124–25.
123 Scheibel, *Zufällige Gedancken*, 62–63: "Was soll aber gemusiciret werden? ... überhaupt man *music*iret etwas/ was sich auff die Zeit schickt: Ihrer eigentlich Beschaffenheit aber/ so müssen sie I. Erbaulich seyn/ II. Den *Affect* wohl *exprim*iren/ III. Nicht undeutliche Redens-Arten in sich halten." The passage is not translated in Scheibel, "Random Thoughts about Church Music."
124 Scheibel, *Zufällige Gedancken*, 66–67: "Doch können wir überhaupt mercken/ daß dieselbe [an appropriate text] von einem guten Meister/ der die Lehre von den *affect*en gut eingesehn/ müsse verfertiget werden. Wenn der Text noch so gutt/ und die *Composition* einfältig/ ob Sie gleich *harmonice* gesetzt/ so wird feine Erbauung folgen. Was ich in demjenigen Capitel dargethan/ wo ich bewiesen daß die Kirchen- und *Theatral*ische *Composition Ratione* der Bewegung der Affecten nichts eignes haben/ wil ich hier erst nicht wiederhohlen. Genung/ daß ein Componiste die Zuhörer in der Kirchen eben so zu *movi*ren suchen muß/ als auf

116   *Liturgy*

The object of both text and music is to "move the hearers"—not simply to please the ears, or divert the mind, but to move the heart. The individual movements of Bach's cantatas, especially the arias, are more than musical expositions of their respective texts, more than simple word-painting, more than theological concepts in sonic form. They are all these things and more. But the primary purpose of these astonishingly well-crafted movements of musical rhetoric is "movere," "to move," to evoke an emotional response from the hearers. The aria "Schlummert ein" in Cantata 82 is a superlative example that continues to "speak to the heart" as effectively as it did when it was first heard.

Excursus: Cantata libretti published in Nuremberg 1728

Stemming from the music collection of the Nuremberg organist Leonard Scholz (1720–1798) there is a volume of cantata libretti covering a complete liturgical year, intended for performance during 1728–1729 in the church in Hersbruck, a small town near Nuremberg: *Gott-geheiligte Sabbaths-Zehnden/ bestehend aus Geistlischen Cantaten auf alle Hohe Fest- Sonn- und Feyer-Tage der Herspruckischen Kirch-Gemeinde zu Gottseeliger Erbauung gewiedmet, von Christoph Bürckmann/ Rev. Minist. Candid.* (Nuremberg: Bieling [1728]); the preface is dated 26 October 1728.[125] The named author, Christoph Birkmann (1703–1771), was born and brought up in Nuremberg, and was later a student in Leipzig between 1724 and 1727, where he first concentrated on mathematics before turning to theology. As stated on the title page, Birkmann was at the time "candidate for the holy ministry," and was tutor to an aristocratic family in Hersbruck.

Music played an important part in Birkmann's life, having studied with Nuremberg's leading musicians, Cornelius Heinrich Dretzel (1697–1775) and Gabriel Fischer (1684–1749), both of whom had reputed connections with Bach. For part of his time in Leipzig Birkmann had stayed in the house of Johann Abraham Birnbaum, rhetorician and friend of Bach, and, according to his autobiography, he "did not neglect music but kept busy with the great master, Herr Director Bach and his choir, and in winter with the *collegia musica*."[126] Birkmann's *Gott-geheiligte Sabbaths-Zehnden* is significant in that it includes libretti of cantatas that Bach had performed in the Leipzig churches between 1724 and 1727, together with the libretto of the second

---

dem *Theatro.*" The passage is not translated in Scheibel, "Random Thoughts about Church Music."

125 See Christine Blanken, "Christoph Birkmanns Kantatenzyklus 'Gott-geheiligte Sabbaths-Zehnden' von 1728 und die Leipziger Kirchenmusik unter J. S. Bach in den Jahren 1724–1727," BJ 101 (2015): 13–74; for a partial translation, see: "A Cantata Text Cycle of 1728 from Nuremberg: A Preliminary Report on a Discovery relating to J. S. Bach's so called 'Third Annual Cycle,'" *Understanding Bach*, 10 (2015): 9–30.

126 Cited in Blanken, "Birkmanns Kantatenzyklus," 19.

Bach and the cantata controversy 117

(1725) version of the St. John Passion (BWV 245[II]). Of these, eight of the libretti appear in print for the first time: BWV 49, 52, 55, 56, 58, 82, 98, 169. It therefore has been assumed that Birkmann was their author. However, that conclusion is undermined by the fact that around eighteen of the libretti in the volume are known to have been written by other authors, such as Salomon Franck, Georg Christian Lehms, Christian Friedrich Henrici (Picander), the author(s) of the anonymous libretti published in Meiningen in 1704, among others. Thus, Birkmann may have been the compiler rather than the author of these libretti. According to the auction catalog of Birkmann's personal library, he owned a sequence of annual cantata libretti printed in Nuremberg, with the title *Sonn– Fest– und Feyertages musicalische Kirchen-Andachten*, that apparently began in 1735—around the time that Birkmann became the senior pastor of the Egidiuskirche, Nuremberg—and continued at least until 1756.[127] If these volumes could be located, perhaps they would present a clearer picture of Birkmann as a possible librettist.

---

127 *Bibliotheca Birckmanniana, seu Catalogus librorum…* (Nuremberg: Bauer, [1772]); the books are classified according to format rather than subject matter.

Part II
Hymnology

6 Bach and Johann Christoph Olearius

Apart from the various rebukes of the consistory in 1705–1706,[1] not a great deal is known about Bach's life in Arnstadt, yet these must have been formative years for the young musician. Between 1703 and 1707 he was organist of the rebuilt Bonifatiuskirche—then known as the "Neuen Kirche."[2] These were years when he was still in his early twenties. As a musician he was already extremely accomplished, but in other respects he was still a very young man gathering knowledge and experience.

Various generations of the Bach family continued to live and work in and around Arnstadt.[3] The family connections were most likely crucial in the invitation being extended to the young Bach, then only nineteen, first to test the new organ built by Johann Friedrich Wender in 1703,[4] and then to become the church's full-time organist later the same year.[5]

Among other Arnstadt extended families were representatives of the numerous Olearius family of pastors, theologians, professors, and lawyers, with branches in Halle, Leipzig, and Weissenfels.[6] The father was Johann Gottfried Olearius (1635–1711),[7] the superintendent and pastor of the

---

1 BDok 2: 15–22 (Nos. 14–17); NBR 43–48 (Nos. 19–21).
2 Since 1935 named the "Johann-Sebastian-Bach-Kirche."
3 See Fritz Wiegand, "Die Arnstädter Bache," *Arnstädter Bachbuch: Johann Sebastian Bach und seine Verwandten in Arnstadt*, ed. Karl Müller and Fritz Wiegand, 2nd ed. (Arnstadt: Arbeitsgemeinschaft für Bachpflege im Kulturbund Arnstadt, 1957), 23–57; Gisela Vogt, "Die Musikerfamilie Bach in Thuringen," *Der junge Bach: weil er nicht aufzuhalten ... Begleitbuch*, ed. Reinmar Emans (Erfurt: Erste Thüringer Landesausstellung, 2000), 108–10.
4 See Christoph Wolff and Markus Zepf, *The Organs of Johann Sebastian Bach: A Handbook*, trans. Lynn Edwards Butler (Urbana: University of Illinois Press, 2012), 9–11.
5 BDok 2: 11–13 (Nos. 8–10); NBR 41 (No. 16); see Konrad Küster, *Der junge Bach* (Stuttgart: Deutsche Verlags-Anstalt, 1996), 123–29; Klaus Hofmann, "Bach in Arnstadt," *Der junge Bach: weil er nicht aufzuhalten*, ed. Reinmar Emans, 239–55; see also, Peter Wollny, "Über die Hintergründe von Johann Sebastian Bachs Bewerbung in Arnstadt," BJ 91 (2005): 83–94.
6 See *Religion in Geschichte und Gegenwart*, 4th ed., ed. Hans Dieter Betz, et al. (Tübingen: Mohr Siebeck, 1998–2007), 6: cols. 547–49. For an English translation, see *Religion Past & Present*, 4th ed. English ed., ed. Hans Dieter Betz, et al. (Leiden: Brill, 2007–2013), 9:304–7.
7 Johann Heinrich Zedler, *Grosses vollständiges Universal-Lexicon aller Wissenschafften und Künste ...* (Halle: Zedler, 1732–1750), 25: cols. 1187–89; Martin Petzoldt, "Bach in theologischer Interaktion. Persönlichkeiten in seinem beruflichen Umfeld," *Über Leben,*

122 *Hymnology*

Barfüsserkirche, and the son was Johann Christoph Olearius (1668–1747),[8] deacon and sometime pastor of the Neuen Kirche.

The father, Johann Gottfried Olearius, as the chair of the church consistory, issued a number of official reprimands to the young organist of the Neuen Kirche.[9] But these were official statements, when Olearius was acting as the spokesman for the decisions of the consistory, and they do not necessarily mean that there could not have been a relationship of mutual respect between the older pastor and the younger organist. Especially so given that J. G. Olearius had also been an accomplished church musician himself, combining the roles of deacon with director of church music at the Marktkirche, Halle, where his father was pastor and superintendent.[10] J. G. Olearius also had connections with the Bach family. For many years Sebastian's great uncle Heinrich Bach (1615–1692) had been the much-respected organist in the town, and when his blindness prevented him from fulfilling his duties, Johann Christoph Bach (1671–1721)—Johann Sebastian's older brother and guardian in Ohrdruf after their parents' deaths—substituted for the ailing organist. On Heinrich Bach's death in 1692 it was Johann Gottfried Olearius who preached the funeral sermon.[11] J. G. Olearius also wrote a number of hymns, one of which appears to have made a particular impact on the young Bach. Thirty years later, when he was working on the music for the Schemelli *Gesangbuch*, he included a melody, probably his own, for Olearius's *Dich bet ich an, mein höchster Gott* (BWV 449).

Johann Christoph Olearius, Arnstadt deacon

Johann Christoph Olearius was born in Halle during the time when his father was doing double-duty as deacon and director of music at the Marktkirche. Therefore, his introduction to music is likely to have come from his father.[12] Just how proficient he was in music is unclear. The extent of his musical library is also uncertain, but he is known to have owned at least two Venice imprints of collected Latin motets, containing works by such Italian composers as

---

    Kunst und Kunstwerke: Aspekte musikalischer Biographie Johann Sebastian Bach im Zentrum, ed. Christoph Wolff (Leipzig: Evangelische Verlagsanstalt, 1999), 148.

  8 Zedler, *Universal-Lexicon*, 25: cols. 1176–84; Martin Petzoldt, "Bach in theologischer Interaktion," 147–48.

  9 See note 1 above.

10 See Robin A. Leaver, "Churches," in *The Routledge Research Companion to Johann Sebastian Bach*, ed. Robin A. Leaver (London: Routledge, 2017), 153–54.

11 Johann Gottfried Olearius, *I.N.J. Der Hier zeitlich- und dort ewiglich Reichbeseligte Lebens-Bach/ Nach seinem Herfliessen/ Ergiessen/ und Geniessen/ Aus des 91sten Psalms letzten Vers: Bey … Leichbestattung Des … Herrn Heinrich Bachs/ An die 51. Jahr Wohlverdient-gewesenen Organisten un[d] Wohlbeliebten Stadt-Musici allhier zu Arnstadt/ Welcher am 10. Iulii … im 77. Jahre seines mit Ehren hochgebrachten Alters …* (Arnstadt: Meurer, 1692). See also Heinrich Beyer, "Leichensermone auf Musiker des 17. Jahrhunderts," *Monatshefte für Musikgeschichte* 7 (1875): 171–75, 177–88, esp. 178–79.

12 Petzoldt, "Bach in theologischer Interaktion," 147.

Claudio Monteverdi, Gasparo Casati, Francesco Cavalli, Nicolò Fontei, Giovanni Battista Treviso, Pietro Tamburini, and Gaspare Filippi.[13] Provenance of these editions is attested by his holograph monogram, which appears without his father's ownership mark, suggesting that he obtained them rather than inherited them. He also owned a set of the partbooks of Johann Walter's *Wittembergisch deudsch geistlich Gesangbüchlein mit 4 u. 5 Stimmen* (Wittenberg Rhaw 1550–1551).[14] While most of his many writings on the Lutheran chorale concern textual matters, Johann Christoph Olearius does not avoid passing judgment on associated melodies, such as in his published discussion of the music associated with the Passion hymn *Jesu, meines Lebens-Leben*, which includes the notation of two of the preferred melodies with their respective figured basses.[15] At the beginning of his preface to the *Arnstädtisches Verbessertes Gesangbuch*, dated 8 December 1700, Olearius states:

> Hymns have their great usefulness as much for their beautiful melodies as for their pleasing poetry and edifying content. The melody, or art of song, is the power of music which has such an undeniable effect that even the devil himself must acknowledge.[16]

The *Arnstädtisches Verbessertes Gesangbuch* includes letter codes to indicate the pitch and key of the melodies to which the hymn texts were to be sung. To create this information implies a particular knowledge of music theory and an understanding of the current practice of accompanying congregational singing. The question is: Was this done by Olearius, the editor of the hymnal?[17]

Johann Christoph Olearius attended the university of Jena (1687–1693), where he studied a wide variety of subjects, becoming something of a polymath, which in later years resulted in a substantial sequence of publications on local history, numismatics,[18] antiquities, homiletics, bibliography, and so

---

13 Both are in the Forschungs- und Landesbibliothek, Gotha: *Sacri Concenti A Voce Sola Di Gasparo Casati Maestro di Capella nel Duomo di Nouara* (Venice: Gardano, 1646), shelfmark Cant.spir 8 00439; and *Motetti A Voce Sola De diuersi Eccellentissimi Autori: Libro Primo* (Venice: Gardano, 1645), shelfmark Mus 8 00081e/02.

14 Johann Christoph Olearius, *Jubilirende Lieder-Freudel Bestehend in erster Aufflage derer allerersten A.C. 1524. und 1525. in Druck gegangenen Lutherischen Gesängen zur Vermehrung schuldigster Devotion und Danckbarkeit, bey dem Andern von Gott verliehenen Lutherischen Reformations-Jubilaeo, nebst einer Vorrede* (Arnstadt: Meurer, 1717), sig. 2(ᵛ) – 3(ʳ).

15 Johann Christoph Olearius, *Betrachtung des bekannten Passion-Liedesl Jesu meines Lebens-Leben ...* (Jena: Bielcke, 1704), 17–22; Zahn 6794 and 6795.

16 *Arnstädtisches Verbessertes Gesangbuch* (Arnstadt: Bachmann, 1705), sig. a 2ʳ: "Lieder haben ihren grossen Nutzen/ sowohl wegen der schönen Melodien/ als auch angenehmen *Poësie* und erbaulichen Innhalts. Die Melodie oder Gesang-Art hat Krafft der Music eine solche unwiedersprechliche Würckung/ daß der Teufel selbst solche bezeugen muß. . ."

17 See the discussion in Chapter 10, especially 210–211.

18 In 1693, on completing his studies at Jena, he became curator of the numismatic collection of Graf Anton Günther II of Schwarzburg-Sondershausen in Arnstadt; see Peter Berghaus,

124 *Hymnology*

forth.[19] But a major part of his publishing output was devoted to the history and use of hymnody,[20] which made him one of the pioneer Lutheran hymnologists of the early eighteenth century.[21]

Hanseatic journeys from Arnstadt

There is an interesting parallel between Johann Christoph Olearius and Johann Sebastian Bach. Between 1694 and 1695, that is, some ten years or so before Bach visited Lübeck in 1705–1706, Olearius the younger made a similar journey from Arnstadt to Hamburg, Lübeck, and Travemünde. He was ordained in Arnstadt in 1694 and, soon after, as Bach did later, set out to further his professional experience at this early stage of his career, but his purpose was to visit pastors and theologians, especially those with extensive libraries. Not only did he go to the same area that Bach was to visit, but Olearius also experienced a similar reaction from the superintendent, his father. When in the Hanseatic region, probably in Hamburg, Olearius the son proposed to continue on to Holland and England. Olearius the father, on hearing of this intent, insisted that his son was taking too much time and that instead he should return to Arnstadt![22] Thus, the obedient son made his way home in 1695 and took up his duties as deacon and librarian of the significant Arnstadt church library.[23]

The superintendent in Lübeck was Georg Heinrich Götze (1667–1728),[24] appointed in 1702. Götze already had an interest in hymnology and, beginning the following year, produced a succession of hymnological publications that would eventually number at least fifty titles. One of the first things he did on taking office was to supervise the creation of the first official hymnal for Lübeck and the surrounding area. It was published as

---

"Numismatiker im Porträt: 38. Johann Christoph Olearius, 17.9.1668 Halle–31.3.1747 Arnstadt," *Geldgeschichtliche Nachrichten* 31 (1996): 276–85.

19 See *Catalogus Scriptorum, welchen, auf Begheren redlich gesinnter Freunde und besonderer Liebhaber der Hist. Literariae, zum Andencken seiner wenigen und geringen Schrifften, wie sie von A. C. 1690. bis A. C. 1727. in Druck gegangen, wohlmeynend communiciren wollen, Io. Christoph. Olearius* ([Arnstadt]: [s.n.], [1727]).

20 The pastors and theologians of the Olearius family made significant contributions to Lutheran hymnody; see Johann Bernhard Liebler, *Hymnopoeographia Oleariana, oder Olearische Lieder-Historie, darinnen unterschiedene Olearii, als berühmte Lieder-Dichter und Lieder-Freunde ...* (Naumburg: Boßögel, [1727]), 11–12 (Johann Gottfried Olearius) and 14–20 (Johann Christoph Olearius).

21 See Martin Rößler, "Die Frühzeit hymnologischer Forschung," *Jahrbuch für Liturgik und Hymnologie* 19 (1975): 123–86, esp. 134–37.

22 Zedler, *Universal-Lexicon*, 25: cols. 1177–78.

23 See Felicitas Marwinski and Konrad Marwinski, "Die Kirchenbibliotheken in Arnstadt, Sondershausen und Schmalkalden," *Laudate Dominum: Achtzehn Beiträge zur thüringischen Kirchengeschichte* (Berlin: Evangelische Verlaganstalt, 1976), 161–64.

24 Zedler, *Universal-Lexicon*, 11: cols. 87–89. Georg Heinrich Götze was apparently not related to Georg Götze, superintendent in Jena.

Lübeckisches Gesang-Buch ... (Lübeck: Wiedemeyer, 1703).[25] The *Gesangbuch* was introduced on the Third Sunday in Advent (16 December 1703), when Buxtehude played the Marienkirche organ and Götze preached an appropriate sermon. When the sermon was published the following year, it included an open letter addressed to Johann Christoph Olearius, who is praised for his hymnological studies: *Christliche Lieder-Predigt* ... (Lübeck: Wiedermeyer, 1704).[26] Given this connection between the Lübeck superintendent and the Arnstadt deacon and librarian, it would not be unreasonable to suppose that Bach took with him a letter of introduction addressed to the Lübeck superintendent, Götze, from Johann Christoph Olearius.

Johann Christoph Olearius, pioneer hymnologist

Johann Christoph Olearius and Bach clearly shared a common interest in the Lutheran chorale, both texts and music. As well as his oversight of the Arnstadt church library,[27] Olearius was at work on creating a substantial library of his own, which included books and manuscripts relating to hymns and hymnody, and especially hymnals—the source material for what would become an extensive list of hymnological publications that established him as one of the earliest Lutheran hymnologists.[28] His editing, writing, and publishing of hymnological works had begun before Bach arrived in Arnstadt, beginning with his editing of the *Neu-verbessertes Arnstädtisches Gesangbuch* (Arnstadt: Bachmann, 1701; further editions in 1703 and 1705, which had a slightly different title).[29] This was followed by *Kurtzer Entwurff einer nützlichen Lieder-Bibliotheck*, published in 1702 by Bielcke in Jena, but printed by Bachmann in Arnstadt in the same duodecimo format as the hymnal, thereby facilitating the possibility of the two titles being bound together. The content of the *Kurtzer Entwurff* was clearly closely connected with Olearius's editorial work on the hymnal; indeed, the volume has the character of being a commentary on the hymns of the *Arnstädtisches Verbessertes Gesangbuch*. The volume has three main sections: the first is a discussion of

25 The earliest known extant imprint dates from 1716.
26 See Martin Rößler, *Die Bibliographie der deutschen Liedpredigt* (Nieuwkoop: de Graaf, 1976), 205; and Rößler, "Die Frühzeit hymnologischer Forschung," 138–39; see also J. C. Olearius, *Betrachtung des bekannten Passion-Liedes/ Jesu meines Lebens-Leben* ... sig. a1ᵛ.
27 Johann Christoph Olearius, *Kurtze doch hinlängliche Nachricht von der öffentlichen Kirchen-Bibliotheck in Arnstadt* (Arnstadt: Schill, 1746).
28 J. C. Olearius continued collecting such sources throughout his career, amassing a remarkable collection of rare and significant hymnals, some of them unique copies; see Johann Jacob Gottschaldt, *Sammlung von allerhand auserlesenen Lieder-Remarqüen* (Leipzig: Martini, 1748), 334–36. Many of them can be found in the Forschungs- und Landesbibliothek, Gotha, including his copy of the Schemelli *Musicalisches Gesangbuch* (Leipzig: Breitkopf, 1736) (shelfmark Cant. spir. 8° 00265), for which Bach was the musical editor.
29 Liebler, *Hymnopoeographia Oleariana*, 15–16; Eduard Emil Koch, *Geschichte des Kirchenlieds und Kirchengesangs der christlichen, insbesondere der deutschen evangelischen Kirche*, 3rd ed. (Stuttgart: Belser, 1866–1877; reprint, Hildesheim: Olms, 1973), 5: 357–58.

126 *Hymnology*

"Geistlichen Liedern" in general; the second, gives brief information on the authors of the hymns, arranged alphabetically—information that was not generally included in hymnals at that time; and third, comments on the hymns, again arranged alphabetically, with cross-references to where sermons on the individual hymns could be found.[30] The volume concludes with an index of first lines and an alphabetical list of authors. Bach must have regularly used the *Arnstädtisches Verbessertes Gesangbuch*, edited by J. C. Olearius, during his time as the organist of the Neuen Kirche, Arnstadt, and similarly it seems more than likely that he not only knew of but also used Olearius's *Kurtzer Entwurff*.

Liedpredigten

Congregational hymnody became a significant feature of the Lutheran Reformation of the sixteenth century. With the many newly written hymns there was the need to ensure that they were understood by those who sang them. Thus, the "Liedpredigt," the hymn-sermon, which explored the biblical and theological meaning of a hymn, was specifically created to meet this need.[31] In the seventeenth century, when the Lutheran chorale had been firmly established, the didactic function of the Liedpredigt was intensified by an increased devotional content, especially when it was used as the homiletic form for funerals and memorial services. But at the same time there was also the occasional use of a hymn as the principal element in the *Exordium* of regular Sunday preaching.[32] Given the fact that a primary hymn was assigned to each day and celebration of the church year, to be sung between the Epistle and Gospel,[33] it was not long before preachers saw the possibility of creating an *Exordia-Jahrgang* based on these Graduallieder throughout the church year. However, it is not exactly clear who was the first to do so. According to Johann Christoph Olearius, his grandfather, Gottfried Olearius, preached such a complete cycle of *Lieder-Exordia* in Halle for the year 1657,[34]

---

30 For a summary of the contents, see Rößler, "Die Frühzeit hymnologischer Forschung," 135–37.

31 For the background, see Martin Rößler, *Die Liedpredigt: Geschichte einer Predigtgattung* (Göttingen: Vandenhoeck & Ruprecht, 1976). While Bach was in Arnstadt Johann Christoph Olearius edited and published a manuscript of a sequence of fifty-four Liedpredigten by Martin Crusius (1526–1598) dating from 1598: *Martini Crusii ... Homiliae hymnodicae, quinquaginta quatuor cantica ecclesiae Lutheranae, bene disposita, verbo Dei puro illustrantes: quas e Manuscripto usui dedit publico*, ed. Johann Christoph Olearius (Arnstadt: Ehrt, 1705); see Rößler, *Die Bibliographie der deutschen Liedpredigt*, 127–28.

32 On the homiletic *exordium*, see Chapter 2.

33 See Detlef Gojowy, "Kirchenlieder im Umkreis von J. S. Bach." *Jahrbuch für Liturgik und Hymnologie*, 22 (1978): 79–123.

34 The claim is made by J. C. Olearius in the preface to *Vollständiges Passion-Lied. Wir dancken dir Herrn Jesu Christ daß du für uns gestorben bist u.s.w. welches nebst einigen Anmerckungen zur Beförderung verständiger Lieder-Andacht folgender Gestallt communiciret M. Joh. Christoph*

Bach and Johann Christoph Olearius   127

but the 71 *dispositionen*[35] were not published, and no manuscript is apparently extant. In Leipzig some thirty years later, 1688–1689, Johann Benedict Carpzov [II] (1639–1699), superintendent and pastor of the Thomaskirche, collaborated with the Thomascantor, Johann Schelle, who composed chorale cantatas on the Graduallieder sung throughout the church year,[36] with Carpzov creating *Exordia*, expositions of the same chorales for the respective Sundays and celebrations. The 69 *Dispositionen* of these sermons were published late in 1689, apparently the first of the genre to appear in print: Johann Benedict Carpzov [II], *Kurtz Verzeichniß derer Anno 1689. von D. Johann Benedict Carpzov, in Leipzig gehaltenen Lehr- und Lieder-Predigten* (Leipzig: Grosse & Scholvien, 1689).[37]

Around the time that Bach arrived in Arnstadt, Olearius edited and published the *Exordia-Jahrgang* that the Jena pastor, Georg Götz (1633–1699), had preached in 1692 on the primary hymns of the church year: *Erbauliche Lieder-Betrachtung* (Jena: Bielcke, 1703). With his experience of editing the *Arnstädtisches Gesangbuch*, and producing the background information to the hymnal in *Kurtzer Entwurff*, together with the examples of Götz's *Lieder-Betrachtung* and Carpzov's *Lieder-Predigten*, Olearius was at work on a much more ambitious project: Johann Christoph Olearius, *Evangelischer Lieder-Schatz darinn allerhand Auserlesene Gesänge, so sich auff alle Sonn- und Fest-Tags Evangelia … und darauff schließlich eine kurtzgefaste Disposition*, published by Bielcke in Jena.[38] The title page gives the year of publication as 1707, but this is somewhat misleading, since the work was issued in four installments, each with its own title page: I (1705), II (1705), III (1706), IV (1707). When the fourth part was issued the complete volume was given a new title page and a new preface that included additions and corrections to the first three parts. The *Evangelischer Lieder-Schatz* included a commentary on each of the primary hymns sung on every Sunday, festival, and celebration throughout the church year (see Table 8.2).

While it was still being published, Olearius's *Evangelischer Lieder-Schatz* exerted a significant influence on the creation and dissemination of the genre of Liedpredigten. After the first two parts were published in 1705 there must have been some contact between Olearius and one of Carpzov's former students,

---

Olearius, Prediger in Arnstadt (Jena: Bielcke, 1710); see Rößler, "Die Frühzeit hymnologischer Forschung," 131, note 29.

35 *Disposition* was the term used for a sermon outline.

36 Most of these chorale cantatas are no longer extant; see Johann Schelle, *Six Chorale Cantatas*, ed. Mary S. Morris, *Recent Researches in the Music of the Baroque Era*, vols. 60–61 (Madison: A-R Editions, 1988).

37 The preface is dated 3 December 1689; see Rößler, *Die Bibliographie der deutschen Liedpredigt*, 112.

38 See Rößler, *Die Bibliographie der deutschen Liedpredigt*, 132–34. On the possible connections between Olearius's comments on *Christ lag in Todesbanden* in *Evangelischer Lieder-Schatz* and Bach's Cantata BWV 4, see the discussion in Chapter 7.

128 *Hymnology*

Friedrich Simon Löffler (1669–1748),[39] concerning Carpzov's Liedpredigten of 1688–1689, which until then had only been published in outline form. The result was the publishing of the complete texts of these sermons: Johann Benedict Carpzov [II], *Lehr- und Lieder-Predigten, an der zahl LXXIV. gehalten an Sonn- Fest- und Buß-Tagen Anno 1689 ...* (Leipzig: Lanckisch, 1706),[40] which must have appeared in the first few months of 1706.[41] By this time Olearius had published the first two parts of his *Evangelischer Lieder-Schatz*[42] and was at work on the third part. Significantly, parts three and four of Olearius's *Evangelischer Lieder-Schatz* contain frequent references to Carpzov's *Lieder-Predigten* as published in full in 1706.

Johann Christoph Olearius's *Dispositionen*

In his *Evangelischer Lieder-Schatz* Johann Christoph Olearius not only included background information on the hymn associated with each Sunday and celebration of the church year, like Carpzov and Olearius's homiletic mentor Georg Götz, but he also included sermon outlines, *dispositionen*. The *exordia* of these outlines focused on the primary hymn sung on each of the days in question, but the substance of the same hymn was frequently woven into the other sections and subsections of the *dispositio*. Some of these *dispositionen* were taken from the published outlines of Götz, Carpzov, Serpilius, and others, but some were Olearius's own synopses of sermons he had preached. In the first part of his *Evangelischer Lieder-Schatz*, but not in the later volumes, Olearius recorded specific dates when he had preached some of these *dispositionen* in Arnstadt (see Table 6.1).

J. C. Olearius explains the pattern of preaching in Arnstadt thus:

---

39 Löffler was pastor of Probstheida, Holtzhausen and Zuckelhausen, near Leipzig, son of Simon Löffler (1627–1674), archdeacon of the Thomaskirche, Leipzig, nephew of the philosopher Gottfried Wilhelm Leibniz, and student of Johann Benedict Carpzov [II] at Leipzig university; see *Disputatio Theologica ex Rom. IX, vers. 5. De Divinitate Christi: Recentissimo Scriptori Anglo eam impugnanti potissimum opposita / ... In Academia Lipsiensi Sub Praesidio Magnifici Domini Rectoris Jo. Benedicti Carpzovi Doctoris & Professoris Theologi ... Solenni Theologorum Examini in Auditorio Principum maiori ad d. XVI. Novembr. MDCXCVII. P. P. a M. Friderico Simone Loeflero, SS. Theol. Baccalaureo & Pastore Ecclesiae Probstheidensis, Holtz- & Zuckelhusanae* (Leipzig: Titius, 1697). Löffler was a respected scholar who was much involved in church affairs in Saxony, such as editing the Saxon *Vollständiges Kirchen-Buch* (Leipzig: Lanckisch, 1707).
40 See Rößler, *Die Bibliographie der deutschen Liedpredigt*, 128–30.
41 Olearius's first reference to Carpzov's sermons is *Evangelischer Lieder-Schatz*, 3: 25. Since the date 27 April 1706 is mentioned on a later page in connection with Carpzov's Liedpredigten (*Evangelischer Lieder-Schatz*, 3: 52), the implication is that Carpzov's sermons were published early in 1706.
42 The dedication of Part 2 is dated 28 September 1705; Olearius, *Evangelischer Lieder-Schatz*, 2: sig. Aii[v]. In his preface Loeffler draws attention to writers on hymnology, notably J. C. Olearius; see Carpzov, *Lieder-Predigten*, sig. a3[r]–b1[r].

Bach and Johann Christoph Olearius 129

Table 6.1 J. C. Olearius's *Dispositionen* preached in Arnstadt, 1698–1704

Sunday	Hymn	Year	Lieder-Schatz
Advent 2	*Gott hat das Evangelium*	1698	1:16–17
Advent 3	*Nun komm, der Heiden Heiland*	1699	1:11
Epiphany	*Gelobet seist du, Jesu Christ*	1700	1:31–33
Advent 3	*Gottes Sohn ist kommen*	1701	1:20–22
Advent 1	*Gott, durch deine Güte*	1702	1:24–25
New Year	*Helft mir Gotts Güte preisen*	1703	1:52–53
S. after Christmas	*Nun danket alle Gott*	1703	1:45, 48–49
Epiphany	*Danksagen wir alle*	1704	1:58–59
Septuagesima	*O Gott, du frommer Gott*	1704	1:123–124

On Sundays there are four sermons, the first, early in the Liebfrauenkirche, from 6 until 7 a.m., given by one of the three deacons in turn … The second is given by the superintendent in the Barfüsserkirche from 9 until 10 o-clock [a.m.] … The third is given in the Neuen Kirche by its own pastor from 9 until 10 o-clock [a.m.]. In the afternoon the fourth, from 1 until 2 [p.m.] in the Barfüsserkirche, is given by a deacon in alternation … Tuesdays early from 7 until 8 o-clock [a.m.] the same deacon preaches in the Barfüsserkirche what he had preached the previous Sunday afternoon. Thursdays early from 6 until 8 [a.m.] a sermon is given in the Neuen Kirche by the deacon who had preached it the previous Sunday at the early [morning] service in the Liebfrauenkirche.[43]

There were five clergy in Arnstadt at this time: the superintendent, the pastor of the Neuen Kirche, and three deacons (sub-deacon, deacon, and arch-deacon), one of whom was Johann Christoph Olearius.[44] The pattern of preaching in the churches by each of the clergy, and how and when each sermon was repeated in each of the churches, have many similarities with a permutation fugue! For example, at the early service in the Liebfrauenkirche on Sundays the three deacons took turns to preach each week. Likewise, the three deacons preached in a similar sequence at the early Sunday afternoon

---

43 Olearius, *Historia Arnstadiensis*, 47–48: "Sonntags geschehen 4. Predigten/ deren die (1.) früh in der Lieben Frauen-Kirche von 6. biß 7. einer von denen drey *Diaconis* wechsels-weise verrichtet … Die (2.) thut der *Superintendens* in der Barfüsser-Kirchen von 9. biß 10. Uhr … Die (3.) geschicht in der Neuen Kirche von ihrem eigenen Prediger von 9. biß 10. Uhr. Nachmittags hält die (4.) von 1. biß 2. in der Barfüsser-Kirchen ein *Diaconus* wechsels-weise… Dienstags früh von 7. biß 8. prediget derjenige *Diaconus* in der Barfüsser-Kirchen/ welcher am vorigen Sonntag Nachmittag geprediget hat… Donnertags früh von 7. biß 8. geschiehet eine Predigt in der Neuen Kirche von dem *Diacono*, welcher am vorigen Sonntag früh in der Lieben Frauen-Kirche geprediget … ."

44 J. C. Olearius had been interim pastor of the Neuen Kirche for some months following his ordination in 1694 (see Olearius, *Historia Arnstadiensis*, 113, 114).

130   Hymnology

service in the Barfüsserkirche. These sermons were also repeated on weekdays so that most sermons were heard preached in all the churches, including the Neuen Kirche, where Bach was organist. Thus, of Olearius's nine *dispositionen* in Table 6.1, the first six were preached by Olearius in the seasons of Advent through Epiphany between 1698–1703, that is, before Bach's arrival. But the remaining three were preached from the Neuen Kirche pulpit when Bach would have been leading the congregation from the Neuen Kirche organ bench. To have access to outlines of what was preached in Bach's presence is a rarity in Bach literature.

Bach, of course, would have heard deacon Olearius preach frequently in the Neuen Kirche. As one of the three deacons Olearius would preach at the early Thursday morning service once or twice each month (preaching the same sermon he had given the previous Sunday in the Liebfrauenkirche), around 17 or 18 times each year. But there may well have been other occasions too, special services such as those for catechism teaching, on days of repentance and prayer, and at weddings and funerals. But deacon Olearius no doubt substituted for the pastor of the Neuen Kirche from time to time, when he was sick or away for any reason. In 1694 Olearius had been the interim pastor of the Neuen Kirche,[45] and it seems likely that he served again in that role when there was an interregnum in this position in 1704.[46]

What is clear is that when deacon Olearius preached he frequently focused on the primary hymns of the Lutheran church, the so-called "Kern-Lieder," the term used in later generations. His *Evangelischer Lieder-Schatz* was in part a homiletic handbook on how to use these hymns in the regular pulpit ministry. Among other hymnological publications Olearius produced is a kind of supplement to his *Evangelischer Lieder-Schatz*. Instead of being based on the hymns of the church year it was based on hymns of the Passion: *Hymnologia Passionalis, i. e. Homiletische Lieder-Remarqves über nachfolgende Passion-Gesänge: I. Da Jesus an dem Creutze stund [et]c. II. O Lam[m] Gottes unschuldig [et]c. III. O Traurigkeit! O Hertzeleid! IV. Ein Läm[m]lein geht und trägt [et]c. V. Wenn meine Sünde mich kräncken [et]c. VI. Ehre sey dir Christe [et]c* (Arnstadt: Ehrt, 1709). Although not published until after Bach had left Arnstadt, Olearius was working on the project during Bach's time at the Neuen Kirche. As before, when working on his *Evangelischer Lieder-Schatz*, Olearius incorporated homiletic *dispositionen* into the new study. In his *Historia Arnstadiensis*, Olearius notes the following concerning Passion sermons in the Arnstadt churches:

---

45 See Olearius, *Historia Arnstadiensis*, 113, 114.

46 In early 1704 it seems probable that Olearius was acting as interim pastor of the Neuen Kirche, as he had done in 1694–1695. Johann Petrus Kreiß, who had been the pastor of the Neuen Kirche since 1699, left Arnstadt in 1704 and was replaced later that year by Justus Christian Uthe; see Olearius, *Historia Arnstadiensis*, 115.

Passion sermons take place during Lent on Sunday afternoons and [repeated] early Tuesdays in the Barfüsserkirche, early on Thursdays in the Neuen Kirche, and also early on Fridays in the Barfüsserkirche.[47]

In his treatment of *O Lamm Gottes unschuldig* in his *Hymnologia Passionalis*, Olearius makes the following statement: "In 1704 I expounded the substance of this Passion-hymn, in place of the customary *Exordia*, in eight Passion sermons."[48] The schematic *dispositionen* of the sermons originally preached in the Arnstadt churches between Estomihi, the Sunday before Lent, and Maundy Thursday in 1704, are given in detail.[49] Thus, over a period of three months, between the end of December 1703 and the end of March 1704, we have access to no less than eleven outlines of sermons that Olearius had preached in the Arnstadt churches, sermons that Bach must have heard. But these sermons were not the usual homiletic offerings; they were different in their exploration of classic Lutheran chorales. This must have intrigued the young organist of the Neuen Kirche, who believed that he was specifically employed to accompany chorales.[50] When Olearius preached on one of these chorales in the Neuen Kirche, Bach would have improvised a prelude on the respective melody before the congregation sang the hymn. Perhaps some of the movements of Bach's partita on *O Gott, du frommer Gott* (BWV 767), which seems to date from this time, may have been linked to Olearius's Septuagesima sermon on the chorale.

An Arnstadt chorale-based organ manual (1704)

Arnstadt provided a musical environment in which Olearius's hymnological writings would have been warmly received. There were close interconnections between the court, the churches, and the school: the Capellmeister, Paul Gleitsmann (1660–1710), successor to Adam Drese (1620–1701), led the music in the principal church, the Barfüsser-Kirche, when Anton Günther II (1653–1716), Count of Schwarzburg-Arnstadt, was present; the court organist, Christoph Herthum (1641–1710), son-in-law of Heinrich Bach (1615–1692), was also the regular organist of the Barfüsser-Kirche; and the Latin school (Lyceum) supplied both the *chorus musicus* for the principal church, directed by the cantor, Ernst Dietrich Heindorff, as well as the student choir for the

---

47 Olearius, *Historia Arnstadiensis*, 49: "Die Passions-Predigten geschehen die Fasten-Zeit über des Sonntags Nachmittag und Dienstags früh in der Barfüsser-Kirchen/ des Donnerstags frühe in der Neuen Kirche/ so auch des Freytags früh in der Barfüsser-Kirchen."

48 Olearius, *Hymnologia Passionalis*, 82: "A. C. 1704. habe ich dieses Paßion-Gesänglein/ statt derer gewöhnlichen *Exordium*, 8, in Paßion-Predigten."

49 Olearius, *Hymnologia Passionalis*, 82–87.

50 NBR 45 (No. 19c); BDok 2: 17 (No.14).

132 *Hymnology*

Neuen Kirche, directed by Bach.[51] There were also the musical connections between generations of the Bachs and the Treibers in and around Arnstadt. Johann Friedrich Treiber (1642–1719), rector of the Arnstadt Latin Lyceum since 1674, was a composer as well as a teacher and author.[52] His son, Johann Philipp Treiber (1675–1727), who had studied philosophy and law at Jena University and music with Adam Drese,[53] was also a composer and music theorist. In 1704, when Bach was the organist of the Neuen Kirche and Olearius was at work on his *Evangelischer Lieder-Schatz*, J. P. Treiber issued (anonymously) the idiosyncratic manual that must have intrigued both the organist and the deacon:

> The Accurate Organist in Thorough-Bass, that is: a new, clear, and Complete Guide to Thorough-Bass, namely of those Chorales: *Was Gott tut, das ist wohlgetan*, and *Wer nur den lieben Gott läßt walten*, are carried through all keys and chords in such a way that, in those two examples, all the chords, and consequently the signatures of all the notes, and, incidently, the most convenient devices for the hand, are shown. Published at Jena by Caspar Junghans, copper engraver. 1704. Printed at Arnstadt by Nicholaus Bachmann.[54]

Although the manual was published by the engraver Junghans in Jena, it was actually printed in Arnstadt by Bachmann, the official book printer to the Arnstadt court, the printer and publisher of the *Arnstädtisches Gesangbuch*.[55]

---

51 See Christoph Wolff, *Johann Sebastian Bach: The Learned Musician* (New York: Norton, 2013), 81–83; Klaus Hofmann, "Bach in Arnstadt," *Der junge Bach: weil er nicht aufzuhalten ... Begleitbuch*, ed. Reimar Emans (Erfurt: Erste Thüringer Landesausstellung, 2000), 239–55.

52 Zedler, *Grosses vollständiges Universal-Lexicon*, 45: cols. 350–51; Johann Christoph Olearius's *Historia Arnstadiensis. Historie der alt-berühmten Schwartzburgischen Residenz Arnstadt* (Arnstadt: Bachmann, 1701; reprint, Arnstadt: Donhof, 1998), 172.

53 Zedler, *Grosses vollständiges Universal-Lexicon*, 45: cols. 351–54; see also NG2 25: 712–13.

54 *Der Accurate Organist Im General-Baß. Das ist: Neue/ deutliche und vollständige Anweisung Zum General-Baß, Worinne/ statt der Exempel/ Nur zweene Geistliche General-Bäße/ nemlich die von denen Choralen: Was Gott thut/ das ist wohlgethan/ u. Wer nur den lieben Gott läst walten/ u. durch alle Tone und Accorde dergestalt durchgeführet sind/ daß in denenselben zweyen Exampeln alle Griffe/ mithin die Signaturen aller Clavium/ anbey die bequemsten Vorthel zur Faust/ gewiesen werden. Jena/ in Verlegung Caspar Junghanßens/ Kupferstechers/ MDCCIV. Arnstadt, druckts Nicolaus Bachmann*. Translation from Frank Thomas Arnold, *The Art of Accompaniment from Thorough-Bass as Practiced in the XVIIth and XVIIIth Centuries* (1931) (New York: Dover, 1965), 1: 243. Only one copy of the first edition is locatable (British Library, Shelfmark D-7896.g.33); a second edition was issued in 1713. For the background, see Robin A. Leaver and Derek Remeš, "J. S. Bach's Chorale-Based Pedagogy: Origins and Continuity," *BACH* 48, no. 2 and 49, no 1. (2018): 132–38.

55 Most eighteenth-century sources identify Arnstadt rather than Jena as the place of publication; see for example, Jacob Adlung, *Anleitung zu der musikalischen Gelahrtheit ...* (Erfurt: Jungnicol, 1758; reprint, Kassel: Bärenreiter, 1953), 639.

Treiber's *Der accurate Organist* is a kind of workbook in which the user could learn to interpret figured bass,[56] based on two familiar chorale melodies: *Was Gott tut, das ist wohlgetan* (major),[57] and *Wer nur den lieben Gott läßt walten* (minor).[58] The notation of the two chorale melodies was not included, since they were regarded as being so well-known that it was unnecessary to notate them. The twenty-four basses, with their figures, alternating between the major and minor melodies, explore different keys, sometimes by simply transposing a figured bass, sometimes with a different bass and figures, and sometimes challenging the reader to distinguish between notes that should be given a new chord and those that should continue with the previous chord. While the primary purpose was to explain the basics of figured bass realization, Treiber's manual was particularly focused on transposition and the ability to play in all keys, major and minor.[59]

Towards the end of the seventeenth century, notably in the writings of Andreas Werckmeister, there were proposals to temper mean-tone tunings of keyboard instruments, especially the organ, that favored common keys (such as C, G, and F) but created dissonant "wolfing" in remote keys. The aim was to reduce the harshness of keys with more than two flats or three sharps. Although this was not yet equal temperament, the modified tunings reduced the dissonance when moving from the common keys. The new organ in the Neuen Kirche, Arnstadt, was built by the Mühlhausen organ-builder Johann Friedrich Wender, a proponent of modified temperament.[60] Thus, Bach, as the organist of the new instrument, surely had more than a passing interest in the possibilities of transposition when accompanying congregational singing, a facility he is known to have relished later in life[61] but which must have manifested itself much earlier. For example, the rebuke of the Arnstadt consistory, dated 21 February 1706, that Bach "made many curious *variations*

---

56 Christoph Gottlieb Schröter (1699–1792), who sided with Bach in the conflict with Scheibe, thought highly of Treiber's manual, a copy of which was given to him, New Year 1708, when he was singing in the Dresden Kreutzchor; see his *Deutlicher Anweisung zum General-Bass* (Halberstadt: Gross, 1772), viii.

57 Zahn 5629.

58 Zahn 2778.

59 Although the title page of Treiber's manual claims to cover all twenty-four keys, only twenty are represented.

60 NBR, 40–41 (Nos. 15–16); BDok, 2: 10–12 (Nos. 7–8); Wieland Meinhold, "Der Mühlhäuser Orgelbauer Johann Friedrich Wender und sein Wirken im Bereich des mitteldeutschen barocken Orgelbaus," *Mühlhäuser Beiträge zu Geschichte, Kulturgeschichte, Natur und Umwelt* 10 (1987): 41, cited Markus Rathey, "Die Temperierung der Divi Blasii-Orgel in Mühlhausen," BJ 87 (2001): 166.

61 In 1739 Bach tested the new Trost organ in the Schlosskirche, Altenburg, when, as part of the worship the hymn *Wir glauben all an einen Gott* was sung. Bach began in D minor but at the end of the first stanza raised it to E-flat minor for the second stanza, and then again to E minor for the third stanza. The ear-witness hinted at the tuning by saying that this was only possible because it was the skilled Bach playing this special instrument; see BDok, 5: 213 (No. C760a).

134   *Hymnology*

in the chorale, and mingled many strange tones in it, and ... the Congregation has been confused,"[62] may have been as much a criticism of his transpositions as it was a complaint about his extravagant harmonizations.

It seems extremely unlikely that Bach would have ignored Treiber's practical, if somewhat unusual, manual on realizing figured basses of chorale melodies published in Arnstadt during his early years as the organist of the Neuen Kirche. Indeed, Treiber's practical approach may well have stimulated Bach in the development of his own pedagogy of using chorales as the basis for the teaching of keyboard harmony and composition.[63]

Olearius's continuing influence in Bach's later years

It was Johann Christoph Olearius with his writings on the history, theology, and homiletic use of the Lutheran chorale that in the first decade of the eighteenth century made Arnstadt recognized as a center for such studies. Being in Arnstadt at that time provided the young Bach with the rare opportunity to be able to explore and understand the Lutheran chorale tradition, both in general and in particular, which could not have been done elsewhere. The influence of this background of working in close proximity to Johann Christoph Olearius in Arnstadt is traceable in Bach's later use of classic Lutheran chorales in his organ and vocal compositions. For example, there is the evidence of his early organ chorale preludes, especially those of the projected *Orgelbüchlein*,[64] which reflect quite closely the selection of hymns found in Olearius's *Evangelischer Lieder-Schatz* (see Table 8.2).

Bach's association with Johann Christoph Olearius can also be seen in the chorale cantatas he composed in Leipzig, mostly between 1724–1725 (Jahrgang II). There is no direct evidence as to why Bach decided to focus on Graduallieder that year, but given that Leipzig had a propensity to celebrate important anniversaries, such as the tricentenary of the founding of Leipzig University in 1709 and the bicentenary of the Lutheran Reformation in 1717,[65] it seems most likely that the intention was to mark the bicentenary of the earliest Lutheran hymnals published between 1524–1525.[66] Many of the chorales of Jahrgang II date from the earliest period of Lutheran hymnwriting, with a particular emphasis on the hymns of Luther. Perhaps the Leipzig clergy—especially Salomon Deyling (1677–1755), superintendent

---

62 NBR 46 (No. 20); BDok 2: 20 (No. 16).

63 See Leaver and Remeš, "J. S. Bach's Chorale-Based Pedagogy," passim.

64 See Chapter 8.

65 See Chapter 15

66 During the bicentenary of the Lutheran Reformation in 1717 Olearius drew attention to the forthcoming bicentenary of the first Lutheran hymnals that was still seven years away. He republished the contents of the earliest Lutheran hymnals, issued in 1524–1525, and observed in the preface that these hymns had been sung continuously in Lutheran churches and homes for "almost two hundred years" (fast auf 200. Jahr); Olearius, *Jubilirende Lieder-Freude*, sig. 8ᵛ.

and pastor of the Nikolaikirche, and Christian Weiss (1671–1737), pastor of the Thomaskirche—drew attention to the precedent of the Carpzov/Schelle collaboration and the publication of Carpzov's *dispositionen* in 1689, and to Carpzov's complete *Lieder-Predigten* published in 1706.[67] But the idea of focusing attention on Graduallieder would not have been a novel concept for Bach, since he had been in Arnstadt when Olearius was not only at work on his *Evangelischer Lieder-Schatz* but was also promoting Carpzov's *Lieder-Predigten*.

The influence on Bach of the Arnstadt Olearius clergy can be traced in other directions. For example, the superintendent and deacon had to have been aware of their family's literary accomplishments, which, together with the facts that Johann Christoph Olearius was the Arnstadt church librarian as well as an avid book collector, makes it seem highly likely that they influenced the young Bach in his choice of books to study and purchase. First and foremost is the Bible commentary written by Johann Olearius (1611–1684), Johann Gottfried's uncle, the Wittenberg theologian and hymn-writer, who was ultimately court preacher and superintendent in Weissenfels. Bach may well have obtained these folio volumes early in his career as a result of his contact with the Olearius family: *Biblische Erklärung Darinnen nechst dem allgemeinen Haupt-Schlüssel Der gantzen heiligen Schrifft* ... (Leipzig: Tarnoven, 1678–1681).[68]

The libretto of the early funeral cantata, *Gottes Zeit ist die allerbeste Zeit*, titled "Actus tragicus" (BWV 106), is comprised of a sequence of Bible verses that were almost certainly extracted from a devotional book written by the same Johann Olearius: *Christliche Bet-Schule: auff unterschiedliche Zeit/ Personen/ Verrichtungen/ Creutz/ Noth und Zufälle im Leben und Sterben* ... (Leipzig: Frommann, 1664; reprinted 1665, 1668, 1669, 1672).[69] Since the libretto can be traced to this book by Johann Olearius, there is the possibility that the cantata may have been composed for the funeral of a relative

---

67 If the sequence of specific chorales of Bach's chorale Jahrgang, 1724–1725, was the result of a collaboration between the pastors of the two principal churches and the cantor, given Bach's position with regard to the choice of hymns at Vespers in 1728 (See BDok 2:182 [No. 246]; BDok 1: 54–57 [No. 19]; NBR 137–39 [Nos. 137–38]), he would not simply have passively accepted the choices of the pastors.

68 Robin A. Leaver, *Bachs theologische Bibliothek: Eine kritische Bibliographie* (Stuttgart: Hänssler, 1983), No. 12. A set of the Olearius volumes was in the Arnstadt church library; see Johann Christoph Olearius, *Kurtze doch hinlängliche Nachricht von der öffentlichen Kirchen-Bibliotheck in Arnstadt . . ., welche nebst dem Verzeichnis der Bücher, so darinnen befindlich* ... ([Arnstadt]: Schill, 1746), 11, Nos. 74–78. It is strange that the title page of the library catalogue describes Olearius as "Diaconus und Bibliothecarius," since he was elevated to archdeacon in 1712, and had been superintendent in Arnstadt since 1736. It is probably an indication that the bibliography was compiled over a long period of time. The library had been founded in 1588 (see Johann Christoph Olearius, *Historia Arnstadiensis. Historie der alt-berühmten Schwartzburgischen Residentz Arnstadt* (Jena: Bielcke, 1701; facsimile, Arnstadt: Donhof, 1998), 71–72, 309–10.

69 See Renate Steiger, "J. S. Bachs Gebetbuch? Ein Fund am Rande einer Ausstellung," *Musik und Kirche* 55 (1985): 231–34.

136　*Hymnology*

of the Olearius family. There is no autograph score of the work, and the earliest dates from the second half of the eighteenth century, but stylistically the music seems to come from 1707–1708, when Bach had recently become organist in Mühlhausen. There is reason to believe that the source of the copy of the *Christliche Bet-Schule* that Bach saw was Johann Christoph Olearius, since the book contained hymn texts by Johann Olearius.[70]

One of Bach's favorite authors was August Pfeiffer (1640–1698), superintendent in Lübeck, which was something he apparently had in common with Johann Christoph Olearius. Bach must have discovered the writings of Pfeiffer fairly early in his career. Sometime after 1722 he listed three of Pfeiffer's books on the title page of the manuscript "Clavier-Büchlein vor Anna Magdelena Bach"[71]: "*Ante* [sic] *Calvinismus* und Christen Schule *item Anti Melancholicy*."[72] At Bach's death in 1750 these three books were still in his possession,[73] together with five more titles by Pfeiffer[74]—more than any other author, except Luther, in his library. Although very few of the theologians that the younger Olearius met during his visit to north Germany in 1694–1695 are named, it is specifically recorded that in Lübeck he had a significant meeting with Pfeiffer.[75] This was just a few years before the latter's death. Therefore, it seems a distinct possibility that Johann Christoph Olearius not only shared an interest in the writings of Pfeiffer but also may have introduced the organist to the works of the published author.

Although Bach was in Arnstadt only for a relatively short time, what he learned and experienced while organist of the Neuen Kirche he was able to draw on in later years. The influence of Johann Christoph Olearius, one of a very small group of leading Lutheran hymnologists of the time, was incalculable and informed his understanding and use of chorales, the texts and their associated melodies, in organ works, cantatas, and especially his Passions.

70　Fischer and Tümpel, *Das deutsche evangelische kirchenlied des 17. Jahrhunderts*, 4: Nos. 372, 376–79, 381–401, 405, 423–26, 428.

71　BB Mus. ms. Bach P 224.

72　BDok 1: 268.

73　Leaver, *Bachs theologische Bibliothek*, Nos. 37, 16, and 39 respectively.

74　Leaver, *Bachs theologische Bibliothek*, Nos. 14–15, 17–18, and 38. No.15, Pfeiffer's *Gazophylacion Evangelicum: Evangelische Schatz-Kammer* (Jena: Rist, 1689), sermons on the Gospels throughout the church year, was cited by J. C. Olearius in his *Evangelischer Lieder-Schatz ... Ander Theil* (Jena: Bielcke, 1705), 117 (on this work, see the discussion below).

75　Zedler, *Universal-Lexicon*, 25: col. 1178: "In Lübeck sprach er dem Herrn D. Pfeiffern."

7 Bach's *Christ lag in Todesbanden* (BWV 4)

Hymnology and chronology

Bach's cantata BWV 4, *Christ lag in Todesbanden*, is by any standard a remarkable composition. Although originally written over a century ago, words concerning this cantata penned by William Gillies Whittaker are worth repeating:

> Bach frequently set himself problems for the [apparent] sheer joy of overcoming difficulties ... The problem Bach set himself in this cantata was ... of founding every number [movement] on a basic chorale, but here it seems exceptionally daring because of the nature of the tune and of the poem. The tune is long, eight-lined, and, moreover, circumscribed in tonality. Half of the lines end on the tonic, half on the dominant. Thrice the cadential tonic is preceded by a descending scale passage. Thrice, too, the cadential dominant is preceded by a descending scale passage. The mere technical problems of avoiding the palling monotony of these oft-recurring ideas in seven settings necessitated by the self-imposed task seems insuperable. And then the poem was not one which could be dealt with lightly. It was not the compilation of some minor rhymester which made no appeal of moment to the minds of the congregation ... It was one of the most popular of Luther's religious poems, esteemed highly by the worshipers of that day and intimately associated with the Festival of Easter. Every line would be critically followed by the congregation.[1]

The origins of the cantata are not entirely clear since the original score is no longer extant; what survives are the Leipzig parts. This has led to speculation as to when the cantata was first composed, a process that has seen the date of composition being gradually assigned to successively earlier years.[2]

---

1 William G. Whittaker, *Fugitive Notes on Certain Cantatas and the Motets of J. S. Bach* (London: Oxford University Press, 1924), 129–30. The collected essays were originally published during the previous ten years in the monthly journal *The Organist and Choirmaster*.

2 See the discussion, under the heading "The Dating of Cantata No. 4," in Gerhard Herz, ed., *Bach, Cantata No. 4, Christ lag in Todesbanden: An Authoritative Score. Backgrounds, Analysis, Views and Comments* (New York: Norton, 1967), 21–23.

138 *Hymnology*

Towards the end of the nineteenth century Philipp Spitta was of the opinion that it was "highly probable" that the first performance of the cantata was on Easter Day, 9 April 1724,[3] a view that was repeated by various writers in subsequent decades. More recently the scholarly consensus has focused on the year 1708: in his study of the early cantatas Alfred Dürr suggested "1708 or a little later" but "before 1714"[4]; Armin Schneiderheinze argued for its origin in Weimar during the years before Bach was appointed concertmaster, that is between 1708 and 1713[5]; Hans-Joachim Schulze and Christoph Wolff have taken the year as a *terminus ad quem* rather than a *terminus post quem* and assert "probably 1708 or earlier."[6] What follows is the case for considering the possibility that the original performance of the cantata was on Easter Day 1706.

The evidence of the extant parts

The original version of Cantata 4, *Christ lag in Todesbanden*, was one of Bach's earliest compositions in the genre, perhaps even the earliest. It displays many similarities with vocal works based on chorales by earlier composers, such as Buxtehude and Pachelbel.[7] For example, it has no secco recitatives, the sinfonia is a separate movement rather than being incorporated into the opening choral movement—Bach's usual practice in Leipzig—the libretto comprises only the text of Luther's Easter hymn, and therefore it lacks the meditative poetic arias of the later cantatas. Since there are stylistic links with Cantata 71, *Gott ist mein König*, composed for the annual installation of the Mühlhausen town council in 1708, and Cantata 150, *Nach dir, Herr, verlanget mich*, which was also composed in Mühlhausen,[8] it is generally thought that the earliest form of *Christ lag in Todesbanden* was composed for and performed in Mühlhausen, possibly at Easter in 1708, or perhaps the previous year as part of his audition for the position of organist at the Blasiuskirche (see further below).

Bach performed the cantata again for his first Easter in Leipzig in 1724 and again at Easter the following year, 1725. For these later performances some adjustments were made to the instrumentation, but the cantata, as far as can

---

3 Spitta 2: 220–21; Spitta ET 2:392.

4 Alfred Dürr, *Studien über die frühen Kantaten J. S. Bachs* (Leipzig: Breitkopf & Härtel, 1951), 210.

5 Armin Schneiderheinze, "'Christ lag in Todes Banden': Überlegungen zur Datierung von BWV 4," *Das Frühwerk Johann Sebastian Bachs: Kolloquium, Rostock, 11.–13. September 1990* (Cologne: Studio, 1995), 267–79.

6 BC 1:237 (A54a).

7 See Kerala Snyder, "Tradition with Variations: Chorale Settings *per omnes versus* by Buxtehude and Bach," *Music and Theology: Essays in Honor of Robin A. Leaver*, ed. Daniel Zager (Lanham: Scarecrow, 2007), 31–50.

8 See Hans-Joachim Schulze, "Rätselhafte Auftragswerke Johann Sebastian Bachs: Anmerkung zu einigen Kantatentexten," BJ 96 (2010): 69–74.

Bach's Christ lag in Todesbanden *(BWV 4)*   139

be judged, remained in substantially the same form as the earlier version. For the performance on Easter Day 1724 the cantata was probably concluded by a four-part chorale (no-longer-extant), probably newly composed, with strings doubling the voice parts. The following year, 1725, Cantata 4 was performed again on Easter Day with an alternative four-part setting of the concluding chorale, with a cornetto and three trombones strengthening the voice parts in movements 2, 3, and 8. What is known for certain about the earliest form of the cantata is deduced from the parts that were prepared for these later Leipzig performances. Unfortunately, neither the score nor the parts of the earliest version of the cantata have survived, and therefore many questions about the nature of the original cantata cannot be fully answered.

Textual variations in Bach's libretto

The libretto is made up of all seven stanzas of Luther's 1524 Easter hymn, without paraphrase or elaboration, and thus parallels earlier *per omnes versus* chorale compositions, such as Pachelbel's *Christ lag in Todesbanden* and Buxtehude's *Jesu meine Freude* (BuxWV 60).[9] Bach's libretto, however, includes a number of textual variants from Luther's original (see Figure 7.1).[10] These variants can be classified into two categories: those that appear to be made by Bach and those that can be found in various hymnals.

Of those variants apparently unique to the manuscript parts of Cantata 4, two are simple transcription errors. In stanza 2, line 5 (movt. 3), Bach wrote "darum" instead of "davon," an error that only occurs in the soprano part.[11] Similarly, in stanza 5, line 5 (movt. 6), Bach wrote "das" instead of "des" into the bass part.[12] In stanza 3, line 3 (movt. 4), Luther's "abgetan" was replaced by the similar word, "weggetan," without an essential change in meaning. Other changes appear to be more significant choices. Line eight of stanza 5 (movt. 6) was expanded from eight to nine syllables: "Der Würger kann uns nicht rühren" became "Der Würger kann uns nicht **mehr** schaden." There is only a slight change in meaning, from "cannot strike us" to "can no more harm us." The reason for the change was almost certainly compositional. Bach wanted to emphasize the negative by the repetition of "nicht," which he does four times (see movt. 6, mm. 76–79). But he was then faced with the problem of completing the cadence with the weak-sounding, two-syllable "rühren." His solution was to change the final word to the stronger-sounding

---

9 Nine other cantatas by Bach are similarly *per omnes versus* settings: BWV 107 (1724), 137 (1724), 177 (1725), 129 (1726/27), 117 (1728/31), 192 (1730), 112 (1731), 100 (after 1732), and 97 (1734).

10 The basic text of Luther's *Christ lag in Todesbanden* in Figure 7.1 is from *Arnstädtisches Verbessertes Gesangbuch*, edited by Johann Christoph Olearius (Arnstadt: Bachmann, 1705), 117–18; cf. the listing of variants in NBA 1/9 KB (Dürr 1986): 22–23.

11 See NBA KB 1/9: 13.

12 See NBA KB 1/9: 14.

140 *Hymnology*

Luther 1524

1. Christ lag in Todes-Banden
  für unser Sünd gegeben/
  der* ist wider erstanden/
  und hat uns bracht das Leben:
   Deß wir sollen frölich seyn/
   Gott loben und danckbar seyn/
   und singen A.[lleluja.
   Alleluja.]
* Bach = *Er*

2. Den Tod niemand zwingen kunt
  bey allen Menschen-Kindern/
  Das macht alles unser Sünd,
  kein Unschuld war zu finden.
   Davon§ kam der Tod so bald/
   und nahm über uns Gewalt/
   hielt uns in seinm Reich gefangen.
   Alleluja.
§ Bach = *Darum* only in soprano part

3. Jesus Christus Gottes Sohn
  an unser Statt ist kommen/
  und hat die Sünde abgetan/†
  damit dem Tod genommen
   all sein Recht und sein Gewalt/
   da bleibet nichts denn Tod's Gestalt/
   den Stachel hat er verloren.
   All.[eluja].
† Bach = *weggetan*

4. Es war ein wunderlicher Krieg/
  da Tod und Leben rungen/
  das Leben behielt‡ den Sieg/
  es hat den Tod verschlungen.
   Die Schrifft hat verkündet das/
   wie ein Tod den andern fraß/
   Ein Spott aus dem Tod ist worden.
   All.[eluja].
‡ Bach = *Leben da[s] behielt* only in tenor and bass parts

5. Hie ist das rechte Oster-Lamm/
  davon Gott hat geboten/
  Das ist an¶ des Creuzes Stam[m]
  in heisser Lieb gebraten:
   desʃ Blut zeichnet unser Thür/
   das hält der Glaub dem Tode für:
   der Würger kan uns nicht rühren.**
   Allel.[uja].
¶ Bach = *Das ist hoch an*
ʃ Bach = *Das*
** Bach = *nicht mehr schaden.*

Figure 7.1 Christ lag in Todesbanden (Luther, 1524)

6. So feyren wir dies hohe Fest
mit Hertzen-Freud und Won[n]e/
das uns der Herre scheinen läst:
Er ist selber die Sonne/
  der durch seiner Gnaden-Glanz/
  erleuchtet uner Hertzen gantz:
  Der Sünden-nacht ist vergangen.[++]
  All.[eluja].

[++] Bach = *verschwunden.*

7. Wir essen und leben wohl
in rechten Oster-Fladen/
Der alte Sauerteig nicht soll
seyn bei dem Wort der Gnaden!
  Christus wil die Koste seyn/
  und speisen die Seel allein/
  der Glaub will keins andern leben.
  Alleluja.

Figure 7.1 (Cont.)

"schaden" and precede it with "mehr" to form an emphatic conclusion before the following "Alleluja": "nicht mehr schaden."

At the end of the following stanza (st. 6, line 8; movt. 7) there is another word change, but without an additional syllable: "der Sünden Nacht ist vergangen" becomes "der Sünden Nacht ist **verschwungen**." Here it is perhaps more difficult to see an obvious reason for the alteration. Both words are of three syllables and have the same pattern of rhythmic stress. However, it is possible that Bach wanted a word that would be more suitable for word-painting, the night of sin "vanishing" rather than simply coming to an end. It is significant that throughout this movement, up until this point, the triplets in the soprano and tenor voice-parts run in parallel thirds. But at "verschwungen" the triplets are displaced and sound alternately against each other, instead of running in parallel thirds, until they dissolve ("vanish") into the same quarter note before the Halleluia begins (movt. 7, mm. 31–34).

There is another addition that has the appearance of being unique to the manuscript parts, since it only occurs in two of the four voice parts of movement 5—a conclusion of both Werner Neumann and Alfred Dürr.[13] In the tenor and bass parts, stanza 4, line 3 is expanded by the addition of "das"; from "Das Leben behielt" to "Das Leben **das** behielt." But when Bach repeats the line in both voice parts he does so without the addition of "das" (movt. 5, mm. 12–16), and conforms to the text found in the soprano and alto parts.

13 Werner Neumann, *Sämtliche von Johann Sebastian Bach vertonte Texte* (Leipzig: VEB Deutscher Verlag für Musik, 1974), 69, n. 4, and Alfred Dürr, NBA KB 1/9: 22.

142   *Hymnology*

Dürr could not find this verbal formula in any of the hymnals he examined:[14] Mühlhausen (1697), Weimar (1713), Weißenfels (1714), Leipzig (1682, 1697, 1721), and Dresden (1725). Since Cantata 4 may have been composed for Mühlhausen, the 1697 Mühlhausen *Gesangbuch* is an obvious source to investigate with regard to Bach's libretto. The Weimar *Gesangbuch* of 1713 might have influenced the text as it occurs in the Leipzig parts of the cantata but, since Bach spent some time in Weimar in 1703, the edition of the Weimar *Gesangbuch* of 1681 might have been a more relevant source to examine, since Bach must have had some experience of using it before he composed the cantata *Christ lag in Todesbanden*. The Leipzig *Gesangbücher* of 1682, 1697, and 1721, together with the 1724 Dresden *Gesangbuch* that was also used in Leipzig, establish the received "Leipzig" text of Luther's hymn (although there is not absolute orthographic unanimity between them), but are only relevant for the text of the final movement of the cantata that originated in Leipzig.

While the 1681 Weimar *Gesangbuch* was included among the hymnals consulted in establishing the sources of Bach's libretto for the NBA, there are some notable omissions from Dürr's list in NBA KB 1/9, including:

1. The *Eisenachisches Gesang Buch* of 1673, which would have had a formative influence on the young Bach, since it was the first hymnal he sang from in church and school in Eisenach as a boy.
2. The *Lüneburgisches Gesangbuch* of 1695 (preface dated 1686), which he would have sung from when he was a member of the choir of St. Michael's, Lüneburg, between 1700 and 1703.
3. The *Arnstädtisches Gesangbuch* of 1701 (preface dated 1700; reissued 1703 and 1705), which he must have used when he was organist of the Neuen Kirche in Arnstadt between 1703 and 1707.
4. Since he made an extended visit to Lübeck in 1705–1706, he presumably must also have encountered the *Lübeckisches Gesang-Buch* of 1703.[15]

These were the hymnals of his formative years, or those that he worked with early in his professional career.

When these hymnals are examined, it becomes clear that the addition of "da" into stanza 4, line 3, did not originate with Bach. It is found, for example, in the Lüneberg *Gesangbuch* (1695),[16] and similarly the *Lübeckisches Gesangbuch* (1703/1716) has "Das leben **das** behielt den sieg."[17] The addition of the extra syllable resolved the metrical irregularity of Luther's text. In the

---

14 NBA KB 1/9: 21–22.
15 The *Gesangbuch* was used for the first time in the Marienkirche, Lübeck, on the Third Sunday in Advent, December 16, 1703.
16 *Lüneburgisches Gesangbuch/ darinnen über 2000/ so wol alte als neue Geistreiche Lieder* (Lüneburg: Stern, 1695), 472.
17 *Lübeckisches Gesang-Buch* (Lübeck: Wiedemeyer, 1716), 83.

way that Bach uses the contour of the chorale melody with the tenor and bass entries at mm. 12 and 14, the extra syllable ensures a regular iambic stress on the alternate syllables: "Das *Le*ben *da* be*hielt* den *Sieg*." But, thereafter, when he repeats the line, he returns to Luther's original text. Undoubtedly the reason for the addition was compositional, but it also suggests that Bach had remembered the form of the line of that stanza from his Lüneburg school-days, when he sang from the *Lüneburgisches Gesangbuch*. It also suggests that, while he was willing to accept a later modification to Luther's text for musical reasons, once the particular difficulty had been surmounted, he returned to the original form of Luther's text.

Then there are the other textual changes that can be traced to various hymnals. The first concerns the small change in stanza 1, line 3, which Bach begins with the personal pronoun "Er" in place of Luther's "Der," essentially a change in spelling rather than a change in meaning. It is an alteration found in some later eighteenth-century hymnals,[18] but all the late seventeenth-century and early eighteenth-century hymnals examined for this chapter were found to have "Der." Interestingly "Er ist wieder erstanden" is the text found in Pachelbel's cantata *Christ lag in Todesbanden*,[19] a cantata that had some influence on the composition of Bach's Cantata 4.[20] Thus, the slight textual modification might be a further link between the two cantatas on Luther's Easter hymn.

Another textual change concerns the additional syllable, added to stanza 5, line 3 (movt. 6). The seven syllables of "Das ist an des Kreutzes Stamm" are expanded to eight: "Das ist **hoch** an des Kreutzes Stamm." The change was clearly made for musical reasons. When the melody is in 4/4 time, even though two quarter notes are tied on an unimportant syllable (see Figure 7.2, A), the result is tolerable. But when the melody is given in 3/4, as in movement 6, then the tie on "des" would distort the meaning of the line by giving it a prominence it should not have (see Figure 7.2, B). But the addition of the extra syllable "hoch" creates a regular iambic stress in which the strong syllables coincide with the first beat of each measure (see Figure 7.2, C).

By including "hoch" Bach was following the example of a number of hymnals that include the modified line, among them Weimar (1681), Lüneburg (1695), Lübeck (1703), Weißenfels (1714), and Leipzig (1721). Bach therefore

---

18 For example, *Das privilegirte Ordentliche und Vermehrte Dreßdnische Gesang-Buch* [1724] (Dresden & Leipzig: Hekel, 1732), 90; *Das privilegirte Vollständige und vermehrte Leipziger Gesang-Buch* [1734] (Leipzig: Barnbeck, 1758), 309.

19 Johann Pachelbel, *Sämtliche Vokalwerk, 8: Concerti II*, ed. Thomas Röder (Kassel: Bärenreiter, 2012), 48–49, 200–201.

20 See Alfred Dürr, *The Cantatas of J. S. Bach, with their Librettos in German-English Parallel Text*, rev. and ed. Richard D. P. Jones (Oxford: Oxford University Press, 2005), 264; Crawford R. Thoburn, "Pachelbel's *Christ lag in Todesbanden*: A Possible Influence on Bach's Work," *American Choral Review* 19/1 (January 1977): 3–16; and Gerhard Herz, "More on Bach's Cantata No. 4: Date and Style—A Reply to Crawford R. Thoburn," *American Choral Review* 21/2 (April 1977): 3–19.

144 *Hymnology*

Figure 7.2 Comparisons of different metrical stress patterns

used a major received text for his libretto at this point, even though other hymnals did not include it, preferring Luther's unaltered 1524 text—apart from orthographic variables—such as Eisenach (1673), Mühlhausen (1697), and Arnstadt (1705), among others.

Olearius on *Christ lag in Todesbanden* and Bach's libretto

If *Christ lag in Todesbanden* was composed for Bach's application for the post of organist at the Blasiuskirche, Mühlhausen and performed there at Easter 1707,[21] then it must have been composed in Arnstadt.[22] It therefore would have been composed within the ambit of one of the most knowledgeable hymnologists of the day, one who had a particular appreciation for the hymns of Martin Luther: Johann Christoph Olearius.[23]

The second part of Olearius's *Evangelischer Lieder-Schatz*, issued in 1705 during Bach's tenure in Arnstadt, includes a discussion of Luther's *Christ lag in Todesbanden*. It begins with a survey of the background of the Easter hymn, and continues with many citations praising this "true masterpiece."[24] Olearius also includes a detailed examination of some of the more important alterations to Luther's text that had been made in various hymnals, mostly in the interests of eliminating metrical irregularities. For example, he draws attention to stanza 3, line 1, "Jesus Christus, Gottes Sohn," which was expanded to "Jesus Christus, **wahr** Gottes Sohn"—an alteration found, for

---

21 BDok 2: 22–23 (No. 19).
22 See, for example, Wolff BLM, 99; Peter Williams, *Bach: A Musical Biography* (Cambridge: Cambridge University Press, 2016), 92.
23 On J. C. Olearius, see Chapter 6.
24 "Ist ein rechtes Meisterstück"; Johann Christoph Olearius, *Evangelischer Lieder-Schatz … Anderer Theil* (Jena: Bielcke, 1705), 96.

Bach's Christ lag in Todesbanden *(BWV 4)* 145

example, in the Weimar *Gesangbuch* of 1681, but not in the libretto of Bach's Cantata 4. Another is the addition of "hoch" in stanza 5, line 3, "Das ist **hoch** an des Kreuzes Stamm," which occurs in some hymnals as well as in Bach's *Christ lag in Todesbanden*. Having recorded such alterations Olearius asks rhetorically, "But what is the purpose of such unnecessary and supposed improvements?"[25] Olearius clearly had great respect for the original form of Luther's Easter hymn, even its rugged metrical irregularities.

Do these censures of such alterations imply a fundamental disagreement between Olearius and Bach? Not necessarily. After all, Bach's revisions were generally minor and, in some cases, not found in all the voice parts. The changes were mostly made for compositional reasons; not one of them undermined the integrity of Luther's text, and some, it could reasonably be argued, intensified Luther's meaning. Olearius was thinking in terms of congregational singing, the expression of the corporate belief of the assembled congregation, whereas Bach was composing a vocal piece for specialized singers in the church. Even though he did make some textual changes, Bach did not stray far from Olearius's concern for Luther's original text, since he only adopted one of the alterations that the Arnstadt hymnologist called into question (stanza 5, movt. 6, line 3)—and Bach did so for good musical reasons—and one of the other modifications was abandoned when the text was repeated (stanza 4, movt. 5, line 3).

In a sense, one can regard the Eisenach *Gesangbuch* of 1673 as Bach's primary source for Luther's text, since this was the hymnal from which he no doubt committed it to memory during his earliest years. The cantata libretto is very close to the text as given in this hymnal, apart from Bach's few verbal variants, notably the substitution of "weggetan" for "abgetan" in stanza 3, and "nicht mehr schaden" for "nicht ruhren" in stanza 5.[26] The text in the Arnstadt *Gesangbuch* is similar to that of the Eisenach *Gesangbuch*, and it would seem to have been the most likely hymnal that Bach would have referred to if he needed to confirm what was embedded in his memory. As indicated above, in addition to the hymnals of Eisenach (1673) and Arnstadt (1705), there are

---

25 "Worzu dient aber solches unnöthiges und vermeintes verbessern?"; Olearius, *Evangelischer Lieder-Schatz ... Anderer Theil*, 100.

26 *Neues vollständiges Eisenachisches Gesangbuch* (Eisenach: Rörer, 1673), 207–208; see Conrad Freyse, "Sebastians Gesangbuch," BJ 45 (1958): 123–26; Conrad Freyse, "Johann Sebastian Bachs erstes Gesangbuch," *Jahrbuch für Liturgik und Hymnologie* 6 (1961): 138–42. The hymnal includes an additional 8th stanza by an unknown author that is identified as not being by Luther by being enclosed in square brackets and in a slightly-different type-size: "[Du Uberwinder Jesu Christ/ der du uns bringst das Leben/ hilf/ daß mit dir zu aller Frist/ wir auferstehen eben. Weck uns auf vom Schlaf und Tod/ und reyß uns aus der Sünden Noht/ daß wir nicht ewig sterben. Alleluja]"; *Eisenachisches Gesangbuch*, 208. A search of many seventeenth-century German hymnals failed to locate the stanza, and therefore it may have been unique to the Eisenach *Gesangbuch*. Strangely, the hymnal heads Luther's Easter hymn thus: "*Hymnus: Surrexit Christus Hodie*. Verbeßert/ durch D.M.L." The reference should have been to the Easter Sequence *Victimae paschali laudes*.

146 *Hymnology*

four other primary hymnals that Bach would have been familiar with early in the eighteenth century: Weimar (1681), Lüneburg (1695), Mühlhausen (1697), and Lübeck (1703/1716). But they contain textual variants different from those found in Bach's cantata libretto, which renders them unlikely to have been used by Bach in connection with the libretto of Cantata 4. Although three sources—Weimar (1681), Lüneburg (1695), and Lübeck (1703/1716)—share with Bach the addition of "hoch" in stanza 5, line 3, all four expand stanza 1, line 6, with "ihm," a revision not found in Bach's libretto: "Gott loben und **ihm** dankbar sein."

Therefore, taking all these details into account, the *Arnstädtisches Gesangbuch* (1705)—notwithstanding the absence of "hoch" in stanza 5, line 3, the addition of which the *Gesangbuch* editor, Johann Christoph Olearius, criticized—was most likely the hymnal that Bach referred to when composing the cantata *Christ lag in Todesbanden*. However, this conclusion has to remain tentative, given the fact that the original score of the cantata has not survived, and the extant sources date from Bach's early years in Leipzig.

The Chorale Cantata (BWV 4)

What is really significant is that Bach chose to write an Easter cantata using only the text of Luther's hymn, *per omnes versus*. The chorale not only constitutes the libretto but also establishes the structure of the cantata. Following the introductory instrumental Sinfonia, the first vocal movement is headed "Versus I," and thereafter all the remaining movements are numbered according to the seven stanzas of Luther's chorale.

Bach clearly understood the chiastic structure of Luther's seven stanzas, which are arranged around stanza 4, the central stanza. After the opening Sinfonia, the cantata is symmetrically arranged around this pivotal stanza:

1. Sinfonia
2. Versus I. Chorus SATB
   3. Versus II. Duet SA
      4. Versus III. Solo T
         5. Versus IV. Chorus SATB
      6. Versus V. Solo B
   7. Versus VI. Duet ST
8. Versus VII. Chorus SATB

The opening chorus balances the closing chorale (movts. 2 and 8); the soprano and alto duet matches the soprano and tenor duet (movts. 3 and 7); and the tenor aria balances the bass aria (movts. 4 and 6). In the middle is a motet-like setting of the chorale (movt. 5).

Most of the paired movements have many features in common, but the weakest pairing is the first chorus and the closing chorale. On the one hand, there is an extended chorale movement, bipartite in form: a chorale fantasia in strict counterpoint, which is followed by a free *alla breve*—almost

Bach's Christ lag in Todesbanden *(BWV 4)* 147

breathless—Alleluja. It seems highly likely that in these two sections of this first vocal movement Bach is giving audible form to the theological distinction between Law and Gospel, the concept that lies at the heart of Luther's and Lutheran theology. The Law condemns; the Gospel gives life. Christ died to fulfil the demands of the Law; Christ rose again to bring life, the heart of the Gospel. But this magnificent movement is balanced by a four-part chorale, which, while it cannot be dismissed as merely "simple," is somewhat restrained and brief when compared with movement 2. From the evidence of the parts, this four-part chorale with instruments doubling the voices, which now concludes the cantata, was composed for the 1725 performance in Leipzig. It is not known what concluded the cantata in 1724, but most writers suggest that it was a different simple four-part setting of the final stanza of Luther's hymn. But the really important question is: What was the concluding movement of the earliest version of the cantata? Alfred Dürr made the following cautious but perceptive comment: "We cannot entirely rule out the possibility that the oldest version ended with an exact reprise of the opening chorus to the text of verse 7."[27]

From time to time in later compositions Bach repeated music within a symmetrical structure, such as in the motet *Jesu, meine Freude*, the St. John Passion, the Christmas Oratorio, and the B-minor Mass. I am convinced that in its original form the cantata was concluded by the repetition of the music of movement 2, with the words of stanza 7 replacing those of stanza 1. The outer movements of the symmetrical structure would then have been unmistakable, with the repetition of the same music, and the meaning of the central movement (movt. 5), which also has a Law/Gospel reference, would have been more strongly underscored by being framed by these outer movements, which employ the same music.[28]

The central movement of the cantata (movt. 5) is quite extraordinary, a vigorous and lively depiction of the struggle between life and death, in which life, resurrection life, is the victor. This is the fulcrum on which both Luther's chorale and Bach's cantata turn. The chorale melody in diminution is used to create an energetic three-voice counterpoint (soprano, tenor, and bass) within which the melody is heard at normal tempo. This rushing counterpoint is a depiction in sound of the duel between life and death that the hymn stanza speaks of, which also incorporates an incredible canonic device to depict the devouring of death by death. Here this central movement links with Bach's setting of the first stanza in movement 2, and with movement 8—if the same music was repeated for the closing movement of the first version of the cantata. If so, then all three movements would be musical expositions of the distinction between Law and Gospel.

---

27 Dürr, *The Cantatas of J. S. Bach*, 265.

28 The impressive recording of Cantata 4 by Cantus Cölln, conducted by Konrad Junghänel, under the title *Actus tragicus* (Harmonia Mundi France HMC 901694, 2000), repeats the music of movement 2 with the text of stanza 7 of Luther's hymn for the final movement.

148 *Hymnology*

It is here that some words of Olearius might support the possibility that in the original version of Cantata 4 Bach repeated the same music he had composed for the first stanza of Luther's Easter hymn at the end of the cantata, but with the text of the seventh and last stanza of the hymn. After his comments on *Christ lag in Todesbanden* in part two of his *Evangelischer Lieder-Schatz* (1705), Olearius gives, as he does for every hymn he discusses, a "*Disposition*," an outline for a sermon on Luther's Easter hymn. At the very end of his outline, he comments, "Here it should be borne in mind, that the first stanza of this hymn contains the whole *Disposition*, which is expanded and expounded in the following stanzas."[29]

Here is justification for the reuse of the music of stanza 1 for the final movement of Bach's Easter cantata. If the first stanza contains the essence of the hymn, that is elaborated in the subsequent stanzas, then there is every reason to repeat the musical setting of this first stanza with the text of the final stanza. The cantata would, therefore, have a more explicit symmetrical structure and would end on a note of resurrection joy with the repeat of the *alle breve* Alleluja.

Christ lag in Todesbanden may well have been performed in Mühlhausen at Easter 1707 in connection with Bach's application for the position of organist at the Blasiuskirche, but was it composed for that occasion? There is a strong possibility that it was originally composed for Easter the previous year, 1706. Towards the end of 1705 Bach journeyed to Lübeck to hear the music of Dieterich Buxtehude. Buxtehude was not only a composer for the organ but also a noted composer of vocal works. Bach stayed longer than he had permission to be absent from Arnstadt. On his return, the consistory called him on 21 February, 1706, to account for his conduct. He was asked where had he been, why had he been away for so long, and who had given him permission. Bach replied that "he had been to Lübeck in order to comprehend one thing and another about his art, but had asked leave beforehand from the superintendent." Superintendent Johann Gottfried Olearius responded that Bach "had asked for only four weeks, but had stayed about four times as long."[30] At the same session of the consistory he was also reproved for having "made many curious *variationes* in the chorale, and mingled many strange tones in it," confusing the congregation.[31] The assumption is that, fresh from hearing Buxtehude in Lübeck, Bach was experimenting with the harmonizations of chorale melodies.

The consistory also raised another matter of concern:

> In addition, it was quite disagreeable that hitherto no concerted music had been performed, for which he was responsible ... accordingly he was to declare whether he was willing to play for concerted music as well as

---

29 "Hierbey ist zu gedencken/ daß der 1. v. dieses Liedes gantze *Disposition* in sich hält/ welche in folgenden erweitert und ausgeführet worden"; Olearius, *Evangelischer Lieder-Schatz ... Anderer Theil*, 102.

30 NBR 46 (No. 20); BDok 2: 19 (No. 16).

31 Ibid.

chorales sung by the students ... If he did not wish to do so, he should
but state that fact *categorice* so that other arrangements could be made
to someone who would.

[Bach responded:] "If he were provided with a competent conductor he
would perform well enough."[32]

In a sense this interchange was a continuation of the difference between Bach
and the consistory that had arisen during the Geyersbach incident the previous year, when Bach had claimed that he was responsible only for "simple
chorale music, and not for concerted pieces." The consistory responded that
he was wrong on this matter and that he "must help out in all music making."[33]

From what is known about Bach's character, he could be somewhat blunt
and belligerent, especially if he thought that he was being unjustly criticized.
Having received this reprimand, his reaction may well have been to demonstrate to the members of the consistory that not only would he participate in
concerted music, he would compose such a piece that would show them his
worth and competence.[34]

Bach had returned to Arnstadt in the middle of February 1706, after
hearing Buxtehude's music in Lübeck—that is, around the beginning of Lent
that year. It is understandable that the young Bach, on his return to Arnstadt,
should want to try his hand at composing a Buxtehude-like cantata. There are
certainly strong links between his cantata and the vocal music of Buxtehude.[35]
For example, even though Bach's cantata also owes something to Pachelbel's
cantata on the same hymn, he does not use Pachelbel's instrumentation of 2
violins, 3 violas and continuo, but rather 2 violins, 2 violas and continuo, as
commonly used by Buxtehude. There was also the further incentive to demonstrate to the church consistory something of what he had learned while he
had been away, and he had the remaining weeks of Lent to work on the composition. Thus, it seems quite likely that Bach composed the cantata, *Christ
lag in Todesbanden*, for Easter Day, 1706.

One way to respond to the criticism of the consistory and impress the
Arnstadt clergy—especially the some-time deacon of the Neuen Kirche,
hymnologist Johann Christoph Olearius, who had a great regard for the
hymns of Martin Luther—would be to use Luther's Easter hymn as the cantata libretto. If this scenario is basically correct it means that *Christ lag in
Todesbanden* is the product of a twenty-one-year-old and, whatever the exact
chronology of its composition, it is an extraordinarily competent work that
foreshadows the contrapuntal complexities of his later years.

---

32 Ibid.

33 NBR 45 (No. 19c); BDok 2: 17 (No. 14).

34 After referring to Cantata 4, Peter Williams writes: "Since it is clear from the complaints
made about Bach in February 1706 that he was expected to participate in the ensemble [in
addition to organ] music, one can suppose that he was already trying his hand at composing
church pieces himself." Williams, *Bach: A Musical Biography*, 67.

35 See note 7 above.

8 Bach's *Orgelbüchlein*

For organists the chorale preludes of Bach's *Orgelbüchlein* are fundamental. As George Stauffer writes in the foreword to Russell Stinson's monograph on the collection:

> No other volume of music is so well known to organists as the *Orgelbüchlein* of Johann Sebastian Bach. For generations of players it has stood as the first resource for honing manual and pedal skills. As Bach's Two-Part Inventions, Three-Part Sinfonias, and *Well-Tempered Clavier* are to pianists and harpsichordists, so the *Orgelbüchlein* is to organists: it is central to the educational process, a pedagogical *vade mecum* that no student or instructor can be without.[1]

It is, therefore, understandable that an extensive body of literature on the collection continues to grow, in which many aspects of performance, pedagogy, analysis, compositional techniques, registration, and so forth, are discussed in detail and at length.[2]

The manuscript: Deutsche Staatsbibliothek, Berlin. Mus. Ms. Bach P 283

Bach's title page, added to the manuscript some years after he had begun work on the project, indicates his pedagogical and practical concerns:

---

1 Russell Stinson, *Bach: The Orgelbüchlein* (New York: Schirmer, 1996), xi.
2 There are two facsimiles of the document: *Johann Sebastian Bach Orgelbüchlein BWV 599–644* (Documenta Musicologica, Zweite Reihe: Handschriften-Faksimiles xi), ed. Heinz-Harald Löhlein (Kassel: Bärenreiter, 1981); and Johann Sebastian Bach, *Orgelbüchlein BWV 599–644. Faksimile nach dem Autograph in der Staatsbibliothek zu Berlin Preußischer Kulturbesitz*, ed. Sven Hiemke (Laaber: Laaber, 2004); see also NBA IV/1, KB (Löhlein 1987). Earlier literature is recorded in Pieter Dirksen, "Bibliografie," *Bachs "Orgel-Büchlein" in nieuw perspectief*, ed. Frans Brouwer, et al. (Utrecht: Hogeschool voor de Kunsten, 1988), 240–44. More recent literature includes Christoph Wolff, "Chronology and Style in the Early Works: A Background for the Orgel-Büchlein," *Bach: Essays on His Life and Music* (Cambridge: Harvard University Press, 1991), 297–305; Sven Hiemke, *Johann Sebastian Bach, Orgelbüchlein* (Kassel: Bärenreiter, 2007); and *Johann Sebastian Bach, The Complete Organ Works*, I/1A: *Pedagogical Works*, ed. George B. Stauffer (Colfax: Leupold, 2012), xvi–xl.

Orgel-Büchlein in which a beginner[3] at the organ is given instruction in developing a chorale in many divers ways, and at the same time in acquiring facility in the study of the pedal since in the chorales contained therein the pedal is treated as wholly obbligato.

In Praise of the Almighty's will,
And for my neighbor's greater skill.
Autore
Joanne Sebast. Bach
p.t. Capellae Magistro
S. P. R. Anhaltini-
Cotheniensis.[4]

One's first encounter with these remarkable organ compositions is usually in one of the many practical editions of the forty-five chorale preludes. But amazement gives way to astonishment when one discovers that Bach intended to compile in excess of one hundred more such concise chorale masterpieces. The evidence is in the original manuscript, the small volume, almost square (15.5 x 19 cm), comprising ninety-two sheets in sixteen fascicles, plus additional sheets to accommodate the final measures of three of the preludes.[5] All the pages are ruled with sets of staves, usually six per page, though some pages have eight, and given at the head of most pages is the first line of the text of the hymn by which the melody is known. The overall scheme that Bach planned was to compose a comprehensive collection of chorale preludes on 164 chorale melodies. In the event, only forty-five were completed (BWV 599–644), together with the brief fragment of the opening of the setting of *O Traurigkeit, o Herzeleid* (BWV Anh. I 200). The proposed remainder of the settings are known only by their headings at the top of their respective pages, which are full of ruled staves that remain empty of notation.

Although a few of the preludes, both completed and projected, are assigned two pages, most are allotted just one page, indicating that perhaps Bach's original intention was to produce concise settings somewhat akin to the cantional style. While he may have begun composing in this way, he soon moved on to more sophisticated compositional techniques and, in consequence, found that it was not easy to keep within the confines of space he had allotted for himself.

Bach was not systematic in his entry of the preludes into the manuscript, nor did he record their dates of composition. Studies of the variations in his general handwriting and specific musical notation suggest that the completed

---

3 Is Bach tongue-in-cheek here? His chorale preludes demand something more advanced than the term "anfahender organist" (beginning organist) conveys.

4 BDok 1: 214 (No. 148); NBR 80–81 (No. 69). The abbreviation "p.t." means either *Pleno titulo* ("with full title") or *pro tempore* ("at this time"); S. P. R. = *Serenissimi Principis Regnantis* ("Serene Prince Reigning").

5 BWV 617, 618 and 624. The later version of BWV 620 was presumably entered on a similar additional sheet, but this has been lost.

152 Hymnology

preludes, with one exception, were entered into the manuscript during his time in Weimar. The editor for the *Neue Bach-Ausgabe*, Heinz-Harald Löhlein, has suggested that Bach began the collection after returning in December 1713 to Weimar from Halle, where he had considered becoming Friedrich Wilhelm Zachaw's successor as the organist of the Liebfrauenkirche. From that time onward, so Löhlein proposes, Bach composed a group of preludes annually, reflecting various seasons of the church year, between 1713 and 1716.[6]

Löhlein's suggestion that the origin of the *Orgelbüchlein* dated from 1713 appears to be supported by several factors, such as the new edition of the Weimar hymnal issued that year (preface dated 19 February 1713): *Schuldiges Lob Gottes/ Oder: Geistreiches Gesang-Buch ... So in Kirchen und Schulen des Fürstenthums Weimar... zu gebrauchen* (Weimar: Mumbach, 1713), edited by the court preacher, Johann Georg Lairitz. At the beginning of November, the new hymn book was accorded a special dignity at the consecration of the Jakobskirche in Weimar. At the head of the procession, in which Bach had his allotted place,[7] were the Lutheran clergy of court and town, each carrying important items to be placed in the new church: a silver crucifix, various Bibles, a copy of the *Formula of Concord*, and liturgical books. The last of these ministers was the assistant pastor of the Jakobskirche, who carried "das neue Weimarische Gesang-Buch."[8]

Ernst Arfken had earlier come to a conclusion similar to that of Löhlein and observed that since all the hymns Bach set, or intended to set, in the *Orgelbüchlein* are to be found in the Weimar *Geistreiches Gesang-Buch* of 1713, this hymnal must have been his primary source.[9] However, it is clear that Bach did not slavishly follow the contents of this book, since a comparison of the sequential pages of both the *Orgelbüchlein* and the 1713 *Gesangbuch* reveals that Bach was working to a different ground plan.[10] Since Bach was a practical musician, he would be expected to choose the chorale melodies assigned to the hymns that were in current use in Weimar, but the order in which he selected them is different from that of the hymnal.[11] While there are

---

6 NBA IV/1, KB, 91–93; see also Löhlein, *Bach Orgelbüchlein* (facsimile), 18.

7 Johann Christian Lünig, *Theatrum Ceremoniale Historico-Politicum, Oder Historisch- und Politischer Schau-Platz Aller Ceremonien, welche so wohl an Europäischen Höfen, als auch sonsten bey vielen Illustren Fällen beobachtet worden ... Anderer Theil* (Leipzig: Weidmann, 1720); facsimile of *Theatrum Ceremoniale* (Vienna: Ahlgrimm-Fiala, 1953), 2: 352–59; BDok 2: 48 (No. 60).

8 Lünig, *Theatrum Ceremoniale*, 353–54; Gottfried Albin Wetten, *Historische Nachrichten von der berühmten Residentz-Stadt Weimar ...* (Weimar: Hoffmann, 1737), 432–34; Robin A. Leaver, "Churches," in *The Routledge Research Companion to Johann Sebastian Bach* (London: Routledge, 2017), 165–66.

9 Ernst Arfken, "Zur Entstehungsgeschichte des Orgelbüchleins," BJ 52 (1966): 41–58.

10 Ibid., 55–58.

11 Terry's earlier attempt to establish Christian Friedrich Witt's *Psalmodia sacra* (Gotha, 1715)— now known to have been published after Bach had begun work on the *Orgelbüchlein*—as Bach's source suffers from the same problem; see Charles Sanford Terry, *Bach Chorals. Part*

Bach's Orgelbüchlein   153

numerous other contemporary hymnals that follow a structure similar to that of the *Orgelbüchlein*, in calling for an equivalent corpus of chorale melodies, the fact is that no contemporary hymnal has been discovered that can definitively be shown to have been Bach's model for his *Orgelbüchlein*. However, an examination of the chorales employed in the early cantatas—especially those composed in Weimar from 1714, when he became "Concertmaster" with the responsibility of composing a cantata each month—reveal that most of them were also planned to be included within the *Orgelbüchlein* (see Table 8.1). The chorales in these cantatas formed part of the corpus of hymnody sung in the Weimar court chapel and presumably represent the specific choices of his respective librettists, where Bach used libretti that had already appeared in print before he composed the cantatas, notably BWV 18 (Neumeister), BWV 199 (Lehms), and BWV 31, 80a, 132, 155, 164, 165, and 168 (Franck). But Salomo Franck was poet to the Weimar court, and some of Bach's cantatas were composed before the libretti were published, such as BWV 70a, 147a, 152, and 186a, together with five unpublished libretti that were most likely the work of Franck: BWV 12, 21, 158, 172, 182. Thus, there is the possibility that Bach might have collaborated in the choice of chorales for these cantata libretti. Whether or not that was the case, what is clear is that the majority of the chorales in these early cantatas were also to be included in Bach's overall plan for the *Orgelbüchlein*.

The question of chronology

According to Wisso Weiß's watermark catalog in NBA, the watermark of the *Orgelbüchlein* manuscript indicates that the paper was made around 1713/ 1714,[12] though there is some confusion as to whether the watermark is identical with that of the paper used for the autograph scores of Cantatas 61 and 152.[13] The question is whether the watermark of the manuscript establishes the beginning of Bach's work on the project, or whether it represents his commitment after having spent some considerable time planning the extent and scope of the project. Arfken, Löhlein, and Berben argue the former, and Wolff, Stinson, and Zehnder the latter.[14] Wolff writes:

III. The Hymns and Hymn Melodies of the Organ Works (Cambridge: Cambridge University Press, 1921), 29–63.

12 NBA IX/1, No. 117.

13 See Russell Stinson, "The Compositional History of Bach's *Orgelbüchlein* Reconsidered," *Bach Perspectives 1*, ed. Russell Stinson (Lincoln: University of Nebraska Press, 1995), 45, note 5; and Léon Berben, "Orgel-Büchlein," in *Bachs Klavier- und Orgelwerke*, ed. Siegbert Rampe, Das Bach-Handbuch 4/1 (Laaber: Laaber, 2007), 518, note 2.

14 See Berben, "Orgel-Büchlein," 517–21; WolffBLM, 130–32; Stinson, "The Compositional History," 43–78; Stinson, *Bach: The Orgelbüchlein*, 12–25; and Jean-Claude Zehnder, *Die frühen Werke Johann Sebastian Bachs* (Basel: Schwabe, 2009), 1:324.

154   *Hymnology*

Table 8.1 Chorales in the early cantatas

BWV	Sunday or Festivals	Year	Details	Orgelbüchlein No.
61	Advent 1	1714	Nun komm, der Heiden Heiland (chorale cantata)	1
			Wie schön leuchtet der Morgenstern	120
70a	Advent 2	1716	Meinem Jesum lass icht nicht	—
186a	Advent 3	1716	Von Gott will ich nicht lassen	93
132	Advent 4	1715	Herr Christ der einig Gotts Sohn	3
147a	Advent 4	1716	Ich dank dir, lieber Herre	144
63	Weihnacht I	ca1716	—	—
152	S. n.Weihnachten	1714	—	—
143	Neujahr	1707/14	Du Friedefürst, Herr Jesu Christ	125
155	Epiphanias 2	1716	Es ist das Heil uns kommen her	77
72	Epiphanias 3	1715	Was mein Gott will, das gescheh allzeit	89
18	Sexagesima	1713/14	Durch Adams Fall ist ganz verderbt	78
54	Oculi	1714	—	—
80a	Oculi	1715	Ein feste Burg ist unser Gott	116
182	Palmarum	1714	Jesu Leiden, Pein und Tod	—
4	Oster I	1706	Christ lag in Todesbanden (chorale cantata)	33
31	Oster I	1715	Wenn mein Stündlein vorhanden ist	127
12	Jubilate	1714	Was Gott tut, das ist wohlgetan	112
172	Pfingstag I	1714	Wie schön leuchtet der Morgenstern	120
165	Trinitatis	1715	Nun lasst uns Gott dem Herren	153
21	Trinitatis 3	1714	Wer nur den Lieben Gott lässt walten	113
185	Trinitatis 4	1715	Ich ruf zu dir, Herr Jesu Christ	91
168	Trinitatis 9	1716	Herr Jesu Christ, du höchstes Gut	72
199	Trinitatis 11	1714	Wo soll ich fliehen hin	74
164	Trinitatis 13	1716	Herr Christ der einig Gotts Sohn	3
161	Trinitatis 16	1714	Herzlich tut mich verlangen	73
162	Trinitatis 20	1714	Alle menschen müssen sterben	130/131
163	Trinitatis 23	1714	Wo soll ich fliehen hin	74

The *Orgel-Büchlein* project originated near the beginning of the composer's appointment as organist and chamber musician at the ducal court in Weimar, effective July 1, 1708. Handwriting and stylistic evidence suggest that Bach must have embarked on the collection soon after settling into his Weimar post. From the outset he must have considered that writing 164 chorale preludes of the kind he had in mind was not a matter of weeks or even months, but would be a long-term undertaking. Indeed, the manuscript evidence demonstrates that the organ chorales were entered in irregular sequence over a period of several years in Weimar, most likely up to 1714/15.[15]

The suggestion, therefore, is that Bach's major involvement in the *Orgelbüchlein* project spanned the Weimar years between 1708 and 1714/1715. But since Bach had been barely a year in Mühlhausen, 1707–1708, the initial planning for such a collection of chorale compositions may well have originated during his Arnstadt years. Indeed, the fact that there are earlier versions of two of the preludes in the so-called Neumeister Collection (BWV 601a and 639a) points in this direction. There were certainly significant influences that would have encouraged him along these lines. His duties as organist of the Neuen Kirche were not particularly onerous, just four services each week,[16] and he had at his disposal the new Wender organ, completed around the time of his appointment as organist in 1703.[17]

Chorales were fundamental in Lutheran life and worship and especially so in Arnstadt around this time. For instance, Bach viewed playing chorales as his primary task in Arnstadt, as he declared at his third appearance before the consistory over the Geyersbach affair: he said "he was engaged only for chorales."[18] He was clearly fascinated by the way in which a simple chorale melody can be expressed harmonically in many different ways. Thus, on his return from his extended visit to Lübeck (February 1706), Bach's harmonic explorations of chorale melodies caused some problems for his congregation, and the consistory had to reprove him "for having hitherto made many curious *variations* in the chorale, and mingled many strange tones in it, and for the fact that the Congregation has been confused by it."[19] Then there is the curious music treatise by Johann Philipp Treiber (1675–1727), *Der Accurate Organist im General-Baß*, published in Arnstadt in 1704, a pedagogical

---

15 Christoph Wolff, *Bach's Musical Universe: The Composer and His Work* (New York: Norton, 2020), 35. In a note (page 349) Wolff adds: "In the earliest entries, Bach's handwriting resembles closely the autograph copies of some instrumental works by Telemann and de Grigny from around 1709 (NBA IX/2: 38–45)." Wolff had earlier noted that Bach used two rastrale to draw the staves of the *Orgelbüchlein* manuscript, which he also used for the score of BWV 152, and the parts of BWV 18, 70a, 182, and 154, which date from 1714–1716; see Christoph Wolff, "Die Rastrierungen in den Originalhandschriften Joh. Seb. Bach und ihre Bedeutung für die diplomatische Quellenkritik," *Festschrift für Friedrich Smend zum 70. Geburtstag* (Berlin: Merseburger, 1963), 90–92.

16 WolffBLM, 78–79.

17 Christoph Wolff and Markus Zepf, *The Organs of J. S. Bach: A Handbook*, trans. Lynn Edwards Butler (Urbana: University of Illinois Press, 2012), 9–11; NBR 40 (No. 14).

18 "Er sey nur auff Choral ... bestellet." Consistory minute, 19 Aug, 1705. BDok, 2: 17 (No. 14); the NBR, 45 (No. 19c), translates it slightly differently.

19 Consistory minute, 21 Feb, 1706. NBR, 46 (No. 20); BDok, 2: 20 (No. 16).

156 *Hymnology*

workbook based on two familiar chorale melodies: *Was Gott tut, das ist wohlgetan* (major), and *Wer nur den lieben Gott läßt walten* (minor).[20] The singularity of Treiber's manual must have attracted the young Bach and may well have inspired him to use chorale melodies in his teaching, and at the same time influenced his own concise approach to composition that is exhibited in his *Orgelbüchlein*.

Of particular significance is the presence of Johann Christoph Olearius in Arnstadt at the same time as Bach. Olearius was the librarian of the Arnstadt church library and one of the three deacons serving the churches of the town, one of which was the Neuen Kirche, where Bach was the organist. Olearius was a distinguished hymnologist who published a number of important and influential works on hymnody.[21] He was particularly concerned to preserve the classic chorales of the Reformation. For example, in the bicentenary year of the Reformation he published *Jubilirende Lieder-Freude bestehend in erster Aufflage, derer allerersten A. C. 1524 und 1525 in Druck gegangenen Lutherischen Gesängen zur Vermehrung schuldeigster Devotion und Danckbarkeit bey dem andern von Gott verliehenen Lutherischen Reformations-Jubilaeo* (Arnstadt: Meurer, 1717). In the preface Olearius traced the history of early Lutheran hymnals and then reprinted the contents of the three earliest published collections of 1524–1525. But Olearius's interest in early Lutheran hymnody was not exclusively antiquarian but also practical. Thus, in 1700 he edited the *Neu-Verbessertes Arnstädtisches Gesangbuch*, a collection of 512 hymns, slightly revised and reissued in 1702, and again in 1705, a collection that Bach must have used almost daily during his Arnstadt years.

With Bach's known and continued interest in hymnody it seems likely that Olearius had some influence on him while he was organist of the Arnstadt Neuen Kirche. In Arnstadt with Olearius, Bach worked in an atmosphere in which the sixteenth-century hymn was regarded as the ideal expression of evangelical faith and piety. This is reflected in the contents of the *Orgelbüchlein*: of the proposed 164 preludes, 70 percent of the chorales date from the sixteenth century—30 were those by Luther—and most of the remainder date from around 1650 or earlier.

In 1705, while Bach was still in Arnstadt, Olearius began to issue a commentary on the *de tempore lieder*, the principal hymns of the church year, a project that took two years to complete: *Evangelischer Lieder-Schatz darinn allerhand Auserlesene Gesänge, so sich auff alle Sonn- und Fest-Tags Evangelia ... und darauff schließlich eine kurtzgefaste Disposition* (Jena: Bielcke, 1707). The work was issued in four printed sections and deals in turn with one hymn for each of the Sundays and Festivals of the church year.[22] In Lutheran

---

20 For details, see Chapter 6: 132.
21 On Johann Christoph Olearius, see Chapter 6. In the introduction to the 2004 facsimile, it is unfortunate that Hiemke confuses the superintendent Johann Gottfried Olearius with deacon Johann Christoph Olearius.
22 The work is discussed from a different perspective in Chapter 6; the significance of the church year is discussed in Chapter 1.

Bach's Orgelbüchlein   157

tradition the Graduallied, that is, the hymn sung between the Epistle and Gospel, was the principal hymn of the day, related to the teaching of the biblical readings, especially the Gospel. Olearius listed these *Graduallieder*, or *de tempore* hymns, of the church year and commented on the background and meaning of the texts. Since a substantial part of Bach's *Orgelbüchlein* is concerned with such hymns, it is instructive to compare Olearius's basic list (Table 8.2) with that of Bach's projected sequence of chorale settings (listed in Table 8.3).

In the main Olearius's listing follows the traditional pattern of *Graduallieder* that had been established throughout Lutheran Germany. Although there were local variations, there was a general consensus as to which hymns should be associated with which Sundays and festivals of the church year.[23] Of the seventy-five hymns given by Olearius only seven cannot be found in Bach's projected manuscript. Of these, two came from the end of the Trinity season, Sundays that tended to produce the greatest local variation since these Sundays occurred only rarely. Two others perhaps represent Olearius's personal choices: *Nun danket alle Gott* for the Sunday after Christmas, and *Danksagen wir alle Gott* for the Feast of the Epiphany. However, apart from the principal festivals of Christmas, Easter, and Pentecost, where the sequence of the two series is very close, it is obvious that Bach did not follow the strict order of these *de tempore* hymns. Thus, Olearius could not have been his immediate source. However, the comparison does demonstrate that Bach included most of the basic *Graduallieder* of the church year in his own projected collection.

The overall plan of the *Orgelbüchlein*

Table 8.3 lists the chorale preludes, completed or planned, as they occur in the manuscript. Editorial additions comprise the consecutive numbering, the BWV numbers, and the headings of the sections within which the preludes are grouped. These headings are conjectural but are typical of those found in contemporary hymnals. They are the result of detailed research. The origin of each chorale text in Bach's manuscript was established by reference to hymnological resources such as the Fischer *Kirchenlieder-Lexicon*,[24] especially establishing the season, Sunday, or occasion for which it was originally written. Other hymnological reference works were then consulted, along with numerous contemporary hymnals, in order to chart the subsequent history of its usage. As each chorale was investigated the ground plan of Bach's choices

---

23 See the composite list, compiled from fifteen hymnals published between 1545 and 1694, given in Rochus Freiherr von Liliencron, *Liturgisch-musikalische Geschichte der evangelischen Gottesdienste von 1523 bis 1700* (Schleswig: Bergas, 1893; reprint, Hildesheim: Olms, 1970), 61–77.

24 Albert Friedrich Wilhelm Fischer, *Kirchenlieder-Lexicon: Hymnologisch-literarische Nachweisungen* (Gotha: Perthes, 1878–1879; facsimile, Hildesheim: Olms, 1967).

158   *Hymnology*

Table 8.2 Graduallieder in J. C. Olearius, *Evangelischer Lieder-Schatz* (1705–1707)

Sunday or Festival		Orgelbuch lein No.	BWV
Erster Theil (Jena 1705)			
Advent 1	Nun komm, der Heiden Heiland	1	599
Advent 2	Gott hat das Evangelium	141	—
Advent 3	Gottes Sohn ist kommen	2	600
Advent 4	Gott durch deine Güte		
	[Melody = Gottes Sohn ist kommen	2	600]
Weihnacht I	Gelobet seist du, Jesu Christ	7	604
Feria II	Vom Himmel hoch, da komm ich her	9	606
Feria III	In dulci jubilo	11	608
S. Nach Weihnacht	Nun danket alle Gott	—	—
Neujahr (Fest. Circ.)	Helft mir Gotts Güte preisen	16	613
S. nach Fest. Circ.	Das alte Jahr vergangen ist	17	614
Epiphanias	Danksagen wir alle Gott	—	—
Epiphanias 1	Ein Kindelein so löbelich		
	[= Der Tag, der ist so freudenreich]	8	605
Epiphanias 2	Wie schön leuchtet der Morgenstern	120	—
Epiphanias 3	Ich ruf zu dir Herr Jesu Christ	91	639
Epiphanias 4	Wenn wir in höchstein Nöten sein	100	641
Epiphanias 5	Ach Gott vom Himmel sieh darein	114	—
Mariae Reinigung	Mit Fried und Freud ich fahr dahin	19	616
Epiphanias 6	Es woll uns Gott genädig sein	117	—
Septuagesima	O Gott du frommer Gott	96	—
Sexagesima	O Herre Gott, dein göttlich Wort	60	—
Quinquagesima	Herr Jesu Christ, wahr Mensch und Gott	128	—
Anderer Theil (Jena 1705)			
Invocavit	Christ, der du bist Tag und Licht	149	—
Reminiscere	Gott der Vater wohn uns bei	52	—
Oculi	Ein feste Burg ist unser Gott	116	—
Laetare	Nun lasst uns Gott, dem Herren	153	—
Judica	Wo Gott der Herr nicht bei uns hält	119	—
Mariae Verkündigung	Herr Christ der einig Gotts Sohn	3	601
Palmarum	Nun freut euch, lieben Christen gmein	85	—
Gründonnerstag	Gott sei gelobet und gebenedeiet	79	—
Charfreitag	Jesu meines Lebens Leben	—	—
Ostern I	Christ lag in Todesbanden	34	625
Feria II	Jesus Christus unser Heiland, der den Tod	35	626
Feria III	Christ ist erstanden	36	627
Quasimodogeniti	Erschienen ist der herrliche Tag	38	629
Misericordias	Von Gott will ich nicht lassen	93	—
Jubilate	Mag ich Unglück nicht wiederstahn	99	—
Cantate	Wär Gott nicht mit uns diese Zeit	118	—
Rogate	Vater unser im Himmelreich	65	636
Himmelfahrt	Christ fuhr gen Himmel		
	[Melody = Christ ist erstanden	36	627]
Exaudi	Verzage nicht o Häuflein	—	—

Bach's Orgelbüchlein 159

Table 8.2 Cont.

Sunday or Festival		Orgelbuch lein No.	BWV
Pfingsten I	Komm, Heiliger Geist, Herre Gott	43	—
Feria II	Komm, Gott Schöpfer, Heiliger Geist	44	631
Feria III	Nun bitten wir den Heiligen Geist	45	—
Trinitatis	Wir glauben all an einen Gott	64	—
Dritter Theil (Jena 1706)			
Trinitatis 1	Herzlich lieb hab ich, o Herr	135	—
Trinitatis 2	Es spricht der Unweisen Mund wohl	115	—
Trinitatis 3	Ach Gott und Herr	71	—
Trinitatis 4	Allein zu dir, Herr Jesu Christ	70	—
Johannis der Taufer	Christ, unser Herr, zum Jordan kam	66	—
Trinitatis 5	Wer nur den lieben Gott lässt walten	113	642
Trinitatis 6	Es ist das Heil uns kommen her	77	638
Trinitatis 7	Danket dem Herren, d. er ist sehr freundlich	152	—
Mariae Heimsuchung	Allein Gott in der Höh sei Ehr	53	—
Trinitatis 8	Erhalt uns, Herr, bei deinem Wort	122	—
Trinitatis 9	Mensch, willst du leben seliglich	62	—
Trinitatis 10	Nimm von uns Herr du treuer Gott [Melody = Vater unser im Himmelreich	65	636]
Trinitatis 11	Erbarm dich mein, o Herre Gott	68	—
Trinitatis 12	Nun lob, mein Seel, den Herren	86	—
Trinitatis 13	Dies sind die heilgen zehn Gebot	61	635
Vierdter Theil (Jena 1707)			
Trinitatis 14	Ach Gott, wie manches Herzeleid	104	—
Trinitatis 15	Warum betrübst du dich, mein Herz	102	—
Trinitatis 16	Nun lasst uns den Leib begraben	133	—
Trinitatis 17	In dich hab ich gehoffet, Herr	97 & 98	640
Trinitatis 18	Ich weiss dass mein Erlöser lebt	—	—
Trinitatis 19	Aus tiefer Not schrei ich zu dir	67	—
Trinitatis 20	Jesu, meine Freude	13	—
Trinitatis 21	Auf meinen lieben Gott	136	—
Trinitatis 22	Ach, was soll ich Sünder machen	158	—
Trinitatis 23	Wer Gott vertraut	94	—
Trinitatis 24	Ach wie flüchtig, ach wie nichtig	159	—
Trinitatis 25	O grosser Gott von Macht	126	—
Trinitatis 26	Es ist gewisslich an der Zeit	—	—
Trinitatis 27	Wachet auf, ruft uns die stimme	—	—
Michaelis	Herr Gott dich loben alle wir	57	—
Aposteltagen	Mir ist ein geistlich Kirchelein [Melody = Erhalt uns, Herr]	122	—

160 *Hymnology*

Table 8.3 Projected contents of the *Orgelbüchlein*

			Tabulaturbuch	Neumeister
	Advent	*BWV*	*1704*	*ca 1700*
1	Nun komm, der Heiden Heiland	599	1	1
2	Gott, durch deine Güte			
	or Gottes Sohn ist kommen	600	2	—
3	Herr Christ, der einig Gotts Sohn	601	10	3/78
	or Herr Gott, nun sei gepreiset			
4	Lob sei dem allmächtigen Gott	602	3	—
	Weihnacht			
5	Puer natus in Bethlehem	603	—	—
6	Lob sei Gott in des Himmels Thron	+	8	—
7	Gelobet seist du, Jesu Christ	604	4	8/9
8	Der Tag, der ist so freudenreich	605	—	11
9	Vom Himmel hoch, da komm ich her	606	5	10
10	Vom Himmel kam der Engel Schar	607	7	—
11	In dulci jubilo	608	—	12
12	Lobt Gott, ihr Christen, allzugleich	609	9	—
13	Jesu, meine Freude	610	—	—
14	Christum wir sollen loben schon	611	—	13
15	Wir Christenleut	612	—	14
	Neujahr			
16	Helft mir Gottes Güte preisen	613	—	—
17	Das alte Jahr vergangen ist	614	11	15
18	In dir ist Freude	615	12	—
	Mariae Reinigung			
19	Mit Fried und Freud ich fahr dahin	616	15	—
20	Herr Gott, nun schleuss den Himmel auf	617	—	16
	Passion			
21	O Lamm Gottes, unschuldig	618	19	19
22	Christe, du Lamm Gottes	619	20	—
23	Christus, der uns selig macht	620	18	—
24	Da Jesus an dem Kreuze stund	621	17	—
25	O Mensch, bewein dein Sünde gross	622	26	—
26	Wir danken dir, Herr Jesu Christ, das du für	623	22	—
27	Hilf, Gott, dass mir's gelinge	624	—	—
28	O Jesu, wie ist dein Gestalt	+	—	18
29	O Traurigkeit, o Herzeleid (fragment)	Anh. 200	24	—
30	Allein nach dir, Herr Jesu Christ	+	—	—
31	O wir armen Sünder	+	—	—
32	Herzliebster Jesu, was hast du verbrochen	+	25	17
33	Nun gibt mein Jesus gute Nacht	+	—	—
	Ostern			
34	Christ lag in Todesbanden	625	31	22
35	Jesus Christus, unser Heiland, der den Tod	626	32	23
36	Christ ist erstanden	627	—	—

Table 8.3 Cont.

			Tabulaturbuch	Neumeister
37	Erstanden ist der heil'ge Christ	628	—	—
38	Erschienen ist der herrliche Tag	629	—	—
39	Heut triumphieret Gottes Sohn	630	—	62
	Himmelfahrt			
40	Gen Himmel aufgefahren ist	+	—	—
41	Nun freuet euch, Gottes Kinder, all	—	—	—
	Pfingsten			
42	Komm, Heiliger Geist, erfüll die Herzen	+	—	—
43	Komm, Heiliger Geist, Herre Gott	+	34	—
44	Komm, Gott Schöpfer, Heiliger Geist	631	—	—
45	Nun bitten wir den Heiligen Geist	+	35	—
46	Spiritus Sancti gratia or Des Heil'gen Geistes reiche Gnad	+	—	—
47	O Heil'ger Geist, du göttlich Feur	+	—	—
48	O Heil'ger Geist, o heiliger Gott	+	—	—
49	Herr Jesu Christ, dich zu uns wend	632	—	—
50	Liebster Jesu, wir sind hier	634	—	—
51	Liebster Jesu, wir sind hier	633	—	—
	Trinitatis			
52	Gott, der Vater, wohn uns bei	+	40	—
53	Allein Gott in der Höh sei Ehr	+	39	27/28
54	Der du bist drei in Einigkeit	+	—	26
	Johannis der Taufer			
55	Gelobet sei der Herr, der Gott Israel	+	—	—
	Mariae Heimsuchung			
56	Meine Seele erhebt den Herren	+	—	2
	Michaelis			
57	Herr Gott, dich loben alle wir	+	43	—
58	Es stehn vor Gottes Throne	+	44	—
	Apostel-Tagen			
59	Herr Gott, dich loben wir	+	72	—
	Reformationsfest			
60	O Herre Gott, dein göttlich Wort	+	—	60
	Catechismus			
	Die zehn Gebot			
61	Dies sind die heil'gen zehn Gebot	635	57	30
62	Mensch, willst du leben seliglich	+	—	—
63	Herr Gott, erhalt uns für und für	+	—	—
	Von Glauben			
64	Wir glauben all an einen Gott	+	58	31
	Das Gebet den Herrn			
65	Vater unser im Himmelreich	636	59	49
	Von der Heiligen Taufe			
66	Christ, unser Herr, zum Jordan kam	+	60	—

(*continued*)

162 *Hymnology*

Table 8.3 Cont.

		Tabulaturbuch	Neumeister
	Von der Beicht, Busse und *Rechtfertigung*		
67	Aus tiefer Not schrei ich zu dir	+	62	32
68	Erbarm dich mein, o Herre Gott	+	63	76
69	Jesu, der du meine Seele	+	—	—
70	Allein zu dir, Herr Jesu Christ	+	61	33/34
71	Ach Gott und Herr	+	—	35
72	Herr Jesu Christ, du höchstes Gut	+	—	67
73	Ach Herr, mich armen Sünder [melody: Herzlich tut mich verlangen]	+	47	36
74	Wo soll ich fliehen hin	+	65	
75	Wir haben schwerlich	+	—	—
76	Durch Adams Fall ist ganz verderbt	637	—	38
77	Es ist das Heil uns kommen her	638	—	—
	Von der Heiligen Abendmahl		
78	Jesus Christus, unser Heiland, der von uns	+	—	—
79	Gott sei gelobet und gebenedeiet	+	—	—
80	Der Herr ist mein getreuer Hirt	+	49	45
81	Jetzt komm ich als ein armer Gast	+	—	—
82	O Jesu, du edle Gabe	+	—	—
83	Wir danken dir, Herr Jesu Christ, daß du das	+	—	—
84	Ich weiss ein Blümlein hübsch und fein	+	—	—
85	Nun freut euch, lieben Christen gmein	+	33	4
86	Nun lob, mein Seel, den Herren	+	—	—
	Vom Christlichen Leben und Wandel		
87	Wohl dem der in Gottes furcht steht	+	—	—
88	Wo Gott zum Haus nicht gibt sein Gunst	+	45	—
89	Was mein Gott will, das gescheh allzeit	+	—	41
90	Kommt her zu mir, spricht Gottes Sohn	+	64	42
91	Ich ruf zu dir, Herr Jesu Christ	639	68	43/44/77
92	Weltlich Ehr und zeitlich Gut	+	—	—
93	Von Gott will ich nicht lassen	+	13	47
94	Wer Gott vertraut	+	74	74
95	Wie's Gott gefällt, so gefällt mir's auch	+	—	—
96	O Gott, du frommer Gott	+	—	—
97	In dich hab ich gehoffet, Herr	+	51	—
98	In dich hab ich gehoffet, Herr (alio modo)	640	—	—
99	Mag ich Unglück nicht widerstahn	+	—	29
100	Wenn wir in höchsten Nöten sein	641	—	—
101	An Wasserflüssen Babylon	+	56	56

Bach's Orgelbüchlein   163

Table 8.3 Cont.

			Tabulaturbuch	Neumeister
102	Warum betrübst du dich, mein Herz	+	76	46
103	Frisch auf, mein Seel, verzage nicht	+	—	—
104	Ach Gott, wie manches Herzeleid	+	—	—
105	Ach Gott, erhör mein Seufzen	+	—	—
106	So wünsch ich nun eine gute Nacht	+	—	—
107	Ach lieben Christen, seid getrost	+	—	—
108	Wenn dich Unglück tut greifen	+	—	50
109	Keinen hat Gott verlassen	+	—	—
110	Gott ist mein Heil, mein Hülf und Trost	+	—	52
111	Was Gott tut, das ist wohlgetan, kein einig	+	—	69
112	Was Gott tut, das ist wohlgetan, es bleibt	+	—	—
113	Wer nur den lieben Gott läßt walten	642	—	—
	Psalmlieder			
114	Ach Gott, vom Himmel sieh darein (Psalm 12)	+	—	53
115	Es spricht der Unweisen Mund wohl (Psalm 14)	+	48	54
116	Ein feste Burg ist unser Gott (Psalm 46)	+	53	—
117	Es wolle uns Gott gnädig sein (Psalm 67)	+	54	—
118	Wär Gott nicht mit uns diese Zeit (Psalm 124)	+	55	—
119	Wo Gott der Herr nicht bei uns hält (Psalm 124)	+	46	55
	Von dem Wort Gottes und den Christlichen Kirche			
120	Wie schön leuchtet der Morgenstern	+	52	61
121	Wie nach einer Wasserquelle	+	—	73
122	Erhalt uns, Herr, bei deinem Wort	+	73	48
123	Lass mich dein sein und bleiben	+	—	—
124	Gib Fried, o frommer, treuer Gott	+	—	—
125	Du Friedefürst, Herr Jesu Christ	+	—	40
126	O grosser Gott von Macht	+	—	—
	Vom Tod und Sterben			
127	Wenn mein Stündlein vorhanden ist	+	78	63
128	Herr Jesu Christ, wahr Mensch und Gott	+	—	—
129	Mitten wir im Leben sind	+	—	—
130	Alle Menschen müssen sterben	+	—	70
131	Alle Menschen müssen sterben (alio modo)	643	—	—
132	Valet will ich dir geben	+	—	—
133	Nun lasst uns den Leib begraben	+	—	64
134	Christus, der ist mein Leben	+	—	65
135	Herzlich lieb hab ich dich, o Herr	+	—	68

(*continued*)

164   *Hymnology*

Table 8.3 Cont.

		Tabulaturbuch	*Neumeister*
136	Auf meinen lieben Gott	+	—	37
137	Herr Jesu Christ, ich weiss gar wohl	+	—	—
138	Mach's mit mir, Gott, nach deiner Güt	+	—	71
139	Herr Jesu Christ, meins Lebens Licht	+	—	—
140	Mein Wallfahrt ich vollendet hat	+	—	—
141	Gott hat das Evangelium	+	—	6/7
142	Ach Gott, tu dich erbarmen	+	—	59
	Morgen			
143	Gott des Himmels und der Erden	+	—	—
144	Ich dank dir, lieber Herre	+	—	—
145	Aus meines Herzens Grunde	+	—	—
146	Ich dank dir schon	+	—	—
147	Das walt mein Gott	+	—	—
	Abend			
148	Christ, der du bist der helle Tag	+	70	—
149	Christe, der du bist Tag und Licht	+	16	20
150	Werde munter, mein Gemüte	+	—	72
151	Nun ruhen alle Wälder	+	—	—
	Nach dem Essen			
152	Danket dem Herren, denn er ist sehr	+	—	—
153	Nun lasst uns Gott dem Herren	+	71	39
154	Lobet dem Herren, denn er ist sehr	+	—	—
155	Singen wir aus Herzensgrund	+	—	—
	Um gut Wetter			
156	Gott Vater, der su deine Sonn	+	—	—
	Anhang			
157	Jesu, meines Herzens Freud	+	—	—
158	Ach, was soll ich Sünder machen	+	66	—
159	Ach wie nichtig, ach wie flüchtig	644	—	—
160	Ach, was ist doch unser Leben	+	—	—
161	Allenthalben, wo ich gehe	+	—	—
162	Hast du denn, Jesu, dein Angesicht			
	or Soll ich denn, Jesu, mein Leben	+	—	—
163	Sei grüsset, Jesu gütig			
	or O Jesu, du edle Gabe	+	29	—
164	Schmücke dich, o liebe Seele	+	—	—

began to emerge, how he brought the chorale melodies together into similar general categories that can be found in contemporary published hymnals.

Most of the section divisions are obvious and straightforward, but there are some ambiguities. First, there is *Liebster Jesu, wir sind hier* (Nos. 50–51). There are two texts that have the same first line and melody, one a baptismal

Bach's Orgelbüchlein   165

hymn by Benjamin Schmolck, and the other a hymn for the beginning of worship by Tobias Clausnitzer. It is not immediately clear which text Bach had in mind. But in either case it seems certain that he intended the associated melody to be included among the Pentecost hymns. The reasoning is that the Schmolck text, being a baptismal hymn, has links with the gift of the Spirit, and baptism is a primary theme of Pentecost; the Clausnitzer text speaks of the Spirit's work in the lives of believers in its second and third stanzas. Further, when *Liebster Jesu* is included among the Pentecost hymns, there follow, appropriately, three Trinitarian hymns (Nos. 52–54), which seems to be Bach's deliberate decision.[25] Then there is *Gott Vater, der du deine Sohn* (No. 156): Is this the last of the original plan, a hymn "For good weather," or the first of the *Anhang*, an appendix of assorted hymns for various occasions?

Generally speaking, the hymns are grouped together in broad categories. While the main seasons, such as Christmas, Passion, Easter, and Pentecost, are well represented, there is no specific section for either Epiphany or Lent. However, as with Olearius's listing given above (Table 8.2), *de tempore* hymns for Epiphany, together with those for the period before Lent and for Lent itself, are included elsewhere in Bach's plan.

Traditional Lutheran hymnals throughout the seventeenth century, like those of the previous century, almost universally began with Advent hymns, Luther's *Nun komm, der Heiden Heiland* usually being the first. But towards the end of the seventeenth century and beginning of the eighteenth century there was a growing tendency to begin a hymnal with a section of general worship hymns before the Advent hymns. For example, the 1705 edition of the Arnstadt *Gesangbuch* followed the older tradition with *Nun komm, der Heiden Heiland* as the first hymn, whereas the Weimar *Gesangbuch* of 1713, while including *Nun komm, der Heiden Heiland* as the first Advent hymn, nevertheless began with a section of hymns under the heading "Beym Anfang des Gottesdiensts" (for the beginning of worship). Bach, however, followed the older tradition and began his *Orgelbüchlein* with *Nun komm, der Heiden Heiland*. Although *Liebster Jesu, wir sind hier* (Nos. 50–51) is an early hymn in the Weimar *Gesangbuch* of 1713, since the melody was composed by Johann Rudolf Ahle, the father of Bach's immediate predecessor as organist of the Blasiuskirche, Mühlhausen, its inclusion in the *Orgelbüchlein* may reflect Bach's Mühlhausen experience. It could be argued that *O Gott, du frommer Gott* (No. 96) might have found a more appropriate place among the *Morgenlieder* (Nos. 143–147),[26] and *Nun freut euch, lieben Christen gmein* (No. 85), which is found among the Communion hymns, might have been given a more usual position among the hymns on justification (Nos. 76, 77). But since

---

25 See Chapter 14.

26 Sections of domestic hymns classified under such rubrics as Morning, Evening, After Eating, and Good Weather, might seem to be out of place in a collection of melodies for use in public worship. But these were where the associated melodies were located in the hymnals, melodies that were also used for other hymn texts found elsewhere in the hymnal.

166   *Hymnology*

the prelude was apparently never composed it is not clear which melody was intended, the *Nun freut euch* that begins with consecutive fourths, or the *Nun freut euch* that is also known as *Es ist gewißlich an der Zeit*? The hymns in the *Anhang*, following the common practice of published hymnals, were presumably added some time after the original scheme had been drawn up, thus forming a varied section of hymns for different needs and occasions.

The *Orgelbüchlein* in relation to a *Choralbuch*

In preparing the manuscript, what had Bach set himself to do? He had cut, folded, and assembled the pages into book form; had planned the sequence that the chorale melodies would follow; inscribed their identifying first lines at the head of most pages; and had ruled the staves on every page. If he were the usual organist of the time his next action would have been to supply figured basses for the prescribed chorale melodies, that is, to create a *Choralbuch* for the accompaniment of congregational singing. But this was clearly not Bach's intention. However, there are significant parallels between the *Orgelbüchlein* and the typical *Choralbuch* that help to reveal both the continuity and discontinuity of what he was doing in creating this collection of chorale preludes.

A *Choralbuch* was generally compiled by (or for) an individual organist for his personal use, a comprehensive repertoire of chorales numbering on average between 150 and 200 or so melodies. There are numerous such manuscript *Choralbücher* in libraries, archives, and private collections, but as yet there is no overall linked bibliographic data for such sources, although there are the individual catalogues of libraries and special collections, as well as specific studies of aspects of the phenomenon.[27] Accessible information remains somewhat sporadic. For example, Zahn was restricted to those manuscripts that he either owned or had located in the libraries he visited, so he only listed twenty manuscript *Choralbücher*, dating from between 1700 and 1750.[28] Similarly RISM is selective in its recording of such manuscripts, though bibliographical descriptions are available online, and some of them include detailed listings of the chorale melodies they contain. Even though the information is not as accessible as one would like, it is still possible to detect traits and traditions of such manuscript *Choralbücher*.

In the attempt to understand Bach's overall plan of the *Orgelbüchlein*, in the past much attention has been given to the possible influence of a specific published *Gesangbuch*, even though no such hymnal has been identified. Perhaps the problem is that our thinking has been too much conditioned by the search for a foundational *Gesangbuch* and not enough by an examination of the *Choralbuch* tradition as it existed in the early eighteenth century. Of

---

27 There were also a few published chorale books, such as *Hoch-Fürstliches Sachsen-Weissenfelsisches Vollständiges Gesang- und Kirchen-Buch* (Weissenfels: Brühl, 1714), and Christian Friedrich Witt, *Psalmodia Sacra, Oder: Andächtige und schöne Gesänge* (Gotha: Reyher, 1715).

28 Zahn 6:535–41.

course, a study of contemporary *Gesangbücher* is necessary in order to understand the structure of the different sections in which the typical *Choralbuch* usually groups its chorale melodies, but a *Gesangbuch* is significantly different from a *Choralbuch*. A *Gesangbuch* is a printed and published anthology of texts for use by individual members of a congregation; a *Choralbuch* is usually a manuscript collection of settings of chorale melodies, with figured basses, for the personal use of the organist.[29] A *Gesangbuch* is a collection of singable religious poetry, but usually has no music and only records the identity of each melody by a textual first line. Conversely a *Choralbuch* is an anthology of chorale melodies that appear without their associated texts, though each one is identified by its primary associated textual first line, and sometimes with an alternative first line. Many of these *Choralbuch* characteristics are shared by Bach's *Orgelbüchlein*.

A particular feature of a significant number of such manuscript chorale collections is that what would have been the title page often remains blank. This is because there was no need for a title when the anthology was intended for personal use. For example, Susan McCormick, whose dissertation is restricted to sources with multiple (rather than single) figured basses, records that out of the thirteen manuscript chorale books she investigated, dating from between ca. 1730 and the end of the century, four were without titles.[30] Of course, some of these manuscripts may have lost their title pages over the course of time. On the other hand, there are other examples of *Choralbücher*, where the title pages were originally blank, but had titles added at a later date. One example is the Sibley Library manuscript *Choral-Buch*, stemming from the circle of Bach's students in Dresden (ca. 1730–1740), which has the title written in a contemporary hand that is different from both that found on the spine of the binding and in the main body of the manuscript.[31] Another example is Johann Philipp Kirnberger's manuscript *Allgemeine Choralbuch* (ca. 1760–1780), which only had its title penned by the later owner, Carl Ferdinand Becker, in 1830.[32] Like such *Choralbücher*, Bach's *Orgelbüchlein* title page was originally blank, and remained so for some years before he added the title during his time in Cöthen. Then the pedagogical purpose was clearly defined: to provide examples by which "a beginner at the organ is given instruction in developing a chorale in many divers ways, and at the same time in acquiring facility in the study of the pedal."[33] But was this as clear in Bach's thinking when he

---

29 There were of course some printed hymnals that included melodies with figured basses, such as Crüger's *Praxis pietatis melica*, but most organists preferred to use their own manuscript compilation of melodies.

30 See the summary tables in Susan Rebecca McCormick, "Johann Christian Kittel and the Long Overlooked Multiple Bass Chorale Tradition" (PhD diss., Queen's University Belfast, 2014), 19–22.

31 Robin A. Leaver, "Bach's Choral-Buch? The Significance of a Manuscript in the Sibley Library," in *Bach and the Organ*, ed. Matthew Dirst, Bach Perspectives, 10 (Urbana: University of Illinois Press, 2016), 16.

32 McCormick, "Kittel and the Long Overlooked Multiple Bass Chorale Tradition," 124, 127.

33 See note 4 above.

168   Hymnology

began working on the project as it was a decade or so later in Cöthen when he inscribed the title page? Since when he began composing the settings he was the court organist in Weimar, was he simply providing the collection for his own liturgical use or was he equally concerned about compositional pedagogy for others? And was he aware that the basic ground plan of the 164 chorale melodies had much in common with the typical *Choralbuch*?

As a representative example of a *Choralbuch* of the time there is the manuscript in the Herzog August Bibliothek, Wolfenbüttel: *Choral-Buch Pro Heinrich Andreas Schünemann. Worinne die in unsern Evangelischen Kirchen gebrauchlichen Melodeyen in nachfolgenden Register können gefunden werden* (Choral-Buch for Heinrich Andreas Schünemann. The Melodies that are used in our Lutheran Churches that can be found in the following index).[34] The manuscript dates from the same period when Bach began working on the *Orgelbüchlein*, that is, approximately during the first decade of the eighteenth century. It contains a similar number of chorale melodies, 170 compared to the *Orgelbüchlein*'s proposed 164. Each melody is supplied with a figured bass. The first eleven unnumbered leaves comprise a detailed index of the melodies, which also includes alternative first lines by which each one was known. But such an index could only be prepared when most of the melodies had been entered into the manuscript. No doubt Bach would have included such a comprehensive index had he completed all the settings of the *Orgelbüchlein*. Like the *Orgelbüchlein* manuscript, each page of the *Choralbuch* was ruled with empty staves in anticipation of notation being added in the future, but unlike the *Orgelbüchlein*, did not include identifying first lines of any proposed forthcoming settings. This is confirmed by the fact that pages 214 through 248 are blank apart from empty staves. This reveals a different approach being pursued in each manuscript. The *Orgelbüchlein* was carefully preplanned, with the complete repertory of chorale melodies being assigned to their respective pages before the composition of the individual settings. In contrast, the *Choralbuch*, as with many similar manuscripts, evolved as each setting was added to the collection. That the settings of the melodies in the early part of the manuscript are grouped together in clearly definable sections suggests that they were entered consecutively around the same period. Later in the manuscript the settings become disparate in content, implying that they were added one at a time, and that the compilation of the corpus as a whole was to some degree a work in progress. It was a flexible approach to a growing repertory, with melodies being added as they were required. The *Orgelbüchlein* was different in that from the very beginning Bach knew what the finished compilation should contain.

---

34 Wolfenbüttel, Herzog August Bibliothek: Cod. Guelf. 209 Novis. 8. The identity of Heinrich Andreas Schünemann is unknown. RISM ID no.: 451509610. The title appears to have been inscribed at the same time as the melodies. One of the reasons for choosing this manuscript for comparative purposes is because RISM online lists the content of the melodies in the sequence they appear.

Following the example of a good many contemporary hymnals, the first section of Schünemann's *Choralbuch* is devoted to the melodies associated with primary worship hymns, those that were frequently sung, often every week, such as the Gloria hymn, *Allein Gott in der Höh sei Ehr*, or the Creedal hymn *Wir glauben all an einen Gott*. Then follow the main sections of the major seasons of the church year, from Advent through to Trinity Sunday, *de tempore* settings, as does the *Orgelbüchlein*. Thereafter the *Choralbuch* has some clearly identifiable groups of similar chorale melodies, such as the significant sections of *Busslieder* (repentance hymns), *Morgen- & Abend-lieder* (morning and evening hymns), and *Tod- und Auferstehungs-lieder* (death and resurrection hymns), but there are also disparate groupings—identified as "Miscellaneous" in the listing below—where the adjacent melodies have been culled from different sections of the typical hymnal:

Schünemann's *Choral-Buch*	*Melodies* (totals)	*Pages*
Gottesdienst	18	1–25
Advent	2	26–27
Weihnachten	11	28–42
Mariae Reinigung	1	43
Passion	12	44–57
Ostern	9	58–69
Pentecost	5	70–75
Trinitatis	1	76–77
Miscellaneous	4	78–85
Psalmlieder	4	86–89
Miscellaneous	14	90–103
Busslieder	13	104–116
Miscellaneous	11	117–127
Morgen- & Abend-lieder	11	128–137
Nach dem Essen	2	138–139
Tod und Auferstehung	10	140–149
Miscellaneous	42	150–213
[Empty staves]	—	214–248

The groupings of the melodies in the two manuscripts are strikingly similar, particularly the major *de tempore* settings between Advent and Trinity, and especially the intention in each to include a similar section of Psalmlieder. Schünemann's *Choral-Buch*:

> Ein feste Burg ist unser Gott (Psalm 46), page 86
> Es spricht der Unweisen Mund wohl (Psalm 14), page 87
> Es wolle Gott uns gnädig sein (Psalm 67), page 88
> Wär Gott nicht mit uns diese Zeit (Psalm 124), page 89

170   *Hymnology*

Bach's *Orgelbüchlein*:

114   Ach Gott, vom Himmel sieh darein (Psalm 12)
115   Es spricht der Unweisen Mund wohl   (Psalm 14)
116   Ein feste Burg ist unser Gott (Psalm 46)
117   Es wolle Gott uns gnädig sein (Psalm 67)
118   Wär Gott nicht mit uns dieser Zeit (Psalm 124)
119   Wo Gott der Herr nicht bei uns hält (Psalm 124)

It is noteworthy that in his proposed section of Psalmlieder Bach planned that they should appear in their biblical order, whereas Schünemann was apparently unconcerned about following such a principle. This difference in approach with regard to Psalmlieder is also apparent elsewhere when the two manuscripts are compared: in his *Orgelbüchlein* Bach was much more careful in the planning and presentation of his settings than Schünemann was in his *Choral-Buch*.

In his choice and organization of chorale melodies Bach's first concern was with compiling a basic repertory that a church organist would require in the course of a year. A compiler of a *Choralbuch* would have had a similar primary concern, but Bach had something different in mind than creating an anthology of figured-bass settings of chorale melodies, the usual content of a *Choralbuch*.

Chorale preambling redefined

Johann Pachelbel (1653–1705) had an enormous influence on German organ music, especially in Thuringia. Around half of his extant compositions are chorale preludes. His contract as the organist of the Predigerkirche in Erfurt, dated 19 June 1678, included the following: "In common with the most approved organists of today, he [the organist] will play the hymns first by preambling them thematically and then accompanying [the singing] throughout."[35] Here is put into words what was generally understood, that the organist's primary responsibility was to introduce and accompany congregational singing.

While he was still the organist in Erfurt, Pachelbel published a kind of sampler of the different ways a chorale melody could be composed for the purpose of preceding congregational singing: *Erster Theil etlicher Choräle welche bey währenden Gottes Dienst zum praeambuliren gebraucht werden können*

---

35 *Denkmäler der Tonkunst in Österreich* 17 (Jahrgang VIII/2) (Vienna: Artaria, 1901; reprint, Graz: Akademische Druck und Verlagsanstalt, 1959), viii: "Die Choralgesänge, welche Er, wie unter den heutigen Bewehrtesten Organisten üblich, vorhero *thematice praeambulando* zu tractiren sich befleissigen wird, durchgehends mitspielen." The same *verbatim* direction was required from Pachelbel's successors as organist of the Predigerkirche, for example: "Instruction für Hrn. Joh. Heinrich Buttstedt ... als Organisten bey der Prediger Kirch" (1693); see Ernst Ziller, *Der Erfurter Organist Johann Heinrich Buttstädt (1666–1727)* (Kassel: Bärenreiter, 1935), 126.

gesetzet, Und dem Clavier-Liebenden zum besten herauß gegeben von Iohann Bachelbeln. Org: Zu St. Sebald in Nürnberg Joh. Christ. Wiegel excudit (The First Part of Several Chorales which have been Composed for Preambling in the Gottesdienst, and for the Best use of the Lover of the Clavier created by Johann Pachelbel, Organist of St. Sebald in Nuremberg. Engraved by Joh. Christ. Wiegel). Despite the reference on the title page to Pachelbel being an organist in Nuremberg, a position he took up in 1690, the collection must have been issued somewhat earlier, while he was still the organist of the Predigerkirche in Erfurt. Johann Mattheson reports that he owned a copy that had the following title page: *Erster Theil etlicher Choräle ... von Johann Pachelbel, Praedic. Organista, in Erfurdt.*[36] Similarly the reference on the title page to the liturgical purpose of such *praeambuliren* strongly echoes the "vorher thematicè praeambulando" of the Erfurt organist contract.

The eight "Choräle zum praeambuliren"[37] illustrate the different ways the chorale can be treated in a prelude: with the chorale melody in the soprano (PTC Nos. 45, 48), tenor (PTC No. 47), and bass (PTC Nos. 46, 52), ornamented (PTC No. 49), in a two-part bicinium (PTC No. 51), or as the subject of a fugue (PTC No. 50, designated "Fuga"). These, together with the broad spectrum of Pachelbel's preludes, were both played and emulated by early eighteenth-century organists who, especially in Thuringia, seem to have had a particular fascination with the chorale fugue.

Of course, chorale fugues were not a novelty and had been and continued to be explored by other composers such as Johann Erasmus Kindermann and Zachaw, as well as other Bachs, such as Johann Christoph's father, Heinrich (1615–1692), and brother, Johann Michael (1648–1694). However, Pachelbel appears to have been particularly influential through the succession of his pupils who seem to have had a particular liking for the chorale fugue. For example, Pachelbel taught Buttstett, and Buttstett taught Kauffmann, and each had their circle of pupils.[38] Kathryn Welter concludes: "In the century that spans Sweelinck to Johann Sebastian Bach, Pachelbel represents the most prominent and sought-after teacher in central Germany in the seventeenth century."[39]

One of the most extensive collections of chorale fugues is the tablature manuscript of 205 settings by Hieronymus Florentinus Quehl (1694–1739),

---

36 Johann Mattheson, *Der vollkommene Capellmeister* (Hamburg: Herold, 1739; facsimile, Kassel: Bärenreiter, 1954), 476.

37 Jean M. Perreault, *The Thematic Catalogue of the Musical Works of Johann Pachelbel*, ed. Donna K. Fitch (Lanham: Scarecrow, 2004) (hereafter cited as PTC; numbers without prefix "No." refer to page numbers), 48–52 (Nos. 45–52).

38 On Pachelbel's influence as a teacher, see Kathryn Welter, "A Master Teacher Revealed: Johann Pachelbel's *Deutliche Anweisung*," *About Bach*, eds. Gregory Butler, George B. Stauffer, and Mary Dalton Greer (Urbana: University of Illinois Press, 2008): 3–13.

39 Welter, "A Master Teacher," 11; see also Michael Kube, "Pachelbel, Erfurt und der Orgelchoral," *Musik und Kirche* 64 (1994): 76–82.

172   *Hymnology*

organist in Suhl, a collection later acquired by Georg Poelchau.[40] There is no evidence that would link the collection directly to Pachelbel's influence, but indirectly these compositions seem to stem from an environment similar to that of Pachelbel's pupils. The melodies are approximately arranged in identifiable sections, such as the *de tempore* chorales of the church year and chorales of the catechism, but as a whole the arrangement is not as carefully organized as is the *Orgelbüchlein*. Little is known of Quehl, except that he was the teacher of Johann Peter Kellner,[41] and that he knew Bach well enough to ask him to be godparent to his son, Johann Carolus Augustus Quehl, on 17 July 1723.[42] But it is Pachelbel who was particularly associated with fugal chorale preludes. For example, in the summer of 1690, before he left Erfurt for Nuremberg, Johann Valentin Eckelt (1675–1732) became his student. Sometime during the early decades of the eighteenth century, when the pupil was teaching his own pupils, Eckelt prepared a treatise on music theory that appears to reflect Pachelbel's teaching.[43] The manuscript is dated 1722 and is in the hand of Eckelt's pupil, Heinrich Nicolaus Gerber (1702–1775), who was later Bach's pupil in Leipzig[44]: *Diesen Kurtzen Unterricht wie man eine Fuga oder Præludium formiren und einrichten soll* (Short Instruction How One should Form and Arrange a Fugue or Prelude).[45] Although it is dated 1722, this only records when Gerber copied the manuscript, and there is no evidence of when the treatise was first written. But it is significant that it includes a section specifically on the composition of chorale fugues and begins by using the chorale melody *Vater unser im Himmelreich* to demonstrate how

---

40 The manuscript (Mus. ms. 40301) was eventually deposited in the Royal Library, Berlin, with Polchau's other manuscripts. For safety during the Second World War, it was evacuated to Poland, and is now in the library of the Jagiellonian University, Kraków; see William Anthony Wojnar, "Hieronymus Florentinus Quehl: 205 Chorale Fugues: Transcription and Commentary" (PhD diss., University of Iowa, 1995). Many chorales in the manuscript are set more than once, thus the total number of preludes is 205 but the repertory of the melodies is 121.

41 See Kellner's autobiography in Friedrich Wilhelm Marpurg, *Historisch-Kritische Beyträge zur Aufnahme der Musik, I. Band* (Berlin: Schütz, 1754–1755), 439–45, here 442: "Hr. Organist Quehl in Suhla; seine Fertigkeit und andere musikalische Eigenschaften, reizten mich, auch da einen Vesuch zu machen" (his skill and other musical qualities encouraged me to emulate him). It seems quite likely that Quehl was instrumental in encouraging Kellner to study with Bach; see Wolff and Zepf, *The Organs of J. S. Bach*, 114.

42 There is another manuscript of chorale fugues, in normal music notation, by Quehl in the Staatsbibliothek, Berlin (Mus. Ms. 18040): *XXXXII Fugen und Choräle von Hieron. Flor. Quehl 1734 nebst VI Vorspielen zu Chorälen von Frid. Christ. Morheim Capelmeister zu Danzig 1742*. Friedrich Christian Samuel Morheim (1719–1780) was a Thomaner, 1733–1736, and a copyist for Bach.

43 See Derek Remeš, "Thoroughbass Pedagogy Near Johann Sebastian Bach: Editions and Translations of Four Manuscript Sources," *Zeitschrift der Gesellschaft für Musiktheorie* 16/2 (2019): 95–165.

44 Alfred Dürr, "Heinrich Nicolaus Gerber als Schüler Bachs," BJ 64 (1978): 7–18.

45 Musikuniversität, Bibliothek, Vienna, shelf-mark 221/27; see Remeš, "Thoroughbass Pedagogy," 98–99 (introduction), 115–26 (transcription and translation).

Bach's Orgelbüchlein   173

the subject, the first line of the chorale melody, makes its second entry a fifth above the initial entry.[46]

Pachelbel, both personally and musically, was well-known among the Bachs. Between 1677 and 1678 he was the organist at the Eisenach court of Prince Johann Georg I. During this time, he is known to have established a close and cordial relationship with Johann Ambrosius Bach, Sebastian's father, who was director of town music in Eisenach. The friendship continued in later years, for example, with Pachelbel standing as godfather to Sebastian's sister, Johanna Juditha, in January 1680,[47] and performing at the wedding of Sebastian's elder brother, Johann Christoph,[48] in the fall 1694.[49] Also, performed at that wedding—attended by the nine-year-old Sebastian—was a cantata composed by a first cousin to Sebastian's father, another Johann Christoph Bach.[50] He was the organist of the Georgenkirche in Eisenach and also court harpsichordist when Pachelbel was court organist in Eisenach. These two "Johann Christoph Bachs"[51] with strong connections with Pachelbel, were effectively Sebastian's first two organ teachers. Johann Christoph (13) (1642–1703), as the organist of the local parish church, must have introduced the young Bach to the instrument, its powers and possibilities. To judge from his known organ compositions (see further below), the Eisenach organist presumably would also have introduced the young Bach to Pachelbel's approach to the composition of chorale preludes. The other Johann Christoph (22) (1671–1721) studied with Pachelbel in Erfurt for three years, between 1686–1689. After the deaths of their parents in 1695 Sebastian went to live with his brother, Johann Christoph, who was then the organist in Ohrdruf. For the next five years the elder brother almost certainly passed on to the younger brother what he had learned from Pachelbel,[52] that is, a transparent and uncomplicated approach

---

46 Remeš, "Thoroughbass Pedagogy," 122–26. There is another treatise on music theory by Eckelt that has a similar content to this manuscript, except that its fugal section is different: *Kurtzer Unterricht was einen Organist[en] nötig zu wißen seÿ* (Brief Instruction on What an Organist Must Know); see ibid., 127–40.

47 WolffBLM 19, 24. Johanna Juditha died at the age of six.

48 Johann Christoph Bach (1671–1721), number 22 in Bach's genealogy; BDok 1: 259 (No. 184); NBR 289 (No. 303); see Hans-Joachim Schulze, "Johann Christoph Bach (1671–1721), 'Organist und Schul Collega in Ohrdruf,' Johann Sebastian Bachs erster Lehrer," BJ 71 (1985): 55–81.

49 WolffBLM, 24, 37.

50 Johann Christoph Bach (1642–1703), number 13 in Bach's genealogy; BDok 1: 258 (No. 184); NBR 288 (No. 303). In the genealogy this Bach is the only one to receive the accolade "a profound composer." See also Fritz Rollberg, "Johann Christoph Bach, Organist zu Eisenach," *Zeitschrift für Musikwissenschaft* 11 (1928/29): 549–61.

51 These were not the only Johann Christoph Bachs, which makes the identity and attribution particularly difficult; see Daniel Melamed, "Constructing Johann Christoph Bach (1642–1703)," *Music & Letters* 80 (1999): 345–65.

52 For example, see Michael Belotti, "Johann Pachelbel als Lehrer," in *Bach und seine mitteldeutschen Zeitgenossen: Bericht über das Internationale Musikwissenschaftliche Kolloquium, Erfurt und Arnstadt, 13. bis 16. Januar 2000*, ed. Rainer Kaiser (Eisenach: Wagner, 2001), 8.

174   *Hymnology*

to counterpoint in which the individual voices are melodically distinct within the harmonic whole.

In the years before he moved to Ohrdruf, Sebastian Bach presumably studied the organ with Johann Christoph (13), which would have been around the same time that the Eisenach organist was preparing a collection of chorale preludes for publication, compositions that were indebted to Pachelbel's chorale fugues. The collection was prepared but never published and only exists in a primary anonymous manuscript copy: *Choraele welche bey während Gottesdienst zum Praeambulieren gebraucht werden können gesetzet und herausgegeben von Johann Christoph Bach Org. in Eisenach* (Chorales which can be Useful for Preluding during the Gottesdienst Composed and Published by Johann Christoph Bach, Organist in Eisenach).[53] The manuscript was once owned by Bach's biographer, Philipp Spitta.[54] On his death it was deposited with other papers in the library of the Berlin Hochschule für Musik.[55] During World War II the manuscript disappeared but resurfaced again in 1998,[56] and is now in the library of the Universität der Kunste Berlin.[57] The 44 *Choraele* comprise the first part of the manuscript (fols. 1^r–22^v), and the second section (fols. 23^r–33^r) is made up of organ music by other composers, such as Briegel, Pachelbel, and Buttstett, including the chorale prelude by Bach, *Der Tag der ist so freudenreich* (BWV 719), which, until the discovery of the Neumeister chorales, was the sole source.[58] The liturgical function of the preludes as expressed on the title page of J. C. Bach's 44 *Choraele* again recalls the Erfurt organists' contract and the title page of Pachelbel's "Choräle zum praeambuliren."

Compared to Johann Christoph's vocal music, Spitta found these organ pieces somewhat mundane and disappointing because they did not realize the potential that he thought they should have.[59] His summary however is useful:

---

53 Johann Christoph Bach, *44 Choräle zum Präambulieren*, ed. Martin Fischer (Kassel: Bärenreiter, 1929).

54 See Spitta 1: 99 and Spitta ET 1: 101.

55 Shelf-mark: Spitta Ms. 1491.

56 See David L. Schulenberg, "Missing Spitta Manuscript Found," *The American Bach Society Newsletter* (Fall 1998): 6–7; Rainer Kaiser, "Johann Christoph Bachs 'Choräle zum Präambulieren'—Anmerkungen zu Echtheit und Überlieferung," BJ 87 (2001): 185–89. There is also a later variant copy of the *44 Choräle* manuscript; see Martin Fischer, *Die organistische Improvisation im 17. Jahrhundert: dargestellt an den "Vierundvierzig Chorälen zum Präambulieren" von Johann Christoph Bach* (Kassel: Bärenreiter, 1929), 5–7.

57 Shelf-mark RH 0093.

58 See Christoph Wolff, "Zum Quellenwert der Neumeister-Sammlung: Bachs Orgelchoral 'Der Tag der ist so freudenreich' BWV 719," BJ 83 (1997): 155–67.

59 Spitta 1: 99–105; Spitta ET 1: 101–7. Zehnder (*Die frühen Werke Johann Sebastian Bachs*, 1: 178) acknowledges that there are stylistic problems with these settings, though regards the treatment of the chorale melodies as remarkable, and tentatively suggests that the composer might have been Bach's brother, Johann Christoph.

Bach's Orgelbüchlein   175

In twenty-one of the preludes the whole melody is taken up; in ten, a mere *complexus* of the first lines; in the others, the first is used ... as the theme of a fugue, and the second line is heard occasionally, or comes in at the close, but not fugally treated. Arrangements of the whole melody always begin with a fugato of the first line or of the first two, quite short interludes sometimes preparing us for the leads; the following lines are then usually worked out in close canon, for which a pedal-point is used as a favourite basis; but we also frequently find an extension or dissection of the theme, thus forming separate subjects, or a more or less characteristic transformation of the principal features of the melody, and between these again freely invented smaller subjects of a more lively character.[60]

Karl Geiringer took Spitta to task for exhibiting "insufficient insight into the meaning and purpose of this part of the composer's music."[61] Geiringer pointed to the liturgical function of these compositions and the need for obvious and direct use of the melody to inform the congregation what it was about to sing. For Geiringer *Wir glauben all an einen Gott* (No.9) "belongs to the most highly developed pieces of the collection"; *Aus meines Herzen Grunde* (No. 41) "has a gay and light character which matches the joyous content of the text"; and *Warum betrübst du dich mein Herz?* (No. 44), is "far ahead of its time" and is specifically compared to the chorale preludes of the *Orgelbüchlein* in the way it expresses the change of emotion from grief to joy.[62]

Another collection with chorale fugues, apparently also prepared for publication but never printed at the time, is *Tabulatur Buch Geistliche Gesänge D. Martini Lutheri und anderer Gottseliger Männer Sambdt beygefügten Choral Fugen Durchs gantze Jahr Allen Liebhabern des Claviers componiret von Johann Pachelbel, Organisten zu S. Sebald in Nürnberg 1704.* (Tablature Book of the Spiritual Hymns of D. Martin Luther and other Godly Men together with Chorale Fugues throughout the Whole Year for all Lovers of the Clavier composed by Johann Pachelbel, Organist of St. Sebald in Nuremberg).[63] The manuscript was created in Nuremberg and was not deposited in the Weimar library until the nineteenth century. However, like Pachelbel's "Choräle zum praeambuliren" that was published in Nuremberg but originated in Erfurt, the Nuremberg manuscript appears to reflect Thuringian traditions. When

---

60 Spitta ET 1: 103; Spitta 1: 102.
61 Karl Geiringer, *The Bach Family: Seven Generations of Creative Genius* (New York: Oxford University Press, 1954), 58.
62 Geiringer, *The Bach Family*, 58–60. The most detailed analysis of these preludes remains Fischer, *Die organistische Improvisation im 17. Jahrhundert*, passim.
63 Die Herzogin Anna Amalia Bibliothek, Weimar, MS Q341b. Suzy Schwenkedel, *La Tablature de Weimar Johann Pachelbel et son école ... 79 fugues et chorals en basse chiffrée* (Arras: Anfol, 1993), text in French, German and English. For a description of the manuscript, see Hans Heinrich Eggebrecht, "Das Weimarer Tabulaturbuch von 1704," *Archiv für Musikwissenschaft* 22 (1965/66): 115–16. Not all the chorale preludes are by Pachelbel; for example, a few are by Buttstett, and some perhaps by Heinrich Bach.

176 *Hymnology*

the manuscript is compared to that of the *Orgelbüchlein*, a number of similarities become apparent. They appear to be organized in much the same way, especially the *de tempore* chorales of the church year, specific liturgical and catechetical chorales, together with hymns expressing various aspects of Christian devotion, life, and death. Interestingly, the *Tabulaturbuch*, like the *Orgelbüchlein*, has a small section of Psalmlieder arranged in biblical sequence, though with a slightly different selection of melodies:

> 53. Ein feste Burg ist unser Gott (Psalm 46)
> 54. Es woll uns Gott gnädig sein (Psalm 67)
> 55. Wär Gott nicht mit uns dieser Zeit (Psalm 124)
> 56. An Wasserflüssen Babylon (Psalm 137)[64]

What is particularly striking is that the two manuscripts either included, or intended to include, many of the same melodies. The second right-hand column of Table 8.3 lists the chorale melodies of the *Tabulaturbuch* that were also intended for inclusion in the projected *Orgelbüchlein*.[65] Out of a total of seventy-nine melodies in the *Tabulaturbuch* Bach planned for sixty-four of them to be included in the *Orgelbüchlein*, which is just a little over 80 percent. This suggests that there was effectively a basic core repertory of chorale melodies in the various *Choralbücher* and manuscript collections of organ chorales used by Thuringian organists of the early eighteenth century. Thus, it is not surprising to find that the so-called Neumeister Collection, discovered as a Bach source in 1985, exhibits a good many of these identifiable features.

The Neumeister Collection

The manuscript Neumeister Collection was compiled in the early 1790s by Johann Gottfried Neumeister (1756–1840), organist in Homburg. Sometime after 1807 it was obtained by Christian Heinrich Rinck (1770–1846),[66] whose extensive music collection was purchased by Lowell Mason in 1852, and following Mason's death was acquired by Yale University in 1873.[67] Neumeister had studied with Georg Andreas Sorge (1703–1778), and he

---

64 Numbering of the contents of the manuscript by earlier scholars is confusing; see PTC 282–285. Numbering here follows Schwenkedel, *La Tablature de Weimar*. For the proposed Psalmlieder section of the *Orgelbüchlein*, see page 170 above.

65 The numbers are again those of Schwenkedel, *La Tablature de Weimar*, and they reveal the location of each melody within the manuscript.

66 Rinck was the pupil of Kittel, who had been a pupil of Bach.

67 For the background of the Rinck collection, see Henry Cutler Fall, "A Critical-Bibliographical Study of the Rinck Collection," master's thesis (Yale University, 1958); for the background of the Neumeister manuscript, see Christoph Wolff, ed., *The Neumeister Collection of Chorale Preludes from the Bach Circle (Yale University Library LM 4708): A Facsimile Edition* (New Haven: Yale University Press, 1986); the introduction is also in Wolff, *Bach Essays*, 107–27,

Bach's Orgelbüchlein   177

copied five chorale preludes from Sorge's published collection, *Erster Theil der Vorspiel vor bekannten Choral Gesängen* (Nuremberg: Schmid, [1750]), four as a kind of appendix at the end of Neumeister's manuscript. But the remainder of the music appears to have been copied from a single source that internal evidence suggests must have dated from sometime around 1700. The fact that of these seventy-seven preludes sixty-six were composed by no less than three members of the Bach family—brothers Johann Christoph (three preludes) and Johann Michael (twenty-five preludes), and Johann Michael's son-in-law, Johann Sebastian (thirty-eight preludes)—strongly suggests that the compilation of the primary source that Neumeister copied came from within the Bach clan. The few other composers represented in the manuscript comprise Zachow (1663–1712) (four preludes), Pachelbel (two preludes[68]), Daniel Erich (ca. 1660–1730) (one prelude), and anonymous (five preludes). The primary interest in the manuscript is the thirty-three previously unknown chorale preludes composed by the young Bach during the period before he began working on the *Orgelbüchlein*.

The structure of the manuscript is similar to the examples of *Choralbücher* and collections of chorale preludes already discussed. It begins with *de tempore* chorales from Advent to Trinity Sunday and is followed by a somewhat freer assortment of chorales on the catechism, various aspects of personal and ecclesial devotion, death and dying, and so forth. Without the Sorge preludes the Neumeister manuscript has a repertory of seventy chorale melodies, fifty-nine of which were to be included in the completed *Orgelbüchlein*,[69] that is, 84 percent, a similar proportion to that of the *Tabulaturbuch* discussed above. Other parallels between the Neumeister Collection and the *Orgelbüchlein* include the fact that, on the one hand, the title page of the Neumeister manuscript is blank, and on the other hand, the Neumeister Collection has a brief section of Psalmlieder arranged in biblical order, as Bach later planned to do in the *Orgelbüchlein*:

53   Ach Gott vom Himmel sieh darein (Psalm 12), Johann Michael Bach

54   Es spricht der Unweisen Mund wohl (Psalm 14), Johann Michael Bach

55   Wo Gott der Herr nicht bei uns hält (Psalm 124), Johann Michael Bach

56   An Wasserflüssen Babylon (Psalm 137), Johann Christoph Bach

---

408 (postscript); NBA IV/9, KB (Christoph Wolff, 2003); Russell Stinson, "Some Thoughts on Bach's Neumeister Chorales," *Journal of Musicology* 9 (1991): 455–77.

68 *Allein zu dir, Herr Jesus Christ* (PTC 13), and *Christe der du bist Tag und Licht* (PTC No. 63, a variant of PTC No. 64). For a time PTC No. 63 was ascribed to Bach and assigned the number BWV 1096. Recent scholarship identifies the variant as by Pachelbel and the BWV number has been withdrawn.

69 See Table 8.3, third right-hand column.

178   *Hymnology*

In five of the hymnals that Bach must have known and used around this time,[70] these hymns are included, with others, under the rubric "Von der Christlichen Kirche," often appearing as a subgroup at the beginning of the section, rather than under a specific "Psalmlieder" rubric. Bach was clearly aware of the established tradition of including biblical sequences of psalm-hymns, which appears to be a feature of collections of chorales by other organists, such as, for example, in Samuel Scheidt's *Görlitzer Tabulaturbuch* (1650).[71]

The connections between Bach's chorale preludes that appear in the Neumeister collection and the *Orgelbüchlein* fall into three categories: first, early versions that were included in the later manuscript; second, those that could have been included but were not; and third, those that were specifically rejected.

Of the first category, earlier versions of preludes that were taken over with some revision into the *Orgelbüchlein*, there are two. The first is the Advent melody, *Herr Christ, der einig Gotts Sohn* (BWV 601a/601), which, appropriately, appears to have been the first prelude that Bach entered into the manuscript of the *Orgelbüchlein*.[72] Stinson sees it as the prototype of the so-called *Orgelbüchlein* type of chorale prelude that Bach created, the main elements of which can be summarized thus:

1. The complete unadorned chorale melody stated once in the soprano without interludes. The melody was stated with clarity in order to prevent confusion among the congregation with regard to which melody was about to be sung;
2. Four-voice texture throughout (except at the final cadence) with obbligato rather than *ad libitum* pedal;
3. Alto and tenor share the same motive(s);
4. Pedal either independent or echoes the alto and tenor motive(s).[73]

However, in the preludes that were subsequently entered into the *Orgelbüchlein* after BWV 601, Bach was not pedantic in applying these criteria but rather creative in using them to set the chorale melodies in a variety of ingenious ways.[74]

The other prelude to be taken over from the Neumeister collection is *Ich ruf zu dir Herr Jesu Christ* (BWV 639a/639), a prelude that epitomizes Bach's practice in the *Orgelbüchlein* of exploring different forms and techniques in

---

70 Eisenach (1673), Lübeck (1703), Arnstädt (1705), Weimar (1713), and Halle (1715).

71 Samuel Scheidt, *Tabulatur-Buch/ Hundert geistlicher Lieder und Psalmen Herrn Doctoris Martini Lutheri und anderer gottseligen Männer/ Für die Herren Organisten/ mit der Christlichen Kirchen und Gemeine auff der Orgel* (Görlitz: Herman, 1650); *Scheidt: Das Görlitzer Tabulaturbuch vom Jahre 1650*, ed. Christhard Mahrenholz (New York: Peters, [1940]), Nos. 53–65.

72 Stinson, *Bach: The Orgelbüchlein*, 77.

73 Based on Stinson, *Bach: The Orgelbüchlein*, 18–19.

74 Stinson, *Bach: The Orgelbüchlein*, 62–75.

Bach's Orgelbüchlein   179

setting chorale melodies. Here instead of an expected four-part texture is a trio: the melody in the soprano is untypically ornamented (at least in the first six measures), the middle voice continuously flows in sixteenth notes, and the insistent bass, sometimes chromatic and sometimes static, makes the prelude sound like an accompanied aria.[75]

The second category is of those preludes in the Neumeister collection that, at least in theory, could have been included in the *Orgelbüchlein*, but for some reason Bach chose not to do so. As can be discovered from Table 8.3, among the chorale melodies for which no prelude was entered into the *Orgelbüchlein*, twenty-one can be found in the Neumeister collection.[76] A significant reason for the non-appearance of these Neumeister chorales in the *Orgelbüchlein* must have been because most were simply too long for the usual single page that Bach assigned for them. These twenty-one Neumeister preludes range in length between 21 measures (BWV 1118) and 79 measures (BWV 1109), with an average length of 38 measures, whereas the average length of the *Orgelbüchlein* preludes range from between 8 and 12 measures for the majority that appear on a single page, and between 13 and 20 measures for those that cover more than one page.

A more telling reason for the omission of Neumeister chorales is that they did not come up to the standard that Bach had set himself in creating this collection of chorale preludes. Since most of the preludes in the Neumeister collection "appear to belong to the earliest stratum of Bach's compositional experience, probably even reaching back into the Ohrdruf study years with his brother,"[77] there were bound to be examples of youthful immaturity and faulty grammar. Thus, it is understandable that Bach would not want to perpetuate such imperfections in the *Orgelbüchlein*, the collection that was clearly intended to break new ground. In order to illustrate his discussion of the defects of Bach's youthful Neumeister chorales, Peter Williams specifically cites three examples from this group of twenty-one preludes that were passed over in the *Orgelbüchlein* (BWV 1109, 1111 and 1117).[78]

The third category is of those preludes in the Neumeister collection that in effect were displaced by later *Orgelbüchlein* compositions. Again, as can be discovered from Table 8.3, there are six such preludes.[79] Bach's decision to exclude them and instead compose new preludes is not difficult to understand. To begin with, most of them, like those in the second category, were too long for the space that Bach had assigned to the melodies. These Neumeister chorales average between 32 and 42 measures, the longest being

---

75 Stinson, *Bach: The Orgelbüchlein*, 119–120; see also Peter Williams, *The Organ Music of J. S. Bach* (Cambridge: Cambridge University Press, 2003), 307–8.

76 *Orgelbüchlein* Nos. 28, 32, 60, 64, 67, 71–73, 108, 110, 111, 121, 122, 125, 130, 133–135, 138, 142, 150.

77 Wolff, "Introduction," *The Neumeister Collection*, 9.

78 Williams, *The Organ Music of J. S. Bach*, 543–44.

79 *Orgelbüchlein* Nos. 15, 17, 20, 21, 65, 76.

180   *Hymnology*

61, the shortest 27, compared with an average of 15 measures for the equivalent *Orgelbüchlein* preludes. It might be argued that Bach could have tipped-in an extra page to the *Orgelbüchlein* to accommodate the extra length of one or more of these Neumeister preludes, as he did for his later prelude on *O Lamm Gottes, unschuldig* (BWV 618). But he did not do so. When the individual Neumeister preludes are compared with the later *Orgelbüchlein* compositions, Bach's decisions become clear. For example, *Herr Gott, nun schleuss den Himmel auf* (BWV 617) is a much more sophisticated composition than its Neumeister equivalent (BWV 1092). Youthful exuberance and infelicities had no place in Bach's masterful collection of the organist's art that he was then in the process of creating.[80]

The influence of Pachelbel

In studies of Bach's early development as a composer of organ music, much is rightly made of the influence of Georg Böhm (1661–1733) in Lüneburg during his school years, and of Dieterich Buxtehude (ca. 1637/1639–1707) in Lübeck during his sabbatical from Arnstadt. But it should not be forgotten that Bach was able to benefit from these experiences because of the solid foundation provided by Johann Christoph Bach (No. 13 in the Bach Genealogy) in Eisenach and Johann Christoph Bach (No. 22 in the Bach Genealogy) in Ohrdruf, the foundation that owed much to the influence of Pachelbel. Indeed, the two organ teachers may have been responsible for transmitting some of Pachelbel's characteristics that effected Sebastian Bach's planning and initial work on the *Orgelbüchlein*.

Whether he was inspired directly or indirectly by Pachelbel, Bach came up with an audacious plan of creating a complete repertoire of chorale preludes for the "ganze Jahr," using the typical *Choral-Buch* as a model—at least for what melodies were to be included and how they were to be organized. The earlier sections of the chorales in the proposed *Orgelbüchlein*, Advent through Trinity, would mostly provide for the weekly Gottesdienst, and many of the sections that followed would be used mainly at the weekly Vespers, such as the section of catechism chorales, since it was customary to teach the catechism on Sundays after Vespers.

In the past I have suggested that, in a sense, the 164 chorale melodies indicate the extent of what amounts to Bach's personal hymnal. But this would be to misunderstand the nature of the proposed collection and to concentrate mainly on hymn texts rather than chorale melodies. Compared to the hymnals of the time, a hymnal comprising 164 hymns would be somewhat meager. What Bach had in mind was much more significant. This is where the *Choral-Buch Pro Heinrich Andreas Schünemann*, discussed above, needs to be looked at again. The *Choral-Buch* contains 170 chorale melodies, but that does not reveal the

---

80 See the technical shortcomings listed in Alfred Dürr, "Kein Meister fällt vom Himmel: Zu Johann Sebastian Bachs Orgelchorälen der Neumeister-Sammlung," *Musica* 40 (1986): 309–12.

extent of the collection. By examining the index (Register) and accounting for the alternative hymns that were sung to each of the melodies, one discovers that 750 hymn texts were sung to the melodies in this *Choral-Buch*. If Bach had finished what he had set out to do in the *Orgelbüchlein*, there would have been more than sufficient chorale preludes to cover every hymn in each of any of the hymnals that he knew and used in the first decades of the eighteenth century, such as the Weimar *Gesangbuch* (1713), with its total of 547 hymn texts.

There is, however, more to Bach's overall plan than simply an anthology of chorale preludes, albeit a rather special one. In brief, his aim was to explore a wide variety of compositional techniques with the utmost brevity. In many respects he seems to be emulating Pachelbel who, in his *Erster Theil etlicher Choräle* (pre-1690), gave eight examples of how individual chorale melodies can be set in different ways.[81] Of course, Bach's anthology is incomplete, which precludes us from knowing his full intentions, but there is enough to detect a similar pattern of different compositional approaches. For example, while most are four-part settings of the *cantus firmus*, BWV 639 is in three voices, and BWV 599 and 619 are in five voices; while most preludes have the *cantus* in the soprano, in BWV 611 it is in the alto voice; and while in most preludes the *cantus* begins in the first measure, in the following examples the accompaniment precedes the *cantus*: BWV 617–619, 637.

The one form that is apparently missing—the form that is associated with Pachelbel and his pupils, and the one that might be expected to be present—is the chorale fugue. A generation later, Johann Mattheson opined that organ preludes "should always be expressive and short rather than long."[82] But it would seem that there were those in these early years of the eighteenth century who thought there were too many long chorale preludes. This is a particular problem with the chorale fugues that Pachelbel composed and stimulated in others. They tended to expand in length in order to accommodate subsequent fugal entries, especially if the first two lines of the chorale melody were the subject of the fugue. And if they were improvised then they were likely to be even longer. However, there is evidence that there were attempts to moderate the length of chorale fugues. The 205 chorale fugues of Quehl and the 44 of Johann Christoph Bach (No. 13 in the Bach Genealogy), with an average of 29 measures in length, are some-what shorter than a good many of Pachelbel's examples, and the chorale fugues in the *Tabulaturbuch* (1704) attributed to Pachelbel are shorter still, averaging between 10 and 15 measures. Bach's aim in the *Orgelbüchlein* was to make the preludes as brief as possible without sacrificing either musical ingenuity or integrity. It was not so much that Bach abandoned the chorale fugue, but rather that he transformed it into a more concise and compact counterpoint: the chorale canon, where the soprano *cantus firmus* is usually in canon with another voice

---

81 See page 170 above.

82 Mattheson, *Der vollkommene Capellmeister*, 472, §22: "Praeludirens, welches immer nachdrücklich, iedoch mehr kurtz, als lang seyn soll."

182   *Hymnology*

(BWV 600, 608, 618–620, 629, 633/634), though in one case the canon is in all voices (BWV 615).

The paradox of the *Orgelbüchlein* is that while it remains but a torso of what Bach originally planned—being 75 percent incomplete—together the composed chorale preludes form the most intriguing collection of compositions for the organ, unrivaled by anything that came before it and unparalleled by anything that has come after it. In his preparation of the manuscript Bach had a very clear view of what he had set himself to do, but as he began composing the preludes the whole process became intensified. In *Der vollkommene Capellmeister*, Johann Mattheson uses the terms *Vorspiel* and *Praeludiren* as interchangeable synonyms for chorale preludes.[83] However, Konrad Küster provides evidence to show that there was a distinction between the two terms: *Vorspielen*, brief settings preceding congregational singing; *Praeludiren*, settings of variable length, sometimes improvised, and not always connected to congregational singing.[84] When Bach planned the project along the lines of a *Choralbuch* he intended the chorale preludes to be *Vorspielen*, short settings preceding congregational singing. But, as he began to compose them, they became *Praeludiren*, settings in which the exploration of compositional techniques became primary and congregational singing secondary.

83 Mattheson, *Der vollkommene Capellmeister*, 472, §21.
84 Konrad Küster, "Choralfantasie als Exegese: Konflikte zwischen musikalischer Realität um 1700 und jüngeren Gattungsbegriffen," *Kirchenmusikalisches Jahrbuch* 94 (2010): 23–34.

9 Bach and the hymnic aria

During the seventeenth century, several movements had a marked effect on the development of hymnody in Germany. There was also the impact of the Thirty Years' War, the devastations of the interminable conflict that engendered poverty and pestilence, death, and destruction. But against these external privations an intense and internalized spirituality was expressed in the hymns that were written during and following the chaos created by the war. Two of the leading poets were Johann Rist (1607–1667) and Paul Gerhardt (1607–1676), who, with others, stimulated the composition of new melodies for this new religious verse.

Rist and Gerhardt

After university in Rostock, which was adversely affected by the Thirty Years' War, Rist was appointed pastor of Wedel, near Hamburg. He made his name first as a dramatist and then as a poet, becoming the leader of a group of local poets.[1] He published several poetic anthologies, his religious hymns appearing especially in *Himlischer* [sic] *Lieder* (Lüneburg: Stern, 1641/1642), and *Neuer Himlischer Lieder* (Lüneburg: Stern, 1651), which were published with newly composed melodies by such composers as Johann Schop (1590–1667) and Andreas Hammerschmidt (1611/1612–1675).[2] Bach used a number of Rist's hymns. For example: *O Ewigkeit, du Donnerwort*, with the associated melody by Schop (modified by Johann Crüger, 1598–1662), for the opening movement of BWV 60 (1723), and as the basis for his chorale cantata BWV 20 (1724). Bach also used Schop's melody for Rist's *Ermuntre dich, mein schwacher Geist* (Zahn 5741), in BWV 43/11 (1726), in BWV 11/6 (1735), and suppled a new figured bass for it in the Schemelli *Gesangbuch*, BWV 454 (1736). In the Christmas Oratorio (1734) Bach used three of Rist's hymns

---

1 Theodor Hansen, *Johann Rist und seine Zeit: Aus den Quellen dargestellt* (Halle: Waisenhaus, 1872; reprint, Leipzig: Zentralantiquariat, 1973).
2 Johann Rist, *Himmlische Lieder (1641/42)*, ed. Johann Anselm Steiger (Berlin: Akademie-Verlag, 2012), and Johann Rist, *Neue Himmlische Lieder (1651)*, ed. Johann Anselm Steiger and Konrad Küster (Berlin: Akademie-Verlag, 2013).

184 Hymnology

with their associated melodies: *Ermuntre dich, mein schwacher Geist* (BWV 248/12), *Jesu, du mein liebstes Lebens* (Zahn 7891) (BWV 248/38 and 40), and *Hilf, Herr Jesu, laß gelingen* (see Zahn 6: 566) (BWV 248/42).

Like Rist, Gerhardt's early career was affected by the unrest of the Thirty Years' War and, instead of immediate ordination following theological studies at the University of Wittenberg, sometime around 1642 he became tutor to a lawyer's family in Berlin. He soon became friends with Crüger, cantor and organist of the Nicolaikirche in Berlin, who had recently published a hymnal: *Neues vollkömliches Gesangbuch, Augspurgischer Confession* (Berlin: Runge, 1640). Later, Gerhardt was appointed an assistant pastor of the Berlin Nicolaikirche. Crüger admired Gerhardt's religious poetry, and the two developed a creative working collaboration that continued for two decades or more, with Gerhardt writing the poetry, and Crüger composing the music. Crüger published Gerhardt's early hymns in what amounts to a revised, expanded edition of his hymnal that was issued with a new title page: *Praxis pietatis melica. Das ist Ubung der Gottseligkeit in Christlichen und Trostreichen Gesängen* ... (Berlin: Runge, 1647). The hymnal proved to be the most successful and widely known Lutheran hymnal of the seventeenth century. By 1737 it had reached a forty-fifth edition, having been published in Frankfurt, Greifswald, Schaffhausen, and Stettin, as well as in Berlin. Crüger's successor in Berlin, Johann Georg Ebeling (1637–1676), brought out a complete edition of Gerhardt's hymns, in which he replaced some of Crüger's melodies and supplied the initial melodies for others: *Pauli Gerhardi Geistliche Andachten Bestehend in hundert und zwantzig Liedern* ... (Berlin: Runge, 1667). Many of the 120 hymns made their first appearance in one of the editions of Crüger's *Praxis pietatis melica*.[3] By the end of the seventeenth century Gerhardt was regarded as the leading Lutheran hymn writer for domestic devotion, but it was not until the eighteenth century that these hymns generally found their way into the hymnals used in public worship.[4]

The new melodies had not yet evolved into the quasi-aria forms that appeared later, but they often exhibited an intimacy and freedom that contrasted with the older chorale melodies.

Bach's use of Gerhardt's hymn texts in his vocal works is confined to his Leipzig years between 1723 and 1736; stanzas from five appeared in the Christmas Oratorio (see Table 9.1).[5] The eleven melodies that Bach employed

---

3 See Albert Fischer and Wilhelm Tümpel, *Das deutsche evangelische Kirchenlied des 17. Jahrhunderts* (Gütersloh: Bertelsmann, 1904–1916; reprint, Hildesheim: Olms, 1964), 3:295–449.

4 For example, only one Gerhardt hymn was included in Gottfried Vopelius, *Neu Leipziger Gesangbuch/ von den schönsten und besten Liedern verfasset* (Leipzig: Klinger, 1682), 553: *Wach auf, mein Herz und singe* (Zahn 159).

5 Six Gerhardt texts were set by Bach in the Schemelli *Gesangbuch* (1736); BWV 441, 448, 451, 460, 469, 489; see Markus Jenny, "Bachische Sololieder mit Gerhardt-Texten," *Musik und Gottesdienst* 13 (1976): 48–51.

Bach and the hymnic aria   185

Table 9.1 Bach's use of Gerhardt's hymns in the vocal works

Gerhardt text	*BWV*	*Melody*	*Zahn*
Barmherzger Vater, höchster Gott	103/6 (1725)	Was mein Gott will	7568
Befiehl du deine Wege	153/5 (1724), 244/44 (1727)	Herzlich tut mich verlangen	5385a
Fröhlich soll mein Herze springen	248/33 (1734)	Warum sollt ich mich denn grämen	6461
Gott Vater, sende deinen Geist	74/8 (1725) 108/6 (1725)	Kommt her zu mir, spricht Gottes Sohn	2496c
Ich hab in Gottes Herz und Sinn	65/7 (1724) 92(1725)	Was mein Gott will	7568
Ich steh an deiner Krippen hier	248/59 (1734)	Es ist gewißlich an der Zeit	4429a
O Haupt voll Blut und Wunden	159/2 (1729) 244/15, 17, 54, 62 (1727)	Herzlich tut mich verlangen	5385a
O Welt, sieh hier dein Leben	244/37 (1727) 245/11 (1724)	O Welt, ich muß dich lassen	2293b
Schaut, schaut, was ist für Wunder	248/17 (1734)	Vom Himmel hoch da komm ich her	346
Schwing dich auf zu deinem Gott	40/6 (1723)	Meine Hoffnung stehet feste	4870
Warum sollt ich mich denn grämen	228 (1726?)	Warum sollt ich mich denn grämen	6461
Was alle Weisheit in der Welt	176/6 (1725)	Es wolle uns Gott genädig sein	7246
Weg, mein Herz, mit den Gedanken	32/6 (1726)	Wie nach einer Wasserquelle	6543
Wie soll ich dich empfangen	248/5 (1734)	Herzlich tut mich verlangen	5385a
Wir singen dir, Immanuel	248/23 (1734)	Vom Himmel hoch da komm ich her	346
Zeuch ein zu deinen Toren	183/5 (1725)	Helft mir Gotts Güte preisen	5267

for these sixteen texts by Gerhardt are revealing. One (*Herzlich tut mich verlangen*) was used with three different texts, and three (*Warum sollt ich mich denn grämen, Was mein Gott will*, and *Vom Himmel hoch*) were each used with two different texts. What is more surprising is that of these eleven melodies no less than eight date from the sixteenth century, with only two from the seventeenth century and just one from the early eighteenth century. This means that while the Crüger melodies for such hymns as Johann Franck's *Schmücke dich* (Zahn 6923) and *Jesu, meine Freude* (Zahn 8032), or Martin Rinckart's *Nun danket alle Gott* (Zahn 5142), appear from time to time in Bach's works,

186 *Hymnology*

the following five Crüger melodies associated with Gerhardt's hymns were displaced by older melodies:

Fröhlich soll mein Herze springen (Zahn 6481)
Schwing dich auf zu deinem Gott (Zahn 6309a)
Warum sollt ich mich denn grämen (Zahn 6455a)
Wie soll ich dich empfangen (Zahn 5438)
Zeuch ein zu deinen Toren (Zahn 5294)

The only contemporary melody Bach used was *Warum sollt ich mich denn grämen* (Zahn 6461), by the organist of the Nikolaikirche, Leipzig, Daniel Vetter (1657/58–1721), which the composer published in his *Musicalischer Kirch- und Haus-Ergötzlichkeit, Anderer Theil* (Leipzig: "Autore," [1713]; the first part was published in 1709).

This preference for the older melodies must have been Bach's, since, as cantor, it was his responsibility to choose which hymns should be sung and to which melodies. This long-standing tradition in Leipzig was challenged in September 1728 when the subdeacon of the Nikolaikirche, Gottlieb Gaudlitz (1670–1745), appealed to the consistory to insist that hymns before and after sermons, especially at Vespers, should be the choice of the preacher, not the cantor.[6] The consistory initially agreed,[7] but Bach objected and reminded the members of the consistory that this would be an innovation that would overturn the traditional practice:

Among these [Leipzig] customs and practices ... the ordering of the hymns before and after sermons ... was always left to me and my predecessors in the Cantorate to determine ... since hitherto the ordering of the hymns has remained for so long a function of the Cantorate.[8]

Although the outcome of these exchanges is unclear, since he was able to appeal to precedent—something that was *sacrosanct* in Leipzig—the responsibility for choosing hymns must have been restored to Bach.

About eighteen months later another question concerning the choice of hymns became an issue. In a letter to Deyling, dated 16 February 1730, the Leipzig consistory issued the following directive to the superintendent:

That also he [superintendent Deyling] shall arrange that in the churches of this town matters shall be regulated accordingly, and new hymns,

---

6 BDok 1: 54–57 (No. 19); NBR 137 (No. 137).
7 BDok 1: 56 (No. 19A).
8 NBR 137–39 (No. 138); BDok 1: 54–55 (No. 19).

Bach and the hymnic aria 187

hitherto not customary, shall not be used in public divine services without his, or if need be our, previous knowledge and approbation.[9]

An interesting feature of the letter is that neither Bach's name, nor the reason for the consistory's concern are mentioned, but the implication is that, as cantor with the responsibility of choosing the hymns, Bach had chosen a "neues Lied" to which some in the respective congregation had objected. Note also that the consistory did not say that new hymns were forbidden but that before they could be introduced into public worship approval of the superintendent must be sought. This was similar to the practice already in place by which Bach regularly submitted the texts of the cantatas he would be performing in upcoming weeks for the approval of the superintendent.[10] The concern was primarily with the texts of such possible "neue Lieder," that they should be theologically sound and appropriate for the specific liturgical service. But the objection may have been as much against a new melody as a new text, and, indeed, may have been directed against both the text and melody of a new hymn.

At the time of the consistory's letter to the superintendent, Bach had presumably begun composing and editing the melodies that would eventually be included in the Schemelli *Musicalisches Gesang-Buch*, though for Zeitz rather than Leipzig. There is something of a paradox here, since on the one hand he was creating new melodies, yet, on the other hand, at least as far as Gerhardt's hymns were concerned, his preference was with traditional chorale melodies of the sixteenth century. But perhaps the church authorities in Leipzig were more cautious about new melodies than were their counterparts in Zeitz.

Hymns and arias

At the beginning of the seventeenth century hymn singing was largely unaccompanied; by the end of the century it was almost always accompanied, organ in church, harpsichord or clavichord at home—at least in those homes that could afford such instruments. During the century the tempo of congregational singing became extremely slow, a process that converted rhythmic elements of chorale melodies into isometric forms and encouraged the improvisation of organ interludes between each melodic line (Zwischenspielen). In contrast, domestic hymn singing, accompanied by figured bass, could be expressed with greater freedom. Thus, in effect, two chorale genres existed in

---

9 NBR 144 (No. 149); Karl Hermann Bitter, *Johann Sebastian Bach*, 2nd ed. (Berlin: Baensch, 1881), 2: 231–32: "Dass auch in denen Kirchen dieser Stadt sich hienach geachtet, und neue, bisshero nicht üblich gewesene Lieder, ohne seinen und bedürffenden Falls unsere Vorbewusst und Approbation, beim öffentlichen Gottesdienste nicht gebrauchet werden."

10 See Martin Petzoldt, *"Texte zur Leipziger Kirchen-Music": Zum Verständnis der Kantatentexte Johann Sebastian Bachs* (Wiesbaden: Breitkopf & Härtel, 1993), 12–19.

188 *Hymnology*

parallel: the congregational hymn in church and the soloistic hymnic aria in the home, though they were not mutually exclusive.

Domestic hymn singing has its roots in the sixteenth-century Reformation. By the seventeenth century the practice had become commonplace, as the following hymnal titles illustrate:

> *Devoti musica cordis, Haus- und Hertz- Musica* (Breslau: Müller, 1630)
> *Zellisches Kirche- Schul- und Hauß-Buch* (Celle: Holwein, 1658)
> *Evangelisch Haus- und Kirchen-Buch* (Jena: Nisius, 1663)
> *Tägliche Haus- und Hertzens-Andacht* (Nurenberg: Endter, 1664)
> *Preußisches... Kirchen- Schul- und Haus- Gesangbuch*
> (Königsberg: Reusner, 1690).
> *Singendes Haus- und Kirchen- Paradeis* (Nördlingen: Rollwagen, 1700).

Thus, the hymnal in the home was afforded a more intimate environment for the singing of hymns, which could be just a single voice, or perhaps a small group of voices—very different from the hymn-singing in public worship, especially in the large congregations of town and city churches that could number as many as one or even two thousand people. Domestic hymn singing is likely to have been influenced by the small-scale sacred concertos that were composed in the wake of the dismantling of the large foundations of musicians and singers as a consequence of the Thirty Years' War. The common assumption is that these solo voice compositions were for the public worship of the church.[11] But since they call for limited musical resources they could also be performed domestically. Indeed, one of Bach's predecessors, Johann Hermann Schein (1586–1630), in the dedication of his *Opella Nova, Ander Theil, Geistlicher Concerten, mit 3. 4. 5. und 6. Stimmen zusampt dem General-Bass, auff ... Italiänische Invention componirt, etc* (Leipzig, 1626) specifically states that his concertos could be performed "not only in public in the church but also in private in the house."[12] Similarly, in a letter to the Nuremberg council, dated 28 April 1634, Samuel Scheidt (1587–1654) stated that his *Geistliche Concerten ... Ander Theil* (Halle and Erfurt, 1634) could be used in church, in house, or even traveling.[13] Many of these small-scale works are settings of chorales. Sometimes the chorale melody is unadorned, as in Schein's *Komm heiliger Geist, Herre Gott* (Zahn 7445) (*Opella Nova* II), where the cantus firmus is sung simply without ornamentation by the soprano, line

---

11 For example, Anne Kirwan-Mott, *The Small-Scale Sacred Concerto in the Early Seventeenth Century*, 2 vols. (Ann Arbor: UMI Research Press, 1981).
12 Johann Hermann Schein, *Neue Ausgabe sämtlicher Werke*, ed. Adam Adrio, et al. (Kassel: Bärenreiter, 1963–1986) 5: xi: "so wol publicè in der Kirchen/ als auch privatim zu Hause."
13 Heinz Zirnbauer, *Der Notenbestand der Reichsstädtisch Nürnberischen Ratsmusik: Eine bibliographische Rekonstruktion* (Nuremberg: Stadtbibliothek, 1959), 30, cited in Stephen Rose, "Daniel Vetter and the Domestic Keyboard Chorale in Bach's Leipzig," *Early Music* 33 (2005): 39.

by line, against an unrestrained instrumental accompaniment.[14] In other Schein settings the cantus firmus is treated in a highly soloistic manner recreating the chorale melody into an aria and disguising its contours by ornamentation. Examples include *Aus tiefer Not* (Zahn 4437) (*Opella Nova* I, 1618), in which two sopranos echo each element of the decorated melody in their impassioned prayer,[15] and *Also heilig ist der Tag* (Zahn 7149) (*Opella Nova* II, 1626), where Schein assigns the cantus firmus to the tenor and does so with great freedom.[16]

Other similar examples can be found in a whole range of music by Lutheran composers in the earlier seventeenth century. Of course, not every household would have the necessary instruments or the skills to play and sing them, but these aria-like settings of preexisting chorale melodies contributed to the development of simpler melodies for the new spiritually intensive texts, many of them inspired by the mysticism of St. Bernard of Clairvaux, and the love poetry of the biblical Song of Songs.[17]

Collections of domestic songs, both secular and religious, began to appear with the prominent word "Arien" on the title page. A few representative examples are reviewed here. An early anthology was published by Heinrich Albert (1604–1651), cousin and pupil of Heinrich Schütz, and organist of the cathedral in Königsberg: *Erster Theil der Arien oder Melodeyen Etlicher theils Geistlicher/ theils Weltlicher/ zu gutten Sitten und Lust dienender Lieder. Jn ein Positiv Clavicimbel/ Theorbe oder anders vollstimmiges Jnstrument zu singen gesetze* (Königsberg: Segebade, 1638). In subsequent years Albert issued a further seven collections, which were published together in a combined edition in 1650. Albert was both poet and composer of these mostly simple strophic songs (118 secular, and 74 sacred), though some were through-composed. A few melodies entered into common use, notably *Gott des Himmels und der Erden*, which Bach used in its later form (Zahn 3614b) to conclude the fifth part of his Christmas Oratorio (BWV 248/ 53).

Adam Krieger (1634–1666) was a pupil of Samuel Scheidt in Halle, organist of the Nikolaikirche, Leipzig, afterwards court organist in Dresden between 1657 and his death in 1666. Like Albert, Krieger was both poet and composer and influential in the development of the solo song in Germany. An earlier edition of his *Arien* was published in 1657 with an expanded edition following ten years later: *Neue Arjen/ Jn 6. Zehen eingetheilet/ Von Einer/ Zwo/ Drey/ und Fünf- Vocal-Stimmen/ benebenst ihren Rittornellen, auf*

---

14 Schein, *Neue Ausgabe sämtlicher Werke*, 5:196–214.

15 Ibid., 4:75–79.

16 Ibid., 5:136–48.

17 For the background see, Ingeborg Röbbelen, *Theologie und Frömmigkeit im deutschen evangelisch-lutherischen Gesangbuch des 17. und frühen 18. Jahrhunderts* (Berlin: Evangelische Verlaganstalt, 1957), and Christian Bunners, *Kirchenmusik und Seelenmusik: Studien zu Frömmigkeit und Musik im Luthertum des 17. Jahrhunderts* (Berlin: Evangelische Verlagsanstalt, 1966).

190   Hymnology

Zwey Violinen, Zwey Violen, und einem Violon, sammt dem Basso Continuo, Zu singen und zu spielen (Dresden: Seyfert, 1676).[18] Some of Krieger's folk-like melodies were widely sung, such as *Nun sich der Tag geendet hat* (Zahn 212b), which Bach harmonized (BWV 396). Krieger's *Eins ist not! ach Herr, dies Eine* (Zahn 7127), originally with a secular text, was first used with religious verse in Joachim Neander, *Glaub- und Liebesübung: Auffgemuntert durch Einfältige Bundes-Lieder und Danck-Psalmen* (Bremen: Brauer, 1680)—a Calvinist/ Reformed rather than Lutheran hymnal—from where it was later incorporated into the Pietist hymnal edited by Johann Anastasius Freylinghausen, *Geistreiches Gesang-Buch* (see further below). Interestingly, the text *Eins ist not!* was included in the Schemelli *Gesangbuch*, but Bach, as the music editor, did not set it with the Krieger melody, and instead composed a new melody with figured bass (BWV 453).

Johann Rudolph Ahle (1625–1673), a predecessor of Bach as the organist of the Blasiuskirche, Mühlhausen, was a prolific composer of church music. He is especially noted for the sacred songs he published in four editions issued under the title *Neuer Geistlicher Arien, So mit 1. 2. 3. 4. und mehr Stimmen* (Mühlhausen: Hüter, 1660–1669). The songs could be performed with or without figured bass, and ritornelli were inserted between the stanzas.[19] Bach set two of Ahle's melodies several times, *Liebster Jesu, wir sind hier* (Zahn 3498b; BWV 373, 633, 634, 706, 730, 731), and *Es ist genug! So nimm, Herr, meinen Geist* (Zahn 7173), which concludes Cantata 60—a melody that in the first few notes encompasses a tritone (the *diabolus in musica*) that is more than matched by Bach's arresting harmonization.[20]

Almost at the end of the century a new hymnal, which was to prove influential, was published in Dresden. Issued posthumously, it was the work of Christoph Bernhard (1628–1692), the Dresden court capellmeister, who had studied with Heinrich Schütz. The hymnal was published in two distinct parts, part one for the church, part two for the home, each with its own title page: [I:] *Geist- und Lehr-reiches Kirchen- und Hauß-Buchl vollerl wie gewöhnlich- alt-Lutherisch- so lieblich- neu- reiner ... Sonn- und Fest-Tags-Gesänge ... für Cantores und Organisten, mit Noten und unterlegtem Bass* (Spiritually and Doctrinally rich Church and House Book Full of the Customary- Old-Lutheran- Lovely- New- Pure ... Hymns) (Dresden: Matthesius, 1694); [II:] *Hundert. ahnmuthig- und sonderbahr geistlicher Arjenl vieler Herzen Verlangenl Zu gefälligem Vergnügenl unter Discant und Bass, herausgegeben und dem Neuen Gesang-Buche wohin die Anweisungen der Melodeien zielenl als ein Anhang*

---

18 Adam Krieger, *Arien*, ed. Alfred Heuss, *Denkmäler deutscher Tonkunst* 19 (Leipzig: Breitkopf & Härtel, 1905).

19 For background and analysis, see Markus Rathey, *Johann Rudolph Ahle 1625–1673: Lebensweg und Schaffen* (Eisenach: Wagner, 1999), 467–506

20 See Alfred Dürr, *The Cantatas of J. S. Bach with their Librettos in German-English Parallel Text*, revised trans. Richard D. P. Jones (Oxford: Oxford University Press, 2005), 634.

(One Hundred Charming- and Especially Spiritual Arias, for the Desire and Pleasure of Many Hearts, with Discant and Bass, edited as an Appendix to the New Hymnal with Instruction on the Melodies) (Dresden: Matthesius, 1694).[21] According to Zahn, the first part included seventy-eight new melodies, and the second part thirty-three new "Arien."[22] The tone of the main title page is somewhat defensive and reflects an Orthodox response to the Pietist turbulence that occurred in the Lutheran Church at the end of the seventeenth century, much of it caused by new hymns that were being sung to new simple aria-like melodies. After the title page established that the double volume was for use in both church and home, on the one hand, it reassured the reader/user that the hymnal contained all the familiar "old-Lutheran" hymns, and, on the other hand, that the new hymns could be trusted for their purity, that is, theological purity. This is specifically made explicit with regard to the new melodies in the preface addressed to the "Pious lovers of spiritual hymns and songs" ("Gottselige Liebhabere Geistliche Lieder und Gesänge"):

> With a few exceptions—which will speak for themselves—the editor thought it to be preferable, for the sake of devotion, to set the new melodies not in the typical Aria manner of today, but in correct church style. This, he hopes, will not displease but rather well please the singer of sacred music.[23]

The "Arien" of the double hymnal were, therefore, generally conservative in style, because of the more secular musical style that was being promoted by the Pietist movement, then creating controversy.[24] Nevertheless, there was some common ground between the opposing factions within Lutheranism, since the Pietists did not have a monopoly on piety, especially with regard to the writings of the medieval mystics and their "Jesus-Lieder." For example, the Dresden *Hundert Arien* included the complete *Jesus dulcis memoria* of Bernard of Clairvaux in both Latin and German.[25] These texts, together

---

21 It was reissued some years later with a new title page and different publisher: *Neu-auffgelegtes Dreßdnisches Gesang-Buch/ Oder Gott-geheiligte Kirchen- und Haus-Andachten/ Darrinen Nicht allein des Hoch-erleuchteten Mannes Gottes D. Martini Lutheri, sondern auch der Kern vieler andern vornehmer Gottselig-gelehrter Leute Geistreiche Lieder zu finden/ Nebst einem Anhang von 100. sonderbahren Arien für Cantores und Organisten, mit Noten und unterlegtem Bass* (Dresden and Leipzig: Miethen, 1707).

22 Zahn 6:270–71.

23 *Geist- und Lehr-reiches Kirchen- und Hauß-Buch* (Dresden: Matthesius, 1694), sig. (a) 2ᵛ: "Die neuen Melodeien aber hat der Editor bis auf etliche wenige/ die sich selbst melden werden/ nicht in heut üblicher Arien-Manier, sondern/ mit gutem Wohlbedacht/ in rechtem Kirchen-Stylo zu setzen/ üm der Andacht willen/ für guht erachtet/ welches hoffendlich dem Geistlichen Sänger nicht mis-sondern vielmehr angenehm fallen wird."

24 On Pietism in general, see Chapter 11.

25 *Hundert Arien*, Nos. 29–40. The associated melodies are not found in Zahn.

192   Hymnology

with their melodies, were taken from Narziss Rauner, *Davidischer Jesus-Psalter: also inn Lateinisch und teutsche Reimen gesangsweiss eingerichtet ... ieden Psalmem in einer besondern neu darzugemachten Melody anstimmen ... Und noch einer Zugab Bernhardinischer Jesus-Lieder* (Augspurg: Goebels, 1670). Philipp Jacob Spener, the founder of Lutheran Pietism and somewhat controversial *Oberhofprediger* at the Saxon court in Dresden between 1686 and 1691, contributed the preface. Thus, hymns promoted by a Pietist were being incorporated into a basically orthodox hymnal.

A notable feature of the Dresden double hymnal is the way in which many of the Arien of the second part are linked directly to hymns in the first part. For example, the section of *Jesus dulcis memoria* beginning *Veni, Veni Rex optime / Komm, König, komm O frömmer Herr!* (Arien Nos. 37–38) is headed by a reference to the melody *Vom Himmel hoch da komm ich Herr* (Hymnal, No. 19); the hymns in the two parts of the hymnal have the same meter: 8.8.8.8. Similarly, *Das ist meine grosste Freude* (Arien No. 63; Zahn 3654a) is linked to *Gott des Himmels und der Erden* (Hymnal, No. 389; Zahn 3614b); again, the two hymns in each part of the hymnal have the same meter: 8.7. 8.7. 7.7. This suggests that the two texts with their respective melodies could be sung at the same time, one after the other, or perhaps the two melodies were used interchangeably with the two texts.

The Pietist hymnal, edited by Johann Anastasius Freylinghausen, was published ten years after the Dresden double hymnal: *Geist-reiches Gesang-Buch/ Den Kern Alter und Neuer Lieder/ Wie auch die Noten der unbekannten Melodeyen* (Halle: Waysenhause, 1704).[26] It included ninety-two melodies culled from various previously published sources together with eighty-two new melodies that confirmed the distinctive musical style.[27] The appearance of the hymnal was met by the adherents of Orthodoxy with trenchant criticism both of its theological content as well as its musical style. However, with the passage of time, Orthodoxy began to weaken, and Pietism had to defend itself on two fronts, not only against Orthodoxy but also against the beginnings of Rationalism that even threatened to take over the University of Halle, which until then had been the center of the Pietist movement. The Freylinghausen *Gesangbuch* became a source for hymnal editors, who culled some of the non-radical hymns and a good many of the melodies. One of the hymnals was the Schemelli *Gesangbuch*, and one of the editors was Johann Sebastian Bach (see Table 9.2 and Table 9.3).

---

26 Johann Anastasius Freylinghausen, *Geistreiches Gesangbuch: Edition und Kommentar*, ed. Dianne Marie McMullen and Wolfgang Miersemann, 7 vols. (Tübingen: Franckesche Stiftungen, 2004–2010); Dianne Marie McMullen, "The Geistreiches Gesangbuch of Johann Anastasius Freylinghausen (1670–1739): A German Pietist Hymnal" (PhD diss., University of Michigan, 1987).

27 Zahn 6:283–84.

Bach and the hymnic aria 193

Table 9.2 Freylinghausen melodies edited by Bach in the Schemelli *Gesangbuch*

BWV	Melody	Text	
	Freylinghausen, 1704		
455	Erwürgtes Lamm! das die verwahrten Siegel	U. B. v. Bonin	1704
456	Es glänzet der Christen inwendiges Leben	C. F. Richter	1704
459	Es kostet viel, ein Christ zu sein	C. F. Richter	1704
474	Jesus ist das schönste Licht	C. F. Richter	1704
486	Mein Jesu dem die Seraphinen	W. C. Deßler	1692
489	Nicht so traurig, nicht so sehr	P. Gerhardt	1648
506	Was bist du doch, o Seele, so betrübet	R. F. v. Schultt	1704
	Freylinghausen, 1708		
451	Die güldne Sonne, voll Freud und Wonne	P. Gerhardt	1666/67
446	Der lieben Sonnen Licht und Pracht	C. Scriver	1684
490	Nur mein Jesus ist mein Leben	Anon.	1697
497	Seelenweide, meine Freude	A. Drese	1695
	Freylinghausen, 1714		
472	Jesu, meines Glaubens Zier	G. W. Sacer	1714
458	Es ist vollbracht! Vergiß ja nicht	J. E. Schmidt	1714
475	Jesus, unser Trost und Leben	E. C. Homburg	1659
482	Liebes Herz bedenke doch	C. J. Koitsch	1714
461	Gott lebet noch. Seele, was verzagst du doch?	J. F. Zihn	1692
503	Steh ich bei meinem Gott	J. D. Herrnschmidt,	1714

Did Bach distance himself from the traditional chorale?

In 1983, in an important contribution to the Alfred Dürr *Festschrift*, Walter Blakenburg investigated Bach's connection with the church hymn of his day, especially the phenomenon of the soloistic strophic aria.[28] Blankenburg made the observation that while Bach composed no example of a truly congregational hymn, he did compose and/or edit a significant group of spiritual arias that are found in the Schemelli *Gesangbuch* (BWV 439–507). The implication that could be drawn from this information is that by the mid-1730s Bach had moved away from a strong commitment to the old congregational chorale in favor of the more intimate and individualistic spiritual aria. Some years earlier, Alfred Dürr, in the Walter Buszin *Festschrift*, had made a similar

---

28 Walter Blankenburg, "Johann Sebastian Bach und das evangelische Kirchenlied zu seiner Zeit," in *Bachiana et alia Musicologica: Festschrift Alfred Dürr zum 65. Geburtstag am 3. März 1983* (Kassel: Bärenreiter, 1983), 31–38. English Translation: "Johann Sebastian Bach and the Protestant Hymn in His Time," *The Hymnology Annual*, vol. 3, ed. Vernon Wicker (Berrien Springs: Vande Vere, 1993), 95–105.

194   *Hymnology*

observation to that of Blankenburg by posing a question at the end of his chapter on Bach's chorale cantatas:

> It would be advisable to ask cautiously whether Bach himself, in the course of his life, was not exposed to a change and in the 1730s turned his interest to an increasing degree to the chorale output [Liedschaffen] of his own time. Already in the *Christmas Oratorio* the hymnody of the 17th century outweighs that of the Reformation period.[29]

Similarly, in a contribution to the Karl Geiringer *Festschrift*, Walter Buszin lamented the fact that Bach made no specific contribution to ecclesiastical congregational hymnody: "The songs in the Schemelli collection are intriguing," he wrote, "but they are arias rather than hymns."[30]

Bach was intimately involved, at various levels, in the process of creating the *Musicalisches Gesang-Buch*, edited by Georg Christian Schemelli, cantor in Zeitz,[31] published by Breitkopf in Leipzig in 1736. First, he was effectively the composer/editor of the music that the *Gesangbuch* contained. As Friedrich Schultze, superintendent in Zeitz, explained in the preface:

> The melodies to be found in this *Musicalische Gesangbuch* have been in part quite newly composed and in part improved in the thorough bass by the most noble Herr Johann Sebastian Bach, Electoral Saxon Capellmeister and *Director Chori Musici* in Leipzig.[32]

Second, as Gregory Butler has effectively demonstrated, Bach was closely involved in the process of engraving these melodies and their basses,[33] which was a selling point for Breitkopf in 1736: "The unfamiliar melodies have either been newly composed or improved as necessary by Herr Capellmeister Bach and then cleanly engraved in copper."[34] Third, Bach had prepared around

---

29 Alfred Dürr, "Bach's Chorale Cantatas," *Cantors at the Crossroads: Essays on Church Music in Honor of Walter Buszin*, ed. Johannes Riedel (St. Louis: Concordia, 1967), 119.

30 Walter E. Buszin, "The Chorale in the Baroque Era and J. S. Bach's Contribution to It," *Studies in Eighteenth-Century Music: A Tribute to Karl Geiringer on His Seventieth Birthday*, ed. H. C. Robbins Landon and Roger E. Chapman (London: Allen and Unwin, 1970), 112.

31 For the Zeitz background, see Chapter 10.

32 NBR 170 (No.179), Georg Christian Schemelli, *Musicalisches Gesangbuch* (Leipzig: Breitkopf, 1736; facsimile, Hildesheim: Olms, 1975), sig. **4ᵛ; BDok 2: 266 (No. 379): "Die in diesem Musicalischen Gesangbuche befindlichen Melodien, sind von Sr. Hochedl. Herrn Johann Sebastian Bach, Hochfürstl. Sächß. Capellmeister und *Directore Chor. Musici* in Leipzig, theils ganz neu componiret, theils auch von Ihm im General-Baß verbessert."

33 Gregory G. Butler, "J. S. Bach and the Schemelli *Gesangbuch* Revisited," *Studi musicali* 13 (1984): 241–57.

34 Leipzig *Oster messkatalog* for 1736, BDok 2: 266 (No. 378): "Die Unbekandten Melodien sind von Herrn Capellmeister Bach entweder neu verfertiget, oder nach Befinden verbessert und so dann sauber in Kupffer gestochen worden."

Bach and the hymnic aria   195

three hundred melodies, old and new, for the *Gesangbuch*, but for economic reasons—copper engraving was expensive—the publisher only included sixty-nine melodies that were either new or less familiar. As Schultze noted in the preface:

> One should not doubt that many more [melodies] would have made the book too expensive. While no extensive edition is made at this time, the hope is that the present example of this *Musicalische Gesangbuch* will soon be sold out. The publisher has around 200 melodies completely prepared and ready for engraving, so that no single hymn, that does not have a known melody, will be found without [musical] notes [in the second edition].[35]

This means that Bach, as the musical editor of the collection, had already prepared an additional 200 or so melodies for publication—traditional chorales as well as newer aria forms—which are no longer extant.[36] Fourth, again in his capacity of music editor of the hymnal, Bach reviewed the assigned melodies for all of the 954 texts, old and new, and for many of them indicated the preferred key in which they should be sung.[37] Fifth, Bach was obviously well aware of the more intimate style of the new contemporary melodies alongside the older chorales, as is described on the title page of the hymnal: "geistreiche, sowohl alte als neue Lieder und Arien, mit wohlgesetzten Melodien, in Discant und Bass" (spiritually rich old as well as new hymns and arias, with well-arranged melodies, in discant and bass).

If the discussion of Bach's contribution to the Schemelli *Gesangbuch* is restricted to the sixty-nine melodies that occur with their figured basses in the hymnal, then the questions raised cautiously by Dürr and Blankenburg will receive inadequate answers. Of course, to use Dürr's words, Bach in the 1730s did "turn his interest to an increasing degree to the chorale output of his own time."[38] As can be seen in Table 9.3, Bach either composed or edited nineteen melodies associated with texts that had been written during his lifetime in the first three decades of the eighteenth century, as well as seven others that apparently made their first appearance in the Schemelli *Gesangbuch* of

---

35 Schemelli, *Musicalisches Gesangbuch*, sig. **4v: "Man hätte deren noch mehrer beyfügen können, wenn man nicht bedencken müssen, daß hiedurch manchem das Buch zu theuer werden mögen. Indem man aber vor dießmal keine große Auflage gemachet, und daher zu hoffen ist, daß die vorhandenen Exemplaren dieses musicalischen Gesangbuches bald abgehen dörften; so ist der Verleger gesonnen, bey 200 Melodien, die zum Stechen bereits fertig liegen, noch hinzu zu thun: Daß alsdenn kein einzig Lied in diesem Gesangbuche, wenn es nicht eine gantz bekannte Melodie hat, ohne Noten wird befindlich seyn."

36 See Markus Jenny, "Zweihundert verschollene Bach-Werke," *Mededelingen van het Instituut voor Liturgiewetenschap van die Rijksuniversiteit te Groningen* 18 (Sept. 1984): 20–29.

37 This is the primary investigation of Chapter 10.

38 See note 29 above.

196 *Hymnology*

Table 9.3 Eighteenth-century texts Bach set in the Schemelli *Gesangbuch*

BWV	Text	Author	
	A. Originating Between 1701 and 1728		
507	Wo ist mein Schäflein, das ich liebe	J. P. v. Schultt	1701
492	O finstre Nacht, wenn wirst du doch vergehen	G. F. Breithaupt	1704
455	Erwürgtes Lamm! das die verwahrten Siegel	U. B. v. Bonin	1704
474	Jesus ist das schönste Licht	C. F. Richter	1704
459	Es kostet viel, ein Christ zu sein	C. F. Richter	1704
456	Es glänzet der Christen inwendiges Leben	C. F. Richter	1704
506	Was bist du doch, o Seele, so betrübet	J. P. v. Schultt	1704
439	Ach, dass nicht die letzte Stunde	E. Neumeister	1705
447	Der Tag ist hin, die Sonne gehet nieder	J. C. Rube	1712
479	Kommt, Seelen, dieser Tag	V. E. Löscher	1713
480	Kommt wieder aus der finstern Gruft	V. E. Löscher	1713
505	Vergiß mein nicht, mein allerliebster Gott	G. Arnold	1714
503	Steh ich bei meinem Gott	J. D. Herrnschmidt	1714
482	Liebes Herz, bedenke doch	C. J. Koitsch	1714
472	Jesu, meines Glaubens Zier	G. W. Sacer	1714
458	Es ist vollbracht! vergiß ja nicht	J. E. Schmidt	1714
478	Komm, süßer Tod, komm, selge Ruh	Anon., Dresden	1724
442	Beglückter Stand getreuer Seelen	U. B. v. Bonin	1727
488	Meines Lebens letzte Zeit	Anon. Gotha	1728
	B. Originating in the Schemelli Gesangbuch, 1736		
471	Jesu, deine Liebes wunden	M. C. W. [Wegleiter?]	
487	Mein Jesu! was vor Seelenweh	S. [Schultze?]	
498	Selig, wer an Jesum denkt	A. G. B.	
462	Gott, wie groß ist deine Güte	G. C. S. [Schemelli?]	
494	O liebe Seele, zieh' die Sinnen	Anon.	
466	Ich halte treulich still und liebe	J. H. Till	
468	Ich liebe Jesum alle Stund	Anon.	

1736. It is undeniable that Bach took a particular interest in the hymnody of his time, especially the aria-like melodies that had first flourished in domestic circles but subsequently had migrated into the public worship of the church. However, he did not emulate those Pietists who advocated that these newer texts with their lighter melodies should replace the older chorales, but rather held that the traditional chorales and the contemporary spiritual arias were complementary—not competing—forms of sacred song. Indeed, in the Schemelli *Gesangbuch* there are two items that are syntheses of the two genres for which Bach supplied new aria-like melodies alongside older chorales. They occur in the Anhang (appendix) at numbers 936 and 938, respectively *Kommt, seelen, dieser Tag* (BWV 479) and *Kommt wieder aus der finstern Gruft* (BWV 480).

Both these texts were written by Valentin Ernst Löscher (1673–1749), consistorial counselor and superintendent in Dresden, pastor of the Kreuzkirche, and prolific author. Like Erdmann Neumeister, with whom he corresponded for around fifty years,[39] Löscher was theologically and unwaveringly Orthodox and strongly anti-Pietist, while at the same time able to write warm devotional poetry that was appreciated by both Pietist and Orthodox alike. But, unlike Neumeister, even though Löscher believed Pietism to be a dangerous movement within Lutheranism, he took the view that Pietists were not to be condemned out of hand. Thus, on the one hand, he was careful to commend Spener where he could and, on the other hand, he did not shrink from criticizing Orthodox theologians for being too heavy-handed and blustering in their opposition to Pietism.[40]

Löscher first published the texts found in the Schemelli *Gesangbuch* in a small volume intended for members of the Kreutzkirche congregation: *Dreyfache Andachts-Übung, Der Gemeinde Christi zum Heil. Creutz in Dreßden: Zur Beförderung des geistlichen Wachsthums überlieffert: Als 1. Geistliche Oden und Lieder so bei der Communion gebraucht werden können. 2. Fest- und Sonntags-Andachten, 3. Erklährung der bißherigen und heurigen Lehr-Art* [Threefold devotional exercises, for Christ's congregation in the Kreuzkirche Dresden: Provided for the promotion of spiritual growth: As 1. Spiritual poems and hymns to be used at Communion. 2. Festival and Sunday devotions, 3. Explanation of the previous and this year's teaching method] (Dresden: Harpeter, 1713). Löscher directed that each of his new texts should be sung to a familiar chorale melody, but after the first stanza of the new text had been sung, the first stanza of an older, well-known chorale was then sung to its well-known melody. Thereafter the stanzas of the two hymn texts were sung in alternation.

The singing of choir and congregation in alternation has a long history in Lutheran tradition. Its roots are in the late medieval *alternatim praxis* of polyphony and plainchant that was customary, for example, in Latin hymns for Vespers, and in settings of the Magnificat, the latter usually for two choirs to express the sequential text. In the early years of the Reformation in Luther's Wittenberg the practice was developed to involve congregational singing of vernacular hymns, especially on the major festivals of the church year. Thus, on Easter Day in Wittenberg, between the Epistle and Gospel, there was a complex, three-way alternation in which the congregation sang stanzas of Luther's hymn *Christ lag in Todesbanden*, and the choir sang and the organ played verses of the Latin Easter Sequence, *Victimae paschali laudes*.[41] In later years a simpler alternation of choir and congregation became the widespread practice. By the time of Bach, it had also become customary

---

39 See Herwarth von Schade, "*Geld ist der Hamburger ihr Gott*": *Erdmann Neumeisters Briefe an Valentin Ernst Löscher* (Herzberg: Bautz, 1998).

40 On Löscher, see Chapter 11.

41 See Adolf Boes, "Die reformatorischen Gottesdienste in der Wittenberger Pfarrkirche von 1523 an," *Jahrbuch für Liturgik und Hymnologie* 6 (1961): 52–53. The stanzas of the older Easter hymn, *Christ ist erstanden* were woven into the polyphonic verses of the Sequence. The melodies *Christ lag in Todesbanden* and *Christ ist erstanden* were developed from the *Victimae paschali laudes* melody.

198   *Hymnology*

for hymnals to print seasonal hymns alternating the stanzas of their Latin and German texts, such as *Puer natus in Bethlehem* with *Ein Kind geborn zu Bethlehem,* and *Quam pastores laudevere* with *Den die Hirten lobten sehre* at Christmas. Each Latin stanza was sung by the choir and was followed by the congregation singing the same stanza in German, the two texts being sung to the same melody. Löscher would have been aware of these examples of alternation, together with the more recent example of the Dresden double hymnal of 1694, or its reprint of 1707, the hymnal that juxtaposed two different hymns, one from each of its two sections.[42] However, the immediate inspiration appears to have been the Pietist hymnal, Freylinghausen's *Geist-reiches Gesang-Buch* (Halle, 1704), in which Löscher found at least two examples of a newly written text coupled with an older chorale, namely: *Seid zufrieden, lieben brüder*, sung in alternation with *Gelobet seist du, Jesu Christ* (Luther), and *Mein Herz soll nun gantz absagen* sung in alternation with *Jesu, meine Freude* (Franck/Crüger).[43] It seems that Löscher saw a useful model in these examples in the Freylinghausen *Gesangbuch* and was encouraged to create his own hymns to be sung in alternation with older chorales. This is a good example of how Löscher, who was very negative of aspects of the Freylinghausen *Gesangbuch*,[44] could nevertheless take something positive from the flagship of the Pietist movement.

In the original 1713 imprint of *Dreyfache Andachts-Übung* there were two Löscher texts paired with two older hymns,[45] but sometime later he added two more pairs:[46]

> *Auf, die ihr Jesum liebt*, melody: *In dulci jubilo* (Zahn 4947), 6 stanzas
>> Paired with text *Vom Himmel kam der Engel Schar*, 6 stanzas
>> and melody: *Vom Himmel hoch da komm ich her* (Zahn 346)
>
> *Mein Jesu! Treuer Hirt*, melody: *Wo soll ich fliehen hin* (Zahn 2177),
> 8 stanzas
>> Paired with text and melody: *O Traurigkeit, o Herzeleid* (Zahn 1915),
>> 8 stanzas
>
> *Kommt wieder aus der finstern Gruft*, melody: *Wenn mein Stündlein*
> *vorhanden ist* (Zahn 4482), 8 stanzas

---

42 See page 190 above.

43 Freylinghausen, *Geist-reiches Gesang-Buch*, Nos. 36 and 330 respectively. *Mein Herz soll nun gantz absagen / Jesu, meine Freude* was also included in the Schemelli *Gesangbuch* (No. 765).

44 See the discussion in Chapter 11.

45 Eduard Emil Koch, *Geschichte des Kirchenlieds und Kirchengesangs der christlichen, insbesondere der deutschen evangelischen Kirche*, 3rd edition, ed. Richard Lauxmann (Stuttgart: Belser, 1866–1890; reprint, Hildesheim: Olms, 1973), 5: 401.

46 Information regarding *Auf, dir Ihr Jesum liebt* and *Mein Jesu! Treuer Hirt* is found in *Auserlesenes und vollständiges Gesangbuch Worinnen 751 der besten und geistreichsten Lieder, Welche In denen ChurSächß. Kirchen pflegen gesungen zu werden* (Dresden: Zimmermann, 1718), but they must have been written sometime earlier, since they are also found in an Ulm *Gesangbuch: Glaubiger Kinder Gottes*, published in 1717 (see further below).

Paired with text and melody: *Heut triumphiret Gottes Sohn* (Zahn 2585), 8 stanzas

Kommt, seelen, dieser Tag, melody: *Nun danket alle Gott* (Zahn 5142), 7 stanzas

Paired with text and melody: *Komm, Gott Schöpfer, Heiliger Geist* (Zahn 295), 8 stanzas

The original *Dreyfache Andachts-Übung* indicates that the paired hymns were to be sung during Communion and, for example, the *Glaubiger Kinder Gottes Englische Sing-Schule hier auf Erden* (Ulm: Bartholomäi, 1717) establishes that they were to be sung during the primary seasons of Christmas, Lent, Easter, and Pentecost:

No. 1088. *Auf, die ihr Jesum liebt/ Vom Himmel kam der Engel Schar*
Headed: "Communions-Lied zur Heil. Weyhnacht-Zeit"

No. 1089. *Mein Jesu! Treuer Hirt / O Traurigkeit, o Herzeleid*
Headed: "Communions-Lied in der Fasten-Zeit"

No. 1090. *Kommt wieder aus der finstern Gruft/ Heut triumphiret Gottes Sohn*
Headed: "Communions-Lied, die Oster-Zeit über"

No. 1091. *Kommt, seelen, dieser Tag / Komm, Gott Schöpfer, Heiliger Geist*
Headed: "Communions-Lied die Pfingst-Zeit über"[47]

All four Löscher texts, together with information on their paired hymns, instruction on the alternation, and assignment of the same melodies, are found in the Leipzig and Dresden hymnals that Bach knew and used.[48] In the Schemelli *Gesangbuch*, Bach only provided new melodies for Löscher's Easter and Pentecost texts, which were to be sung with the specific older hymns. The hymnal omitted Löscher's Christmas text, with its paired hymn, but did include his text for Lent, *Mein Jesu! Treuer Hirt*, paired with *O Traurigkeit, o Herzeleid* (No. 153)—headed: "Paßions- and abendmahlslied" (Passion and Communion hymn). But there was no new Bach melody for this Löscher text. Why, remains something of a mystery, though it is possible that Bach did compose a new melody for the text, and it was among the 200 or so melodies that Breitkopf had ready for engraving in 1736, if a second edition was warranted, but which were subsequently lost.

---

47 *Glaubiger Kinder Gottes Englische Sing-Schule hier auf Erden* (Ulm: Bartholomäi, 1717), 820–21. A few years later Löscher created another text to be sung in alternation with a Luther hymn, discussed in Chapter 15.

48 *Das Privilegirte Ordentliche und Vermehrte Dreßdnische Gesang-Buch* (Dresden and Leipzig: Hekel, 1724, and later reprints) and *Das privilegirte Vollständige und vermehrte Leipziger Gesangbuch* (Leipzig: Barnbeck, 1734, and later reprints). Unlike the Ulm 1717 hymnal, in which the Löscher texts are grouped together, these hymnals include them individually in the section of the respective festival, or with Communion hymns.

200   *Hymnology*

Although there is no direct reference in the Schemelli *Gesangbuch* that *Kommt wieder aus der finstern Gruft* (BWV 480) (see Example 9.1A and B), and *Kommt, seelen dieser Tag* (BWV 479) (see Example 9.2A and B) were to be sung during the distribution of Communion, other sources make this clear, such as: Löscher's original booklet *Dreyfache Andachts-Übung* that has on the title page, "Geistliche Oden und Lieder so bei der Communion gebraucht werden können" (Spiritual poems and hymns to be used at Communion); the Ulm *Gesangbuch* of 1717 heads the four items as "Communions-Lieder"; and the Dresden *Gesangbuch* of 1724 (and later) includes *Mein Jesu! Treuer Hirt* (to be sung with *O Traurigkeit, o Herzeleid*) among the Communion hymns.

The distribution of Communion could be quite protracted, especially at the major festivals of the church year, when *musica sub communione*, in the form of a motet or concerted music, preceded the customary hymn singing in alternation with organ chorale preludes, as Bach noted on the reverse of the title pages of the original scores of the Advent cantatas *Nun komm der Heiden Heiland* (BWV 61 and 62): "Preluding on the [concerted] music. After the same, alternate preluding and singing of chorales until the end of the Communion."[49] For the major festivals Löscher created this hymnic form in which two hymns— one a newly written text that expanded and expounded the text of an older, well-known hymn—were sung in alternation to different familiar melodies during the distribution of Communion. Pietists in the early eighteenth century, who generally wanted to simplify public worship, probably would have been extremely unhappy with the ritual context that Löscher intended for this composite hymnic form.

Bach's two settings witness to the way in which simple, aria-like melodies, a form that had originated in domestic circles during the seventeenth century, found their way into public worship in the eighteenth century. Before Bach came to set these texts, it was customary for a solo voice to sing Löscher's text in alternation with the congregation singing a well-known chorale. In the Colditz *Gesangbuch* of 1724 *Kommt wieder aus der finstern Gruft* was specifically headed an "Aria"—"Communion-Arie zur Osterzeit"[50]—indicating a solo voice. The nature of these two melodies by Bach (BWV 480 and 479) is that they are small-scale strophic arias intended for a single voice rather than a congregation. Both are written in the emerging galant style and appeared the year before Scheibe published his criticism of Bach's "turgid and confused style"![51] What could be more immediate than these two delightful arias?

In these two cases Bach composed a new melody for each of the two aria texts. He replaced Löscher's choice of the melody *Wenn mein Stündlein*

---

49 NBR 113–14 (No. 113); BDok 1: 248 (No. 178): "Praelud. Auf die Music. Und nach selbiger wechselweise praelud. v. Choräle gesungen, biß die Communion zu Ende & sic porrò." See also BDok 1: 251 (No. 181), and the discussion of *musica sub communione* in Chapter 2.

50 *Colditzer Kirchen-, Schul- und Hauß-Gesang-Buch* (Rochlitz: Lange, 1724), 536; cited Albert Friedrich Wilhelm Fischer, *Kirchenlieder Lexicon* (Gotha: Perthes, 1878–1879; reprint Hildesheim: Olms, 1967), 2:17.

51 NBR 338 (No. 343); BDok 2: 286 (No. 400).

Example 9.1 Communion hymns for Easter

A. *Kommt wieder aus der finstern Gruft* (BWV 480). Text: Löscher, 1713. Melody: Bach, 1736.

B. *Heut triumphiret Gottes Sohn*. Text: Kaspar Stolzhagen, 1591. Melody: Bartolomäus Gesius, 1601.

202 *Hymnology*

Example 9.2 Communion hymns for Pentecost
A. *Kommt, seelen dieser Tag* (BWV 479). Text: Löscher, 1713. Melody: Bach, 1736.
B. *Komm, Gott Schöpfer, Heiliger Geist*. Text and melody *Veni creator Spiritus*, adapted by Martin Luther 1524/1529.

vorhanden ist with his own melody, *Kommt wieder aus der finstern Gruft* (BWV 480; Example 9.1A), which was to be sung by a single voice in alternation with the congregation singing *Heut triumphiret Gottes Sohn* (Example 9.1B). Similarly, Bach replaced Löscher's choice of the melody *Nun danket alle Gott* for his own *Kommt, seelen, dieser Tag* (BWV 479; Example 9.2A), again sung by a solo voice in alternation with the combined voice of the congregation singing the text and melody of Luther's *Komm, Gott Schöpfer, Heiliger Geist* (Example 9.2B). It was a new expression of hymnody that brought together the texts and melodies of new and old hymns, arias and chorales. In a sense, these two examples epitomize the aim of the Schemelli *Gesangbuch* as a whole, which announced on its title page that it contained old and new "Lieder und Arien."

10 Bach and the letter codes of the Schemelli *Gesangbuch*

Text-only hymnals are frequently overlooked by musicologists because it is thought that they contain very little of musical interest. However, this is not very different from assuming that opera libretti have little musical significance because they deal only with words, plots, and narratives. These anthologies of congregational song may be comprised entirely of words, but they are thoughts and emotions expressed in rhymes, rhythms, and meters that have particular musical implications. A chorale melody must have the same number of lines as the poetic text, with or without repetition. A chorale melody must have the same number of poetic feet per line as the text. A chorale melody must have the same stress patterns as the text, be they iambic, trochaic, dactylic, or whatever. A chorale melody must express the same emotion as the text, be it mournful or joyful, reflective or celebratory. This chapter explores some of the ways in which musical matters are addressed in text-only German hymnals—especially the phenomenon of indicating pitch and key by letter codes—and Bach's knowledge and use of such coding in the Schemelli *Gesangbuch* (1736).

Identification of chorale melodies

The long-standing German tradition in text-only hymnals has been to give, as a heading to the whole hymn, the textual incipit of the associated chorale melody to which the following text is to be sung. This is usually given in the form: "Mel. Nun freuet euch etc." If, however, the hymn text has its own melody then it is unnecessary to repeat the first line as the melody because the information is already known. Sometimes the melody is identified with "In bekandter Melodey" (to the known melody), or the place simply left blank. Thus, the chorale repertoire of a particular church or town was defined by the associated chorale incipits/names in the *Gesangbuch* that was in use. When these identifiers are compared with those found in the hymnals used by other churches and towns at the same period it becomes clear that there was agreement only on the most familiar melodies. Indeed, the situation often appears somewhat chaotic, since one melody was often known by many different names, and one identity could be assigned to multiple melodies in

204 *Hymnology*

these different hymnals. This is reflected in Jacob Adlung's comment penned in the early 1750s:

> Concerning the disunity in the melodies there would also be much to recall. No village in the present territory is identical to another in all pieces of music: in fact no church in this city [Erfurt,] sings the [chorale] melodies in the same way as another. Either they use completely different ones, or they are so greatly altered that no player is capable of playing a hymn on other organs outside his own church if someone does not set in front of him a chorale book that has been introduced in that place. And when an honest citizen attends another church, he must quite often remain a mere listener.[1]

But for the people who regularly attended these churches and sang from the common hymnal there was no problem, since within that community everyone knew what melodies were designated by these chorale incipits/names at the head of most hymn texts in their *Gesangbuch*.

Multiple texts and melodies

Some text-only hymnals include what amounts to a metrical index of the melodies. A typical example is *Neues Vollständiges Gesang-Buch* (Berlin: Kunst, 1757).[2] Preceding the alphabetical index of textual incipits at the end of the volume there is an index of the sixty-three different meters of the associated melodies:

> *Melodies Index*
> Information how one may sing a hymn to many melodies, as follows:
>   All the hymn texts given under a number [in this index] can be sung to one melody. For example, under Number 1 the first hymn is named: *Ach ein Wort von grosser Treue*, etc. All the following hymns under this number can be sung to this melody [33 of them]; and the same applies to all the other [numbered] melodies and their first hymn.

---

1 Jacob Adlung, *Anleitung zu der musikalischen Gelahrtheit* (Erfurt: Jungnicol, 1758; facsimile, Kassel: Bärenreiter, 1953), 664: "Von der Uneingkeit in den Melodien wär gleichfalls viel zu erinnern. Kein Dorf des hiesigen Gebietes ist in allen Stücken dem andern gleich; ja keine Kirche dieser Stadt singt die Melodien wie die andere. Entweder sie haben ganz andere, oder sie sind doch so sehr geändert, daß kein Spieler im Stande ist auf andern Orgeln ausser seiner Kirche einen Choral mit zu spielen, wo man ihm nicht ein Melodienbuch vorlegt, welches allda eingeführt. Und wenn ein ehrlicher Bürger in eine andere Kirche kommt, muß er sehr oft einen blossen Zuhörer abgeben." Trans. based on Joseph Herl, *Worship Wars in Early Lutheranism: Choir, Congregation, and Three Centuries of Conflict* (New York: Oxford University Press, 2004), 138.
2 It was first published as *Neues Vollständiges Gesang-Buch, Vor die Königlich-Preußischel Auch Chur-Fürstl. Brandenburgische und andere Lande* (Berlin: Rüdiger, 1725).

The significance of this information is that one need know only a minimum of melodies, thus: all the hymns listed under a given number can be sung to one known melody. But where many melodies are known then one has the advantage of making a fine choice and all the others can be sung.[3]

This index of melodies assisted the smaller, rural congregations that sang without organ accompaniment, being led by the single voice of the cantor. These congregations needed to know only sixty-three melodies to be able to sing every text in the Berlin hymnal, but if they knew only twenty tunes they would be still be able to sing a substantial portion of the hymns. By contrast, in town and city churches when there were organs and choirs, a much richer repertoire of chorale melodies was possible.

Hymnals linked to specific chorale books

A somewhat rare phenomenon in German text-only hymnals is when a direct connection is made to a specific published hymnal or *Choralbuch* as the primary source for associated melodies. Thus, the Meiningen *Gesangbuch* of 1683 cites Johann Crüger's *Praxis Pietatis Melica, Das ist: Übung der Gottseligkeit in Christlichen und trostreichen Gesangen*—the most widely known and used hymnal during the seventeenth and early eighteenth centuries—as the primary source for chorale melodies, in which they are given with simple figured basses. For example, "12. Mel. Crüger p. 158. Wie sol ich dich empfangen…,"[4] though it is not clear which of the different Berlin and Frankfurt editions of Crüger's *Praxis* is being cited. Another notable example is the hymnal edited by Johann Jacob Rambach: *Neu-eingerichtetes Hessen- Darmstädtisches Kirchen-Gesang-Buch* (Darmstadt: Fortner, 1733). In the preface Rambach draws attention to the "Darmstädtischen Choral-Buch" edited "with great diligence," by the Darmstadt capellmeister.[5] This is the chorale collection of Christoph Graupner (1683–1760), court capellmeister in Darmstadt

---

3 *Neues Vollständiges Gesang-Buch, Für die Königlich-Preußische, auch Churfürstlich-Brandenburgische und andere Lande … Siebente verbesserte Auflage* (Berlin: Kunst, 1757), sig. Xx5ʳ: "Melodeyen-Register Zum Unterricht, wie man ein Lied nach vielen Melodeyen singen könne, dienet folgendes: Alle diejenigen Lieder, die unter einer No. stehen, können alle nach einer Melodey gesungen werden. Z. E. Unter No. 1. heißt das erste Lied: *Ach ein Wort von grosser Treue*, etc. Nach dessen Melodey nun können alle in dieser No. nachstehende Lieder gesungen werden; deßgleichen kan man auch nach aller folgender Melodeyen solches erste Lied singen. Der Nutzen dieses Unterrichts ist für diejenigen, so wenig Melodeyen wissen, folgender: daß sie alle unter einer No. stehende Lieder nach der Weise singen können, die ihnen bekannt ist. Für diejenigen aber, denen viel Melodeyen bekannt sind, ist dieß der Vortheil: daß sie sich können die schönsten wählen, und alle andere Lieder darnach singen."
4 *Geistliches neu-vermehrtes Gesang-Buch* (Meiningen: Hassert, 1683), 12.
5 *Neu-eingerichtetes Hessen-Darmstädtisches Kirchen-Gesang-Buch* (Darmstadt: Fortner, 1733), sig.) 6ʳ.

206   *Hymnology*

between 1711 and 1754: *Neu vermehrtes Darmstädtisches Choral-Buch …*
zum Nutzen und Gebrauch vor Kirchen und Schulen hießiger Hoch-Fürstl.
Landen (Darmstadt: [s.n.], 1728). The melodies are given in isometric forms,
almost exclusively half-notes, with uncomplicated basses and minimal figures. Although Rambach does use the established custom of referring to the
associated melody, such as "Mel. Christus der uns selig macht" (No. 89), or
"In voriger Melodey" (to the previous melody) (No. 56), a significant number
are given with page numbers in Graupner's *Choral-Buch*, usually in the
form: "Darmst. Choral-Buch p. 6." (No. 159).

Encoded keys

An interesting phenomenon that has not received the attention it deserves
is the use of letter codes to indicate starting and ending notes, thereby
establishing both pitch and mode (or key) of the melody to be sung with
a specific text. The earliest I have discovered thus far[6] is the hymnal edited
by Christian Demelius (1644–1711), cantor in Nordhausen: *Schrifftmässiges*
Gesangbuch/ zu nützlichem Gebrauch Evangelischer Christen/ absonderlich
der Kirchen-Gemeinden in Nordhausen … (Nordhausen: [Demelius], 1687).
By 1699 it had reached its fifth edition, with at least a further seven editions
appearing by 1737, and the *Gesangbuch* was still in print in 1777.[7] Following
the Vorrede, issued by the Nordhausen clergy, dated Michaelmas Day 1687,
there is a brief explanation of the letter codes:

> *Information concerning the melodies and their collation.*
>
> First, on the left next to the roman numeral before the hymn [text] there is
> a capital letter, which informs the learned singer on which note the hymn
> should begin. The letter at the end of the hymn informs the organist of
> the concluding bass.[8]

---

6 Research for this article has meant the examination of many hundreds of Gesangbücher, both
   print and digital. The results, however, can only be representative rather than exhaustive, given
   the sheer magnitude of hymnal editions and imprints and the incomplete nature of holdings
   of libraries and special collections. The *Gesangbuchbibliographie* at the Johannes Gutenberg
   Universität Mainz is extremely useful, but the letter codes discussed here are not among its
   database categories. <www.gesangbucharchiv.uni-mainz.de/104.php>
7 See Werner Braun, "Christian Demelius und der 'Schrifftmässige' Gesang in Nordhausen um
   1700," *Pietismus und Liedkultur*, ed. Wolfgang Miersemann and Gudrun Busch (Halle: Verlag
   der Franckeschen Stiftungen, 2002), 159–79.
8 *Schrifftmässiges Gesangbuch/ zu nützlichem Gebrauch Evangelischer Christen/ absonderlich*
   der Kirchen-Gemeinden in Nordhausen … Zum fünfften mal … heraus gegeben
   (Nordhausen: [Demelius], 1699), Sig. (8 ᵛ: "Der Bericht Von den Melodeyen und derselben
   Vergleichung. Erstlich stehet vor dem lied neben der Römerzahl zur lincken ein einzeler
   lateinischer Buchstabe/ der deutet dem gelehrten Sänger an/ in welchem ton das lied anzufangen
   ist. Der buchstabe nach dem Lied weiset dem Organisten das *Bass final.*")

Most of the hymn texts are assigned two capital letters, as in the following example:

D. XIV. Luc 2. D. M. L.[9]
Vom himmel hoch da komm ich her/
Ich bring euch gute neue mähr/ der
guten mähr bring ich so viel/ davon
ich singen und sagen will ...

15. Lob/ ehr sey Gott in höchsten
thron/ der uns schenckt seinen eingen
Sohn/ des freuet sich der Engel schaar/
und singen uns solch neues Jahr. C.[10]

Thus, the melody of *Vom Himmel hoch*, like other melodies, is assigned two letters, the former of importance to "the learned singer," that is, the cantor, and the latter to the organist. But in this case one would have expected that if the first note was D then the last would also be D, since the melody ends exactly an octave lower than its first note. It may be a simple error, since many other examples in the *Gesangbuch* give the same note at the beginning as at the end. However, organs were customarily tuned to Chorton, approximately a step higher than Kammerton. Thus, in this case the discrepancy might be explained by Chorton C equalling Kammerton D.

Rietschel interpreted the two letters found in Demelius's *Schrifftmässiges Gesangbuch* to mean that the singing was *a capella* unison throughout, and that the organ only played a postlude after the singing.[11] Silberborth argued that the starting pitch was meant for village congregations where there were no organs, and the concluding pitch was for town churches that had organs and where the singing was accompanied.[12] But neither viewpoint is convincing without corroborating evidence.

Demelius's use of letters to designate beginning and ending pitches of chorale melodies appears to be a development of the Latin formula *in fine videbitur, cuius toni*—"at the end it will be seen which Tone [it is]." Towards the end of the fifteenth century Adam von Fulda quoted it as an established saying in his treatise *De musica*[13]; it was also known to Luther[14]; and it was still sufficiently well-known in the later eighteenth century to be cited in popular

---

9 D. M. L. = Doctor Martin Luther.

10 *Schrifftmässiges Gesangbuch* (1699), 17–19.

11 See Georg Rietschel, *Die Aufgabe der Orgel im Gottesdienste bis in das 18. Jahrhundert* (Leipzig: Dürr, 1893), 64.

12 See Hans Silberborth, *Geschichte des Nordhäuser Gymnasiums* (Nordhausen: Wimmer, [1923]), 15.

13 Martin Gerbert, *Scriptores ecclesiastici de musica sacra potissimum* (St. Blaise: Typis San Blasius, 1784; reprint Hildesheim: Olms, 1963), 3: 355.

14 WA TR No. 76 (1531).

208 *Hymnology*

literature.[15] The saying provides the key to establishing the tone/mode of a Gregorian chant, that is, by going to the end of the *Gloria Patri*, where the vowels from *seculorum amen* (*euouae*) appear with the notation of the particular ending, from which the specific tone/mode can be established.[16] Here Demelius applies the concept to establishing the mode or key of respective chorale melodies as well as providing their starting pitch.

The *Eisenachisches Neu-revitirt und beständiges Gesang-Buch*, first published in 1725 and still in print in 1776, follows the Nordhausen model by giving letter codes at the beginning and end of each hymn text.[17] In 1725 this was perhaps considered an innovation, since the latest imprint of the previous edition of a local hymnal—*Der fröliche Dienst ... Oder Geist-reiches Gesangbuch ... zum 3 mahl herausgegeben* (Eisenach: Boetius, 1723)—does not observe the practice.

Other hymnals modify the Nordhausen model by arranging the starting and ending pitches together at the head of the respective text, rather than one at the beginning and the other at the end. One example is the *Hällisches Neu-eingerichtetes Gesang-Buch/ Voll Alter und Neuer Vor andern Geistreicher Lieder ... heraus gegeben Von einem Sämmtlichen Ministerio der Stadt Halle* (Halle: Schütze, 1711).[18] In its list of the features of this particular collection of hymns it notes that "identification of well-known melodies is given above the hymn texts," and that it also records "The *tonus initialis* and *finalis*, good information for those who understand music."[19] Thus the heading of the first hymn text appears thus:

> G. *Tonus initialis*. 1. G. *Tonus finalis*.
> In bekandter Melodey.
> Allein Gott in der höh sey ehr, Und ...[20]

But thereafter only the letters, without the explanation, are given:

---

15 For example, Jakob Michael Reinhold Lenz, *Der Hofmeister oder Vortheile der Privaterziehung: Eine Komödie* (Leipzig: Weigand, 1774), 79.

16 See further, Robin A. Leaver, *Luther's Liturgical Music: Principles and Implications* (Minneapolis: Fortress, 2017), 34–35.

17 *Eisenachisches Neu-revitirt und beständiges Gesang-Buch ... Achte Auflage* (Eisenach: Kruge, 1753) was examined.

18 This hymnal was the product of the Halle clergy Ministerium and is not to be confused with the *Geistreiches Gesang-Buch*, edited by Johann Anastasius Freylinghasuen, first published by the Halle orphanage in 1704, a hymnal that included music.

19 *Eines Sämmtlichen Stadt-Ministerii zu Halle Neu eingerichtetes Und mit einem Anhang vermehrtes Gesang-Buch/ Voll Alter und Neuer Vor andern Geistreicher Lieder ...* (Halle: Schütze, 1715), 28: "5. Eine Darstellung lauter bekannter Melodien über denen Liedern. 6. Der *Tonus initialis* und *finalis*, denen Music-Verständigen zu guter Nachricht."

20 Ibid., 29.

Bach and the Schemelli letter codes 209

D.   2.   G.
Mel. Nun dancket alle Gott.
Dreyeinig höchster Gott! Gott, der du nie ...[21]

The *Neu-vermehrtes Ratzeburgisches Gesang-Buch* (Ratzeburg: Hartz, 1715)[22] is similar, except that explanation of the letter codes is given in German at the head of the first hymn:

B. (Anfangs-Ton.)   B. (Schluß-Ton).
1. Wach auf, mein hertz, und singe/...[23]

The *Neuvermehrtes und verbessertes Gesang-Buch*, first issued in Eisleben in 1720 and in print at least until 1738, similarly adopts the same letter codes at the beginning of each hymn text but has no explanation of their meaning.[24]

The *Sondershäusisches Gesang-Buch*, first published in 1692 and issued in eleven editions by 1726, also adopts letter codes for beginning and ending pitches of the chorale melodies. They appear one after the other, before the identity of the melody is given, with the beginning pitch given in lower case and the ending in upper case. However, in a number of cases alternative pitches are suggested. Examples:

Christus, der uns selig macht	e.C. [oder] d.B.	No.62[25]
Nun komm, der Heiden Heiland	g.G. oder a.A.	No.2
O Mensch, bewein dein Sünde groß	c.C. od[er]. d.D.	No.61
O wir armen Sünder	a.D. [oder] d.G.	No.58
Von Gott will ich nicht lassen	g.G. oder a.A.	No.90

Following the eleventh edition of the *Sondershäusisches Gesang-Buch* (1726), the next hymnal—*Vollständiges Neu aufgelegtes und vermehrtes Evangelisches Gesang-Buch* ... (Sondershausen: Bock, 1730)—discontinued the practice.

The *Wittenbergisches Gesang-Buch* of 1733 also adopts a lowercase-uppercase coding at the beginning of each hymn text but instead of a second uppercase letter registering the final pitch it identifies the key, major or minor,

---

21 Ibid., 30.
22 It reached an 8th edition by 1752, as well as being the basis for later editions. The earlier *Vollständiges Gesang-Buch* (Ratzeburg: Hoffmann, 1704) included the identification of respective chorale melodies but without reference to starting or ending letter codes.
23 *Neu-vermehrtes Ratzeburgisches Gesang-Buch ... bey nahe 900. Gesänge. ... Die dritte ... Auflage* (Ratzeburg: Hartz, 1725), 1. Thereafter, like the Nordhausen model, the letter codes appear without explanation at the head of each hymn.
24 *Neuvermehrtes und verbessertes Gesang-Buch* (Eisleben: Hüllmann, 1724) was examined.
25 Numbers are those of *Sondershäusisches Gesang-Buch ... zum Eilfftenmal nach fleißiger Revision gedruckt* (Sondershausen: Bock, 1726).

210 *Hymnology*

rather than suggesting mode, which seems to imply that organ accompaniment was normative. Examples:

e.	M[el]. Ach! Du edler Gast	E. moll.	No. 1
g.	In eigner Melodie [Auf, auf mein Herz]	G. dur	No. 2
g.	In eigner Melodie [Herr Jesu Christ, dich zu uns]	Gd.	No. 3
h.[= b]	Mel. Liebster Jesu, wir sind hier	Gd.	No. 4
h.[= b]	In eigner Melodie [Liebster Jesu, wir sind hier]	Gd.	No. 5
a.	M[el]. Jesu, meine Freude	Dm.	No. 6[26]

This 1733 edition is the latest in a succession of editions of the Wittenberg *Gesangbuch* and includes the prefaces of four successive Wittenberg general superintendents: Abraham Calov (1612–1686), Caspar Löscher (1636–1718), Gottlieb Wernsdorf (1668–1729), and Johann Georg Abicht (1672–1740). Wernsdorf's preface, dated November 1719, reveals that the practice of including letter codes with major-minor tonality indications had been introduced in the 1719 edition of the *Gesangbuch*. Wernsdorf also indicates that this was devised by the Director of Music and Cantor of the Stadtkirche, Johannes Gottfried Thomae (fl. 1715–1730), and was unique to the Wittenberg *Gesangbuch* of 1719.[27]

Two contemporary pioneering Lutheran hymnologists produced sequences of local hymnal editions utilizing letter codes for pitch and key, which, since each was aware of the other's hymnological publications, suggests some kind of connection: Johann Christoph Olearius (1668–1747), deacon and later superintendent in Arnstadt, and Johann Martin Schamelius (1668–1742), pastor primarius in Naumburg.

Olearius produced a new hymnal for Arnstadt at the beginning of the eighteenth century (the Vorrede is dated 8 December 1700): *Neu-Verbessertes Arnstädtisches Gesangbuch … Vorrede … Joh. Christoph. Olearius* (Arnstadt: Bachmann, 1701). It was reissued in 1703 and a slightly revised imprint was published in 1705—which was presumably the edition Bach worked with when he was organist of the Neue Kirche in Arnstadt between 1703 and 1707[28]—and further issues appeared retaining the letter codes at least until 1726 or perhaps a little later. These Arnstadt hymnals use a single-letter code, ranged left at the head of nearly every hymn text, rather than the two-letter codes of earlier hymnals. The reason might be that since the *tonus initialis* and *tonus finalis* were frequently identical in earlier hymnals that employed

---

26 Numbers are those of *Wittenbergisches Gesang-Buch … Privilegio und ordentlicher Theologischer Censur* (Wittenberg: Zimmermann 1733). After the first two numbers "moll" is given as "m." and "dur" as "d."

27 *Wittenbergisches Gesang-Buch* (1733), sig.)()(3ᵛ: "Samt Beschaffenheit des *Toni,* ob er dur, oder *mol* sey … gesetzet, welches wohl auf solche Art in keinem Gesang-Buche wird gefunden werden."

28 For the background, see Chapter 6.

letter codes, there was only the need to include one letter code, which could serve both for the cantor, leading unaccompanied singing, and the organist leading accompanied singing. But it could also signify the transition of the shift away from designating the starting pitch of a modal melody to indicating the key of the melody to be sung, since they appear to cover common keys, such as C, D, F, G, A, though major and minor are not identified as they are in the later Wittenberg hymnals.[29] Congregational singing appears to have been supported by organ accompaniment in Arnstadt, to judge from the complaints from the congregation relating to Bach's harmonic adventures during the hymn singing,[30] and the few examples that have been preserved of his organ chorale accompaniments dating from an early period.[31]

Naumburgisches Gesang-Buch, bestehend Aus denen Alten Lutherischen Kern- und Kirchen- wie auch den bekantesten Neuen Liedern ... Vorrede ... Joh. Martinus Schamelius (Naumburg: Boßögel, 1712–1714)[32] went through a number of editions, notably the fourth edition of 1720, entitled *Naumburgisches glossirtes Gesangbuch nebst einer kurzgefaßten Geschichte der Hymnopoeorum*, which set new standards of hymnological content. Like the Arnstadt hymnals, these Naumburg hymnals utilize the single-letter code that was still being used in the 1735 edition.[33]

Bach, Schemelli, and codes

A number of misleading assumptions have been made with regard to the *Musikalisches Gesang-Buch* of 1736, usually referred to as the Schemelli *Gesangbuch*, and of Bach's involvement in the project. For example, it is assumed that because it was published in Leipzig it was intended for use there. As the title page makes clear, it was compiled for Naumburg-Zeitz, edited by the Naumburg-Zeitz cantor, with a preface by the Naumburg-Zeitz superintendent:

> Musical Hymn Book, wherein 954[34] spiritual songs and arias, old as well as new, with well-set melodies, in soprano and bass are to be found. Specially dedicated to the Evangelical [Lutheran] congregations of the

---

29 See, for example, *Arnstädtisches Verbessertes Gesangbuch ... Vorrede ... Joh. Christoph. Olearius* (Arnstadt: Bachmann, 1705), 1, 2, 4, 5, etc.

30 See BDok 2: 20 (No. 16); NBR, 46 (No. 20); dated 21 February 1706.

31 See, for example, *Allein Gott in der Höh sei Ehr* (BWV 715), *Herr Jesu Christ dich zu uns wend* (BWV 726), and *In dulci jubilo* (BWV 729).

32 See Andreas Lindner, *Leben im Spannungsfeld von Orthodoxie, Pietismus und Frühaufklarung: Johann Martin Schamelius, Oberpfarrer in Naumburg* (Gießen: Brunnen, 1998), 216–53.

33 *Neuvermehrtes und wohleingerichtetes Naumburgisches Gesang-Buch*, 6th ed. (Naumburg: Boßögel, 1735). For the background, see Johann Christian Stemler, *Historie und Führung des Lebens Johann Martin Schamelii* (Leipzig: Lanckisch, 1743), 84–91.

34 In the Leipzig *Oster messkatalog* for 1736 Breitkopf gave the number of hymns and arias as 950; see BDok 2: 266 (No. 378).

212   Hymnology

diocese of Naumburg-Zeitz and with a foreword by the Most Reverend Herr Friedrich Schulz, Preacher at the Castle [and] Superintendent ... edited by Georg Christian Schemelli, cantor at the castle [Schloß] in that place ... Leipzig 1736. Published by Bernhard Christoph Breitkopf, Bookprinter.[35]

Bach had significant connections with Zeitz. His second wife, Anna Magdalena Wilcke (1701–1760), whom he married in 1721, was born there, youngest daughter of Johann Caspar Wilcke (ca. 1662–1731), Zeitz court trumpeter until 1718. Georg Christian Schemelli (ca. 1676–1762), Zeitz Cantor from 1727, sent his son, Christian Friedrich Schemelli (1713–1761), to study with Bach in Leipzig between 1731 and 1734. The Leipzig superintendent and professor of theology, Salomon Deyling (1677–1755), was also Zeitz Domherr (canon) between 1713 and 1745.

During the Reformation the Catholic diocese of Naumburg, in which Zeitz is situated, was secularized by the dukes of Saxony and administered from the Naumburg Schloß. Following disputes among the dukes, the area became a second-geniture possession in 1657, under Moritz of Saxe-Zeitz (1619–1681), who spent the next twenty years building his baroque Schloß in Zeitz as his official residence. Therefore, both Naumburg and Naumburg-Zeitz had claims to prominence in the territory of Saxe-Zeitz. This is reflected in the ecclesiastical life of the two towns: both had superintendent ministers, and both produced their own hymnals. The sequence of eighteenth-century Naumburg hymnals, referred to above, is paralleled by similar hymnals published in Zeitz, such as *Das Gott lobende Zion; Oder Zeitzisches- Kirchen-Schul- und Haus- Gesang-Buch, zur Übung der Gottseligkeit ...* (Zeitz: Hucho, 1729), which was the third edition, with further editions issued in 1734 and 1736 (none with letter codes). Thus, even though Naumburg and Naumburg-Zeitz had recently published hymnals (the former in 1735 and the latter in 1734 and 1736), the Schemelli *Gesangbuch* was offered to all the churches of ducal Saxe-Zeitz. Thus, in the mid-1730s these churches had no less than three possible hymnals to choose from, which is probably a primary reason why the *Musikalisches Gesang-Buch* of Schemelli and Bach never appeared in the possible second expanded edition referred to in its preface.[36]

Another assumption is that Bach's involvement with the project was confined to the sixty-nine melodies he edited with figured bass, the corollary assumption being that Bach made a significant shift away from traditional chorale melodies. While it is true that none of the published melodies are the older traditional chorale tunes, the title page nevertheless states that the hymnal contains old and new hymns (texts and tunes). That only newer melodies were included in the hymnal suggests that at a fairly late stage in the production of the hymnal a decision was made to exclude the more

---

35 NBR, 170 (No.178).
36 See the discussion in Chapter 9.

Bach and the Schemelli letter codes   213

familiar melodies. The paragraph at the end of the preface explaining this gives the impression of being a late addition, since it is separated from the main text with a row of asterisks. The sixty-nine melodies are representative of the more recent freer style of melody, epitomized in Freylinghausen's *Geistreiches Gesangbuch* published in Halle between 1704 and 1714, indeed, some of the melodies for which Bach supplied figured basses first appeared in the Freylinghausen hymnal (see Table 9.2). They are by nature more "Arien" rather than "Lieder," the two terms that occur on the Schemelli title page. This has led some to regard the *Musicalisches Gesangbuch* as evidence that in the 1730s Bach was moving away from the traditional chorale. Some of the sixty-nine melodies, however, were offered as alternatives to older chorales, not as substitutes but as alternatives for melodies that were over-used with many different texts. Thus, *Lasset uns mit Jesu ziehen* (BWV 481) was an alternative to *Lasset uns den Herren preisen* (Zahn 7886b), and *Mein Jesu was vor Seelenweh* (BWV 487) an alternative to the over-used *Wie schön leuchtet der Morgenstern* (Zahn 8359).

Bach's involvement in the Schemelli *Gesangbuch* did not end with the provision of the sixty-nine figured-bass melodies. Following the example of the hymnals reviewed earlier in this chapter, Bach carefully edited the older and more familiar melodies so that many of the texts are not only given the first line of the intended melody—and sometimes an alternate melody—to which the text can be sung, but many also have an uppercase letter ranged to the left of the hymn number. Thus, hymn 185, *Dieß ist der Nacht*, is assigned the melody *Wer nur den lieben Gott läßt walten* and has the letter "D" placed before the hymn number, which might indicate D-hypodorian or d minor – probably the latter, given the nature of the melodies included in the *Gesangbuch*. The popular melody *Wer nur den lieben Gott läßt walten* (Zahn 2778) is assigned to no less than fifty-six texts in the Schemelli *Gesangbuch*; not all are assigned keys, but those that do have either "D" or "G" (two have both).[37] Thus, throughout the Schemelli *Gesangbuch*, a complete range of keys are thus designated by C, D, E, F, Fis (=F♯), G, B (=B♭), H (= B). As with *Wer nur den lieben Gott läßt walten*, when a melody is associated with more than one text it is often assigned to different keys. Thus, the melody *Ach Gott, wie manches Herzeleid* at No. 155 (Zahn 533) is designated in F, but in G at No. 773. When the melody *Es ist das Heil uns kommen her* (Zahn 4430) is sung with its associated text at No. 113, it is to be in G; but at No. 244 in F; at No. 384 in C; and at No. 433 in B (=B♭).[38] The use of these letter codes implies the practice of improvised accompaniments. Since Bach was the musical editor

---

37 Schemelli *Gesangbuch*, Nos. 14, 25, 26, 43, 56, 83(D.G), 85, 114, 166(D&G), 185(D), 300, 402, 482, 483, 492, 510, 511, 512(G), 513, 517, 528, 529, 530, 547, 559, 566, 586(G), 591, 603, 607, 651, 653, 655, 658, 659, 662, 663, 708, 714(D), 715(G), 718, 719, 728, 729(D), 730, 735, 738, 762, 763, 774, 784(G), 797, 822, 823, 864, 886(G).

38 The melodies for which Bach supplied figured basses are treated in a similar manner; for example, *Ermuntre dich, mein schwacher Geist* (BWV 454), is assigned to no less than nine different texts: Schemelli *Gesangbuch*, Nos. 10, 129, 187, 201, 233, 349(F), 448(H), 450(H), 485.

214　*Hymnology*

of the Schemelli *Gesangbuch*, these letter codes must, therefore, represent his careful choices.

Even though the Schemelli *Gesangbuch* was published by Breitkopf in Leipzig, the use of letter codes was not a practice followed in Leipzig hymnals. Earlier eighteenth-century unofficial Leipzig hymnals, one way or another based on Vopelius's *Neu Leipziger Gesangbuch* (1682), do not include them, and when the Saturday preacher in the Thomaskirche and Vesper preacher at the Nikolaikirche, Carl Gottlob Hofmann, edited the official hymnal, *Das privilegirte Vollständige und vermehrte Leipziger Gesangbuch* (Leipzig: Barnbeck, 1734), no letter codes were included. Similarly, when Hofmann moved to Wittenberg, as professor and general-superintendent, he re-edited the Wittenberg hymnal in 1742 and letter codes that had appeared in earlier Wittenberg editions were excluded.[39] However, Bach was well-aware of letter-codes, as they were included in the hymnal he used in his first professional employment as organist in Arnstadt. It is also possible that he was aware of the use of letter codes in the 1735 edition of the Naumburg *Gesangbuch*, published in the period when the Schemelli *Gesangbuch* was being prepared.

Although the evidence for text-only hymnals with letter codes at this stage can only be regarded as representative rather than exhaustive,[40] a number of tentative conclusions can be drawn.

First, the proportion of hymnals with letter codes appears to be relatively small. In most of the hymnals examined such codes are absent.

Second, chronologically such editions appear to date from the last decades of the seventeenth century and decline in usage from around the middle of the eighteenth century. The following list is based on the apparent first editions of hymnals with letter codes: Nordhausen, 1687; Sondershausen, 1692; Arnstadt, 1701; Arnstadt, 1711; Halle, 1711; Naumburg, 1712; Ratzeburg, 1715; Wittenberg, 1719; Eisleben, 1720; Eisenach, 1725; and Naumburg-Zeitz, 1736.

Third, geographically such hymnals were published in a relatively small area. With one exception—Ratzeburg in Schleswig-Holstein—all the other places of publication can be enclosed within a circle of an approximately 45-mile radius, centered on Erfurt. Thus, letter codes appear to be essentially a Thuringian phenomenon.

Fourth, a development can be detected in which the codes shift from establishing pitches and modes to conveying keys, which differ according to the content of the hymn texts to which they are assigned.

Fifth, Bach was made aware of letter codes early in his career in Arnstadt and was apparently one of the last editors to employ them in a hymnal: in the Schemelli *Gesangbuch* of 1736, where his use of such codes is perhaps the most sophisticated of all.

39　*Das Wittenbergische Kirchen-Gesang-Buch* (Wittenberg: Zimmermann, 1742).
40　See note 6 above.

Coda

Bach's contribution to hymnody, especially in the Schemelli *Gesangbuch*, was recognized in 1742 on the death of Johann Martin Schamelius, Naumburg superintendent and noted hymnologist. A memorial poem, presumably read as part of Schamelius's funeral rites, was published as *Die Verdienste der Lieder-Dichter und Erklärer* (Naumburg: Boßögel, 1742).[41] The purpose of the poem was to honor the eminence of Schamelius as a hymnologist, so the Naumburg poet presents an overview of the history of hymnody, beginning with biblical singers—Moses, Miriam, Barak, David, Mary, and Zachariah—then continuing with primary Lutheran hymn writers of the sixteenth and seventeenth centuries. The poet then moves on to later generations and presents names in groups of threes—three composers of chorale melodies and three poets of chorale texts, though the author found that there was a fourth name that could not be omitted from the group of poets. The unknown poet then turns to a number of leading hymnologists, especially Schamelius. Significantly, Bach is mentioned as the first of the three composers:

> Des Luthers Glaub und Gerhards[42] Geist,
> Bachs, Hermanns[43] und der Franken[44] Triebe
> erwecken das was christlich heist,
> und zeugen Hoffnung, Glaub und Liebe.
> Neumeisters,[45] Schmolkens,[46] Brokes[47] Gluht,
> in der Andacht Stärke ruht,
> verewiget durch Rambachs[48] Feuer,
> und lenkt der Neuern Harfen-Spiel[49]

41 The only recorded copy of the four-page leaflet was in the Herzogin Anna Amalia Bibliothek, Weimar, shelf-mark 32, 1: 69 [item 63], but appears to have been destroyed in the library fire of 2004. Fortunately, a substantial proportion of the poem is cited in Lindner, *Leben im Spannungsfeld von Orthodoxie, Pietismus und Frühaufklärung*.

42 Paul Gerhardt (1607–1676), widely regarded as the hymn-writer second only to Luther.

43 Nikolaus Hermann (ca. 1480–1561), Joachimsthal Cantor, hymn-writer, and composer.

44 There are a number of Francks who might be intended, but the most likely would seem to be Melchior Franck (ca. 1579–1639), Coburg court Capellmeister.

45 Erdmann Neumeister (1671–1756), Hamburg pastor, poet, and cantata librettist.

46 Benjamin Schmolck (1672–1737), pastor and prolific author of devotional poetry and hymnody.

47 Presumably Barthold Heinrich Brockes (1680–1747), Hamburg poet, especially known for his Passion oratorio libretto *Der für die Sünde der Welt gemarterte und sterbende Jesus* (1712), set to music by Keiser (1712), Telemann (1716), Handel (1716), Mattheson (1718), Fasch (1723), Stölzel (1725), as well as partially by Bach in 1724.

48 Johann Jakob Rambach (1693–1735), theologian, poet, and cantata librettist.

49 Contemporary hymnody seen as the continuation of Biblical psalmody

216 *Hymnology*

auf das von Gott bestimmte Ziel
und macht ihr Dichten werth und theuer.[50]

Luther's faith and Gerhardt's spirit,
Bach's, Hermann's and Franck's inspiration
awaken Christian ardor,
and summon hope, faith and love.
Neumeister's, Schmolck's and Brockes's warmth
in the strong calm of devotion,
immortalized in Rambach's fire,
and expressed in the new playing of the harp
according to God's appointed design
is what makes their poetry worthy and valued.

"Bach" can only be Johann Sebastian, whose figured-bass melodies had been published for Naumburg-Zeitz six years earlier in the *Musikalisches Gesang-Buch*. His name appears here in this poem among a most select company, and it is a measure of how well his Schemelli settings had been received, especially in Naumburg and Naumburg-Zeitz. His reputation as a superlative recitalist on harpsichord and organ had frequently been reported in newspapers published in such cities as Dresden, Hamburg, Kassel, and Leipzig, and similar periodicals had applauded his concerted music composed in honor of the Saxon royal family in Dresden. His biography had been published in Johann Gottfried Walther's *Musicalisches Lexicon* (Leipzig, 1732), and Johann Mattheson had drawn attention to the intricacies of his compositions in his *Grosse General-Baß-Schule* (Hamburg, 1731), *Kern melodischer Wissenschaft* (Hamburg, 1737), and *Der vollkommene Capellmeister* (Hamburg, 1739). Similarly, those who had worked with Bach in Leipzig wrote glowingly of his gifts, both as a composer and performer, including Lorenz Christoph Mizler in his *Musikalische Bibliothek* (Leipzig, 1738), Johann Matthias Gesner in his edition of Quintillian's *De Institutione Oratoria* (Göttingen, 1738),[51] and Johann Christoph Gottsched in his *Beyträge zur critischen Historie der deutschen Sprache, Poesie und Beredsamkeit* (Leipzig, 1740). Here, in this poem of 1742, written to memorialize the deceased Naumburg superintendent, is apparently the earliest reference to Bach's distinctive contribution to German hymnody.

---

50 Cited in Lindner, *Leben im Spannungsfeld von Orthodoxie, Pietismus und Frühaufklarung*, 308. The following stroph of the poem begins with a reference to "Olears," that is, Johann Christoph Olearius with whom Bach had worked in Arnstadt.
51 See further, Chapter 12.

Part III
Theology

11 Bach and Pietism

The subject matter is controversial: controversial regarding Bach; controversial concerning Pietism; and controversial with respect to Bach's relationship to Pietism as presented in Bach studies. The basic problem is that there is much misperception of what Pietism was and much misunderstanding of Bach's relation to Pietism. The literature on Pietism is confusing in that different and conflicting opinions are propounded concerning the nature of the movement and its relation to Lutheran Orthodoxy. Similarly, there are conflicting accounts in the Bach literature on the relationship of the Thomascantor to Pietism. This chapter sets out: to review some of the presuppositions regarding both Pietism and Bach's relation to it; to examine basic features of the Pietist movement of the seventeenth and eighteenth centuries; to investigate contemporary representative personalities on both sides of the divide; and to reexamine relevant aspects of Bach's career and compositions.

Some views of Bach and Pietism

The subject of Bach and Pietism has generated a significant literature.[1] In his book, *Church Music and Theology*, originally published in 1959, Erik Routley wrote about Bach and his music, including a section on "Bach and Pietism." Twenty years later the book was substantially revised and reissued as *Church Music and the Christian Faith*,[2] but the paragraphs about Bach and Pietism remained virtually unchanged. Routley first summarized his understanding of Pietism:

> In modern terms [Pietism] adds up to a fundamentalist outlook, a layman's religious movement, a contempt for the academic and cerebral

---

1 Representative German writers include: Martin Petzoldt, "Zwischen Orthodoxie, Pietismus und Aufklärung: Überlegungen zum theologiegeschichtlichen Kontext Johann Sebastian Bachs," in: *Johann Sebastian Bach und die Aufklärung* (Leipzig: Breitkopf & Härtel, 1982), 66–108; and Martin Geck, "Bach und der Pietismus," in his *"Denn alles findet bei Bach statt": Erforschtes und Erfahrenes* (Stuttgart: Metzler, 2000), 88–108.
2 Erik Routley, *Church Music and the Christian Faith* (Carol Stream: Agapé, 1978), 54–58.

220   *Theology*

aspects of Christian practice, a stress on interdenominationalism, a preference for prayer over instruction, and a system of conversion.[3]

He then expressed the following judgment regarding Bach and Pietism:

It is helpful in understanding Bach's religious background to note that he was, to all intents and purposes, moving among and faithful to groups of loyal Inter-Varsity Christian Fellowship adherents; for that is exactly what, in its day, pietism was.[4]

Routley saw Bach in terms of the conservative Christian affiliations, evident on many campuses of higher education, that promote informal meetings for Bible study and prayer and exist beyond the boundaries of denominational Christianity. For his evidence of Bach's Pietism Routley looked to the libretti of the vocal works, especially the cantatas and Passions, and came to the astonishing—demonstrably untrue—conclusion that they were "innocent of any rejoicing in the resurrection."[5] He states further that "pietism reserves all its expository energies for the passion, all its theological attention for the atonement, and all its sense of liturgical drama for this one occasion." He concluded, that "we must ascribe to this religious culture everything distinctive about the Bach Passions." Several paragraphs further on he made the categorical statement: "Bach's Passions are entirely unliturgical," and this was to be explained by the fact that "pietism was unliturgical."[6] For Routley, Bach was a Pietist, little interested in the outward forms of liturgical worship, one who was much more concerned with inward religion, which he expressed in his music with consummate skill and artistry.

Jaroslav Pelikan, the distinguished Yale theologian, in his book *Bach Among the Theologians*, wrote a fairly substantial chapter entitled: "Pietism, Piety, and Devotion in Bach's Cantatas."[7] Like Routley's, Pelikan's analysis of Pietism dealt primarily with the hallmarks of the spirituality of the movement. One of these was the awareness of sin as "Angst" (anxiety), in contrast to Luther's "Anfechtung" (temptation). This anxiety over sin represented a theological shift from an understanding of sin as a state of being to a preoccupation with sins as acts of volition. Pietism is viewed in many respects as a new kind of Puritanism. Pelikan quoted the "Rules for the Protection of Conscience and for Good Order in Conversation or in Society," written by August Hermann Francke in 1689:

---

3 Ibid., 54–55.
4 Ibid., 55.
5 Ibid.
6 Ibid., 56–57.
7 Jaroslav Pelikan, *Bach Among the Theologians* (Philadelphia: Fortress Press, 1986), 56–71.

Games and other pastimes such as dancing, jumping, and so forth, arise from an improper and empty manner of life, and common and unchaste postures in speech are associated with them.[8]

Another hallmark perceived by Pelikan was

the way Pietism came to interpret the relation of the soul to Jesus [which] entailed a shift of emphasis from objective to subjective, from the idea of "Christ *for* us," which had predominated in orthodox interpretations both before and after the Reformation, to a primary interest in "Christ *in* us," which had never been absent from orthodoxy but which had been pronouncedly subordinated to the primary concern with the objectivity of the Gospel history and of the redemptive transaction on the historic cross.[9]

Before continuing with Pelikan's exposition, it should be noted that here is an example of the difficulty in coming to terms with the issue, because when the viewpoints of Routley and Pelikan are compared, one is found to insist that the emphasis on the Passion was the hallmark of Pietism, while the other is equally persistent in stressing that the Passion was central to Lutheran Orthodoxy. Pelikan examined the cantatas of Bach and found that "Angst" was a common theme, as was the emphasis on "Christ in us," especially in the frequent use of the Bride–Bridegroom imagery that occurs from time to time in the cantatas. For Pelikan these were illustrations of the position he adopted earlier in his chapter, where, though carefully avoiding calling Bach a Pietist, he states the following:

All the attempts by Orthodox Lutheran confessionalists, in his time or in ours, to lay claim to Bach as a member of their theological party will shatter on the texts of the cantatas and the *Passions*, many (though by no means all) of which are permeated by the spirit of Pietism. Above all, the recitatives and arias ... ring all the changes and sound all the themes of eighteenth-century Pietism: all the intense subjectivity, the moral earnestness, and the rococo metaphors of Pietist homiletics, devotion, and verse.[10]

Despite their differences, Routley and Pelikan were agreed on the basic presupposition that Pietism was essentially a movement for renewed spirituality,

---

8 *Pietists: Selected Writings*, ed. Peter C. Erb (New York: Paulist Press, 1983), 111; cited in Pelikan, *Bach Among the Theologians*, 61. Gustav Kramer, *August Hermann Francke: Ein Lebensbild* (Halle: Waisenhauses, 1880–1882), 1: 271: "XXX Regeln zur des Gewissens und guter Ordnung in der Conversation oder Gesellschaft."

9 Pelikan, *Bach Among the Theologians*, 64–65.

10 Ibid., 57.

222   *Theology*

that the intrinsic characteristics of Pietist devotion were to be found in the cantatas and Passions of Bach, and that, therefore, Bach must have been a Pietist. But it is not only Bach who is interpreted in this way. A similar reasoning is applied to other baroque composers. For example, Martin Geck portrays Buxtehude as a Pietist, largely on the basis of the spirituality expressed in his libretti.[11] But the question is: Do such analyses really expose the heart of Pietism and, therefore, do they provide the adequate background to explain the true nature of Bach's relationship with this movement?

Lutheran Pietism

Pietism is a problematic term to use without qualification because so many different things can be denoted by it.[12] It is frequently used today as a general term for any kind of subjective spirituality. When it is used in an historical context it is usually employed to designate the widespread movement of subjective piety that extended throughout Europe from the seventeenth century onwards, the movement that has its roots in Reformed theology but which developed in parallel, though in different ways, in various denominations such as Anglican, Presbyterian, Moravian, Lutheran, Methodist, and so forth, as well also within Roman Catholicism.[13] But in relation to Bach, the term needs to be used in a much more restricted and nuanced way. Pietism in this context denotes the specific movement within the German Lutheran churches that began around 1675, created a controversial division within Lutheranism—especially during the first two decades of the eighteenth century—later became accepted into German society, and by the middle of the nineteenth

11 Martin Geck, *Die Vokalmusik Dietrich Buxtehudes und die frühe Pietismus* (Kassel: Bärenreiter, 1965); see the critique of Geck's interpretation, Kerala J. Snyder, *Dieterich Buxtehude: Organist in Lübeck*, 2nd ed., (Rochester: University of Rochester Press, 2007), 146–49.

12 Pietism in general was extraordinarily diverse, involving different countries, language groups, and denominational affiliations. German Pietism as it relates to Bach is specific with regard to time, place, and confession. This volume follows the convention that when the general European movement is intended the term "pietism" is employed, in contrast to the specific German Lutheran manifestation, which is designated "Pietism."

13 English studies include: Douglas H. Shantz, *An Introduction to German Pietism: Protestant Renewal at the Dawn of Modern Europe* (Baltimore: Johns Hopkins University Press, 2013), see especially Shantz's review of the different ways Pietism is understood and promoted, ibid., 1–11; Douglas H. Shantz, ed., *A Companion to German Pietism, 1660–1800* (Leiden: Brill, 2015); F. Ernest Stoeffler, *The Rise of Evangelical Pietism* (Leiden: Brill, 1965); F. Ernest Stoeffler, *German Pietism during the Eighteenth Century* (Leiden: Brill, 1973). German studies include: Martin Schmidt, et al., eds., *Geschichte des Pietismus* (Göttingen: Vandenhoeck & Ruprecht, 1993–2004), especially volume 1, *Der Pietismus vom siebzehnten bis zum frühen achtzehnten Jahrhundert*, ed. Martin Brecht (Göttingen: Vandenhoeck & Ruprecht, 1993); *Der Pietismus im achtzehnten Jahrhundert*, ed. Martin Brecht and Klaus Deppermann (Göttingen: Vandenhoeck & Ruprecht, 1995); and the articles that have appeared in the yearbook, *Pietismus und Neuzeit: Ein Jahrbuch zur Geschichte des neueren Protestantismus* (Göttingen: Vandenhoeck & Ruprecht, 1974–), especially those of Johannes Wallmann.

Bach and Pietism 223

century emerged as a dominant, mainstream force in Prussian nationalism.[14] Hence the significant number of studies of pietism published around the mid-nineteenth century, whose authors were as much involved with their own contemporary issues as they were with those of earlier generations, whose history they were attempting to chart.[15]

What is not always made clear is that in the early seventeenth century, long before the specific Pietist movement, there was a particularly creative period of Lutheran theological literature that included both personal and subjective devotional handbooks as well as erudite objective works of dogmatic theology; indeed, some of the authors wrote both types of books. Yet the claim has frequently been made, especially by later Pietists, that the preaching and teaching of the clergy at this time was universally intellectually dry, lifeless, and spiritually moribund, and thus needed the revival that the Pietists eventually brought.[16] The most influential book to come from this period was Johann Arndt's *Wahres Christentum* (True Christianity), in six books, initially published between 1605 and 1609, and continuously reprinted and translated over the following centuries, a book that was to be found in Bach's personal library.[17] Arndt's meditations were inspired by the medieval mysticism of a number of authors, such as Bernard of Clairvaux and Johannes Tauler.[18] Another influential writer of devotional literature in the early seventeenth century was Johann Gerhard, who wrote the small-scale *Meditationes sacrae ad veram pietatem excitandam*, first published in 1606, with many later reprints and translations. Gerhard followed it with his more extensive work, *Schola Pietatis* (School of Piety), published in five books between 1622 and 1623, a

---

14 See, for example, *Der Pietismus im neunzehnten und zwanzigsten Jahrhundert*, ed. Ulrich Gäbler (Göttingen: Vandenhoeck & Ruprecht, 2000); Richard L. Gawthrop, *Pietism and the Making of Eighteenth-Century Prussia* (Cambridge: Cambridge University Press, 1993); Koppel S. Pinson, *Pietism as a Factor in the Rise of German Nationalism* (New York: Columbia University, 1934).

15 See, for example, Heinrich Schmid, *Die Geschichte des Pietismus* (Nordlingen: Beck, 1863), translated as *History of Pietism*, trans. James L. Langebartels (Milwaukee: Northwestern, 2007); August Tholuck, *Geschichte des Rationalismus, Erste Abtheilung: Geschichte der Pietismus und des ersten Stadiums der Aufklärung* (Berlin: Wiegandt und Grieben, 1865; reprint, Aalen: Scientia-Verlag, 1970); Albrecht Ritschl, *Geschichte des Pietismus* (Bonn: Marcus, 1880–1886; reprint, Berlin: de Gruyter, 1966).

16 A Leipzig professor of theology, writing in the mid-nineteenth century, noted that Pietists, especially August Hermann Francke, "manifested a rather strong feeling of overbearing superiority to Orthodoxy"; Karl Friedrich August Kahnis, *Internal History of German Protestantism since the Middle of Last Century*, trans. Theodore Meyer (Edinburgh: Clark, 1856), 102.

17 See Robin A. Leaver, *Bachs theologische Bibliothek: Ein kritische Bibliographie* (Stuttgart: Hänssler, 1983), No. 51; see the abbreviated translation, Johann Arndt, *True Christianity*, trans. and ed., Peter Erb (New York: Paulist Press, 1979).

18 Bach owned a copy of the sermons of Tauler; Leaver, *Bachs theologische Bibliothek*, No. 9, see also No. 51f.

224 *Theology*

work that in many ways parallels Arndt's *Wahres Christentum*.[19] Between 1610 and 1625 Gerhard produced his magisterial *Loci theologici*, in nine volumes, one of the most significant expositions of Lutheran dogmatics.[20] Thus, the two types of literature, on the one hand, heart-warming devotion, and on the other, intellectually challenging theology, were not antithetically opposed, as has been frequently asserted, but were rather two sides of the same coin.

Seventeenth-century Germany was devastated by the privations of the Thirty Years' War (1618–1648) that ruined much of the countryside and decimated the population. As is common in such times when the externals of life are collapsing, the natural response is to turn inward to find consolation and spiritual strength. Such comfort was supplied by the spiritual writings current at the beginning of the war, such as those of Gerhard and especially the *Wahres Christentum* of Arndt. To these were added the consolation of newly written sensitive hymns reflecting the times, by such poets as Johann Heermann, Martin Rinckart, Johann Rist, and especially Paul Gerhardt,[21] together with new devotional literature written by other authors, notably the books by Heinrich Müller, who wrote in the immediate aftermath of the war.[22] But this is where the whole terminology of pietism becomes difficult to unravel. If you are looking at the general European development of pietism, of which these authors were definitely a part, then it is important that they should be considered within this larger pietist movement. But if you are dealing with the specific phenomenon of Lutheran Pietism itself, it is misleading to categorize these authors as generally "Pietist," since the particular Pietist movement within Lutheranism is a later seventeenth-century development that had not yet come into being. Yet the term "Pietist" is frequently applied to them, or such cognate terms as "Pre-Pietists," "Proto-Pietists," or as representatives of "frühe-Pietismus" (early Pietism). The problem with such categorization is that it defines these earlier writers in terms of the later movement and implies that in the later Orthodox/Pietist divide within Lutheranism they are to be included among the Pietists rather than the Orthodox. But this is ana-chronistic since it reads back into an earlier time the later specific controversy that had not yet arisen.[23] These authors wrote as Orthodox Lutherans; they could not do otherwise, and simply to equate piety with Pietism obscures the

---

19 Bach owned a set of the five volumes of Gerhard's *Schola Pietatis*; Leaver, *Bachs theologische Bibliothek*, No. 45.

20 Johann Gerhard, *Locorum Theologicorum Cum Pro Adstruenda Veritate, Tum Pro Destruenda quorumvis contradicentium falsitate, per theses nervose, solide & copiose explicatorum Tomus …* (Jena: Steinmann, 1622–1625); Johann Gerhard, *Theological Commonplaces*, trans. Richard J. Dinda (St. Louis: Concordia, 2009–).

21 Rist and Gerhardt are discussed in Chapter 9.

22 Bach owned five different books by Heinrich Müller: *Apostolische Schluss-Kette, Evangelische Schluss-Kette, Evangelisches Praeservativ, Göttliche Liebes-Flamme*, and *Geistliche Erquickstunden*; Leaver, *Bachs theologische Bibliothek*, Nos. 8, 20, 19, 41, 42, respectively.

23 That is not to imply that there were no divisions among Lutheran pastors and theologians; they were a rather quarrelsome lot. Arndt was accused of heresy, though was strenuously

Bach and Pietism   225

significance of the long line of Lutheran devotional writings that existed ages before there was the specific Lutheran Pietist movement. The tradition began with Luther himself—such as in his use of the bride-bridegroom imagery in his treatise *On Christian Freedom* (1520)—which continued in the following generations, the *Erbauungsliteratur*, the devotional handbooks and sermons that are distinctive in Lutheranism in general.

Instead of cognates derived from "Pietist/Pietism" it would be more helpful to refer to this earlier literature in terms of Lutheran *mysticism*. In other words, instead of defining this earlier literature by what succeeded it, that is, Lutheran Pietism, it should rather be understood by what preceded it, that is, the *unio mystica* (the mystical union between the individual and Jesus), the reinterpretation of medieval mysticism. One of the earliest to draw attention to the importance of this insight with regard to such literature in relation to Bach studies was Wolfgang Herbst in his Erlangen dissertation,[24] a work that has not been given the attention it deserves. Arndt and his contemporaries drew heavily on the writings of Bernard of Clairvaux (11th century), Angela of Foligno (13th century), Johannes Tauler (14th century), and Thomas à Kempis (15th century).[25] Lutheran mysticism developed from these medieval writers, and its influence is traceable on both sides of the later Orthodox/Pietist divide. For example, the resultant *ordo salus* (order of salvation), as expounded by Arndt, remained constant throughout later Lutheranism, not only among Pietists but also among Orthodox dogmaticians, such as David Hollatz in his *Examen theologicum acroamaticum,* originally published in 1707 and still in print in the later eighteenth century.[26] Among those who have followed the lead of Herbst by exploring the *unio mystica* background to the

---

    supported by Johann Gerhard; and both Arndt and Heinrich Müller were critical of clergy who overstressed outward formality while neglecting spirituality; but this was a long way from the Orthodox/Pietism controversy that developed towards the end of the century; see Arndt/ Erb, *True Christianity*, 4–5; Timothy Schmeling, *Lives and Writings of the Great Fathers of the Lutheran Church* (St. Louis: Concordia, 2016), 305.

24 Wolfgang Herbst, "Johann Sebastian Bach und die lutherische Mystik" (PhD diss., Friedrich-Alexander-Universität Erlangen, 1958). The original title of the dissertation was: "Die Bedeutung der spätorthodoxen Lehre von der *unio mystica*: Ein Beitrag zur Frömmigkeitsgeschichte des beginnenden 18. Jahrhunderts."

25 For the detail of Arndt's medieval sources, see Edmund Weber, *Johann Arndts vier Bücher vom Wahren Christentum als Beitrag zur protestantischen Irenik des 17. Jahrhunderts: Eine quellenkritische Untersuchung*, 3rd ed. (Hildesheim: Gerstenberg, 1978); Johannes Wallmann, "Johann Arndt und die protestantische Frömmigkeit: Zur Rezeption der mittelalterlichen Mystik im Luthertum," in *Frömmigkeit in der frühen Neuzeit: Studien zur religiösen Literatur des 17. Jahrhunderts in Deutschland*, ed. Dieter Breuer (Amsterdam: Rodopi, 1984), 50–74; see also the introduction in Arndt/Erb, *True Christianity*, esp. 6–16.

26 See the comparative table in Arndt/Erb, *True Christianity*, 7–8, note 22. A new edition was edited by Romaus Teller—Bach's Beichtvater (Father-confessor) between 1738 and 1740— published in Leipzig in 1750; see Robin A. Leaver, ed., *The Routledge Research Companion to Johann Sebastian Bach* (New York: Routledge, 2017), 176–77.

226   *Theology*

music of Bach include Jörg Herchet and Jörg Milbradt, Walter Blankenburg, Elke Axmacher, and Markus Rathey.[27]

The beginning of specific Lutheran Pietism is usually seen in the new edition of Arndt's *Wahres Christentum* published in Frankfurt in 1675. It included a fairly lengthy new introduction written by the city's senior pastor, Philipp Jakob Spener, published separately the following year as *Pia Desideria* (Pious Desires).[28] Spener included a six-point agenda for spiritual renewal, which in many respects was similar to other calls for spiritual awakening that had been made in earlier generations. Of Spener's six-fold agenda the first proved to be the most radical and had an impact far wider than simply the intensification of spiritual life.[29] Spener began with the need for "a more extensive use of the Word of God [the Bible] among us."

> Although solitary reading of the Bible at home is in itself a splendid and praiseworthy thing, it does not accomplish enough for most people. It should therefore be considered whether the church would not be well advised to introduce the people to Scripture in still other ways than through the customary sermons on the appointed lessons.[30]

The criticism is, of course, directed at the annual cycle of Epistles and Gospels throughout the church year, which formed the basis of preaching and was a fundamental element of Lutheran worship.[31]

> In addition to our customary services with preaching, other assemblies would be held in the manner in which Paul describes them in I Corinthians 14:26–40. One person would not rise to preach (although

27 Jörg Herchet and Jörg Milbradt, "Bach als Mystiker," in *Bach als Ausleger der Bibel: theologische und musikwissenschaftliche Studien zum Werk Johann Sebastian Bachs*, ed. Martin Petzoldt (Berlin: Evangelische Verlags-Anstalt, 1985), 207–22; Walter Blankenburg, "Mystik in der Musik J. S. Bachs," in *Theologische Bach Studien 1: Beiträge zur theologischen Bachforschung*, ed. Walter Blankenburg and Renate Steiger (Stuttgart: Hänssler, 1987), 47–66; Elke Axmacher, "Mystik und Orthodoxie im Luthertum der Bachzeit?," in *Theologische Bachforschung heute: Dokumentation und Bibliographie der Internationalen Arbeitsgemeinschaft für Theologische Bachforschung, 1976–1996*, ed. Renate Steiger (Berlin: Galda & Wilch, 1998), 215–36; Markus Rathey, "Bach's Christmas Oratorio and the Mystical Theology of Bernard of Clairvaux," in Robin A. Leaver, ed., *Bach and the Counterpoint of Religion* (Urbana: University of Illinois Press, 2018), 84–103, esp. 89–94. See also the more broadly-based study, Isabella van Elferen, *Mystical Love in the German Baroque* (Lanham: Scarecrow, 2009).

28 Philipp Jakob Spener, *Pia Desideria: Oder Hertzliches Verlangen/ nach Gottgefalliger Besserung der wahren evangelischen Kirchen* (Pia Desideria: or Heartfelt Desire for a God-pleasing Reform of the True Evangelical Church) (Frankfurt: Zunner, 1676), *Pia Desideria*, trans. and ed., Theodore G. Tappert (Philadelphia: Fortress, 1964).

29 The six points, and their elaboration, form the third part of Spener's book; Spener/Tappert, *Pia Desideria*, 87–118.

30 Spener/Tappert, *Pia Desideria*, 88.

31 For the background, see Chapter 1.

Bach and Pietism 227

this practice would be continued at other times), but others who have been blessed with gifts and knowledge would also speak and present their pious opinions on the proposed subject ... [They then could] take up the Holy Scriptures, read aloud from them, and fraternally discuss each verse in order to discover its simple meaning and whatever may be useful for the edification of all.[32]

Again, this call for informal Bible studies was hardly a new idea; for example, Luther's Small Catechism (1529) calls for the head of the household to direct daily prayer and Bible reading, morning and evening, in the home. In later generations there were many publications of handbooks for such daily Bible readings and devotions. For example Salomon Glass, general superintendent in Gotha, compiled his *Christliches Haus-Kirch-Büchlein* in 1654, which, like Spener's six-point agenda, begins with the need to read and understand the Bible as the key to the spiritual health of the family and the individuals within it.[33] But whereas these exercises were kept within the family circle, Spener's informal gatherings, soon called *collegia pietatis* (schools of piety), were comprised of a variety of people who met in private homes, and, although Spener intended that they should come under ministerial supervision, as the movement became popular this became impractical.

At the beginning the *collegia pietatis* achieved broad acceptance as a movement of spiritual renewal in many places, including Leipzig from 1689.[34] But as time passed, it became clear that Pietism had implications that raised ecclesiological questions that went far beyond the renewal of spiritual life. The *collegia pietatis* that met for weekly Bible study and prayer in the pursuit of holiness of life, marked a modification of the doctrine of the church: they were *ecclesiola in ecclesia*, little churches in the Church, and this appeared to go much further than the definition in the Augsburg Confession (1530), that states (Article VII):

[The] one holy, Christian church ... is the assembly of all believers among whom the gospel is purely preached and the holy sacraments are administered according to the gospel.[35]

In other words, the Church is the visible community of faith at worship, within which the Word is read and expounded, and at which the sacraments

---

32 Spener/Tappert, *Pia Desideria*, 89.
33 Salmon Glass, *Christliches Haus-Kirch-Büchlein, Darinnen gelehret und gezeiget wird, Wie ein Christ nit allein für sich, in der Wissenschafft derer zur Seligkeit nohtwendigen Stück, sich gründe[n], und in der waaren Gottseligkeit üben, sondern auch die Seinen hierinn recht anführen und aufferziehen solle* (Nuremberg: Endter, 1654).
34 Tanya Kevorkian, *Baroque Piety: Religion, Society, and Music in Leipzig, 1650–1750* (Aldershot: Ashgate, 2007), 169–91.
35 BC-K/W, 42.

228 *Theology*

of Baptism and Eucharist are observed. In the following article (Art. VIII) there is the further clarification that within this visible community there may well be "false Christians, hypocrites, and even public sinners,"[36] but their presence within does not undermine the doctrine of the church, nor invalidate the efficacy of the sacraments.

The Pietists were not so sure. They argued that their call for holiness of life on the part of individual Christians was a means of purifying the corporate church. But this purification did not take place through the activity of liturgical worship Sunday by Sunday, but rather through the exercises of the *collegia pietatis*, the small informal groups that met for Bible study and prayer. Those who met in the *collegia pietatis* were those who had experienced the "new birth" of conversion and were thus "true Christians." It was but a small step in logic to conclude that if the *collegia pietatis* were made up of true Christians, then the *collegia pietatis* comprised the true church; and if they were the true church, then the outward manifestation of public worship within Lutheranism would be purified when the activities of the *collegia pietatis* were transferred into the local parish churches. Thus, the nature of the conflict between Orthodoxy and Pietism was not about spirituality, over which there was much agreement, but rather about two different approaches to the nature of the church, which came to a head after August Hermann Francke effectively became the leader of Pietism after he was appointed professor at Halle and pastor in Glaucha around the turn of the eighteenth century.

Francke argued that the Reformation of the sixteenth century had never been completed; it was good as far as it went, but there was more reforming to be done.[37] Indeed, this was the primary purpose of the wider pietist movement, as Douglas Shantz summarizes: "Pietism sought to bring reformation to the Reformation."[38] But for Orthodox Lutherans the Reformation of the sixteenth century had clearly defined what should be eliminated and what should be retained. Thus, the Augsburg Confession stated (Art. XV) that the holy days and festivals of the church year could be observed "without sin," and (Art. XXIV) "no noticeable changes have been made in the public celebration of the Mass ... For after all, all ceremonies should serve the purpose of teaching the people what they need to know about Christ."[39] The Pietists demurred and argued that such ceremonies, together with various practices associated with them, were still in need of reform. Their program of reformation was essentially a process of elimination. Eucharistic vestments and exorcism at Baptism they considered to be remnants of unreformed Catholicism and

---

36 Ibid.

37 *August Hermann Franckes Schrift über eine Reform des Erziehungs- und Bildungswesens als Ausgangspunkt einer geistlichen und sozialen Neuordnung der Evangelischen Kirche des 18. Jahrhunderts: der Grosse Aufsatz. Mit einer quellenkundlichen Einführung* (1704), ed. Otto Podczeck (Berlin: Akademie, 1962).

38 Shantz, *An Introduction to German Pietism*, 1.

39 BC-K/W, 48 and 68.

Bach and Pietism   229

should be discontinued. Similarly, the rigidity of the annual cycle of Epistles and Gospels of the church year should give way to a more thorough sequence of biblical readings. Most elaborate music in worship was considered to be worldly ostentation that should be replaced by simple, devotional hymnody, to be sung not to the "heavy" chorale melodies of Luther's generation, but to the lighter and more accessible tunes that the Pietists sang in their *collegia pietatis*.[40] These were the areas of conflict between the Pietists and the Orthodox, not differences in their piety, which was often indistinguishable from each other.

Some comparisons of Pietists and Orthodox

Christian Gerber (1660–1731)

Christian Gerber, author and chronicler of Saxon affairs, born and bred in Saxony, studied at the universities of Jena, Leipzig, and Wittenberg, and then, like his father, became a pastor, serving one or two parishes around Dresden before becoming the pastor of Lockwitz in 1690, where he served for the rest of his life, more than forty years.[41] He published sermons and other devotional works, as well as writing on various aspects of church and society in Saxony. He also wrote poetry, and one of his hymns entered into common use in that part of Germany: *Wohl dem, der Gott zum Freunde hat*, which first appeared in a Dresden hymnal of 1698, then in later Saxon hymnals, especially those published in Dresden and Leipzig, including the *Dreßdnische Gesang-Buch* (Dresden and Leipzg, 1724), and the so-called Schemelli *Gesangbuch* (Leipzig, 1736) for which Bach was the musical editor.[42] Bach was probably unaware that Gerber was its author, since at this time the hymn generally appeared anonymously in the hymnals,[43] but if he consulted recently published hymnological studies he would have discovered that Gerber had written this text.[44]

---

40 For the background, see Joyce Irwin, *Neither Voice nor Heart Alone: German Lutheran Theology of Music in the Age of the Baroque* (Bern: Lang, 1993);Tanya Kevorkian, "Pietists and Music" in Shantz, *A Companion to German Pietism, 1660–1800*, 171–200, esp. 171–86.

41 On Gerber, see: Johann Heinrich Zedler, ed., *Grosses vollständiges Universal-Lexicon aller Wissenschafften und Künste* (Halle & Leipzig: Zedler, 1732–1750), 10 (1735): cols. 1071–72; Eduard Emil Koch, *Geschichte des Kirchenlieds und Kirchengesangs der christlichen, insbesondere der deutschen evangelischen Kirche*, 3rd ed. (Stuttgart: Belser, 1866–1877), 4: 275–77; Friedrich Wilhelm Bautz, ed., *Biographisch-Bibliographisches Kirchenlexikon* (Hamm: Bautz, 1990-), 2 (1990): col. 212.

42 On the Schemelli *Gesangbuch*, see Chapters 9 and 10

43 See Albert Fischer, *Kirchenlieder-Lexicon* (Gotha: Perthes, 1878–1879; reprint, Hildesheim: Olms, 1967), 2: 407.

44 See Johannes Martinus Schamelius, *Des Evangelischen Lieder-Commentarii Anderer Theil: Darinnen Die neuern Lieder nebst beygefügten Anmerckungen ... enthalten* (Leipzig: Lanckisch, 1725), 194; Johann Caspar Wetzel, *Hymnopoeographia, oder historische Lebens-Beschreibung der berühmtesten Lieder-Dichter* [4] (Herrnstadt: Roth-Scholtz, 1728), 156.

230   *Theology*

A turning point came in Gerber's life in the years immediately before his appointment to Lockwitz when he made the acquaintance of Philipp Jacob Spener, the founder of Lutheran Pietism, then the *Oberhofprediger* in Dresden. From this time on Gerber's publications became strongly Pietistic in content. In sequence they include the following: *Der unerkannten Sünden der Welt: nach Gottes heiligem Wort* (The Unknown Sins of the World: According to God's Holy Word) (Dresden: Winckler, 1690–1706); *Die unerkannten Wohlthaten Gottes in dem Churfürstenthum Sachsen* ... (The Unknown Goodness of God in Electoral Saxony) (Dresden: Winckler, 1704–1711); *Historia derer Wiedergebohrnen in Sachsen* (History of the Re-born in Saxony) (Dresden: Winckler, 1726); and the posthumously published *Historie der Kirchen-Ceremonien in Sachsen* (History of Church Ceremonies in Saxony) (Dresden: Saueressig, 1732). His scholarship is not always secure, and it is difficult to decide whether the many mistakes in his citations of source materials are simply carelessness or whether they are cavalier attempts to massage the information.[45] Similarly, his personal anecdotal style and tendency for overstatement make one suspect the veracity of some of his claims. Nevertheless, many of his eyewitness accounts of church practices in Saxony are extremely valuable—indeed, some are the only sources for such information.[46]

This is particularly true of his *Historie der Kirchen-Ceremonien in Sachsen*, which is descriptive of all kinds of ecclesiastical observances in Saxony, with special reference to churches in Dresden and Leipzig. Throughout there is a clear pro-Pietist promotion of internalized spirituality, set against an anti-Orthodox stance that is dismissive of most external liturgical forms as being examples of worthless worldliness. Yet for all his criticisms of Lutheran Orthodoxy, especially liturgical practices, Gerber nevertheless had a great respect for the preaching of the churches in Leipzig. Leipzig at this time, while it did have pockets of Pietism among some of the leading laypeople, in its churches and university, was essentially a center of Orthodoxy. It was a lively Orthodoxy, illustrated by the fact that in the first two decades of the eighteenth century formerly disused churches were opened up for worship, and existing churches had new galleries built to accommodate the large numbers of people wishing to attend.[47] And, of course, it was in the principal churches of this city that Johann Sebastian Bach was later the director of music. Gerber writes about this time:

---

45 George J. Buelow charged him with "overzealous criticisms and ... faulty citations from the Bible and Luther"; "Gerber, Christian," NG2, 9: 685.

46 For example, the following studies make effective use of Gerber's writings: Charles Sanford Terry, *Joh. Seb. Bach Cantata Texts, Sacred and Secular: With a Reconstruction of the Leipzig Liturgy of His Period* (London: Constable, 1926; reprint, London: Holland, 1964); Günther Stiller, *Johann Sebastian Bach and Liturgical Life in Leipzig*, English trans. ed. Robin A. Leaver (St. Louis: Concordia, 1984); Joseph Herl, *Worship Wars in Early Lutheranism: Choir, Congregation, and Three Centuries of Conflict* (New York: Oxford University Press, 2004); and Kevorkian, *Baroque Piety*.

47 See Stiller, *Johann Sebastian Bach and Liturgical Life in Leipzig*, 39–48.

Bach and Pietism 231

In the world-renowned city of Leipzig there are very many sermons held on Sundays and feast days. In the morning in the St. Thomas and St. Nicholas churches there are two "Amts-Predigten"[48] ... At the same time sermons are also held in the great St. Paul's, St. Peter's, and the so-called New or Franciscan, churches. Then at midday the same is done for domestic servants, and also for many other people of similar standing, and at 2-o-clock follows the Vesper-sermon. We may surely call this the riches of divine goodness!: "The Lord gave the Word: great was the company of the preachers". [Psalm 68:11].[49]

Gerber was not only impressed by the preaching on Sundays and feast days in Leipzig, but also by the fact that sermons were to be heard on every day of the week in the churches of the city.

He is particularly blessed who lives in a city where public worship is held every day. In this respect the inhabitants of Dresden and Leipzig are fortunate, because in these two cities preaching and prayer services are held every day, so that they are enriched with all doctrine and all understanding and are not lacking in any [spiritual] gift. [1 Cor. 1:5–7]

And in the following sentences Gerber implies that Leipzigers were more fortunate than Dresdeners because they could attend Saturday Vesper preaching, an omission from the practice of the Dresden churches that Gerber hoped would soon be rectified.[50]

48 Gerber explains that this is the term for the eucharistic Hauptgottesdienst (Divine Service). "Predigten" (sermons) did not mean only what was delivered from the pulpit but rather the complete order of service at which a sermon would be preached.

49 Christian Gerber, *Historie der Kirchen-Ceremonien in Sachsen* (Dresden: Saueressig, 1732), 398–99: "In der Welt-berühmten Stadt Leipzig werden an Sonn- und Fest-Ta[ge] auch sehr viel Predigten gehalten: In der Thomas und Nicolai-Kirche sind des Morgens zween Amts-Predigten, die daher den Nahmen haben, weil die Communion dabey gehalten, diese aber aus Gewohnheit das Amt genennet wird. Zu gleicher Zeit wird aber auch in der grossen Pauliner-in der Peters- und in der so gennanten Neuen-weiland Barfüsser-Kirche Predigt gehalten. Zu Mittage geschiehet dergleichen vor das Gesinde, dabey aber gleichwol viel andere Leute von *Condition* erscheinen, und um 2. Uhr gehen wieder die Vesper-Predigten an. Das mag ja wol ein Reichthum der Göttlichen Güte heissen! Und hier giebt der Herr das Wort mit grossen Schaaren Evangelisten."

50 Gerber, *Historie der Kirchen-Ceremonien in Sachsen*, 355–56: "Der ist glückselig, der in einer Stadt wohnen kan, wo alle Tage Gottesdienst öffentlich gehalten wird. Und in diesem Stück sind die Einwohner in der Stadt Dreßden und Leipzig glückselig, als in welchen beyden Städten alle Tage Predigten und Bet-Stunden gehalten werden, daß sie also reich gemacht sind an aller Lehre, und in aller Erkänntniß, und keinen Mangel haben an irgend einer Gabe: Nur ist zu wünschen, daß auch die Predigt von Christo bey allen kräftig worden sey. In Dreßden zwar mangelt des Sonnabends eine Predigt, doch wird eine so genannte Vesper oder Bet-Stunde bey dem Beicht-Sitzen gehalten. Und möchte man sich wundern, da einige Jahre her von guten

232   *Theology*

For Gerber, preaching throughout the week was one thing; specific liturgical observances on weekdays was quite another. Many feasts of the church year were assigned to specific dates and therefore frequently occurred on weekdays. In the first paragraph of his chapter on minor feasts Gerber includes the following:

> [In Luther's] *Kirchen-Postille* we find many sermons for various feast-days that are no longer observed today, but have long since ceased, such as the Invention of the Cross, Exaltation of the Cross, Nativity of Mary, Assumption of Mary, &c., feast days that are still now today richly celebrated in the Roman Church. It is therefore to be wondered why the Festival of the Wise Men from the East, the Purification of Mary, St. John's Day, the Visitation of Mary, and St. Michael's Day have not been eliminated as well.[51]

Gerber's objections are twofold. On the one hand, he thinks that evangelical Lutherans should not be celebrating feast days invented under the Papacy.[52] On the other hand, such celebrations should be eliminated because of the frequent abuse of such holidays, when they are made into "days of drinking, dancing, and gaming," as Gerber says in his treatment of John the Baptist's Day.[53]

By suggesting the elimination of these observances Gerber is certain that he is correctly reflecting Luther's intentions, such as the following passage from the *Formula Missae* of 1523:

> We therefore first assert: It is not now nor ever has been our intention to abolish the liturgical service of God completely, but rather to purify the one that is now in use from the wretched accretions which corrupt it and to point out an evangelical use.[54]

When Gerber draws attention to the discontinuance of the celebration of the Invention of the Cross and the Exaltation of the Cross, he is at one with

---

Hertzen neue Predigten sind gestifftet worden, als am Char-Freytage eine Vesper-Predigt zum Gedächtniß der Begräbniß Christi, eine Mittags-Predigt und Catechismus-Examen, in der Frauen-Kirche."

51 Gerber, *Historie der Kirchen-Ceremonien in Sachsen*, 160: "Und in dieser Kirchen-Postill finden wir auch unterschiedliche Predigten auf etliche Fest-Tage, die doch heutiges Tages nicht mehr gehalten werden, sonder längst abgekommen sind, als Creutz-Erfindung, Creutz-Erhebung, Mariä Geburt, Mariä Himmelfahrt, &c. Wie man nun die Feste, die in der Römischen Kirche noch heutiges Tages hochfeyerlich begangen warden … So ist zuverwundern, warum nicht immer auch daß Fest der Waisen aus Morgenland, Mariä Reinigung, Johannis-Fest, Mariä Heimsuchung und *Michaelis*-Fest sind abgeschaffet worden… "

52 See also Gerber, *Historie der Kirchen-Ceremonien in Sachsen*, 156.

53 Gerber, *Historie der Kirchen-Ceremonien in Sachsen*, 155: "einen Sauff- Tanz- und Spiel-Tage." He makes a similar argument for the elimination of the Visitiation, ibid., 156.

54 LW, 53: 19.

Luther, who, again in the *Formula Missae*, declared categorically: "The feasts of the Holy Cross shall be anathema."[55] But Gerber is clearly out of step with Luther when he goes on to call for the abolition of other celebrations. In the same paragraph that Luther condemns the observances of the Holy Cross, he also states: "We regard the feasts of Purification, and Visitation as feasts of Christ, as also the Epiphany."[56] Here were three Christocentric feasts for Luther and Orthodox Lutherans, but three feasts that Gerber, together with other Lutheran Pietists, thought should be eliminated. However, these celebrations continued to be observed throughout Saxony, and in Leipzig over the years Bach produced some of his finest cantatas for these three celebrations.

For the Feast of the Epiphany (January 6) Bach composed three magnificent cantatas: Cantata 65, *Sie werden aus Saba alle kommen*, that begins with a glorious chorus in which the three gifts are depicted by three different wind instruments at three different pitches; Cantata 123, *Liebster Immanuel, Herzog der frommen*, a chorale cantata on the "Cross and Comfort" hymn by Ahasverus Fritsch, a fairly new hymn at the time, being first published in Leipzig in 1670; the sixth cantata of the Christmas Oratorio (BWV 248^{VI}), which is a musical exposition of the contrast between true and false faith, the faith of the wise men being contrasted with the falsity of Herod.

For the Purification (February 2) no less than seven Bach cantatas were associated with the celebration: Cantata 161, *Komm, du süße Todesstunden*; Cantata 83, *Erfreute Zeit im neuen Bunde*; Cantata 125, *Mit Fried und Freud ich fahr dahin*, a chorale cantata on Luther's German *Nunc dimittis*; Cantata 82, *Ich habe genung*, a particularly beautiful solo cantata that exists in several different versions[57]; Cantata 157, *Ich lasse dich nicht*; Cantata 200, *Bekennen will ich seinen Namen*; and Cantata 158, *Der Friede sei mit dir*.

For the Visitation (March 25) Bach composed two cantatas, each one stunning in its own way: Cantata 182, *Himmelskönig*; Cantata 1, *Wie schön leuchtet der Morgenstern*, a chorale cantata on Philipp Nicolai's familiar hymn.

The other two celebrations that Gerber believed should also be eliminated, that is, St John the Baptist's Day and St. Michael's Day, were also provided with some splendid music composed by Bach. For St. John the Baptist's Day (June 24), which Gerber states that, because of abuses, "it would be much better if this day was absolutely not celebrated,"[58] there are three fine cantatas by Bach: Cantata 167, *Ihr Menschen, rühmet Gottes Liebe*; Cantata 7, *Christ unser Herr zum Jordan kam*, a chorale cantata on Luther's catechism hymn on Baptism; and Cantata 30, *Freue dich, erlöste Schar*.

---

55 LW, 53: 22.

56 LW, 53: 22; slightly modified.

57 See the discussion in Chapter 5.

58 Gerber, *Historie der Kirchen-Ceremonien in Sachsen*, 155–56: "Wäre also in Ansehen solcher Leute viel besser, dieser Tag würde gar nicht gefeyert." See also note 53 above.

234 *Theology*

Gerber is particularly incensed by St. Michael's Day: "the current left over, the so-called St. Michael's Festival of whose dissolute, wretched and idolatrous origin in the Roman Church should long ago have been shamed."[59] Bach apparently did not agree, since he composed a series of significant cantatas for the celebration of the *Michaelis-Fest*: Cantata 130, *Herr Gott, dich loben alle wir*, a chorale cantata on Paul Eber's familiar hymn; Cantata 19, *Es erhub sich ein Streit*; Cantata 149, *Man singet mit Freuden vom Sieg*.[60] Somehow Gerber got it into his head that on St. Michael's Day the people were accustomed to worshiping angels, therefore the feast should be eliminated. What he apparently did not know is that in some parts of Saxony, especially in Leipzig, before the celebration of the Reformation festival on 31 October became an annual event, it was customary to celebrate the beginnings of the Reformation on St. Michael's Day each year. The struggle between Michael and the devil was seen as emblematic of Luther's struggle against the papacy, an interpretation that owed much to Bugenhagen's funeral sermon for Luther in which he identified Luther as the angel with an eternal gospel to proclaim in Revelation 14:6.[61] Gerber is apparently unaware of this, but if he did know about it, he would not have endorsed the kind of music that Bach composed for the celebration. Elsewhere, Gerber writes of the centenary of the Reformation in 1617, and he is very dismissive of the musical celebrations that took place:

> At the Reformation festival of 1617 a loud noise was made with instrumental music, drums and trumpets, pipes and strings, but such extravagance is approved and praised by no one except vain minds. Of course, church music should be conducted with moderation, only cantors for their part take great freedom so that their art is heard with every instrument, as only they can bring together; long and theatrical music, according to their own fancy and pleasure, that is better suited to an opera and comedy than to worship.[62]

---

59 Gerber, *Historie der Kirchen-Ceremonien in Sachsen*, 156–57: "Nun ist noch übrig, das sogenannte *Michaelis*-Fest dessen leiderlichen, elenden und abgöttischen Ursprungs sich die Römische Kirche längst hätte schämen sollen."

60 Cantata 50, *Nun ist das Heil und die Kraft*, has been regarded as a composition for St. Michael's Day. In Chapter 15 I argue that it was more likely composed for a Reformation festival.

61 On celebrations of the Reformation, see Chapter 15.

62 Gerber, *Historie der Kirchen-Ceremonien in Sachsen*, 225–26: "Daß bey dem Jubel-Fest 1617. ein grosser Lermen mit *Instrumental-Music*, Paucken und Trommeten, Pfeiffen und Geigen gemacht worden, kan wol seyn, solche Ubermaß aber wird von niemand, als nur von eiteln Gemüthern, gebilliget und gelobet. Es solte freylich mit der Kirchen-*Music* eine Maß gehalten werden: allein die *Cantores* nehmen ihnen zum Theil so große Freyheit hinaus, daß sie ihre Kunst hören zu lassen, mit allen *Instrumenten*, die sie nur zusammen bringen können, lange und *theatralische Musiquen* nach ihren Phantasien und Gefallen machen, die sich besser in eine *Opera* und *Comœdie* schickten, als zum Gottesdienst."

Bach and Pietism   235

This sounds very much like another passage in Gerber that for a long time was thought to be a comment on the first performance of a Bach Passion in Leipzig. However, Gerber says that it was the first time such Passion music was heard, but in Leipzig that was in 1721, three years before Bach's St. John Passion was performed. Also suspect is the fact that Gerber does not name the city in which the Passion was heard. To judge from his writing elsewhere, if it had been in either Leipzig or Dresden he would have said so. Indeed, the "large town" may not have been in Saxony, otherwise, again, he presumably would have named it. The fairly familiar passage runs:

> When in a large town ... Passion music was done for the first time, with twelve violins, many oboes, bassoons, and other instruments, many people were astonished and did not know what to make of it ... But when this theatrical music began, all these people were thrown into great bewilderment, looked at each other, and said, "What will become of this?" An old widow of the nobility said, "God save us, my children! It's just as if one were at an Opera Comedy."[63]

The references in these two passages to "theatrical," "opera," and "comedy" are coded language. In Pietist literature there is much condemnation of theatrical performances in general, and of opera and comedies in particular; those who attended them were regarded as unregenerate and worldly people. Thus, the clear message from these references is that such secular-sounding music should be kept out of the sanctuary. Apparently the abuses of the minor feasts that Gerber feared were in large measure attributable to the elaborate music with which they were celebrated.[64]

In many different places Gerber is very critical of concerted music in worship, and he appeals to a number of theologians in support of his contention. For example, his reference to words of the "famous Dannhauer," which are cited in both the original Latin and in German translation: "The best we can say for instrumental music is that it is a decorative element in our church, but in no way does it belong to the essence of worship."[65] Gerber's logic is that

---

63 NBR 327 (No. 324); Gerber, *Historie der Kirchen-Ceremonien in Sachsen*, 283–84: "Als in einer vornehmen Stadt diese Passions-*Music* mit 12. *Violin*en, vielen *Hautbois*, *Fagots* und andern Instrumenten mehr, zum erstenmal gemacht ward, erstaunten viel Leute darüber, und wusten nicht, was sie daraus machen sollen ... Als nun diese *theatral*ische *Music* angieng, so geriethen alle diese Personen in die gröste Verwunderung, sahen einander an und sagten: Was soll daraus werden? Eine alte adelische Wittwe sagte: Behüte Gott ihr Kinder! Ist es doch, als ob man in einer *Opera* oder Comödie wäre." For an alternative, and more extensive, translation from this section in Gerber, see Stiller, *Johann Sebastian Bach and Liturgical Life in Leipzig*, 264–65.

64 However, some Pietists did not object to cantatas, and some Orthodox resisted "theatrical" music; see the discussion in Chapter 5.

65 Gerber, *Historie der Kirchen-Ceremonien in Sachsen*, 282: "Der berühmte *Theologus*, Herr D. *Dannhauer* schreibet in seiner *Hodomorr. Spir. Calv. Ph.* 6, p. 1253. *Organicam musicam*

236 *Theology*

if such music is not essential it cannot be necessary, and therefore should be dispensed with.

Here, Gerber is consistent. In the first part of his earlier work *Der unerkannten Sünden der Welt*, published some forty years earlier in 1690, there is a chapter devoted to "The Abuse of Performed Music in Church":

> Look at the present-day manner of making music in our church, God help us, what a clamor and din that is! One hears organs, violins, trumpets, trombones, cornetti, and kettle drums, often all together, and at the same time several voices yelling now and then, and one chases the other, trying to outdo the other, striving to be heard with all diligence, artistry, and loveliness; but the listeners seldom understand a word of it, and the text is generally chopped up and mutilated that one cannot make any sense out of it, even if one can catch several words. Such music is considered quite splendid and is highly praised, but if a stranger were to attend who had not previously heard anything like it, he would think that people had lost their senses or that they wanted to prepare for battle.[66]

Gerber's opinions on church music in this earlier work were challenged point by point in print by Georg Motz, cantor of Tilsit in Prussia,[67] which seems to have influenced Gerber into moderating his language in his subsequent writings but not his basic objection to elaborate church music. For him only simple strophic hymns were needed in worship. Organs were to be tolerated because they kept congregational singing on pitch and, while chorale preludes were useful in this regard, they should certainly not be very long.[68]

For Gerber and many other Pietists, outward ceremonial and elaborate music in worship were seen as vestiges of Roman Catholic practice that should be done away with. For them, the Reformation of Luther was great as far as

---

altiori censu non habemus, quam ut sit ecclesiæ ornamentum, nec ipsam cultus divini substantiam intret. Die *Instrumental-Music* achten und halten wir nicht höher, als daß sie eine Zierde unserer Kirche sey, keinesweges aber zum Wesen des Gottesdienstes gehöre."

66 Christian Gerber, *Die unerkanten Sünden der Welt*, Vol. 1., "Das LXXXI. Capitel. Von dem Mißbrauch der KirchenMusic" (Dresden: Hekel 1690), 1065–66: "Da sehe man aber die heutige Art zu musiciren in unsern Kirchen an/ hilff Gott/ welch ein Geschrey und Gethön ist das! Da höret man Orgeln/ Geigen/ Trompeten/ Posaunen/ Zincken/ und Paucken offt alles zugleich/ und auf einmahl/ etliche Stimmen schreyen denn mit unter/ und jaget eines den andern/ es will es auch einer immer besser machen als der andere/ und trachten mit allem Fleiß/ Kunst und Lieblichkeit hören zu lassen/ es verstehen aber die Zuhörer selten ein Wort davon/ und wird auch gemeiniglich der Text so zuhacket und zerstümmelt/ daß man keinen Verstand draus nehmen kan/ ob man schon etliche Worte erschnappet. Eine solche Music wird denn für sehr herlich gehalten/ und hoch gelobet/ wenn aber ein Fremder dazu käme/ der dergleichen noch nie gehöret/ der würde dencken/ man sey unsinnig/ oder man wollte sich zum Streit rüsten." English trans., Herl, *Worship Wars*, 201.

67 See the discussion in Herl, *Worship Wars*, 120–22.

68 Gerber, *Historie der Kirchen-Ceremonien in Sachsen*, 279–81; see also Herl, *Worship Wars*, 134–35.

Bach and Pietism 237

it went but needed to be completed by sweeping away these continuing abuses. For Pietists like Gerber, contemporary Christianity was seen as totally antithetical to almost everything that had gone before it, and entirely new ways of worship and spirituality must be discovered, developed, and promoted, displacing the old.

Valentin Ernst Löscher (1673–1749)

Valentin Ernst Löscher, the son of a famous Wittenberg professor of theology, studied at the universities of Wittenberg and Jena and was ordained into the Lutheran ministry.[69] From 1696 he lectured at Wittenberg for two years, then served as superintendent, first at Jüterbog then at Delitzsch (1698–1707); he returned to Wittenberg as professor of theology for two years (1707–1709) and then became the pastor of the Kreuzkirche and superintendent in Dresden, where he remained for the rest of his life. Löscher was a prolific author, publishing devotional works, sermons, compilations of Reformation documents, and so forth, but above all in founding, editing, and substantially writing the first German theological journal: *Unschuldige Nachrichten von alten und neuen theologischen Sachen* (Innocent Reports of Old and New Theological Subjects), first published in Leipzig in 1701. The journal continued in print, under slightly different titles until 1761.[70] It was issued every month or so and included older and newer theological writings. The older material included excerpts from previously published books, which by that time had become inaccessible by their rarity, or of manuscripts that had not been previously published. The newer material was mostly in the form of reviews of recently published theological literature, though it also included commentary on current theological events and trends. The most pressing issue during the early years was the disturbing effect that the Pietist movement was having throughout Lutheran Germany, and it became a primary focus of Löscher's contributions to the journal. Part of the reason for the changing title of the journal was because Löscher was effectively banned

---

69 On Löscher, see: Zedler, ed., *Grosses vollständiges Universal Lexicon* 18 (1738): cols. 174–92; August Tholuck, *Der Geist der lutherischen Theologen Wittenbergs im Verlaufe des 17. Jahrhunderts* (Hamburg: Perthes, 1852), 297–308; Moritz von Engelhardt, *Valentin Ernst Löscher nach seinem Leben und Wirken: Ein geschichtlicher Beitrag zu den Streitfragen über Orthodoxie, Pietismus und Union*, 2nd ed. (Stuttgart: Liesching, 1856); Koch, *Geschichte des Kirchenlieds und Kirchengesangs* 5: 388–401; Martin Greschat, *Zwischen Tradition und neuem Anfang: Valentin Ernst Löscher und der Ausgang der lutherischen Orthodoxie* (Witten: Luther Verlag, 1971); Bautz, ed., *Biographisch-Bibliographisches Kirchenlexikon*, 5 (1993): cols. 175–77.

70 *Altes und Neues aus dem Schatz theologischer Wissenschaften* (Leipzig: Gross, 1701); *Unschuldige Nachrichten von alten und neuen theologischen Sachen* (Leipzig: Braun, 1702–1719); *Fortgesetzte Sammlung von alten und neuen theologischen Sachen* (Leipzig: Braun, 1720–1750); *Neue Beiträge von alten und neuen theologischen Sachen* (Leipzig: Braun, 1751–1761).

238   *Theology*

from editing it for around ten years from 1719, the direct consequence of his anti-Pietist stance.[71]

From the beginning, the *Unschuldigen Nachrichten* included the responses of Orthodoxy to the aims, objective, claims, and counterclaims of Pietism, Löscher being the primary author. During 1711 Löscher began a more systematic critique of Pietism in the journal, writing under the pseudonym of "Timotheus Verinus" (True Timothy). This led in turn to a continuous point-by-point refutation by Joachim Lange (1670–1744), Pietist pastor in Berlin.[72] These responses appeared in Lange's journal, *Auffrichtige Nachricht* (Honest News), specifically created to oppose Löscher's *Unschuldige Nachrichten*.[73] The charges and countercharges continued in the two journals over the years, and then between 1718 and 1721 Löscher reedited and expanded his contributions to *Unschuldige Nachrichten* into a two-volume definitive Orthodox answer to Pietism (as defined by Lange) under the title *Vollständiger Timotheus Verinus* (Complete True Timothy).[74]

In these volumes Löscher gives a blow-by-blow account of Lange's depiction of Pietism and his attacks on Orthodoxy. Lange often resorted to sharp invective and *ad hominem* attacks, whereas Löscher by contrast was in large measure irenic and conciliatory on many matters. For Lange the Orthodox were unregenerate and therefore at fault on every issue. For Löscher the Pietists, even though they were exposing what he saw as dangerous developments within Lutheranism, were not always to be considered in the wrong.[75] On the one hand, he was careful to discover points of agreement with Spener, and on the other hand, he criticized Orthodox theologians for being totally negative in their treatment of Pietism. Löscher's position is succinctly summarized by his biographer, Moriz von Engelhardt: "Until now, the [Orthodox] leaders

---

71 The ban was almost certainly engineered by the Oberhofprediger in Dresden, Bernhard Walther Marperger (1682–1746), who strongly favored Pietism; see Zedler, ed., *Grosses vollständiges Universal-Lexicon* 19 (1739): cols. 1651–58.

72 Lange was a fierce critic of Orthodoxy and effectively excommunicated himself from the Lutheran church and its sacraments; see Martin Kühnel, ed., *Joachim Lange (1670–1744), der "Hällische Feind," oder, Ein anderes Gesicht der Aufklärung: Ausgewählte Texte und Dokumente zum Streit über Freiheit-Determinismus* (Halle: Hallescher Verlag, 1996).

73 *Auffrichtige Nachricht von der Unrichtigkeit der so genanten unschuldigen Nachrichten* (Leipzig: Heinichen, 1707–1714).

74 D. *Valentin Ernst Löschers ... Vollständiger Timotheus Verinus, oder, Darlegung der Wahrheit und des Friedens in denen bisherigen pietistischen Streitigkeiten nebst christlicher Erklärung und abgenöthigter Schutz-Schrifft ...* (Wittenberg: Hannauer, 1718–1721); Valentin Ernst Löscher, *The Complete Timotheus Verinus, or a Statement of the Truth and Call for Peace in the Present Pietistic Controversy . . . ,* trans. James L. Langebartels and Robert J. Koester (Milwaukee: Northwestern, 1998).

75 Representative literature discussing the Löscher/Lange debate includes: August Tholuck, *Der Geist der lutherischen Theologen Wittenbergs im Verlaufe des 17. Jahrhunderts: theilweise nach handschriftlichen Quellen* (Hamburg: Perthes, 1852), 297–308; Hans-Martin Rotermund, *Orthodoxie und Pietismus: Valentin Ernst Löschers "Timotheus Verinus" in der Auseinandersetzung mit der Schule August Hermann Franckes* (Berlin: Evangelische Verlagsanstalt, 1959); Stoeffler, *German Pietism*, 63–71.

Bach and Pietism   239

forgot the Church or the Communion of Saints in their concern for pure doctrine; now the Church is forgotten [by the Pietists] in their zeal for Christian life."[76]

Neither piety itself, nor its intensity, were the real issues that separated the Pietists and the Orthodox. Löscher explained that Pietists were not the only ones who promoted piety:

> Piety is necessary for the comprehensive fullness of true religion as a necessary result of it. Piety is necessary, not for salvation, but for those who want to be saved, who strive for salvation, as a part of the divine order. Piety is necessary for true Christianity as its fruit and life. Piety is absolutely necessary for the active Christian life, or, much more, it is the active Christian life itself. Piety is not necessary for the means of grace, but very necessary for the one who wants to use the means of grace according to God's order without harm to his soul, or danger to his life.[77]

Thus, expressions of piety by both Pietists and Orthodox are often indistinguishable. Consider the following two examples.

Johann Jacob Rambach (1693–1735)

Johan Jacob Rambach emerged from the Halle Pietism of August Hermann Francke, and on Francke's death in 1727, succeeded him as professor and leader of the movement.[78] However, he did not stay long in Halle; it seems that other Pietists at the university were either jealous of him, or, perhaps, thought that some of his views were suspect. In 1731 he therefore accepted the invitation of Landgrave Ernst Ludwig of Hessen to become superintendent and first professor of theology in Giessen, and some years later became professor of theology in Göttingen.

Rambach wrote many collections of sermons and devotional books that circulated beyond Pietist circles. Bach owned three of his volumes,[79] one of them almost certainly Rambach's *Betrachtungen über das gantze Leiden Christi* (Jena: Hartung, 1730). It must have been a book that the Bach household treasured, since in 1741 Bach's wife, Anna Magdelena, gave to a friend a copy of the second edition of this sequence of devotions on the Passion.[80] Rambach was also a poet, wrote a good many hymns, and published collections

---

76 Engelhardt, *Valentin Ernst Löscher*, 25: "Bisher hatten die Führer der Kirche über der reinen Lehre die Kirche oder die Gemeinschaft der Gläubigen vergessen; jetzt vergaßen sie der Kirche in ihrem Eifer für christliches Leben."

77 Löscher, *The Complete Timothy Verinus*, 1: 251.

78 Koch, *Geschichte des Kirchenlieds und Kirchengesangs* 4: 521–35.

79 Leaver, *Bachs theologische Bibliothek*, Nos. 26, 27, 40.

80 See Hans-Joachim Schulze, "Anna Magdalena Bachs 'Herzens Freündin.' Neues über die Beziehungen zwischen den Familien Bach und Böse, BJ, 83 (1997): 151–53.

240   *Theology*

of verse.[81] Some of his hymns express the concerns of Pietism, such as *Mein Schöpfer, steh mir bei,* but others, such as *Ich bin getauft auf deinen Namen,* were acceptable to Orthodox sensibilities.

Rambach, however, was apparently not like Christian Gerber and other Pietists who disliked what they termed the "theatricality" of concerted music within worship. He worked closely with the Hessen *Kapellmeister,* Christoph Graupner (who had been a student with Telemann in Leipzig), in compiling the *Neu-eingerichtetes Hessen-Darmstädtisches Kirchen-Gesang-Buch* of 1733.[82] At least two of Rambach's collections of poetry include cantata libretti; indeed, the first part of his *Geistliche Poesien* (Halle, 1720) comprised a complete cycle of seventy-two libretti for all the Sundays and festivals of the church year.[83] These texts were written for Johann Gotthilf Ziegler (1688–1747), organist and director of music at the Ulrichskirche, Halle (from 1718), who composed a complete cycle of cantatas of these Rambach texts. Significantly, Ziegler was a pupil of Bach, having studied with him in Weimar around 1715. Bach must have known the cantata libretti by Rambach, and maybe even at one time owned a copy of Rambach's *Geistliche Poesien,* because the text of his Cantata 25, *Es ist nichts Gesundes an meinem Leibe,* composed for the fourteenth Sunday after Trinity, 1723, is a reworking of Rambach's libretto written for the same Sunday.[84] Pietist he may have been, but Rambach was respected and appreciated by many non-Pietists, and among Pietists he did not toe the line in opposing concerted music in worship.

Erdmann Neumeister (1671–1756)

Erdmann Neumeister, pastor, theologian, author, and poet of strong Orthodox views, was in large measure the architect of the so-called "reform" cantata that Bach exploited with consummate skill.[85] Because of the warm devotional style of his hymn texts and the intimate nature of his cantata libretti, Neumeister is frequently referred to as a Pietist. But nothing could be further from the truth. He certainly knew of Pietism firsthand. When he was a student at Leipzig university late in the seventeenth century, he was deeply impressed by August Hermann Francke, who was conducting informal Pietist gatherings among

---

81 Koch, *Geschichte des Kirchenlieds und Kirchengesangs* 4: 521–35.

82 *Neu-eingerichtetes Hessen-Darmstädtisches Kirchen-Gesang-Buch ... von D. Joh. Jacob Rambach* (Darmstadt: Forter, 1733), fol.)(6ʳ.

83 Johann Jacob Rambach, *Geistliche Poesien: Davon Der erste Theil Zwey und siebenzig Cantaten über alle Sonn- und Fest-Tags-Evangelia; Der ander Theil Einige erbauliche Madrigale, Sonnette und geistliche Lieder in sich fasset* (Halle: Neue Buchhandlung, 1720; later editions: 1734, 1735, 1753.

84 The two texts are given in parallel in Martin Petzoldt, *Bach-Kommentar: theologisch-musikwissenschaftliche Kommentierung der geistlichen Vokalwerke Johann Sebastian Bachs* (Kassel: Bärenreiter, 2004–), 1: 388–93.

85 Koch, *Geschichte des Kirchenlieds und Kirchengesangs* 5: 371–81. On Bach and Neumeister, see Chapter 13.

Bach and Pietism 241

students in the city at that time. But when Francke suggested that the Lutheran church was defective because it had not gone far enough in its Reformation— implying that sanctification was more important than justification, that corporate church practice was secondary to individual lifestyle, and so forth—it was then that Neumeister became an ardent adversary of Pietism; indeed, he has been called "the last Orthodox opponent of Pietism."[86] He did not object to its piety but fiercely rejected its theological implications and ecclesiology. He wrote a whole sequence of anti-Pietist pamphlets and booklets, sometimes under his own name and at other times pseudonymously. They include: *Idea Pietismi, Oder Kurtzer Entwurff Von der Pietisten Ursprung, Lehr und Glauben: Durch ein Send-Schreiben in gebundener Rede gezeiget / von Orthodoxophilo* [i.e., Erdmann Neumeister] (Fictional imprint: "Lichtenberg/ d. 12 Mart. Anno 1712"; 2nd ed. Frankfurt: [s.n.], 1714; 3rd "verbesserte" ed. ca. 1720); *Kurtzer Auszug Spenerischer Irrthümer, welche in den Articuln von der heiligen Schrifft ... von Christo ... der erkänntnis der Wahrheit zur Gottseligkeit nachtheilig fallen* ([s.l.]: [s.n.], 1727); *Das Ungebührliche Verhalten Der Pietisten Gegen die Weltliche Obrigkeit* (Hamburg: [s.n.], 1734). However, he did not confine himself to print but used the pulpits of the churches he served to express his opposition. For example, when he was superintendent in Sorau he preached a whole year's worth of sermons (1712–1713) exploring in each one three types of people: "I. A right-believing Lutheran (with a teaching-point from our Lutheran church); II. A fanatic enthusiast (with the most egregious fanatical and Pietist errors); III. A distressed heart (with a physical or spiritual concern)."[87] In 1736 a comedy was published anonymously in Leipzig that ridiculed Pietists: *Die Pietisterey in Fischbeinrock* (Pietism in a Whalebone Corset). It was the work of Luise Adelgunde Victorie Gottsched, wife of the Leipzig professor of poetry, but it was assumed that it must have been written by Neumeister, and so a crowd took action and smashed the windows of his house in Hamburg.[88]

The Pietist hymnal was the *Geistreiches Gesang-Buch* (Halle: Waysenhaus, 1704), edited by Francke's son-in-law, Johann Anastasius Freylinghausen.[89]

---

86 Johannes Wallmann, "Erdmann Neumeister, der letzte orthodoxe Gegner des Pietismus," in *Erdmann Neumeister (1671–1756): Wegbereiter der evangelischen Kirchenkantate*, ed. Henrike Rucker (Rudolstadt: Hain, 2000), 27–37.

87 Erdmann Neumeister, *Priesterliche Lippen in Bewahrung der Lehre; Das ist: Son[n]- und Festtags-Predigten durchs gantze Jahr. Darinnen I. Ein Rechtgläubiger Lutheraner, (Mit einem gewissen Lehr-Puncte unserer Evangelischen Kirche) II. Ein Fanatischer Schwärmer, (Mit den vornehmsten Fanat- und Pietistischen Jrrthümern) III. Ein bekümmertes Hertz, (Mit einem leiblichen oder geistlichen Anliegen) vorgestellet wird.* (Leipzig: Laurentius, 1714).

88 Carol K. Baron, *Bach's Changing World: Voices in the Community* (Rochester: University of Rochester Press, 2006), 64–66. For the background, see Bettina Bannasch, "Von Menschen und Meerkatzen. Luise Adelgunde Victorie Gottscheds *Pietisterey im Fischbein-Rocke*," *Pietismus und Neuzeit* 35 (2009): 253–68.

89 For the background, see Gudrun Busch, ed., *"Geist-reicher" Gesang: Halle und das pietistische Lied* (Halle: Franckeschen Stiftungen, 1997).

242   *Theology*

Much of the controversy between Orthodoxy and Pietism centered on this hymnal. In 1716 the Wittenberg theological faculty issued an assessment of the hymnal and declared, on theological grounds, that it was suspect and therefore could not be recommended for use either in church or in the home.[90] On the one hand, Orthodox Wittenberg theologians criticized the omission of classic hymns that dealt with the fundamentals of Lutheran theology, such as Luther's *Erhalt uns, Herr, bei deinem Wort*,[91] which was sung especially at Reformation celebrations. On the other hand, they took issue with texts that undermined church practice, such as Ludwig Andreas Gotter's *Treuer Vater und deine Liebe*, which expressed the following in stanza 3:

Da ich dacht/ ich wär ein Christe/	Since I thought I was a Christian
und davon zu reden wuste/	and knew how to speak about it,
brauchte kirch/ altar dabey	I needed the church and altar,
sung und guts den armen thate/	I sang and gave to the poor.
keine grobe laster hatte/	I had no terrible vices,
war es doch nur heucheley.[92]	and yet it was only hypocrisy.[93]

Here services of public worship and acts of charity are denigrated as outward formalism that is deemed harmful for spiritual life.

Lutheran Pietism, therefore, had theological and liturgical, as well as musical, implications; being pious was not the issue, since both Pietists and Orthodox expressed their spirituality in a similar manner. This is seen in the somewhat surprising fact that, when the second part of the Freylinghausen *Gesangbuch* was published in 1714,[94] it included the following hymns written by the anti-Pietist and pro-Orthodox Erdmann Neumeister:

O Jesu, willst du noch so gnädig (No. 283)
Machs, lieber Gott, wie dirs gefällt (No. 618)
Mein Herz, warum betrübst du dich (No. 620)

Being pious was not the issue, but, when personal piety was presented as the condition for salvation, rather than its fruit, when Pietist meetings for prayer and Bible study were considered as essential and the public worship of the church unimportant and even dispensable, then Orthodox pastors and theologians objected.

---

90 The document is given in both German and English translation in Dianne Marie McMullen, "The *Geistreiches Gesangbuch* of Johann Anastasius Frelinghausen (1670–1739): A German Hymnal" (PhD diss., University of Michigan, 1987), 567–631.

91 The hymn was included in the second section of the hymnal, issued in 1714.

92 Johann Anastasius Freylinghausen, *Geist-reiches Gesang-Buch/ Den Kern alter und neuer Lieder* ... (Halle: Waysenhaus, 1706), 369 (No. 249).

93 Loc. cit.

94 Johann Anastasius Freylinghausen, *Neues Geist-reiches Gesang-Buch* ... (Halle: Waysenhaus, 1714).

Pietism and Bach

The answer to the direct question, "Was Bach a Pietist?" has to be an emphatic negative. Where we have evidence during Bach's lifetime of tensions between Orthodoxy and Pietism, Bach will always be found on the side of Orthodoxy. With the possible exception of Mühlhausen, in all of his professional church appointments Bach found himself in Orthodox environments.

In Arnstadt between 1703 and 1707 he was the organist of the Neuen Kirche where he worked with two members of the distinguished Olearius family of Orthodox theologians: Johann Gottfried and Johann Christoph.[95]

Between 1707 and 1708 Bach was the organist of the Blasiuskirche in Mühlhausen. Among his predecessors were the father and son, Johann Rudolf and Johann Georg Ahle, musicians with Pietist sympathies, and the pastor of the church, Johann Adolph Frohne, with whom Bach worked, was a dedicated Pietist. During Bach's short time in the town, it is significant that he appears to have become a close associate of Georg Christian Eilmar, the Orthodox pastor of the Marienkirche in Mühlhausen, with whom Frohne was in frequent conflict. Bach's Cantata 131 was commissioned by Eilmar, who may have been responsible for the libretto, and it was performed in the Marienkirche rather than the Blasiuskirche, where Bach was organist. The Orthodox pastor was also godfather to Bach's firstborn child, Catharina Dorothea, during this time.[96] Having been in Mühlhausen for just about a year, Bach requested permission to leave, in a letter dated 25 June 1708.

> Even though I should always have liked to work toward the goal, namely, a well-regulated church music, to the glory of God … and would, according to my small means, have helped out as much as possible with the church music that is growing up in almost every township, and often better than the harmony that is fashioned here … yet it has not been possible to accomplish all this without hindrance, and there are, at present, hardly any signs that in the future a change may take place … Now, God has brought it to pass that an unexpected change should offer itself to me, in which I see the possibility of a more adequate living and the achievement of my goal of a well-regulated church music without further vexation.[97]

The vexations and hindrances to his "goal" of "a well-regulated church music"—significantly mentioned twice in almost the same words—are almost certainly references to the difficulties he had with working in the antagonistic environment that existed between the two pastors. However, treatment of the

---

95 See Chapter 6.
96 BDok 1:37.
97 BDok 1:19–20; NBR 57.

244   *Theology*

conflict between the two men needs to be much more nuanced than Spitta's characterization of the conflict in black-and-white terms, a view that has conditioned much of subsequent scholarship.[98] For example, although both pastors had their supporters in Mühlhausen, it was never a simple, two-sided conflict. There was, in fact, a third group, led by the pastor of a parish on the outskirts of Mühlhausen, which sought to mediate between the other two.[99]

In Weimar between 1708 and 1717, first as organist then as concertmaster, Bach was immersed in the Orthodoxy that the deeply religious duke, Wilhelm Ernst, carefully oversaw for his court. It was a lively Orthodoxy that was theologically and liturgically led by the *Oberhofprediger* and superintendent, Johann Georg Lairitz, and for which the consistorial secretary and ducal librarian, Salomon Franck, wrote cantata libretti, following the models of Erdmann Neumeister, for Bach to set to music.[100]

During his twenty-seven years in Leipzig, 1723–1750, apart from one or two minor disputes over principle rather than theology, Bach appears to have been on good terms with the Orthodox clergy of the principal churches he served.[101] Some of the leading clergy were also members of the theological faculty of the university, which was at this time noted for its Orthodoxy, notable examples being Salomon Deyling (1677–1755), pastor of the Nikolaikirche and superintendent of Leipzig for the whole of Bach's time in the city, and Johann Gottlob Carpzov (1679–1767), archdeacon of the Thomaskirche until 1730.

In 1723, before his appointment in Leipzig could be ratified, Bach's Orthodoxy had to be established, and Deyling was one of the two theological professors who conducted the *viva voce* examination and was satisfied with Bach's responses.[102] Deyling's own commitment to Orthodoxy is without question. He was an alumnus, then a professor, of Wittenberg University, a prolific author of mostly erudite theological studies. While he was superintendent of Eisleben he oversaw a new edition of the *Kirchen-Agenda*, with its liturgical content, for the use of the churches in Mansfeld,[103] and within a few years of becoming superintendent in Leipzig produced a devotional handbook for worshipers in the Leipzig churches[104]—a publication that appears to have been issued in competition with a similar volume by Bernhard Walther

---

98 Spitta 1: 354–65; Spitta ET 1: 358–66.

99 See Leaver, *Routledge Research Companion to ... Bach*, 159–63; see also Johannes Wallmann, "Neues Licht auf die Zeit Johann Sebastian Bachs in Mühlhausen. Zu den Anfängen des Pietismus in Thüringen," *Pietismus und Neuzeit* 35 (2009): 46–114.

100 See Leaver, *Routledge Research Companion to ... Bach*, 163–70.

101 See Leaver, *Routledge Research Companion to ... Bach*, 174–79.

102 BDok 2:99–100 (No. 134); NBR 103 (No. 101).

103 Salomon Deyling, *Kirchen-Agenda ... Für die Prediger der Graffschafft Mannßfeld Jezund zum drittenmahl gedruckt* (Eisleben: Hüllmann, 1718).

104 Salomon Deyling, *Der Wohlunterrichtete und würdiglich zubereitete Communicant, Oder Evangelisches Com[m]union-Büchlein, Worinnen I. Die reine Lehre vom H. Abendmahl ...* (Leipzig: Boetius, 1726).

Bach and Pietism   245

Marperger,[105] Dresden *Oberhofprediger* from 1724, a known supporter of Pietism.[106] Deyling also wrote a book on pastoral theology, first published in 1734, in which he upheld the Orthodox position on liturgical worship and the importance of the classic Lutheran hymns of the sixteenth century.[107] In his personal library Deyling had twelve significant volumes of hymnological studies of key hymns of the sixteenth and seventeenth centuries,[108] including Johann Christoph Olearius's four-volume study of the primary hymns of the church year, published when Bach was working with him in Arnstadt,[109] which may well have been a source for Deyling's preaching during 1724–1725, Bach's second year in Leipzig, when he was composing and performing chorale cantatas. Again, Deyling's personal library confirms his Orthodoxy in connection with Pietism, since he owned a number of specifically anti-Pietist titles, including Löscher's *Timotheus Verinus* (1718–1721) and Neumeister's *Spenerische Irrthümer* (1727).[110]

Johann Gottlob Carpzov, professor of Hebrew and one of the clergy of the Thomaskirche, belonged to the distinguished family of Leipzig Orthodox theologians and jurists. His father, Samuel Benedikt Carpzov (1647–1707), studied at Leipzig and Wittenberg, where he was a close associate of Abraham Calov, and later became pastor and superintendent of the Kreuzkirche and Oberhofprediger in Dresden, where Johann Gottlob was born and brought up. In Dresden Samuel Benedikt was an opponent of Pietism, perhaps not quite as strident as his brother, Johann Gottlob's uncle, Johann Benedikt

---

105 Bernhard Walther Marperger, *Neues Communion-Büchlein/ für die Liebhaber des rechtschaffenen Wesens in Christo Jesu* (Nuremberg and Leipzig: Hoffmann, 1724).

106 Johann Georg Walch, *Historische und Theologische Einleitung in die Religions-Streitigkeiten … der Evangelisch-Lutherischen Kirche* (Jena: Meyer, 1733), 1: 1013–17.

107 Salomon Deyling, *Institutiones Prudentiae Pastoralis … edition seconda* (Leipzig: Lanckisch, 1739), 589–618.

108 They include: Cyriacus Spangenberg, *Cithara Lutheri* (Wittenberg: Seuberlich, 1601), 4 vols; Daniel Seiffart, *Christholds Deliciarum Melicarum Centuria Prima, Oder Christ-erbaulichen Lieder-Ergötzlichkeiten Erstes Hundert: Darinnen so wol des Autoris selbsteigene, als anderer Lehrer zufällige Andachten … enthalten …* (Nürnberg : Zieger, 1704); Georg Serpilius, *Anmerckungen Uber D. Pauli Sperati Geistlich- und liebliches Lied: Es ist das Heyl uns kommen her …* (Regensburg: Seidel, 1707); Johann Christoph Olearius, *Evangelischer Lieder-Schatz: darinn allerhand Auserlesene Gesänge, so sich auff alle Sonn- und Fest-Tags Evangelia schicken, angezeiget, zugleich auch Von jedes Liedes Autore, …* (Jena: Bielcke, 1707), 4 vols. issued between 1705–1707; Johann Avenarius, *Evangelischer Lieder-Catechißmus; darinnen die gantze Christliche Lehre nach Anweisung der Sechs Hauptstücke des H. Catechismi Lutheri durch erbauliche Lieder erläutert und raren Historien auch andere nachdencklichen Remarquen erkläret …* (Frankfurt and Leipzig: Stössel, 1714); Thomas Paul Steger, *Heilige Meditationes und Andachten über das schöne, Geistreiche Glaubens-Lied, So alle Sonn- und Feyertage in denen Christlichen Kirchen und Gemeinen, bald beym Anfang des Gottes-Diensts, gesungen wird: Allein Gott in der Höh sey Her …* (Dresden: Zimmermann & Gerlach, 1725). See *Catalogus Bibliothecae Deylingiae auctionis lege in collegii rubri vaporario die xxi Iunii seqq vendendae* (Leipzig: Cruciger, 1756), 104, 145.

109 For the background, see Chapter 6.

110 *Catalogus Bibliothecae Deylingiae*, 124, 136–37.

246   *Theology*

Carpzov II (1639–1699), who, as a student in Leipzig, like Neumeister, was at first impressed by August Hermann Francke, but later, again like Neumeister, strenuously resisted Pietism. In the years after Johann Gottlob Carpzov became pastor of the Marienkirche and superintendent in Lübeck in 1730, he resisted both Pietists within Lutheranism and Pietists without, especially the Moravians.[111] A short time before J. G. Carpzov moved to Lübeck, his daughter, Sophia Benedicta, stood as godparent to Bach's daughter, Christiana Benedicta,[112] implying a connection between the two families. A sermon on church music that Carpzov gave in the Thomaskirche in 1714, though not published until 1733,[113] together with his relationship with Caspar Ruetz (1708–1755), music director and cantor of the Marienkirche in Lübeck,[114] suggests that he most likely appreciated Bach's musical leadership during the time he was archdeacon of the Thomaskirche. He also owned a copy of an influential treatise on church music, Caspar Calvör's *De musica ac sigillatim de ecclesiastica* (Leipzig: König, 1702), and he may have had keyboard skills, since he owned at least one hymnal with figured bass, Johann Crüger's *Praxis pietatis melica: Das ist: Ubung der Gottseligkeit* (Frankfurt: Wust, 1680), and a copy of the anonymous *Kurtze Anführung zum General-Bass: darinnen die Regeln, welche bey Erlernung des General-Basses zu wissen nöthig; Kürtzlich*

---

111 Carpzov's personal library included a good many anti-Pietist books and pamphlets, notably titles by Erdmann Neumeister; see Johann Franck, *Catalogus Bibliothecae Iohannis Gottlob Carpzovii, SS. Theol. quondam D. & Minist. Lubec. Superintendentis: exhibens Libros ex omni Theologia, Philosophia, Philologia, praesertim sacra, Antiquitatibus, Historia tam sacra quam profana selectissimos; multos etiam rariores; Lubecae die X. Octob. An. MDCCLXVIII. in Auditorio Catharianiano plus licitantibus addicendos* (Lübeck: Green, 1768), 69, 75–76, 157–58, and passim. Much of the controversy in Lübeck, as elsewhere, centered around Pietists calling for the displacement of older hymnody by the new; see the pamphlets and booklets J. G. Carpzov accumulated, *Catalogus Bibliothecae Iohannis Gottlob Carpzovii*, 157–58.

112 BDok 2:200 (No. 273). Johann Gottlob Carpzov baptized Ernestus Andreas Bach on 30 October 1728, who survived only two days; see Martin Petzoldt, *Bachs Leipziger Kinder: Dokumente von Johann Sebastian Bachs eigener Hand* (Leipzig: Evangelische Verlagsanstalt, 2008), 55.

113 Johann Gottlob Carpzov, *Unterricht vom Unverletzten Gewissen beyde gegen Gott und Menschen, in vier und achtzig Predigten, Vormahls der Gemeine Gottes zu St. Thomas in Leipzig vorgetragen, und nun auf vielfältiges Verlangen in Druck gegeben* (Leipzig: Martini, 1733), 409–34; see Leaver, *Routledge Research Companion to ... Bach*, 178–79.

114 J. G. Carpzov's personal library included Caspar Ruetz's three volumes with similar titles on church music, Caspar Ruetz, [I.] *Widerlegte Vorurtheile vom Ursprunge der Kirchenmusic, und klarer Beweis, daß die Gottesdienstliche Music sich auf Gottes Wort gründe, und also göttliches Ursprungs sey, der Gleichgültigkeit in Ansehung dieser Art des Gottesdienstes entgegen gesetzet*; [II.] *Widerlegte Vorurtheile von der Beschaffenheit der heutigen Kirchenmusic und von der Lebens-Art einiger Musicorum*; [III.] *Widerlegte Vorurtheile von der Wirkung der Kirchenmusic, und von den darzu erforderten Unkosten* (Lübeck: Schmidt und Böckmann, 1751, 1752, and Rostock and Wismar: Berger und Boedner, 1753); see *Catalogus Bibliothecae Iohannis Gottlob Carpzovii*, 261–62. Carpzov also owned fifteen librettti books of "Lübecker Abendmusiken" from various years; see *Catalogus Bibliothecae Iohannis Gottlob Carpzovii*, 324.

und mit wenig Worten enthalten / Allen Anfängern des Claviers zu nützlichen Gebrauch zusammen gesetzet (Leipzig: Martini, 1728).[115]

At the end of Bach's life things were changing intellectually, philosophically, culturally, and religiously, and they would continue to do so throughout the rest of the century. Pietism was increasing its influence at the expense of Orthodoxy, and Rationalism was undermining both Orthodoxy and Pietism with the expansion of secularism.[116] Orthodoxy was under pressure from both Pietism and Rationalism, but, notwithstanding their significant differences, both Pietists and Rationalists pursued similar agendas: the elimination of elaborate music from the liturgy in favor of more simple music, and the reduction of the complex liturgical form into a basic sequence of hymns, prayers, and biblical readings, with a plain-spoken sermon. In Bach's day the liturgy in Leipzig was an intricate amalgam of the traditional structure of the old Lutheran Mass with all its Propers, Ordinary—some of it still in Latin— congregational hymnody, ecclesiastical monody, a one-hour sermon, and the cantata, itself a rich combination of choral, vocal, and instrumental sound, but which functioned as a liturgical Proper for the day. These were the elements that the Orthodox strived to retain within the worship of the church, while Pietists, along with Rationalists, worked to simplify or eliminate them. Without the liturgical and theological framework to contain it, the cantata form did not make much sense—at least to those who encountered it in the following century—and, isolated as they were from their liturgical roots, it took time for all of Bach's cantatas to be appreciated and published.

In sum: although the contents of Bach's cantatas have the appearance of Pietism in imagery and expression, it was the liturgical purpose, eucharistic context, and theological content of Orthodoxy that provided the environment that brought the cantatas into existence.

---

115 *Catalogus Bibliothecae Iohannis Gottlob Carpzovii*, 316, 303–4 and 325 respectively.

116 For the background, see Kahnis, *Internal History of German Protestantism*, and Jeffrey S. Sposato, *Leipzig after Bach: Church and Concert Life in a German City* (New York: Oxford University Press, 2018).

12 Bach, Gesner, and Johann August Ernesti

In eighteenth-century Germany there were two acclaimed philologists. For some years both were colleagues together in the Thomasschule in Leipzig, as rector and conrector, where Bach served as the school's cantor and the city's director of music.[1] One was Johann Matthias Gesner, noted for his editions of Claudian, Pliny the Younger, Horace, and especially Quintilian, among others, and the other was Johann August Ernesti, famous for editions that included Suetonius, Tacitus, Homer, and notably Cicero. Both philologists were also educationalists intent on expanding the traditional school core curriculum, augmenting the study of classic literature in the original languages, along with the Bible and basic theology, to include such subjects embraced by history, natural history, science, geography, and art, though there was some dissonance between them with regard to the continued role of music. In their collaboration with Bach both profoundly affected his career, one positively, the other negatively.

Johann Matthias Gesner (1691–1761)

Gesner's father, a pastor, died when Johann Matthias was 13, leaving him and his family in somewhat straitened circumstances. His education was fostered by his stepfather and, especially, by the rector of the Ansbach gymnasium, who gave him extra coaching and loaned him books.[2] Gesner matriculated as

---

1 For the history of the Thomasschule, see Michael Maul, *Bach's Famous Choir: The Saint Thomas School in Leipzig, 1212–1804*, trans. Richard Howe (Woodbridge: Boydell, 2018), and Andreas Glöckner, ed., *Dokumente zur Geschichte des Leipziger Thomaskantorate, II: Vom Amtsantritt Johann Sebastian Bachs bis zum Beginn des 19. Jahrhunderts* (Leipzig: Evangelische Verlagsanstalt, 2018).

2 A modern account of Gesner can be found in Reinhold Friedrich, *Johann Matthias Gesner: Sein Leben und sein Werk* (Roth: Genniges, 1991); see also the summary in Michael C. Legaspi, *The Death of Scripture and the Rise of Biblical Studies* (Oxford: Oxford University Press, 2010), 61–68. However, a primary account of Gesner's life and works was written by Johann August Ernesti after Gesner's death in 1761, published in Leipzig and Leiden in1762. Thirty years later it was published in German in Johann August Ernesti, *Denkmäler und Lobschriften auf gelehrte, verdienstvolle Männer, seine Zeitgenossen nebst der Biographie Johann Matthias Geßners, in einer Erzählung für David Ruhnken* (Leipzig: Schwickert, 1792), 190–244.

a theological student at Jena University in 1710, and his brilliance combined with his impecuniosity led the theological professor, Johann Franz Buddeus, to give him room and board in his own house. In spite of Buddeus's support, no Jena University position was offered to Gesner on his graduation. In 1715 he combined the responsibilities of ducal librarian, keeper of the ducal coin and medal collection, and conrector of the Latin gymnasium in Weimar. The position of conrector was no doubt awarded on the strength of the treatise that Gesner had published earlier that year, *Institutiones rei scholasticae* (Jena: Bielcken, 1715), with a preface by Buddeus. In his treatise Gesner outlined the abilities and expertise of the ideal teacher and expounded a number of proven teaching methods.[3] In Weimar, between 1715 and 1717, he was an associate of Bach, who was then the court organist, concertmaster, and composer. The relationship between Gesner and Bach was by all accounts a cordial one. Indeed, there appears to have been quite a comfortable working relationship between the gymnasium faculty and Bach in Weimar: the rector was Johann Christoph Kiesewetter, who had been the rector of the Ohrdruf Lyceum when Bach was a pupil there; the conrector was Gesner; and the cantor was Georg Theodor Reineccius, who oversaw boys from the school who sang Bach's cantatas in the court chapel. Thus, Gesner had two full years of firsthand knowledge and experience of Bach as a performer before the latter left Weimar to become capellmeister in Cöthen.

Gesner continued with his joint positions in Weimar until 1729, when he became the rector of the gymnasium in Ansbach, the school he had attended as a boy. But this only lasted a few months because the following year he was appointed the successor of the recently deceased rector of the Thomasschule in Leipzig, Johann Heinrich Ernesti (1652–1729). For the second time in his career Gesner found himself a close colleague of Bach, and for a further four years was able to regularly observe Bach in performance.

In order to understand the Leipzig environment that Gesner entered, it is necessary to review some of the tensions that had simmered for decades between the city council and the faculty of the Thomasschule. From the early years of the eighteenth century, the Leipzig city council was concerned to modernize the curriculum of its two schools.[4] In 1716 the regulations of the

---

3 See Ulrich Schindel, "Johann Matthias Gesners aufgeklärte Pädagogik," in Ulrich Leisinger and Christoph Wolff, eds., *Musik, Kunst und Wissenschaft im Zeitalter J. S. Bachs*, Leipziger Beiträge zur Bach-Forschung, 7 (Hildesheim: Olms, 2005), 39–49; Markus Rathey, "Schools," in Robin A. Leaver, ed., *The Routledge Research Companion to Johann Sebastian Bach* (New York: Routledge, 2017), 137–38. For the general background, see Peter Lundgreen, "Schulhumanismus, pädagogischer Realismus und Neuhumanismus: Die Gelehrtenschule zur Zeit J. S. Bachs," in Leisinger and Wolff, *Musik, Kunst und Wissenschaft*, 25–38. Much of the background of Lundgreen's essay is based on Friedrich Paulsen, *Geschichte des gelehrten Unterrichts auf den deutschen Schulen und Universitäten vom Ausgang des Mittelalters bis zur Gegenwart, mit besonderer Rücksicht auf den klassischen Unterricht*, 3rd ed. (Leipzig: de Gruyter, 1919–1921; reprint Berlin: de Gruyter, 1965).

4 Maul, *Bach's Famous Choir*, 149–65.

250   *Theology*

Nikolaischule were revised to expand the number of different subjects taught, and the following year, 1717, an inspection of the Thomasschule was undertaken, also with the aim of revising its curriculum. The first question put to the rector, Johann Heinrich Ernesti, and cantor, Johann Kuhnau, revealed a preexisting difference of opinion that would only increase in intensity as time passed: "How to divide the time for singing and music so that the students' academic work doesn't suffer?"[5] The rector's response was direct:

> The St. Thomas School was of a completely different nature from the St. Nicholas School ... The former was a *Schola pauperum* [charity school], and its students had to spend most of their time not only learning music, which had been the chief intention of the school's founders, but on singing at the services, the funerals, the rounds of street singing [*Currende*], and other musical events [in order to raise money for the school], as a result of which the remaining hours were insufficient for the lessons and the authors introduced at the St. Nicholas School.[6]

The basic curriculum that had been in place for generations was largely based on memorization, and everything had to be learned according to the rules of grammar, style, and rhetoric, and written up in exercise books.[7] The Thomasschule faculty resisted pressure from the city council for educational reforms—though much of their opposition was apparently based on fear of losing additional income from the extracurricular activities of the students rather than for any pedagogical principle[8]—and the content of the newly published *Schulordnung* of 1723, like the *Schulordnungen* issued during the seventeenth century, dealt mostly with daily life in the school.[9] However, there were significant changes to the regulations: the dominance of Latin was moderated, in that reading and speaking the German language was now to be taught—thus daily prayers morning and evening were in future to be in German rather than Latin[10]—and it was hoped, but left unspecified, that history, geography, and logic, would be introduced into the curriculum.[11] But more significant were the changes made to the admissions procedure. In the past the financial stability of the school depended on admitting boys who had demonstrated musical ability, decisions that were made jointly by the rector and cantor. The new regulations claimed (erroneously) that the intention of the founders of the school had been to create a charity school for the

---

5 Cited ibid., 156.
6 Cited ibid., 157–58.
7 Lundgreen, "Schulhumanismus," 31.
8 Schindel, "Gesners aufgeklärte Pädagogik," 44.
9 *E. E. Hochw. Raths der Stadt Leipzig Ordnung der Schule zu S. Thomae* ([Leipzig]: Tietzen, 1723; facsimile in Hans-Joachim Schulze, *Die Thomasschule Leipzig zur Zeit Johann Sebastian Bachs: Ordnungen und Gesetze 1634. 1723. 1733* (Leipzig: Zentralantiquariat, 1987).
10 *Ordnung Der Schule zu S. Thomae* (1723), 27–28 (IV, § iii).
11 Ibid., 22 (II, § xxx).

Bach, Gesner, and Ernesti   251

poor rather than a music school, and effectively added a third person to the admissions process:

> Because ... this school was principally founded and endowed for the improvement of the poor, but also with regard for the provision of church music, so the rector is free to admit our local little boys [the "external" or "day" students in the lower grades], the children of townspeople ... and none are to be refused [admission] without some particularly good reason; whereas neither the rector nor the cantor has the authority to admit someone to ... the boarding school without the prior knowledge and consent of the school overseer [Vorsteher].
>
> If boys come here from out of town, and request admission as boarders, then the rector must first of all report this to the school overseer, and then examine them diligently, but not as regards musical aptitude alone but principally as having a good intelligence inclined to study, and if he [the rector] finds them sufficiently qualified ... then, with the approval of the overseer, to accept them into the school.[12]

Thus, right from Bach's first year in Leipzig, instead of having an equal voice with that of the rector concerning who should be accepted into the school—as was the experience of his predecessor, Kuhnau—he could be outvoted by the rector and Vorsteher. However, with rector Johann Heinrich Ernesti's resistance to changes in the way the school was being run, he and Bach were apparently able to establish a workable relationship with Gottfried Conrad Lehmann (1661–1728), the city councilor who had been the Vorsteher since 1709. But it was hardly plain sailing.

Between 1728 and 1729 this *status quo* came to an abrupt end with the deaths of both rector and Vorsteher that occurred within a few months of each other. The significance of the new Vorsteher becomes clear when the career of Johann August Ernesti is reviewed (see below). Great interest was shown in the vacancy of rector, which attracted many applications and recommendations. These were reduced to three possibilities and eventually on 6 June 1730 Gesner was elected the new rector.[13] The prospect of having his old Weimar colleague as the new rector must have been encouraging for Bach, especially as the outline of his concerns for the future of music in the school was penned just three days before Gesner's arrival in Leipzig.[14] But it was clearly an unsettling time for Bach, since within two months of writing the

---

12 *Ordnung Der Schule zu S. Thomae* (1723), 37–38 (VI, § i–ii); Maul, *Bach's Famous Choir*, 167.

13 Maul, *Bach's Famous Choir*, 209–10.

14 Bach's memorandum to the city council: "Kurtzer, iedoch höchstnöthiger Entwurff einer wohlbestallten Kirchen Music" (Short but Necessary Draft for a Well-Appointed Church Music), BDok 1: 60–66 (No. 22); NBR 145–51 (No. 151). The "Entwurff" was dated 23 August 1730; Gesner arrived in Leipzig on 26 August 1730.

252   *Theology*

"Entwurff" he was then writing to his school friend, Georg Erdmann, looking for an alternative position.

> The [Leipzig] authorities are odd and little interested in music, so that I must live amid almost continual vexation, envy, and persecution; accordingly I shall be forced, with God's help, to seek my fortune elsewhere.[15]

Surely something must have happened in these months that removed the gloss from the prospect of working with his Weimar colleague, who had been officially installed on 14 September, just a few weeks before Bach had written to Erdmann? A distinct possibility may have been the conditions that Gesner was required to accept, in writing, before being confirmed as the new rector. These were that he would immediately resign as the rector of the Thomasschule if he accepted a professorship in the university, and, further, that he would "not take up writing books." It seems that Gesner was unaware of these conditions until after he had submitted his resignation as the rector of the Ansbach gymnasium, when it was too late for any change of heart.[16] Did Gesner share with Bach the conditions of his appointment? And if so did he indicate that his stay in Leipzig might therefore not be long? No doubt the reasoning of the city councilors was that they believed that Johann Heinrich Ernesti's effectiveness as rector was undermined by his responsibilities as the university's professor of poetry, a situation they did not want to see repeated with Gesner—the new rector was, therefore, expected to devote all his attention to leadership of the Thomasschule.

When Gesner arrived in 1730 there was much to be done. The school building was in a dilapidated state and had become cramped for lack of space. Much of his first two years were taken up with overseeing the complete renovation of the building, which included the provision of additional floors. The reconstruction took place between May 1731 and April 1732, during which time the daily life of the school had to function in different buildings, and the rector and cantor, with their families, had to live in temporary accommodation. On the completion of the reconstruction and the resumption of the use of the school building, Gesner's next task was to produce a new version of the *Schulordnung*.[17] Like earlier examples of such regulations the main function was to deal with the details of the daily life of the school: defining what was expected from each student, rules for meals, conduct in the dormitories, penalties for misdemeanors, and so forth. When compared with the 1723 *Ordnungen*, what is missing from the 1733 *Gesetze* are the directives

---

15 BDok 1: 67–70 (No. 23); NBR, 151–52 (No. 152). The letter is dated 28 October 1730.

16 Maul, *Bach's Famous Choir*, 209–10.

17 *E. E. Hochweisen Raths der Stadt Leipzig Gesetze der Schule zu S. Thomae* (Leipzig: Breitkopf, 1733; facsimile in Schulze, *Die Thomasschule Leipzig … Ordnungen und Gesetze*), 39: "Das vornehmste Gesetz ist: Befördere das Wohl der Schule" (The primary rule is: To promote the well-being of the school).

Bach, Gesner, and Ernesti 253

concerning the admission of students. Although no longer included, it did not mean that the process had been abandoned.[18] From what happened after Gesner left Leipzig, it is clear that admissions were continuing to be decided by the triumvirate of rector, cantor, and Vorsteher—at least in theory (see further below).

Another omission was that the 1733 *Gesetze* made no specific reference to curriculum matters other than music, which was treated at some length in a complete section under the heading "Von der Music." It began thus:

> Our forefathers intended that music should be taught in the Thomasschule in order that its alumni [boarders] should provide music in all the city churches. Therefore they should diligently fulfil their calling and duty to practice as much as possible in this art, and to bear in mind by so doing they participate in a work that even the heavenly hosts undertake with the greatest pleasure.[19] Therefore they should apply all their powers with utmost earnestness in learning to sing well. Not only should they not miss the [daily] hour dedicated to this practice, but also apply that time to this permitted enjoyment of mind, in which they have nothing proper to do, and which others ruin with disgraceful idleness and play.[20]

Bach must have been encouraged to read this, since it was a reaffirmation of the role of music in the Thomasschule. First, Gesner corrects the statement of the 1723 *Ordnungen*, which had suggested that it was primarily a school for the poor and only secondarily a school for music.[21] Gesner's 1733 *Gesetze* state clearly that the school was founded in the first place as a music school

---

18 In 1737 Bach complained about the continuation of the provisions of the 1723 *Ordnungen* that had never been ratified by the Leipzig consistory; see BDok 1: 98 (No. 40); NBR 192 (No. 194).

19 Here there is a cross-reference to a similar statement made near the beginning of the document: *Gesetze der Schule zu S. Thomae* (1733), 5–6 (I, § 5). The passage is translated in Markus Rathey, *Johann Sebastian Bach's Christmas Oratorio: Music, Theology, Culture* (New York: Oxford University Press, 2016), 191.

20 *Gesetze der Schule zu S. Thomae* (1733), 22 (VI, § 1): "Es haben unsere Vorfahren angeordnet, daß die Musik auf der Thomas-Schule getrieben, und von den dasigen *Alumnis* in allen Stadt-Kirchen besorget werden soll. Daher sollen diese fleißig an ihren Beruff und an ihr Amt gedencken, und sich in dieser Kunst auf das möglichste zu üben suchen, und bedencken, daß sie ein Werck thun, welches selbst die himmlischen Heerschaaren mit dem grösten Vergnügen treiben. Sie sollen also mit höchstem Ernste alle ihre Kräfte anwenden, daß sie wohl singen lernen. Sie sollen nicht nur keine Stunde versäumen, welche zu dieser Ubung bestimmet ist, sondern auch dieienige Zeit zu diesem erlaubten Gemüths-Vergnügen anwenden, in welcher sie nichts ordentliches zu thun haben, und welche andere mit dem schändlichen Müßiggange und Spielen verderben."

21 "Weil ... diese Schule vornehmlich denen Armen zum best an angeleget and gestifftet, zugleich auch das Absehen die Bestellung der Music gerichtet worden" (This school was principally founded and endowed for the improvement of the poor, but also with regard for the provision of church music); *Ordnung Der Schule zu S. Thomae* (1723), 37 (VI, § i); Maul, *Bach's Famous Choir*, 167.

254   *Theology*

in order to serve the Leipzig churches. Second, because the role of supplying music for the churches demanded an appropriate level of musicianship, it was imperative for the alumni to attend the daily singing lessons. Third, the alumni were also encouraged to use their spare time in furthering their musical expertise.

The 1733 *Gesetze* reflected Gesner's interest in music, an interest found in many of his other writings. His support for music-making in the Thomasschule is specifically recorded in the manuscript history of the Leipzig schools compiled in the later eighteenth century by theologian Johann Friedrich Köhler. Köhler cites the following words about Gesner written by an anonymous admirer:

> Gesner was highly approachable and tender in his relationships with the students, visited them even in their singing lessons (which was unusual for a rector), and heard with pleasure the pieces of church music that were performed.[22]

Unfortunately, from Bach's point of view, Gesner's tenure as rector of the school came to an end a year or so after the publication of the *Gesetze*. In 1734 Gesner was appointed professor of poetry and eloquence at the newly founded University of Göttingen where, in the following decades, he pursued an illustrious career.

In Göttingen Gesner continued his interest in music, especially in connection with a former Leipzig student who transferred to Göttingen in 1735, the year after Gesner had taken up his appointment at the new university. This was Johann Friedrich Schweinitz (1708–1780) who, while a student in Leipzig between 1732 and 1735 had been a private pupil of Bach.[23] As soon as Schweinitz arrived in Göttingen he applied for, and was granted, permission to found a Collegium Musicum along the lines of Bach's Collegium in Leipzig. He directed the music (including his "Festkantate") for the official inauguration service of the university, in September 1737, as the *"Director Musices bey dortiger Universität."*[24] In 1745 he applied for the position of cantor in Celle, and Gesner wrote a letter of recommendation

---

22 "Historia Scholarum Lips. collecta a Joh. Frid. Köhlero, pastore Tauchensi. 1776." Sächsische Landesbibliothek Staats und Universitätsbibliothek Dresden, Ms. L 443; cited Maul, *Bach's Famous Choir*, 215.

23 See Daniela Garbe, "Der Director musices, Organist und Kantor Johann Friedrich Schweinitz. Ein Beitrag zur Musikgeschichte Göttingens im 18. Jahrhundert," *Göttinger Jahrbuch* 37 (1989): 71–90; and Hans-Joachim Schulze, "Johann Friedrich Schweinitz, 'A Disciple of the Famous Herr Bach in Leipzig,'" *About Bach*, ed. Gregory G. Butler, George B. Stauffer, and Mary Dalton Greer (Urbana: University of Illinois Press, 2008), 81–88.

24 Jörg Baur, "Die Anfänge der Theologie an der 'wohl angeordneten evangelischen Universität' Göttingen," in Jürgen v. Stackelberg, ed., *Zur geistigen Situation der Zeit der Göttinger Universitätsgründung 1737* (Göttingen: Vandenhoeck & Ruprecht, 1988), 9.

in which he described Schweinitz as "a disciple[25] of the famous Herr Bach in Leipzig."[26]

Johann August Ernesti (1707–1781)

Like Gesner, Ernesti was the son of a pastor and studied philology, philosophy, theology, and mathematics, first at Wittenberg University (1726–1728) and then at Leipzig University (1728–1730). While still a student in Leipzig he was also private tutor to the children of Christian Ludwig Stieglitz (1677–1758), a powerful man in Leipzig politics: city councilor from 1715, judge from 1725, lawyer to the royal Polish and electoral Saxon courts in Dresden, and six times Leipzig Burgermeister between 1741 and 1757.[27] In 1729, that is, during the time Ernesti was tutoring his children, Stieglitz was appointed the Thomasschule Vorsteher, replacing Gottfried Conrad Lehmann, who had died the previous year. One of Stieglitz's first actions was to raise questions about admissions to the school and the status of the choirs.[28] It was revealed that only half the vacancies in the boarding school were filled with musically gifted students[29]—a situation that helps to explain both Bach's "Entwurff" addressed to the city council and his letter addressed to Erdmann, both written the following year.

In 1731 Johann Christian Hebenstreit (1686–1756)—who like Gesner seems to have been contractually obliged to resign his position in the Thomasschule if he accepted a professorship in the university—stepped down as conrector on being appointed professor of Hebrew in the theological faculty. His chosen replacement was Karl Friedrich Pezold (1678–1731), who had been the *Tertius* (the most senior teacher after the conrector and cantor) in the Thomaschule since 1704, but he died before the end of the year. This unforeseen opportunity was not lost on Vorsteher Stieglitz. In August 1731 he proposed to the city council that his children's tutor, Johann August Ernesti, who had only just obtained his masters degree and was barely 24 years old, be appointed as the new conrector. Ernesti was elected unanimously and apparently without debate.[30] Thus, Stieglitz's protégé became the conrector alongside the rector, Gesner, and the cantor, Bach. In the first few years there seemed to be an amicable relationship between the three leading faculty. Examples include: the cantata (probably BWV 36c) Bach performed on 8 April 1731 celebrating

---

25 "Disciple" because he was not a Thomaner.
26 BDok 3: 422–23 (No. 541); BDok 5: 168 (No. B 527a): "Discipul von den berühmten Herrn Bach in Leipzig."
27 Karin Kühling and Doris Mundus, eds., *Leipzigs Regierende Bürgermeister vom 13. Jahrhundert bis zur Gegenwart: Eine Übersichtsdarstellung mit biographischen Skizzen* (Beucha: Sax, 2000), 44.
28 See BDok 2: 192–93; NBR 140 (No. 141).
29 Maul, *Bach's Famous Choir*, 193.
30 Maul, *Bach's Famous Choir*, 217.

256 *Theology*

Gesner's birthday[31]; Ernesti and Gesner's wife, Elisabeth Charitas, on 5 November 1733 stood as godparents at the baptism of Bach's son, Johann August Abraham[32]; and Gesner's 1733 *Gesetze* included words of praise for Vorsteher Stieglitz.[33]

Since Gesner was effectively blocked from a Leipzig professorship, when the prospect of such a position at the new University of Göttingen presented itself he took it, though it seems that health issues were an important factor in his decision.[34] Gesner made his formal farewell to the school on 4 October 1734, an occasion for which Bach composed a suitable cantata (BWV Anh. I, 210; music lost[35]). A month later, 3 November, a full session of the city council considered the vacancy of the position of rector of the Thomasschule. Stieglitz reported that Gesner had warmly commended the 27-year-old Ernesti as his successor. As before, when he became the conrector, Ernesti was elected unanimously. The previous day Stieglitz had declared, "I vote for Herr Magister Ernesti for rector, he is tireless in his studies, has also introduced and maintained discipline"; but he went on to add, "incidently, my office as overseer [Vorsteher] of the school of St. Thomas's is made very difficult by the cantor in that the latter does not do what he is obligated to do at the school."[36] This negative assessment of what had taken place in the past cast an ominous shadow on what would happen in the future. A few weeks later, on 21 November, Ernesti was inaugurated in a ceremony that included the performance of a cantata by Bach (BWV Anh. I, 19; music lost). During the next year or so a tolerable working relationship continued between Ernesti and Bach, which included personal connections, such as Ernesti standing as godfather to Johann Christian Bach at his baptism on 7 September 1735,[37] but it would not continue.

Different approaches to curriculum reform

The two philologists, one in Leipzig and the other in Göttingen, developed their own approaches to curriculum reform. In Leipzig Ernesti had the support of Stieglitz, who arranged for the young rector to be excused from obligatory menial duties, a privilege that was denied to Bach.[38] No doubt the reason for

---

31 The Canon a 2 perpetuus (BWV 1075), dated 10 January 1734, is sometimes stated to have been dedicated to Gesner, but this is based on a misunderstanding; see Hans-Joachim Schulze, "Johann Sebastian Bachs Kanonwidmungen," BJ 53 (1967): 87–88.

32 BDok 2: 242 (No. 340) and 5: 95–96 (No. A92i); Martin Petzoldt, *Bachs Leipzger Kinder: Dokumente von Johann Sebastian Bachs eigener Hand* (Leipzig: Evangelische Verlagsanstalt, 2008), 83–92. Johann August Abraham died the day after his baptism.

33 See the conflated citation in Maul, *Bach's Famous Choir*, 213–14.

34 Maul, *Bach's Famous Choir*, 216.

35 BDok 5: 153 (No. B 359a).

36 BDok 2: 252 (No. 355); Maul, *Bach's Famous Choir*, 218.

37 BDok 5: 96–97 (No. A92i); Petzoldt, *Bachs Leipzger Kinder*, 92–101.

38 See NBR 172 (No. 180); BDok 3: 314 (No. 820).

freeing up his time was so that Ernesti could work on creating a new curriculum for the school, something that a good many on the city council in general, and Stieglitz in particular, had for years wanted to see accomplished—that is, a change in the educational philosophy of the school by reducing its primary focus on music and by expanding the curriculum beyond traditional classical studies. Ernesti's detailed curriculum, *Initia doctrinae solidioris*, was published by Christian Martini in Leipzig in two parts, part one in 1734 and part two in 1735. Since Ernesti only became the rector at the beginning of November 1734, the imprint of the first part implies that he had probably been working on the project before being appointed rector. The complete curriculum was reprinted in a single volume in 1736—an octavo amounting to more than seven hundred pages—followed by a further nine or ten editions by the end of the century, all of them published in Leipzig, three of them appearing after Ernesti's death. The curriculum covered the following subjects: arithmetic, geometry, philosophy, natural theology, dialectics, natural law, moral philosophy, physics, and, some years later, rhetoric.[39] Music is mentioned only once in Ernesti's curriculum, and then only in passing, within the context of mathematics and acoustics.[40] If he had been challenged concerning the omission no doubt he would have responded by pointing out that it was unnecessary to include music since the 1733 *Gesetze* dealt with the matter. Nevertheless, it was clear that as soon as the subjects of the new curriculum were implemented there would be less time for music, and therefore sooner rather than later a conflict between rector and cantor was inevitable.

In Göttingen Gesner continued to be involved in school curricula. In addition to his professorship Gesner was also the inspector of schools for the electorate of Braunschweig-Lüneburg, in which capacity, during his early years in Göttingen, he was involved in preparing a general *Schulordnung* for the schools of the electorate.[41] The document was drafted by Johann Andreas Buttstedt (or Buttstett) (1701–1765), who was at the time rector of the gymnasium in Osterode, but the final form was the work of Gesner.[42] The regulations

---

39 Johann August Ernesti, *Initia rhetorica* (Leipzig: Wendler, 1750), with numerous reprints. It took some years for the curriculum to work its way through the school and for a Thomaner to have benefitted from it for the whole of his time in the school. When Johann August Bach (no relation) left the school in 1741 Ernesti wrote the following note: "Dismissus est cum optimis omnibus Iuvenis ingenio, doctrina, moribus, superior omnibus, in quibus disciplina nostra elaboravit" (Discharged with the best of all the young talent, learning, behavior, above all, in which system we developed); Bernard Friedrich Richter, "Stadtpfeifer und Alumnen der Thomasschule in Leipzig zu Bachs Zeit," BJ 4 (1907): 72 (No. 172).

40 Johann August Ernesti, *Initia doctrinae solidioris* (Leipzig: Wendler, 1745), 7.

41 Ibid., 211–12.

42 See Reinhold Vormbaum, ed., *Die evangelischen Schulordnungen des achtzehnten Jahrhunderts* (Gütersloh: Bertelsmann, 1864), 359. It is possible that J. A. Buttstedt was related to the noted writer on music, Johann Heinrich Buttstedt (1766–1727), since it is reported that his father was a cantor and that he was born near Erfurt, where J. H. Buttstedt was organist; see *Fortsetzung und Ergänzungen zu Christian Gottlieb Jöchers allgemeinem Gelehrten-Lexicon … Erster Band*, ed. Christoph Adelung (Leipzig: Gleditsch, 1784), cols. 2472–73.

258 *Theology*

were completed in 1737 and published the following year: *Schulordnung vor die Churfürstl. Braunschweig-Lüneburgische Lande* ... (Göttingen: Vandenhoeck, 1738). Unlike Ernesti's detailed curriculum that was intended primarily for the use of one school, these *Schulordnungen* were to be used by many schools throughout the electorate. They were, therefore, more broadly drawn but had much in common with the 1733 *Gesetze* that Gesner had prepared for the Leipzig Thomasschule. Covered were various practical issues, such as discipline, duties of teachers, responsibilities of rectors, and so forth. Latin still dominated the curriculum, with an emphasis on grammar (7),[43] reading (9), writing (13), and the study of the Latin poets (12). But basic Greek (15) and Hebrew (16) were also included, as well as the study of German (14), something that Latin schools had tended to omit in the past. But there were other subjects to be taught, for example: arithmetic (4), surveying (5), nature and art (6), geography (10), history (11), philosophy (17), and music (22). Here, as in the Leipzig 1733 *Gesetze*, Gesner stressed the daily singing lesson:

> Music fundamentals should, as far as possible, be taught to each and all in the hour immediately following the midday meal. Where a school has two teachers, the singing-hour should be held in two classes simultaneously; but if this is not the case, half of the time is to be devoted to beginners and the other half to those who have progressed further, so that not only those who have a voice and natural ability can eventually express the notes; but that others may also at least understand the significance of the [musical] terms and signs [notation].[44]

For Gesner the long-standing practice of the daily music lesson was of primary importance in the education of students.

At the same time that he was working on the 1737 *Schulordnung* Gesner was also at work on a much larger project, a new critical edition of and commentary on the treatise of the Roman rhetorician Marcus Fabius Quintilian (ca. 35–ca. 100): *De Institutione oratoria libri duodecim collatione codicis Gothani et Iensonianae editionis aliorumque librorum ac perpetuo commentario illustrati a Io Matthia Gesnero accedit praefatio et indices copiosissimi* (Göttingen: Vandenhoeck, 1738). The continuing significance of Quintilian's treatise was based on the understanding that society in every

---

43 The numbers in parentheses refer to the sections of the *Schulordnung*.
44 *Schulordnung vor die Churfürstl. Braunschweig-Lüneburgische Lande* ... (Göttingen: Vandenhoeck, 1738), 142: "Die Anfangs-Gründe der Music sollen, so viel möglich, allen und jeden bekant gemachet, und dazu die nächste Stunde nach der Mittags-Mahlzeit angewendet werden. Wo an einer Schulen zwey Docenten zu haben sind, wird in zwey Classen zugleich Sing-Stunde gehalten; wo aber dieses nicht angehet, wird die Hälfte der Stunden vor die Anfänger und die andere Hälfte vor die, so etwas weiter gekommen sind, gehalten, und darauf gesehen, daß nicht nur diejenigen, so eine Stimme und natürliche Fähigkeit haben, nach und nach etwas treffen lernen; sondern auch die andern zum wenigsten die Bedeutung der Kunst-Wörter und Zeichen begreifen mögen."

generation depends on good orators such as politicians, lawyers, preachers, and teachers. The twelve books set out the theory and practice of rhetoric and are explorations of the fundamental premise that to be a good orator one must first be a good person. Quintilian's primary questions explored in Book I are: How are good orators created? What and where should they be taught? As to the location of teaching, while aware of the significance of the home, Quintilian sees the advantages of a school education, where an integrated curriculum can be followed. There the students should be taught reading, writing, and grammar, then such intellectual subjects as logic, geometry, mathematics, and history—studies to be complemented by physical exercises taught by actors and gymnasts. Music was fundamentally important in Quintilian's curriculum,[45] as was well-known at the time.[46] The section on music begins thus:

> Everyone knows that music ... was not only so much studied in ancient times but also so much venerated that Orpheus and Linus (not to mention others) were regarded both as musicians and as prophets and wise men ... no one can doubt that some men famous for wisdom have been students of music.[47]

Gesner in Göttingen endorsed what he read in Quintilian; Ernesti in Leipzig had a different mindset.

The so-called "Präfektenstreit"

In August 1736 Ernesti apparently deliberately set out to undermine Bach's authority in the Thomasschule by appointing prefects without reference to the cantor, which was a fundamental break from the traditional practice of such appointments. Up until that time the choice had always been made solely by the cantor, because a major part of the prefects' responsibilities was to direct the music in the other churches in the city, while Bach was directing the music in one or other of the two principal churches. These prefects therefore needed to be chosen by the cantor for their musical skills. The long, drawn-out dispute continued for years, with claims and counterclaims in which Bach complained to various authorities in Leipzig and Dresden, but the matter was never really resolved.[48] The following is a summary of its beginnings written some years later.

---

45 Quintilian, *De Institutione oratoria*, Bk. 1, 10: 9–34; Gesner, 50–55; Quintilian, *The Orator's Education*, trans. and ed. Donald A. Russell [The Loeb Classical Library] (Cambridge: Harvard University Press, 2001), 1:216–29.

46 See the 1683 petition of church musician Johann Caspar Horn to the Dresden city council for financial support that also makes reference to the music tradition of the Thomasschule in Leipzig, cited Maul, *Bach's Famous Choir*, 217.

47 Quintilian, *De Institutione oratoria*, Bk. 1, 10, 9–12; Gesner, 50–51; Russell, 1:216–19.

48 For the documents 1736–1737, see: BDok 1: 82–91, 95–106 (Nos. 32–35, 39–41, 99), 3: 268–76, 293 (Nos. 382–83, 406); NBR 172–86, 189–96 (Nos. 181–86, 192–96).

260 *Theology*

With Ernesti Bach fell out completely. The occasion was the following. Ernesti removed the general prefect [Gottfried Theodor] Krause for having chastised one of the younger students too rigorously, expelled him from the school when he fled [to avoid the corporal punishment that Ernesti sought to administer] and chose another student [who also had the same surname: Johann Gottlieb Krause] in his place as general prefect—a prerogative that really belongs to the cantor, whom the general prefect has to represent. Because the student chosen was of no use in the performance of the church music, Bach made a different choice. The situation between him and Ernesti developed to the point of charge and countercharge, and the two men from that time on were enemies. Bach began to hate those students who devoted themselves completely to the *humaniora* and treated music as a secondary matter, and Ernesti became a foe of music. When he came upon a student practicing on an instrument, he would exclaim "What? You want to be a beer-fiddler too?" By virtue of the high regard in which he was held by the Burgomaster [and school Versteher], Stieglitz, he managed to be released from the duties of the special inspection of the school and have them assigned to the fourth colleague. Thus when it was Bach's turn to undertake the inspection, he cited the precedent of Ernesti and came neither to table nor to prayers, and his neglect of duty had the worst influence on the moral training of the students. From that time on, though there have been several incumbents of both posts, little harmony has been observed between the rector and cantor.[49]

There are several details in this account that need to be noted. First is the reference to Stieglitz, which implies that Ernesti acted with his full support and suggests that the admissions procedure of the 1723 *Ordnungen* that gave the opportunity for the Vorsteher and rector to outvote the cantor, was now being applied to the appointment of prefects within the school. There is the interesting comment in Johann Joachim Quantz's treatise, *Versuch einer Anweisung die Flöte traversiere zu spielen*, written about ten years or so after the dispute began, that although it purports to be a general statement the details nevertheless reflect with some accuracy the situation in Leipzig, especially the role of the Vorsteher:

If a cantor is found here and there who understands his duties, and wants to administer his musical office honestly, at many places the authorities of the school ... seek to hinder the practice of music. And even in

---

49 "Historia Scholarum Lips. collecta a Joh. Frid. Köhlero, pastore Tauchensi. 1776," 94; BDok 3: 314 (No. 820); NBR 172 (No. 180). See, for example, the conflict between rector Johann Friedrich Fischer, who "hated music," and the successive cantors Johann Andreas Doles and Johann Adam Hiller, Maul, *Bach's Famous Choir*, 253–59, 267–76.

those schools which, as their laws attest, have been established principally with the aim that music should be taught and learned, and *musici eruditi* should be trained, the rector supported by the director [Vorsteher] is often the most open enemy of music.[50]

Second, although the dispute began as a disciplinary matter dealing with an overbearing prefect, one suspects that it was the excuse for which Ernesti and Stieglitz were waiting. The timing of the outbreak of the dispute in 1736 is significant, since Ernesti's *Initia doctrinae solidioris* was issued in a single volume for the first time that year. This suggests that the detailed curriculum had been introduced into the Thomasschule and that it was part of Ernesti's plan to use the prefects to ensure the implementation of the new curriculum, which meant that the role of music in the school had to be curtailed. Indeed, Bach appears to have registered a negative attitude towards the new curriculum: "Bach began to hate those students who devoted themselves completely to the *humaniora* [the humanities, the new curriculum] and treated music as a secondary matter."[51]

Third, Ernesti's demeaning discouragement of students using their free time for instrumental practice specifically contravened the 1733 *Gesetze* drawn up by Gesner.[52]

The intensity and bitterness of the dispute was no doubt exacerbated by the different personalities of the two stubborn protagonists: Ernesti the nitpicking pedant and Bach the mercurial genius, both somewhat pugnacious in asserting their points of view. Bach's conflicts with various authorities are well known, but Ernesti also seems to have been a rather quarrelsome person. For example, in the decades after Bach's death, Ernesti was in open conflict with another Leipzig professor, Christian August Crusius (1715–1775). They scolded and mocked each other in public, both attracting their partisan supporters and neither willing to back down or compromise. This later conflict sheds light on the dispute between Ernesti and Bach.[53]

---

50 Johann Joachim Quantz, *Versuch einer Anweisung die Flöte traversiere zu spielen* (Berlin: Boß, 1752; facsimile, Wiesbaden: Breitkopf & Härtel, 1988), 326 (Hauptstück XVIII, § 80); Johann Joachim Quantz, *On Playing the Flute*, trans. and ed. Edward R. Reilly, 2nd ed. (Boston: Northeastern University Press, 2001), 336–37.

51 See note 49 above.

52 See note 20 above.

53 See Karl Friedrich August Kahnis, *Internal History of German Protestantism since the Middle of Last Century* (1854), trans. Theodore Meyer (Edinburgh: Clark, 1856), 119–20. Kahnis's opinion of Ernesti is devastating: "Ernesti spoke Ciceronian Latin, but wanted Cicero's eloquence. He had good Latin words, but not very bright thoughts. With poor faculties of mind, he was astonishingly learned; but he owed his glory more to his industry than to his genius, more to his memory than to his depth. He was a great philologist, but not a great philosopher." Kahnis, *Internal History*, 120.

262   *Theology*

Was the cause of the conflict about theology or music?

The conflict in the 1730s between Bach and Ernesti has generally been viewed as illustrative of the collision of the tectonic plates of Orthodoxy and Rationalism that was occurring during the eighteenth century. On the one hand was Ernesti, the founder of the so-called grammatical-historical methodology that had significant rationalistic implications for New Testament hermeneutics,[54] and on the other hand there was Bach, whose choice of books in his personal library,[55] as well as the libretti of his church music,[56] displayed a much more conservative understanding of theology. The focus of attention has been Ernesti's important study, *Institutio interpretis novi testamenti* in which he expounded and explained his methodology of treating the scriptural text, that it should be studied in the same way as one would study the letters and treatises of Cicero or any other classical writer. But this was seen to devalue and undermine the status of the Bible. Thus, Paul Minear portrayed the animosity between the two Leipzig educators as being an "exegetical and theological conflict" that revealed "two approaches to the Bible," from which other dichotomies arose, such as, "two avenues towards Catholicity," and "two types of secularization."[57] The New Testament scholar, William Baird, summarizes the generally accepted view of the dispute as expounded by Stevenson, Minear, Pelikan, and others:

> Johann August Ernesti was a noted classical philologist ... In 1734, he was appointed principal of the Thomasschule at Leipzig ... There Ernesti had the misfortune of having on his staff a genius—J. S. Bach. Bach had been the cantor and instructor of music at St. Thomas since 1723, and when the young Ernesti (age twenty-seven) assumed leadership, conflict

---

54 William Baird, *History of New Testament Research: From Deism to Tübingen* (Minneapolis: Fortress, 1992), 108–15.

55 Robin A. Leaver, *Bachs theologische Bibliothek: Eine kritische Bibliographie* (Stuttgart: Hänssler, 1983).

56 See Melvin P. Unger, *Handook to Bach's Sacred Cantata Texts: An Interlinear Translation with Reference Guide to Biblical Quotations and Allusions* (Lanham: Scarecrow, 1996).

57 Paul S. Minear, "J. S. Bach and J. A. Ernesti: A Case Study in Exegetical and Theological Conflict," in *Our Common History as Christians: Essays in Honor of Albert C. Outler*, ed. John Deschner, et al. (New York: Oxford University Press, 1975), 131–55; a slightly revised version appears as chapter 1 of Paul S. Minear, *The Bible and the Historian: Breaking the Silence About God in Biblical Studies* (Nashville: Abingdon, 2002), 25–36. Minear is cited by Pelikan in his chapter "Rationalism and Aufkärung in Bach's Career," in Jaroslav Pelikan, *Bach Among the Theologians* (Philadephia: Fortress, 1986), 29–41; see also Robert M. Stevenson, "Bach's Quarrel with the Rector of the St. Thomas School," in Robert M. Stevenson *Patterns of Protestant Church Music* (Durham: Duke University Press, 1953), 67–77; Martin Petzoldt, "Zwischen Orthodoxie, Pietismus und Aufklärung : Überlegungen zum theologiegeschichtlichen Kontext Johann Sebastian Bachs," *Johann Sebastian Bach und die Aufklärung*, ed. Reinhard Szeskus, Bach-Studien, 7 (Leipzig: Breitkopf & Härtel, 1982), 78–81.

between the two strong personalities was inevitable. Actually, Bach, a devout Lutheran, was suspicious of Ernesti's Enlightenment sympathies, while Ernesti, who was preoccupied with philology, had little appreciation of music. A dispute arose between them in 1736 concerning the authority to appoint and discipline the student musical assistants, an authority each claimed as his. The dispute ... raged for months.[58]

The conflict between Ernesti and Bach has thus been characterized as the collision of two theologies, with Bach as the backward-looking Orthodox Lutheran and Ernesti as the forward-looking exponent of the emerging Enlightenment.[59] The key document, Ernesti's *Institutio interpretis novi testamenti*, first published in 1761—eleven years after Bach's death—called for the writings of the New Testament to be studied in the same way as Greek and Latin classics were studied. The treatise became foundational in biblical studies of the nineteenth century. But the edition of Ernesti's *Institutio* widely used in the nineteenth century was the fourth, edited by Christoph Ammon in 1792 (with later reprints), in which Ernesti's original 276 pages were expanded to 452 pages.[60] It is Ammon's copious annotations rather than Ernesti's original text that exhibit untrammeled rationalism. Ernesti's views were thus filtered through Ammon's Enlightenment interpretations. Ernesti himself preferred a more literal, grammatical interpretation of the biblical text, and his own views had more in common with Salomon Glassius's *Philologia sacra* (first published in 1623 with many later reprints)[61]—the classic Lutheran textbook on biblical linguistics—than with the later editor of his *Institutio*.

Then there is his call for the New Testament to be treated like any classic document, which offended the more conservative biblical scholars. But their offense was misplaced because he was not advocating what they thought he was advocating. Ernesti was seen to be devaluing the Scriptures by regarding them as no different from any other books. But that is not what he meant. In April 1736—the year that saw the publication of Ernesti's new curriculum in a single volume, and a few months before the prefect dispute broke out—he gave an oration in the Thomasschule. In it Ernesti denounced the generally accepted practice, what he termed the *stupor paedagogicus*, that is, the stupidity of teaching a fragmented reading of Latin authors with the single aim of developing a superior Latin style. In contrast he called for the reading of complete texts, or at least substantial portions of them, so that one could

---

58 Baird, *History of New Testament Research*, 108.

59 See, note 57 above.

60 Johann August Ernesti, *Institutio Interpretis Novi Testamenti. Editionem quintam suis observationibus auctam curavit Christoph Frider Ammon* (Leipzig: Weidmann, 1792).

61 Editions in print during Bach's time included an additional treatise by Glassius on sacred logic, edited by Johann Gottfried Olearius, superintendent in Arnstadt during Bach's time there; for example: Salomon Glass, *Philologiae sacrae* (Amsterdam: Wolters, 1711), 975–90.

264 *Theology*

learn the substance rather than simply the style of these documents.[62] His later call for reading the New Testament like non-sacred literature was the same methodology he had applied to the study of classic literature, that is, to encourage people to read substantial and consecutive passages of Scripture rather than relying solely on the fragmented Epistle and Gospel passages assigned to Sundays and celebrations of the church year.[63]

While later New Testament scholars praised Ernesti for pioneering the historical-grammatical method, they criticized him for his adherence to the Orthodox Lutheran position on biblical inspiration and the primacy of Scripture.[64] For example, Ernesti wrote this in his *Institutio interpretis novi testamenti*:

> Since the books of Scripture were written by inspired men, it is clear that no real contradiction can exist in them ... All interpretation, both of profane, and still more of the sacred books, ought to harmonize with the spirit of the author, and with the context. For men may, through ignorance or carelessness, insert that which is foreign to their purpose; the Holy Spirit cannot.[65]

Thus, to speak of Ernesti's "Enlightenment sympathies"[66] rather overstates the case and conflates later Enlightenment thinking with Ernesti's original position. The conflict between the two men, Bach and Ernesti, was not over differences in theology, since they both held substantially the same basic beliefs. It was rather, as explored in this chapter, a fundamental disagreement over the role of music in education, which had significant ramifications for the Leipzig churches as well as the Thomasschule.

Gesner's footnote on Bach

For centuries Quintilian's *De Institutione oratoria* was considered a fundamental educational treatise and was issued in numerous imprints and reprints

---

62 "De intereuntium humaniorum literarum caussis," Johann August Ernesti, *Opuscula varii argumenti* (Leipzig: Fritsch, 1794), 36–50; see also Lundgreen, "Schulhumanismus," 31–32, however, the year is wrongly recorded as 1738 instead of 1736.

63 For the background, see Chapter 1.

64 See John H. Sailhamer, "Johann August Ernesti: The Role of History in Biblical Interpretation," *Journal of the Evangelical Theological Society* 44/2 (2001): 206.

65 Johann August Ernesti, *Principles of Biblical Interpretation*, trans. Charles H. Terrot (Edinburgh: Clark, 1843), 38–39; Johann August Ernesti, *Institutio Interpretis Novi Testamenti, editio tertia* (Leipzig: Weidmann, 1775), 15: "Quoniam autem libri sacri scripti sunt a viris Θεοπνεύςις, facile intelligitur, veram dictorum repugnantiam in iis esse non posse ... omnis interpretatio, ut in libris humanis, sie multo magis in divinis, debebit consentire consilio scribentis, et orationi reliquae, contextum vocant. Nam homines possunt negligentia aut inscitia ponere, quae consilio non conveniant: Spiritus sanctus nullo modo." (I. sect. I. Cap.I. §23–24).

66 See note 58 above.

from the end of the fifteenth century.[67] Gesner's edition was published in 1738, a large quarto volume amounting to almost 850 pages, which must have taken some years to complete. It therefore seems highly likely that he would still be working on his edition during the early years of the Präfektenstreit in Leipzig, especially when it first erupted, 1736–1738. Since the dispute was noisy and controversial—involving the school, the city council, the consistory, and even the royal court of the King of Poland—the issue and the protagonists were certainly known by the people in these institutions, and even further afield. Thus, it is more than likely that Gesner was well aware of what was going on in Leipzig, and that it may have provided the impetus for him to add the footnote describing Bach in performance, especially as he mentions that a few years earlier they were colleagues together at the Thomasschule in Leipzig:

To Marcus Fabius Quintilianus

You would think but slightly, my dear Fabius, of all these [accomplishments of the citharists], if, returning from the underworld, you could see Bach (to mention him particularly, since he was not long ago my colleague at the Leipzig St. Thomas School), either playing our clavier [*polychordum*], which is many citharas in one, with all the fingers of both hands, or running over the keys of the instrument of instruments [*organon organorum*], whose innumerable pipes are brought to life by bellows, with both hands and, at the utmost speed, with his feet, producing by himself the most various and at the same time mutually agreeable combinations of sounds in orderly procession. If you could see him, I say, doing what many of your citharists and six hundred of your tibia players together could not do, not only, like a citharist, singing with one voice and playing his own parts, but watching over everything and bringing back to the rhythm and the beat, out of thirty or even forty musicians [*symphoniaci*], the one with a nod, another by tapping with his foot, the third with a warning finger, giving the right note to one from the top of his voice, to another from the bottom, and to a third from the middle of it—all alone, in the midst of the greatest din made by all the participants, and, although he is executing the most difficult parts himself, noticing at once whenever and wherever a mistake occurs, holding everyone together, taking precautions everywhere, and repairing any unsteadiness, full of rhythm in every part of his body—this one man taking in all these harmonies with his keen ear and emitting with his voice alone the tone of all the voices. Favorer as I am of antiquity, the accomplishments of my Bach,[68] and of any others

---

67 See Johannes Albertus Fabricius, *Bibliotheca Latina Sive Notitia Auctorum Veterum Latinorum* ... (Hamburg: Schiller, 1721–1722), 1: 421–31.

68 Gesner presents a contrast between "my Bach" (singular) and "your Orpheuses and Arions" (plural): "multus unum Orpheas & viginti Arionas complexum Bachium meum & si quis illi similis sit forte, arbitror."

266 *Theology*

who may be like him, appear to me to effect what not many Orpheuses, nor twenty Arions, could achieve.[69]

The footnote is not, as one might expect, appended to words in Quintilian's section on music but rather to a later passage where he deals with the possibility of multitasking, and does so by describing musicians in performance. Gesner's footnote is a commentary on the phrase "et haec pariter omnia" (all this goes on simultaneously). Quintilian wrote the following:

> The power of the human mind ... is so nimble and quick ... that it cannot even concentrate exclusively on one thing at a time, but applies its powers to many objects, not only on the same day but at the same moment. Singers to the lyre simultaneously attend to their memory and to the sound and various inflexions of the voice, meanwhile running over certain strings with the right hand, and plucking, stopping, or releasing others with the left; even the foot is kept occupied in beating time; and all this goes on simultaneously.[70]

Gesner's footnote is a superlative illustration of Quintilian's description of the various levels of simultaneous activity that music-making requires. It describes Bach as the consummate virtuoso both in his own performance and in his direction of the performance of others. When these words first appeared in print the dispute in Leipzig was still raging. Gesner must have been aware that whatever he said about one of the key people in the conflict in Leipzig would carry much weight, since, as the former rector of the Thomasschule, he had firsthand knowledge of the institutions of school, church, and city and was personally acquainted with the protagonists involved. The image of Bach that Gesner presents is far different from that held by Stieglitz and Ernesti, among others, in Leipzig. Quintilian presents musicians "as prophets and wise men"[71]; Gesner describes Bach as a remarkable musician who belongs alongside other famous and wise men. Gesner's edition of Quintilian is supplied with three indexes: the first a very full and detailed index of "Verborum, Phrasium, ac Rerum" (words, phrases, and subjects); the second is of authors quoted by Quintilian; and the third is of "Auctorum veterum ac recentium qui in Notis laudantur" (authors old and new who are praised in the notes).

---

69 Quintilian, *De Institutione oratoria*, Gesner, 61; BDok 2: 331–33 (No. 432); NBR 328–29 (No. 328). It is interesting to note that, the year before, in an anonymous letter published in *Der Critische Musicus*, 14 May 1737, Johann Adolph Scheibe also noted the dexterity of Bach's performances: "I have heard this great man play on many occasions. One is amazed at his ability, and one can hardly conceive how it is possible for him to achieve such agility, with his fingers and with his feet, in the crossings, extensions, and extreme jumps that he manages, without mixing in a single wrong tone, or displacing his body by any violent movement"; NBR 338 (No. 343); BDok 2: 286 (No. 400).

70 Quintilian, *De Institutione oratoria*, Bk. 1, 12, 2–4; Gesner, 61; Russell, 1:244–47.

71 See note 47 above.

Among contemporary (or near contemporary) authors in this third index are found, among others, such names as Jean Le Clerc (1657–1736), theologian; Johannes Albertus Fabricius (1688–1736), philologist; Johann Friedrich Gronovius (1611–1671), classical scholar; and Johann Heinrich Kromayer (1689–1734), philologist. Somewhat surprisingly Ernesti's name does not appear in this index, even though he had recently published a new edition of Cicero's *Opera omnia* in four volumes (dedicated to Stieglitz).[72] But Bach's name, even though he was not an author, is indexed along with these and other wise and worthy men, such as Juvenal, Plato, Seneca, Socrates, and Tacitus: "Bachii, Musici Lips. laus" (In praise of Bach, musician in Leipzig).[73]

Whatever the antagonism between Bach and Ernesti, the two philologists appear to have maintained a cordial friendship after Gesner left Leipzig. Ernesti's account of Gesner's life and works is notable for the respect and admiration Ernesti had for his former colleague. He speaks of their unbroken friendship (*unverbrüchliche Freundschaft*) over the twenty-seven years of Gesner's life after he left Leipzig,[74] and of their frequent correspondence during these years.[75] But Gesner also had a deep respect and admiration for Bach, as is clear from his Quintilian footnote. The Präfektenstreit therefore presented him with a personal dilemma: How could he support Bach without offending Ernesti? Or vice versa? Perhaps his Quintilian footnote was the solution?

Gesner's footnote in Leipzig

Ernesti's biographical account of Gesner[76] was originally written in Latin shortly after the latter's death in 1761. The following year David Ruhnken (1723–1798), professor of history and eloquence at Leiden University— classicist and admirer of Ernesti—edited and published a collection of Ernesti's Latin speeches and other writings, reprinted from individual imprints issued in Leipzig. Ernesti's account of Gesner is the only item in the volume to be specifically named on the title page: Johann August Ernesti, *Opuscula oratoria, orationes, Prolusiones et Elogia. Accessit Narratio de Jo. Matthia Gesnero ad Davidem Ruhnkenium* (Leiden: Luchtmans, 1762). The volume has three sections. The first comprises eight *Orationum* (orations), the second, five *Prolusionum* (introductions), and the third, twelve *Elogiorum* (elegies) on deceased Leipzig professors and scholars. Ernesti's memoir of Gesner appears at the end of the volume as a kind of appendix that is much longer than any of the preceding elegies.[77]

---

72 *M. Tullii Ciceronis Opera omnia*, ed. Johann August Ernesti (Leipzig: Martini, 1737).

73 Quintilian, *De Institutione oratoria*, Gesner, Index III, sig. Mmmmm3r.

74 Ernesti, *Denkmäler und Lobschriften auf gelehrte*, 192.

75 Ibid., 214, 218, 241.

76 See note 2 above.

77 Each of the elegies averages between 10 and 12 pages; the *Biographie* of Gesner covers 35 pages.

268   *Theology*

In 1792 the third section comprising these memorial tributes was published separately in German translation, and again only the Gesner biography is referred to on the title page: Johann August Ernesti, *Denkmäler und Lobschriften auf gelehrte, verdienstvolle Männer, seine Zeitgenossen nebst der Biographie Johann Matthias Geßners, in einer Erzählung für David Ruhnken* (Leipzig: Schwickert, 1792). The aim of this German volume was to celebrate these academics and scholars and the significance of their contributions not only for Leipzig but for Germany as a whole. The German versions appear in the same sequence as in the 1762 Latin volume:

> Johann Friedrich Christ (1701–1756), professor of poetry, sometime rector of the university
> Johann Christian Hebenstreit (1686–1756), professor of theology
> Johann Florenz Rivinus (1681–1755), professor of law,[78] sometime rector of the university
> Benjamin Gottlieb Bosseck (1676–1758), jurist and professor of law
> Johann Ernst Hebenstreit (1703–1757), professor of medicine, sometime dean of the medical faculty
> Christian Gottlieb Jöcher (1694–1758), professor of history and university librarian[79]
> Friedrich August Sandel (1688–1759), medical doctor
> Carl Gottfried Winckler (1691–1758), lawyer and judge
> Heinrich Dietrich Nedderhof (1730–1758), student of medicine
> Georg Gottfried Zehmisch (1735–1759), master of philosophy and fine art
> Johann Zacharias Platner (1694–1747), professor of anatomy and surgery
> Justus Gottfried Günsten (1714–1754), professor of medicine
> Johann Matthias Gesner

All these men had strong connections with Leipzig, mostly with the university, but a good many of them also simultaneously held other positions in the city, as councilors or burgermeisters, or had responsibilities in the churches, schools, or consistory. Some also held positions in the electoral Saxon and royal Polish courts in Dresden. Although Gesner was never a professor in Leipzig, he had been well received as the rector of the Thomasschule, and his subsequent reputation in Göttingen was widely respected.

The translator and editor of the German volume was Gottlob Friedrich Rothe (1733–1813), who had spent most of his life in Leipzig: Born in Grimma, where his father was cantor, Rothe was a Thomaner between

---

78 With Johann August Ernesti, Johann Florenz Rivinus was godfather to Johann Christian Bach in 1735; see note 37 above.

79 Jöcher was the editor of the *Allgemeines Gelehrten-Lexicon*, 4 vols. (Leipzig: Gleditsch, 1733–1751). In 1730 Jöcher was considered for the position of rector of the Thomasschule but was passed over in favor of Gesner; see Maul, *Bach's Famous Choir*, 209.

Bach, Gesner, and Ernesti 269

1744–1752; in private service for a decade before becoming the *custos* (sexton) of the Johanneskirche, 1763–1772; from 1772 he was the custos of the Thomaskirche.[80] Rothe supplied an introduction to the volume—entitled, "Etwas über Ernesti, über und für die Übersetzung" (Something on Ernesti, and about the translation), and began with the words "Ernesti der Große" (Ernesti the great). The introduction is partly a panegyric honoring Ernesti's multifaceted expertise and his "good and elegant Latin," and partly a celebration of the worthiness of the notables whose lives and works are recorded in the volume, eight of whom had been students of Ernesti in Leipzig, either in the Thomasschule or the university or both.[81]

In translating these Ernesti essays, Rothe was concerned not only to reveal the details of the lives of these illustrious men but also to record connections with the churches in Leipzig. To begin with he dedicated the volume to four individuals who held primary responsibilities in the two principal churches: Burgermaster Carl Wilhelm Müller (1728–1801), Vorsteher of both the church and the school of St. Nicholas;[82] Burgermaster Adolph Christian Wendler (1734–1794), Vorsteher of the church of St. Thomas;[83] Johann Georg Rosenmüller (1736–1815), professor of theology, superintendent, and pastor of the St. Thomas church;[84] and Christian Gottlieb Kühlnöl (1736–1805), pastor of the St. Nicholas church.[85] Since all of the people who were memorialized by Ernesti had died more than a generation earlier, and also some of the people mentioned in these writings were similarly distant or unknown figures, Rothe added some footnotes giving relevant information that made Ernesti's prose more accessible in the later eighteenth century. Significantly a number of the individuals who are highlighted in these footnotes were connected with the Leipzig churches. They include, Christoph Wolle (1700–1761), professor of theology and archdeacon of the Thomaskirche, who is described as the "beloved preacher" (beliebtesten Canzelredner);[86] Salomon Deyling (1677–1755), professor of theology, superintendent and pastor of the

---

80 Stefan Altner and Martin Petzoldt, eds., *800 Jahre Thomana: Glauben, Singen, Lernen* (Wettin-Löbejün: Stekovics, 2012), 462.

81 Ernesti, *Denkmäler und Lobschriften*, iii–xxvi; see also note 2 above. In a list of important personalities "Bach" is mentioned (ibid., xi), but this is a reference to Johann August Bach (1721–1758), legal historian who had been a Thomaner and a student at Leipzig University; Richter, "Stadtpfeifer und Alumnen der Thomasschule," 72 (No. 172).

82 Kühling and Mundus, *Leipzigs Regierende Bürgermeister*, 50–51.

83 Ibid., 52; Maul, *Bach's Famous Choir*, 305.

84 Altner and Petzoldt, *800 Jahre Thomana*, 445. Burgermaster Müller promoted Rosenmüller for the position of superintendent against local opposition; see Maul, *Bach's Famous Choir*, 268.

85 Altner and Petzoldt, *800 Jahre Thomana*, 449.

86 Ernesti, *Denkmäler und Lobschriften*, 16; Altner and Petzoldt, *800 Jahre Thomana*, 448. Wolle was Bach's last Beichtvater (confessor); for Wolle's interaction with the Bach family, see Robin A. Leaver, "Churches," in Leaver, *The Routledge Research Companion to Johann Sebastian Bach*, 177.

270   Theology

Nikolaikirche;[87] and Johann Gottfried Körner (1726–1785), professor of theology, superintendent, and pastor of the Thomaskirche.[88]

A noticeable though understandable feature of Ernesti's biographical account of Gesner, given the Leipzig prefect controversy that had begun in the mid-1730s, is that there is no mention of Bach, who was a colleague of Gesner for two years at the Weimar court and a colleague of both Gesner and Ernesti for four years in the Thomasschule in Leipzig. But Rothe, while he was too young to have had personal experience of Gesner, had been a Thomaner for five years under both Bach and Ernesti.[89] Rothe thus supplied what was lacking in Ernesti's account of Gesner by adding a complete German translation of Gesner's Quintilian description of Bach in performance in a footnote to Ernesti's biographical memoire of Gesner.[90] Rothe introduced Gesner's words with the following:

> Gesner's philanthropic character, benevolent kindness, and friendship with those who had been in a collegial relationship with him, not least his recognition and appreciation of their merits, find strong evidence in a note in his Quintilian no. 1–3, concerning his former colleague, the famous Johann Sebastian Bach, Fürstl. Cöthen Capellmeister[91] and cantor of the St. Thomas school in Leipzig, and thus honors Gesner's sympathy. In the location, where Quintilian speaks of and admires the skill and art of the ancient cithara players, Gesner says in the note … [Then follows Rothe's German translation of Gesner's note].[92]

It is doubtful that Rothe translated the footnote directly from Gesner's Quintilian. His most likely source is the brief biography of Bach—based on the obituary by C. P. E. Bach and Johann Friedrich Agricola[93] and the entry on Bach in Johann Gottfried Walther's *Musikalisches Lexicon*[94]—that Johann Adam Hiller included in his *Lebensbeschreibungen berühmter Musikgelehrten und Tonkünstler neuerer Zeit* (Leipzig, 1784),[95] which concludes with the

---

87 Ernesti, *Denkmäler und Lobschriften*, 31. Altner and Petzoldt, *800 Jahre Thomana*, 443. Deyling was superintendent during the whole of Bach's 27 years in Leipzig; see also Leaver, "Churches," 175–76.

88 Ernesti, *Denkmäler und Lobschriften*, 154; Altner and Petzoldt, *800 Jahre Thomana*, 444–45.

89 Between 1744 and 1750; Richter, "Stadtpfeifer und Alumnen der Thomasschule," 75 (No. 260).

90 Ernesti, *Denkmäler und Lobschriften*, 191–92.

91 Interesting that Rothe should refer to the title of Cöthen Capellmeister that ended with the death of Leopold of Anhalt-Cöthen in 1728, rather than more prestigious Hofcompositeur to the royal court in Dresden, awarded to Bach in 1736.

92 BDok 5: 257–58 (No. C 978b).

93 BDok 3: 80–93 (No. 666); NBR 297–307 (No. 306).

94 BDok 2: 231 (No. 323); NBR 294–95 (No. 304).

95 Johann Adam Hiller, *Lebensbeschreibungen berühmter Musikgelehrten und Tonkünstler neuerer Zeit … Erster Theil* (Leipzig: Dykisch, 1784; facsimile, Leipzig: Peters, 1975), 9–29. On Hiller see further below.

Bach, Gesner, and Ernesti 271

complete Latin footnote.[96] Given the nature of the anthology that Rothe translated, the addition of Gesner's footnote effectively aligns Bach with the other important names from Leipzig's immediate past.

Rothe's translations of Ernesti's biographical essays were published at a time when far-reaching reforms of church life in the city were taking place. It was a movement of modernization as the leaders of the Leipzig churches attempted to move away from what was perceived to be lifeless formalism inherited from Orthodoxy in favor of a more expressive religious environment, what has been described as "pious enlightenment," an amalgam of elements of Pietism and Rationalism. In many respects Leipzig was among the last cities to undertake similar reforms; elsewhere in Germany such changes had generally taken place much earlier.[97] In Leipzig the prime mover was Burgermeister Carl Wilhelm Müller who, as Vorsteher of the Nikolaikirche, advocated and oversaw the reconstruction of the interior of the church in a neoclassical style between 1784 and 1797, completely disguising the medieval structure of the building. In 1785 Müller was instrumental in securing the appointment of Johann Georg Rosenmüller as superintendent and pastor of the Thomaskirche, and around three years later, in 1789, was similarly involved in securing Johann Adam Hiller (1728–1804) as the Thomascantor.

Almost immediately after his appointment Rosenmüller, encouraged by Burgermeister Müller, began to make changes in the liturgical practice of the churches in the city, mostly by curtailing as much as possible in order to make the services shorter, more accessible, and more "modern." These changes included the elimination of most of the Latin hymns and other liturgical texts, the introduction of new liturgical formularies, exchanging many of the older hymns of the sixteenth and seventeenth centuries with newer more accessible hymns with lighter melodies, the abandonment of eucharistic vestments, public confession replacing private confession, and so forth.[98] However, such changes were not made without controversy, opposition, and some decline in congregational attendance. Rosenmüller directed the changes that were to be made, and Rothe, as custos of the Thomaskirche, recorded them in detail in the manuscript notebook begun by Johann Christoph Rost in 1716.[99] Cantor Hiller supported the changes by supplying appropriate music in the fashionable Galant/Empfindsamer style.

---

96 Hiller, *Lebensbeschreibungen*, 27–29.
97 For the general background, see Paul Graff, *Geschichte der Auflösung der alten gottesdienstlichen Formen in der evangelischen Kirche Deutschlands. 2. Band. Die Zeit der Aufklärung und des Rationalismus* (Göttingen: Vandenhoeck & Ruprecht, 1939).
98 See Günther Stiller, *Johann Sebastian Bach and Liturgical Life in Leipzig*, trans. Herbert J. A. Bouman, et al., ed. Robin A. Leaver (St. Louis: Concordia, 1984), 158–67.
99 Johann Cristoph Rost, "Nachricht, Wie es, in der Kirchen zu St: Thom: alhier, mit dem Gottesdienst, jährlichen sowohl an Hohen Festen, als andern Tagen, pfleget gehalten zu werden. Auffgezeichnet von Johann Christoph Rosten, Custode ad D. Thomae. Anno 1716." Thomaskirche Archiv, uncataloged manuscript.

272   *Theology*

Music was extremely important in the liturgical reforms, and all the men who spearheaded the introduction of the changes had impressive musical pedigrees. Burgermeister Müller was an accomplished musician who played violin, viola d'amore, and clavier, and was involved in the founding of the Gewandhaus Orchestra, for which he served as an early director. According to Hiller, superintendent Rosenmüller had a "warm love of music" that was "grounded in understanding and knowledge."[100] Custos Rothe had been a Thomaner and must have been a gifted singer, since, on entering the Thomasschule at the age of ten or eleven in 1744, he went straight into Bach's "erste Kantorei."[101] Such an occurrence did not happen very often;[102] it was usual for a new boy to enter one of the other choirs (IV or III), gaining experience before moving up into the next highest choir. Hiller had already been a leading figure in the musical life of Leipzig for many decades before he became the Thomascantor in 1789.[103] He had been successively music director of the university's Paulinerkirche, music director of the Neuekirche, conducted performances of the orchestra of the Großes Concert that morphed into the Gewandhaus Orchestra, of which he was its first conductor, and so forth. Although no longer a young man, he was nevertheless vigorous and effective in reestablishing the Thomasschule, preeminently as a music school that served the needs of the Leipzig churches.[104] Thus, Hiller's reforms had the opposite effect compared with Ernesti's curricular changes made in the later 1730s, which had diminished the role of music in school and church.

On becoming cantor Hiller was faced with having to deal with the disorganization and low morale in the school that had been created by the open antagonism between the rector, Johann Friedrich Fischer (1726–1799), and Hiller's predecessor, cantor Johann Friedrich Doles (1715–1797).[105] A visitor in 1784 observed the situation:

> The school has a worthy man in Rector Fischer. But he does not get along with any of his colleagues. Cantor Doles is an implacable foe of his.

---

100 "Die warme, auf Einsicht und Kenntniß gegründete Liebe zur Musik"; from the extended dedication to Rosenmüller in the revision of his 1761 settings of Gellert's hymns: Johann Adam Hiller, *Fünf und zwanzig neue Choralmelodien zu Liedern von Gellert* (Leipzig: Breitkopf, 1792), [iii]. Custos Rothe was a subscriber to this collection; see ibid, [vi].

101 See Bernhard Friedrich Richter, "Stadtpfeifer und Alumnen der Thomasschule in Leipzig zu Bachs Zeit," BJ 4 (1907): 77, and 75 (No. 260); Andreas Glöckner, "'The ripienists must also be at least eight, namely two for each part': The Leipzig Line of 1730—Some Observations," *Early Music* 39 (2011): 576–77 (Table 1).

102 See BDok 3: 429 (No. 916); and Glöckner, "'The ripienists," 580.

103 See his autobiography: Hiller, *Lebensbeschreibungen*, 286–320.

104 See Maul, *Bach's Famous Choir*, 259–72; Jeffrey S. Sposato, *Leipzig After Bach: Church and Concert Life in a German City* (New York: Oxford University Press, 2018), 157–88.

105 Maul, *Bach's Famous Choir*, 246–59; Sposato, *Leipzig After Bach*, 114–34.

I don't know whether it is even possible for young people to learn anything at all when teachers quarrel with one another in the classrooms.[106]

Hiller was now the cantor, but Fischer—who had begun his career at the Thomasschule in 1751, being appointed conrector on the recommendation of Ernesti—was still the rector. What had been the fractious norm between Fischer and Doles continued between Fischer and Hiller. There is a certain irony in the similarity of this later rector–cantor conflict with the earlier Praefektenstreit that had occurred between Ernesti and Bach a half-century before. Hiller presumably must have been aware of that conflict, since his teacher, Gottfried August Homilius (1714–1785), had been a law student at Leipzig University between 1735 and 1742, during which time he also studied with Bach, that is, during the initial years of the conflict between Bach and Ernesti. Similarly, it seems likely that custos Rothe, who had sung under Bach and studied under Ernesti, was aware of what had begun a few years before he became a Thomaner. Rothe and Hiller may have respected Ernesti as an erudite educator and scholar, but perhaps their current situation with regard to rector Fischer gave them a different perspective on Bach, who had continued to teach and perform under difficult circumstances. What is most interesting is that Gesner's footnote, first published in Latin during the immediate aftermath of the Praefektenstreit, should reappear in German during a similar period of conflict between rector and cantor towards the end of the eighteenth century.

---

106 Helmut Banning, *Johann Friedrich Doles: Leben und Werke* (Leipzig: Kister & Siegel, 1939), 79; cited in Maul, *Bach's Famous Choir*, 255–56.

13 Bach and Erdmann Neumeister

Erdmann Neumeister was a dominant personality in the first half of eighteenth-century Germany. His primary function was that of pastor—preaching, teaching, and writing devotional books. But he was also known for his religious and other poetry, having taught poetics for a time in Leipzig. His devotional verse, which could be warm and sensitive, was frequently at variance with his polemical writings, which fiercely and unremittingly upheld the tenets of Lutheran Orthodoxy against the views of Pietists, Calvinists, Moravians, Roman Catholics, Jews, and others. A Weissenfels historian had to admit: "The man is a psychological riddle when I see the poet of pious songs and the man of biting satire united in his person."[1] But the paradox was often not recognized because he did not always write under his own name, using at least fifteen or more different pseudonyms, such as Hildebrand Eschinger, Christian Lauterwahr, Menippus, Adami Martini, Georg Meuerstein, Orthodoxophilius, among others. Some of this has already surfaced in this book, notably in Chapter 5, which explores the large part he played in the importation of operatic musical genres into the church, thus creating a new liturgical cantata form—something that was not acceptable to all his coreligionists—and in Chapter 11, which makes reference to his primary role as an ardent anti-Pietist. From time to time Bach and Neumeister were in contact with each other, and Bach is known to have used a number of Neumeister's cantata libretti. This chapter seeks to explore the significance of these encounters and to discover whether there might have been other connections between the two men. The evidence is often sporadic and incomplete, but at least it presents the opportunity to draw attention to the extensive involvement in music that was characteristic of the court of Saxe-Weissenfels.

---

1 Friedrich Gerhardt, *Geschichte der Stadt Weissenfels a. S. mit neuen Beiträgen zur Geschichte des Herzogtums Sachsen-Weissenfels* (Weissenfels: Urlaub, [1907]), 374–75: "Der Mann ist ein psychologisches Rätzel, wenn ich den Dichter frommer Lieder und den Mann der beissenden Satire in seiner Person vereinigt sehe."

Neumeister and Weissenfels

Exactly when Bach and Neumeister became known to each other is not entirely clear, because the evidence is somewhat sparse. Nevertheless, the fact that both had close and continuing connections with the court of Weissenfels suggests that this was where they first became aware of each other.

Neumeister was born in Uichteritz, three or four miles from Weissenfels, in 1671.[2] After attending schools in Weissenfels and Schulpforta, he matriculated in theology at the University of Leipzig in 1689. A man of pious conviction, he spent much of his time cultivating poetry, a major part of which was religious in content. In 1695 he published his thesis, *De poetis Germanicis huius seculi praecipuis dissertatio compendiaria*, a pioneering work on German poetry. Between 1695 and 1697 he taught poetics in Leipzig, and some years later the substance of these lectures was published—without his consent—by Christian Friedrich Hunold (1680–1721),[3] under the pseudonym Menantes, as *Die Allerneueste Art/ Zur Reinen Galanten Poesie zu gelangen* (Hamburg: Liebernickel, 1707). In 1696 Neumeister married Johanna Elisabeth Meister, who was the second daughter of the head chef of the Weissenfels court. The marriage produced a number of children who, like their parents, retained their contacts with Saxe-Weissenfels. For example, in later years, when the children had grown up and married, Neumeister's son and a son-in-law served the principality as church councilors (Fürstl. Sachsen-Weissenfelsischen Kirchen-Rath).

The year following his marriage, 1697, Neumeister took on his first pastorate, as the substitute pastor in Bibra, about twenty miles from Weissenfels. Here he quickly advanced from substitute to permanent pastor, and then to superintendent. But at the same time he was attending to these responsibilities in Bibra he maintained contacts with the Weissenfels court. For example, a cycle of sermons on the Gospels of the church year that he preached in Bibra were later issued by the court publisher in Weissenfels, Johann Friedrich Wehrmann.[4] Around the same time as he was preaching these Bibra sermons

---

2 On Neumeister, see Zedler 24 (1740): cols., 259–73; Eduard Emil Koch, *Geschichte des Kirchenlieds und Kirchengesangs der christlichen, insbesondere der deutschen evangelischen Kirche*, 3rd ed. (Stuttgart: Belser, 1866–1877), 5: 371–81; Hans Schröder, *Lexikon der hamburgischen Schriftsteller bis zur Gegenwart* (Hamburg: Verein für hamburgische Geschichte, 1851–1883), 5: 494–512. Henrike Rucker, "Kurze Lebensbeschreibung Erdmann Neumeisters," in *Erdmann Neumeister (1671–1756): Wegbereiter der evangelischen Kirchenkantate*, ed. Henrike Rucker (Rudolstadt: Hain, 2000), 19–23; Ute Poetzsch-Seban, "Bach und Neumeister—Bach und Telemann," in *Telemann und Bach: Telemann-Beiträge*, ed. Brit Reipsch and Wolf Hobohm, Magdeburger Telemann-Studien XVIII (Hildesheim: Olms, 2005), 54–62; Hans-Joachim Schulze, "Wege und Irrwege: Erdmann Neumeister und die Bach-Forschung," in *Bach-Facetten* (Leipzig: Evangelische Verlagsanstalt, 2017), 403–09.

3 Hunold would later supply Bach with libretti for five Cöthen cantatas: BWV 66a, 134a, BWV Anh. 5, 6, 7.

4 Erdmann Neumeister, *Worte der Weisen Statt eines Leit-Sterns Zum Wort der mannichfaltigen Weisheit Gottes. Oder: Hoher Personen Christliche Symbola, Bey Schrifftmäßiger und Lehrreicher*

276   Theology

he was involved in two projects for the Weissenfels court. One that significantly contributed to the content of worship in the court chapel was Neumeister's cycle of cantata libretti for the church year, written for the Capellmeister, Johann Philipp Krieger (1649–1725), who composed and performed them in the court chapel either in 1700 or 1701. These libretti were published anonymously a year or so later as *I. N. I. Geistliche Cantaten Uber alle Sonn- Fest- und Apostel-Tage/ Zu einer denen Herren Musicis sehr bequemen Kirchen -Music In ungezwungenen Teutschen Versen ausgefertiget. Anno 1702*.[5] A second edition was issued under Neumeister's name: *Geistliche Cantaten statt einer Kirchen-Music. Die zweyte Auflage Nebst einer neuen Vorrede/ auf Unkosten Eines guten Freundes* ([s. l.]: [s.n.], 1704). Thus, the identity of the author of these libretti was revealed, and the new preface Neumeister wrote unequivocally stated that the religious recitatives and arias were modeled on secular operatic forms.[6]

The Weissenfels court was noted for its extensive music, both secular and religious. Operas of various types were performed regularly alongside a fully developed program of sacred music, all under the direction of Capellmeister Krieger.[7] This was the musical environment that stimulated Neumeister to develop a new approach to the cantata form. But the cantatas were not regarded as secondary in importance when compared with the operas presented at the court. Krieger kept an inventory of his sacred music performed in the court chapel that, over the years, totaled an astonishing 2,250 cantatas or more, though virtually none of the music has survived.[8]

The second project for the Weissenfels court that Neumeister worked on in Bibra was a devotional handbook to be used in connection with attending Confession and participating in the Lord's Supper: *Der Zugang zum Gnaden-Stuhl Jesu Christo, Das ist: Christliche Gebete und Gesänge Vor, bey und*

Erklärung aller Sonn- und Fest-Tags Evangelien, Wie auch am Reformations- und Kirch-Weyhungs-Feste, so anmuthig, als erbaulich angewendet. Hiebevor einer Christlichen Gemeine im Stifft Bibra geprediget ... (Weissenfels: Wehrmann, 1706). A second edition of these sermons was published, again by the court publisher in Weissenfels, seventeen years later, when he was the pastor of the Jacobikirche Hamburg: *Worte der Weisen* (Weissenfels: Wehrmann, 1723).

5 See Chapter 5, note 29.

6 See Wolfgang Miersemann, "Erdmann Neumeisters 'Vorbericht' zu seinen 'Geistlichen Cantaten' von 1704: ein literatur- und musikprogrammatisches 'Meister-Stück,'" Rucker, *Neumeister ... Wegbereiter der evangelischen Kirchenkantate*, 51–74.

7 See Arno Werner, *Städtische und fürstliche musikpflege in Weissenfels bis zum ende des 18. Jahrhunderts* (Leipzig: Breitkopf & Härtel, 1911), esp. 51–147; Adolf Schmiedecke, "Zur Geschichte der Weißenfelser Hofkapelle," *Die Musikforschung* (1961), 416–23; Klaus-Peter Koch, "Das Jahr 1704 und die Weißenfelser Hofoper: Zu den Umständen der Aufführung von Reinhard Keisers Oper *Almira* anläßlich des Besuches des Pfälzischen Kurfürsten am Weißenfelser Hof," in *Weißenfels als Ort literarischer und künstlerischer Kultur im Barockzeitalter*, ed. Roswitha Jacobsen (Amsterdam: Rodopi, 1994), 75–95; Wolfgang Ruf, "The Courts of Saxony-Weißenfels, Saxony-Merseburg, and Saxony-Zeitz," in Samantha Owens, Barbara M. Reul, and Janice B. Stockigt, eds., *Music at German Courts, 1715–1760: Changing Artistic Priorities* (Woodbridge: Boydell, 2011), esp. 227–35.

8 Ruf, "The Courts of Saxony-Weißenfels," 232.

nach der Beichte und Heil. Abendmahl; Nebst Morgen- und Abend-Seegen und dergleichen neuen Liedern. Auf gottseliges Ansinnen und Vorschrift Sr. Hochfürst. Durchlaucht Johannis Georgii, Herzogen zu Sachsen-Weissenfels. Anno 1703. (Access to the Throne of Grace[9] of Jesus Christ, that is: Christian Prayers and Hymns Before, During and After Confession and the Holy Sacrament; together with Morning and Evening Prayers and similar New Hymns. At the Godly Request and Direction of his Serene Highness, Johann Georg, Duke of Saxe-Weissenfels).[10] But it was apparently not published at that time. However, the contents of this devotional book, together with his cantata libretti, must have impressed the duke greatly, since in 1704 he appointed Neumeister as court deacon in Weissenfels, with the special responsibility to "instill spiritual matters" (Aufricht in geistlichen Dingen) into his princess daughter.[11]

Probably during his first year in Weissenfels, Neumeister preached sermons on all the Epistles of the church year in the court chapel, according to custom, at Sunday Vespers. Approaching fifteen years later they were published: *Epistolische Nachlese/ Derjenigen Predigten/ Welche er* [Neumeister] *ehedessen In der Fürstlichen Schloß-Kirche zu Weissenfelß/ Uber die Sonn- und Fest-Tags Epistel-Texte/ gehalten/ Und nebst Sechs Paßions-Predigten* (Hamburg: Liebezeit, 1720). The sermons were dedicated to Duke Christian, who had succeeded his brother in 1712 and was, therefore, not the duke during whose time these sermons of Neumeister were given in the court chapel. Thus, it witnesses to the way in which he continued his connections with the Weissenfels court in later years, which was marked by the succession of congratulatory epistles in Neumeister's publications issued between 1736 and 1741, addressed to Christian's brother, Johann Adolf II, who regularly personally responded to Neumeister.[12]

The Epistle for the Twentieth Sunday after Trinity, Ephesians 5: 15–21, in *Epistolische Nachlese* includes words about singing, which elicits from Neumeister the following comment in the sermon he preached on the passage in the Weissenfels court chapel:

---

9 An alternative translation is "Mercy Seat," the gold covering of the Ark of the Covenant; see Exodus 25: 10–22. The Ark represented the presence of God, and on the Day of Atonement sins were covered by the sprinkling of blood on the "Gnaden-Stuhl"; Leviticus 16.

10 For the background, see Wolfgang Miersemann, "Lieddichtung im Spannungsfeld zwischen Orthodoxie und Pietismus: zu Erdmann Neumeisters Weißenfelser Kommunionbuch *Der Zugang zum Gnaden-Stuhl Jesu Christo*," in Jacobsen, *Weißenfels als Ort literarischer und künstlischer Kultur*, 177–216. In 1718 Neumeister preached a sermon in the Jacobikirche, Hamburg, on *Der Zugang zum Gnaden-Stuhl Jesu Christo*, in which he confirmed that it was written for Duke Johann Georg of Saxe-Weissenfels; Erdmann Neumeister, *Geistliche Bibliothec, Bestehend und Predigten auf alle Sonn- und Fest-Tage des Jahrs, Nach Anleitung allerhand Geistlicher Bücher gehalten, und mit Neuen Liedern beschlossen* (Hamburg: Liebezeit, 1719), 1025.

11 Zedler 24 (1740): col., 260.

12 Spitta 1: 466; Spitta ET 1: 471.

278 *Theology*

The apostle exhorts to spiritual music: "Speak to each other in psalms and hymns and spiritual songs. Singing and playing to the Lord in your heart" [Ephesians 5:19]. Spiritual hymns in church and at home are the devil's greatest annoyance, but to God a pleasant offering. It is only to be lamented that some corrupt the beautiful hymns so shamefully with false words and faulty understanding. It all comes down to the fact that people only memorize them by listening and are ashamed to open the *Gesang-Buch* and look at the words. So continue on the way of strength and devotion ... What the mouth sings must be harmonized in the heart.[13]

The passage underscores, as one would expect, that Neumeister put a great value on the integrity of poetry, and especially religious poetry. But it is his choice of the Latin term, "componiren"—commonly used to designate musical composition, in order to convey the harmony or agreement that should exist between mouth and heart when singing—that is particularly striking. It is perhaps a reflection of the extensive role music enjoyed at the Weissenfels court, as well as a measure of Neumeister's sensitivity to the way in which language has to carry deep meanings, especially when sung, as in his cantata libretti and his devotional handbook.

In 1705 one hundred copies of Neumeister's *Der Zugang zum Gnaden-Stuhl Jesu Christo* were printed by the court publisher, Wehrmann, for use by the ducal family and others at court.[14] It was to prove to be Neumeister's most popular publication. By locating copies in libraries and taking note of the numbering of editions as stated on their title pages, it is obvious that there must have been at least a minimum of thirty editions published between 1705 and 1772.[15]

Der Zugang zum Gnaden-Stuhl Jesu Christo conforms to a distinctive literary tradition that was closely intertwined with activities that expressed

---

13 Erdmann Neumeister, *Epistolische Nachlese* (Hamburg: Liebezeit, 1720), 2: 275: "Im übrigen ermahnet der Apostel zur Geistlichen Music: Und redet untereinander von Psalmen und Lobgesängen/ und geistlichen Liedern. Singet und spielet dem Herrn in eurem Hertzen. Geistliche Lieder in der Kirche und zu Hause/ sind des Teufels grösteer Verdruß/ Gotte aber ein angenehmes Opfer. Nur ist zu beklagen/ daß manche die schönen Lieder so gar schändlich radebrechen/ mit falschen Worten und verkehrten Verstande. Es kömmt alles daher/ daß man sie nur vom Hören auswendig gelernet/ und sich schämet/ das Gesang-Buch aufzuschlagen/ und die Worte anzusehen. So bleibet dann Krafft und Andacht weg ... Was der Mund singt/ das muß das Hertz componiren." Neumeister wrote something similar on the title page of a collection of libretti he published in 1708: "To musicians who like to sing to God with heart and mouth appropriate church music"; see note 44 below.

14 Letter, Neumeister to Löscher, dated 31 July 1708; Herwarth von Schade, ed., *"Geld ist der Hamburger ihr Gott"; Erdmann Neumeisters Briefe an Valentin Ernst Löscher* (Herzberg: Bautz, 1998), 72; see also Miersemann, "Lieddichtung im Spannungsfeld zwischen Orthodoxie und Pietismus," 186.

15 Many of these editions are recorded in Koch, *Geschichte des Kirchenlieds und Kirchengesangs* 5: 377–78; and Miersemann, "Lieddichtung im Spannungsfeld zwischen Orthodoxie und Pietismus," 186.

Bach and Erdmann Neumeister 279

Lutheran identity. This literary tradition disappeared almost completely in the nineteenth century when one of the important activities became rarely if ever observed. Alexander Wieckowski writes about this tradition:

> Along with preaching, Baptism and Holy Communion, Confession is one of the most sought after official acts of the Lutheran Church, even if it currently occupies a modest place within this quartet. Traditional use of individual Confession that continued up to the 19th century is rarely found today. The waning practice almost led to forgetfulness, so knowledge about it is rather rare.[16]

The physical manifestation of these Lutheran activities is found in pulpit, font, altar, and confessional, and during the nineteenth century it was the confessional that was either abandoned or removed from older churches or not installed into new churches. Because it is a practice that is all but forgotten it is necessary here to outline some of its main features, especially as the religious sentiments expressed in the devotional handbooks are similar to those found in the cantata libretti of Neumeister and his contemporaries.

Confession and Absolution

While rejecting the Roman Catholic sacrament of penance, Luther nevertheless retained private Confession and Absolution in a reinterpreted form. He saw these as the necessary preparation for participation in the Lord's Supper: in the privacy of the confessional (Beichtstuhl) the individual declared his or her repentance in the presence of their father confessor (Beichtvater, one of the clergy) who then declared to the penitent the assurance of forgiveness using words from scripture.[17] It was the devotional exercise that bridged personal piety expressed in the privacy of one's home with the corporate piety manifested in the public worship of the church. It became the custom for Confession to be administered individually after corporate Vespers on

---

16 Alexander Wieckowski, "Evangelische Privatbeichte und Beichtstühle. Beobachtungen zu einem fast vergessenen Kapitel lutherischer Frömmigkeitsgeschichte in Leipzig und Umgebung," in Markus Cottin, Detlef Döring, and Cathrin Friedrich, eds. *Stadtgeschichte: Mitteilungen des Leipziger Geschichtsvereins, Jahrbuch 2006* (Beucha: Sax, 2012), 67: "Die Beichte gehört neben der Predigt, der Taufe und dem heiligen Abendmahl zu den wichtigsten Amtshandlungen der lutherischen Kirche, auch wenn sie zur Zeit innerhalb dieses Quartetts einen bescheidenen Platz einnimt. Stand die Privat-bzw. Einzelbeichte bis zum 19. Jahrhundert hinem in traditionellem Gebrauch, wird sie heute eher selten in Anspruch genommen. Ihre abnehmende Praxis führte fast Vergessen und so sind Kenntnisse über eher selten."

17 For the background, see Wieckowski, "Evangelische Privatbeichte und Beichtstühle," 67–76, and the literature cited there; Alexander Wieckowski, *Evangelische Beichtstühle in Sachsen* (Beucha: Sax, 2005).

280   *Theology*

a Saturday afternoon, in preparation for participation in Communion the following Sunday morning.

The practice of individual Confession and Absolution as the necessary rite for admission to the Lord's Supper became a significant flash point in the Lutheran controversy between Pietists and Orthodox in the late seventeenth and early eighteenth centuries. As was outlined in Chapter 11, principal protagonists in print on each side were Valentin Ernst Löscher, pastor of the Kreuzkirche, Dresden, for Orthodoxy, and Joachim Lange (1670–1744), assistant pastor of the Neue Kirche, Berlin, close friend of August Herman Francke, for Pietism.[18] While the Pietists attacked many of the external rites of the church as corrupt and in need of purification and simplification, a particular focus, especially in Berlin, was on the attempted abolition of private Confession and Absolution.[19] Lange declared: "the private use today of Confession and Absolution is unscriptural." Löscher complained that "Lange writes that the joining of confession to the Lord's Supper and to each and every person is a misuse ... He has written that the confessional is nothing more than a human ordinance introduced in the papacy, cleansed somewhat at the time of the Reformation, and thus retained in use. He calls confession and absolution not only a 'mere ecclesiastical rite,' but also 'a completely ruined work.'" Löscher insisted that "the special arrangement of confession and absolution is a necessary and highly treasured part of the church orders. However, it is well known in what way many have up to now, under the appearance of piety, rushed against it." Lange believed "Confessional matters as things in themselves [are] improper and harmful." Löscher responded with "where the pietistic-minded gain the upper hand, there they strive to do away with the confessional." It did not help either when the deacon of the Nicolaikirche, Berlin, Johann Caspar Schade (1666–1698)—who had been a theological student in Leipzig at the same time as Neumeister, but was banished because of his Pietism—published a tract in which he characterized the confessional as "Satan's firepit."[20]

What was at stake here was not simply a different approach to piety, but nothing less than a radical and fundamental change to the Lutheran belief and practice of that time. In that light something of Neumeister's vehemence against Pietism can be understood, if not condoned. His title, *Der Zugang*

---

18 See Chapter 11, page 238.

19 For the background, see Helmut Obst, *Der Berliner Beichtstuhlstreit: Die Kritik des Pietismus an der Beichtpraxis der lutherischen Orthodoxie* (Witten: Luther, 1972); Claudia Drese, "Der Berliner Beichtstuhlstreit oder Philipp Jakob Spener zwischen allen Stühlen?" *Pietismus und Neuzeit* 31 (2005): 60–97. Unless otherwise notated, the citations in the following sentences are from Valentin Ernst Löscher, *The Complete Timotheus Verinus* (Milwaukee: Northwestern, 1998), 1: 203–4, a translation of Valentin Ernst Löscher, *Vollständiger Timotheus Verinus Oder Darlegung der Wahrheit und des Friedens in denen bißherigen Pietistischen Streitigkeiten ... Erster Theil* (1718) (Wittenberg: Hannauer, 1726), 625–27. Löscher is careful to cite and identify his sources.

20 See Obst, *Der Berliner Beichtstuhlstreit*, 23–26, 31–44.

zum Gnaden-Stuhl Jesu Christo, strongly implies that for him access to the "Gnaden-Stuhl" of Jesus Christ is the "Beichtstuhl" of the church. What was then being called into question had long been the belief and practice of Lutherans, as well as expressed in the specific literary genre of books of prayers and devotions for the penitents to use in their preparation for, participation in, and evaluation of Confession and Communion, such as Neumeister's *Der Zugang zum Gnaden-Stuhl Jesu Christo*, prepared in the first place for the court of Weissenfels.

Many such devotional handbooks were in circulation,[21] similar in content but with some differences in detail. They usually comprised three main sections: first, daily prayers for use both before making one's confession and in preparation for participation in Communion; second, a selection of verbal formulae of confession to be used by the penitent in the confessional; third, daily prayers following the reception of Communion; to which was often added a small selection of hymns, usually around thirty in number.[22] These devotional handbooks were often written and published locally by parish clergy, though some had wider circulation, such as the following examples.

Johann Friedrich Mayer, *Würdiger Com[m]unicant: Wie Er sich zu verhalten Vor dem Abendmahl/ Bey dem Abendmahl/ und nach dem Abendmahl … Samt einem Beicht- und Com[m]union- Gebet-Buch* (Leipzig: Grosse, 1684), reprinted many times by 1735.[23] Mayer (1650–1712) studied in Leipzig, taught at Wittenberg University, where he was a colleague of theologians Abraham Calov and Johann Andreas Quenstedt, and later a predecessor of Neumeister as the pastor of the Jacobikirche, Hamburg; Mayer was a strong opponent of Spener's Pietism.

Johann Rittmeyer, *Himmlisches Freuden-Mahl der Kinder Gottes auff Erden. Oder Geistreiche Gebete, so vor/ bey und nach der Beicht und heiligem Abendmahl, kräfftig zu gebrauchen … wie auch einiger Geistreichen Gesänge und Lieder* (Helmstedt: Hamm, 1684), one of the most popular of such handbooks, reprinted numerous times in Berlin, Helmstedt, Lüneburg, Magdeburg, et al., by a variety of publishers, well into the nineteenth century. Rittmeyer (1636–1698) was a pastor and professor in Helmstedt, where he seems to have imbibed something of the irenic nature of Calixtus's theology without its particular contentious content.

Benjamin Schmolck, *Der mit rechtschaffenem Hertzen zu seinem Jesu sich nahende Sünder: In auserlesenen Buß- Beicht- und Communion-Andachten*

---

21 The volumes of Deyling and Marpurger mentioned in Chapter 11 are of this type; see pages 244–45.

22 For the background, see Inge Mager, "Beicht und Abendmahl nach lutherischen Beicht- und Kommunionbüchern aus vier Jahrhunderten," *Makarios-Symposium über das Gebet: Vorträge der dritten Finnisch-deutschen Theologentagung im Amelungsborn 1986*, ed. Jouko Martikainen and Hans-Olof Kvist (Turku, Finland: Åbo Akademi University Press, 1989), 169–85.

23 In 1718 Neumeister based his Maundy Thursday sermon at the Jacobikirche, Hamburg, on Mayer's *Würdiger Communicant*; Neumeister, *Geistliche Bibliothec*, 506–21.

282 *Theology*

... (Chemnitz: Stößel, 1730), perhaps the most widely disseminated handbook of all, being reprinted scores of times in Chemnitz, Danzig, Hamburg, Königsberg, Liegnitz, Wernigerode, Zwickau, and so forth, deep into the nineteenth century. Schmolck (1672–1737) studied at Leipzig; pastor in Schweidnitz (now Świdnica) for most of his life; poet, prolific hymn-writer, and author of cantata libretti; used the language of Pietism but was rooted in Orthodoxy.

Confession and Absolution were not abolished at that time—that came later when the Enlightenment joined forces with Pietism—thus those with Pietist sentiments, if they were to continue as Lutherans, had to endure a practice in which they had varying degrees of reservation. With their suspicion of liturgical forms, no doubt they chose to use Confession and Communion handbooks that had little or no liturgical content alongside the devotional prayers. Many of these devotional aids included varying levels of liturgical matter, and some overflowed with such details. One example is the *Leipziger Kirchen Andachten* (1694), a primary source for details concerning the liturgy of the Leipzig churches and their use of music, but which is somewhat modest in its prayers for Confession and Communion.[24]

In *Der Zugang zum Gnaden-Stuhl Jesu Christo*, Neumeister presents a series of spiritual exercises that continue over a period of two weeks, theologically Orthodox but verbalized in expressive, pious language. It began with prayer on Sunday morning, which was followed by set prayers, morning and evening, every day throughout the following week as the individual moved daily closer to the climax of the first week, that is, Vespers on Saturday afternoon, at the close of which each individual made Confession and received Absolution. Significantly Neumeister included the liturgical order of Vespers and supplied a cantata libretto that was to be performed within the liturgy:

Beicht-Vesper	**Confession Vesper**
1. Intoniret der Priester: *Deus in adjutorium meum intende.*	Intoned by the pastor: "O God come to my aid."
2. Das *responsorium* vom Chor: *Deus ad adjuvandum me festina &c.*	*Responsorium* from the choir: "Make haste to deliver me."

---

24 *Leipziger Kirchen-Andachten/ Darinnen Der Erste Theil das Gebetbuch/ Oder Die Ordnung des gantzen öffentlichen Gottes-Dienstes durchs gantze Jahr/ Nebst Gebet/ Fürbitt/ Collecten/ Dancksagungen/ Abkündigungen etc. oder was sonst an Sonn- und Fest-Tagen/ Wochen-Predigten und Betstunden etc. vorkömmt/ begreiffet/ Der Ander Theil Das Gesangbuch ...* (Leipzig: Würdig, 1694), 1: 245–84. What is fascinating is that the volume includes a collection of "pious" emblematic images of "Jesus in the heart," which are very similar to those found in the Lüneburg editions of Rittmeyer's *Himmlisches Freuden-Mahl der Kinder Gottes* that similarly originate from Leipzig engravers; see Markus Rathey, *Johann Sebastian Bach's Christmas Oratorio: Music, Theology, Culture* (New York: Oxford University Press, 2016), 74–75.

Bach and Erdmann Neumeister   283

3. Gesungen: *Erbarm dich mein, o Herre Gott.* Oder: *Aus tiefer Not schrei ich zu dir.*

Sung: [one of the two hymns]

4. Ein Buß-Psalm musiciret.

A penitential Psalm is sung.

5. Vor dem Altar gelesen die Beicht-Ermahnung; Hierauf gelesen der XXV. oder der CXLIII. Psalm. Sodenn das Gebet und Vater Unser.

Before the altar is read the confession exhortation; thereafter is read Psalm 25 or Psalm 143. Followed by prayer and the Lord's Prayer.

6. Musiciret folgende Cantata.

Musical setting of the following Cantata.

CANTATA
Ach! Wo bin ich hingerathen?. . .

7. Gesungen: *O Jesu Christ, du höchstes Gut.* Oder: *Nimm von uns, Herr, Gott.* Oder: *Ach Gott und Herr.*

Sung: [one of the three hymns]

8. Collecte und Seegen.

Collect and Benediction.

9. Gesungen: *Christe, du Lamm Gottes.*[25]

Sung [German *Agnus Deï*]

At the close of the service of Vespers came the individual visits to the confessionals, for which Neumeister gave three verbal formulas for the individual to choose from and indicated that Psalms of contrition should be read before Confession, and Psalms of thanksgiving read after receiving Absolution.

The next day, Sunday, began with the Lord's Supper, and Neumeister provided prayers before and during the Eucharistic service, together with the liturgical order in outline, which again included a cantata libretto:

Gottes-Dienst bey der Communion

God's Service with Communion

1. Wird das Kyrie musiciret.

Musical setting of the Kyrie

2. Gesungen: *Allein zu dir, Herr Jesu*

Sung: [one of the three hymns]

---

25 *Der Zugang zum Gnaden-Stuhl Jesu Christo, Das ist: Christliche Gebete und Gesänge Vor, bey und nach der Beichte und Heil. Abendmahle* ... (Weissenfels: Wehrmann, 1721), 227–31.

284   *Theology*

Christ. Oder: *Nun lob, mein Seel,*
den Herren. Oder: *Wie schön*
leuchtet der Morgenstern.

3. Vor dem Altar gelesen die Beicht-Ermahnung; Hierauf gelesen der XXIII. oder der CIII. Psalm.	Before the altar is read the confession exhortation; thereafter is read Psalm 23 or Psalm 103.
4. Musiciret folgende Cantata.	Musical setting of the following Cantata.

CANTATA
O Seelig Vergnügen!

5. Erfolget die gewöhnliche Consecration.	Then follow the customary consecration [Words of Institution]
6. Währender Communion wird gesungen: *Jesus Christus unser Heyland [der von uns].*	During Communion is sung *Jesus Christus* *unser Heyland.*
7. Collecte und Seegen.	Collect and Blessing
8. *Gott sei gelobet und gebenedeiet* [wird gesungen].[26]	*Gott sei gelobet und gebenedeiet* is sung.

In Neumeister's handbook the first week of devotion worked towards the climax of Confession and Absolution, so the second week began with the high point of participation in the Lord's Supper, with specific devotions throughout the following week, morning and evening, dealing with aspects of the meaning and significance of what had taken place in the confessional and at the altar. Neumeister also included hymns of his own composition, and later editions of *Der Zugang zum Gnaden-Stuhl* often included more of his hymn texts, some of which were parodies of preexisting hymns by others.[27] In his hymns Neumeister expresses the same basic religiosity that is found in his cantata libretti: imagery from the biblical Song of Songs, echoes of medieval mysticism, expressions of gratitude for the love of Christ, and the

---

26 Neumeister, *Der Zugang zum Gnaden-Stuhl Jesu Christo,* 314–18.

27 For an outline of Neumeister's parody technique see, Ute Poetzsch-Seban, *Die Kirchenmusik von Georg Philipp Telemann und Erdmann Neumeister: Zur Geschichte der protestantischen Kirchenkantate in der ersten Hälfte des 18. Jahrhunderts* (Beeskow: Ortus, 2006), 272; for a more detailed analysis, see Ada Kadelbach, "'Jesu, meine Freude, Purpur, Gold und Seide': Zitat und Parodie in Erdmann Neumeisters 'Lieder-Andachten' 1743," in Rucker, *Neumeister … Wegbereiter der evangelischen Kirchenkantate*, 147–70.

Bach and Erdmann Neumeister 285

Passion intertwined with its commemoration in Communion. To give just one example, the hymn *Angenehme Fasten-Zeit*:

4.   ...

Was aus Christi Wunden quillt	What flows from Christ's wounds
Das soll mich erquicken;	will revive me;
Und ich will sein blutig Bild	and I will his bloody image
Mir ins Hertze drücken.	imprint in my heart.

5. Jesu, Jesu, du allein   Jesus, Jesus, you alone

Bleibest mein Ergötzen.	remain my joy.
Ich will dein Creutzes-Pein	I will make your cross-pain
Mir zur Freude setzen,	my settled joy,
Ach aus Liebe ließt du dich	Ah, out of love you let yourself
Martern und zuschlagen,	be tortured and beaten,
Ja, aus Liebe[28] gegen mich	Yes, out of love for me
Lidtst du alle Plagen . . .	you suffered every torment . . .

12. Jesu, tausend-tausend mahl   Jesus a thousand-thousand times

Danck ich dir voll Freuden.	I thank you full of joy.
Danck sey dir vor Blut und Qual,	Thank you for your blood and anguish,
Danck vor alles Leiden!	thank you for all [your] suffering!
Danck sey die mein Lebelang,	I will thank you all of my life
Daß du bist gestorben!	that you have died!
Vor den Himmel sey dir Danck,	Thank you for heaven
Den du mir erworben.[29]	which you have won for me.[30]

The liturgical orders for Vespers on Saturday afternoon and Gottesdienst on Sunday morning in the Weissenfels court chapel were not devised by Neumeister but represent the customary use that had been in place for some time. This is confirmed by the orders included in the new hymnal commissioned by Duke Christian on inheriting the dukedom: *Hoch-Fürstliches Sachsen-Weissenfelsisches Vollständiges Gesang- Und Kirchen-Buch* ...

---

28 The phrase "Aus Liebe" occurs twice in this stanza, declaring that it is out of love the Savior dies. It is an echo of its occurrence in earlier hymns—such as Johann Heermann's *O Jesu, du mein Bräutigam* (1630), st. 1, line 2; Johann Rist's *O Traurigkeit, o Herzeleid* (1641), st. 2, line 5; Paul Gerhardt's *Auf, auf, mein Herz, mit Freuden* (1647), st. 3, line 8—as well as its later occurrence in three of Bach's cantatas: BWV 116/3 (1724), anonymous librettist; BWV 110/4 and BWV 151/4 (both 1725), both libretti by Georg Christian Lehms—and supremely in the key aria of the St. Matthew Passion, BWV 244/49: "Aus Liebe will mein Heiland sterben" (Picander).

29 Neumeister, *Der Zugang zum Gnaden-Stuhl Jesu Christo*, 575–77.

30 Translation slightly modified: Isabella van Elferen, *Mystical Love in the German Baroque: Theology, Poetry, Music* (Lanham: Scarecrow, 2009), 189–90.

286   *Theology*

(Weissenfels: Brühl, 1714). The hymnal includes detailed liturgical outlines for the Sundays, festivals, and celebrations of the church year, together with other observances. The orders for these two services in the 1714 hymnal confirm the basic sequences presented by Neumeister, as well as supply additional details.

In the hymnal the Vesper service is headed, "Von denen Sonnabends- oder Beicht-Vespern" (Of the Saturday- or Confession-Vespers) and follows the same detailed order as is given in Neumeister, with minor variations, such as the Buß-lied (No. 3) that is unspecified, and the Buß-Psalm (No. 4) that is identified as one of the "Seven Penitential Psalms."[31] The major difference between the two sources is that the hymnal indicates that following the Lord's Prayer there was to be "Ein Buß-Lied gesungen" (No. 6), whereas Neumeister has "Musiciret folgende Cantata" (No. 6), and includes the seven-movement libretto, beginning *Ach! Wo bin ich hingerathen*. Since the later editions of Neumeister's *Der Zugang zum Gnaden-Stuhl* published in Weissenfels continued to include the libretto, the implication is that the cantata (with Krieger's music?—or another's?) continued to be an option at this juncture of the Beichtvesper service, especially since the cantata in effect replaced the Magnificat, the usual Vespers canticle, which was sometimes sung concerted, sometimes hymnic.

Neumeister's first cycle of cantata libretti was written mostly for the Sundays of the church year, but here he is writing a cantata for the Saturday Beichtvesper, which by all accounts was not a common occurrence. Nevertheless, Werner unearthed information, clearly incomplete, that from time to time special music was performed at the Saturday Beichtvesper in the court chapel, such as in 1682, when a composition for two choirs comprising fifty-six voices was included, or a *Miserere à 12*, five voices and seven instruments, performed in 1685 and again in 1703.[32] Perhaps this is something that happened elsewhere but has gone unnoticed. Special Buss-Tagen, repentance days, are known for which special music was composed, but perhaps there were occasional Beichtvesper services that also included appropriate music. Thus, while the specific occasion for Bach's early cantata, *Aus der Tiefen rufe ich* (BWV 131), composed in Mühlhausen, 1707–1708, is unspecified, its content made it particularly appropriate to have been included in a Saturday Vesper service that concluded with Confession and Absolution.

When it came to Communion on Sunday morning, following the Saturday Beicht-Vespers, it was a very full service. On most Sundays in the Weissenfels court chapel Communion was not celebrated. The Hauptgottesdienst— beginning with the Introit, continuing with Kyrie and Gloria, Collect, Epistle,

---

31 *Sachsen-Weissenfelsisches Vollständiges Gesang- Und Kirchen-Buch* (Weissenfels: Brühl, 1714), 494. The prose texts of the seven penitential Psalms (6, 32, 38, 51, 102, 130, 143) are given with a single harmonized chant, ibid., 495–507.

32 Werner, *Musikpflege in Weissenfels*, 135.

Bach and Erdmann Neumeister 287

Gospel, cantata, Creed, sermon—came to a close with a collect, benediction, and a hymn.[33] But on Communion days the service continued with the basic order as given by Neumeister. The 1714 Weissenfels hymnal fills out some of the details, including the heading "Gottes-Dienst. Bey der Hoch-Fürstlichen Communion" (Worship. At the High-Princely Communion).[34] Similar to the way that the earlier part of the Sunday morning service had included the Kyrie in the traditional place near its beginning, so the Communion part of the service continued with another "Kyrie eleison," this time the capella sang a three-section *Kyrie, Christe, Kyrie eleison* in alternation with the congregation singing the three stanzas of Luther's hymn *Gott der Vater wohn uns bei*.[35] Both Neumeister's handbook and the 1714 hymnal mention the singing of the hymn *Allein zu dir, Herr Jesu Christ* and the reading of Psalm 23. However, Neumeister records that the confession exhortation that had been read at Vespers the day before, was read again (before Psalm 23), thereby linking the Communion with the Confession and Absolution of the day before. After the reading of Psalm 23 Neumeister indicates "Musiciret folgende Cantata," and includes the seven-movement libretto, beginning *O Seelig Vergnügen!* Instead of the cantata the hymnal directs that Johann Heermann's Communion hymn, *O Jesu, du mein Bräutigam* (1630), should be sung at this juncture.[36] As was argued with the Vesper cantata, since the libretto of Neumeister's Communion cantata continued to be included in later Weissenfels imprints of *Der Zugang zum Gnaden-Stuhl*, the implication is that either this libretto (with Krieger's music?), or another suitable cantata, was likely to have been performed in the court chapel from time to time in place of Heermann's hymn.

What is particularly significant is that this cantata was to be performed before rather than after the Consecration/Words of Institution. The usual position for a Communion cantata (or aria) was after the Consecration during the distribution, and indeed was frequently referred to as *musica sub communione* (music during Communion).[37] Both the 1714 hymnal and Neumeister's *Der Zugang zum Gnaden-Stuhl* indicate that only Luther's hymn, *Jesus Christus unser Heiland, der von uns*, was to be sung during the distribution of Communion. Here, before the Consecration, Neumeister's cantata libretto anticipates the presence of Christ in the sacrament, registering the emotion it evokes, the theology it expresses, and the relationship it establishes. It begins with an emotional awareness of what is about to take place (note that the first two lines are repeated at the end of the movement):

---

33 For the order for the First Sunday in Advent, see *Sachsen-Weissenfelsisches Vollständiges Gesang- Und Kirchen-Buch*, 1–21.

34 Ibid., 486.

35 Ibid.; Werner, *Musikpflege in Weissenfels*, 135.

36 *Sachsen-Weissenfelsisches Vollständiges Gesang- Und Kirchen-Buch*, 486–88, set to the melody *Ach Gott, wie manches Herzeleid*.

37 See Chapter 2, pages 39–41.

288   *Theology*

[1.] O Seelig Vergnügen!   O blissful pleasure!
      O heilige Lust!   O holy delight!
      Ich gehe bey meinem Erlöser zu   I go to my Savior's table,
        Tische,
      Damit mich ein himmlisches Labsal   so that I have a heavenly
        erfrische.   refreshment.
      Mich speiset und träncket sein Leib   I eat and drink his
        und sein Blut.   body and his blood.
      Diß machet den Glauben voll Feuer   This makes faith full of fire and
        und Muth.   courage.
      Diß stärcket die Seele, diß tröstet die   This strengthens the soul, consoles
        Brust,   the breast,
      Und lässet mich Teufel und Hölle   and lets devil and hell be defeated.
        besiegen.
      O seelig Vergnügen!   O blissful pleasure!
      O heilige Lust!   O holy delight!

The second movement incorporates the classic Lutheran eucharistic definition, that Christ is present "in, with, and under" the bread and wine. (Notice
again that the movement ends with the same words that begin and end the
first movement):

[2.] ...
      In, mit und unter Brodt und   In, with and under bread and wine
        Weine
      Ist wesentlich dasselbe Fleisch   is essentially the same flesh and
        und Blut,   blood,
      Das unser Jesus angenommen.   that our Jesus accepted.
      Der Jesus, der am Creutze hieng,   The Jesus that hung on the cross,
      Der lebend aus der Grabe   the living from the grave
      Und sichbarlich gen Himmel   who visibly went to heaven,
        gieng,
      Ist selber hier dieselbe Gabe,   is the same who is gifted here,
      Die lieblich unser Mund genießt,   who loves our mouth,
      Und geistlich in die Seele   and is spiritually enclosed in the
        schließt.   soul.
      ...   ...
      O seelig Vergnügen!   O blissful pleasure!
      O heilige Lust!   O holy delight!

Throughout all the movements the relationship between Jesus and the
communicant is expressed in the baroque imagery of mystical love, of the
Bride and Bridegroom, the lover and the beloved, that is characteristic of

much religious poetry and music of late seventeenth- and early eighteenth-century Germany.[38]

Du bist mein, und ich bin dein ... (mvt. 3)	You are mine and I am yours ...
Denn ich bin dein, und du bist mein ... (mvt. 5)	Because I am yours and you are mine ...
Daß ich mich gantz an dich ergebe,	That I totally surrender to you
Und mehr in dir, als in mir selber, lebe ... (mvt. 6)	and live in you more than myself ...
Herr Jesu, dir leb ich, dir will ich auch sterben.	Lord Jesus, I live for you; and to you I will also die.
So will ich dein ewiges Eigenthum seyn ... (mvt.7)[39]	So shall I be yours eternally ...

Neumeister's time in Weissenfels was abruptly curtailed with the death of the duke's daughter, whose spiritual welfare was the reason for his appointment as court deacon. Since there were already two more-senior clergy at the court, it was necessary for him to look for a suitable position elsewhere. However, even though he had only been at the Weissenfels court for barely two years Neumeister nevertheless made a lasting impression on many aspects of the liturgical, devotional, and musical life of the court.[40] In his later dealings with the court, Bach must have noticed these things even if he was not entirely aware of the extent of Neumeister's influence.

Neumeister in Sorau and Hamburg

On New Year's Day 1706 Neumeister became *Oberhofprediger*, Consistorial-Rath and Superintendent in Sorau (now Żary), Upper Silesia, appointed by Balthasar Erdmann (1683–1745), Count von Promnitz, who had succeeded his father a few years earlier in 1703. The suggestion is that these positions were made available to Neumeister through the influence of duke Johann Georg of Saxe-Weissenfels, since in 1705 Erdmann had married the duke's sister, Anna Maria. It seems that Erdmann in Sorau was keen to emulate the court in Weissenfels. His cantor was the music historian Wolfgang Caspar Printz (1641–1717), and in 1705, just a few months before the arrival of Neumeister, he appointed the twenty-four-year-old Georg Philipp Telemann (1681–1767) as his court Capellmeister. Telemann had already made a name for himself

---

38 The background and multifaceted nature of this rich tradition, from its roots in Petrarchan poetry, through medieval mysticism, and Baroque poetry and music of the seventeenth century, to the music of Bach and his librettists, is fully discussed in van Elferen, *Mystical Love in the German Baroque*, passim.

39 These two lines begin and end the movement.

40 See Werner, *Musikpflege in Weissenfels*, 144–46.

290   *Theology*

by directing the Leipzig opera.[41] It seems most likely that Telemann and Neumeister already knew each other before they arrived in Sorau. In his later autobiography, published by Mattheson, Telemann writes about the twenty or so operas he had directed in Leipzig, adding, "For the Weissenfels court I made about four operas."[42] This was in 1703 and 1704 when documentation in Weissenfels records that singers (unnamed) came from Leipzig on several occasions, with one entry specifically referring to Telemann, "*Mons. Delemann und 3 Sänger,*" on 14 August 1704,[43] that is, when Neumeister was at the Weissenfels court. Now in Sorau was the opportunity of a permanent working relationship. It seems likely that Telemann's settings of Neumeister's two cantata libretti included in *Der Zugang zum Gnaden-Stuhl* date from his Sorau years: *Ach! Wo bin ich hingeraten* (TVWV 1:42) and *O Seelig Vergnügen, o heilige Lust* (TVWV 1:1212).[44]

Telemann and Neumeister formed a bond of mutual respect, a creative partnership that continued for forty years or so.[45] During this time Neumeister supplied Telemann with at least five, complete or partial, annual cantata cycles, together with numerous odes, arias, and other occasional poetry. But they were only together for three years in Sorau before Telemann left in 1708 to become Concertmeister, then Capellmeister, to the court in Eisenach. In 1712 Telemann became the city music director and Capellmeister for the two main churches in Frankfurt, which lasted for nine years. In the meantime, Neumeister continued with his pastoral duties in Sorau, with much writing and editing of sermons and other publications, together with cantatas, odes, hymns, and other poetry. In 1715 he was called to be *pastor primarius* of the Jacobikirche, Hamburg, where he remained for the rest of his life.

41 See Michael Maul, *Barockoper in Leipzig (1693–1720)* (Freiburg: Rombach, 2009). 1:617–817.

42 Johann Mattheson, *Grundlage einer Ehren-Pforte* (Hamburg: [Mattheson], 1740), 359; the operas have not survived. Telemann also indicates that some of the operas originated in Sorau.

43 Werner, *Musikpflege in Weissenfels*, 109.

44 The libretti were reprinted together in [Erdmann Neumeister,] *Geistliche Cantaten Oder Außerlesene Kirchen-Gesängel Über alle Sonn- Fest- und Apostel-Tagel Ingleichen Bey jedermahliger Beicht und H. Communionl Zu einer Denen Herren Musicis und jedweden mit Hertz und Mund zu Gott gern singenden Christen bequemen Kirchen-Music (In ungezwungenen Teutschen Versen ausgefertiget)* (Augsburg: Lotter, 1708), 173–79. They were again reprinted in Erdmann Neumeister, *Fortgesetzte Fünffache Kirchen-Andachten, in Drey neuen Jahrgängen* ... (1717) (Hamburg: Kißner, 1726), *173–*176 (*Ach! Wo bin ich hingeraten*) and *179–*182 (*O Seelig Vergnügen, o heilige Lust*); see Ute Poetzsch, "Telemanns Vertonungen von Texten aus Neumeisters Andachtsbuch 'Der Zugang zum Gnaden-Stuhl Jesu Christo,'" in Rucker, *Neumeister ... Wegbereiter der evangelischen Kirchenkantate*, 135–45.

45 In a letter, dated 27 December 1714, Teleman called Neumeister the "beste Poet in geistlichen Sachen" (the best poet for sacred things), and in the preface to his *Freytags-Andachten* (Hamburg, 1726) Neumeister viewed Telemann as an "unvergleichen Componisten" (unparalleled composer); both cited in Poetzsch-Seban, *Die Kirchenmusik von Georg Philipp Telemann und Erdmann Neumeister*, 45.

Bach and Erdmann Neumeister 291

In 1720 there appears to have been some concern in Hamburg about the health of Joachim Gerstenbüttel, cantor of the Johanneum and director of music for the five principal churches. The worry was the possibility that a successor might have to be sought. Gerstenbüttel did indeed die in the spring of the following year, and after the customary auditions Telemann was chosen as the appointed successor, remaining in Hamburg for the rest of his life. Thus, a close working relationship, such as the one they had known in Sorau, was now made possible in Hamburg for Neumeister and Telemann.

This raises an interesting question. Given Telemann's respect for Neumeister, was he influential in any way in commending Neumeister to Bach? Or vice versa? In his letter to Forkel, dated 13 January 1775, C. P. E. Bach writes about his father and states that "in his younger days he saw a good deal of Telemann."[46] But when was this? Around the time of C. P. E.'s baptism in 1714, or earlier, such as between 1708 and 1712, when Telemann was in Eisenach, and where they could have met when Sebastian was in the town visiting family? Or did the Bach/Neumeister connection predate these possibilities?

Bach and Weissenfels

In the summer of 1702 Sangerhausen—which came under the jurisdiction of the dukes of Saxe-Weissenfels, where they maintained a secondary ducal residence—was faced with the need to find a new town organist to replace Gottfried Christoph Gräffenhayn, who had died in early July. The seventeen-year-old Johann Sebastian Bach applied for the position, auditioned, and was unanimously elected to be Gräffenhayn's successor. The information comes from the letter Bach directed to the Sangerhausen town council, in November 1736, commending his son, Johann Gottfried Bernhard, for the same position that was then again vacant. Bach wrote that in 1702: "all of the votes were cast for my humble self."[47] But Bach was never appointed because of the intervention of duke Johann Georg of Saxe-Weissenfels, who insisted that Johann Augustin Kobelius (1674–1731), should be the new Sangerhausen organist.

Kobelius was clearly being groomed by the Weissenfels court. He had studied keyboard with the court organist and cantor, Johann Christoph Schieferdecker, composition with court Capellmeister Krieger, and had spent some time in Italy. The way that his later career developed confirms this early intention. In 1713 as the primary organist in Sangerhausen he took over the direction of music in the newly constructed ducal chapel,[48] later

46 NBR 400 (No. 395); BDok 3: 289 (No. 803).
47 NBR 187 (No. 189); BDok 1: 93–94 (No. 38): "obwohln damahln die sämtlichen *vota* ... meine Wenigkeit betraffen."
48 The *Sachsen-Weissenfelsisches Vollständiges Gesang- Und Kirchen-Buch*, was inaugurated in the Sangerhausen chapel in 1714 and included the following on the title page: "Gnädigste Anordnung, Zum Gebrauch so wohl Dero Hoch-Fürstlichen Residence, Und der

292   Theology

assumed managerial responsibilities at the Weissenfels court, composed and directed many operas between 1712 and 1729, and became Krieger's successor as Capellmeister after the latter's death in 1725.[49] In 1702 it therefore must have been something of a surprise for the duke when the seventeen-year-old, with no track record at this stage, was preferred to the twenty-eight-year-old experienced musician with an impeccable musical pedigree and promising future. Likewise, the town and church officials, pillars of the local community, may well have been equally surprised at their own unanimous vote for the young Bach to replace the respected Gräffenhayn, since he was not only the town organist but also Sangerhausen's judge. As Christoph Wolff explains,

> whatever audition Bach had to pass, he must have exhibited professionalism of the highest caliber in his performance, improvisation, composition, and knowledge of organ technology. He must also have been judged qualified to supervise an assistant organist and to take over, sooner or later, the direction of the chorus musicus, the vocal-instrumental ensemble of the church.[50]

But the duke had his way, and Kobelius was appointed Sangerhausen's town organist in November 1702.

Presumably the Bach family was involved in Sebastian's bid to become the organist in Sangerhausen. When this was unsuccessful it appears that they then turned to the Weimar court organist, Johann Effler, with whom they had a long history of collaboration.[51] Because of ill-health Effler was to resign, somewhat abruptly, as Weimar court organist in 1708 (when Bach became his successor), so the suggestion is that in 1702 he was possibly already in some need of assistance. Thus, from the end of December 1702—that is within a matter of weeks of being denied the Sangerhausen position—Bach was paid as a footman at the Weimar court[52] but his primary duties were as Effler's assistant.

The position apparently lacked permanence, and the Bach family would have been aware that Sebastian's Weimar position did not have the visibility that the Sangerhausen position would have given him, and that it was

---

neu-erbautem Schloß-Capelle, zur Heil. Dreyfaltigkeit in Sangerhusen" (Most gracious arranged, for use in the High Princely Residence [in Weissenfels], and the newly built castle chapel of the Holy Trinity in Sangerhusen).

49 Werner, *Musikpflege in Weissenfels*, 78.

50 WolffBLM, 68.

51 See Michael Maul, "Frühe Urteile über Johann Christoph und Johann Nikolaus Bach," BJ 90 (2004): 157–68; WolffBLM, xviii–xix.

52 BDok 5: 289, additional note to BDok 5: No. 6. Much has been made of the lowly position that Bach was given at the Weimar court—in the relevant account book he is identified as "Laquey Baachen" (Lackey Bach); BDok 2: 10 (No. 6); NBR 39 (No. 13). But it was common for supporting court musicians to hold various practical positions, which justified their payments, but their presence at court in the first place was for their musical abilities.

important for his skills and abilities to be seen and heard. In Arnstadt's Neue Kirche in 1703, after four years' work, Johann Friedrich Wender had completed building a new organ, which not only needed examining and demonstrating, but also a full-time organist. There were similarities between the position in Sangerhausen and the position in Arnstadt, not least the opportunity for music-making in the residence of Anton Günther II, duke of Schwartzburg-Sonderhausen. Again, given Bach's young years, it would seem likely that it was the Bach family who approached the consistory for him to be engaged to inspect and demonstrate the new instrument. The Arnstadt consistory settled Bach's fee and expenses for inaugurating the new organ on 13 July 1703,[53] and just three weeks later, on 9 August, the certificate was signed confirming Bach's appointment as the organist of the Neue Kirche.[54]

These possibilities that opened up in fairly quick succession in Weimar and Arnstadt were in large measure due to the remarkable musical gifts and abilities that Bach had demonstrated at his audition in Sangerhausen, especially as he was chosen in preference to the candidate of the duke of Saxe-Weissenfels. Although the position went to the duke's choice, Bach nevertheless made a distinctive impression, not only on the Sangerhausen town officials, but presumably also on the duke and others of the Weissenfels court. The Sangerhausen audition must have alerted duke Johann Georg—and most likely his brother Christian, who would succeed to the dukedom in 1712—from then on to keep track of Bach's developing career.

One suspects that members of the Weissenfels capella also took an interest in Bach's professional progress. They were in a unique position to be able to do this in that there was an informal network of communication between the musicians of the various courts. On the one hand, from time to time there were occasional performances of music that required additional voices and instruments to augment those of the resident capella.[55] The visiting musicians brought with them news of what was happening in the wider world of music. On the other hand, there were the dynastic families with their specialized expertise, such as the Bachs as organists and town musicians; the Hoffmanns as violinists; the Abels as gambists; and the Altenburgs, Nicolais, and Wilckes as trumpeters. The different members of these families served various courts and therefore facilitated the interchange of information with members of their family who served in other courts.

After a few years in Arnstadt, "the nerve center of the Bach family,"[56] Bach was keen to assert his independence beyond the immediate influence of the

---

53 NBR 40 (No. 15); BDok 2: 10 (No. 7): "Bach, Fürstlich Sächsischer HoffOrganiste zu Weimar." In his genealogy of the Bach family he records his first professional position as "HoffMusicus in Weimar bey Herzog Johann Ernsten, An. 1703." (Court Musician, in Weimar, to Duke Johann Ernst, Anno 1703); BDok 1: 259 (No. 184); NBR 290 (No. 303). The description of Bach as "HoffOrganiste zu Weimar" is not entirely incorrect; see the previous note.
54 NBR 41 (No. 16); BDok 2: 11–12 (No. 8).
55 For the court of Weissenfels, see Werner, *Musikpflege in Weissenfels*, passim.
56 WolffBLM, 89.

294   *Theology*

family, and took the position of organist of the Blasiuskirche in Mühlhausen, in succession to Johann Georg Ahle (1651–1706).[57] However, while pursuing his professional independence he nevertheless consolidated his family ties by marrying Maria Barbara (1684–1720),[58] daughter of his father's cousin, Johann Michael Bach (1648–1694), organist and town scribe in Gehren.[59] But in little over a year (June 1708) he was on the move again, this time to Weimar as chamber musician and court organist on the retirement of Johann Effler. No doubt this appointment was made on the strength of his abbreviated presence at the court at the end of 1702 and the beginning of 1703, but perhaps this was the plan all along, that Bach would be Effler's successor when the time came?

Bach now had the increased visibility as a court musician and was in a position to further his own branch of the Bach family, with the births of Catharina Dorothea (29 December 1708), Wilhelm Friedemann (22 November 1710), and Carl Philipp Emanuel (8 March 1714), as well as twins that did not survive. By this time Bach was apparently well known to Duke Christian of Saxe-Weissenfels, an association that may have begun before he succeeded his brother Johann Georg in March 1712, but which cannot be charted since there is, frustratingly, no documentary evidence. The only hint is found in the letter C. P. E. Bach wrote to Forkel, dated 13 January 1775, which has this comment about his father: "Duke Christian in Weissenfels particularly loved him, and rewarded him appropriately."[60] The rewards came for music composed for the duke, such as the cantata for the duke's birthday, 23 February 1713, *Was mir behagt, ist nur die muntre Jagd* (BWV 208), performed in the duke's hunting lodge.[61] He also composed a birthday cantata for the duke in 1725, *Entfliehet, verschwindet, entweichet, ihr sorgen* (BWV 249a), and another in 1729 (see further below), which suggests that there might have been others that have not survived.

In his earlier Weimar years Bach had been composing occasional cantatas, which were well received, and as a result his position at court was intensified in early 1714 when, in addition to his position as court organist, he was appointed concertmaster. This involved the regular composition of cantatas and the direction of the court capella. His librettist was usually the court poet, Salomon Franck, but significantly two cantatas composed around this time were to libretti written by Erdmann Neumeister:

---

57 Bach's successor as organist of the Neue Kirche, Arnstadt, was his cousin Johann Ernst Bach (1683–1739); BDok 2: 25 (No. 22).
58 17 October 1707; NBR 51–52 (No. 26); BDok 2: 28 (No. 28).
59 WolffBLM, 89.
60 NBR 399 (No. 395); BDok 3: 289 (No. 803).
61 NBR 64–65 (No. 44); BDok 2: 45 (No. 55). The occasion would have allowed Bach to meet up with Adam Immanuel Weldig (1667–1716), falsettist and master of the pages at Weimar, who had just recently moved to similar positions at the court of Weissenfels. Weldig had also been Bach's landlord in Weimar, and, with Telemann, was godfather to C. P. E. Bach; Werner, *Musikpflege in Weissenfels*, 84–85.

Gleichwie der Regen und Schnee vom Himmel fällt.
Cantata for Sexagesima in Neumeister's third cycle of cantata libretti.[62]
TVWV I: 160 (1711); BWV 18 (1713 or 1714).

Nun komm, der Heiden Heiland.
Cantata for Advent Sunday in Neumeister's fourth cycle of cantata
   libretti.[63]
TVWV I: 1174 (1717); BWV 61 (1714).

Here is Bach, whose responsibilities now include the monthly composition of
a cantata, working with libretti written by arguably the most influential poet
of such texts at that time. The intriguing question is: How did these libretti
come into his hands? The time frame is revealing, since these cantatas were
composed around the time of C. P. E. Bach's baptism (14 March 1714), for
whom Telemann was godfather. Some have questioned whether Telemann was
actually present in the Weimar parish church for this occasion. For example,
Siegbert Rampe believes that Telemann was not there; Hans-Joachim Schulze
is simply doubtful that he was there.[64] On the other hand, both Steven Zohn
and Ellen Exner have independently argued that Telemann was already present at the Weimar court when C. P. E. was born.[65] The same would be true
for the other godfather, Adam Immanuel Weldig—previously falsettist at
the Weimar court but at that time falsettist at the Weissenfels court—whose
presence in Weimar may have been in connection with the possible first performance of Bach's *Widerstehe doch der Sünde* (BWV 54) on Oculi Sunday,
4 March 1714.[66] This was a time of family complication for Weldig because
his wife gave birth to a son about a week or so after C. P. E. Bach's baptism. Johann Friedrich Immanuel Weldig was baptized on 22 March in

---

62 [Erdmann Neumeister], *Geistliches Singen und Spielen/ Das ist: Ein Jahrgang von Texten …*
   bey öffentlicher Kirchen Versam[m]lung in Eisenach musicalisch aufgeführet werden von Georg.
   Philipp. Telemann, Capellmeister (Gotha: Reyher, 1711), 49–52.
63 Erdmann Neumeister, *Geistliche Poesien/ mit untermischten Biblischen Sprüchen und Choralen*
   auf alle Sonn- und Fest-Tage durchs gantze Jahr (Eisenach: Boetius, 1717), 1 2; this is a reprint
   of the original edition that appeared in Frankfurt am Main in 1714.
64 Siegbert Rampe, *Carl Philipp Emanuel Bach und seine Zeit* (Laaber: Laaber, 2014), 86–87;
   Hans-Joachim Schulze, "'Fließende Leichtigkeit' und 'arbeitsame Vollstimmigkeit': Georg
   Philipp Telemann und die Musikerfamilie Bach," in *Telemann und seine Freunde: Kontakte–*
   Einflüsse–Auswirkungen (Magdeburg: Zentrum für Telemann-Pflege und -Forschung,
   1986), 34.
65 Steven Zohn, *Music for a Mixed Taste: Style, Genre, and Meaning in Telemann's Instrumental*
   Works (New York: Oxford University Press, 2008), 193–206; Ellen Exner, "The Godfather:
   Georg Philipp Telemann, Carl Philipp Emanuel Bach and the Family Business," BACH 47/1
   (2016): 1–20.
66 See Exner, "Godfather … Telemann," 12–13; see also Ellen Exner, "Is Resistance Futile?
   Telemann, Konzertmeister Bach, and 'Widerstehe doch der Sünde' BWV 54," forthcoming
   in *Telemann Studies*, ed. Wolfgang Hirschmann and Steven Zohn (Cambridge University
   Press).

296 *Theology*

Weissenfels, and Johann Sebastian Bach was one of the two godfathers.[67] But he was not present at the baptism and, following the usual custom, was represented by proxy, as the Weissenfels register clearly states: "Bach ... Loco Herr Secr. Eylenberg" (Bach ... In his place Herr Secretary [Johann Christian] Eylenberg).[68] What is significant about the entry in the Weimar church register of C. P. E.'s baptism is that neither godfather has the name of a proxy alongside his own name, indicating that both Telemann and Weldig were present at the baptism.[69]

Was Telemann Bach's source for these Neumeister libretti, and what was their format? There is some ambivalence with regard to the Sexagesima libretto since this is the only one that Bach ever used from this source, and therefore it could have been supplied in manuscript. But the case of the Advent libretto is different, and Bach almost certainly used Neumeister's annual cycle that had just been published. This appears confirmed by the fact that he later used three further libretti from the same published source, one in each of his first three years in Leipzig, suggesting that he still owned the copy of the Neumeister libretti that had come into his hands some ten or more years earlier:

> *Ein ungefärbt Gemüte*, BWV 24, Fourth Sunday after Trinity, 1723.
> *Wer mich liebet, der wird mein Wort halten*, BWV 59, Pentecost
>   Sunday, 1724.
> *Gottlob! nun geht das Jahr zu Ende*, BWV 28, First Sunday after
>   Christmas, 1725.

If Neumeister's new cycle of cantata libretti was to be publicized and circulated in time for composers to plan for their next year's program of composition, with performances that began at Advent, the collection would need to be printed early in the calendar year. Therefore, advance copies of Neumeister's *Geistliche Poesien*—printed and published in Frankfurt, where Telemann was Capellmeister—were likely to have been available by early March 1714. Thus, did Telemann, bring Bach the gift of an advance copy of Neumeister's *Geistliche Poesien*? And was the gift from Telemann? Or did Neumeister in Sorau instruct Telemann to pick up a copy from the Frankfurt publisher and take it to Bach in Weimar?

---

67 It might be considered that the Weissenfels baptism was too soon after the Weimar baptism for the father, Weldig, to have been at C. P. E. Bach's baptism and then to be present at his son's baptism in Weissenfels, implying that Weldig did not attend the Weimar baptism so he could be back in Weissenfels in time for his son's baptism. However, it is a specious argument because the custom of the time was that the godparents took the child to the font, not the parents, who customarily did not attend the baptism of their children; see Exner, "Godfather ... Telemann," 5.

68 BDok 2: 54–55 (No. 68).

69 BDok 2: 54 (No. 67). The manuscript entry is reproduced in Exner, "Godfather ... Telemann," 4.

As concertmaster in Weimar Bach was *de facto* Capellmeister, though in rank he was below both the appointed Capellmeister and Vice-Capellmeister. When the elderly Capellmeister, Johann Samuel Drese, died in December 1716, Bach must have thought that there was a possibility that he could become Drese's successor. After some delay the duke announced that Drese's son, the Vice-Capellmeister, Johann Wilhelm Drese (1677–1745), would succeed his father. For Bach this meant that Weimar was no longer as attractive to him as it had been in the past, and he almost immediately set about seeking a new position. By the end of 1717, he was in Cöthen with his family as Capellmeister to Prince Leopold of Anhalt-Cöthen.

Here Bach worked with an experienced capella, which had at its core a group of virtuosi instrumentalists who had come to Cöthen in 1713 when the Berlin court capella was dissolved. From time to time, Prince Leopold brought his capella with him to "take the waters" at Carlsbad. The third visit during Bach's tenure began in May 1720.[70] When they returned from Carlsbad early in June Bach was devastated to discover that his wife, Maria Barbara, who was apparently in good health when he had left, had been taken ill, died, and was buried. Thus, in addition to his responsibilities at court he was now also a widower with children to look after.

It is here that one becomes frustrated with the paucity of available information. What there is amounts to disjointed fragments that are separated by connected unknowns. What is known is that there were just eighteen months between the death of Maria Barbara and Bach's marriage to Anna Magdalena Wilcke towards the end of 1721, and that connections with the court of Weissenfels were important and close, but exactly how is difficult to define.

Weissenfels was particularly noted for its trumpet players. Sometime around 1718 a leading trumpeter at the court of Zeitz, Johann Caspar Wilcke (1660–1731), joined the court trumpeters in Weissenfels.[71] Wilcke had one son and four daughters: the son, Johann Caspar Wilcke, Jr., was trumpeter at the court of Zerbst. Three of the daughters were married to trumpeters:

Daughter	Husband	Court Trumpeter
Johanna Christina	Johann Andreas Krebs	Zerbst
Anna Katharina Georg	Christian Meissner	Weissenfels
Dororthea Erdmunthe	Christian August Nicolai	Weissenfels

The fourth and youngest daughter, Anna Magdalena, was unmarried and an experienced singer who had sung regularly in both the courts of Zeitz and

---

70 Maria Hübner, "Neues zu Johann Sebastian Bachs Reisen nach Karlsbad," BJ 92 (2006): 105–7.

71 For the background, see Ruf, "The Courts of Saxony-Weißenfels," 230–31; WolffBLM, 216–17.

298   *Theology*

Weissenfels,[72] as well as making a recorded guest appearance at the court of Zerbst, 24 June 1721, in which her fee was twice that of her trumpeter father.[73] But by this time Anna Magdalena appears to have moved to Cöthen. Her name appears in the list of communicants (as does Bach's) at the Lutheran Jacobskirche, Cöthen, under the date 15 June 1721: "Mar. Magd. Wilkin."[74] The implication is that she had already become a member of the capella at the Cöthen court, a decision that Bach, as Capellmeister, would have made.

In August 1721 Bach traveled to the court of count Heinrich XI in Schleiz, Thuringia, a route that took him through Weissenfels on both the outward and inward journeys.[75] Did he use this contact to confirm their betrothal with Anna's father? Were there other formalities that had to be attended to? Did he feel it necessary to inform Duke Christian about his impending marriage, especially as Anna Magdalena had been a prominent singer in the court capella in Weissenfels? A little over a month later (25 September 1721) Anna Magdalena joined Johann Sebastian as godparents at the baptism of the son of a footman, in the Lutheran Jacobskirche, Cöthen: "Jungfer Magdalena Wilckens. fürstl. Sängerin allhier" (Miss Magdalena Wilckens, singer at the princely court here).[76] Around two months after this (3 December) Johann Sebastian Bach and Anna Magdalena Wilcke were married, according to custom for second marriages, "in Hause."[77]

Bach now had relatives in the court capella in Weissenfels: three trumpeters, that is, his father-in-law, and two brothers-in-law, who were married to Anna Magdalena's sisters. There were probably regular visits to Weissenfels in later years, especially in connection with family matters, such as the death of Anna Magdalena's father, 30 November 1731. That there were such visits is hinted at by Anna Magdalena in a letter to the Weissenfels chamberlain, Johann Leberecht Schneider, September 1741, when she wrote of "the pleasure that I may always promise myself in advance from a visit to our beloved Weissenfels."[78] But only one such visit can be documented for certain. Johann Sebastian and Anna Magdalena visited the court of Weissenfels in early November 1739, when chamber music was performed in Chamberlain Schneider's house.[79]

Early in 1729, when Bach was cantor in Leipzig, Duke Christian of Saxe-Weissenfels visited the New Year's Fair in the city. Bach honored the duke by

---

72 Christoph Schubart, "Anna Magdalena Bach: Neue Beiträge zu ihrer Herkunft und ihren Jugendjahren," BJ 40 (1953): 48; Werner, *Musikpflege in Weissenfels*, 67. Anna Magdalena studied voice with the celebrated operatic soprano, Pauline Kellner, who had been at the Weissenfels court since 1716; Werner, *Musikpflege in Weissenfels*, 77.

73 Schubart, "Anna Magdalena Bach," 48.

74 BDok 2: 71 (No. 92).

75 BDok 2: 81–82 (No. 107); NBR 93 (No. 85).

76 BDok 2: 82 (No. 108).

77 BDok 2: 83 (No. 110); NBR 86.

78 NBR 214 (No. 224); BDok 2: 394 (No. 493).

79 BDok 2: 373; NBR 205–206 (No. 212).

Bach and Erdmann Neumeister 299

composing and performing a homage cantata: *O! Angenehme Melodie* (BWV 210a).[80] Early the next month Bach visited the court of Weissenfels to celebrate the birthday of the duke. This is when, most likely, the duke honored Bach by conferring on him the honorary title *Hochfürstlich Sæchßisch Weißenfelßischen Capellmeistern*[81] (Capellmeister to the Prince of Saxe-Weissenfels).

Of course, while both Neumeister and Bach maintained their individual connections with the Weissenfels court over the years, there is no evidence whether any of their visits overlapped. However, there is at least one occasion when it is certain that they were both in the same place at the same time, and that was in Hamburg towards the end of 1720.

Hamburg 1720

The year 1720 was transitional: for Bach as he coped with being a widower and wondering whether the changed conditions meant that he should be looking for a different position; for Hamburg and its music leadership, since its city cantor, Joachim Gerstenbüttel, was chronically ill, and the organist of the Jacobikirche, Heinrich Friese, had died on 12 September. Neumeister was then well established as the pastor of the Jacobikirche, having been there for five years. One wonders whether it was already in his mind to lure Bach as the new Jacobi organist and Telemann as the new city cantor, should Gerstenbüttel's ill-health lead to his demise. If so, his hopes with regard to Bach remained unfulfilled, while those connected with Telemann proved to be well placed.

Heinrich Friese had succeeded Matthias Weckmann as Jacobi organist in 1674, and had, therefore, held the position for almost fifty years.[82] Preparations began to secure the new organist, a position that also included the role of church secretary. According to the church minutes, on 21 November, "The pastor," that is Erdmann Neumeister, representatives of the congregation, several beadles, and other officers of the church, met in the church chamber (KirchenSahl). It was reported that eight candidates had applied, including Vincent Lübeck, Jr., Johann Joachim Heitmann, and Johann Sebastian Bach. It was decided that all the "competent" candidates should take part in the audition, and that "everything should be done again this time according to the procedure of November 26, Anno 1674,"[83] when Friese was chosen as Weckmann's successor. The main points of this process were that the organists of the churches of St. Petri, St. Nikolai, and St. Katharine should be the principal adjudicators, and that the fugal themes and Psalm melodies

---

80 BDok 5: 143 (No. B 253a).
81 As Bach signed himself on testimonials and on the title pages of *Clavier-Übung* I and II; NBR 153–54 (Nos. 154–55); BDok 1: 235 (No. 168); see also BDok 2: 187–88 (No. 254).
82 Dorothea Schröder, "Die Organisten der Hauptkirche St. Jacobi," in *Die Arp Schnitger-Orgel der Hauptkirche St. Jacobi in Hamburg*, ed. Heimo Reinitzer (Hamburg: Christians, 1995), 78.
83 BDok 2: 77–78 (No. 102); NBR 89 (No. 81).

300 *Theology*

as the basis for improvisations should be taken at random out of a hat.[84] It was decided that the auditions should take place on 28 November, after the hour of prayers (Betstunde). But that was not the end of these preliminary deliberations. The minutes continue:

> The question was raised whether it was desired that money should be given for the organist's post; on which point it was decided that: There were many reasons not to introduce the sale of an organist's post, because it was part of the ministry of God; accordingly the choice should be free, and the capacity of the candidates should be more considered than the money. But if, after the selection had been made, the chosen candidate of his own free will wished to give a token of his gratitude, the latter could be accepted for the benefit of the Church.[85]

It apparently was not recorded who raised the issue, but the most likely person was the pastor, Erdmann Neumeister. It was apparently the custom in Hamburg for important positions of the city council to be sold to the highest bidder. In his correspondence Neumeister often decried the mercenary nature of the way that Hamburg conducted its business. To Löscher he wrote, 21 June 1724: "Money is the Hamburger's God."[86] To Ernst Salomon Cyprian he wrote, in 1731: "The Hamburger sings 'We all believe in one God' but means money."[87]

Bach had probably arrived in Hamburg by 21 November. In the obituary, in a section that must have been penned by C. P. E. Bach, the following appears:

> During this time ... [Bach] made a journey to Hamburg and was heard for more than two hours on the fine organ of St. Catherine's before the Magistrate and many other distinguished persons of the town, to their general astonishment. The aged Organist of this Church, Johann Adam Reinken ... listened to him with particular pleasure. Bach, at the request of those present, performed extempore the chorale *An Wasserflüssen Babylon* at great length (for almost half an hour) and in different ways, just as the better organists of Hamburg in the past had been used to do at Saturday vespers. Particularly on this, Reinken made Bach the following compliment: "I thought that this art was dead, but I see that in you it still lives."[88]

The implication is that Bach's presence at the organ created something that was rarely heard in the Hamburg churches at that time.

---

84 See Schröder, "Die Organisten der Hauptkirche St. Jacobi," 78.
85 NBR 90 (No. 81); not in BDok.
86 Schade, *"Geld ist der Hamburger ihr Gott,"* 182: "Denn Geld ist der Hamburger ihr Gott."
87 Ibid, 182, note 174: *"Wir glauben all an einen Gott* singen die Hamburger, der heißt Geld."
88 NBR 302 (No. 306); BDok 3: 84 (No. 666).

Bach and Erdmann Neumeister 301

Since Johann Mattheson included specific details of the cantata *Ich hatte viel Bekümmernis* (BWV 21), in his *Critica Musica*, published in Hamburg in 1725,[89] that means Bach must have performed the cantata in Hamburg during his visit in connection with his bid to become the Jacobi organist. Notwithstanding Mattheson's complaints about the repetitions of the text of the first movement of the cantata, the performance was probably as well received as his organ playing. However, Bach could not take part in the auditions arranged for 28 November because of his need to return to Cöthen, probably in preparation for Prince Leopold's upcoming birthday, which meant that he left Hamburg on 23 November.

Four candidates gave auditions on 28 November, and the original plan was for the choice to be made and announced at a special gathering scheduled for 12 December. However, because of Bach, the meeting was held a week later. On 19 December, as reported in the minutes of the Jacobikirche, the pastor—by name "Erdmann Neumeister" rather than by function—together with officials and trustees of the church were gathered in the church chamber (KirchenSahl). The minutes explain:

> The choice [of the new organist] had been set for December 12. But Mr. Luttas [a trustee] had sought a postponement until he should receive a letter from Mr. Johann Sebastian Bach, Capellmeister in Cöthen, in which the Pastor [Neumeister] and Gentlemen of the Congregation had acquiesced. Since Mr. Luttas had now received a letter, he had already communicated the same to the Pastor and Gentlemen of the Congregation, and it was thereupon read aloud in full.[90]

Clearly there was considerable support for Bach, otherwise there would not have been the agreement for a postponement of the decision. Equally clearly there was something troubling Bach, almost certainly his inability to donate a substantial "thanks offering" if selected. Perhaps Bach, after returning to Cöthen, had requested the expected thanks offering to be waived in his case if he was chosen, and Luttas, on behalf of the church, had communicated the response to Bach, which would have been negative. But before the people of the Jacobikirche made their choice, they needed to know whether Bach's name was to remain on the roster of candidates, hence the need to wait for the reception of Bach's letter to Luttas. Unfortunately, Bach's letter has not survived, but it almost certainly must have expressed his withdrawal from consideration.[91] Thus, his letter was read, and the election followed:

89 BDok 2: 153–54 (No. 2000; NBR 325 (No. 319).
90 NBR 90 (No. 81); BDok 2: 78 (No. 102).
91 BDok 1: 27 (No. 7); BDok 2: 78 (No. 102).

302　*Theology*

Whereupon it was resolved in God's Name to proceed to the choice, and thus Johann Joachim Heitmann was chosen by a majority vote, *viva voce*, as organist and clerk of the St. Jacobi Church.[92]

Heitmann accordingly, "of his own free will," in due course gave the Jacobikirche a thanks offering of 4,000 marks. This was a substantial sum, several times Bach's annual salary as Capellmeister in Cöthen.[93]

The election had taken place just a few days before Christmas and by all accounts Neumeister, who had obviously supported Bach's candidacy, was not pleased with the outcome, as was revealed a few years later. The source was Hamburg's leading musician, composer, and music critic, Johann Mattheson, who was an eyewitness to the events surrounding the choice of the new organist. Mattheson was also on personal terms with Neumeister, who, for example, supplied him with libretti over the years, such as oratorios for Pentecost (1719) and Christmas (1725).[94] The account was published in Mattheson's *Der Musikalische Patriot* (Hamburg, 1728). The delay in publishing was undoubtedly due to the fact that Heitmann was still the organist of the Jacobikirche, and even if no names were mentioned it would be obvious that it was about him. But he had died in May 1727[95] so the story could then be told.

The whole affair had upset Erdmann Neumeister, so much so that his feelings overflowed into his preaching, according to Mattheson:

I recall, as many others will too, that some years ago a certain great musician [Bach], whose merits have since earned him an important cantorate [in Leipzig], competed for the post of organist in a town of no small size [Hamburg], and exhibited his mastery on several of the finest organs, arousing universal admiration. But there was also present, among other incompetent journeymen, the son of a wealthy tradesman [Heitmann] who could prelude better with talers than with his fingers, and it was he (as might easily be guessed) who was given the post, although most people were furious about it. It was Christmastide, and the eloquent chief preacher [Neumeister], who had not consented to the simony, expounded magnificently the gospel of the music of the angels at the birth of Christ [Luke 2:1–14, the Gospel for Christmas Day], which in connection with the recent incident naturally gave him the opportunity to reveal his thoughts, and ended his sermon with a remarkable pronouncement something like

---

92　NBR 90 (No. 81); BDok 2: 78 (No. 102).

93　The exchange rate in Hamburg in the eighteenth century was 3 Marks to 1 Reichstaler [rtl]. Heitmann's thankoffering was therefore around 1,340rtl. Bach's basic annual salary as Capellmeister in Cöthen, without the ancillary benefits, was 400rtl; see WolffBLM, 540.

94　Beekman C. Cannon, *Johann Mattheson: Spectator in Music* (New Haven: Yale University Press, 1947), 171 and 184 respectively.

95　See Schröder, "Die Organisten der Hauptkirche St. Jacobi," 80.

Bach and Erdmann Neumeister 303

this: He was quite certain that if one of the angels at Bethlehem had come down from heaven and played divinely to become organist at St. J. [Jacobikirche], but had no money, he might just as well fly away again.[96]

Hamburg and Leipzig

In connection with the organist vacancy at the Jacobikirche, Bach is known to have been in Hamburg by 21 November 1720, though it is possible that he arrived a day or so earlier. He left to return to Cöthen on 23 November, so he was probably in the Hanseatic port for four or five days, during which time he was quite busy. The Obituary only mentions him playing one organ, the Stellwagen in the Katharinenkirche, but Mattheson indicates that Bach played on "several" organs, which of course must have included the Schnitger in the Jacobikirche, but there were others no doubt. There was also the rehearsal and performance of Cantata 21 which presumably would have been in the Jacobikirche. But what did he do with any spare time, especially in the evenings? There is a strong possibility that some of it must have been spent with Neumeister; after all, if Bach became the organist of the Jacobikirche they would be working closely together on an almost daily basis. The possibility of such an informal meeting becomes stronger if, as seems likely, the pastor and the Capellmeister were already known to each other through their connections with the court of Weissenfels. There were many things they could have discussed, practical issues, such as how things were done in the Jacobikirche, or philosophical matters, such as the nature and purpose of church music—each expressing their views from within their particular expertise, Bach from the perspective of a composer and director of music, and Neumeister from the viewpoint of a poet and pastor. Of course, one can only speculate. However, there is an activity that they are both known to have shared, and that is book collecting, and this may well have provided more than a simple talking point between them.

Neumeister had an extensive library, as can be judged from the titles he cited in the many books that he wrote. Many of these quoted sources were theological tomes, specialist works not for the average reader. But there is an intriguing collection of sermons that Neumeister preached that were mostly based on popular religious literature, books that had to have been in his personal library. The sermons were later published in 1719 as *Geistliche Bibliothek* (*Spiritual Library*),[97] and they were on the Gospels for the Sundays and celebrations of a complete church year. Each sermon was based on a different published book, which was used to expound the Gospel of the day.

---

96 Johann Mattheson, *Der Musicalische Patriot* (Hamburg: [s.n.], 1728), 316; BDok 2:186–87 (No. 253); translation based on Malcolm Boyd, *Bach*, 3rd ed., The Master Musicians (New York: Oxford University Press, 2000), 74; an alternative translation is in NBR 91 (No. 82).

97 See note 10 above.

304   *Theology*

In content these books were generally either devotional, biblical, or specifically Lutheran, very similar to the kind of books found in Bach's personal library.[98] Indeed, some of the volumes that Neumeister used in these *Geistliche Bibliothek* sermons were also to be found in Bach's collection[99]:

J. Gerhard, *Schola Pietatist* (Nuremberg, 1622–23)	45	Advent 1
A. Pfeiffer, *Lutherthum vor Luthern* (Dresden, 1683)	38	Epiphany
H. Bünting, *Itinerarum Sacra Scripturae* (Helmstedt, 1582)	11	Easter 2nd day
H. Müller, *Geistliche Erquickstunden* (Rostock,1664)	42	Easter 2
H. Müller, *Göttliche Liebes-Flamme* (Frankfurt, 1659)	41	Pentecost 2nd day
J. C. Adami, *Güldige Aepffel* (Leipzig, 1708)	31	Trinity
J. Arndt, *Paradies-Gärtlein* ([s. l.], 1612)[100]	51	John the Baptist
M. Luther, *Tischreden* (Eisleben, 1566)	4	Trinity 17

Thus, there was a commonality in the kind of books they collected and read, and this was something that they might well have discussed in Hamburg in 1720.

Sometime later Bach added two books by Neumeister into his collection, which were apparently kept side by side on his bookshelves[101]:

> Erdmann Neumeister, *Tisch des Herrn. Jn LII. Predigten über 1. Cor. XI., 23–32.: Da zugleich in dem Eingange unterschiedliche Lieder erkläret worden.* (Hamburg: Kißner, 1722)

> Erdmann Neumeister, *Das Wasserbad im Worte, Oder: Die Lehre von der Heil. Tauffe: so in LII. Predigten; und zugleich in dem Eingange derselben Unterschiedliche Lieder erkläret worden.* (Hamburg: Kißner, 1731)

Both volumes were anthologies of sermons on the two Sacraments, one on the Lord's Supper, and the other on Baptism. Each volume began its life as an annual series of fifty-two sermons on one of the chief sections of Luther's

---

98 See Robin A. Leaver, *Bach's theologische Bibliothek: Eine kritische Bibliographie* (Stuttgart: Hänssler, 1983).

99 In the following short-title listing of the books in Neumeister's *Geistliche Bibliothek*, the original publication date is used; the numbers in the second column refer to those in Leaver, *Bach's theologische Bibliothek*; and the third column gives the Sunday or celebration on which Neumeister's sermon was preached.

100 Often appended or bound with Arndt's *Wahres Christentum*.

101 Leaver, *Bach's theologische Bibliothek*, Nos. 46 and 47, respectively.

Small Catechism.[102] All of the fifty-two sermons of *Tisch des Herrn* were expositions of the same Scriptural passage: 1 Corinthians 11: 23–32. The resultant massive book of almost fifteen hundred pages presents a thorough exposition of Lutheran eucharistic theology and practice, as can be seen in the detailed "Register der vornehmsten Sachen" (Index of Important Things).

Did Bach purchase the Neumeister volumes, or did he receive them as gifts? These two volumes were the first titles of what would become Neumeister's extensive commentary on all five sections of Luther's Small Catechism. Presumably, they were obtained soon after they were published (1722 and 1731), but the other three did not join them on Bach's bookshelves when they were published (1734, 1735, and 1737). If Bach had bought the first two volumes in the series, why did he not purchase the other three volumes when they appeared? It was not because he had stopped acquiring books, since he is known to have bought the Altenburg edition of Luther's *Schriften*, bound in seven volumes in 1742,[103] and a copy of the Merian Bible in 1744.[104] This suggests that he probably received the two Neumeister volumes as gifts and, if so, then the most likely person to have given them to Bach was the author himself, Erdmann Neumeister.

A distinctive feature of many of Neumeister's published works is the repetition of the Bible verse: "Gott der Herr ist Sonn und Schild" (God the Lord is Sun and Shield; Psalm 84:12). For example, in *Tisch des Herrn* the verse appears three times near the beginning of the book: on the title page, as a heading before the preface, and before the first sermon. The following list is a random selection of Neumeister's books published in Hamburg, with the number of times the verse is repeated, usually on the title page and other prelims:

Geistliche Bibliothek (1719)	2
Der allerheiligste Glaube (1723)	2
Freytags-Andachten (1724)	3
Der Leidende Christus (1728)	2
Das Wasserbad im Worte (1731)	3
Die Lehre vom Glauben (1735)	3

It was customary at that time, especially among pastors and theologians, to choose a Biblical verse as a personal motto. Thus, Neumeister chose

---

102 Over the years, Neumeister published collections of sermons on the five main sections of Luther's *Small Catechism*, each volume comprising fifty-two sermons: [I.] *Die Lehre von dem Gesetz Gottes* (Hamburg, 1737): [II.] *Die Lehre vom Glauben* (Hamburg, 1735); [III.] *Geistliche Rauchwerck; oder die Lehre vom Gebet* (Hamburg, 1734); [IV.] *Wasserbad im Worte* (Hamburg, 1731); [V.] *Tisch des Herrn* (Hamburg, 1722).

103 Robin A. Leaver, "Bach und die Lutherschriften seiner Bibliothek." BJ 61 (1975): 124–32.

104 Peter Wollny, "Fundstücke zur Lebensgeschichte Johann Sebastian Bachs 1744–1750," BJ 97 (2011): 37–39, 47–48.

306   *Theology*

Psalm 84:12 as the personal summary of his attitude towards his faith and life and as the keynote of his ministry, and therefore he used it extensively in his published works. In some of the frontispieces, which were engraved portraits of himself, a visual form of the motto is included,[105] and he also wrote a personal hymn in which the motto is repeated in each of the six stanzas.[106]

Bach's cantata 79, a Reformation Day cantata composed for 31 October 1725, begins with the same Psalm verse. There is no known librettist, but the fact that the first two movements begin with Neumeister's personal motto is a strong suggestion that he was most likely the author:

[1.]	Gott der Herr is Sonn und Schild.	God the Lord is sun and shield.
	Der Herr gibt Gnade und Ehre,	The Lord gives grace and honour;
	er wird kein Gutes mangeln	he will not withhold any good thing
	lassen den Frommen.	from the devout. [Psalm 84: 12].
[2.]	Gott ist unsre Sonn und Schild!	God is our sun and shield!
	Darum rühmet dessen Güte	Therefore our grateful spirit
	Unser dankbares Gemüte	praises the goodness he shows
	Die er für sein Häuflein hegt.	for his little body of men.
	Denn er will uns ferner schützen	For he will protect us further,
	Ob die Feinde Pfeile schnitzen	Though our enemies sharpen arrows
	Und ein Lästerhund gleich billt.	and the dog Blasphemy should bark.[107]

The imagery of the "hound of blasphemy" in the aria (movt. 2) is typical of Neumester's reference to those he regards as enemies and opponents.

The choice of the first stanza of *Nun danket alle Gott* as the 3rd movement is obvious in this context and is not a marker for identifying the librettist, since it could have been added by almost anyone, being a popular hymn, frequently sung throughout the year, especially at times of thanksgiving. Yet it was a hymn that Neumeister parodied with his own stanzas at least four times, his common method being to take the first line of each stanza of

---

105 The image is circular, and the motto appears around the circumference enclosing the design; rays of light stream from the sun of the Divine Name in Hebrew (in the center at the top) onto a double shield; see the examples reproduced in Werner Neumann, *Auf den Lebenswegen Johann Sebastian Bachs* (Berlin: Verlag der Nation, 1962), 93; and Leaver, *Bach's theologische Bibliothek*, 172.

106 See Erdmann Neumeister, *Psalmen, und Lobgesänge und Geistlicher Lieder, aus seinen Poetischen und andern seinen Schrifften* (Hamburg: Beneke, 1755), 641–42.

107 Alfred Dürr, *The Cantatas of J. S. Bach with their Librettos in German-English Parallel Text*, rev. and trans. Richard D. P. Jones (New York: Oxford University Press, 2005), 711–12.

a preexisting hymn but then to write new lines for the rest of each stanza.[108] The chorale meant something significant to Neumeister.

The vocabulary and imagery of the following recitative and duet (movts. 4–5) are similar to what one finds in the collected edition of Neumeister's hymns, especially in the section under the heading, "Vom Worte Gottes. Wo zugleich von der Reformation und den Kirchen Jubelfesten" (Of the Word of God as well as Reformation and church anniversaries),[109] the category that would embrace Cantata 79.

The chorale at the end of the cantata is the final (8th) stanza of Ludwig Helmbold's *Nun lasst uns Gott, dem Herren* (1575). Much of Neumeister's *Tisch des Herrn* is an exposition of the Lutheran understanding of the Sacrament of the Lord's Supper. Throughout these sermons Neumeister used eight primary Lutheran hymns, one stanza in each sermon, as a fundamental part of his exposition of the Sacrament. In the second half of the volume all eight stanzas of *Nun lasst uns Gott, dem Herren* are employed.[110] Reformation Day was often used by contemporary preachers to remind their congregations of the Word and Sacraments, the essence of Lutheran faith and practice. It is significant that when Neumeister embarked on his massive preaching marathon, instead of following the sequence of the Small Catechism, beginning with sermons on the Ten Commandments, he goes instead to the last section of the Catechism and preaches on the Lord's Supper, because it is the Sacrament that essentially seals Lutheran identity. The hymn was important to Neumeister. Cantata 79 ends thus:

Erhalt uns in der Wahrheit,	Preserve us in the truth:
Gib ewigliche Freiheit,	Grant us eternal freedom
Zu preisen deinen Namen,	to praise your Name
Durch Jesum Christum. Amen.	through Jesus Christ. Amen.[111]

The evidence may not be conclusive, but it does point to Neumeister as the probable author of the libretto of Cantata 79, composed for the celebration of the Reformation in 1725. The fact that the links between the two men were at their strongest during the 1720s, when Bach composed a number of other cantatas to Neumeister texts; that Neumeister was deeply committed to the Lutheran Reformation; that the structure, form, and content are similar to Neumeister's other cantata libretti; and especially that his personal motto is the keynote of the cantata—these would all seem to point to the *pastor primarius* in Hamburg as the librettist.

---

108 Neumeister, *Psalmen, und Lobgesänge und Geistlicher Lieder*, 63, 84, 87, 233. Neumeister also wrote new hymn texts to be sung to the *Nun danket* melody.

109 Neumeister, *Psalmen, und Lobgesänge und Geistlicher Lieder*, 201–34.

110 Neumeister's *Tisch des Herrn*, 621, 648, 672, 699, 702, 728, 748, 767.

111 Dürr, *The Cantatas of J. S. Bach*, 712.

14 Bach's *Clavierübung III*

The year 1739 was important in Leipzig: it marked the bicentenary of the introduction of the Reformation into the city. During that year there were no less than three Reformation festivals. The first was at Pentecost, since it was the reformer, Martin Luther, himself who heralded the introduction of Reformation doctrine and practice by preaching in the Thomaskirche on the Feast of Pentecost, 25 May 1539. The second was held on 12 August celebrating the bicentenary of the acceptance of the Augsburg Confession by Leipzig University.[1] The third celebration was the usual, annual Reformation festival held on 31 October each year. It is significant indeed that this important Reformation year in Leipzig saw the publication of the third part of Bach's *Clavierübung*.

It is known that Bach was working on the project in January of that year, intending it to be published at the Easter book fair in Leipzig, that is, just before the first of the three Reformation celebrations.[2] However, the collection was not published until much later in the year.[3] But it was clearly Bach's intention to bring out this collection just prior to the Reformation celebration at Pentecost, and there are grounds for believing that this anniversary of the introduction of the Reformation into Leipzig provided him with the inspiration to compose and compile *Clavierübung III*.

1 Salomon Deyling, Superintendent and professor of theology in Leipzig, gave a Latin oration on each of these occasions; Salomon Deyling, *Observationum Sacrarum Pars V* (Leipzig: Lanckisch, 1748), 407–32.
2 *Die Briefentwürfe des Johann Elias Bach* (1705–1755), ed. Evelin Odrich and Peter Wollny, Leipziger Beiträge zur Bach-Forschung, 3, 2nd ed. (Hildesheim: Olms, 2005), 99–100 (No. 13); BDok 2: 335 (No. 434); NBR 202 (No. 205).
3 *Leipziger Zeitungen*, 30 Sept. 1739, 624; BDok 2: 370 (No. 456). See also the letter of Johann Elias Bach of 28 Sept. 1739, *Die Briefentwürfe des Johann Elias Bach*, 118–19 (No. 33); BDok 2: 370.

Bach's Clavierübung III   309

Reformation in Leipzig

The House of Wettin was a dynasty of electors, dukes, princes, and counts who ruled in Saxony and Thuringia. Towards the end of the fifteenth century the family divided into two ruling branches: Ernestine and Albertine. Luther's Reformation in Wittenberg took place in Ernestine territory and was protected at first by Duke Frederick the Wise (1463–1525), but especially by his brother, Duke Johann the Steadfast (1468–1532). In contrast, Albertine Saxony, under Duke Georg (1471–1539), remained loyal to Catholicism. However, on his death in 1539 he was succeeded by his brother, Duke Henry (1473–1541), who set out to change the religious affiliation of Albertine Saxony from Catholic to Lutheran. It was Luther who personally introduced the far-reaching changes.

Luther's visit to Leipzig in May 1539 led to two interrelated activities: a reformation of belief (doctrine) and a reformation of practice (worship).[4] The Elector, Duke Henry, summarized the significance of what happened in Leipzig at Pentecost 1539: "Papal abuses were abolished from all the churches, the Word of God was preached in all of them (may God be praised), and the Sacrament was administered and celebrated as a Christian Mass."[5] This reference to the celebration of the Sacrament as a Christian Mass embraces Luther's liturgical reforms, especially the *Deudsche Messe und ordnung Gottesdiensts* of 1526.[6] A new *Gesangbuch* was issued in Leipzig for the use of the newly reformed congregations, and it included Luther's *Deutsche Messe: Geistliche lieder, auffs new gebessert und gemehrt zu Witte[n]berg. D. Marti. Luther ... Ite[m] Die ordnu[n]g der deutsche[n] Mess* (Leipzig: Schumann, 1539).[7] In the *Deutsche Messe* Luther speaks of a doctrinal need. He writes that in a "truly evangelical order ... for ... those who want to be Christians in earnest and who profess the gospel ... Here one would need a good short catechism on the Creed, the Ten Commandments, and the Our Father."[8] Luther is here

---

4 For the background, see Carl Gottlob Hofmann, *Ausführliche Reformations-Historie der Stadt und Universität Leipzig* (Leipzig: Breitkopf, 1739); Georg Buchwald, *Reformationsgeschichte der Stadt Leipzig* (Leipzig: Richter, 1900).

5 Veit Ludwig von Seckendorf, *Commentarius Historicus et Apologeticus De Lutheranismo, sive De Reformatione Religionis ductu D. Martini Lutheri in magna Germaniae parte aliisque religionibus, & speciatim in Saxonia recepta & stabilita* (Frankfurt and Leipzig: Gleditsch, 1692), 2: 218: "abusus Pontificii in omnibus templis cessarunt, praedicato in omnibus (Deus sit laus) verbo Dei & administrato secundum ejus praescriptum Sacramento, celebrataque Missa Christiana." Deyling, *Observationum Sacrarum Pars V*, 415, specifically adds the information that the vernacular Reformation hymns were also introduced into the liturgy at that time.

6 WA 19: 72–113; LW 53: 61–90.

7 The *Deutsche Messe* appears on fols. 108ʳ–112ᵛ; see Philipp Wackernagel, *Bibliographie zur Geschichte des Deutschen Kirchenlieds* (Frankfurt: Hender & Zimmer, 1855; reprint, Hildesheim: Olms, 1961), 470–71.

8 LW 53, 63–64; WA 19: 75: "die rechte art der Evangelischen ordnunge haben solte ... so mit ernst Christen wollen seyn und das Evangelion ... bekennen ... Hie muste man eynen guten kurtzen Catechismum haben uber den glauben. zehen gebot und vater unser."

310   *Theology*

introducing the German *Gottesdienst,* which was to be a musical service, but as he does so he speaks of the need to teach the fundamentals of the Christian faith in a catechism. Significantly, these are the two main elements of Bach's *Clavierübung III,* with the reformed way of worship being expressed by the pieces that comprise the Mass settings (BWV 669–77), and the reformed doctrine by the catechism preludes (BWV 678–89).

Many scholars have been puzzled by this juxtaposition of liturgical and doctrinal concerns in Bach's publication. Clearly the Thomascantor saw no distinction between dogmatics and liturgics, and in so doing he was following the fundamental Lutheran position. The classic Lutheran theologians of the seventeenth century discuss liturgical matters in the course of their dogmatic works and speak of theological principles when discussing particular liturgical forms.[9] In the worship of the Leipzig churches, stemming from the sixteenth century, liturgical forms and doctrinal considerations, as expressed in Luther's catechism, were intertwined.

Later in 1539 an *Agenda,* or *Kirchen-Ordnung,* was compiled and published in Leipzig, slightly revised in 1540, and thereafter was continuously reprinted in every subsequent generation: *Agenda, Das ist, Kirchen-Ordnung … Für die Diener der Kirchen In Hertzog Heinrichs zu Sachsen Fürstenthum gestellet* (Leipzig: Lanckisch, 1712).[10] It provided basic forms of worship, though it was more of a directory rather than a fully worked-out sequence of liturgies. It contained Luther's orders for Baptism, marriage, and so forth, but was mainly concerned with the weekly *Gottesdienst* for Sunday worship, which was basically Luther's *Deutsche Messe.* It is significant to note that it was customary to bind with the *Kirchen-Ordnung* a copy of Luther's Small Catechism. This was because the catechism formed the basis of much of ecclesiastical life. In Leipzig in Bach's day on every weekday there was at least one teaching session on the various sections of the catechism in one or other of the Leipzig churches,[11] and it was part of Bach's responsibility as cantor to teach the Latin version of Luther's Small Catechism in the Thomasschule on Saturday mornings.[12]

On Sundays there were two principal services, the *Hauptgottesdienst* and the *Vespergottesdienst.* The *Hauptgottesdienst* was the main service

---

9 See Friedrich Kalb, *Theology of Worship in 17th-Century Lutheranism,* trans. Henry P. A. Hamann (St. Louis: Concordia, 1965), 16–17.

10 The preface was dated 19 Sept. Anno 1539. However, sometime in the seventeenth century the year was misprinted as "1536." This incorrect year was repeated in many of the later reprints. The *Kirchen Agenda* was widely accessible, being available separately, but was also incorporated within such official Saxon publications as *Corpus Juris Ecclesiastici Saxonici, Oder Churfl. Sächs. Kirchen- Schulen- wie auch andere darzu gehörige Ordnungen* (Dresden: Winckler, 1708), and *Vollständiges Kirchen-Buch …* (Leipzig: Lanckish, 1743).

11 Günther Stiller, *Johann Sebastian Bach und das Leipziger gottesdienstliche Leben seiner Zeit* (Kassel: Bärenreiter, 1970), 42–43; Günther Stiller, *Johann Sebastian Bach and Liturgical Life in Leipzig,* trans. Herbert J. A. Bouman, et al. (St. Louis: Concordia, 1984), 51–52.

12 Spitta 2: 6, 13; Spitta ET 2: 185, 191.

of worship, held on Sunday mornings and was a celebration of the Lord's Supper. The *Vespergottesdienst* was an afternoon service of hymns, readings, and preaching, at the close of which a part of the catechism was read and expounded.[13] It would seem that Bach had these two services in mind when he composed the *Clavierübung III*. Enshrined within these pieces is the distinctive Lutheran understanding of worship and theology, which had been introduced into Leipzig by Luther himself at Pentecost 1539. With the exception of the four Duets (BWV 802–805), all the pieces are appropriate for either liturgy. Both began with organ music[14] and therefore the majestic prelude (BWV 552/1) was suitable for beginning either service. Similarly, both services conclude with the blessing. The great three-section fugue (BWV 552/2), with all its Trinitarian associations, appears to be the musical counterpart of the verbal Trinitarian benediction that customarily brought worship to an end, and therefore was appropriate to conclude either service. The following listing indicates the aptness for both services of the hymns on which Bach has written chorale preludes. The columns on the right give either the liturgical position of the hymn in the *Hauptgottesdienst* or the Sunday in the church year for which Vopelius prescribes its use[15]:

BWV	Cantus firmus	Hauptgottesdienst	Vespergottesdienst
669–674	3-fold, Trinitarian Kyrie-Christe-Kyrie	Kyrie	Penitential hymn
675–677	Allein Gott in der Höh sei Ehr	Gloria	Hymn of praise
678–679	Dies sind die heil'gen zehn Gebot	Trinity 4, 6, 13, 18	Catechism Pt. I
680–681	Wir glauben all an einen Gott	Creed	Catechism Pt. II

---

13 *Agenda, Das ist, Kirchen-Ordnung*, 81: "Und wenn die Vesper aus ist, nehme man ein Stück aus dem Catechismo vor, und lege daselbige dem Volck aufs einfältigste aus, und was man des Sonntags aus dem Catechismo vorgeleget hat, dasselbige soll man den Kindern in der Woche ... Man soll aber nicht an einem jeden Ort einen sonderlichen Catechismum vornehmen, sondern durchaus einerley Form halten, wie solche zu Wittenberg durch D. Martin Luthern gestelet ist." ("At the end of Vespers, let one of the chief parts of the Catechism be selected and expounded in the simplest way to the people. The section from the Catechism which has been explained on the Sunday can be brought forward in the week for the children's instruction ... There shall not be taught a different catechism in every locality, but one and the same form, as presented by Dr. Martin Luther at Wittenberg, shall be observed everywhere." For the background, see Hans-Jürgen Fraas, *Katechismustradition: Luthers kleiner Katechismus in Kirche und Schule* (Göttingen: Vandenhoeck & Ruprecht, 1971); Bruno Jordahn, "Katechismus-Gottesdienst im Reformationsjahrhundert," *Luther. Mitteilungen der Luther-Gesellschaft* 30 (1959): 64–77.

14 See Chapter 2.

15 Gottfried Vopelius, *Neu Leipziger Gesangbuch* (Leipzig: Klinger, 1682); see also Jürgen Grimm, *Das Neu Leipziger Gesangbuch des Gottfried Vopelius (Leipzig 1682)* (Berlin: Merseburger, 1969).

312 Theology

BWV	Cantus firmus	Hauptgottesdienst	Vespergottesdienst
682–683	Vater unser im Himmelreich	Septuages., Lent 1, Trinity 5, 7, 11, 15, 22, 25	Catechism Pt. Ill
684–685	Christ unser Herr zum Jordan kam	St. John the Baptist	Catechism Pt. IV
686–687	Aus tiefer Noth schrei ich zu dir	Epiphany 4, Palm Sunday, Trinity 11, 19, 21, 22	Catechism Pt. V
688–689	Jesus Christus unser Heiland	Communion hymn	Catechism Pt. VI

Christoph Wolff is of the opinion that, while these organ pieces were liturgical in concept, they were unliturgical in practice. He writes, "Despite their unquestionably liturgical background and character, the organ chorales of *Clavier-Übung* III were in fact not designed to be played at services."[16] I am not so sure. Earlier he had characterized *Clavierübung III* as "A German *Livre d'Orgue*," recalling the collections of liturgical organ music by Girolamo Frescobaldi (Rome 1635) that Bach had copied in 1714, and by Nicolas de Grigny (Paris 1699) that Bach had copied around 1710.[17] But these collections were of practical Catholic liturgical organ music, mostly for the Mass, and thus if Bach was inspired by them to create a Lutheran *Livre d'Orgue,* then the expectation would be that these pieces had practical use. But, of course, not for the average organist.

Luther's preaching

Luther introduced the Reformation in Leipzig by preaching in the Thomaskirche on Pentecost, 1539, but unfortunately the actual sermon was not preserved. However, the sermon that he preached on the previous evening in Leipzig's Pleissenburg castle has survived. In this sermon Luther states that the true Christian church is to be found where the commandments are obeyed, where the Lord's Prayer is truly prayed, where Baptism is rightly understood, where the distressed sinner receives the assurance of forgiveness, where the Sacrament is rightly administered, and where, above all, the Trinitarian faith is confessed.[18]

16 Christoph Wolff, *Bach's Musical Universe: The Composer and His Work* (New York: Norton, 2020), 177.
17 See Kirsten Beißwenger, *Johann Sebastian Bachs Notenbibliothek* (Kassel: Bärenreiter, 1991), 284–85, and 287–89. Wolff could also have referred to the *Livre d'Orgue* by Pierre Du Mage (St. Quintin 1708), which Bach encountered in his early years; see Beißwenger, *Bachs Notenbibliothek*, 351.
18 WA 47: 722–79; LW 51: 303–12.

Just before rehearsing these main teachings of the catechism on that significant occasion, Luther makes the following key statement: "It is true that Christ wants to have his home where the Father and the Holy Spirit want to be and to dwell. The entire Trinity dwells in the true church; what the true church does and directs is done and directed by God."[19] Thus, Luther speaks of two things: the Trinity of God and the substance of the teaching of the catechism.

Bach was a man who had a deep regard for the writings of Luther. He owned two multivolume editions of the works of the reformer, the Jena and Altenburg editions,[20] as well as a single volume of the Wittenberg edition.[21] He also owned the three-volume commentary on the whole of the Bible, which Abraham Calov edited from the writings of Luther,[22] two different copies of the *Hauspostille*,[23] and an edition of the *Tischreden* (Table Talk).[24] Even though Luther's sermon preached in the Pleissenburg was not included in any of the volumes in Bach's library at this date,[25] it is difficult to believe that he had no knowledge of it. It would have been a natural source to quote from the pulpits of the Leipzig churches at Pentecost, 1739, and it would have been referred to, well in advance of the day, by all those involved in the celebrations. For example, Bach's contemporary, Carl Gottlob Hofmann, then the pastor of the Petrikirche in Leipzig, reprinted the sermon in full in his 1739 account of the Reformation in Leipzig.[26] That the same two elements—the doctrine of the Trinity and the substance of the catechism— are stressed in both Luther's 1539 sermon and Bach's 1739 collection of organ compositions seems to suggest that the sermon strongly influenced the compositions.

---

19 LW 51: 305; WA 47: 773: "Und ist wahr, Christus wil seine Wohnung haben, wo der Vater und heilige Geist seyn und wohnen wollen, die gantze Dreyfaltigkeit wohnet in der wahren Kirchen, was die warhafftige Kirche thut und ordnet, das thut und ordnet Gott."

20 Robin A. Leaver, *Bachs theologische Bibliothek: Ein kritische Bibliographie* (Stuttgart: Hänssler, 1983), Nos. 3 and 2 respectively.

21 Leaver, *Bachs theologische Bibliothek*, No. 6.

22 Leaver, *Bachs theologische Bibliothek*, No. 1. These three volumes are the only ones from Bach's library that have survived; they are in the library of Concordia Seminary, St. Louis; see Robin A. Leaver, *J. S. Bach and Scripture: Glosses from the Calov Bible Commentary* (St. Louis: Concordia, 1985; reprinted 2017).

23 Leaver, *Bachs theologische Bibliothek*, Nos. 7 and 28.

24 Leaver, *Bachs theologische Bibliothek*, No. 4.

25 The first collected edition to include the sermon was the Altenburg edition: *Der Siebende Teil aller Deutschen Bücher und Schrifften der theuren/ seeligen Mannes Gottes/ Doctor Martini Lutheri ...* (Altenburg: Fürst. Sachs. Offizin, 1662), fols. 297^r–300^v. However, Bach purchased the volumes of the Altenburg edition of Luther's works at an auction in 1742; see Robin A. Leaver, "Bach und die Lutherschriften seiner Bibliothek," BJ 61 (1975): 124–32; Robin A. Leaver, "Bach and Luther," *BACH* 9/3 (July 1978): 9–12, 25–32.

26 Hofmann, *Ausführliche Reformations-Historie der Stadt und Universität Leipzig*, 350–66.

314   *Theology*

The Trinitarian preludes

Trinitarian associations are to be found in abundance throughout the whole set. It is the *third* part of the *Clavierübung*; it begins with a prelude in the Trinitarian key of *three* flats; the prelude is followed by *three* groups of *three* preludes in honor of the Trinity; many of the catechism preludes—notably the larger settings—have strong Trinitarian associations; it concludes with the massive fugue in *three* sections; and it was published in the Trinitarian year of "9"in which there were *three* Reformation celebrations in Leipzig.

The doctrine of the Trinity was no theological abstraction to orthodox Lutheran theologians. They regarded any weakening of the doctrine as

> deviation from the Christian faith. The doctrine of the Trinity was considered by the Lutheran teachers to be not only a touchstone for Christian orthodoxy but a fundamental article of the Christian faith, an article necessary to know for salvation. For to know and worship God as triune means to know Him and worship Him as a gracious God who through His Spirit seeks and saves sinners for Christ's sake.[27]

Reflecting this Lutheran understanding, Bach, after the opening prelude, produces nine pieces, in three groups of three, in honor of the Trinity:

BWV

669	Kyrie, Gott Vater in Ewigkeit:	2 Clav. e. Ped.
670	Christe, aller Welt Trost:	2 Clav. e. Ped.
671	Kyrie, Gott heiliger Geist:	Con Organo pleno
672	Kyrie, Gott Vater in Ewigkeit:	Manualiter
673	Christe, aller Welt Trost:	Manualiter
674	Kyrie, Gott heiliger Geist:	Manualiter
675	Allein Gott in der Höh' sei Ehr:	Manualiter
676	Allein Gott in der Höh' sei Ehr:	2 Clav. e. Ped.
677	Allein Gott in der Höh' sei Ehr:	Manualiter

In the first group—the larger settings of the three stanzas of the German version of the Latin *Kyrie fons bonitatis*—each person of the Trinity is represented by a different voice. In the first the chorale melody, representing God the Father, appears in the soprano; in the second, God the Son, the middle person of the Trinity, is represented by the melody in the middle voice, the tenor; and in the third, God the Holy Spirit is symbolized by the melody in the bass. Of the three preludes the one on *Kyrie, Gott heiliger Geist* is singled out for a particularly powerful treatment. Why should Bach thus

27 Robert D. Preus, *The Theology of Post-Reformation Lutheranism* (St. Louis: Concordia, 1970–1972), 2: 213–14.

Bach's Clavierübung III   315

seek to emphasize the third person of the Trinity? If his inspiration for the whole set was indeed the bicentenary of the introduction of the Reformation into Leipzig, then the reason is clear. It would have been natural for him to wish to emphasize the Holy Spirit since it was at Pentecost, the festival of the Holy Spirit, that Luther preached in order to begin the reforming movement in Leipzig.

The second group, based on the same three stanzas, is simple and straightforward, comprising settings for manuals only. There may well be Trinitarian significance in the progression of the time signatures: 3/4, 6/8, and 9/8.

The third and final group is comprised of three preludes on the Trinitarian hymn, *Allein Gott in der Höh' sei Ehr.* A brilliant trio movement, reminiscent of the organ sonatas, is placed within two fughettas for manuals alone, and each is written in three basic parts. The hymn on which the preludes are based has associations with the introduction of the Reformation into Leipzig. The first High German version of the words and the melody both appeared for the first time in the Leipzig *Gesangbuch* of 1539,[28] and it is likely that Bach would have been aware of the fact. The hymn would have had further Leipzig connections for him. Although the author of the hymn was actually Nikolaus Decius, contemporary hymnals known to Bach record the author as Nikolaus Selnecker.[29] Selnecker was an eminent Lutheran theologian in Leipzig, professor of theology and pastor of the Thomaskirche in the second half of the sixteenth century. He was also an accomplished musician, an organist before he was a theologian, who helped to establish the reputation of the *Thomanerchor*, and wrote both the texts and melodies of hymns.[30]

Bach represents the doctrine of the Trinity in these three groups of three pieces, and there may well be a reference here to the confessional writings of the Lutheran church. The doctrinal position of the church is enshrined in the documents contained in *The Book of Concord.*[31]

---

28 See page 309 above.

29 For example, Vopelius, *Neu Leipziger Gesangbuch*, 425; *Das Privilegirte Ordentliche und Vermehrte Dreßdnische Gesang-Buch* (Dresden and Leipzig: Hekel, 1732), 118. The same attribution is found in the eight-volume hymn anthology that Bach owned (Leaver, *Bachs theologische Bibliothek*, No. 52): Paul Wagner, *Andachtiger Seelen geistliches Brand- und Gantz Opfer ...* (Leipzig: Zedler, 1697), 1: 298. Incidentally, the two hymns that Bach uses, *Kyrie-Christe-Kyrie* and *Allein Gott in der Höh sei Ehr*, appear in both Vopelius and Wagner following each other (as Bach has them) under the general heading: "Von der Heiligen dreyfaltigkeit."

30 Selnecker (1528–1592) was one of the authors of the Formula of Concord, a primary Lutheran confessional document. His hymnological compositions are to be found in his *Christliche Psalmen/ Lieder/ und Kirchengesenge/ Jn welchen die Christliche Lehre zusam gefasset und erkleret wird ...* (Leipzig: Beyer, 1587), which includes his six hymns on the six chief parts of Luther's Catechism.

31 *Die Bekenntnisschriften der evangelisch-lutherischen Kirche*, 11th ed. (Göttingen: Vandenhoeck & Ruprecht, 1992); BC-K/W. It includes such documents as the Augsburg Confession (1530), the two Catechisms (1529), and the Formula of Concord (1577). The collection was first issued in 1580.

316　*Theology*

It begins with the three historic creeds (Apostolic, Nicene, and Athanasian), which are the three classic statements of Trinitarian belief and stand behind Bach's planning of three groups of three.[32] In these nine preludes on *Hauptgottesdienst* melodies Bach has presented two basic approaches: four that demand the resources of a large organ with pedals, and five that can be played on a small, two-manual instrument. The *Saxon Agenda* draws a distinction between the more elaborate form of service that would be used in the churches of cities and towns and the simpler forms suitable for village churches with their more limited resources.[33] In these preludes Bach has provided compositions for both situations.

Luther's catechisms

Luther wrote his catechisms in 1529, and it is difficult for a non-Lutheran to appreciate fully the impact and later influence that these documents had in the church that was to bear his name.[34] The catechism exists in two forms: the Large Catechism, intended for pastors and teachers, and the Small Catechism, written for children and young people. Both were included in *The Book of Concord* and thus form part of the confessional writings of Lutheranism. Indeed, the Formula of Concord speaks of them thus:

> And because these matters also concern the laity and the salvation of their souls, we pledge ourselves also to the Small and Large Catechisms of Dr. Luther, as both catechisms are found in Luther's printed works as a Bible of the Laity, in which everything is summarized that is treated in detail in Holy Scripture and that is necessary for a Christian to know for salvation.[35]

In his longer Preface to the Large Catechism, Luther declared that "the Catechism ... is a brief digest and summary of the entire Holy Scriptures."[36]

Bach especially draws attention to the catechism in the title of the collection: *Dritter Theil der Clavier Ubung bestehend in verschiedenen Vorspielen über die Catechismus und andere Gesaenge vor die Orgel* (Third Part of the Keyboard Practice consisting in Various Preludes on the Catechism and Other Hymns for the Organ). *Clavierübung III* can be divided theologically into two parts: the doctrine of God and the doctrine of Holy Scripture.

32　BC-K/W 19–25. Note also that the first article of the Augsburg Confession is a statement of the fundamental importance of the doctrine of the Trinity; BC-K/W 36–37.

33　*Agenda, Das ist, Kirchen-Ordnung*, 77–82 and 83–85 respectively.

34　Johann Georg Walch, *Bibliotheca Theologica Selecta* (Jena: Cröcker, 1757–1765), 4: 1064–1072, lists some 85 titles of volumes of sermons based on Luther's catechisms. The list is by no means exhaustive but includes many names of the most distinguished Lutheran theologians.

35　BC-K/W 487, see also 528.

36　BC-K/W 382.

Bach's Clavierübung III   317

These were the two basic considerations in Lutheran dogmatic theology,[37] and Bach has given them musical expression.

In his short Preface to the Large Catechism Luther had requested that the basic teachings of the catechism be taught not only in sermons but also in appropriate hymns,[38] and later he himself completed hymns on all the six[39] chief parts of the catechism.[40] It is these catechism hymns of Luther that Bach has used in the second main section of his collection. Each melody is treated twice; a simple setting for manuals alone and a more extensive setting for manuals and pedal. Undoubtedly Bach intended to represent the two Catechisms of Luther: the Small Catechism (in simple form for children) and the Large Catechism. This is borne out by the fact that the larger preludes precede the smaller. Logically and psychologically, one would expect the smaller settings to precede the larger, but Bach, the attentive student of Luther, knows that the Large Catechism was written before the Small Catechism.

The Large Catechism settings

The solid prelude on *Dies sind die heil'gen zehn Gebot* (BWV 678) is a trio, representing the Trinity, which produces from within itself the Law, the Ten Commandments, symbolized by the canonic form of the melody, which appears in the middle stave. It is a two-part canon at the octave representing the two tablets of stone on which the commandments were inscribed. The

---

37 These were the first two *loci* of Leonhard Hutter, *Compendium Locorum Theologicorum Ex Scripturis sacris, & libro Concordiae* (Wittenberg: Helwig, 1610); modern edition, *Compendium locorum theologicorum*, ed. Wolfgang Trillhaas (Berlin: de Gruyter, 1961), 1–8. This was the basic theological manual used in schools throughout Germany. It was the primer that Bach would have known in the schools he attended in Eisenach, Ohrdruf, and Lüneburg, as well as in the Thomasschule during his cantorate.

38 BC-K/W, 386.

39 There is some confusion over the exact number of the chief parts of the catechisms. They are variously quoted as being in five parts or six parts. Luther was responsible for the subsequent confusion. The Large Catechism was written first and consisted of five main parts: Commandments, Creed, Lord's Prayer, Baptism, and the Lord's Supper. The Small Catechism, written later the same year, had six chief parts. The extra section being a consideration of Confession that was inserted between Baptism and the Lord's Supper. However, Luther had dealt with Confession in the Large Catechism as an appendix to his section on the Lord's Supper. Thus, the catechism comprised of six main topics, even though it was often referred to as "the teaching of the five chief parts of the catechism." The confusion is best illustrated in the most influential commentary on the Lutheran Confessions in Bach's day where it states that there are five chief parts of the catechism, yet when the teaching of the catechism is discussed in detail, it is treated under the six headings of the Small Catechism; Johann Benedict Carpzov, *Isagoge in Libros Ecclesiarum Lutheranarum Symbolicos* (Dresden: Zimmermann, 1725), 950–1128.

40 For a detailed discussion of Luther's catechism hymns, see Robin A. Leaver, *Luther's Liturgical Music: Principles and Implications* (Minneapolis: Fortress Press, 2017), 116–60.

318   *Theology*

individual Ten Commandments are suggested by the ten basic periods into which the prelude can be divided.[41]

Before Luther's time it was customary to divide the Creed into twelve articles, one section supposedly written by each of the twelve Apostles. The reformer swept this division aside in favor of a more simple Trinitarian formula. He says,

> We shall briefly sum up the entire Creed in three main articles, according to the three persons of the Godhead, to whom everything that we believe is related. Thus the first article, concerning God the Father, explains creation; the second, concerning the Son, redemption; the third, concerning the Holy Spirit, being made holy.[42]

So Bach, in the prelude on *Wir glauben all an einen Gott* (BWV 680), modifies the first line of the melody and sets out on a three-part Trinitarian fugue. Underneath the fugue appears the powerful ostinato bass, with its six emphatic statements. Some commentators see in this an allusion to a firm faith in God. This may well be so, but as the first words of the first stanza are "Wir glauben all an einen Gott *Schöpfer*" (We all believe in one God, *Creator*), it is likely that Bach had in mind the six days of creation in Genesis, chapter 1, the so-called *Hexameron*. Bach had been brought up to believe that "the creation is an external action of the entire Trinity, in which God created all things, visible and invisible, in a period of six days, and, according to his completely free and good will, made them from nothing."[43] When Bach set the Trinitarian creedal hymn, his first thought was for the creativity of God in giving and sustaining life.[44]

As with BWV 678, the setting of *Vater unser im Himmelreich* (BWV 682) is a trio within which the melody is set. Also, like the prelude on *Dies sind die heil'gen zehn Gebot*, the chorale melody appears in canon with itself at the octave. This seems to be an expression of the words of Luther in the Large Catechism on the Lord's Prayer: "We are in such a situation that no one can keep the Ten Commandments perfectly, even though he or she has begun to believe."[45] So, Bach gives a reminder of the commandments by the octave canon. Luther goes on to say:

41 Bach uses a similar canonic device to symbolize the two tables of the commandments, using this same melody, in the opening chorus of Cantata 77.

42 BC-K/W, 432.

43 Hutter, *Compendium locorum theologicorum*, 19: "Creatio est actio externa totius Trinitatis, qua Deus res omnes creatas, visibiles et invisibiles, sex dierum intervallo, liberrima optimaque sua voluntate ex nihilo condidit."

44 Luther, Large Catechism: 'For here we see how the Father has given to us himself with all creation and has abundantly provided for us in this life, apart from the fact that he has also showered us with inexpressible eternal blessings through his Son and the Holy Spirit." BC-K/W, 433.

45 BC-K/W, 440–41.

Bach's Clavierübung III   319

Consequently, nothing is so necessary as to call upon God incessantly and to drum into his ears our prayer that he may give, preserve, and increase in us faith and the fulfillment of the Ten Commandments and remove all that stands in our way and hinders us in this regard. That we may know what and how to pray, however, our Lord Christ himself has taught us both the way and the words.

The accompaniment is an embellished version of the melody in canon at the fifth with a persistently repeated dotted rhythm suggestive of the Lord's Prayer being repeated again and again.

Like earlier settings the prelude on *Christ unser Herr zum Jordan kam* (BWV 684) is a trio against which the melody is set (in this case, in the bass). Baptism is administered according to the Trinitarian formula: "In the name of the Father, and of the Son, and of the Holy Spirit." So, Bach represents this in the three-part setting. The symbolism can be taken further. No doubt the running sixteenth notes illustrate the waters of Baptism, as many have noted, but they probably have another significance as well. In Lutheran theology the regeneration that the rite of Baptism represents is essentially the work of the Holy Spirit, whose presence is indicated by the "sound of a rushing, mighty wind" in the New Testament.[46] In the order of Baptism in the *Saxon Agenda*, the final prayer speaks of the one baptized as having been "regenerated through water and the Holy Spirit."[47] The sixteenth notes no doubt have this double significance: the waters of Baptism and the operation of the Holy Spirit. However, the symbolism does not end here. Christoph Albrecht has made a good case for supposing that the opening four notes in the upper stave represent the sign of the cross[48] (see Figure 14.1).

This figure is appropriately used at the beginning of the prelude as the order of Baptism began, following an exhortation from the pastor, with the sign of the cross. The pastor declared: "N. N. receive the sign of the holy cross on both thy forehead ✠ and thy breast ✠."[49]

The hymn *Aus tiefer Not schrei ich zu dir* is not included among catechism hymns in Vopelius or Wagner but, instead, appears among their *Psalmlieder.* Luther's metrical version of Psalm 130 is the classic penitential hymn, and of all the reformer's hymns this is the most suitable for this section of the catechism. The vast, architectural prelude on *Aus tiefer Not schrei ich zu dir*

---

46 Acts 2:2; see also John 3:8.

47 *Agenda, Das ist, Kirchen-Ordnung*, 20: "Der dich anderweit gebohren hat durchs Wasser und den Heiligen Geist ..." See also John 3:5.

48 Christoph Albrecht, "J. S. Bachs *Clavier Übung, Dritter Theil*. Versuch einer Deutung," BJ 55 (1969): 52–54. Albrecht gives four other examples that demonstrate Bach's use of the figure in association with verbal references to the cross or crucifixion. The same configuration is used in the successive entries of the tenor, soprano, bass and alto in mm. 9–13 of the Crucifixus in the B-minor Mass; see pages 70–71.

49 *Agenda, Das ist, Kirchen-Ordnung*, 7: "N. N. Nimm das Zeichen des heiligen Creutzes, beyde an der Stirn ✠ an der Brust ✠."

Figure 14.1

(BWV 686) is unique among Bach's organ works in its true six-part writing. Confession is linked to the Ten Commandments and the Lord's Prayer; the purpose of the Law, the commandments, is to expose sin; sin, once brought to light, needs to be dealt with, hence, the necessity for prayer and confession. Luther links confession with the Lord's Prayer directly:

> Indeed, the entire Lord's Prayer is nothing else than such a confession. For what is our prayer but a confession that we neither have nor do what we ought and a plea for grace and a joyful conscience? This kind of confession should and must take place continuously as long as we live.[50]

Bach's three preludes on the commandments, Lord's Prayer, and confession are related to each other by their use of canonic forms. The austerity of *Aus tiefer Not* is relieved in the final thirteen measures by the introduction of a rhythmic figure that works its way through most of the voices. This seems to symbolize that after confession comes the assurance of forgiveness in absolution.[51] This masterly piece of work—arguably the finest in the set—reflects one of the key themes of Luther's Reformation. The opening words of the first of the *Ninety-Five Theses*, which sparked the Reformation debate, were, "When our Lord and Master Jesus Christ said, 'Repent' (Matt. 4:17), he willed the entire life of believers to be one of repentance."[52]

The theme of Bach's treatment of *Jesus Christus unser Heiland, der von uns den Zorn Gottes wand* (BWV 688) has an unusual, widely spaced figure. Schweitzer saw it as a sure-footed progress through the theological controversy regarding the nature of the Lord's Supper.[53] Certainly the figure suggests determined walking. It is possible that Bach had in mind the passage from Isaiah, 63:2–3:

---

50 BC-K/W, 477 (Large Catechism: "A Brief Exhortation to Confession")
51 "Confession consists of two parts. One is that we confess our sins. The other is that we receive the absolution, that is, forgiveness." (Small Catechism); BC-K/W, 360.
52 LW 31: 25; WA 1: 233.
53 Albert Schweitzer, *J. S. Bach* (1911), trans. Ernest Newman (London: Black, 1962), 2: 61.

Figure 14.2

> Why is thy apparel red, and thy garments like his that treads in the wine press? "I have trodden the wine press alone ... I trod them in my anger and trampled them in my wrath."[54]

This passage was interpreted by Lutheran preachers and theologians as a prophecy regarding Christ's victory of the cross[55] and, indeed, Bach was familiar with the interpretation as it occurs in two of his Cantatas: Cantata 31/5, tenor recitative, "So stehe dann, du gottergebne Seele"; and Cantata 43/7, bass aria, "Er ists, der ganz allein." Therefore, the widely spaced step-motive of measures 1–5 seems to represent the treading of the winepress, which in turn is an image of Christ's victory over death and sin. The thought of the triumph of the cross is emphasized by the first four notes that form a cross motive (see Figure 14.2).

The running sixteenth notes that follow (mm. 6ff.) suggest the wine produced from the winepress, an aural image of the fruit of salvation that is made available through this Sacrament of the Lord's Supper. There may well be further symbolism here in that the prelude is a large-scale, two-part invention, under which the melody appears, representing the two elements of bread and wine.

If the six large settings are considered together, they can be divided into two musical groups: those written in a strict contrapuntal form, grave in mood, with various canonic devices (BWV 678, 682, 686), and those that are somewhat freer in form and lighter in mood (BWV 680, 684, 688). This division appears to be a conscious expression of the fundamental Lutheran understanding of the distinction between the Law and the Gospel. It is a distinction that lies at the heart of the doctrine of justification, and it was this doctrine that was the storm-center of the Reformation debate. Lutherans

---

54 The thought may have been suggested by some words of Luther in the Large Catechism: "Moreover, you will surely have the devil around you, too. You will not entirely trample him underfoot because our Lord Christ could not entirely avoid him." BC-K/W, 475.
55 For example, Johann Gerhard refers to the image several times in his exposition of the Passion narratives; see Johann Gerhard, *Erklärung der Historien des Leidens unnd Sterbens unsers Herrn Christi Jesu nach den vier Evangelisten (1611)*, critical edition and commentary, Johann Anselm Steiger (Stuttgart: Frommann-Holzboog, 2002).

Figure 14.3

teach that sinful humanity cannot, by its own efforts, fulfil the demands of the Law and be put into a right relationship with God. This only comes about by the grace of God in the Gospel, who forgives for Christ's sake.[56]

	BWV	Catechism	Subject	Implication
Law	678	I	Commandments	Law exposes sin
	682	III	Lord's Prayer	Sinner needs to pray
	686	V	Confession	Law demands repentance
Gospel	680	II	Creed	Gospel, belief
	684	IV	Baptism	Beginning faith
	688	VI	Lord's Supper	Continuing faith

The Law condemns sin: the Gospel offers salvation through faith in Christ and his sacrifice on the cross. As indicated above, two of Bach's "Gospel" preludes (BWV 684, 688) begin with a cross motive. If the prelude on *Wir glauben* (BWV 680) is now reconsidered, it is revealing to discover that the ostinato bass also begins with such a motive (see Figure 14.3).

Therefore, all three of these "Gospel" preludes are linked by the use of a cross motive, which occurs at the beginning of a different voice in each prelude: in the bass in BWV 680, alto in BWV 684, and soprano in BWV 688.

The Small Catechism settings

The small settings of the catechism melodies are on a more limited scale, but it would do them an injustice to call them simple. The subject of the fughetta on *Dies sind die heil'gen zehn Gebot* (BWV 679) occurs ten times, entries five to eight being inverted. This might be an allusion to the two tables on which the Ten Commandments were written. In the answers to each of the commandments in the Small Catechism, Luther begins with these words: "We are to fear, love, and trust God above all things."[57] This is the recurring theme that appears in the explanation of each of the commandments, and Bach represents this with the ten appearances of the theme, which is based on the first line of the chorale melody. The generally lighthearted nature of the piece

---

56 See Apology of the Augsburg Confession, Art. IV (BC-K/W, 120–73); Formula of Concord. Solid Declaration, Art. V (BC-K/W, 581–86).
57 BC-K/W, 351.

Bach's Clavierübung III   323

can be explained by Luther's words that stand at the end of his exposition of the Ten Commandments: "Therefore we also are to love and trust him [God] and gladly act according to his commands."[58]

The setting of *Wir glauben all an einen Gott* (BWV 681) is a majestic little piece, a diminutive French overture. Luther's Small Catechism has three straightforward paragraphs dealing with the persons of the Trinity. So, Bach constructs a three-voiced fughetta in honor of the Triune God.

The prelude on *Vater unser im Himmelreich* (BWV 683) is a direct, confident little piece, reflecting Luther's opening words in his treatment of the Lord's Prayer in the Small Catechism:

> With these words God wants to entice us, so that we come to believe he is truly our Father and we are truly his children, in order that we may ask him boldly and with complete confidence, just as loving children ask their loving father.[59]

In contrast, the setting of the Baptism hymn, *Christ unser Herr zum Jordan kam* (BWV 685), is more profound. The theme appears three times, and each time is answered by its inversion. Christoph Albrecht argues that this symbolizes Christ and John the Baptist, who are both mentioned in the first stanza of the hymn.[60] However, Bach is not simply concerned here to comment on the hymn text, but rather to symbolize something of the meaning of Baptism. Baptism is administered with the Trinitarian formula, and this is reflected in the three voices of the piece. The theme is stated three times: first in the soprano, second in the tenor, and third in the bass. In the large settings of the Kyrie-Christe-Kyrie (BWV 669–671) Bach has symbolized the persons of the Trinity: Father, Son, and Holy Spirit, each being successively represented by the chorale melody in the soprano, tenor, and bass. It appears that Bach has used the same device here. Furthermore, it is traditional practice in Baptism that, as the name of each person of the Trinity is pronounced in the baptismal formula, it is followed by immersing or sprinkling the candidate in Baptism. So, here the persons of the Trinity are represented by the three appearances of the theme, and its three inversions symbolize the threefold act of Baptism.

Aus tiefer Not schrei ich zu dir (BWV 687) is a skillful piece of work. Luther says:

> Confession consists of two parts. One is that we confess our sins. The other is that we receive the absolution, that is, forgiveness, from the confessor as from God himself and by no means doubt but firmly believe that our sins are thereby forgiven before God in heaven.[61]

---

58 BC-K/W, 354.
59 BC-K/W, 356.
60 Albrecht, "Bachs *Clavier Übung, Dritter Theil*," 57.
61 BC-K/W, 360 (Small Catechism).

Figure 14.4

Each phrase of the chorale melody is imitated in the three lower parts before being introduced in augmentation above, and in every instance the second imitation is by inversion, illustrating that confession of sin is answered by the assurance of forgiveness. It also represents the act of repentance itself, by which the negative effect of sin is counteracted by the positive power of forgiveness (see Figure 14.4).

The Communion hymn, *Jesus Christus unser Heiland, der von uns den Zorn Gottes wand* (BWV 689), is given a fugal treatment. The theme is based on the first line of the chorale melody. The fact that it is a four-voice fugue may represent the four biblical sources that are conflated to form the Words of Institution. Luther writes in the Small Catechism: "Where is this written? Answer: The holy evangelists, Matthew, Mark, and Luke, and St. Paul write thus: 'Our Lord Jesus Christ, on the night in which he was betrayed,'" then follow the familiar words from the four passages: 1 Corinthians 11:23–25[62]; Matthew 26:26–28; Mark 14:22–24; and Luke 22:19–20.[63]

In his double treatment of the six chorale melodies Bach has sought not simply to emphasize the catechisms themselves but rather the doctrines presented in them; he groups them in appropriate pairs, following the order of the six chief parts of the catechisms.

The four Duets

The enigma of the *Clavierübung III* has always been the four Duets (BWV 802–805), and various suggestions have been made as to (1) why these harpsichord pieces were included in a collection of organ music, and (2) what they might symbolize. They have been regarded as music suitable for playing during the distribution of Communion and have been thought to represent the four Gospels or the four elements. But all these explanations are unsatisfactory, because (1) it was customary to sing hymns during the distribution of Communion, and (2) the Duets cannot symbolize either the Gospels or the elements because such ideas do not readily fit into the pattern set by

---

62 Erdmann Neumeister preached for a whole year on this basic passage: Erdmann Neumeister, *Tisch des Herrn, In LII Predigten über I. Cor. XI. 23–32* (Hamburg: Kißner, 1722). Bach owned a copy of the volume; see Leaver, *Bachs theologische Bibliothek*, No. 46; see also Chapter 13.
63 BC-K/W, 362.

Bach's Clavierübung III   325

the other pieces in the collection. The most popular explanation is that these clavier pieces were included simply to fill up available space and therefore have nothing to do with the rest of the *Clavierübung III*. But this is so unlike Bach with his passion for order and completeness, which is so evident from the structures of individual works and the ground plans of works issued in groups.[64] Some other explanation is needed.

Luther's Large Catechism simply deals with the basic teachings, but his Small Catechism includes additional material of a different nature. Following the six doctrinal divisions, there are four prayers: a morning prayer, an evening prayer, a grace before meals, and a thanksgiving for after meals.[65]

Taken together the Small Catechism has a tenfold structure, which Vopelius used to classify sections in his *Gesangbuch*. The relevant sections, under the primary heading, "Aus dem Heiligen Catechismo,"[66] follow consecutively:

	Pages in Vopelius
Die Zehn Gebot	490–497
Vom Glauben	497–504
Das Gebet des Herrn	505–507
Von der Heiligen Taufe	507–510
Von der Beicht und Busse	511–524
Vom Heiligen Abendmahl	524–539
Morgengesange	540–570
Abendgesange	570–585
Vor dem Essen	585–587
Nach dem Essen	587–602

If one takes Bach's Small Catechism settings with the Duets, one is presented with ten pieces, six of which are expositions of the doctrinal parts of the catechism and four, in an entirely different style, which represent the prayers included at the end of the catechism. The idea of prayer is reinforced by Bach's title for these four pieces. Each one is called "Duetto," which is a somewhat unconventional term to use for such clavier pieces. They are two-part inventions, but Bach avoids the term he had used earlier for such works and prefers a term usually associated with vocal music. This is significant since a number of the duet movements in the cantatas—especially those that have the title "Dialogus"[67]—are conversations between the believer and Christ, and thus epitomize the activity of prayer.

---

64 Even the six Schübler Chorales (BWV 645–650), which have been regarded as a collection of independent pieces arranged from cantata movements, have been seen to possess ordered interconnections; see Randolph N. Currie, "Cyclic Unity in Bach's *Sechs Chorale*: A New Look at the 'Schüblers,'" *BACH* 4/1 (1973): 26–38, and 5/1 (1974): 25–39.

65 BC-K/W, 363–64.

66 The running head at the top of the page is "Catechismus-Lieder."

67 Particularly Cantatas 32, 49, 57, and 58.

Figure 14.5

Figure 14.6

The teaching of the six main parts of the Small Catechism was an important part of *church* life—although every head of the household was also expected to continue the teaching in his own *home*, hence the ambiguity of the small preludes that can be played on both organ and harpsichord—and so Bach writes his musical exposition of them with the churchly instrument in mind: the organ. However, prayer on rising from bed or on retiring to bed, and grace before and after meals, are activities which one performs in the intimacy of the home. So, Bach writes four pieces for the instrument that was likely to be in the home: a harpsichord or a clavichord.

Whether or not the themes of the four duets are based on specific chorale melodies is a moot point. Klaus Ehricht identified a number of melodies hidden within the themes,[68] but such associations are not too difficult to find, and it is not always clear whether they are intentional or accidental.

The opening four notes of the fourth Duet (BWV 805) recall the opening phrase of the longer prelude on the Baptism (BWV 684) in that they form a sign of the cross (See Figure 14.5).

This is the only occurrence of such a device in the cycle of ten pieces based on the Small Catechism, and it comes appropriately at the end of the series. It also prepares for the opening four notes of the final fugue (BWV 552:2), which also form a cross motive (See Figure 14.6).

The cross motive is very appropriate in the Duet, for when Luther speaks of daily prayer in the Small Catechism, he encourages the use of the sign of the cross. Furthermore, the connection with the Baptism hymn makes the sign doubly suitable because the sign of the cross is closely associated with Baptism.

The recurring theme of both Luther's catechisms is of the necessity of a constant daily practice of the Christian faith, hence the importance of these

---

68 Klaus Ehricht, "Die zyklische Gestalt und die Auffuhrungsmöglichkeit des III.Teiles der Klavieriibung von Joh. Seb. Bach." BJ 38 (1949/50): 40–56.

prayers at the beginning, during, and at the end of the day. Christianity was presented not as a set of precepts to be grasped with the mind but something that was also to be lived out in all the complications of daily life. The Lutheran preachers used to call this learning and living out the principles of the catechism, the *Catechismus-Übung*. To be a proficient keyboard player one needs not only head knowledge but also finger knowledge, which only comes through daily practice. So, Bach has provided his *Clavierübung,* Parts I *and* II for the purpose. But the person who wishes to be an organist or cantor of the church that bears Luther's name needs both disciplines of *Catechismus-Übung* and *Clavier-Übung*.

15 Bach and anniversaries of the Reformation

The Reformation festival was regularly celebrated throughout Lutheran Germany on 31 October each year, the anniversary of Luther's protest of 1517, when specially composed music was presented within services of worship. In addition, there were other anniversary occasions connected with Reformation events, such as the presentation of the Augsburg Confession (1530), or the settlement of the Peace of Augsburg (1555) that gave the emerging Lutheran church a measure of security, events that also called for appropriate celebrations. Yet when one examines Bach's extant cantatas only two (BWV 79 and 80) were specifically composed for the annual *Reformationsfest*, and one of those was originally composed for another occasion. To these can be added the three cantatas that Bach provided for the bicentenary of the Augsburg Confession in 1730, for which much of the music is lost (BWV 120b, 190a, and Anh. 4). Given the fact that Bach clearly composed more music than is currently extant, it is highly likely that he created other such vocal music that has not survived. On the other hand, it is equally possible that some of his known compositions may have Reformation connections. Some of these connections have been noticed, but there are others that need to be considered.

Historical background

The beginning of the Reformation was often connected with Luther's posting of his Ninety-five Theses on the door of the Allerheiligenkirche [All Saints Church, also known as the Castle Church], Wittenberg, on the Eve of All Saints, 31 October 1517. Luther opposed the sale of indulgences and raised the fundamental question of the Reformation debate: Where does authority lie, with the Church (the Catholic position) or with Scripture (what emerged as the Protestant position)? In later years Luther and his colleagues occasionally marked the anniversary informally with Wittenberg beer, as he did on the tenth anniversary in 1527.[1] Some of the early Lutheran *Kirchenordnungen*,

---

1 Letter to Nicholas Amsdorf, 1 November 1527; WA *Briefwechsel*, 4: 275. For the background, see Volker Leppin and Timothy J. Wengert, "Sources for and against the Posting of the Ninety-five Theses," *Lutheran Quarterly* 29 (2015): 373–98; Martin Treu, "Luther's Posting of the

Bach and anniversaries of the Reformation   329

especially those drawn up by Luther's colleague Johannes Bugenhagen for north German areas, indicated that anniversaries of the introduction of the Reformation could be held on various days of the year, such as Trinity Sunday, the Sunday after St. Aegidius Day (September 1), or St. Martin's Day (November 11—Luther was born on the eve of St. Martin's Day). A common characteristic of these celebrations was that the *Te Deum laudamus* was sung.[2] In Wittenberg, and probably elsewhere in Saxony, 31 October/1 November were the preferred days for celebrating the beginnings of the Lutheran Reformation. For example, sometime after Luther's death, though the specific year is unrecorded, there is a manuscript report that on 31 October Wittenberg professors met early in the day in Luther's study to sing appropriate hymns (Luther's *Es wolle uns Gott genädig sein* [Psalm 67] is particularly noted), before proceeding to the Castle Church, where a sermon was preached to mark the anniversary.[3] Such anniversaries were apparently local and not widespread, but the centenary of 1617 was different.

In a document dated Dresden 12 August 1617, the Saxon Elector, Johann Georg I, issued his "Instruction und Ordnung" directing how the centenary was to be observed throughout Saxony. Announcements were made in the churches on Sunday, 26 October, that beginning at Vespers on 30 October, the anniversary was to be celebrated on the following three days, 31 October–2 November.[4] These services should be

> held with singing in good order. Without doubt in towns where there are superintendents and pastors excellent figural music should be prepared, but with this we esteem it advisable and profitable that for the sake of the congregation familiar German hymns should also be sung, before and after sermons, in villages as well as in towns, such as the following: *Herr Gott, dich loben wir ...* [Luther's German Te Deum (1529)], *Nun lob, mein Seel, den Herren, Allein Gott in der Höh sei Ehr, Ein feste Burg ist unser Gott, Wo Gott der Herr nicht bei uns hält, O Herre Gott, dein göttlich Wort, Erhalt uns, Herr, bei deinem Wort, Wär Gott nicht mit uns diese Zeit, Mag ich Unglück nicht widerstahn.*[5]

Ninety-five Theses: Much Ado About Nothing?" *Martin Luther and the Reformation: Essays*, ed. Katrin Herbst (Dresden: Sandstein, 2016), 92–97.

2 Paul Graff, *Geschichte der Auflösung der alten gottesdienstlichen Formen in der Evangelischen Kirche Deutschlands...* (Göttingen, Vandenhoeck & Ruprecht, 1937–1939), 1: 144–45.

3 Johann Christian August Grohmann, *Annalen der Universität zu Wittenberg* (Meissen: Erbstein, 1801–1802), 1: 72.

4 The document is reprinted in full in the extended "Vorrede" (sig. a2ʳ–e8 ᵛ = 60 pages) by Ernst Salomon Cyprian in Wilhelm Ernst Tentzel, *Historischer Bericht vom Anfang und ersten Fortgang der Reformation Lutheri, zur Erläuterung des Hn. v. Seckendorff Historie des Lutherthums* (Gotha: Reyhern, 1717; reprinted three times in Leipzig by Gleditsch & Weidmann, 1717–1718), here cited from "Der dritte Druck," Leipzig, 1718, sig. c4ᵛ–d1ʳ.

5 Cyprian, "Vorrede," sig. c7ᵛ–c8ʳ: "Mit den Gesengen auch gute Ordnung gehalten werden. So zweiffelt Uns zwar nicht, daß in den Städten die *Superintendenten* und Pfarrer, die *Figural-Music* auffs beste bestellen werden, hierneben aber achten Wir rathsam und nützlich zu

330   *Theology*

In Dresden the centenary was marked in the same way as the principal festivals of the church year, such as Christmas Day, Easter Day, and Pentecost, by the ringing of church bells and firing of cannons,[6] as well as the prescribed liturgical services, during which the specified hymns were sung—especially Luther's German Te Deum—sermons preached, and special music by Heinrich Schütz and Michael Praetorius was heard.[7] Other cities beyond Saxony, such us Nuremberg in Bavaria[8] and Ulm in Württemberg,[9] held similar celebrations. In some areas the celebration was extended to include Luther's birthday on November 10, while others anticipated the anniversary by some weeks. For example, in the Paulinerkirche, Leipzig, the university's Aula—a Latin oration marking the centenary—was given on St. Michael's Day, 29 September 1617.[10]

> seyn, daß man umb des gemeinen Volcks willen, gewisse deutsche Lieder, vor und nach den Predigten, wie in den Dörffern, also auch in den Städten singe, nemlich nachfolgende: Herr Gott dich loben wir ... Nun lob mein Seel den Herren. Allein Gott in der Höhe sey Ehr. Eine feste Burg ist unser Gott. Wo Gott der Herr nicht bei uns helt ... O Herre Gott, dein Göttlich Wort ... Erhalt uns Herr bey deinem Wort. Wer Gott nicht mit uns diese Zeit. Mag ich Unglück nicht widerstahn."

6 See Gina Spagnoli, *Letters and Documents of Heinrich Schütz 1656–1672: An Annotated Translation* (Ann Arbor: UMI Research Press, 1990), German text: 179, 184 and 186; English text: 197, 202 and 204.

7 The basic source is Matthias Hoë von Hoënegg, *Chur Sächsische Evangelische JubelFrewde: In der Churfürstlichen Sächsischen SchloßKirchen zu Dreßden/ theils vor/ theils bey wehrendem/ angestalten Jubelfest/ neben andern Solenniteten, auch mit Christlichen Predigten ... gehalten ... Nach der Vorrede/ findet der Christliche Leser/ mit was für Solenniteten das Evangelische Jubelfest/ in ... Dreßden/ seye gehalten worden.* (Leipzig: Lamberg, 1618). Subsequent discussions rely on this account: see, for example, Graff, *Geschichte der Auflösung der alten gottesdienstlichen Formen*, 1: 238–40; Christhard Mahrenholz, "Heinrich Schütz und das erste Reformationsjubiläum 1617," in *Musicologica et Liturgica; gesammelte Aufsätze*, ed. Karl Ferdinand Müller (Kassel: Bärenreiter, 1960), 196–204; Siegfried Vogelsänger, "Michael Praetorius: Festmusiken zu zwei Ereignissen des Jahres 1617: zum Kaiserbesuch in Dresden und zur Jahrhundertfeier der Reformation," *Die Musikforschung* 40 (1987): 97–109, esp. 101–9; Helga Robinson-Hammerstein, "Sächsische Jubelfreude," in *Die lutherische Konfessionalisierung in Deutschland: Wissenschaftliches Symposion des Vereins für Reformationsgeschichte 1988*, ed. Hans-Christoph Rublack (Gütersloh: Mohn, 1992), 460–94; Robin A. Leaver, "Lutheran Vespers as a Context for Music," in *Church, Stage, and Studio: Music and Its Contexts in Seventeenth-Century Germany*, ed. Paul Walker (Ann Arbor: UMI Research Press, 1990), 143–61, esp. 155–56.

8 Max Herold, *Alt-Nürnberg in seinen Gottesdiensten: ein Beitrag zur Geschichte der Sitte und des Kultus* (Gütersloh: Bertelsmann, 1890), 301–3; cited Graff, *Geschichte der Auflösung der alten gottesdienstlichen Formen*, 1: 238: "[Sunday, 2 November 1617] Vor oder nach der Predigt mit Musik und Figuralgesang etliche Gesänge Luthers gesungen werden, auch nach der Predigt das *Te Deum* [= *Herr Gott, dich loben wir*]."

9 Conrad Dieterichs, *Sonderbarer Predigten von unterschiedenen Materien: Hiebevor zu Ulm im Münster gehalten/ deren theils im Truck allbereit außgangen ... Theil. Auff sonderbar Begehren zusammen gedruckt* (Franckfurt: Schürer & Götze, 1669), 69–71; Graff, loc. cit.: "[2 November 1617] Der Hauptgottesdienst am Sonntag verlief wie an hohen Festtagen mit Musik und Abendmahlsfeier, während welcher *Herr Gott, dich loben wir* also Wechselgesang zwischen zwei Chören, der eine auf der Orgel, der andere 'im Singstuhl' gesungen wurde."

10 *Academiae lipsiensis pietas in sacrosanctam reformationi divi Lutheri memoriam: exhibita quinquaginta dissertationibus ab ordinis theologici decanis separatis temporibus publico nomine*

Bach and anniversaries of the Reformation 331

The centenary celebrations were important for Lutherans to assert and delineate their independence from Roman Catholicism, and much of the preaching and associated publications of 1617 had a strong anti-Catholic polemic, casting the Lutheran Reformation in terms of the rediscovery of the light of the Gospel that had dispelled the darkness of Catholicism, which was identified as the "Antichrist," whose "Babylonian Captivity"[11] was brought to an end by Luther's preaching of God's grace. These themes, together with the hymns, biblical readings, and so forth, prescribed by the Elector of Saxony, became the model for later observances of Reformation anniversaries. In the years following 1617 such observances were not yet universally annual events, though some churches and areas did hold celebrations on 31 October, as is obvious, for example, from the hymn written by Johann Rist, *O Finsterniss! O Dunkelheit!* that appeared in Lüneburg in 1655, with a melody composed by Thomas Selle, with the following heading:

> Joyful thanks- and remembrance-hymn on the day of Dr. Martin Luther, on which God is heartily praised and lauded, that He has called and awakened such a treasured man to bring the bright and blessed-making light of the precious Gospel to dispel the thick darkness.[12]

Other Reformation anniversaries celebrated in Dresden, as elsewhere in Lutheran Germany, were the centenaries of the Augsburg Confession in 1630[13] and the Peace of Augsburg in 1655,[14] while individual towns and cities marked the centenaries of the introduction of the Reformation into their areas, such as Leipzig in 1639 and Halle in 1641. Although earlier records of the Dresden court are no longer extant, it seems that an annual Reformationsfest was observed. Elector Johann Georg II drew up a document outlining the various

---

conscriptis et nunc iunctim editis, ed. Christian Friedrich Börner (Leipzig: Gleditsch, 1717), 1–7, esp. 7: "P. P. Lipsiae, ipso die festo S. Michaelis Archangeli, Victoris & Triumphatoris gloriosissimi; anno a nativitate Christi M. DC. XVII, a Romani Antichristi manifestatione, Centesimo."

11 *De captivatate Babylonica ecclesiae praeludium* (1520) is Luther's classic treatise against Catholicism.

12 Johann Rist, *Neue Musikalische Fest-Andachten* (Lüneburg: Stern, 1655), 330; Albert Fischer and Wilhelm Tümpel, *Das deutsche evangelische kirchenlied des siebzehnten jahrhunderts* (Gütersloh: Bertelsmann, 1904–1916; reprint Hildesheim: Olms, 1964), 2: 299–300: "Frölisches Dank- und Gedächtnis-Lied am Tage D. Martini Lutheri, In welchem Gott hertzlich gelobet und gepreisen, daß Er Einen solchen theüren Mann, der das helle, seligmachende Licht des wehrten Evangeliums aus so dikker Finsternisse wider herführ gebracht, hat beruffen und erwekket." Rist wrote his text to be sung to the melody *An Wasserflüssen Babylon*, an oblique but obvious allusion to Luther's treatise *The Babylonian Captivity*.

13 See Eberhard Schmidt, *Der Gottesdienst am Kurfürstlichen Hofe zu Dresden* (Berlin, Evangelische Verlaganstalt, 1961), 71.

14 Outlines of the Dresden services are given in Mary E. Frandsen, *Crossing Confessional Boundaries: The Patronage of Italian Sacred Music in Seventeenth-Century Dresden* (New York: Oxford University Press, 2006), 356–57.

332   *Theology*

services held in the Dresden court chapel throughout the church year. It is undated but probably originated sometime around 1660 and may well reflect the practice of earlier years. It includes the following directions for the Eve of All Saints:

> On whatever day it falls, 31 October [is a day of] remembrance because on this day the holy Gospel was again brought to light by Luther, shall be observed and celebrated in the following manner: If it falls on a Sunday, however, the court ensemble shall participate as is customary as on other Sundays.
>
> The Mass [= Kyrie and Gloria, the first followed by 2. below; the second by 3.] and the Credo [8. below].
>
> 1. Introit: *Ein feste Burg ist unser Gott.*
> 2. *Kyrie, Gott Vater in Ewigkeit.*
> 3. *Allein Gott in der Höh sei Ehr.*
> 4. Collect, and a text rather than the Epistle which shall be selected by the senior court preacher [in Dresden].
> 5. *O Herre Gott, dein göttlich Wort.*
> 6. A text instead of the Gospel, also selected by the senior court preacher.
> 7. *Nun lob, meine Seel, den Herren* [the same Graduallied appointed for St.Michael's Day[15]].
> 8. *Wir glauben all an einen Gott.*
> 9. Sermon.
> 10. *Erhalt uns, Herr, bei deinem Wort.*
> 11. Collect and Benediction.
> 12. *Ach bleib bei uns, Herr Jesu Christ.*[16]

Such an observance is recorded in the Dresden court diaries as taking place on Wednesday, 31 October 1666—the year before the sesquicentennial of the Reformation—when the preacher was Valentin Heerbrandt, "mittler Hof-Prediger."[17]

The following year—the 150th anniversary of the beginning of the Reformation—Elector Johann Georg II made an annual celebration on 31 October mandatory for all the Lutheran churches of Saxony:

> henceforth 31 October, on whichever day of the week it falls, is to be observed and celebrated annually, before midday as a half festival, throughout the Electoral principality and associated regions, in towns

---

15 See Spagnoli, *Letters and Documents of Heinrich Schütz*, German: 189; English: 207.

16 Spagnoli, *Letters and Documents of Heinrich Schütz*, German: 191–92; English: 209. There is also the added note that on St. Martin's Day, on either 10 or 11 November, Luther should be remembered by observing it as an Apostle's Day.

17 Frandsen, *Crossing Confessional Boundaries*, 433–34.

Bach and anniversaries of the Reformation 333

and villages, with singing and preaching, to honor and hold in great remembrance blessed Herr Luther who on this day began the work of the Reformation.[18]

The Dresden celebration of 31 October 1667 was reported thus:

Thursday the 31st [of October]. In the morning, in the presence of the entire assembled Most Gracious Electoral and Princely Royal Family, an annual sermon of thanksgiving and commemoration was delivered by the senior court preacher, Dr. Martin Geier, on a text drawn from the prophet Isaiah, chapter 6, verse 23, in which God's great blessing and goodness, which He began to allow to shine forth in this land in the year 1517, on this very day, with the blessed Dr. Martin Luther's nailing of the theses in opposition to the papist indulgence peddler, Tetzel, to the castle church in Wittenberg, through which Christian act of reformation was accomplished, was recalled and reflected upon in an elegant and detailed account and sermon, and at the conclusion, the German *Te deum laudamus* [*Herr Gott, dich loben wir*] was sung.[19]

Thereafter the Reformationsfest was celebrated annually on 31 October throughout Saxony and beyond. Bach was no doubt familiar with the observance from his earliest years in Eisenach, and participated in such observances in the churches of Arnstadt and Mühlhausen as well as in the court chapel in Weimar.

A Weimar Reformation Day cantata?

Although no specific Reformation cantata by Bach dating from his Weimar years is known, there is one that may well have been originally composed for such an annual celebration: Cantata 63, *Christen, ätzet diesen Tag In Metall und Marmorsteine!*, performed in the Weimar court chapel on Christmas Day 1714.[20] Three years later a different form of the libretto was utilized by Gottfried Kirchhoff—Friedrich Wilhelm Zachow's successor as organist

---

18 Johann Jacob Vogel, *Leipzigisches geschicht-buch, oder, Annales, das ist: jahr- und tage-bücher der weltberühmten königl. und churfürstlichen sächsischen kauff- und handels-stadt Leipzig* (Leipzig: Lanckischens erben, 1714), 733, cited Hans-Joachim Schulze, "Reformationsfest und Reformationsjubiläen im Schaffen Johann Sebastian Bach," *Bach-fest Buch* [Leipzig] 64 (1989): 38: "forthin den 31. Octobr. er falle auff welchen Tag in der Wochen sey, zu Ehren und zum Gedächtnüß des grossen von Hrn. Luthero sel. am selbigen Tage angefangenen Reformations-Wercks, jährlich vor Mittage, als einen halben Feyertag, durchn unser Chur-Fürstenthum und desselben incorporirten Landen, in Städten und Dörffern mit singen und predigen, ... feyerlich begehen zu lassen."
19 Frandsen, *Crossing Confessional Boundaries*, 88; German text: 448–49.
20 Alfred Dürr, *The Cantatas of J. S. Bach with their Librettos in German-English Parallel Text*, rev. & trans. Richard D. P. Jones (Oxford: Oxford University Press, 2005), 93.

334   *Theology*

of the Marktkirche, Halle—for the Reformation bicentenary in the city (1717).[21] As has often been noticed, Bach's Christmas cantata is somewhat unusual: there is no solo aria, no direct biblical *dictum*, no concluding chorale, and none of the usual elements of the observance of Christmas—the inn, the shepherds, the angelic hymn *Gloria in excelsis Deo*, or any of the familiar hymns of the Christmas season. The same symmetrical structure of seven movements is apparent in both libretti, the primary difference being that the central movement in Bach's cantata is a recitative, whereas in Kirchhoff's it is an arioso:

Weimar, Christmas, 1714	*Halle, Reformation, 1717*
|4| Rezitativ	**|4| Arioso 22 voc.**
So kehret sich nun heut	Ach nimm doch großer Gott
Das bange Leid,	Das Opffer gütig an,
Mit welchem Israel geängstet und beladen,	So unsre Schwachheit dir
In lauter Heil und Gnaden.	Vor solche Liebe bringen kan.
Der Löw aus Davids Stamme ist erschienen,	
Sein Bogen ist gespannt, das Schwert	
ist schon gewetzt,	
Womit er uns in vor'ge Freiheit setzt.	

Movements 2 and 6 of both libretti are recitatives, different in terms of structure and length, with Kirchhoff's being somewhat longer than Bach's. But the other movements of the two cantatas are very closely related:

Weimar, Christmas, 1714	*Halle, Reformation, 1717*
[1] Chor	[1] Aria a Tutti
Christen ätzet diesen Tag	**Christen ätzet diesen Tag**
In Metall und Marmorsteine!	**In Metall und Marmorsteine!**
Kommt und eilt mit mir zur Krippen	Kommt und eilt mit frohen Weisen,
Und erweist mit frohen Lippen	Gott vor seine Huld zu preisen.
Euren Dank und eure Pflicht;	Der aus einer finstern Nacht,
Denn der Strahl, so da einbricht,	Uns hat an das Licht gebracht,
Zeigt sich auch zum **Gnadenschein**.	Und zu seinem **Gnaden-Schein**.
[Da Capo]	Da Capo

---

21 See Walter Serauky, *Musikgeschichte der Stadt Halle* (Halle: Buchhandlung des Waisenhauses, 1935–1943; reprint, Hildesheim: Olms, 1971), 2/1: 500–3. Serauky, following Spitta, understood Cantata 63 as a Leipzig work and therefore considered Bach's libretto a variant of Kirchhoff's. The libretto was reprinted in Johann Michael Heineccius, *Hundertjähriges Denckmahl der Reformation: bestehend in denen von einem gesammten Ehrwürdigen Ministerio der Stadt Halle bey dem Zweyten Ivbileo Reformationis gehaltenen Predigten* ... (Halle: Neuem Buchhandlung, 1718), 89–91; facsimile in Werner Neumann, *Sämtliche von Johann Sebastian Bach vertonte Texte* (Leipzig: VEB Deutsche Verlag für Musik, 1974), 303.

Bach and anniversaries of the Reformation   335

[3] Arie (Duett)	[3] Duetto
Gott, du hast es wohl gefüget,	**Gott, du hast es wohl gefüget,**
Was uns itzo widerfährt.	Deine Lieb ist ungemein!
Drum laß uns auf ihn stets trauen	Gib, daß wir von gantzer Seelen
Und auf seine Gnade bauen,	Deines Namens Ruhm erzehlen,
Denn er hat uns dies beschert,	Weil so ein vollkommner Schein
Was uns ewig nun **vergnüget.**	Deiner Gnade uns **vergnüget.**
[Da Capo]	Da Capo

[5] Arie (Duett)	[5] Duetto
Rufft und fleht den Himmel an,	**Rufft und fleht den Himmel an,**
Kommt, ihr Christen, kommt zum	**Kommt, ihr Christen, kommt**
Reihen,	zusammen,
Ihr sollt euch ob dem erfreuen,	Zeiget eure Andachts-Flammen,
Was Gott hat anheut **getan!**	Denckt, **was Gott** an euch **gethan!**
Da uns seine Huld verpfleget	Der sein Hertz uns zugelencket,
Und mit so viel Heil beleget,	Und uns so viel Heyl geschencket,
Daß man nicht g'nug danken kann.	**Daß man nicht g'nug danken kann.**
[Da Capo]	Da Capo

[7] Chor	[7] Aria a Tutti
Höchster, schau in Gnaden an	**Höchster, schau in Gnaden an**
Diese Glut gebückter Seelen!	**Diese Glut gebückter Seelen!**
Laß den Dank, den wir dir bringen,	**Laß den Dank, den wir dir bringen,**
Angenehme vor dir klingen,	**Angenehme vor dir klingen,**
Laß uns stets in Segen gehn,	**Laß uns stets in Segen gehn,**
Aber niemals nicht geschehn,	**Aber niemals nicht geschehn,**
Dass uns Satan möge quälen.	**Dass uns Satan möge** können.

Bach's libretto suggests that it is a parody, whereas Kirchhoff's appears more directly suitable for its Reformationsfest context. For example, although the concept of rays of light emanating from the manger in the opening movement of Bach's libretto is a suitable Christmas image, Kirchhoff's "Der aus einer finstern Nacht, | Uns hat an das Licht gebracht, | Und zu seinem Gnaden-Scheine" (He [God] from darkest night | has brought us to the light, | the shining of his grace) is directly in line with Reformation Day preaching that customarily contrasted the light of the Gospel, as rediscovered by Luther, as against the darkness of error. Thus, although he composed his cantata at a later time, the strong impression is that Kirchhoff's libretto predates that of Bach, and that Bach's is a parody of the Reformation libretto. If that is the case, then it would seem that Cantata 63 is a parody not simply of a preexisting libretto but rather a parody of a previously composed cantata by Bach.

Towards the end of 1712 the organ builder Christoph Contius was contracted to build a new large instrument for the Marktkirche, Halle, and

336 *Theology*

had begun work on the project in the spring of the following year, 1713.[22] Towards the end of November 1713 there was some kind of contact between the authorities in Halle and Bach, which resulted in Bach's visit to the city in early December to investigate the proposals for the new organ. The Halle authorities took the opportunity to invite Bach to audition for the position of organist of the Marktkirche, as Zachow's successor. The result was that Bach was offered the position, and a contract was drawn up. There was clearly miscommunication, since Bach never signed the contract, and over the following months there was correspondence between the Halle authorities, and Bach paid another visit to the city.[23] Ultimately the matter was amicably resolved between the Halle authorities and Bach, and Kirchhoff was elected "*Director Musices* und Marienorganisten" at the end of July 1714, taking up the appointment at the end of August,[24] but it was another two years before the new instrument was finished.

Although conjectural, the following scenario seems plausible. Given the variance between Bach and the Halle authorities and his failure to sign the contract, together with his apparent concern to see how the new Halle organ was progressing, perhaps he made the offer to compose the cantata for the Marktkirche, or, alternatively, the Halle authorities, who wanted to continue to have access to Bach's widely acknowledged expertise in organ building,[25] invited him to compose a cantata for Reformation Day, 31 October 1714. The libretto was most likely by Johann Michael Heineccius, the Halle superintendent and author of hymns and other poetry, who published the sermons he preached at the 1717 Reformationsfest, a publication that also included the libretto as set by Kirchhoff in 1717. But the original libretto predated the bicentenary of the Reformation, having been previously set by Bach. Thus, Bach's cantata may have been performed in the Marktkirche, Halle, on Reformation Day, 31 October 1714, and over the following eight weeks he presumably recreated his music as a cantata for Christmas Day (BWV 63), performing it in the Weimar court chapel on 25 December 1714. Three years later, for the bicentenary of the Reformation in 1717, Kirchhoff used the original libretto for his cantata—perhaps making the point to his employers that he was the equal of Bach. There is, therefore, a strong case for considering the Halle libretto as evidence of an earlier version of *Christen ätzet diesen Tag*, a Reformation Day cantata, to be designated BWV 63a.

---

22 For the background, see Christoph Wolff and Markus Zepf, *The Organs of J. S. Bach: A Handbook*, trans. Lynn Edwards Butler (Urbana: University of Illinois Press, 2012), 30–31.

23 BDok 1: Nos. 2, 4; 2 (Nos. 62, 64, 65). Perhaps Bach's hesitance was conditioned by the uncertainty of when the new instrument would be completed.

24 Serauky, *Musikgeschichte der Stadt Halle*, 2/1: 479.

25 Bach tested the completed organ in April 1716; BDok 2: 59–62 (Nos. 76, 78).

The bicentenary of the Reformation, 1717

The celebration of the two-hundredth anniversary of the Reformation throughout Lutheran Germany was a momentous occasion. It was prepared for many years in advance, at least as early as 1699, the year that Roman Catholics observed their year of jubilee. Polemics between Catholics and Lutherans had intensified in the last quarter of the century, especially after 1697 in Saxony, when the Elector Friedrich Augustus, "the Strong," converted to Catholicism in order to become simultaneously King of Poland.

In preparation for the bicentenary, an enormous amount of literature was published on the history and progress of the Lutheran Reformation and its theology; detailed orders of worship were drawn up for the churches to observe; and preparations were made for special orations and academic promotions in the universities to be presented during the three days of the celebration. One suspects that the new organs in the Marktkirche, Halle, completed in 1716, and the Paulinerkirche, Leipzig, completed in 1717, were planned to be ready for the celebration of the bicentenary.[26] After the event Ernst Salomon Cyprian, director of the ducal library in Gotha (author and editor of many works associated with the Reformation) compiled a massive volume of more than fifteen hundred folio pages, which reprinted preparatory documents, the texts of sermons given, cantata libretti, and other literature, as well as descriptions of commemorative coins and medals that had been produced to mark the 1717 bicentenary: *Hilaria evangelica, oder Theologisch-Historischer Bericht vom andern Evangelischen Jubel-Fest. Nebst III. Büchern darzu gehöriger Acten und Materien, deren das erste, die obrigkeitlichen Verordnungen, und, viele historische Nachrichten, das andere, Orationes und Programmata Jvbilaea, das dritte, eine vollständige Beschreibung der Jubel-Medaillen begreiffet* (Gotha: Weidmann, 1719).[27]

---

26 Bach tested both instruments; BDok 1: 157–61 (No. 85) (Halle); 1: 163–68 (Nos. 87) and 189 (No. 109) (Leipzig).

27 Not to be confused with the earlier work with a similar title from the same publisher but in Leipzig: Ernst Salomon Cyprian, *Hilaria evangelica: oder Historische Beschreibung des andern evangel. Jubel-Festes, mit beygefügten Instructionen ... der evangelischen Könige ..., auch denen programmatibus der Universitäten ... abgefasset* (Leipzig: Weidmann, 1718). This is a smaller work of some 531 pages in octavo, which was replaced by the more extensive work when it became clear that there was more extensive material that had to be included. For a discussion of the larger work, see Harm Cordes, *Hilaria evangelica academica: das Reformationsjubiläum von 1717 an den deutschen lutherischen Universitäten* (Göttingen: Vandenhoeck & Ruprecht, 2006). Cordes's focus is on the universities rather than the churches, and his main discussion is of how the Reformation was understood. Cyprian's anthology contains a great deal of music-related material, such as cantata libretti, that requires further investigation. Although Cyprian attempted to be comprehensive in his republication of pertinent documents, his anthology is not exhaustive, and there are other documents concerning the 1717 Jubelfest that require investigation.

338　Theology

Bach could hardly have avoided being aware of the bicentenary because it was so widespread, prominent, and touched most levels of society. But there is evidence that he must have taken a close interest in the details of one of the most extraordinarily important events in the Lutheran church that occurred during his lifetime. One of the documents emanating from Leipzig that Cyprian includes in his extensive anthology is a list of sixty books on various aspects of the Reformation, either newly published, or reissued for the bicentenary.[28] Although it is not known when most books came into his possession, it is significant that two titles from this list were to be found in Bach's personal library at his death: Franz Klinge, *Errette Deine Seele Das ist: Treuhertzige Warnung Für Abfall Von Der Lutherischen Zur Papistischen Lehrel Und Ernstliche Vermahnung an die Abgefallene zu Wiederkehre*, originally published in Leipzig in 1700, reissued in Halle in 1717[29]; and August Pfeiffer, *Lutherthum vor Luthern, oder das alte evangelische durch Lutherum erneuerte Christenthum und das neue römische durch Lutherum auffgedeckte Pabstthum*, originally published in Dresden in 1683,[30] a work that pursues the argument (as did Luther himself) that the Lutheran faith was not a new invention but the recovery of the original and authentic Christian faith. It therefore seems likely that the attention given these books at the time of the Reformation bicentenary in 1717 may have influenced Bach to obtain these volumes for himself.

These were not the only volumes of a similar nature that Bach possessed. In addition to these works he also owned Martin Chemnitz's *Examen concilii Tridenti*, originally published in Frankfurt 1566–1573, with many reprints,[31] the classic and extensive Lutheran response to the decrees of the Council of Trent; the double volume of Johann Müller, *Lutherus defensus*, published in Hamburg in 1634, and *Defensio Lutheri defensi*, published in Hamburg in 1659, after which time the two titles were usually issued together[32]—defenses

---

28 Cyprian, *Hilaria evangelica: oder Historische Beschreibung des andern evangel. Jubel-Festes*, 1:115–28; also given in Christoph Ernst Sicul, *Siculs Leipziger Jahr-Geschichte 1719. Oder Des bisherigen Leipziger Jahr-Buchs Zu dessen Andern Bande Erste Fortsetzung*. [bis Vierte Fortsetzung] ... *Auch unterm schwartzen Brete zu finden*. [= *Annales Lipsienses*, Bd. II] (Leipzig: Autor, 1719–1721), 127–35.

29 Robin A. Leaver, *Bachs theologische Bibliothek: Eine kritische Bibliographie* (Stuttgart: Hänssler, 1983), No. 50.

30 Leaver, *Bachs theologische Bibliothek*, No. 38. Since there are two octavo books by Pfeiffer with "Christenthum" on the title page, I argued, against Wilhlemi, that Bach probably owned the other title, *Verus Christianismus, Das ist: das wahre Christenthum*, originally published in Rostock in 1693. On reflection I believe that Wilhelmi's suggestion that Bach more likely owned *Lutherthum vor Luther*, supported by Johannes Wallmann, is the stronger possibility; see Thomas Wilhelmi, "Bachs Bibliothek: Eine Weiterführung der Arbeit von Hans Preuß," BJ 65 (1979): 121, and Johannes Wallmann, "Johann Sebastian Bach und die 'Geistlichen Bücher' seiner Bibliothek," *Pietismus und Neuzeit* 12 (1986): 172.

31 Leaver, *Bachs theologische Bibliothek*, No. 5.

32 Ibid., No. 44.

of Luther against attacks by Catholic authors; the double volume of sermons by Philipp Jacob Spener, *Gerechter Eifer wider das antichristische Pabstthum, welchen er bei unterschiedlicher Gelegenheit in seinen Predigten*, Frankfurt, 1714, and *Geistreiche Vorstellung des Ungrundes unterschiedlicher päbstischen Lehren: als eine Fortsetzung des Tractats Gottseliger und gerechter Eifer wider das Pabstthum*, Halle, 1714 (both parts usually issued together)[33]— many of these sermons were preached on annual Reformation festivals in Dresden, Berlin, and Frankfurt; and Nicolaus Hunnius's much-quoted study, *Apostasia Ecclesiæ Romanæ, Oder Abfall Der Römischen Kirchen von Der alten Apostolischen/ und warhafften Christlichen Reinigkeit der heilsamen Glaubens-Lehre/ Gottesdienst und Religion*, originally published in Latin in Lübeck 1631, and in German translation from the 1670s.[34] This was in addition to the two different collected editions of Luther's works, as well as other writings of the reformer, which Bach obtained over the years.[35] The bicentenary of the Reformation in 1717 must, therefore, have been of great interest to Bach, though there was the major distraction that it occurred at a significant transitional point in his life (see below).

Detailed instructions were published concerning how the bicentennial Reformationsfest was to be celebrated over three days in the duchy of Sachsen-Weimar:[36]

Vespers on the eve of the Celebration, 30 October.

Opening hymn: *Nun freut euch, lieben Christen gmein* sung in a polyphonic setting ["figuraliter gesungen"]
Reading: Psalm 147.
Concluding hymn: *Der du bist drei in Einigkeit*.

---

33 Ibid., No. 48.
34 Leaver, *Bachs theologische Bibliothek*, No. 49. It is significant that the three volumes with a similar content by Spener, Hunnius, and Klinge were kept together on Bach's bookshelves; op. cit., Nos. 48, 49, 50.
35 Leaver, *Bachs theologische Bibliothek*, Nos. 2, 3, 4, 6, 7, 28.
36 Cyprian, *Hilaria evangelica: oder Historische Beschreibung des andern evangel. Jubel-Festes*, 1:209–10; see also the summary in Gottfried Albin de Wette, *Kurzgefasste Lebens Geschichte der Herzoge zu Sachsen, welche vom Churfürst Johann Friedrich an, bis auf den Herzog Ernst August Constantin, zu Weimar regieret haben* (Weimar: Hoffmann, 1770), 445, cited in Carl Hermann Bitter, *Johann Sebastian Bach*. 2nd rev. ed. (Berlin: Baensch, 1881; reprint, Leipzig: Zentralantiquariat der Deutschen Demokratischen Republik, 1978), 1: 121–22. For the musicians at the Weimar court at this time, see Christian Ahrens, *Die Weimarer Hofkapelle 1683–1851: Personelle Ressourcen, Organisatorische Strukturen, Künstlerische Leistungen* (Sinzig: Studio, 2015). For the background, see also Christopher Spehr, Michael Haspel, Wolfgang Holler, eds., *Weimar und die Reformation: Luthers Obrigkeitslehre und ihre Wirkungen* (Leipzig: Evangelische Verlaganstalt, 2016).

340   *Theology*

First Day of the Festival

The early service begins with the singing of a Latin motet, or a German
hymn, according to the list of appropriate hymns (see below)
Kyrie & Gloria etc.
For the Epistle: 2 Thess. 2:1–12
Gradual hymn: *Nun lob, mein Seel, den Herren.*
For the Gospel: Matt. 24:23–26.
Cantata, newly composed, in the Weimar "Residentz" ["in hiesiger
Residentz das neu-componirte … Stück … zu musiciren"]; churches
in the duchy to perform an appropriate composition ["schickendes
Stück"].
Creedal hymn: *Wir glauben all an einen Gott.*
Pulpit hymn: *Liebster Jesu, wir sind hier.*
Sermon, followed by the general confession and the special
Jubilaeums prayer specially prepared for the occasion, concluding
with the Lord's Prayer.
Te Deum laudamus, sung either in Latin or German: *Herr Gott, dich
loben wir.*
During Communion customary hymns are to be sung.

On the following two days, the liturgical order remained the same but with
different readings for the Epistle and Gospel, different motets and cantatas,
and hymns chosen from the following list:

1. *Wo Gott der Herr nicht bei uns hält.*
2. *Wär Gott nicht mit uns diese Zeit.*
3. *Es ist das Heil uns kommen her.*
4. *O Herre Gott, dein göttlich Wort.*
5. *Allein Gott in der Höh sei Ehr.*
6. *Ein feste Burg ist unser Gott.*
7. *Erhalt uns, Herr, bei deinem Wort.*[37]

There would, therefore, have been at least three cantatas performed in the
ducal chapel in Weimar, in addition to other music, in connection with the
bicentenary of the Reformation in 1717.[38]

The aged Weimar kapellmeister, Johann Samuel Drese, had died on 1
December 1716. According to court protocol he would be succeeded by the
vice-kapellmeister, his son, Johann Wilhelm Drese, though it took a year to
confirm the younger Drese in the position, by which time Bach had moved

---

37 This list is very similar to the hymns prescribed by the Saxon Elector in Dresden in 1617; see
note 5 above.
38 And there would have been another cantata celebrating the birthday of Duke Wilhelm Ernst
of Saxe-Weimar on 30 October.

Bach and anniversaries of the Reformation   341

to Cöthen. In 1714, when Bach assumed the status of concertmaster, in addition to being court organist, even though he effectively took over much of the leadership of music at court, in terms of official status he was subordinate to the vice-kapellmeister. Whether he hoped that with the passage of time he could impress Duke Wilhelm Ernst enough to be promoted to become the successor of the aged kapellmeister cannot be asserted with certainty. What is known about Bach's compositional output in Weimar seems to suggest that it diminished significantly in 1717, though he is known to have composed considerably more during his Weimar years than the extant corpus implies, thus the paucity of music in 1717 could be due to lack of transmission as well as with loss of incentive.

On the other hand, Bach was clearly on the lookout for a new position during these months. In Holy Week 1717 he presented a Passion at the court of Gotha, substituting for the kapellmeister, who was terminally ill, possibly with the view to replacing him.[39] By early August he visited Prince Leopold of Anhalt-Cöthen and may have agreed to become the next court kapellmeister,[40] though the obituary indicates that the formal invitation to become kapellmeister was not made until after Bach had been in Dresden and had returned to Weimar.[41] Sometime during the fall, presumably September/October, he was in Dresden, where he met with the court musicians and gave his famous keyboard recital after Louis Marchand's infamous defection. Since the proposed contest was between two famed organists it seems highly likely that Bach played on the various Dresden church organs during this visit. If so, he could not have been unaware of the extensive preparations that were then being made for the *Jubelfest* that was to take place in the churches a few weeks later.[42] For example, the cantor of the Kreutz-Kirche, Johann Zacharias Grundig, was probably already composing his setting of the specially prepared version of Luther's German *Te Deum, Herr Gott, dich loben wir*, with an additional text by the senior pastor and superintendent, Valentin Ernst Löscher, to be sung in alternation with Luther's verses at the close of Löscher's sermon on 31 October.[43]

---

39 See Andreas Glöckner, "Neue Spuren zu Bachs 'Weimarer' Passion," *Leipziger Beiträge zur Bach-Forschung*, 1 (Hildesheim: Olms, 1995): 33–46.

40 See BDok 2: 67 (No. 86).

41 BDok, 3: 84 (No. 666): "Nachdem unser Bach wieder nach Weymar zurück gekommen war, berief ihn, noch in eben deisem Jahre, der damalige Fürst Leopold von Anhalt Cöthen ... zu seinem Capellmeister." NBR 302 (No. 306): "In this same year [1717], after our Bach had returned to Weymar, the reigning Prince Leopold of Anhalt-Cöthen ... called him to be his Capellmeister."

42 Cyprian, *Hilaria evangelica: oder Historische Beschreibung des andern evangel. Jubel-Festes*, 1:105–7.

43 Cyprian, *Hilaria evangelica: oder Historische Beschreibung des andern evangel. Jubel-Festes*, 1:107. It was thus included in the text book for the celebration: *Gott-geheiligte Jubel-Freude Bestehend In denjenigen Musicalischen Texten Welche Bey dem Andern Evangelischen Jubel- und Danck-Feste den 31. Octobr. und folgenden 1. und 2. Nov. Anno 1717 In der Kirche zum Heil. Creutz allhier zu Dreßden auffgeführet worden von Joh. Zachar. Grundig, Schol. Cruc. Cantore et Colleg. Dreßden gedruckt in der Kön. privileg. Hof-Buchdruckerey*; cited in Karl Held, "Das

342 Theology

Bach returned to Weimar from Dresden and soon after received the formal invitation to become kapellmeister to the Cöthen court, which he was moved to accept, an intention that annoyed the duke. However, the duke seems not to have acted immediately. It is extremely significant that Bach was not arrested and detained until a few days after the bicentenary celebrations were completed, that is, on 6 November.[44] The implication is that he must have participated in some way in the Jubelfest celebrations at the Weimar court. Although Bach appears to have hardly composed anything for Weimar since the end of the previous year, given the prominence and importance of the celebration, the duke is likely to have insisted that Bach provide something for the Jubelfest, even if most of the music was prepared by Johann Wilhelm Drese, who had not yet been elevated to the position of kapellmeister.

One possibility might be Bach's setting of Luther's German Te Deum, *Herr Gott, dich loben wir* included in the organ works among the chorale preludes as BWV 725. But it is obviously not a chorale prelude to be played before the singing of the congregation but rather an accompaniment for choral and congregational singing. It is a sturdy, five-voice setting of the Phrygian chant melody that Luther adapted for the rhymed couplets of his vernacular Te Deum. The setting surfaced somewhat late in a non-holograph manuscript owned by Forkel, which makes it difficult to date with certainty, but the modal harmonies and five-part setting suggest a pre-Leipzig origin.[45] Although the vernacular Te Deum was sung on various occasions during the church year, such as New Year and Trinity Sunday, it was a particular feature of specific thanksgivings, especially those connected with Reformation anniversaries, when it was customary for it to be accompanied with trumpets and timpani— embellishments to convey special solemnity at three specific junctures, as was the practice in Dresden:

> The Te Deum laudamus in German for which the trumpets and timpani are used and three salutes are sounded, namely: The first during the words: "Heilig ..., Heilig ..., Heilig ...," the second: "Taglich Herr Gott, etc."—the third occurring with the final "Amen."[46]

Kreuzkantorat zu Dresden," *Vierteljahrschrift für Musikwissenschaft*, 10 (1894): 320–21. The text was published sometime before the event in Valentin Ernst Löscher, *Dreyfacher Beytrag zur heiligen und rechtschaffenen Jubel-Freude, bey dem 200jährigen grossen Reformations-Fest* (Dresden: Harpeter, 1717), 45–50. On Löscher's other poetry that was to be sung alternately with the stanzas of Luther's hymns, see Chapter 9.

44 BDok 2: 65–66 (No. 84).

45 "If one looks for a suitable occasion for a festive performance—a celebration in 1730, or the Thanksgiving on 9 January 1746 after a recent Prussian win ... —more than one can be found, including much earlier occasions around the time of the *Orgelbüchlein*"; Peter Williams, *The Organ Music of Bach*, 2nd ed. (Cambridge: Cambridge University Press, 2003), 468. On the question of its authenticity, BWV 725 has strong affinities with the four-part setting BWV 328.

46 Spagnoli, *Letters and Documents of Heinrich Schütz*, German: 188; English: 207.

Bach and anniversaries of the Reformation   343

The Reformation bicentenary of 1717 especially demanded such a grand and impressive setting of the Te Deum.

Although there are many problematic issues surrounding it, the double chorus, *Nun ist das Heil und die Kraft* (BWV 50)[47] may well have originated in Weimar as part of the celebrations of the bicentenary of the Reformation. That it is a permutation fugue, a form that Bach had largely abandoned by 1724, suggests a pre-Cöthen origin, and its emphatic grandeur implies a special event, and the most likely occasion would appear to be the Reformation bicentenary of 1717.

The single movement, which (like BWV 725) is transmitted only in later manuscripts, could either be the opening or closing movement of a larger work. In the second half of the eighteenth century, when cantatas as such were seldom performed, copyists only transcribed the movements that interested them, mostly choruses. This double-chorus is complete in itself but is usually taken to be a movement from an otherwise unknown cantata for St. Michael's Day,[48] on the grounds that its text, Revelation 12:10 occurs in the prescribed Epistle for St. Michael's Day (Revelation 12:7–12). This is logical enough but not necessarily conclusive. The biblical text is the emphatic statement of the outcome of the war of Michael against the dragon, rather than of the war itself, as is found in other St. Michael's Day cantatas, such as those beginning with a similar text by Johann Christoph Bach[49] and Johann Sebastian Bach (BWV 19): *Es erhub sich ein Streit.*

St. Michael's Day had apparently been celebrated with distinctive Reformationsfest overtones for quite a long time. To begin with, St. Michael's Day and Reformation Day were observed as consecutive Apostle Days, one month apart, at the end of the ecclesiastical year in the Lutheran calendar. Thus, for example, there was a Reformation oration given on St. Michael's Day in the Paulinerkirche, Leipzig, in 1617.[50]

---

47 The problematic issues include its uncertain provenance, unusual voice leading, the second chorus being mostly homophonic in contrast to the polyphonic first chorus, that, for example, have led Joshua Rifkin to question its authenticity, and William H. Scheide to propose that the original version was in five parts rather than for double chorus, and that the expansion was done by someone other than Bach. The basic literature includes: William H. Scheide, "'Nun ist das Heil und die Kraft' BWV 50: Doppelchörigkeit, Datierung und Bestimmung," BJ 68 (1982): 81–96; Klaus Hofmann, "Bachs Doppelchor 'Nun ist das Heil und die Kraft' (BWV 50): Neue Überlegungen zur Werkgeschichte," BJ 80 (1994): 59–73; Klaus Stein, "Stammt 'Nun ist das Heil und die Kraft' (BWV 50) von J. S. Bach?" BJ 85 (1999): 51–66; Joshua Rifkin, "Siegesjubel und Satzfehler: zum Problem von 'Nun ist das Heil und die Kraft' (BWV 50)," BJ 86 (2000): 67–86; William H. Scheide, "Nochmals BWV 50 'Nun ist das Heil und die Kraft'," BJ 87 (2001): 117–30.

48 The *Bach Compendium* does not include BWV 50 with the St. Michael's Day cantatas but among those whose original occasion is uncertain; see BC 2: No. A194; See also Hans-Joachim Schulze, *Die Bach-Kantaten: Einführung zu sämtlichen Kantaten Johann Sebastian Bachs* (Leipzig: Evangelische Verlaganstalt, 2006), 574.

49 Karl Geiringer, *Music of the Bach Family: An Anthology* (Cambridge: Harvard University Press, 1955), 36–52.

50 See note 10 above.

344 *Theology*

There was, however, another connection between the celebration of the action of archangel Michael as recorded in Revelation and Luther's act that brought about the Reformation that can be traced back to the sermon Johannes Bugenhagen preached in Wittenberg at Luther's funeral in 1546. In that sermon Bugenhagen made the following identification:

> For there is no doubt that he [Luther] was the angel of whom it is written in Revelation 14 [:6–8] that he was flying through the midst of the heavens, having an eternal Gospel, etc., as the text says: "And I saw an angel flying through the midst of the heavens, having an eternal Gospel to proclaim to those who reside and dwell on earth, and to all nations and tribes and languages and peoples, saying with a loud voice: 'Fear God and give Him glory, for the time of His judgment has come ...'" This angel who says, "Fear God and give Him glory," was Dr. Martin Luther. And the words here written—"Fear God and give Him glory"—are the two parts of Dr. Martin Luther's doctrine: the Law and the Gospel, through which all of Scripture is laid open and Christ is known as our Righteousness ... and eternal life.[51]

Luther identified as this angel became the Lutheran interpretation,[52] and thus Revelation 14:6–8, after the sesquicentennial of 1667, was the prescribed scripture to be read in place of the liturgical Gospel and preached upon at the annual Reformationsfest thereafter.

If Luther is the "other angel" of Revelation 14:6, then he must also be included in the statement of Revelation 12:7, which speaks of Michael "and his angels" contending against the dragon and his fallen angelic retinue. This is the argument that August Pfeiffer makes at the beginning of his *Lutherthum vor Luthern*,[53] a book in Bach's library. For Pfeiffer, Luther, "the cherished implement and man of God," is to be identified with Michael and his angels because he is one of them, the angel who brought evangelical truth to light again.[54]

---

51 *Sixteenth-Century Biographies of Martin Luther*, ed. Christopher Boyd Brown, Luther's Works Companion Volume (St. Louis: Concordia, 2018), 27–28.

52 See, for example, Caspar Heunisch, *Haupt-Schlüssel über die hohe Offenbahrung S. Johannis* (Scheusingen: Göbel, 1684), 196–98; and Johannes Olearius, *Biblische Erklärung: Darinnen nechst dem allgemeinen Haupt-Schlüssel der gantzen heiligen Schrifft* (Leipzig: Tarnov, 1678–1681), 5: 1975–1976. Both these titles were in Bach's library; Leaver, *Bachs theologische Bibliothek*, Nos. 33 and 1 respectively. Olearius goes one stage further than the usual interpretation and identifies the second angel of Revelation 14:8 as "*D. Mart. Chemnicius* mit seinem *Examine*," Olearius, op. cit., 5: 1976. The Chemnitz volume was also in Bach's library; see note 31 above.

53 August Pfeiffer, *Lutherthum vor Luthern/ Oder Das alte Evangelische durch Lutherum erneuerte Christenthum und Das neue Römische durch Lutherum auffgedeckte Pabstthum* (Dresden: Hübner, 1683), 73–77; see also note 30 above.

54 Pfeiffer, *Lutherthum vor Luthern*, 74–75: "Die Evangelische Wahrheit/ welche in diesen letzten Zeiten durch den theuren Rüstzeug und Mann Gottes *Lutherum* wieder ans Licht gebracht."

Bach and anniversaries of the Reformation   345

Revelation 12:10b (the text of BWV 50) is defined by Olearius as "ein herrliches Triumph-Lied" (a splendid triumph song).[55] It was therefore an appropriate text for the Weimar observance of the Reformation Jubelfest in 1717, along with the hymns specified for use during the three-day festival in Sachsen-Weimar, such as *Es ist das Heil uns kommen her*,[56] which is a strong echo of Revelation 12:10b: "Nun ist das Heil."

The motto of the Reformation, either expressed as "VDMA" or fully spelled out, "Verbum Domini Manet in Aeternum" (the Word of the Lord abides in eternity),[57] appeared everywhere in the literature connected with the 1717 bicentenary of the Reformation. The text that Bach sets in BWV 50, Revelation 12:10b, is the "Word" of "eine große Stimme, die sprach im Himmel" (A great voice that spoke in heaven; Revelation 12:10a) and therefore highly appropriate for the celebration of the two-hundredth anniversary of the Reformation in 1717.

The permutation fugue (BWV 50), when approached purely from a musical point of view, seems to be oddly constructed in the way in which its various elements are worked out (see Figure 15.2[58]). But if, as seems most likely, Bach had another, non-musical ground plan in mind, then most of the anomalies can be explained. Klaus Stein, writing in the *Bach-Jahrbuch* in the year 2000, argues that the context suggests that the text is "a voice from heaven,"[59] that the first chorus represents heaven addressing earth and the second chorus as earth responding to heaven. The "two choirs" concept, the heavenly choir(s) above and the earthly choir(s) beneath, is a common image expressed in a variety of ways in sermons, devotional books, poetry, hymns, cantata libretti, and so forth, as illustrated in the following examples:

Dein Lob im Himmel hoch erklingt/	Your praise in heaven high resounds,
kein Chor ist/ der nicht von dir singt . . .	there is no choir that does not sing to you . . .

Martin Moller's *O Jesu süß, wer dein gedenkt* (1584), st. 16.[60]

Des freuen sich die Engelein/	The little angels rejoice at this
Die gerne um und bey uns seyn,	and gladly join with and around us,
Und singen in den Lüften frey,	singing freely in the air,
daß Gott mit uns versöhnet sey.	that God is reconciled with us.

Cyriakus Schneegaß's *Das neugeborne Kindelein* (1597), st.2.[61]

---

55 Olearius, *Biblische Erklärung*, 5: 1966.
56 See note 37 above.
57 See E. J. Stopp, "Verbum Domini Manet in Aeternum: The Dissemination of a Reformation Slogan 1522–1904," *Lutheran Quarterly* 1 (1987): 54–71.
58 The diagram is based on that of Hofmann, "Bachs Doppelchor," 61.
59 Stein, "Siegesjubel und Satzfehler," 63.
60 *Schuldiges Lob Gottes/ Oder Geistreiches Gesang-Buch* (Weimar: Mumbach, 1713), 676.
61 *Geistreiches Gesang-Buch* (Weimar: Mumbach, 1713), 45.

346 *Theology*

Gloria sey dir gesungen	Glory to you is sung
mit Menschen- und	with the tongues of humans and
Englischen-Zungen/	angels,
mit Harffen und mit Cymbeln schön.	with harps and cymbals fine.
Von zwölff Perlen sind die Pforten	Twelve pearls are at the door
an deiner Stadt/ wir sind Consorten	of your city, we are consorts
Der Engel hoch in deinem Thron.	with angels high before your throne.
Kein Aug hat je gespürt/	No eye has seen
kein Ohr hat mehr gehört/	no ear has heard more
solche Freude/	of such joy.
Des sind wir froh/ jo! jo!	We rejoice and sing
ewig *in dulci jubilo*.[62]	eternally *in dulci jubilo*.

Philipp Nicolai, *Wachet auf, ruft uns die Stimme* (1599), st. 3.

Die Engel, welche sich zuvor	The angels, who formerly shrank away
Vor euch als vor Verfluchten scheuen,	from you, as from the damned,
Erfüllen nun die Luft im höhern Chor,	now fill the air in the higher choir
Um über euer Heil sich zu erfreuen.	to rejoice over your salvation.
Gott, so euch aus dem Paradies	God, who cast you out of Paradise,
Aus englischer Gemeinschaft stieß,	out of the communion of the angels,
Läßt euch nun wiederum auf Erden	now lets you once more on earth
Durch seine Gegenwart vollkommen	become perfectly blessed through his
selig werden:	presence:
So danket nun mit vollem Munde	then be thankful now in full voice
Vor die gewünschte Zeit im neuen	for the desired age of the new
Bunde.	Covenant.[63]

BWV 122/3, *Das neugeborne Kindelein* (1724).[64]

Ach! nimm das arme lob auf erden/	Ah, take this poor praise from earth,
mein Gott, in allen gnaden hin:	my God, in all graces;
Im himmel soll es besser werden,	in heaven it will be better,
wenn ich ein schöner Engel bin;	when I become a fine angel;
da sing ich dir im höhern chor	to sing with you in the higher choir
viel tausend Halleluja vor.	many thousand Alleluias.

Johann Mentzer's *O daß ich tausend Zungen hätte* (1704), st. 15.[65]

Öffne meinen schlechten Liedern,	Open to my poor songs
Jesu, dein Genadenohr!	O Jesus, your ear of grace!
Wenn ich dort im höhern Chor	When there in the choir on high

---

62 Ibid., 533.

63 Dürr, *Cantatas*, 138.

64 The recitative is an expansion of the second stanza of Schneegaß's *Das neugeborne Kindelein*.

65 Johann Anastasius Freylinghausen, *Geist-reiches Gesang-Buch* (Halle: Wäysen-Hause, 1704), 775.

Werde mit den Engeln singen, / I shall sing with the angels.
Soll mein Danklied besser klingen. / My song of thanks shall then sound better.[66]

BWV 25/5. *Es ist nichts Gesundes in meinem Liebe* (1723).

Es freue sich, wer immer kann, / Rejoice, who ever can,
Und stimme seinem Gott zu Ehren / and give voice to God's glory
Ein Loblied an, / a song of praise,
Und das im höhern Chor, / and in a higher choir
Ja, singt einander vor! / indeed sing it to one another![67]

BWV 30/2. *Freue dich, erlöste Schar* (1730s).

Vergnügt man sich hier an einer schönen Music, / If one enjoys beautiful music here, especially when
zumahl wenn in einem Gottes-Hause auf / different choirs sing in a house of God, then how
unterschiedlichen Chören gesungen wird, ey wie / should the chosen ones [in heaven] not be moved by
solten sich die Auserwehlten nicht belustigen an der / the heavenly music, since more than a thousand
himmlischen Music, da mehr als von tausend / choirs will glorify God's name.
Chören der Nahme Gottes wird gerühmet werden.

Friedrich Werner, *Himmels-Weg* (1704).[68]

One way or another these references to heavenly and earthly choirs can be traced back to the account of the birth of Jesus in St. Luke's Gospel (Luke 2:14), with the multitude of angels singing "Gloria in excelsis Deo," the song that was incorporated into the weekly Eucharistic liturgy on earth. In the seventeenth century the choir above and the choir below were often depicted in visual terms in the frontispieces of Lutheran publications that dealt in some way with the music of worship. The most notable is the title page woodcut that Michael Praetorius used for a number of different publications (see Figure 15.1). The two locations of the choirs are presented visually. Above is the polychoral music of heaven, angels on the left and the redeemed on the

---

66 Dürr, *Cantatas*, 521.

67 Dürr, *Cantatas*, 689.

68 Friedrich Werner, *Der richtige und unbetrügliche Himmels-Weg eines Christen ... Zwanzigste Auflage* (Leipzig: Weidmann, 1755), 867. Werner's *Himmels-Weg*, originally published in 1704, was an extremely popular devotional book in and around Leipzig and was reprinted numerous times. It was probably known in the Bach family since Wilhelm Friedemann Bach owned a copy of the 1710 edition; see Peter Wollny, "Fundstücke zur Lebensgeschichte Johann Sebastian Bachs 1744–1750," BJ 97 (2011): 36; Robin A. Leaver, *The Routledge Research Companion to Johann Sebastian Bach* (New York: Routledge, 2017), 184.

Figure 15.1 Michael Praetorius's title page block

right. The content of this heavenly music is distinguished by its use of the same liturgical texts—Gloria in excelsis Deo, Sanctus, Agnus Dei—that are heard on earth. The heading of the woodcut is "Pleni sunt coeli gloria tua" (heaven is full of your glory). This, of course, is a quotation from the Sanctus, but it is incomplete. The words "et terra" are omitted from the heading, but not from the image. They occur at the bottom of the page and undergird the polychoral music of earth, "et terra," that is characterized by psalmody, "Psallite Domino qui habitat in Sion" (Psalm 9:11. Sing praises to the Lord, who dwells in Zion). Thus, the music of earth occurs simultaneously with the

Example 15.1 BWV 50: fugue subject and its inversion

music of heaven, and both are incorporated into the same activity: "Pleni sunt coeli *et terra* gloria tua." The heavenly music is heard on earth, and the earthly music is incorporated into heaven. The quotations cited earlier in this chapter not only establish the two locations of the choirs but also underscore the ultimate aim of the earthly singers, that is, to be incorporated into the heavenly choir(s). This is illustrated in the Praetorius woodcut, with the redeemed singing alongside the angels in heaven, and discussed in the brief treatise of the elderly Johann Mattheson, who looked forward to joining in the heavenly singing.[69] But it is also the ground plan of the double-chorus fugue, BWV 50.

In Cantata 50, Bach's monumental permutation fugue, the homophonic lower choir (Chorus II) is gradually transformed and incorporated into the counterpoint of the upper choir (Chorus I), and its emphatic triple-time fugue subject underscores the important words of the text, which fall on the strong beats: "Nun" (now), "Heil" (salvation), "Kraft" (power), "Reich" (kingdom), "Macht" (strength), and "[unsere] Gott[es]" (see Example 15.1).

The fugue is in two equal sections: I = mm. 1–68; II = mm. 69–136 (see Figure 15.2). In the first section the subject is introduced in ascending order (B, T, A, S) in Chorus I (mm. 1–28). When all the voices have entered, one would expect the subject to be taken up by Chorus II (m. 29), but instead it is

---

[69] Johann Mattheson, *Behauptung der Himmlischen Musik aus den Gründen der Vernunft, Kirchen-Lehre und heiligen Schrift* (Hamburg: Herold, 1747), translated in Joyce L. Irwin, trans. and ed., *Foretastes of Heaven in Lutheran Church Music Tradition: Johann Mattheson and Christoph Raupach on Music in Time and Eternity* (Lanham, MD: Rowman & Littlefield, 2015), esp. 89–91.

350   *Theology*

Measures		Section I									Section II				
		1	8	15	22	29	36	43	50	69	76	83	90	97	104	111
Instruments		–	–	–	–	1 Tr	5 Ob	–	1 Vl	–	–	–	–	–	1 Tr	–
CHOR I	S	–	–	–	1	2	3	4	2	1*	1	2	3	4	6	5
	A	–	–	1	2	3	4	6	6	+	–	1	2	3	4	+
	T	–	1	2	3	4	2	3	4	+	–	–	1	2	3	+
	B	1	2	3	4	0	1	2	3	+	–	–	–	1	2	+
CHOR II	S	–	–	–	–	5	–	1	–	1*	2	3	4	4	1	2
	A	–	–	–	–	+	–	+	–	+	–	5	6	3	+	6
	T	–	–	–	–	+	–	+	–	+	–	–	5	2	+	3
	B	–	–	–	–	+	–	+	–	+	–	–	–	5	+	4

1 = Primary subject   2–6 = Countersubjects   NB 5 = 1 inverted

Figure 15.2 Diagrammatic representation of BWV 50

given to Trumpet I, and the soprano of Chorus II begins a new subject, which is the inversion of the primary subject, being supported chordally by the other three voices of Chorus II. The homophonic texture of Chorus II contrasts with the polyphony of Chorus I. Thus, the theme on "earth" is the mirror image of the theme of "heaven" but is a simple, chordal statement compared with the polyphony above it. At m. 43 the soprano of Chorus II is given the "heavenly" subject, but the underparts of Chorus II continue with homophonic support. The first section is brought to a conclusion with antiphonal effects between the two choruses. The second section begins (m. 69) with the primary subject being split between the two choirs, with the theme broken up antiphonally between the sopranos of Chorus I and Chorus II (indicated by asterisks in Figure 15.2), each being supported chordally by their respective under parts—"earth" echoing "heaven." Then at m. 76 the soprano of Chorus I begins the fugue again, followed by the other voices, this time in descending order (S, A, T, B), while the soprano of Chorus II in the same measure (m. 76), continues with the first countersubject that had been introduced by the bass of Chorus I in m. 8—the first time it has been heard in Chorus II. The other voices of Chorus II join in, again in descending order, first with the "earthly" inversion of the primary subject, followed by "heavenly" countersubjects, but it is only in the soprano of Chorus II that the primary "heavenly" fugue subject is heard. Nevertheless, in this second section both choruses are involved in the polyphony, and at m. 111 the "earthly" inversion of the subject at last appears for its final statement in the soprano of Chorus I. Again, there are antiphonal effects between the two choruses before coming together for the final emphatic statement that the enemies of God have been vanquished. For all its complexities it is a tour de force that, to quote Alfred Dürr, "creates the impression of enormous spacial breadth and splendor ... a work ... of breathtaking power."[70]

Luther's Reformation was not simply a question of theology alone: it was as much to do with how that theology was expressed in practice, and especially in worship. Given the monumental nature of Bach's double-chorus fugue it seems more likely to have been composed for the Reformation Jubelfest in 1717, rather than as part of a cantata for an annual celebration of St. Michael's Day.

---

70 Dürr, *The Cantatas of J. S. Bach*, 704, 706.

Bibliography

Primary sources, before 1800

Academiae lipsiensis pietas in sacrosanctam reformationi divi Lutheri memoriam: exhibita quinquaginta dissertationibus ab ordinis theologici decanis separatis temporibus publico nomine conscriptis et nunc iunctim editis. Edited by Christian Friedrich Börner. Leipzig: Gleditsch, 1717.

Adlung, Jacob. *Anleitung zu der musikalischen Gelahrheit ...* Erfurt: Jungnicol, 1758. Reprint, Kassel: Bärenreiter, 1953.

Agenda: Das ist, Kirchen-Ordnung, Wie sich der Pfarrherren und Seelsorger in ihren Ämtern und Diensten verhalten sollen. Leipzig: Lanckisch, 1712.

Albrecht, Georg. *Geistreicher Evangelischer Schatz-Kammer ... Darinnen über ein jedes Sonn- und Festtägliches Evangelium durchs gantze Jahr.* Ulm: Görlin, 1662–1663.

Allgemeines gelehrten-Lexikon. Edited by Christian Gottlieb Jöcher. Leipzig: Gleditsch, 1733–1751.

Altes und Neues aus dem Schatz theologischer Wissenschaften. Leipzig: Gross, 1701.

Arnstädtisches Verbessertes Gesangbuch. Arnstadt: Bachmann, 1705.

Auffrichtige Nachricht von der Unrichtligkeit der so genanten unschuldigen Nachrichten. Leipzig: Heinichen, 1707–1714.

Auserlesenes und vollständiges Gesangbuch. Dresden: Zimmermann, 1718.

Avenarius, Johann. *Evangelischer Lieder-Catechißmus.* Frankfurt and Leipzig: Stössel, 1714.

Biblia, Das ist: Die gantze Heil. Schrifft Alten und Neuen Testaments/ Verdeutscht durch D. Martin Luthern. Eisenach: Urban, 1704.

Biblia, Das ist: Die gantze Heilige Schrifft Altes und Neues Testaments/ Teutsch/ Herrn D. Martin Luthers ... Ulm: Kühn, 1688.

Burmeister, Joachim. *Musica Poetica.* Rostock: Myliander, 1606. Facsimile, Kassel: Bärenreiter, 1955.

Buttstedt, Johannn Heinrich. *Ut, Mi, Sol, Re, Fa, La, tota Musica et Harmonia Aeterna.* Erfurt: Werther, ca. 1715.

Calvisius, Seth. *Exercitatio musica tertia.* Leipzig: Schürerus, 1611; facsimile, Hildesheim: Olms, 1973.

Carpzov, Johann Benedict. *Hodegeticum Brevibus Aphorismis Olim pro Collegio Concionatorio.* Leipzig: Riese, 1652.

——. *Hodegetici Ad Artem Concionatoriam.* Edited by Tilemannn Andreas Rivinus. Leipzig: [s.n.], 1689.

Bibliography 353

———. *Isagoge in Libros Ecclesiarum Lutheranarum Symbolicos.* Dresden: Zimmermann, 1725.

Carpzov, Johann Gottlob. *Unterricht vom Unverletzten Gewissen beyde gegen Gott und Menschen, in vier und achtzig Predigten, Vormahls der Gemeine Gottes zu St. Thomas in Leipzig vorgetragen* ... Leipzig: Martini, 1733. [See also under Franck, *Catalogus ... Carpzovii.*]

Catalogus Bibliothecae Deylingiae auctionis ... Leipzig: Cruciger, 1756.

Catalogus Scriptorum ... Io. Christoph Olearius. [Arnstadt]: [s.n.], [1727].

Colditzer Kirchen-, Schul- und Hauß-Gesang-Buch. Rochlitz: Lange, 1724.

Corpus Juris Ecclesiastici Saxonici, Oder Churfl. Sächs. Kirchen- Schulen- wie auch andere darzu gehörige Ordnungen. Dresden: Winckler, 1708.

Crusius, Martin. *Martini Crusii ... Homiliae hymnodicae* ... Edited by Johann Christoph Olearius. Arnstadt: Ehrt, 1705.

Cyprian, Salomon. *Hilaria evangelica: oder Historische Beschreibung des andern evangel. Jubel-Festes, mit beygefügten Instructionen ... der evangelischen Könige ..., auch denen programmatibus der Universitäten ... abgefasset.* Leipzig: Weidmann, 1718.

———. *Hilaria evangelica, oder Theologisch-Historischer Bericht vom andern Evangelischen Jubel-Fest. Nebst III. Büchern darzu gehöriger Acten und Materien, deren das erste, die obrigkeitlichen Verordnungen, und viele historische Nachrichten, das andere, Orationes und Programmata Jvbilaea, das dritte, eine vollständige Beschreibung der Jubel-Medaillen begreiffet.* Gotha: Weidmann, 1719.

Deyling, Salomon. *Institutiones Prudentiae Pastoralis ... edition seconda.* Leipzig: Lanckisch, 1739.

———. *Kirchen-Agenda ... Für die Prediger der Graffschafft Mannßfeld Jezund zum drittenmahl gedruckt.* Eisleben: Hüllmann, 1718.

———. *Observationum Sacrarum Pars V.* Leipzig: Lanckisch, 1748.

———. *Der Wohlunterrichtete und würdiglich zubereitete Communicant, oder evangelisches Com[m]union-Büchlein.* Leipzig: Boetius, 1726. [See also under *Catalogus ... Deylingiae.*]

Dieterichs, Conrad. *Sonderbarer Predigten von unterschiedenen Materien: Hiebevor zu Ulm im Münster gehalten/ deren theils im Truck allbereit außgangen ... Theil. Auff sonderbar Begehren zusammen gedruckt.* Frankfurt: Schürer & Götze, 1669.

E. E. Hochw. Raths der Stadt Leipzig Ordnung der Schule zu S. Thomae. Leipzig: Tietzen, 1723. Facsimile in *Die Thomasschule Leipzig zur Zeit Johann Sebastian Bach: Ordnungen und Gesetze 1634, 1723, 1733.* Edited by Hans-Joachim Schulze. Leipzig: Zentral-antiquariat, 1987.

E. E. Hochweisen Raths der Stadt Leipzig Gesetze der Schule zu S. Thomae. Leipzig: Breitkopf, 1733. Facsimile in *Die Thomasschule Leipzig zur Zeit Johann Sebastian Bach: Ordnungen und Gesetze 1634, 1723, 1733.* Edited by Hans-Joachim Schulze. Leipzig: Zentral-antiquariat, 1987.

Eisenachisches Neu-revidiert und beständiges Gesang-Buch. Eisenach: Kruge, 1753.

Episteln und Evangelia, Mit Nutzbaren und erbaulichen Summarien auf alle Sonntage und fürnehmste Feste durchs gantze Jahr ... Dresden & Leipzig: Hekel, 1732.

Ernesti, Johann August. *Denkmäler und Lobschriften auf gelehrte, verdienstvolle Männer, seine Zeitgenossen nebst der Biographie Johann Matthias Geßners, in einer Erzählung für David Ruhnken.* Leipzig: Schwickert, 1792.

354 Bibliography

——. *Initia doctrinae solidioris.* Leipzig: Wendler, 1745.

——. *Initia rhetorica.* Leipzig: Wendler, 1750.

——. *Institutio Interpretis Novi Testamenti. Editio tertia.* Leipzig: Weidmann, 1775.

——. *Institutio Interpretis Novi Testamenti: Editionem quintam suis observationibus auctam curavit Christoph Frider. Ammon.* Leipzig: Weidmann, 1792.

——, ed. *M. Tullii Ciceronis Opera Omnia.* Leipzig: Martini, 1737.

——. *Opuscula varii argumenti.* Leipzig: Fritsch, 1794.

Fabricius, Johannes Albertus. *Bibliotheca Latina Sive Notitia Auctorum Veterum Latinorum* ... Hamburg: Schiller, 1721–1722.

Fortgesetzte Sammlung von alten und neuen theologischen Sachen Leipzig: Braun, 1720–1750.

Fortsetzung und Ergänzungen zu Christian Gottlieb Jöchers allgemeinem Gelehrten-Lexicon. Edited by Christoph Adelung. Leipzig: Gleditsch, 1784.

Franck, Johann. *Catalogus Bibliothecae Iohannis Gottlob Carpzovii* ... Lübeck: Green, 1768.

Freylinghausen, Johann Anastasius. *Geist-reiches Gesang-Buch: Den Kern alter und neuer Lieder.* Halle: Wäysen-Hause, 1706.

——. *Neues Geist-reiches Gesang-Buch.* Halle: Wäysen-Hause, 1714.

Fuhrmann, Martin Heinrich. *Die an der Kirchen Gottes gebauete Satans-Capelle Darin dem Jehova Zebaoth zu Leid und Verdruß, Und dem Baal-Zebub zur Freud und Genuß* ... Berlin, 1729.

Geist- und Lehr-reiches Kirchen- und Hauß-Buch. Dresden: Matthesius, 1694.

Geistliche Cantaten Über alle Sonn- Fest- und Apostel-Tage/ zu einer/ denen Herren Musicis sehrbequemen Kirchen-Music In ungezwungenen Teutschen Versen ausgefertiget. [s.l] : [s.n.], 1702.

Geistliches neu-vermehrtes Gesang-Buch. Meiningen: Hassert, 1683.

Gerber, Christian. *Historie der Kirchen-Ceremonien in Sachsen.* Dresden: Saueressig, 1732.

——. *Die unerkanten Sünden der Welt.* Dresden: Hekel, 1690.

Gerbert, Martin. *Scriptores eccelsiastici de musica sacra potissimum.* St. Blaise: Typis San Blasius, 1784. Reprint, Hildesheim: Olms, 1963.

Gerhard, Johann. *Locorum Theologicorum* ... Jena: Steinmann, 1622–1625.

Gesner, Johann Matthias, ed. *M. Fabii Quinctiliani de Institutione oratoria libri duodecim collatione codicis Gothani et Iensonianae editionis aliorumque librorum ac perpetuo commentario illustrate Io Matthia Gesnero accedit praefatio et indices copiossime.* Göttingen: Vandenhoeck, 1738.

Glass, Salomon. *Christliches Haus-Kirch-Büchlein* ... Nuremberg: Endter, 1654.

——. *Philologiae sacrae.* Amsterdam: Wolters, 1711.

Gläubiger Kinder Gottes Englische Sing-Schule hier auf Erden. Ulm: Bartholomäi, 1717.

Gottschaldt, Johann Jacob. *Sammlung von allerhand auserlesenen Lieder-Remarqüen.* Leipzig: Martini, 1748.

Grohmann, Johann Christian August. *Annalen der Universität zu Wittenberg.* Meissen: Erbstein, 1801–1802.

Die Heilige Schrift/ Neuen Testaments unsers Herrn Jesu Christi: Nach der Teutschen Übersetzung D. Martin Luthers. Lemgo: Meyer, 1734.

Heineccius, Johann Michael. *Hundertjähriges Denckmahl der Reformation: bestehend in denen von einem gesammten Ehrwürdigen Ministerio der Stadt Halle bey dem Zweyten Ivbileo Reformationis gehaltenen Predigten.* Halle: Neuem Buchhandlung, 1718.

Henrici, Christian Friedrich. *Picanders Ernst-Schertzhaffte und Satyrische Gedichte. Dritter Theil*. Leipzig: Boetius, 1732.

——. *Sammlung Erbaulicher Gedancken über und auf die gewöhnlichen Sonn- und Fest-Tage*. Leipzig: Boetius, [ca. 1725].

Heunisch, Caspar. *Haupt-Schlüssel über die hohe Offenbahrung S. Johannis*. Schleusingen: Göbel, 1684.

Hiller, Johann Adam. *Fünf und zwanzig neue Choralmelodien zu Liedern von Gellert*. Leipzig: Breitkopf, 1792.

——. *Lebensbeschreibungen berühmter Musikgelehrten und Tonkünstler neuerer Zeit ... Erster Theil*. Leipzig: Dykisch, 1784. Facsimile, Leipzig: Peters, 1975.

Hoch-Fürstliches Sachsen-Weissenfelsisches Vollständiges Gesang- und Kirchen-Buch. Weissenfels: Brühl, 1714.

Hoënegg, Matthias Hoë von. *Chur Sächsische Evangelische JubelFrewde: In der Churfürstlichen Sächsischen SchloßKirchen zu Dreßden/ theils vor/ theils bey wehrendem/ angestalten Jubelfest/ neben andern Solenniteten, auch mit Christlichen Predigten ... gehalten ... Nach der Vorrede/ findet der Christliche Leser/ mit was für Solenniteten das Evangelische Jubelfest/ in ... Dreßden/ seye gehalten worden*. Leipzig: Lamberg, 1618.

Hoffmann, Carl Julius Adolph. *Die tonkünstler Schlesiens: Ein Beitrag zur Kunstgeschichte Schlesiens vom 960 bis 1830*. Breslau: Aderholz, 1830.

Hofmann, Carl Gottlob. *Ausführliche Reformations-Historie der Stadt und Universität Leipzig*. Leipzig: Breitkopf, 1739.

——. *Die in der Evangelischen Kirche gewöhnlichen Sonn- und Festtäglichen Episteln und Evangelia Mit kurtzen summarischen Betrachtungen ...* Leipzig: Barnbeck, 1743.

Hunold, Christian Friedrich. *Academische Neben-Stunden allerhand neuer Gedichte*. Halle & Leipzig: Zeitler, 1713.

——. *Die Allerneueste Art/ Zur Reinen and galannten Poesie zu gelangen*. Hamburg: Liebernickel, 1707.

Hutter, Leonhard. *Compendium Locorum Theologicorum Ex Scripturis sacris & libro Concordiae*. Wittenberg: Helwig, 1610.

——. *Compendium Locorum Theologicorum*. Wittenberg: Zimmermann, 1728.

Das jetzt lebende und florinde Leipzig, Welches die Nahmen, Characteren, Chargen, Professionen und Wohnungen derer Persone ... Leipzig: Boetius, 1723.

Johannes Bugenhagens Braunschweiger Kirchenordnung 1528. Edited by Hans Lietzmann. Bonn: Marcus & Webber, 1912.

Lehms, Georg Christian. *Gottgefälliges Kirchen-Opffer, In einem gantzen Jahr-Gange*. Darmstadt: Bachmann, 1711.

Leipziger Adreß-, Post- und Reise-Kalender, Auf das Jahr Christi M.DCC. LXVIII. Leipzig: Löper, [1757].

Leipziger Kirchen-Andachten/ Darinnen der Erste Theil Das Gebetbuch/ Oder Die Ordnung des gantzen öffentlichen Gottes-Dienstes durchs gantze Jahr/ ... Der Ander Theil Das Gesangbuch/ ... Leipzig: Würdig, 1694.

Leipziger Kirchen-Staat/ Das ist Deutlicher Unterricht vom Gottes-Dienst in Leipzig/ ... Leipzig: Groschuff, 1710.

Lenz, Jakob Michael Reinhold. *Der Hofmeister oder Vortheile der Privaterziehung: Eine Komödie*. Leipzig: Weigand, 1774.

Liebler, Johann Bernhard. *Hymnopoeographia Oleariana, oder Olearische Lieder-Historie, darinnen unterschiedene Olearii, als berühmte Lieder-Dichter und Lieder-Freunde ...* Naumburg: Boßögel, [1727].

356   *Bibliography*

Lippius, Johannes. *Synopsis musicae novae.* Strassburg: Ledertz, 1612. Facsimile, Hildesheim: Olms, 2004.

Löscher, Valentin Ernst. *Dreyfacher Beytrag zur heiligen und rechtschaffenen Jubel-Freude, bey dem 200jährigen grossen Reformations-Fest.* Dresden: Harpeter, 1717.

———. *Vollständiger Timotheus Verinus, oder, Darlegung der Wahrheit und des Friedens in denen bisherigen pietistischen Streitigkeiten nebst christlicher Erklärung und abgenöthigter Schutz-Schrifft ...* Wittenberg: Hannauer, 1718–1721.

Lübeckisches Gesang-Buch. Lübeck: Wiedemeyer, 1716.

Lüneburgisches Gesangbuch/ darinnen über2000/ so wol alte als neue Geistreiche Lieder. Lüneburg: Stern, 1695.

Lünig, Johann Christian. *Theatrum Ceremoniale Historico-Politicum, Oder Historisch- und Politischer Schau-Platz Aller Ceremonien, welche so wohl an Europäischen Höfen, als auch sonsten bey vielen Illustren Fällen beobachtet worden ... Anderer Theil.* Leipzig: Weidmann, 1720. Facsimile of *Theatrum Ceremoniale.* Vienna: Ahlgrimm-Fiala, 1953.

Luther, Martin. *Der Siebende Teil aller Deutschen Bücher und Schrifften der theuren seeligen Mannes Gottes Doctor Martini Lutheri.* Altenburg: Fürst. Sachs. Offizin, 1662.

———. *Tischreden Oder Colloquia Doct. Mart. Luthers.* Edited by Johann Aurifaber. Eisleben: Gaubisch, 1566. Facsimile, St. Louis: Concordia, 1968.

Marperger, Bernhard Walther. *Neues Communion-Büchlein für die Liebhaber des rechtschaffenen Wesens in Christo Jesu.* Nuremberg and Leipzig: Hoffmann, 1724.

Marpurg, Friedrich Wilhelm. *Historisch-Kritische Beyträge zur Aufnahme der Musik, I Band.* Berlin: Schütz, 1754–1755.

———. *Kritische Briefe über die Tonkunst.* Berlin: Birnstiel, 1760–1764.

Mattheson, Johann. *Behauptung der Himmlischen Musik aus den Gründen der Vernunft, Kirchen-Lehre und heiligen Schrift.* Hamburg: Herold, 1747.

———. *Das Beschützte Orchestre.* Hamburg: [Mattheson], 1717.

———. *Critica Musica, I/2.* Hamburg: [Mattheson], 1722.

———. *Grundlage einer Ehren-Pforte.* Hamburg: [Mattheson], 1740.

———. *Der Musicalische Patriot.* Hamburg: [Mattheson], 1728.

———. *Das Neu-Eröffnete Orchestre.* 1713. Reprint, Hildesheim: Olms, 1993.

———. *Der neue Göttingische aber viel schlechter, als die alten Lacedämonischen, urtheilende Ephorus, wegen der Kirchen-Music eines andern belehret.* Hamburg: [Mattheson], 1727.

———. *Die neueste untersuchung der Singspiele, nebst beygefügter musikalischen Geschmachsprobe.* Hamburg: Herold, 1744.

———. *Der Vollkommene Capellmeister, Das ist Gründliche Anzeige aller derjenigen Sachen, die einer wissen, können, und vollkommen inne haben muß, der Capelle mit Ehren und Nutzen vorstehen will.* Hamburg: Herold, 1739. Facsimile, Kassel: Bärenreiter, 1954.

Mayer, Johan Friedrich. *Würdiger Com[m]unicant: Wie Er sich zu verhalten Vor dem Abendmahl/ Bey dem Abendmahl/ und nach dem Abendmahl ... Samt einem Beicht- und Com[m]munion- Gebet-Buch.* Leipzig: Grosse, 1684.

Melanchthon, Philipp. *De rhetorica libri tres.* Basel: Froben, 1519.

———. *Elementorum rhetorices libri duo.* Wittenberg: Schleich, 1582.

Meyer, Joachim. *Der anmaßliche Hamburgische Criticus sine crisi entgegen gesetzet dem so genannten Göttingschen Ephoro Joh. Matthesons, und dessen vermeyntlicher*

Bibliography 357

Belehrungs-Ungrund der Verthädigung der Theatralischen Kirchen-Music. Lemgo: [s.n.], 1728.

——. *Unvorgreiffliche Gedancken über die neulich eingerissene theatralische Kirchen-Music und denen darinnen bishero üblich gewordenen Cantaten mit Vergleichung der Music voriger Zeiten vorgestellt von J. M. D.* [Lemgo]: [s.n.], 1726.

Neu-auffgelegtes Dreßdnisches Gesang-Buch. Dresden and Leipzig: Miethen, 1707.

Neue Beiträge von alten und neuen theologischen Sachen. Leipzig: Braun, 1751–1761.

Das Neue Testament unsers Herrn und Heylandes Jesu Christi/ Verteutschet D. Mart. Luthern. Hamburg: Holle, 1707.

Neu-eingerichtetes Hessen-Darmstädtisches Kirchen-Gesang-Buch. Darmstadt: Forter, 1733.

Neues vollständiges Eisenachisches Gesangbuch. Eisenach: Rörer, 1673.

Neues vollständiges Gesang-Buch, vor die Königlich-Preußische auch Chur-Fürstl. Brandenburgische und andere Lande. Berlin: Rüdiger, 1725.

Neumeister, Erdmann. *Epistolische Nachlese*. Hamburg: Liebezeit, 1720.

——. *Fortgesetzte Fünffache Kirchen-Andachten, in Drey neuen Jahrgängen*. Hamburg: Kißner, 1726.

——. *Fünfffache Kirchen-Andachten bestend In theils eintzeln, theils niemahls gedruckten Arien, Cantaten und Oden Auf alle Sonn- und Fest-Tage des gantzen Jahres*. Edited by Gottfried Tilgner. Leipzig: Groß, 1716.

——. *Geistliche Bibliothec, Bestehend und Predigten auf alle Sonn- und Fest-Tage des Jahrs, Nach Anleitung allerhand Geistlicher Bücher gehalten, und mit Neuen Liedern beschlossen*. Hamburg: Liebezeit, 1719.

——. *Geistliche Cantaten Oder Außerlesene Kirchen-Gesänge/ Über alle Sonn- Fest- und Apostel-Tage/ Ingleichen Bey jedermahliger Beicht und H. Communion/ Zu einer Denen Herren Musicis und jedweden mit Hertz´und Mund zu Gott gern singenden Christen bequemen Kirchen-Music (In ungezwungenen Teutschen Versen ausgefertiget)*. Augsburg: Lotter, 1708.

——. *Geistliche Cantaten statt einer Kirchen-Music. Die zweyte Auflage Nebst einer neuen Vorrede*. [Hamburg]: [s.n.], 1704.

——. *Geistliche Cantaten Uber alle Sonn- Fest- und Apostel-Tage/ Zu beförderung Gott geheiligter Hauß- Und Kirchen-Andacht: In ungezwungenen Teutschen Versen ausgefertigt*. Halle: Renger, 1705.

——. *Geistliche Poesien mit untermischten Biblischen Sprüchen und Choralen auf alle Sonn- und Fest-Tage durchs gantze Jahr*. Eisenach: Boetius, 1717.

——. *Geistliche Rauchwerk; oder die Lehre vom Gebet*. Hamburg, 1734.

——. *Geistliches Singen und Spielen/ Das ist: Ein Jahrgang von Texten ... beyöffentlicher Kirchen Versam[m]lung in Eisenach musicalisch aufgeführet werden von Georg Philipp Telemann, Capellmeister*. Gotha: Reyher, 1711.

——. *Die Lehre vom Glauben*. Hamburg, 1735.

——. *Die Lehre von·dem Gesetz Gottes*. Hamburg, 1737.

——. *Priesterliche Lippen in Bewahrung der Lehre; Das ist: Son[n]- und Festtags-Predigten durchs gantze Jahr*. Leipzig: Laurentius, 1714.

——. *Psalmen und Lobgesänge und Geistlicher Lieder, aus seinen Poetischen und andern seinen Schrifften*. Hamburg: Beneke, 1755.

——. *Tisch des Herrn, In LII Predigten über I. Cor. XI. 23–32*. Hamburg: Kißner, 1722.

——. *Wasserbad im Worte*. Hamburg, 1731.

——. *Worte der Weisen Statt eines Leit-Sterns Zum Wort der mannichfaltigen Weisheit Gottes. Oder: Hoher Personen Christliche Symbola, Bey Schrifftmäßiger*

358   *Bibliography*

und Lehrreicher Erklärung aller Sonn- und Fest-Tags Evangelien, Wie auch am Reformations- und Kirch-Weyhungs-Feste, so anmuthig, als erbaulich angewendet. Hiebevor einer Christlichen Gemeine im Stifft Bibra geprediget ... Weissenfels: Wehrmann, 1706.

———. *Der Zugang zum Gnaden-Stuhl Jesu Christo, Das ist: Christliche Gebete und Gesänge Vor, bey und nach der Beichte und Heil. Abendmahle.* Weissenfels: Wehrmann, 1721.

Neu-vermehrtes Ratzeburgisches Gesang-Buch. Ratzeburg: Hartz, 1725.

Neuvermehrtes und verbessertes Gesang-Buch. Eisleben: Hüllmann, 1724.

Neuvermehrtes und wohleingerichtetes Naumburgisches Gesang-Buch. Naumburg: Boßögel, 1735.

Olearius, Johann Christoph [1668–1747]. *Betrachtung des bekannten Passion-Liedes/ Jesu meines Lebens-Leben* ... Jena: Bielcke, 1704.

———. *Evangelischer Lieder-Schatz.* 4 vols. Jena: Bielcke, 1705–1707.

———. *Historia Arnstadtiensis. Historie der alt-berühmten Schwartzburgischen Residenz Arnstadt.* Arnstadt: Bachmann, 1701. Reprint, Arnstadt: Donhof, 1998.

———. *Jubilirende Lieder-Freude.* Arnstadt: Meurer, 1717.

———. *Kurtze doch hinlängliche Nachricht von der öffentlichen Kirchen-Bibliotheck in Arnstadt.* Arnstadt: Schill, 1746.

———. *Vollständiges Passion-Lied.* Jena: Bielcke, 1710. [See also under Liebler, and under *Catalogus ... Olearius.*]

Olearius, Johann Gottfried [1635–1711]. *I. N. J. Der Hier zeitlich- und dort ewiglich Reichbeseligte Lebens-Bach ... Herrn Heinrich Bachs ...* Arnstadt: Meurer, 1692.

Olearius, Johannes [1611–1684]. *Biblische Erklärung: Darinnen nechst dem allgemeinen Haupt-Schlüssel der gantzen heiligen Schrifft.* Leipzig: Tarnov, 1678–1681.

Oratorium, Welches Die heilige Weynacht über In beyden Haupt-Kirchen zu Leipzig musiciret wurde, Anno 1734. Facsimile, Stuttgart: Carus, [2000].

Pfeiffer, August. *Gazophylacion Evangelicum: Evangelische Schatz-Kammer.* Jena: Rist, 1689.

———. *Lutherthum vor Luthern, Oder Das alte Evangelische durch Lutherum erneuerte Christenthum und Das neue Römische durch Lutherum auffgedeckte Pabstthum.* Dresden: Hübner, 1683.

Das Privilegirte Ordentliche und Vermehrte Dreßdnische Gesang-Buch. Dresden & Leipzig; Hekel, 1732.

Das privilegirte Vollständige und vermehrte Leipziger Gesangbuch. Leipzig: Barnbeck, 1758.

Quantz, Johann Joachim. *Versuch einer Anweisung die Flöte traversiere zu spielen.* Berlin: Boß, 1752. Facsimile, Wiesbaden: Breitkopf & Härtel, 1988.

Quintilian, Marcus Fabius, see under Gesner.

Rambach, Johann Jacob. *Geistliche Poesien.* Halle: Neue Buchhandlung, 1720.

Des Raths zu Leipzig, Vornewerte Schul-Ordnung. Leipzig: Köler, 1634. Facsimile in *Die Thomasschule Leipzig zur Zeit Johann Sebastian Bach: Ordnungen und Gesetze 1634, 1723, 1733.* Edited by Hans-Joachim Schulze. Leipzig: Zentral-antiquariat, 1987.

Rist, Johann. *Neue Musikalische Fest-Andachten.* Lüneburg: Stern, 1655.

Rittmeyer, Johann. *Himmlisches Freuden-Mahl der Kinder Gottes auff Erden. Oder Geistreiche Gebete, so vor/ bey und nach der Beicht und heiligem Abendmahl, kräfftig zu gebrauchen . . .wie auch einiger Geistreichen Gesänge und Lieder.* Helmstedt: Hamm, 1684.

Bibliography   359

Rost, Johann Christoph. *Nachricht, Wie es, in der Kirchen zu St: Thom: alhier, mit dem Gottesdienst, jährlichen sowohl an Hohen Festen, als andern Tagen, pfleget gehalten zu werden auffgezeichnet von Johann Christoph Rosten, Custode ad D. Thomae, Anno 1716.* [Manuscript in the Thomaskirche archive, no shelfmark].

Ruetz, Caspar. [I.] *Widerlegte Vorurtheile vom Ursprung der Kirchenmusic . . .*; [II.] *Widerlegte Vorurtheile von der Beschaffenheit der heutigen Kirchenmusic . . .*; [III.] *Widerlegte Vorurtheile von der Wirkung der Kirchenmusic* ... Lübeck: Schmidt und Böckmann, 1751, 1752, and Rostock and Wismar: Berger und Boedner, 1753.

Sachsen-Weissenfelsisches Vollständiges Gesang- und Kirchen-Buch. Weissenfels: Brühl, 1714.

Eines Sämmtlichen Stadt-Ministerii zu Halle neu eingerichtetes und mit einem Anhang vermehrtes Gesang-Buch voll alter und neuer vor andern geistreicher Lieder. Halle: Schütze, 1715.

Schamelius, Johannes Martinus. *Des Evangelischen Lieder-Commentarii Anderer Theil: Darinnen Die neuern Lieder nebst beygefügten Anmerckungen ... enthalten.* Leipzig: Lackisch, 1725.

Scheibel, Gottfried Ephraim. *Andachts-Blumen Der zu Ehren Gottes Blühenden Jugend Oder Gedenck-Reime Uber alle Son[n]- und Festtags-Evangelien ...* Breslau: Korn, 1750.

——. *Die Geschichte der Kirchen-Music alter neuer Zeiten.* Breslau: Korn, 1738. Facsimile, Stuttgart: Cornetto, 2002.

——. *Musicalisch-Poetische Andächtige Betrachtungen über alle Sonn- und Fest-Tags Evangelien Durchs gantze Jahre Andächtigen Seelen zur Erbauung ans Licht gestellt.* Breslau: Korn, 1738.

——. *Poetische Andachten Über alle gewöhnliche Sonn- und Fest-Tage, durch das gantze Jahr/ Allen Herren Componisten und Liebhabern der Kirchen-Music zum Ergötzen, Nebst einer Vorrede von der Hindernüssen derselben.* Leipzig & Breslau: Rohrlach, 1725.

——. *Die Unerkannte Sünden der Poeten Welche man Sowohl in ihren Schrifften als in ihrem Leben wahrnimmt. Nach den Regeln des Christenthums und vernüngfftiger Sittenlehre geprüfet.* Leipzig: Teubner, 1734. Facsimile, Munich: Kraus, 1981.

——. *Zufällige Gedancken von der Kirchen-Music.* Frankfurt & Leipzig: "Authore," 1721. Facsimile, Stuttgart: Cornetto, 2002.

Scheidt, Samuel. *Tabulatur-Buch/ Hundert geistlicher Lieder und Psalmen Herrn Doctoris Martini Lutheri und anderer gottseligen Männer/ Für die Herren Organisten/ mit der Christlichen Kirchen und Gemeine auff der Orgel.* Görlitz: Herman, 1650.

Schemelli, Georg Christian. *Musicalisches Gesangbuch.* Leipzig: Breitkopf, 1736.

Schieferdecker, Johann David. *Auserlesene aus Fürstlichen Gedancken ... Nach Ordnung der Sonn- und Festtäglichen Evangelien, in Geistliche Cantaten verfasset.* Eisleben: [s.n.], [1716].

Schmolck, Benjamin. *Der mit rechtschaffenem Hertzen zu seinem Jesu sich nahende Sünder: In auserlesenen Buß- Beicht- und Communion-Andachten.* Chemnitz: Stößel, 1730.

Schrifftmässiges Gesangbuch zu nützlichem Gebrauch Evangelischer Christen absonderlich der Kirchen-Gemeinden in Nordhausen. Nordhausen: Demelius, 1699.

Schuldiges Lob Gottes, Oder Geistreiches Gesang-Buch. Weimar: Mumbach, 1713.

Schulordnung vor die Churfürstl. Braunschweig-Lünebergische Lande ... Göttingen: Vandenhoeck, 1738.

360 Bibliography

Seckendorf, Veit Ludwig von. *Commentarius Historicus et Apologeticus De Lutheranismo, sive De Reformatione Religionis ductu D. Martini Lutheri in magna Germaniae parte aliisque religionibus & speciatim in Saxonia recepta & stabilita.* Frankfurt and Leipzig: Gleditsch, 1692.

Seiffart, Daniel. *Christholds Deliciarum Medicarum Centuria Prima, Oder Christerbaulichen Lieder-Ergötzlichkeiten Erstes Hundert ...* Nürnberg: Zieger, 1704.

Selnecker, Nikolaus. *Christliche Psalmen Lieder und Kirchengesenge Jn welchen die Christliche Lehre zusam gefasset und erkleret wird.* Leipzig: Beyer, 1587.

Serpilius, Georg. *Anmerckungen Uber D. Pauli Sperati Geistlich- und liebliches Lied: Es ist das Heyl uns kommen her ...* Regensburg: Seidel, 1707.

Sicul, Christoph Ernst. *Neo-annalium Lipsiensium Continuatio II: Oder des mit dem 1715ten Jahre neu angefangenen Leipziger Jahr-Buchs Dritte Probe.* Leipzig: Autore, 1717.

——. *Siculs Leipziger Jahr-Geschichte 1719. Oder Des bisherigen Leipziger Jahr-Buchs Zu dessen Andern Bande Erste Fortsetzung... Auch unterm schwartzen Brete zu finden.* Leipzig: Autor, 1719–1721.

Sondershäusisches Gesang-Buch. Sondershausen: Bock, 1726.

Spangenberg, Cyriacus. *Cithara Lutheri.* Wittenberg: Seuberlich, 1601.

Spener, Philipp Jakob. *Pia desideria: Oder Hertzliches Verlangen nach Gottgefalliger Besserung der wahren evangelischen Kirchen.* Frankfurt: Zunner, 1676.

Steger, Thomas Paul. *Heilige Meditationes und Andachten über das schöne, Geistreiche Glaubens-Lied ...* Dresden: Zimmermann & Gerlach, 1725.

Stemler, Johann Christian. *Historie und Führung des Lebens Johann Martin Schamelii.* Leipzig: Lanckisch, 1743.

Tentzel, Wilhelm Ernst. *Historischer Bericht vom Anfang und ersten Fortgang der Reformation Lutheri, zur Erläuterung des Hn. v. Seckendorff Historie des Lutherthums.* Gotha: Reyhern, 1717; Leipzig: Gleditsch & Weidmann, 1717–1718.

Texte Zur Leipziger Kirchen-Music, Auf den Andern, dritten vierdten Sonntage nach der Erscheinung Christi, Das Fest Maria Reinigung, Und die Sonntage Septuagesimae, Sexagesiame, esto mihi, Ingleichen Auf das Fest der Verkündigung Maria, 1724. Facsimile, Stuttgart: Carus, [2000].

Unschuldige Nachrichten. Wittenberg: Ludwieg, 1701; Leipzig: Grosse, 1702–1719; Leipzig: Braun, 1720–1761.

Vogel, Johann Jacob. *Leipzigisches geschicht-buch, oder, Annales, das ist: jahr- und tage-bücher der weltberühmten königl. und churfürstlichen sächsischen kauff- und handelsstadt Leipzig.* Leipzig: Lanckisch, 1714.

Vollständigen Kirchen- und Haus-Music. Breslau: Baumann, 1663.

Vollständiges Kirchen-Buch. Leipzig: Lanckisch, 1707.

Vollständiges Kirchen-Buch, darinnen die Evangelia und Episteln auf alle Fest-, Sonn- und Apostel-Tage durchs gantze Jahr, die Historien von dem schmertzlichen Leiden, und der fröhlichen Auferstehung des Herrn Christi: samt der erbärmlichen Zerstörung der Stadt Jerusalem, die drey Haupt-Symbola und Augspurgische Confeßion ... Leipzig: Lanckisch, 1743.

Vopelius, Gottfried. *Neu Leipziger Gesangbuch/ von den schönsten und besten Liedern verfasset.* Leipzig: Klinger, 1682.

Vulpius, Melchior. *Pars prima Cantionum sacrarum.* Jena: Richtzenhan, 1602.

——. *Pars secunda selectissimarum Cantionum sacrarum.* Jena: Richtzenhan, 1603.

Wagner, Paul. *Andachtiger Seelen geistliches Brand- und Gantz Opfer.* Leipzig: Zedler, 1697.

Walch, Johann Georg. *Bibliotheca Theologica Selecta*. Jena: Cröcker, 1757–1765.

——. *Historische und Theologische Einleitung in die Religions-Streitigkeiten ... der Evangelisch-Lutherischen Kirche*. Jena: Meyer, 1733.

Walther, Johann Gottfried. *Musicalisches Lexicon oder Musicalische Bibliothec*. Leipzig: Deer, 1732. Facsimile, Kassel: Bärenreiter, 1967.

Weiz, Anton. *Verbessertes Leipzig, oder Die vornehmsten Dinge/ so von Anno 1698. an biß hieher bey der Stadt Leipzig verbessert worden, mit Inscriptionibus erlautert*. Leipzig: Lanckisch, 1728.

Werner, Friedrich. *Der richtige und unbetrügliche Himmels-Weg eines Christen*. Leipzig: Weidmann, 1755.

Wette, Gottfried Albin de. *Historische Nachrichten von der berühmten Residentz-Stadt Weimar*. Weimar: Hoffmann, 1737.

——. *Kurzgefasste Lebens Geschichte der Herzoge zu Sachsen, welche vom Churfürst Johann Friedrich an, bis auf den Herzog Ernst August Constantin, zu Weimar regieret haben*. Weimar: Hoffmann, 1770.

Wetzel, Johann Caspar. *Hymnopoeographia, oder historische Lebens-Beschreibung der berühmtesten Lieder-Dichter*. Herrnstadt: Roth-Scholtz, 1728.

Witt, Christian Friedrich. *Psalmodia Sacra, Oder: Andächtige und schöne Gesänge*. Gotha: Reyher, 1715.

Das Wittenbergische Kirchen-Gesang-Buch. Wittenberg: Zimmermann, 1742.

Wittenbergisches Gesang-Buch. Wittenberg: Zimmermann, 1733.

Zarlino, Gioseffo. *Le Istitutioni Harmoniche*. Venice: Senese, 1562.

Zedler, Johann Heinrich. *Grosses vollständiges Universal-Lexikon aller Wissenschafften und Künste*. Leipzig & Halle: Zedler, 1731–1754.

Secondary sources

Ahrens, Christian. *Die Weimarer Hofkapelle 1683–1851: Personelle Ressourcen, Organisatorische Strukturen, Künstlerische Leistungen*. Sinzig: Studio, 2015.

Albrecht, Christoph. "J. S. Bachs *Clavier Übung, Dritter Theil*. Versuch einer Deutung." BJ 55 (1969): 46–66.

Altner, Stefan and Martin Petzoldt, eds. *800 Jahre Thomana: Glauben, Singen, Lernen*. Wettin-Löbejün: Stekovics, 2012.

Alwes, Chester L. "Georg Otto's 'Opus musicuum novum' (1604) and Valentin Geuck's 'Novum et Insigne Opus' (1604): A Musico-Liturgical Analysis of Two Collections of Gospel Music from the Court of Hesse-Kassel." PhD diss., University of Illinois, 1982.

Arfken, Ernst. "Zur Entstehungsgeschichte des Orgelbüchlein." BJ 52 (1966): 41–58.

Arndt, Johann. *True Christianity*. Translated and edited by Peter Erb. New York: Paulist Press, 1979.

Arnold, Frank Thomas. *The Art of Accompaniment from Thorough-Bass as Practiced in the XVIIth and XVIIIth Centuries*. 1931. Reprint, New York: Dover, 1965.

August Hermann Franckes Schrift über eine Reform des Erziehung—und Bildungwesens als Ausgangspunkt einer geistlichen und sozialen Neuordnung der Evangelischen Kirche des 18. Jahrhunderts. Edited by Otto Podczeck. Berlin: Akademie, 1962.

Aulen, Gustaf. *Christus Victor: An Historical Study of the Three Main Types of the Idea of Atonement*. Translated by Arthur Gabriel Herbert. London: SPCK, 1931.

362   Bibliography

Aune, Michael B. "'A Heart Moved': Philip Melanchthon's Forgotten Truth About Worship." *Lutheran Quarterly* 12 (1998): 393–416.

——. *To Move the Heart: Philip Melanchthon's Rhetorical View of Rite and Its Implications for Contemporary Ritual Theory*. San Francisco: Christian Universities Press, 1994.

Axmacher, Elke. *"Aus Liebe will mein Heyland Sterben": Untersuchungen zum Wandel des Passionsverständnisses im frühen 18. Jahrhundert*. Stuttgart: Hänssler, 1984.

——. "Mystik und Orthodoxie im Luthertum der Bachzeit?" In *Theologische Bachforschung heute: Dokumentation und Bibliographie der Internationalen Arbeitsgemeinschaft für Theologische Bachforschung, 1976–1996*, ed. Renate Steiger, 215–36. Berlin: Galda & Wilch, 1998.

Bach, Johann Christoph. *44 Choräle zum Präambulieren*. Edited by Martin Fischer. Kassel: Bärenreiter, 1929.

Bach, Johann Sebastian. *Cantata No. 4, Christ lag in Todesbanden: An Authoritative Score. Backgrounds, Analysis, Views and Comments*. Edited by Gerhard Herz. New York: Norton, 1967.

——. *The Complete Organ Works*, I/1A: *Pedagogical Works*. Edited by George B. Stauffer. Colfax, N.C.: Leupold, 2012.

——. *Klavierbüchlein für Anna Magdalena Bach 1725*. Facsimile edited by Georg von Dadelsen. Kassel: Bärenreiter, 1988.

——. *Mass in B Minor*. Edited by Joshua Rifkin. Wiesbaden: Breitkopf & Härtel, 2006.

——. *Orgelbüchlein BWV 599–644*. Documenta Musicologica, Zweite Reihe: Handschriften-Faksimiles, xi. Edited by Heinz-Harald Löhlein. Kassel: Bärenreiter, 1981.

——. *Orgelbüchlein BWV 599–644. Faksimile nach dem Autograph in der Staatsbibliothek zu Berlin Preußischer Kulturbesitz*. Edited by Sven Hiemke. Laaber: Laaber, 2004.

——. *Das geistliche Vokalwerk/ The Sacred Vocal Music*. Edited by Ulrich Leisinger and Uwe Wolf. Stuttgart: Carus, 2017.

——. *Gesamtausgabe der Bachs Werke der Bachgesellschaft*. Leipzig: Bachgesellschaft, 1851–1899.

Bach. Edited by Yo Tomita. Farnham: Ashgate, 2010.

Bach Compendium. Analytisch-bibliographisches Repertorium der Werke Johann Sebastian Bachs (BC). Edited by Hans-Joachim Schulze and Christoph Wolff. 4 vols. Leipzig: Peters, 1985–1989.

Bach-Dokumente. Edited by Andreas Glöckner, Anselm Hartinger, Karen Lehmann, Michael Maul, Werner Neumann, Hans-Joachim Schulze, Christoph Wolff. 7 vols. Kassel: Bärenreiter; Leipzig: Deutscher Verlag für Musik, 1953–2008.

Baird, William. *History of New Testament Research: From Deism to Tübingen*. Minneapolis: Fortress, 1992.

Bannasch, Bettina. "Vom Menschen und Meerkatzen, Luise Adelgunde Victorie Gottscheds *Pietisterey im Fischbein-Rocke*." *Pietismus und Neuzeit* 35 (2009): 253–68.

Banning, Helmut. *Johann Friedrich Doles: Leben und Werke*. Leipzig: Kistner & Siegel, 1939.

Baron, Carol K., ed. *Bach's Changing World: Voices in the Community*. Eastman Studies in Music, 37. Rochester: University of Rochester, Press, 2006.

Bartel, Dietrich. *Musica Poetica: Musical-Rhetorical Figures in German Baroque Music*. Lincoln: University of Nebraska Press, 1997.

Baur, Jörg. "Die Anfänge der Theologie an der 'wohl angeordneten evangelischen Universität' Göttingen." In *Zur geistigen Situation der Zeit der Göttinger*

Bibliography 363

Universitätsgründung 1737, edited by Jürgen v. Stackelberg. Göttingen: Vandenhoeck & Ruprecht, 1988.

Bautz, Friedrich Wilhelm. *Biographisch-Bibliographisches Kirchenlexikon*. Hamm: Bautz, 1975.

Beißwenger, Kirsten. *Johann Sebastian Bachs Notenbibliothek*. Kassel: Bärenreiter, 1992.

———. "Other Composers." In *The Routledge Research Companion to Johann Sebastian Bach*, edited by Robin A. Leaver, 237–64. London: Routledge, 2017.

Belotti, Michael. "Johann Pachelbel als Lehrer." In *Bach und seine mitteldeutschen Zeitgenossen: Bericht über das Internationale Musikwissenschaftliche Kolloquium Erfurt und Arnstadt. 13 bis 16. Januar 2000*, edited by Rainer Kaiser, 8–44. Eisenach: Wagner, 2001.

Berben, Léon. "Orgel-Büchlein." In *Bachs Klavier- und Orgelwerke*. Edited by Siegbert Rampe. Das Bach-Handbuch 4/1. Laaber: Laaber, 2007.

Berghaus, Peter. "Numismatiker im Porträt: 38. Johann Christoph Olearius, 17.9.1688 Halle–31.3.1747 Arnstadt." *Geldgeschichtliche Nachrichten* 31 (1996): 276–85.

Beyer, Heinrich. "Leichensermone auf Musiker des 17. Jahrhunderts." *Monatshefte für Musikgeschichte* 7 (1875): 171–79.

Bitter, Karl Hermann. *Johann Sebastian Bach*. 2d ed. Berlin: Baensch, 1881. Reprint, Leipzig: Zentral-antiquariat, 1987.

Blanken, Christine. "Christoph Birkmanns Kantatenzyklus 'Gott-geheiligte Sabbaths-Zehnden' von 1728 und die Leipziger Kirchenmusik unter J. S. Bach in den Jahren 1724–1727," BJ 101 (2015): 13–74; partially translated as "A Cantata-Text Cycle of 1728 from Nuremberg: A Preliminary Report on a Discovery relating to J. S. Bach's so-called 'Third Annual Cantata Cycle,'" *Understanding Bach*, 10 (2015): 9–30.

Blankenburg, Walter. "Die innere Einheit von Bachs Werk." PhD diss., Georg-August-Universität, 1942.

———. "Johann Sebastian Bach und das evangelische Kirchenlied zu seiner Zeit." In *Bachiana et alia Musicologica: Festschrift Alfred Dürr zum 65. Geburtstag am 3. März 1983*. ET: "Johann Sebastian Bach and the Protestant Hymn in His Time." In *The Hymnology Annual* 3, edited by Vernon Wicker, 95–105. Berrien Springs: Vande Vere, 1993.

———. "Mystik in der Musik J. S. Bachs." In *Theologische Bach Studien I: Beiträge zur theologischen Bachforschung*, edited by Walter Blankenburg and Renate Steiger, 47–66. Stuttgart: Hänssler, 1987.

Boes, Adolf. "Die reformatorischen Gottesdienste in der Wittenberger Pfarrkirche von 1523 an." *Jahrbuch für Liturgik und Hymnologie* 6 (1961): 49–61.

Boyd, Malcolm. *Bach*. 3d ed. The Master Musicians. New York: Oxford University Press, 2000.

———. ed. *Oxford Composer Companions: J. S. Bach*. Oxford: Oxford University Press, 1990.

Braun, Werner. "Christian Demelius und der 'Schrifftmässige' Gesang in Nordhausen um 1700." In *Pietismus und Liedkultur*, edited by Wolfgang Miersemann and Gudrun Busch. Halle: Verlag der Franckeschen Stiftungen, 2002, 159–79.

———. "Kompositionen von Adam Gumpelzhaimer im Florilegium Portense." *Die Musikforschung* 33 (1980): 131–35.

Die Briefentwürfe des Johann Elias Bach (1705–1755). 2d ed. Edited by Evelin Odrich and Peter Wollny. Leipziger Beiträge zur Bach-Forschung, 3. Hildesheim: Olms, 2005.

Buchwald, Georg. *Reformationsgeschichte der Stadt Leipzig*. Leipzig: Richter, 1900.

364 Bibliography

Bugenhagen, Johannes. *Selected Writings*. Edited by Kurt K. Hendel. Minneapolis: Fortress, 2015.

Bullemer, Karl. *Quellenkritische Untersuchungen zum I. Buche der Rhetorik Melanchthons*. Würzburg: Becker, 1902.

Bunners, Christian. *Kirchenmusik und Seelenmusik: Studien zu Frömmigkeit und Musik im Luthertum des 17. Jahrhunderts*. Berlin: Evangelische Verlagsanstalt, 1966.

———. "Musiktheologische Aspekte im Streit um den Neumeisterschen Kantatentyp." In *Erdmann Neumeister (1671–1756): Wegbereiter der evangelischen Kirchenkantate*, edited by Henrike Rucker, 39–50. Rudolstadt: Hain, 2000.

Busch, Gudrun, ed. *"Geist-reicher" Gesang: Halle und das pietistische Lied*. Halle: Franckeschen Stiftungen, 1997.

Buszin, Walter. "The Chorale in the Baroque Era and J. S. Bach's Contribution to It." In *Studies in Eighteenth-Century Music: A Tribute to Karl Geiringer on His Seventieth Birthday*, edited by H. C. Robbins Landon and Roger E. Chapman, 108–16. London: Allen and Unwin, 1970.

Butler, Gregory G. "J. S. Bach and the Schemelli *Gesang-Buch* Revisited." *Studi musicali* 13 (1984): 241–57.

Butt, John. "Emotion in the German Lutheran Baroque and the Development of Subjective Time Consciousness." *Musical Analysis* 29 (2010): 19–36.

Cammarota, Robert. "The Repertoire of Magnificats in Leipzig at the time of J. S. Bach: A Study of the Manuscript Sources." PhD diss., New York University, 1986.

Cannon, Beekman C. *Johann Mattheson: Spectator in Music*. New Haven: Yale, 1947.

Chafe, Eric. *J. S. Bach's Johannine Theology: The St. John Passion and the Cantatas for Spring 1725*. New York: Oxford University Press, 2014.

Cordes, Harm. *Hilaria evangelica academica: das Reformationsjubiläum von 1717 an den deutschen lutherischen Universitäten*. Göttingen: Vandenhoeck & Ruprecht, 2006.

Currie, Randolph N. "Cyclic Unity in Bach's *Sechs Chorale*: A New Look at the 'Schüblers.'" BACH 4/1 (1973): 26–38, and 5/1 (1974): 25–39.

Dirksen, Pieter. "Bibliografie." In *Bachs "Orgel-Büchlein" in nieuw Perspectief*. Edited by Frans Brouwer, et al., 240–44. Utrecht: Hogeschool voor de Kunsten, 1988.

Dockhorn, Klaus. "*Rhetorica movet*: Protestantische Humanismus und karolingische Renaissance." In *Rhetorik: Beiträge zu ihrer Geschichte in Deutschland vom 16.–20. Jahrhundert*, edited by Helmut Schanze, 17–42. Frankfurt: Athenäion, 1974.

Dokumente zur Geschichte des Leipziger Thomaskantorats. Band 1: *Von der Reformation bis zum Amtsantritt Johann Sebastian Bachs*. Edited by Michael Maul. Band 2: *Vom Amtsantritt Johann Sebastian Bach bis zum Beginn des 19. Jahrhunderts*. Edited by Andreas Glöckner. Leipzig: Evangelische Verlagsanstalt, 2018–.

Drese, Claudia. "Der Berliner Beichtstuhlstreit oder Philipp Jakob Spener zwischen allen Stühlen?" *Pietismus und Neuzeit* 31 (2005): 60–97.

Dürr, Alfred. "Bach's Chorale Cantatas." In *Cantors at the Crossroads: Essays on Church Music in Honor of Walter Buszin*, edited by Johannes Riedel, 111–20. St. Louis: Concordia, 1967.

———. *The Cantatas of J. S. Bach with their Librettos in German-English Parallel Text*. Revised and translated by Richard D. P. Jones. Oxford: Oxford University Press, 2005.

———. "'Entfernet euch, ihr kalten Herzen': Möglichkeiten und Grenzen der Rekonstruktion einer Bach-Arie." *Die Musikforschung* 39 (1986): 32–36.

———. "Heinrich Nicolaus Gerber als Schüler Bachs." BJ 64 (1978): 7–18.

———. *Die Kantaten von Johann Sebastian Bach*. 2 vols. Kassel: Bärenreiter, 1971.

Bibliography   365

——. "Kein Meister fällt vom Himmel: Zu Johann Sebastian Bachs Orgelchorälen der Neumeister-Sammlung." *Musica* 40 (1986): 309–12.

——. *Studien über die frühen Kantaten J. S. Bachs.* Leipzig: Breitkopf & Härtel, 1951.

——. "Zur Bach-Kantate *Halt im Gedächtnis Jesum Christ*, BWV 67." *Musik und Kirche* 53 (1983): 74–77.

Ehricht, Klaus. "Die zyklische Gestalt und die Aufführungsmöglichkeit des III. Teiles der Klavierübung von Joh. Seb. Bach." BJ 38 (1949/50): 40–56.

Eichhorn, Holger. "Ein Sammeldruck vom Beginn des Dreißigjährigen Krieges: Das Florilegium Portense." In *Musik zwischen Leipzig und Dresden: Zur Geschichte der Kantoreigesellschaft Mügeln 1571–1996*, edited by Michael Heinemann and Peter Wollny, 60–84. Oschersleben: Zeithen, 1996.

Elferen, Isabella van. *Mystical Love in the German Baroque: Theology, Poetry, Music.* Lanham, MD: Scarecrow, 2009.

Engelhardt, Moritz von. *Valentin Ernst Löscher nach seinem Leben und Wirken: Ein Geschichtlicher Beitrag zu den Streitfragen über Orthodoxie, Pietismus und Union.* 2d ed. Stuttgart: Liesching, 1856.

Exner, Ellen. "The Godfather: Georg Philipp Telemann, Carl Philipp Emanuel Bach and the Family Business." BACH 47/1 (2016): 1–20.

Fall, Henry Cutler. "A Critical-Bibliographical Study of the Rinck Collection." MA thesis, Yale University, 1958.

Fischer, Albert and Wilhelm Tümpel. *Das deutsche evangelische Kirchenlied des 17. Jahrhunderts.* Gütersloh: Bertelsmann, 1904–1916. Reprint, Hildesheim: Olms, 1964.

Fischer, Albert. *Kirchenlieder Lexicon: Hymnologisch-literarische Nachweisungen.* Gotha: Perthes, 1878–1879. Reprint, Hildesheim: Olms, 1967.

Fischer, Martin. *Die organistische Improvisation im 17. Jahrhundert: dargestellt an den "Vierundvierzig Chorälen zum Präambulieren" von Johann Christoph Bach.* Kassel: Bärenreiter, 1929.

Forchert, Arno. "Polemik als Erkenntnisform: Bemerkung zu den Schriften Matthesons." In *New Mattheson Studies*, edited by George J. Buelow and Hans-Joachim Marx, 199–212. Cambridge: Cambridge University Press, 1983.

Fraas, Hans-Jürgen. "Katechismus-Gottesdienst im Reformationsjahrhundert." *Luther. Mitteilungen der Luther-Gesellschaft* 30 (1959): 64–77.

For Francke, August Hermann, see under *August Hermann Francke.*

Frandsen, Mary E. *Crossing Confessional Boundaries: The Patronage of Italian Sacred Music in Seventeenth-Century Dresden.* New York: Oxford University Press, 2006.

Freylinghausen, Johann Anastasius. *Geistreiches Gesangbuch: Edition und Kommentar.* Edited by Dianne Marie McMullen and Wolfgang Miersemann. 7 vols. Tübingen: Franckesche Stiftungen, 2004–2010.

Freyse, Conrad. "Johann Sebastian Bachs erstes Gesangbuch." *Jahrbuch für Liturgik und Hymnologie* 6 (1961): 138–42.

——. "Sebastians Gesangbuch." BJ 45 (1958): 123–26.

Friedrich, Reinhold. *Johann Matthias Gesner: Sein Leben und sein Werk.* Roth: Genniges, 1991.

Garbe, Daniela. "Der Director musices, Organist und Kantor Johann Friedrich Schweinitz: Ein Beitrag zur Musikgeschichte Göttingens im 18. Jahrhundert." *Göttinger Jahrbuch* 37 (1989): 71–90.

Gawthrop, Richard L. *Pietism and the Making of Eighteenth-Century Prussia.* Cambridge: Cambridge University Press, 1993.

366 *Bibliography*

Geck, Martin. "Bach und der Pietismus." In *"Denn alles findet bei Bach statt:"* *Erforschtes und Erfahrenes*, 88–108. Stuttgart: Metzler, 2000.

———. "Bachs Probestück." In *Quellenstudien zur Musik: Wolfgang Schmieder zum 70. Geburtstag,* edited by Kurt Dorfmüller, 55–68. Frankfurt: Peters, 1972.

———. *Die Vokalmusik Dietrich Buxtehudes und die frühe Pietismus.* Kassel: Bärenreiter, 1965.

Geiringer, Karl. *The Bach Family: Seven Generations of Creative Genius.* New York: Oxford University Press, 1954.

———. *Music of the Bach Family: An Anthology.* Cambridge: Harvard University Press, 1955.

Gennrich, Friedrich. *Die Kontrafaktur im Liedschaffen des Mittelalters.* Frankfurt: Gennrich, 1965.

Gerhard, Johann. *Erklärung der Historien des Leidens unnd Sterbens unsers Herrn Christi Jesu, nach den vier Evangelisten (1611).* Critical edition and commentary by Johann Anselm Steiger. Stuttgart: Frommann-Holzboog, 2002.

———. *Theological Commonplaces.* Translated by Richard J. Dinda. St. Louis: Concordia, 2009–.

Gerhardt, Friedrich. *Geschichte der Stadt Weissenfels a. S. mit neuen Beiträgen zur Geschichte des Herzogtums Sachsen-Weissenfels.* Weissenfels: Urlaub, [1907].

Glöckner, Andreas. *Die Musikpflege an der Leipziger Neukirche zur Zeit Johann Sebastian Bachs.* Beitrage zur Bach-Forschung, 8. Leipzig: Nationale Forschungs- und Gedenkstätten Johann Sebastian Bach, 1990.

———. "Neue Spuren zu Bachs 'Weimarer' Passion." *Leipziger Beiträge zur Bach-Forschung,* 1. Hildesheim: Olms, 1995.

———. "'The Ripienists Must also Be at Least Eight, Namely Two for Each Part:' The Leipzig Line of 1730—Some Observations." *Early Music* 39 (2011): 575–85.

Gojowy, Detlef. "Kirchenlieder im Umkreis von J. S. Bach." *Jahrbuch für Liturgik und Hymnologie* 22 (1978): 79–123.

Graff, Paul. *Geschichte der Auflösung der alten gottesdienstlichen Formen in der Evangelischen Kirche Deutschlands.* 2 vols. Göttingen: Vandenhoeck & Ruprecht, 1937–1939.

Greschat, Martin. *Zwischen Tradition und neuem Anfang: Valentin Ernst Löscher und der Ausgang der lutherischen Orthodoxie.* Witten: Luther Verlag, 1971.

Grimm, Hans-Jürgen. *Das Neu Leipziger Gesangbuch des Gottfried Vopelius (Leipzig 1682).* Berlin: Merseburger, 1969.

Grün-Oesterreich, Andrea and Peter L. Oesterreich. *"Dialectica docet, rhetorica movet*: Luthers Reformation der Rhetorik." In *Rhetorica Movet: Studies in Historical and Modern Rhetoric in Honor of Heinrich F. Plett*, edited by Peter L. Oesterreich and Thomas O. Sloane, 25–41. Leiden: Brill, 1999.

Hansen, Theodor. *Johann Rist und seine Zeit: Aus den Quellen dargestellt.* Halle: Waisenhaus, 1872. Reprint, Leipzig: Zentral-antiquariat, 1973.

Heidrich, Jürgen. *Der Meier-Mattheson-Disput: Eine Polemik zur deutschen protestantischen Kirchenkantate in der ersten Hälfte des 18. Jahrhunderts.* Göttingen: Vandenhoeck & Ruprecht, 1995.

Held, Karl. "Das Kreuzkantorat zu Dresden." *Vierteljahrschrift für Musikwissenschaft* 10 (1894): 320–21.

Herbst, Wolfgang. "Johann Sebastian Bach und die lutherische Mystik." PhD diss., Friedrich-Alexander-Universität Erlangen, 1958.

Bibliography 367

Herchet, Jörg and Jörg Milbradt. "Bach als Mystiker." In *Bach als Ausleger der Bibel: Theologische und musikwissenschaftliche Studien zum Werk Johann Sebastian Bachs*, edited by Martin Petzoldt, 207–22. Berlin: Evangelische Verlagsanstalt, 1985.

Herl, Joseph. *Worship Wars in Early Lutheranism: Choir, Congregation, and Three Centuries of Conflict*. New York: Oxford University Press, 2004.

Herold, Max. *Alt-Nürnberg in seinen Gottesdiensten: Ein Beitrag zur Geschichte der Sitte und des Kultus*. Gütersloh: Bertelsmann, 1890.

Herz, Gerhard. "More on Bach's Cantata No. 4: Date and Style—A Reply to Crawford R. Thoburn." *American Choral Review* 21/2 (April 1977): 3–19 [see also under Bach, *Cantata No. 4*].

——. "Yoshitake Kobayashi's Article, 'On the Chronology of the Last Phase of Bach's Work, Compositions and Performances: 1736 to 1750': An Analysis with Translated Portions of the Original Text." BACH 21/1 (1990): 3–25.

Hiemke, Sven. *Johann Sebastian Bach, Orgelbüchlein*. Kassel: Bärenreiter, 2007.

Hobohm, Wolf. "Ein unbekannter früher Textdruck der *Geistliche Cantaten* von Erdmann Neumeister." *Jahrbuch. Ständige Konferenz Mitteldeutsche Barockmusik in Sachsen, Sachsen-Anhalt und Thüringen, 2000* (2001): 182–86.

Hofmann, Klaus. "Bach in Arnstadt." In *Der junge Bach: weil er nicht aufzuhalten...; Begleitbuch*, edited by Reinmar Emans, 239–55. Erfurt: Erste Thüringer Landesausstellung, 2000.

——. "Bachs Doppelchor 'Nun ist das Heil und die Kraft' (BWV 50): Neue Überlegungen zur Werkgeschichte." BJ 80 (1994): 59–73.

Hübner, Maria. "Neues zu Johann Sebastian Bachs Reisen nach Karlsbad." BJ 92 (2006): 93–107.

Hutter, Leonhard. *Compendium locorum theologicorum*. Edited by Wolfgang Trillhaas. Berlin: de Gruyter, 1961.

Irwin, Joyce. "Bach in the Midst of Religious Transition." In *Bach's Changing World: Voices in the Community*, edited by Carol K. Baron, 108–26. Rochester: University of Rochester Press, 2006.

——. *Foretastes of Heaven in Lutheran Church Music Tradition: Johann Mattheson and Christoph Raupach on Music in Time and Eternity*. Translated and edited by Joyce L. Irwin. Lanham, MD: Rowman & Littlefield, 2015.

——. *Neither Voice nor Heart Alone: German Lutheran Theology of Music in the Age of the Baroque*. New York: Lang, 1993.

Jenny, Markus. "Bachische Sololieder mit Gerhardt-Texten." *Musik und Gottesdienst* 13 (1976): 48–51.

——. "Zweihundert verschollene Bach-Werke." In *Mededelingen van het Instituut voor Liturgiewetenschap van die Rijksuniversiteit te Groningen* 18 (September 1984): 20–29.

Kadelbach, Ada. "'Jesu, meine Freude, Purpur, Gold und Seide': Zitat und Parodie in Erdmann Neumeisters 'Lieder-Andachten' 1743." In *Erdmann Neumeister (1671– 1756): Wegbereiter der evangelischen Kirchenkantate*, edited by Henrike Rucker, 147–70. Rudolstadt: Hain, 2000.

Kahnis, Karl Friedrich August. *Internal History of German Protestantism since the Middle of Last Century*. Translated by Theodore Meyer. Edinburgh: Clark, 1856.

Kaiser, Rainer. "Johann Christoph Bachs 'Choräle zum Präambulieren— Anmerkungen zu Echtheit und Überlieferung." BJ 87 (2001): 185–89.

368   *Bibliography*

Kalb, Friedrich. *Theology of Worship in 17th-Century Lutheranism.* Translated by Henry P. A. Hamann. St. Louis: Concordia, 1965.

Kevorkian, Tanya. *Baroque Piety: Religion, Society, and Music in Leipzig, 1650–1750.* Aldershot: Ashgate, 2007.

Kirwan-Mott, Anne. *The Small-Scale Sacred Concerto in the Early Seventeenth Century.* Ann Arbor: UMI Research Press, 1981.

Kobayashi, Yoshitake. "Zur Chronologie der Spätwerke Johann Sebastian Bachs, Kompositions- und Aufführungstätigkeit von 1736 bis 1750." BJ 74 (1988): 7–72. [See also under Herz, Gerhard.]

Koch, Eduard Emil. *Geschichte des Kirchenlieds und Kirchengesangs der christlichen, inbesondere der deutschen evangelischen Kirche.* 3d ed. Stuttgart: Belser, 1866–77. Reprint, Hildesheim: Olms, 1973.

Koch, Klaus-Peter. "Das Jahr 1704 und die Weißenfelser Hofoper: Zu den Umständen der Aufführung von Reinhard Keisers Oper *Almira* anläßlich des Besuches des Pfälzischen Kurfürsten am Weißenfelser Hof." In *Weißenfels als Ort literarischer und künstlerischer Kultur im Barockzeitalter*, edited by Roswitha Jacobsen, 75–95. Amsterdam: Rodopi, 1994.

Kramer, Gustav. *August Hermann Francke: Ein Lebensbild.* Halle: Waisenhauses, 1880–1882.

Krausse, Helmut K. "Erdmann Neumeister und die Kantatentexte Johann Sebastian Bachs." BJ 72 (1986): 7–31.

Krēsliņš, Jānis. *Dominus narrabit in scriptura populorum: A Study of Early Seventeenth-Century Lutheran Teaching on Preaching and the Lettische lang-gewünschte Postill of Georgius Mancelius."* Wolfenbütteler Forschungen 54. Wiesbaden: Harrassowitz, 1992.

Krieger, Adam. *Arien.* Edited by Alfred Heuss. Denkmäler deutscher Tonkunst, 19. Leipzig: Breitkopf & Härtel, 1905.

Kube, Michael. "Pachelbel, Erfurt und der Orgelchoral." *Musik und Kirche* 64 (1994): 76–82.

Kühling, Karin and Doris Mundus, eds. *Leipzigs Regierende Bürgermeister vom 13. Jahrhundert bis zur Gegenwart: Eine Übersichtsdarstellung mit biographischen Skizzen.* Beucha: Sax, 2000.

Kühnel, Martin, ed. *Joachim Lange (1670–1744), der 'Hällische Feind,' oder, Ein anderes Gesicht der Aufklärung: Ausgewählte Texte und Dokumente zum Streit über Freiheit-Determinismus.* Halle: Hallescher Verlag, 1996.

Kümmerle, Salomon. *Encyklopädie der evangelischen Kirchenmusik.* Gütersloh: Bertelsmann, 1888–1895. Reprint, Hildesheim: Olms, 1974.

Küster, Konrad. "Choralfantasie als Exegese: Konflikte zwischen musikalischer Realität um 1700 und jüngeren Gattungsbegriffen." *Kirchenmusikalisches Jahrbuch* 94 (2010): 23–34.

———. *Der junge Bach.* Stuttgart: Deutsche Verlags-Anstalt, 1996.

———. " 'Theatralisch vorgestellt': zur Aufführungspraxis höfischer Vokalwerke in Thüringen um 1710/20." In *Barockes Musiktheater im mitteldeutschen Raum im 17. und 18. Jahrhundert*, edited by Friedhelm Brusniak, 118–41. Cologne: Studio, 1994.

La Fontaine, Mary Joan. "A Critical Translation of Philip Melanchthon *Elementorum rhetorices libri duo.*" PhD diss., University of Michigan, 1968.

Leaver, Robin A. "Bach and Luther," BACH 9/3 (July 1978): 9–12, 25–32.

———. "Bach und die Lutherschriften seiner Bibliothek." BJ 61 (1975): 124–32.

Bibliography 369

——. "Bach's Choral-Buch? The Significance of a Manuscript in the Sibley Music Library." In *Bach and the Organ*, Bach Perspectives, 10, edited by Matthew Dirst, 16–38. Urbana: University of Illinois Press, 2016.

——. *Bachs theologische Bibliothek: eine kritische Bibliographie/Bach's Theological Library: A Critical Bibliography.* Stuttgart: Hänssler, 1983.

——. *J. S. Bach and Scripture: Glosses from the Calov Bible Commentary.* St. Louis: Concordia, 1985.

——. "J. S. Bach's Parodies of Vocal Music: Conservation or Intensification?" In *Compositional Choices and Meaning in the Vocal Music of J. S. Bach*, edited by Mark A. Peters and Reginald L. Saunders, 177–203. Lanham, MD: Lexington, 2018.

——. "Lutheran Vespers as a Context for Music." In *Church, Stage, and Studio: Music and Its Contexts in Seventeenth-Century Germany*, 143–61. Edited by Paul Walker. Ann Arbor: UMI Research Press, 1990.

——. *Luther's Liturgical Music: Principles and Implications.* Grand Rapids, MI: Eerdmans, 2017.

——. *The Routledge Companion to Johann Sebastian Bach*, edited by Robin A. Leaver. London: Routledge, 2017.

Leaver, Robin A. and Derek Remeš. "J. S. Bach's Chorale-Based Pedagogy: Origins and Continuity." BACH 48, no. 2 and 49, no. 1 (2018): 116–50.

Ledbetter, David. *Bach's Well-tempered Clavier: The 48 Preludes and Fugues.* New Haven: Yale University Press, 2002.

Legaspi. Michael C. *The Death of Scriptures and the Rise of Biblical Studies.* Oxford: Oxford University Press, 2010.

Leisinger, Ulrich. "Die zweite Fassung der Johannes-Passion von 1725." In *Bach in Leipzig—Bach und Leipzig*, Leipziger Beiträge zur Bach-Forschung 5, edited by Ulrich Leisinger, 29–44. Hildesheim: Olms, 2002.

Leppin, Volker and Timothy J. Wengert. "Sources for and against the Posting of the Ninety-five Theses." *Lutheran Quarterly* 29 (2015): 373–98.

Lester, Joel. "Major-Minor Concepts and Modal Theory in Germany, 1592–1680." *Journal of the American Musicological Society* 30 (1977): 208–53.

The Letters of a Leipzig Cantor, Being the Letters of Moritz Hauptmann to Franz Hauser, Ludwig Spohr, and Other Musicians. Edited by Alfred Schöne and Ferdinand Hiller. Translated and arranged by A. D. Coleridge. 2 vols. London: Novello, 1892.

Liliencron, Rochus Freiherr von. *Liturgisch-musikalische Geschichte der evangelischen Gottesdienste von 1523 bis 1700.* Schleswig: Bergas, 1893. Reprint, Hildesheim: Olms, 1970.

Lindner, Andreas. *Leben im Spannungsfeld von Orthodoxie, Pietismus und Frühaufklärung: Johann Martin Schamelius, Oberpfarrer in Naumburg.* Gießen: Brunnen, 1998.

Lölkes, Herbert. "Gottfried Ephraim Scheibel als Autor kirchenmusikalischen Schriften." *Jahrbuch für Schlesische Kirchengeschichte* 74 (1996): 257–81.

Löscher, Valentin Ernst. *The Complete Timotheus Verinus, or a Statement of the Truth and Call for Peace in the Present Pietistic Controversy.* Translated by James L. Langebartels and Robert J. Koester. Milwaukee: Northwestern, 1998.

Lundgreen, Peter. "Schulhumanismus, pädagogischer Realismus und Neuhumanismus: Die Gelehrtenschule zur Zeit J. S. Bachs." In *Musik, Kunst und Wissenschaft im Zeitalter J. S. Bachs*, edited by Ulrich Leisinger and Christoph Wolff, Leipziger Beiträge zur Bach-Forschung, 7, 25–38. Hildesheim: Olms, 2005.

370   Bibliography

Luthers geistliche Lieder und Kirchengesänge. Archiv zur Weimarer Ausgabe der Werke Martin Luthers, 4. Edited by Markus Jenny. Cologne: Böhlau, 1985.

Mager, Inge. "Beicht und Abendmahl nach lutherischen Beicht- und Kommunionbüchern aus vier Jahrhunderten." In *Makarios-Symposium über das Gebet: Vorträge der dritten Finnisch-deutschen Theologentagung im Amelungsborn 1986,* edited by Jouko Martikainen and Hans-Olof Kvist, 169–85. Turku, Finland: Åbo Akademi University Press, 1989.

Mahrenholz, Christhard. "Heinrich Schütz und das erste Reformationsjubiläum 1617." In *Musicologica et Liturgica: Gesammelte Aufsätze,* 196–204. Edited by Karl Ferdinand Müller. Kassel: Bärenreiter, 1960.

Mann, Alfred. "Missa Brevis and Historia: Bach's A Major Mass." BACH 16 (January 1985): 6–11.

Marshall, Robert L. *The Compositional Process of J. S. Bach: A Study of the Autograph Scores of the Vocal Works.* Princeton: Princeton University Press, 1972.

Marwinski, Felicitas and Konrad Marwinski. "Die Kirchenbibliotheken in Arnstadt, Sondershausen und Schmalkalden." In *Laudate Dominum: Achtzehn Beiträge zur thüringischen Kirchengeschichte,* 161–68. Berlin: Evangelische Verlagsanstalt, 1976.

Marx, Hans Joachim. "Bach and the 'theatralische Stil'." Translated by Andrew Talle. *Bach Notes: The Newsletter of the American Bach Society* 5 (Spring 2006): 1–6.

———. "Bach und der 'theatralische Stil'." In *Johann Sebastian Bachs Spätwerk und dessen Umfeld. Bericht über das wissenschaftliche Symposion des 61. Bachfestes der Neuen Bachgesellschaft, Duisburg, 28.–30. Mai 1986,* edited by Christoph Wolff, 148–54. Kassel: Bärenreiter, 1988.

———. "Johann Matthesons Nachlaß zum Schicksal der Musiksammlung der alten Stadtbibliothek Hamburg." *Acta Musicologica* 55 (1983): 108–24.

Maul, Michael. *Bach's Famous Choir: The Saint Thomas School in Leipzig, 1212–1804.* Translated by Richard Howe. Woodbridge: Boydell, 2018.

———. *Barockoper in Leipzig (1693–1720).* 2 vols. Freiburg i.Br.: Rombach, 2009.

———. "Frühe Urteile über Johann Christoph und Johann Nikolaus Bach." BJ 90 (2004): 157–68.

———. "Neues zum Kontext einer musikalischen Debatte: Johann Adolph Scheibes Bach-Kritik." BACH *Magazin* 17 (2011): 9–11.

McCormick, Susan Rebecca. "Johann Christian Kittel and the Long Overlooked Multiple Bass Chorale Tradition." PhD diss., Queen's University Belfast, 2014.

McMullen, Dianne Marie. "The Geistreiches Gesangbuch of Johann Anastasius Freylinghausen (1670–1739): A German Pietist Hymnal." PhD diss., University of Michigan, 1987.

Meinhold, Wieland. "Der Mühlhauser Orgelbauer Johann Friedrich Wender und sein Wirken in Bereich des mitteldeutschen barocken Orgelbaus." In *Mühlhauser Beiträge zu Geschichte, Kulturgeschichte, Natur und Umwelt* 10 (1987), 36–41.

Melamed, Daniel. "Constructing Johann Christoph Bach (1642–1703)." *Music & Letters* 80 (1999): 345–65.

Messerli, Carlos R. "The 'Corona harmonica' (1610) of Christoph Demantius and the Gospel Motet." PhD diss., University of Iowa, 1974.

———. "Gospel Motet." In *Key Words in Church Music.* Rev. ed. Edited by Carl Schalk. St. Louis: Concordia Publishing House, 2004.

Miersemann, Wolfgang. "Erdmann Neumeisters 'Vorbericht' zu seinen 'Geistlichen Cantaten' von 1704: Ein literatur- und musikprogrammatisches 'Meister-Stück.'" In

Bibliography 371

Erdmann Neumeister (1671–1756): Wegbereiter der evangelischen Kirchenkantate, edited by Henrike Rucker, 51–74. Rudolstadt: Hain, 2000.

———. "Lieddichtung im Spannungsfeld zwischen Orthodoxie und Pietismus: Zu Erdmann Neumeisters Weißenfelser Kommunionbuch *Der Zugang zum Gnaden-Stuhl Jesu Christo*." In *Weißenfels als Ort literarischer und künstlerischer Kultur im Barockzeitalter*, edited by Roswitha Jacobsen, 177–216. Amsterdam: Rodopi, 1994.

Minear, Paul S. *The Bible and the Historian: Breaking the Silence about God in Biblical Studies*. Nashville: Abingdon, 2002.

———. "J. S. Bach and J. A. Ernesti: A Case Study in Exegetical and Theological Conflict." In *Our Common History as Christians: Essays in Honor of Albert C. Outler*, edited by John Deschner, 131–55. New York: Oxford University Press, 1975.

Neumann, Werner. *Auf den Lebenswegen Johann Sebastian Bachs*. Berlin: Verlag der Nation, 1962.

———. *Johann Sebastian Bach: Sämtliche Kantatentexte; unter Mitbenutzung von Rudolf Wustmans Ausg. der Bachschen Kirchenkantatentexte*. Leipzig: Breitkopf & Härtel, 1967.

———. *Sämtliche von Johann Sebastian Bach vertonte Texte*. Leipzig: VEB Deutscher Verlag für Musik, 1974.

The New Bach Reader: A Life of Johann Sebastian Bach in Letters and Documents. Edited by Hans T. David and Arthur Mendel. Revised and enlarged by Christoph Wolff. New York: Norton, 1998.

Nocent, Adrian. "The Roman Lectionary for Mass." In *Handbook for Liturgical Studies, III: The Eucharist*, edited by Anscar J. Chupungco, 177–83. Collegeville, Minn.: Liturgical Press, 1999.

Obst, Helmut. *Der Berliner Beichtstuhlstreit: Die Kritik des Pietismus an der Beichtpraxis der lutherischen Orthodoxie*. Witten: Luther, 1972.

Pachelbel, Johann. *Sämtliche Vokalwerk, 8: Concerti II*. Edited by Thomas Röder. Kassel: Bärenreiter, 2012.

Palisca, Claude. "The Genesis of Mattheson's Style Classification." In *New Mattheson Studies*, edited by George J. Buelow and Hans-Joachim Marx, 409–23. Cambridge: Cambridge University Press, 1983.

Paulsen, Friedrich. *Geschichte des gelehrten Unterrichts auf den deutschen Schulen und Universitäten vom Ausgang des Mittelalters bis zur Gegenwart, mit besonderer Rücksicht auf den klassischen Unterricht*. 3d ed. Leipzig: de Gruyter, 1919–1921. Reprint, Berlin: de Gruyter, 1965.

Pelikan, Jaroslav. *Bach Among the Theologians*. Philadelphia: Fortress Press, 1986.

Perreault, Jean M. *The Thematic Catalogue of the Musical Works of Johann Pachelbel*. Edited by Donna K. Fitch. Lanham, MD: Scarecrow, 2004.

Petzoldt, Martin. "Bach in theologischer Interaktion. Persönlichkeiten in seinem beruflichen Umfeld." In *Über Leben, Kunst und Kunstwerke: Aspekte musikalischer Biographie Johann Sebastian Bach im Zentrum*, edited by Christoph Wolff, 133–59. Leipzig: Evangelische Verlagsanstalt, 1999.

———. *Bach-Kommentar: theologisch-musikwissenschaftliche Kommentierung der geistlichen Vokalwerke Johann Sebastian Bachs*. Stuttgart: Internationale Bachakademie, 2004–2019.

———. *Bachs Leipziger Kinder: Dokumente von Johann Sebastian Bachs eigener Hand*. Leipzig: Evangelische Verlagsanstalt, 2008.

372 Bibliography

——. "Liturgie und Musik in den Leipziger Hauptkirchen." In *Die Welt der Bach-Kantaten, Bd. III: Johann Sebastian Bachs Leipziger Kirchenkantaten*, edited by Christoph Wolff, 69–93. Stuttgart: Metzler, 1998.

——. *Texte zur Leipziger Kirchen-Music: Zum Verständnis der Kantatentexte Johann Sebastian Bachs.* Wiesbaden: Breitkopf & Härtel, 1993.

——. "Thomasküster Rost, seine Familie und der Leipziger Gottesdienst zur Zeit Johann Sebastian Bachs." In *800 Jahre Thomana: Glauben, Singen, Lernen: Festschrift zum Jubiläum von Thomaskirche, Thomanerchor und Thomasschule*, edited by Stefan Altner and Martin Petzoldt, 163–81. Wettin-Löbejün: Stekovics, 2012.

——. "'Ut probus & doctus reddar.' Zum Anteil der Theologie bei der Schulausbildung Johann Sebastian Bachs in Eisenach, Ohrdruf und Lüneburg." BJ 71 (1985): 7–42.

——. "Zwischen Orthodoxie, Pietismus und Aufklärung: Überlegungen zum theologiegeschichtlichen Kontext Johann Sebastian Bachs." In *Johann Sebastian Bach und die Aufklärung*, ed. Reinhard Szeskus, 66–108. Leipzig: Breitkopf & Härtel, 1982.

Der Pietismus vom siebzehnten bis zum frühen achtzehnten Jahrhundert. Edited by Martin Brecht. Göttingen: Vandenhoeck & Ruprecht, 1993.

Der Pietismus im achtzehnten Jahrhundert. Edited by Martin Brecht and Klaus Deppermann. Göttingen: Vandenhoeck & Ruprecht, 1995.

Der Pietismus im neunzehnten und zwanzigsten Jahrhundert, Edited by Ulrich Gäbler. Göttingen: Vandenhoeck & Ruprecht, 2000.

Pietismus und Neuzeit: Ein Jahrbuch zur Geschichte des neueren Protestantismus. Göttingen: Vandenhoeck & Ruprecht, 1974–.

Pietists: Selected Writings. Edited by Peter C. Erb. New York: Paulist Press, 1983.

Pinson, Koppel S. *Pietism as a Factor in the Rise of German Nationalism.* New York: Columbia University Press, 1934.

Poetzsch-Seban, Ute. "Bach und Neumeister—Bach und Telemann." In *Telemann und Bach: Telemann-Beiträge*, edited by Brit Reipsch and Wolf Hobohm, Magdeburger Telemann-Studien, XVIII, 54–62. Hildesheim: Olms, 2005.

——. *Die Kirchenmusik von Georg Philipp Telemann und Erdmann Neumeister: Zur Geschichte der protestantischen Kirchenkantate in der ersten Hälfte des 18. Jahrhunderts.* Beeskow: Ortus, 2006.

——. "Telemanns Vertonungen von Texten aus Neumeisters Andachtsbuch 'Der Zugang zum Gnaden-Stuhl Jesu Christo.'" In *Erdmann Neumeister (1671–1756): Wegbereiter der evangelischen Kirchenkantate*, edited by Henrike Rucker, 135–45. Rudolstadt: Hain, 2000.

——. "Weitere Aspekte zu den Geistlichen Kantaten von Erdmann Neumeister." *Jahrbuch. Ständige Konferenz Mitteldeutsche Barockmusik in Sachsen, Sachsen-Anhalt und Thüringen, 2004* (2005): 343–47.

Preus, Robert D. *The Theology of Post-Reformation Lutheranism.* 2 vols. St. Louis: Concordia, 1970–1972.

Prinz, Ulrich. *Johann Sebastian Bachs Instrumentarium: Originalquellen, Besetzung, Verwendung.* Stuttgart: Internationale Bachakademie, 2005.

Quantz, Johann Joachim. *On Playing the Flute.* Translated and edited by Edward R. Reilly. 2d ed. Boston: Northeastern University Press, 2001.

Quintilian. *The Orator's Education.* Translated and edited by Donald A. Russell. Loeb Classical Library. Cambridge: Harvard University Press, 2001.

Rampe, Siegbert. *Carl Philipp Emanuel Bach und seine Zeit.* Laaber: Laaber Verlag, 2014.

Rathey, Markus. "Bach's Christmas Oratorio and the Mystical Theology of Bernard of Clairvaux." In *Bach and the Counterpoint of Religion*, edited by Robin A. Leaver, 84–103. Urbana: University of Illinois Press, 2018.

———. *Johann Rudolph Ahle 1625–1673: Lebensweg und Schaffen*. Eisenach: Wagner, 1999.

———. *Johann Sebastian Bach's Christmas Oratorio: Music Theology, Culture*. New York: Oxford University Press, 2016.

———. "Schools." In *The Routledge Companion to Johann Sebastian Bach*, edited by Robin A. Leaver, 116–41. New York: Routledge, 2017.

———. "Die Temperierung der Divi Blasii-Orgel in Mühlhausen." BJ 87 (2001): 163–71.

———. "Zur Datierung einiger Vokalwerke Bachs in den Jahren 1707 und 1708." BJ 92 (2006): 65–92.

Reckow, Fritz. "Zwischen Ontologie und Rhetorik: Die Idee des *movere animos* und der Übergang vom Spätmittelalter zur frühen Neuzeit in der Musikgeschichte." In *Traditionswandel und Traditionsverhalten*, edited by Walter Haug, 145–78. Tübingen: Niemeyer, 1991.

Remeš, Derek. "Thoroughbass Pedagogy Near Johann Sebastian Bach: Editions and Translations of Four Manuscript Sources." *Zeitschrift der Gesellschaft für Musiktheorie* 16/2 (2019): 95–165. [See also under Leaver, Robin A.]

Richter, B. F. "Stadtpfeifer und Alumnen der Thomasschule in Leipzig zu Bachs Zeit." BJ 4 (1907): 32–78.

Riemer, Otto. *Erhard Bodenschatz und sein Florilegium Portense*. Leipzig: Kistner & Siegel, 1928.

Rietschel, Georg. *Die Aufgabe der Orgel im Gottesdienste bis in das 18. Jahrhundert*. Leipzig: Dürr, 1893.

Rifkin, Joshua. "Siegesjubel und Satzfehler: Zum Problem von 'Nun ist das Heil und die Kraft' (BWV 50)." BJ 86 (2000): 67–86.

Rist, Johann. *Himmlische Lieder (1641/42)*. Edited by Johann Anselm Steiger. Berlin: Akademie-Verlag, 2012.

———. *Himmlische Lieder (1651)*. Edited by Johann Anselm Steiger and Konrad Küster. Berlin: Akademie-Verlag, 2013.

Ritschl, Albrecht. *Geschichte des Pietismus*. Bonn: Marcus, 1880–1886. Reprint, Berlin: de Gruyter, 1966.

Röbbelen, Ingeborg. *Theologie und Frömmigkeit im deutschen evangelisch-luthersichen Gesangbuch des 17. und frühen 18. Jahrhunderts*. Berlin: Evangelische Verlagsanstalt, 1957.

Robinson-Hammerstein, Helga. "Sächsische Jubelfreude." In *Die lutherische Konfessionalisierung in Deutschland: Wissenschaftliches Symposion des Vereins für Reformationsgeschichte 1988*, 460–94. Edited by Hans-Christoph Rublack. Gütersloh: Mohn, 1992.

Rollberg, Fritz. "Johann Christoph Bach, Organist zu Eisenach." *Zeitschrift für Musikwissenschaft* 11 (1928/29): 549–61.

Rößler, Martin. *Die Bibliographie der deutschen Liedpredigt*. Nieuwkoop: de Graaf, 1976.

———. "Die Frühzeit hymnologischer Forschung." *Jahrbuch für Liturgik und Hymnologie* 19 (1975): 123–86.

———. *Die Liedpredigt: Geschichte einer Predigtgattung*. Göttingen: Vandenhoeck & Ruprecht, 1976.

374 Bibliography

Rotermund, Hans-Martin. *Orthodoxie und Pietismus: Valentin Ernst Löschers "Timotheus verinus" in der Auseinandersetzung mit der Schule August Hermann Franckes*. Berlin: Evangelische Verlagsanstalt, 1959.

Routley, Eric. *Church Music and the Christian Faith*. Carol Stream, IL: Agapé, 1978.

Rucker, Henrike. "Kurze Lebensbeschreibung Erdmann Neumeisters." In *Erdmann Neumeister (1671–1756): Wegbereiter der evangelischen Kirchenkantate*, 19–23. Rudolstadt: Hain, 2000.

Ruf, Wolfgang. "The Courts of Saxony-Weißenfels, Saxony-Merseburg, and Saxony-Zeitz." In *Music at German Courts, 1715–1760: Changing Artistic Priorities*, edited by Samantha Owens, Barbara M. Reul, and Janice B. Stockigt, 223–55. Woodbridge: Boydell, 2011.

Sailhamer, John H. "Johann August Ernesti: The Role of History in Biblical Interpretation." *Journal of the Evangelical Theological Society* 44/2 (2001): 193–206.

Saunders, Zoe. "Hidden Meaning in Agnus Dei Canons: Two Cases from the Alamire Manuscripts." *Early Music* 44 (2017): 593–606.

Schade, Herwarth von. *"Geld ist der Hamburger ihr Gott": Erdmann Neumeisters Briefe an Valentin Ernst Löscher*. Herzberg: Bautz, 1998.

Scheibel, Gottfried Ephraim. "Random Thoughts about Church Music in Our Day (1721)." Translated by Joyce Irwin. In *Bach's Changing World: Voices in the Community*, edited by Carol Baron, 227–49. Rochester: University of Rochester Press, 2006.

Scheide, William H. "'Nun ist das Heil und die Kraft' BWV 50: Doppelchörigkeit, Datierung und Bestimmung." BJ 68 (1982): 81–96.

———. "Nochmals BWV 50 'Nun ist das Heil und die Kraft.'" BJ 87 (2001): 117–30.

Scheidt, Samuel. *Das Görlitzer Tabulaturbuch vom Jahre 1650*. Edited by Christhard Mahrenholz. New York: Peters, 1940.

Scheitler, Irmgard. "Zwei weitere frühe Drucke von Neumeisters *Geistlichen Cantaten*." *Jahrbuch. Ständige Konferenz Mitteldeutsche Barockmusik in Sachsen, Sachsen-Anhalt und Thüringen, 2003* (2005): 365–67.

Schelle, Johann. *Six Chorale Cantatas*. Edited by Mary S. Morris. Recent Researches in the Music of the Baroque Era, 60–61. Madison: A-R Editions, 1988.

Schering, Arnold. *Johann Sebastian Bach und das Musikleben Leipzigs im 18. Jahrhundert, Der Musikgeschichte Leipzig Dritter Band, Das Zeitalter Johann Sebastian Bachs und Johann Adam Hillers (von 1723 bis 1800)*. Leipzig: Siegel, 1941.

———. *Johann Sebastian Bachs Leipziger Kirchenmusik*. Leipzig: Breitkopf & Härtel, 1936.

Schindel, Ulrich. "Johann Matthias Gesners aufgeklärte Pädagogik." In *Musik, Kunst und Wissenschaft im Zeitalter J. S. Bachs*, edited by Ulrich Leisinger and Christoph Wolff, Leipziger Beiträge zur Bach-Forschung, 7, 39–49. Hildesheim: Olms, 2005.

Schmeling, Timothy, ed. *Lives and Writings of the Great Fathers of the Lutheran Church*. St. Louis: Concordia, 2016.

Schmid, Heinrich. *Die Geschichte des Pietismus*. Nordlingen: Beck, 1863. Translated by James L. Langebartels, *History of Pietism*. Milwaukee: Northwestern, 2007.

Schmidt, Eberhard. *Der Gottesdienst am Kurfürstlichen Hofe zu Dresden*. Berlin: Evangelische Verlagsanstalt, 1961.

Schmiedecke, Adolf. "Zur Geschichte der Weißenfelser Hofkapelle." *Die Musikforschung* (1961): 416–23.

Bibliography 375

Schneiderheinze, Armin. "'Christ lag in Todes Banden': Überlegungen zur Datierung von BWV 4." In *Das Frühwerk Johann Sebastian Bachs: Kolloquium, Rostock, 11.–13. September 1990*, 267–79. Cologne: Studio, 1995.

Schröder, Dorothea. "Die Organisten der Hauptkirche St. Jacobi." In *Die Arp Schnitger-Orgel der Hauptkirche St. Jacobi in Hamburg*, 67–93. Edited by Heimo Reinitzer. Hamburg: Christians, 1995.

Schröder, Hans. *Lexikon der hamburgischen Schriftsteller bis zur Gegenwart*. Hamburg: Verein für hamburgische Geschichte, 1851–1883.

Schubart, Christoph. "Anna Magdalena Bach: Neue Beiträge zu ihrer Herkunft und ihren Jugendjahren." BJ 40 (1953): 29–50.

Schulenberg, David L. "Missing Spitta Manuscript Found." *The American Bach Society Newsletter* (Fall 1998): 6–7.

Schulze, Hans-Joachim. "Anna Magdalena Bachs 'Herzens Freündin.' Neues über die Beziehungen zwischen den Familien Bach und Böse." BJ 83 (1997): 151–54.

———. *Bach-Facetten: Essays, Studien, Miszellen*. Leipzig: Evangelische Verlagsanstalt; Stuttgart: Carus, 2017.

———. *Die Bach-Kantaten: Einführungen zu sämtlichen Kantaten Johann Sebastian Bachs*. Leipzig: Evangelische Verlagsanstalt, 2006.

———. "'Fließende Leichtigkeit' und 'arbeitsame Vollstimmigkeit': Georg Philipp Telemann und die Musikerfamilie Bach." In *Telemann und seine Freunde: Kontakte—Einflüsse—Auswirkungen*, 34–40. Magdeburg: Zentrum für Telemann-Pflege und -Forschung, 1986.

———. "Johann Christoph Bach (1671–1721), 'Organist und Schul Collega in Ohrdruf,' Johann Sebastian Bachs erster Lehrer." BJ 71 (1985): 55–81.

———. "Johann Friedrich Schweinitz, 'A Disciple of the Famous Herr Bach in Leipzig.'" In *About Bach*, edited by Gregory G. Butler, George B. Stauffer, and Mary Dalton Greer, 81–88. Urbana: University of Illinois Press, 2008.

———. "Johann Sebastian Bachs Kanonwidmungen." BJ 53 (1967): 82–92.

———. "Parody and Text Quality in the Vocal Works of J. S. Bach." In *Compositional Choices and Meaning in the Vocal Music of J. S. Bach*, edited by Mark A. Peters and Reginald L. Saunders, 167–76. Lanham, MD: Lexington, 2018.

———. "The Parody Process in Bach's Music: An Old Problem Reconsidered." BACH 20 (Spring 1989): 7–21.

———. "Rätselhafte Auftragswerke Johann Sebastian Bachs: Anmerkung zu einigen Kantatentexten." BJ 96 (2010): 69–93.

———. "Reformationsfest und Reformationsjubiläen im Schaffen Johann Sebastian Bach." *Bach-fest Buch* [Leipzig] 64 (1989).

———. ed. *Die Thomasschule Leipzig zur zeit Johann Sebastian Bachs: Ordnungen und Gesetze 1634, 1723, 1733*. Leipzig: Zentral-antiquariat, 1987.

———. "Wege und Irrwege: Erdmann Neumeister und die Bach-Forschung." In *Bach-Facetten*, 403–409. Leipzig: Evangelische Verlagsanstalt, 2017.

Schweitzer, Albert. *J. S. Bach*. Translated by Ernest Newman. London: Black, 1962.

Schwenkedel, Suzy. *La Tablature de Weimar Johann Pachelbel et son école ... 79 fugues et chorals en basse chiffrée*. Arras: Anfol, 1993.

Serauky, Walter. *Musikgeschichte der Stadt Halle*. Halle: Buchhandlung des Waisenhauses, 1935–1943. Reprint, Hildesheim: Olms, 1971.

Shantz, Douglas H., ed. *A Companion to German Pietism, 1660–1800*. Leiden: Brill, 2015.

376   *Bibliography*

——. *An Introduction to German Pietism: Protestant Renewal at the Dawn of Modern Europe*. Baltimore: Johns Hopkins University Press, 2013.

Silberborth, Hans. *Geschichte des Nordhäuser Gymnasiums*. Nordhausen: Wimmer, 1923.

Sixteenth-Century Biographies of Martin Luther. Edited by Christopher Boyd Brown. LW Companion Volume. St. Louis: Concordia, 2018.

Smend, Friedrich. *Bach in Köthen*. Translated by John Page. Edited by Stephen Daw. St. Louis: Concordia Publishing House, 1985.

——. *Bach in Köthen*. Berlin: Christlicher Zeitschriftenverlag, 1951.

Snyder, Kerala. *Dieterich Buxtehude: Organist in Lübeck,* 2d ed. Rochester: University of Rochester Press, 2007.

——. "Tradition with Variations: Chorale Settings *per omnes versus* by Buxtehude and Bach." In *Music and Theology: Essays in Honor of Robin A. Leaver*, edited by Daniel Zager, 31–50. Lanham, MD: Scarecrow, 2007.

Spagnoli, Gina. *Letters and Documents of Heinrich Schütz 1656–1672: An Annotated Translation*. Ann Arbor: UMI Research Press, 1990.

Spener, Philipp Jakob. *Pia desideria*. Translated and edited by Theodore G. Tappert. Philadelphia: Fortress, 1964.

Spitta, Philipp. *Johann Sebastian Bach*. Leipzig: Breitkopf & Härtel, 1873–1880. Reprint, Wiesbaden: Breitkopf & Härtel, 1964.

——. *Johann Sebastian Bach: His Work and Influence on the Music of Germany, 1685–1750*. Translated by Clara Bell and J. A. Fuller-Maitland. London: Novello, 1884. Reprint, New York: Dover, 1951.

Sposato, Jeffrey S. *Leipzig after Bach: Church and Concert Life in a German City*. New York: Oxford University Press, 2018.

Steiger, Lothar and Renate Steiger. *Sehet! Wir gehn hinauf gen Jerusalem. Johann Sebastian Bachs Kantaten auf den Sonntag Estomihi*. Göttingen: Vandenhoeck & Ruprecht, 1992.

Steiger, Renate. "J. S. Bachs Gebetbuch? Ein Fund am Rande einer Ausstellung." *Musik und Kirche* 55 (1985): 231–34.

Stein, Klaus. "Stammt 'Nun ist das Heil und die Kraft' (BWV 50) von J. S. Bach?" BJ 85 (1999): 51–66.

Stevenson, Robert M. "Bach's Quarrel with the Rector of the St. Thomas School." In *Patterns of Protestant Church Music*, 67–77. Durham: Duke University Press, 1953.

Stiller, Günther. *Johann Sebastian Bach and Liturgical Life in Leipzig*. Translated by Herbert J. A. Bouman, et al. Edited by Robin A. Leaver. St. Louis: Concordia Publishing House, 1984.

——. *Johann Sebastian Bach und das Leipziger gottesdienstliche Leben seiner Zeit*. Berlin: Evangelische Verlagsanstalt, 1970.

Stinson, Russell. *Bach: The Orgelbüchlein*. New York: Schirmer, 1996.

——. "The Compositional History of Bach's *Orgelbüchlein* Reconsidered." In *Bach Perspectives I*, 43–78. Edited by Russell Stinson. Lincoln: University of Nebraska Press, 1995.

——. "Some Thoughts on Bach's Neumeister Chorales." *Journal of Musicology* 9 (1991): 455–77.

Stoeffler, F. Ernest. *German Pietism during the Eighteenth Century*. Leiden: Brill 1973.

——. *The Rise of Evangelical Pietism*. Leiden: Brill, 1965.

Stolt, Birgit. *Martin Luthers Rhetorik des Herzens*. Tübingen: Mohr Siebeck, 2000.

Stopp, E. J. "Verbum Domini Manet in Aeternum: The Dissemination of a Reformation Slogan 1522–1904." *Lutheran Quarterly* 1 (1987): 54–71.

Strohm, Reinhard. *Dramma per Musica: Italian Opera Seria of the Eighteenth Century*. New Haven: Yale University Press, 1997.

Strunk, Oliver. *Source Readings in Music History*. Rev. ed. Edited by Leo Treitler. New York: Norton, 1998.

Terry, Charles Sanford. *Bach Chorals. Part III. The Hymns and Hymn Melodies of the Organ Works*. Cambridge: Cambridge University Press, 1921.

———. *Joh. Seb. Bach Cantata Texts Sacred and Secular, With a Reconstruction of the Leipzig Liturgy of his Period*. 1926. Reprint, London: Holland, 1964.

Thoburn, Crawford R. "Pachelbel's *Christ lag in Todesbanden*: A Possible Influence on Bach's Work." *American Choral Review* 19/1 (January 1977): 3–16.

Tholuck, August. *Der Geist der lutherischen Theologen Wittenbergs im Verlaufe des 17. Jahrhunderts*. Hamburg: Perthes, 1852.

———. *Geschichte des Rationalismus, Erste Abtheilung: Geschichte des Pietismus und des ersten Stadiums der Aufklärung*. Berlin: Wiegandt und Grieben, 1865. Reprint, Aalen: Scientia-Verlag, 1970.

Tovey, Donald Francis. *Essays in Musical Analysis*. 7 vols. London: Oxford University Press, 1935–1944.

Treu, Martin. "Luther's Posting of the Ninety-five Theses: Much Ado about Nothing?" In *Martin Luther and the Reformation: Essays*, 92–97. Edited by Katrin Herbst. Dresden: Sandstein, 2016.

Unger, Hans-Heinrich. *Die Beziehung zwischen Musik und Rhetorik im 16.–18. Jahrhundert*. 1941. Reprint, Hildesheim: Olms, 2000.

Unger, Melvin P. *Handbook to Bach's Sacred Cantata Texts: An Interlinear Translation with Reference Guide to Biblical Quotations and Allusions*. Lanham, MD: Scarecrow, 1996.

Vickers, Brian. "Figures of Rhetoric/Figures of Music?" *Rhetorica: A Journal of the History of Rhetoric* 2 (1984):1–44.

Vogelsänger, Siegfried. "Michael Praetorius: Festmusiken zu zwei Ereignissen des Jahres 1617: Zum Kaiserbesuch in Dresden und zur Jahrhundertfeier der Reformation." *Die Musikforschung* 40 (1987): 97–109.

Vogt, Gisela. "Die Musikerfamilie Bach in Thuringen." In *Der junge Bach: weil er nicht aufzuhalten … Begleitbuch*, edited by Reinmar Emans, 108–10. Erfurt: Erste Thüringer Landesausstellung, 2000.

Vormbaum, Reinhold, ed. *Die evangelischen Schulordnungen des achtzehnten Jahrhunderts*. Gütersloh: Bertelsmann, 1864.

Wackernagel, Philipp. *Bibliographie zur Geschichte des Deutschen Kirchenlieds*. Frankfurt: Hender & Zimmer, 1855. Reprint, Hildesheim: Olms, 1961.

Wallmann, Johannes. "Erdmann Neumeister, der letzte orthodoxe Gegner des Pietismus." In *Erdmann Neumeister (1671–1756): Wegbereiter der evangelischen Kirchenkantate*, edited by Henrike Rucker, 27–37. Rudolstadt: Hain, 2000.

———. "Johann Arndt und die protestantische Frömmigkeit: Zur Rezeption der mittelalterlichen Mystik im Luthertum." In *Frömmigkeit in der frühen Neuzeit: Studien zur religiösen Literatur des 17. Jahrhunderts in Deutschland*, edited by Dieter Breuer, 50–74. Amsterdam: Rodopi, 1984.

———. "Johann Sebastian Bach und die 'Geistlicher Bücher' seiner Bibliothek." *Pietismus und Neuzeit* 12 (1986): 162–81.

378 *Bibliography*

———. "Neues Licht auf die Zeit Johann Sebastian Bachs in Mühlhausen. Zu den Anfängen des Pietismus in Thüringen." *Pietismus und Neuzeit* 35 (2009): 46–114.

Weber, Edmund. *Johann Arndts vier Bücher vom Wahren Christentum als Beitrag zur protestantischen Irenik des 17. Jahrhunderts: Eine quellenkritische Untersuchung*. 3d ed. Hildesheim: Gerstenberg, 1978.

Weimar und die Reformation: Luthers Obrigkeitslehre und ihre Wirkungen. Edited by Christopher Spehr, Michael Haspel, and Wolfgang Holler. Leipzig: Evangelische Verlagsanstalt, 2016.

Welter, Kathryn. "A Master Teacher Revealed: Johann Pachelbel's *Deutliche Anweisung*." In *About Bach*, edited by Gregory Butler, George B. Stauffer, and Mary Dalton Greer, 3–13. Urbana: University of Illinois Press, 2008.

Werner, Arno. *Städtische und fürstliche Musikpflege in Weissenfels bis zum Ende des 18. Jahrhunderts*. Leipzig: Breitkopf & Härtel, 1911.

Whittaker, William G. *Fugitive Notes on Certain Cantatas and the Motets of J. S. Bach*. London: Oxford University Press, 1924.

Wieckowski, Alexander. *Evangelische Beichtstuhle in Sachsen*. Beucha: Sax, 2005.

———. "Evangelische Privatbeichte und Beichtstühle. Beobachtungen zu einem fast vergessenen Kapitel lutherischer Frömmigkeitsgeschichte in Leipzig und Umgebung." In *Stadtgeschichte: Mitteilungen des Leipziger Geschichtsvereins, Jahrbuch 2006*, edited by Markus Cottin, Detlef Döring, and Cathrin Friedrich, 67–108. Beucha: Sax, 2012.

Wiegand, Fritz. "Die Arnstädter Bache." In *Arnstädter Bachbuch: Johann Sebastian Bach und seine Verwandten in Arnstadt*, edited by Karl Müller and Fritz Wiegand, 23–57. 2d ed. Arnstadt: Arbeitsgemeinschaft für Bachpflege im Kulturbund Arnstadt, 1957.

Wilhelmi, Thomas. "Bachs Bibliothek: Eine Weiterführung der Arbeit von Hans Preuss." *BJ* 65 (1979): 107–29.

Williams, Peter. *Bach: A Musical Biography*. Cambridge: Cambridge University Press, 2016.

———. *The Organ Music of J. S. Bach*. 2d ed. Cambridge: Cambridge University Press, 2003.

Wojnar, William Anthony. "Hieronymus Florentinus Quehl: 205 Chorale Fugues: Transcription and Commentary." PhD diss., University of Iowa, 1995.

Wolff, Christoph. "The Agnus Dei of the B Minor Mass: Parody and New Composition Reconciled." In *Bach: Essays on His Life and Music*, 332–39. Cambridge: Harvard University Press, 1991.

———. "Bach's Audition for the St. Thomas Cantorate: The Cantata 'Du wahrer Gott und Davids Sohn.'" In *Bach: Essays on His Life and Music*, 128–40. Cambridge: Harvard University Press, 1991.

———. *Bach's Musical Universe: The Composer and His Work*. New York: Norton. 2020.

———. "Chronology and Style in the Early Works: A Background for the Orgel-Büchlein." In *Bach: Essays on His Life and Music*, 297–305. Cambridge: Harvard University Press, 1991.

———. *Johann Sebastian Bach: The Learned Musician*. "Updated Edition." New York: Norton, 2013.

———. *The Neumeister Collection of Chorale Preludes from the Bach Circle (Yale University Library LM 4708): A Facsimile Edition*. New Haven: Yale University Press, 1986.

Bibliography 379

——. "Die Rastrierungen in den Originalhandschriften Joh. Seb. Bach und ihre Bedeutung für die diplomatische Quellenkritik." In *Festschrift für Friedrich Smend zum 70. Geburtstag*, 80–92. Berlin: Merseburger, 1963.

——. *Der Stile Antico in der Musik Johann Sebastian Bachs: Studien zu Bachs Spätwerk*. Wiesbaden: Steiner, 1968.

——. "Zum Quellenwert der Neumeister-Sammlung: Bachs Orgelchoral 'Der Tag der ist so freudenreich' BWV 719." BJ 83 (1997): 155–67.

Wolff, Christoph and Markus Zepf. *The Organs of Johann Sebastian Bach: A Handbook*. Translated by Lynn Edwards Butler. Urbana: University of Illinois Press, 2012.

Wollny, Peter. "Dokumente und Erläuterungen zum Wirken Johann Elias Bachs in Schweinfurt (1743–1755)." *Die Briefentwürfe des Johann Elias Bach (1705–1755)*, edited by Evelin Odrich and Peter Wollny. 2d ed. Hildesheim: Olms, 2005.

——. "Fundstucke zur Lebensgeschichte Johann Sebastian Bachs 1744–1750." BJ 97 (2011): 35–50.

——. "Über die Hintergründe von Johann Sebastian Bachs Bewerbung in Arnstadt." BJ 91 (2005): 83–94.

Wustmann, Rudolf. *Joh. Seb. Bachs Kantatentexte*. Veröffentlichungen der Neuen Bachgesellschaft, Jahrgang 14, Heft 1. Leipzig: Breitkopf & Härtel, 1913.

Yearsley, David. *Bach and the Meanings of Counterpoint*. Cambridge: Cambridge University Press, 2002.

Zehnder, Jean-Claude. *Der frühen Werke Johann Sebastian Bachs*. Basel: Schwabe, 2009.

Ziller, Ernst. *Der Erfurter Organist Johann Heinrich Buttstädt (1666–1727)*. Kassel: Bärenreiter, 1935.

Zirnbauer, Heinz. *Der Notenbestand der Reichsstädtisch Nürnbergischen Ratsmusik: Eine bibliographische Rekonstruktion*. Nuremberg: Stadtbibliothek, 1959.

Zohn, Steven. *Music for a Mixed Taste: Style, Genre, and Meaning in Telemann's Instrumental Works*. New York: Oxford University Press, 2008.

Index

Abicht, Johann Georg 210
Ach Gott, wie manches Herzeleid (BWV 58) 117
Adlung, Jacob 204
affectus exprimere 102
affectus movere 102
Affektenlehre 100–102
Agnus Dei: Bach's *Estomihi* cantatas 53–59; Bach's settings of 49–66; in the B-minor Mass 63–66; combined with *Kyrie* 59–60; German 41, 51, 54–56, 58–59, 61, 62, 71; in the *Hauptgottesdienst* 41; historical context 49; in Lutheran eucharistic theology 50–53; in the Roman Mass 49, 53; Tone I 52; visual representation of 63; *see also* hymns, *Christe, du Lamm Gottes*; hymns, *O Lamm Gottes, unschuldig*
Agricola, Johann Friedrich 270
Ahle, Johann Georg 243, 294
Ahle, Johann Rudolf 165, 190, 243
Allerheiligenkirche (Wittenberg) 328
Alles, was von Gott geboren (BWV 80a) 153
Ammon, Christoph 263
Angela of Foligno 225
Apostolic Creed 316
Arfken, Ernst 152, 153
Ärgre dich, o Seele, nicht (BWV 186a) 153
Arndt, Johann 223, 226
Arnstadt, Bach in 6, 121, 125–26, 127, 131–36, 142, 144, 148, 149, 155–56, 214, 243, 293–94, 333
Arnstädtisches Gesangbuch 142, 146
Arnstädtisches Verbessertes Gesangbuch 125
Ascension Oratorio (BWV 11) 63–64

Athanasian Creed 316
atonement 73–74
Augsburg Confession 227–28, 308, 328, 331
Aulén, Gustaf 73
Aus der Tiefen rufe ich (BWV 131) 243, 286
Axmacher, Elke 226

Bach, Anna Magdalena 83–84, 136, 212, 239, 297–98
Bach, Carl Philipp Emanuel 270, 294, 295–96, 300
Bach, Catharina Dorothea 243, 294
Bach, Christiana Benedicta 246
Bach, Heinrich 122, 131, 171
Bach, Johann Ambrosius 173
Bach, Johann August Abraham 256
Bach, Johann Christian 256
Bach, Johann Christoph (brother of Sebastian) 122, 173, 180
Bach, Johann Christoph (cousin of Sebastian's father) 173–75, 180, 181, 343; chorale preludes 177
Bach, Johann Elias 113
Bach, Johann Gottfried Bernhard 291
Bach, Johann Michael 171, 294; chorale preludes 177
Bach, Johann Sebastian: in Arnstadt 6, 121, 125–26, 127, 131–36, 142, 144, 148, 149, 155–56, 214, 243, 293–94, 333; books in library 11–14, 338–39, 344; books of collected sermons 304–5; chorale preludes 177; collaboration with librettists 113–16; compared to Handel 15; conflict with Ernesti 259–64, 273; in Cöthen 56, 104–5, 107, 151, 167–68, 249, 270, 297–98, 301–2, 303, 341–42; in

Index 381

Hamburg 299–303; in Leipzig 6, 22–26, 35, 39–41, 46–48, 55, 56–57, 59, 61, 66, 71, 76, 83, 92, 104, 106, 107, 116, 134, 137–38, 146, 147, 184–85, 187, 212, 216, 233, 244–45, 247, 248, 251–52, 256, 265, 267, 296, 298–99, 308, 310, 313; librettists 107–13; in Mühlhausen 6, 136, 138, 144, 148, 155, 165, 243–44, 286, 294, 333; and Olearius 121–36; parody process of 67–82; and Pietism 219–22, 225–26, 243–47; in Sangerhausen 291–92; and the Schemelli *Gesangbuch* 194–96, 211–14; and the "*theatralische Stil*" 104–7; and the traditional chorale 193–202; use of *stile antico* 67; in Weimar 6, 57, 60, 61, 63, 71, 104–6, 107, 142, 152–55, 168, 240, 244, 249, 270, 292–97, 333, 336, 341–42; at Weissenfels 291–99
Bach, Maria Barbara 294, 297
Bach, Wilhelm Friedemann 294
Bach-Gesellschaft, cantatas in 15–16
Bach-Werke-Verzeichnis (BWV) 15
Baird, William 262–63
Barfüsserkirche (Arnstadt) 130, 131
Bassani, Giovanni Battista 35
Becker, Carl Ferdinand 167
Bekennen will ich seinen Namen (BWV 200) 233
Benediction 42, 46
Benedictus 39
Berben, Léon 153
Bereitet die Wege, bereitet die Bahn (BWV 132) 153
Bernard of Clairvaux (saint) 188, 191, 223, 225
Bernhard, Christoph 190
Birkmann, Christoph 116–17
Birnbaum, Johann Abraham 116
Blakenburg, Walter 193, 226
Blasiuskirche (Mühlhausen) 139, 165, 190, 243, 294
B-minor Mass (BWV 232) 147; *Agnus Dei* 63–66, 76; *Confiteor* 65; *Credo* 71; *Crucifixus* 57, 70; *Domine Deus* 65; *Dona nobis pacem* 66, 76; *Gloria* 64–65, 68; use of trumpets in 79
Bodenschatz, Erhard 29, 30, 47
Böhm, Georg 180
Bonifatiuskirche (Arnstadt) 121–22
Braun, Werner 29
Briegel, Wolfgang Carl 20

Brockes Passion (Telemann) 88
Buddeus, Johann Franz 249
Bugenhagen, Johannes 329, 344
Burmeister, Joachim 101
Buszin, Walter 193–94
Butler, Gregory 194
Buttstedt (Buttstett), Johann Andreas 257
Buttstett, Johann Heinrich 94–95, 114–15, 171
Buxtehude, Dieterich 125, 148–49, 180, 222; *Jesu, Meine Freude* 139

Calov, Abraham 210, 245
Calvisius, Sethus 101
Calvör, Caspar 246
Canonic Variations on *Vom Himmel hoch* (BWV 769) 57–58
Cantata (Anh. 1) (*Gesegnet ist die Zuversicht*) 19, 210, 256
Cantata (Anh. 5) (*Lobet den Herrn, alle seine Heerscharen*) 105
Cantata (Anh. 6) (*Dich loben die lieblichen Strahlen der Sonne*) 105
Cantata (Anh. 7) (*Heut ist gewiss ein guter Tag*) 105
Cantata 1 (*Wie schön leuchtet der Morgenstern*) 233
Cantata 4 (*Christ lag in Todesbanden*) 74, 137–49; chiastic structure 146; comparisons of metrical stress patterns 144; extant parts 138–39; first performances 137–39, 148; Olearius on 144–46; structure of 146–49; textual variations 139–44
Cantata 7 (*Christ unser Herr zum Jordan kam*) 233
Cantata 11 (*Lobet Gott in seinen Reichen*) 183
Cantata 12 (*Weinen, Klagen, Sorgen, Zagen*) 70–71
Cantata 18 (*Gleichwie der Regen und Schnee vom Himmel fällt*) 106, 153, 295
Cantata 19 (*Es erhub sich ein Streit*) 110–11, 234, 343
Cantata 20 (*O Ewigkeit, du Donnerwort*) 183
Cantata 21 (*Ich hatte viel Bekümmernis*) 301
Cantata 22 (*Jesus nahm zu sich die Zwölfe*) 54–55
Cantata 23 (*Du wahrer Gott und Davids Sohn*) 53–58, 61

382 Index

Cantata 24 (*Ein ungefärbt Gemüte*) 106, 296

Cantata 25 (*Es ist nichts Gesundes an meinem Liebe*) 106, 240, 346–47

Cantata 27 (*Wer weiß wie nahe mir mein Ende?*) 86, 113

Cantata 28 (*Gottlob! nun geht das Jahr zu Ende*) 106, 296

Cantata 29 (*Wir danken dir*) 66

Cantata 30 (*Freue dich, erlöste Schar*) 233, 347

Cantata 31 (*Der Himmel lacht! Die Erde jubilieret*) 153

Cantata 36c (*Schwingt freudig euch empor*) 255–56

Cantata 43 (*Gott fähret auf mit Jauchzen*) 75, 183

Cantata 49 (*Ich geh und suche mit Verlangen*) 117

Cantata 51 (*Jauchzet Gott in allen Landen*) 86

Cantata 52 (*Falsche Welt, dir trau ich nicht*) 117

Cantata 54 (*Widerstehe doch der Sünde*) 105, 295

Cantata 55 (*Ich armer Mensch, ich Sündenknecht*) 113, 117

Cantata 56 (*Ich will den Kreuzstab gerne tragen*) 117

Cantata 58 (*Ach Gott, wie manches Herzeleid*) 117

Cantata 59 (*Wer mich liebet, der wird mein Wort halten*) 106, 296

Cantata 60 (*O Ewigkeit, du Donnerwort*)183, 190

Cantata 61/62 (*Nun komm, der Heiden Heiland*) 29, 76, 106, 295, 200

Cantata 63 (*Christen, ätzet diesen Tag*) 333–36

Cantata 65 (*Sie werden aus Saba alle kommen*) 233

Cantata 66a (*Der Himmel dacht auf Anhalts Ruhm und Glück*) 105

Cantata 67 (*Halt im Gedächtnis Jesum Christ*) 71–73, 76–77; compared to BWV 234 79, 81; discarded "Corno" part 80; similarities to BWV 158 and BWV 234 78

Cantata 70a (*Wachet! betet! betet! wachet!*) 153

Cantata 71 (*Gott ist mein König*) 139

Cantata 79 (*Gott der Herr ist Sonn und Schild*) 306–7, 328

Cantata 80a (*Alles, was von Gott geboren*) 153

Cantata 80 (*Ein feste Burg ist unser Gott*) 328

Cantata 82 (*Ich habe genung*) 83–85, 113, 116, 117, 233

Cantata 83 (*Erfreute Zeit im neuen Bunde*) 233

Cantata 98 (*Was Gott tut, das ist wohlgetan*) 117

Cantata 106 (*Gottes Zeit ist die allerbeste Zeit*) 20, 135–36

Cantata 123 (*Liebster Immanuel, Herzog der frommen*) 233

Cantata 125 (*Mit Fried und Freud ich fahr dahin*) 233

Cantata 127 (*Herr Jesu Christ, wahr Mensch und Gott*) 53–54, 58–59, 153

Cantata 130 (*Herr Gott, dich loben alle wir*) 234

Cantata 131 (*Aus der Tiefen rufe ich*) 243, 286

Cantata 132 (*Bereitet die Wege, bereitet die Bahn*) 153

Cantata 134a (*Die Zeit, die Tag und Jahre macht*) 105

Cantata 147a (*Herz und Mund und Tat und Leben*) 153

Cantata 149 (*Man singet mit Freuden vom Sieg*) 234

Cantata 150 (*Nach dir, Herr, verlanget mich*) 139

Cantata 152 (*Tritt auf die Glaubensbahn*) 153

Cantata 155 (*Mein Gott, wie lang, ach lange?*) 153

Cantata 157 (*Ich lasse dich nicht*) 105, 233

Cantata 158 (*Der Friede sei mit dir*) 76–78, 153, 233

Cantata 159 (*Sehet, wir gehn hinauf gen Jerusalem*) 54

Cantata 161 (*Komm, du süße Todesstunden*) 233

Cantata 164 (*Ihr, die ihr euch von Christo nennet*) 153

Cantata 165 (*O heiliges Geist und Wasserbad*) 153

Cantata 167 (*Ihr Menschen, rühmet Gottes Liebe*) 233

Cantata 168 (*Tue Rechnung! Donnerwort*) 153

Index 383

Cantata 169 (*Gott soll allein mein Herze haben*) 117
Cantata 172 (*Erschallet, ihr Lieder, erklinget, ihr Saiten!*) 153
Cantata 182 (BWV 182) (*Himmelskönig sei willkommen*) 153, 233
Cantata 186a (*Ärgre dich, o Seele, nicht*) 153
Cantata 199 (*Mein Herze schwimmt im Blut*) 153
Cantata 200 (*Bekennen will ich seinen Namen*) 233
Cantata 204 (*Ich bin in mir vergnügt*) 107, 109–10
Cantata 208 (*Was mir behagt, ist nur die muntre Jagd*) 294
Cantata 210a (*O! Angenehme Melodie*) 299
Cantata 214 (*Tönet, ihr Pauken!*) 85, 153
Cantata 249a (*Entfliehet, verschwindet, entweichet, ihr sorgen*) 294
cantatas: for Advent Sunday 295; anonymous libretti 109; arranged by sequence of church year 16; chorale cantatas 134; chorales in the early cantatas 154; development of 19–21; in the eighteenth century 83–117; *Estomihi* cantatas 53–59; function of 21; in the *Hauptgottesdienst* 35–36, 39, 44; libretti 84–87, 90–91, 107–17, 240, 244; libretti from three printed sources 108; libretti from two printed sources 108; and the liturgical year 3–21; in Lutheran worship 67–82, 286–89; numbering of 15; for Reformation festivals 306, 328, 333–36; sequence between Epiphany 2 and Annunciation 44; for Sexagesima 295; for St John the Baptist's Day 233; for St. Michael's Day 234, 343; in the *Vespergottesdienst* 44–45; for the Visitation 233; *see also Christmas Oratorio* (BWV 248)
Carpzov, Christiana Benedicta 246
Carpzov, Johann Benedict 127, 128, 135
Carpzov, Johann Benedikt II 245–46
Carpzov, Johann Gottlob 244, 245–46
Carpzov, Samuel Benedikt 245
Catechismus Examen 46–47
Chemnitz, Martin 338
choirs 24–25
Choralbücher 166–70, 177, 205; *Neu vermehrtes Darmstädtisches*

Choral-Buch 206; *see also Gesangbücher*
chorale fugues 171, 174–76, 181
chorale preludes 40, 46, 151; *Aus tiefer Not schrei ich zu dir* (BWV 686) 319–20; *Aus tiefer Not schrei ich zu dir* (BWV 687) 323–24; *Christ unser Herr zum Jordan kam* (BWV 684) 319; *Christ unser Herr zum Jordan kam* (BWV 685) 323; *Der Tag der ist so freudenreich* (BWV 719) 174; *Dies sind die heil'gen zehn Gebot* (BWV 678) 317; *Dies sind die heil'gen zehn Gebot* (BWV 679) 322–23; "Gospel" preludes (BWV 684, 688) 322; *Herr Christ, der einig Gotts Sohn* (BWV 601a/601) 178; *Herr Gott, dich loben wir* (BWV 725) 342–43; *Herr Gott, nun schleuss den Himmel auf* (BWV 1092) 180; *Ich ruf zu dir Herr Jesu Christ* (BWV 639a/639) 178; *Jesus Christus unser Heiland, der von uns* (BWV 688) 320–21; *Jesus Christus unser Heiland, der von uns* (BWV 689) 324; *O Lamm Gottes, unschuldig* (BWV 618) 180; by Sorge 177; *Vater unser im Himmelreich* (BWV 683) 323; *Vater unser in Himmelreich* (BWV 682) 318; *Vorspielen* vs. *Praeludiren* 182; *Wir glauben all an einen Gott* (BWV 680) 318, 322; *Wir glauben all an einen Gott* (BWV 681) 323; *see also Orgelbüchlein* (BWV 599–644)
chorales: *Aus meines Herzen Grunde* 175; in the early cantatas 154; indicated in text-only hymnals 203–4; in the Lutheran services 51, 155; *Vater unser im Himmelreich* 172–73; *Vom Himmel hoch da komm ich her* 185, 192, 198, 207; *Warum betrübst du dich mein Herz?* 175; *Was Gott tut, das ist wohlgetan* 132–33, 156; *Wer nur den lieben Gott läßt walten* 132–33, 156, 213; *Wir glauben all an einen Gott* 20, 37, 169, 175, 311, 318, 322, 323, 332, 340; *see also* hymns; Psalmlieder
Christ lag in Todesbanden (BWV 4) 74, 137–49; chiastic structure 146; comparisons of metrical stress patterns 144; extant parts 138–39; first performances 137–39, 148; Olearius on 144–46; structure of 146–49; textual variations 139–44

384 *Index*

Christ unser Herr zum Jordan kam
(BWV 7) 233
Christe, du Lamm Gottes (BWV 23/4) 60
Christe, du Lamm Gottes (BWV 233a)
60; *see also* hymns, *Christe, du
Lamm Gottes*
Christen, ätzet diesen Tag (BWV
63) 333–36
Christmas Oratorio (BWV 248) 45, 75,
85, 147, 183–84, 194, 233
Christus Victor theme 73–75
Cicero 101
Clausnitzer, Tobias 165
Clavierbüchlein 83–84, 136
Clavierübung III 32, 47, 308–27, 312;
catechism preludes (BWV 678–89)
310; four Duets (BWV 802–805) 311,
324–27; *Large Catechism* settings
317–22, 325; Mass settings (BWV
669–7) 310; organ chorales 311–12;
prelude (BWV 552/1) 311; *Small
Catechism* settings 322–24, 325–26;
three-section fugue (BWV 552/2) 311;
Trinitarian preludes 314–16; *see also*
organ preludes
Colditz *Gesangbuch* 200
collects: in the *Hauptgottesdienst* 42; in
the *Vespergottesdienst* 46
collegia pietatis (schools of piety) 227–29
Contius, Christoph 335
Cöthen, Bach in 56, 104–5, 107, 151,
167–68, 249, 270, 297–98, 301–2,
303, 341–42
Cranach, Lucas 63
Credo 71
Creedal hymn 37
Crüger, Johann 183, 184–86, 205, 246
Cyprian, Ernst Salomon 337

Das neugeborne Kindelein (BWV
122) 346
*Das privilegirte Vollständige und
vermehrte Leipziger Gesangbuch* 214
Das Wohltemperirte Clavier 115
Decius, Nikolaus 315
Demantius, Christoph 38
Demelius, Christian 206, 207
Der accurate Organist im General-Baß
(Treiber) 132–34, 155–56
Der Friede sei mit dir (BWV 158) 76–78,
153, 233
*Der Himmel dacht auf Anhalts Ruhm und
Glück* (BWV 66a) 105

Der Himmel lacht! Die Erde jubilieret
(BWV 31) 153
Deyling, Salomon 134–35, 186, 212,
244–45, 269–70
*Dich loben die lieblichen Strahlen der
Sonne* (BWV Anh. 6) 105
Die Zeit, die Tag und Jahre macht (BWV
134a) 105
Doles, Johann Friedrich 36, 59, 272–73
Dresden *Gesangbuch* 142, 200
Drese, Adam 131, 132
Drese, Johann Samuel 297, 340
Drese, Johann Wilhelm 297, 340
Dretzel, Cornelius Heinrich 116
Dreyfache Andachts-Übung (Löscher)
197–99, 200
Du wahrer Gott und Davids Sohn (BWV
23) 53–58, 61
Dürr, Alfred 138, 141–42, 147, 193–94

Ebeling, Johann Georg 184
Eber, Paul 58, 234
Eckelt, Johann Valentin 172
Effler, Johann 292, 294
Ehricht, Klaus 326
Eilmar, Georg Christian 243
Ein feste Burg ist unser Gott (BWV
80) 328
Ein ungefärbt Gemüte (BWV 24)
106, 296
Eisenachisches Gesang Buch 142, 145
*Eisenachisches Neu-revitirt und
beständiges Gesang-Buch* 208
encoded keys 206–11
Engelhardt, Moriz von 238
*Entfliehet, verschwindet, entweichet, ihr
sorgen* (BWV 249a) 294
Epistles: in almanacs 17–18; and the
dissemination of Bach's cantatas
14–16; in the *Hauptgottesdienst* 33–34;
in Lutheran culture and worship 5–14,
16–18; and Pietism 229
Erdmann, Balthasar 289
Erdmann, Georg 252
Erfreute Zeit im neuen Bunde (BWV
83) 233
Erich, Daniel 177
Erlebach, Philipp Heinrich 92
Ernesti, Johann August 36, 248, 255–64,
271; collected writings 267–70, 271;
conflict with Bach 259–64, 273; work
on curriculum reform 257
Ernesti, Johann Heinrich 249–52

Erschallet, ihr Lieder, erklinget, ihr Saiten! (BWV 172) 153
Es erhub sich ein Streit (BWV 19) 110–11, 234, 343
Es ist nichts Gesundes an meinem Liebe (BWV 25) 106, 240, 346–47
Estomihi Sunday 54–55; and Good Friday 55, 61–63
Evangelienmotette 19
Evangelischer Blümengarten (Briegel) 20
Evangelischer Lieder-Schatz (Olearius) 127–28, 130, 132, 134–36, 144, 148, 156–59
Eylenberg, Johann Christian 296

Falsche Welt, dir trau ich nicht (BWV 52) 117
figured bass 123, 133–34, 166–67, 168, 170, 183, 187, 190, 195, 205, 212–13, 216, 246
Fischer, Gabriel 116
Fischer, Johann Friedrich 272–73
Florilegium Portense (Bodenschatz) 29–30
Franck, Johann 185
Franck, Salomo 86, 98, 105–6, 107, 117, 153, 244, 294
Francke, August Hermann 220–21, 228, 239, 240–41, 246
Frescobaldi, Girolamo 312
Freue dich, erlöste Schar (BWV 30) 233, 347
Freylinghausen, Johann Anastasius 190, 192, 193, 198, 213, 242
Friese, Heinrich 299
Fritsch, Ahasverus 233
Frohne, Johann Adolph 243
Fuga über das Magnificat (BWV 733) 46
Fuhrmann, Martin Heinrich 97
Fulda, Adam von 207

Gaudlitz, Gottlieb 186
Geck, Martin 222
Geier, Martin 14
Geiringer, Karl 175, 194
Geistliche Poesien (Neumeister) 105, 240
Geistreiches Gesang-Buch (Weimar) 152, 190, 213, 241–42
Geist-reiches Gesangbuch Den Kern Alter und Neuer Lieder 192, 198
Georgenkirche (Weisenhauskirche; Leipzig) 23

Gerber, Christian 93, 229–37
Gerber, Heinrich Nicolaus 172
Gerhard, Johann 223–24
Gerhardt, Paul 58, 183–87, 224; hymns used by Bach 185
Gerstenbüttel, Joachim 291, 299
Gesangbücher 166–67; *Arnstädtisches Gesangbuch* 142, 146; *Arnstädtisches Verbessertes Gesangbuch* 125; *Das privilegirte Vollständige und vermehrte Leipziger Gesangbuch* 214; *Eisenachisches Gesang Buch* 142, 145; *Eisenachisches Neu-revitirt und beständiges Gesang-Buch* 208; *Geistreiches Gesang-Buch* (Weimar) 152, 190, 213, 241–42; *Geist-reiches Gesangbuch Den Kern Alter und Neuer Lieder* 192, 198; *Hällisches Neu-eingerichtetes Gesang-Buch* 208; Leipzig *Gesangbücher* 142, 315; *Lübeckisches Gesang-Buch* 125, 142; *Lüneburgisches Gesangbuch* 142–43; Mühlhausen *Gesangbuch* 142; Naumburg *Gesangbuch* 214; *Naumburgisches Gesang-Buch* 211; *Neu-eingerichtetes Hessen-Darmstädtisches Kirchen-Gesang-Buch* 205–6; *Neues vollkömliches Gesangbuch, Augspurgischer Confession* 184; *Neues Vollständiges Gesang-Buch* 204; *Neu-Verbessertes Arnstädtisches Gesangbuch* 210; *Neu-vermehrtes Ratzeburgisches Gesang-Buch* 209; *Neuvermehrtes und verbessertes Gesang-Buch* 209; *Neu Leipziger Gesangbuch* (Vopelius) 41–42; Reformation 309; *Schrifftmässiges Gesangbuch* 206–7; *Sondershäusisches Gesang-Buch* 209; Ulm *Gesangbuch* 200; *Vollständiges Neu aufgelegtes und vermehrtes Evangelisches Gesang-Buch* 209; Vopelius 325; *Wittenbergisches Gesang-Buch* 209–10; *see also Choralbücher*; hymnals; Schemelli *Gesangbuch* (BWV 454)
Gesegnet ist die Zuversicht (BWV Anh. 1) 19, 210, 256
Gesner, Elisabeth Charitas 256
Gesner, Johann Matthias 248–55, 265–67; footnote on Bach 264–67; at Göttingen 254–55; involvement with school curricula 257–58; in Leipzig

386 *Index*

267–73; and Quintilian 258–59, 264–67; at Thomasschule 251–54
Glass, Salomon 227
Gleichwie der Regen und Schnee vom Himmel fällt (BWV 18) 106, 153, 295
Gleitsmann, Paul 131
Gloria: Bach's settings of 75–77, 79; in the B-minor Mass 64–65, 68; in the *Hauptgottesdienst* 32–33; in the Lutheran Masses 68–69; in Missa in A (BWV 234) 71–72
Görlitzer Tabulaturbuch (Scheidt) 178
Görner, Johann Gottlieb 25
Gospel motets 19–20
Gospels: in almanacs 17–18; and the dissemination of Bach's cantatas 14–16; in the *Hauptgottesdienst* 34; in Lutheran culture 16–18; in Lutheran worship 5–14; and Pietism 229
Gott der Herr ist Sonn und Schild (BWV 79) 306–7, 328
Gott fähret auf mit Jauchzen (BWV 43) 75, 183
Gott ist mein König (BWV 71) 139
Gott soll allein mein Herze haben (BWV 169) 117
Gotter, Ludwig Andreas 242
Gottes Zeit ist die allerbeste Zeit (BWV 106) 20, 135–36
Gottesdienst 310; *see also Hauptgottesdienst*; *Vespergottesdienst*
Gottlob! nun geht das Jahr zu Ende (BWV 28) 106, 296
Gottsched, Johann Christoph 216
Götz, Georg 127, 128
Götze, Georg Heinrich 124
Graduallieder 134, 157; in *Evangelischer Lieder-Schatz* (Olearius) 158–59; in the *Hauptgottesdienst* 34
Gräffenhayn, Gottfried Christoph 291
Graupner, Christoph 205–6, 240
Gregorian chant 208
Gregory of Nyssa 73
Grigny, Nicolas de 312
Grundig, Johann Zacharias 341
Gumpelzhaimer, Adam 30
Günther, Anton II 131

Hällisches Neu-eingerichtetes Gesang-Buch 208
Halt im Gedächtnis Jesum Christ (BWV 67) 71–73, 76–77; compared to BWV 234 79, 81; discarded "Corno" part

80; similarities to BWV 158 and BWV 234 78
Hammerschmidt, Andreas 183
Handel, George Frideric 15
Handl, Jakob (Gallus) 29
Hauptgottesdienst 27–43, 286–87; Benediction and Benediction response 42; cantatas 35–36, 54–55; Creedal hymn 37; Dismissal 42–43; Epistle 33–34; Gospel 34; Graduallied 34; hymns 29–32, 43–44; Introit 29–32; Kyrie and Gloria 32–33; Lord's Prayer 38–41; Ministry of the Sacrament 38–42; Ministry of the Word 33–38; motet 29–32; music for 310–11, 316; Nicene Creed 34–35; organ postlude 44; organ prelude 28–29; outline 28; post-communion collects 42; Preparation 28–33; sermon 37–38
Hauptmann, Moritz 14–15
Hebenstreit, Johann Christian 255
Heermann, Johann 224, 287
Heindorff, Ernst Dietrich 131
Heineccius, Johann Michael 336
Heitmann, Johann Joachim 299, 302
Helbig, Johann Friedrich 105, 107
Helmbold, Ludwig 307
Henrici, Christian Friedrich (Picander) 107, 111–12, 117
Herbst, Wolfgang 225
Herchet, Jörg 226
Herr Christ, der einig Gotts Sohn (BWV 601a/601) 178
Herr Gott, dich loben alle wir (BWV 130) 234
Herr Gott, nun schleuss den Himmel auf (BWV 1092) 180
Herr Jesu Christ, wahr Mensch und Gott (BWV 127) 53–54, 58–59, 153
Herthum, Christoph 131
Herz und Mund und Tat und Leben (BWV 147a) 153
Heut ist gewiss ein guter Tag (BWV Anh. 7) 105
Hiller, Johann Adam 59–60, 270, 271, 272–73
Himmelskönig sei willkommen (BWV 182) 153, 233
Himmels-Weg (Werner) 347
Hofmann, Carl Gottlob 214, 313
Hollatz, David 225
Homilius, Gottfried August 273
Hunnius, Nicolaus 339

Hunold, Christian Friedrich (Menantes) 105, 107, 275

hymn singing: alternation of choir and congregation 197–98, 200; in the home 187–89

hymn titles: *Ach bleib bei uns, Herr Jesu Christ* 332; *Ach! Du edler Gast* 210; *Ach Gott, wie manches Herzeleid* 213; *Allein Gott in der Höh sei Ehr* 32, 111–12, 169, 311, 314, 315, 329, 332, 340; *Allein zu dir, Herr Jesu Christ* 287; *Also heilig ist der Tag* 188; *Angenehme Fasten-Zeit* 285; *Auf, auf mein Herz* 210; *Auf, die ihr Jesum liebt* 198, 199; *Aus tiefer Notschrei ichzu dir* 188, 312, 319–20, 323–24; *Christ lag in Todesbanden* 74, 197; *Christ unser Herr zum Jordan kam* 312, 319, 323; *Christe, aller Welt Trost* 314; *Christe, du Lamm Gottes* 51, 53, 55–62, 71; *Christus, der uns selig macht* 209; *Danksagen wir alle Gott* 157; *Das ist meine grosste Freude* 192; *Das neugeborne Kindelein* 345; *Den die Hirten lobten sehre* 198; *Der du bist drei in Einigkeit* 339; *Dies sind die heil'gen zehn Gebot* 311, 317, 322–23; *Dieß ist der Nacht* 213; *In dulci jubilo* 198; *Ein feste Burg ist unser Gott* 329, 332, 340; *Ein Kind geborn zu Bethlehem* 198; *Eins ist not! ach Herr, dies Eine* 190; *Erhalt uns, Herr, bei deinem Wort* 242, 329, 332, 340; *Ermuntre dich, mein schwacher Geist* 183–84; *Es ist das Heil uns kommen her* 213, 340, 345; *Es ist genug! So nimm, Herr, meinen Geist* 190; *Es ist gewißlich an der Zeit* 166; *Es wolle uns Gott genädig sein* 329; *Frölich soll mein Herze springen* 186; *Gelobet seist du, Jesu Christ* 198; *Gott der Vater wohn uns bei* 287; *Gott des Himmels und der Erden* 192; *Gott Vater, der du deine Sohn* 165; *Herr Gott, dich loben wir* 329; *Herr Jesu Christ, dich zu uns wend* 210; *Herzlich tut mich verlangen* 58, 184–85; *Heut triumphiret Gottes Sohn* 199, 201, 202; *Hilf, Herr Jesu, laß gelingen* 184; *Ich bin getauft auf deinen Namen* 240; *Jesu, du mein liebstes Lebens* 184; *Jesu, meine Freude* 186, 198, 210; *Jesu, meines Lebens-Leben* 123; *Jesu Leiden, Pein und Tod*

40; *Jesus Christus unser Heiland, der von uns* 287, 312, 320–21, 324; *Jesus dulcis memoria* 191–92; *Komm, Gott Schöpfer, Heiliger Geist* 199, 202; *Komm heiliger Geist, Herre Gott* 188; *Kommt, seelen, dieser Tag* 196, 199, 200, 202; *Kommt wieder aus der finstern Gruft* 196, 198, 199, 200, 201, 202; *Kyrie, Gott heiliger Geist* 314; *Kyrie, Gott Vater in Ewigkeit* 32, 314, 332; *Lasset uns den Herren preisen* 213; *Lasset uns mit Jesu ziehen* 213; *Liebster Jesu, wir sind hier* 164–65, 190, 210, 340; *Machs, lieber Gott, wie dirs gefällt* 242; *Mag ich Unglück nicht widerstahn* 329; *Mein Herz soll nun gantz absagen* 198; *Mein Herz, warum betrübst du dich* 242; *Mein Jesu! Treuer Hirt* 198, 199, 200; *Mein Jesu was vor Seelenweh* 213; *Mein Schöpfer, steh mir bei* 240; *Nun danket alle Gott* 46, 157, 185, 199, 202; *Nun freut euch, lieben Christen gmein* 165–66, 339; *Nun komm, der Heiden Heiland* 165, 209; *Nun lob, mein Seel, den Herren* 329, 332, 340; *Nun sich der Tag geendet hat* 190; *O daß ich tausend Zungen hätte* 346; *O Ewigkeit, du Donnerwort* 183; *O Finsterniss! O Dunkelheit!* 331; *O Gott, du frommer Gott* 165; *O Haupt voll Blut und Wunden* 58; *O Herre Gott, dein göttlich Wort* 329, 332, 340; *O Jesu süß, wer dein gedenkt* 345; *O Jesu, willst du noch so gnädig* 242; *O Lamm Gottes, unschuldig* 53, 61–62, 131; *O Mensch, bewein dein Sünde groß* 209; *O Traurigkeit, o Herzeleid* 198, 199, 200; *O wir armen Sünder* 209; *Puer natus in Bethlehem* 198; *Quam pastores laudevere* 198; *Schmücke dich* 185; *Schwing dich auf zu deinem Gott* 186; *Seid zufrieden, lieben brüder* 198; *Te Deum, Herr Gott, dich loben wir* 340, 341, 342–43; *Treuer Vater und deine Liebe* 242; *Vater unser im Himmelreich* 312, 318, 323; *Victimae paschali laudes* 74, 197; *Vom Himmel hoch da komm ich her* 185, 192, 198, 207; *Vom Himmel kam der Engel Schar* 198, 199; *Von Gott will ich nicht lassen* 209; *Wachet auf, ruft uns die Stimme* 62, 346; *Wär Gott nicht mit uns diese Zeit* 329, 340; *Warum*

388 Index

sollt ich mich denn grämen 185, 186;
Was mein Gott will 185; *Wenn mein
Stündlein vorhanden ist* 198, 200, 202;
Wer nur den lieben Gott läßt walten
132–33, 156, 213; *Wie schön leuchtet
der Morgenstern* 213, 233; *Wie soll ich
dich empfangen* 186; *Wir glauben all an
einen Gott* 20, 37, 169, 175, 311, 318,
322, 323, 332, 340; *Wo Gott der Herr
nicht bei uns hält* 329, 340; *Wo soll ich
fliehen hin* 198; *Wohl dem, der Gott
zum Freunde hat* 229; *Zeuch ein zu
deinen Toren* 186
hymnals: Arnstadt 210–11; Calvinist/
Reformed 190; commissioned by Duke
Christian 285–86; *Davidischer Jesus-
Psalter* 192; for domestic use 188;
Dresden *double* 192, 198; *Dreyfache
Andachts-Übung* 197–99, 200;
encoded keys in 206–11; *Geist- und
Lehr-reiches Kirchen- und Hauß-Buch*
190–91; *Geistreiches Gesang-Buch*
241–42; Leipzig 214; linked to chorale
books 205–6; metrical index 204–5;
Naumburg 211, 212, 214; Pietist 192,
198; text-only 203–16; Wittenberg
209–10; *see also Choralbücher*;
Gesangbücher
hymnic arias 183–202
hymns: Creedal 37; in the
Hauptgottesdienst 29–32, 37–44; and
hymnic arias 183–202; Lutheran
134–35; for Olearius's *Dispositionen*
129; of the Passion 130; pulpit 37;
responsibility for selection of 186–87;
in the *Vespergottesdienst* 43, 45, 46;
see also chorales; hymn singing; hymn
titles; Psalmlieder

Ich armer Mensch, ich Sündenknecht
(BWV 55) 113, 117
Ich bin in mir vergnügt (BWV 204)
107, 109–10
Ich geh und suche mit Verlangen (BWV
49) 117
Ich habe genung (BWV 82) 83–85, 113,
116, 117, 233
Ich hatte viel Bekümmernis (BWV
21) 301
Ich lasse dich nicht (BWV 157)
105, 233
Ich will den Kreuzstab gerne tragen
(BWV 56) 117

Ihr, die ihr euch von Christo nennet (BWV
164) 153
Ihr Menschen, rühmet Gottes Liebe
(BWV 167) 233
Introits, in the *Hauptgottesdienst* 29–32
Irenaeus 73

Jacobikirche (Hamburg) 93, 299,
301, 303
Jacobskirche (Cöthen) 298
Jakobskirche (Weimar) 152
Jauchzet Gott in allen Landen
(BWV 51) 86
Jesus nahm zu sich die Zwölfe (BWV
22) 54–55
Johannespassion (BWV 245/245b) 53, 61,
75, 117, 147, 235
Johanniskirche (Leipzig) 22–23, 47,
113, 269

Kanzeldienst service 45
Katharinenkirche (Hamburg) 303
Kauffmann, Georg Friedrich 171
Kellner, Johann Peter 172
Kevorkian, Tanya 88
keyboards: *Clavierübung* intended for
187; mean-tone tuning of 133
Kinderman, Johann Erasmus 171
Kirchen-Ordnung 310
Kirchenordnung (Braunschweig 1528)
51
Kirchhoff, Gottfried 333–36
Kirnberger, Johann Philipp 167
Klinge, Franz 338
Knauer, Johann Oswald 105
Kobelius, Johann Augustin 291–92
Köhler, Johann Friedrich 254
Komm, du süße Todesstunden (BWV
161) 233
Köpping, Christian 36
Körner, Johann Gottfried 270
Krausse, Helmut 86
Krebs, Johann Andreas 297
Kreuzkirche (Dresden) 237, 245
Krieger, Adam 189–90
Krieger, Johann Philipp 86, 90–92,
276, 291–92
Kühnöl, Christian Gottlieb 269
Kuhnau, Johann 22, 25, 88, 92, 250,
251
Kyrie: Bach's settings of 71; combined
with *Agnus Dei* 59–60; in the
Hauptgottesdienst 32–33; Tone I 52

Index   389

Lairitz, Johann Georg 152, 244
Lange, Joachim 238, 280
Lasset uns mit Jesu ziehen (BWV
481) 213
Lassus, Orlandus 29
Lazarethkirche (Leipzig) 23
lectionary readings: chanted 19–20; and
the dissemination of Bach's cantatas
14–16; in Lutheran culture 16–18;
sermons based on 11–14; vocal works
correlated to 7–11
Lehmann, Gottfried Conrad 251, 255
Lehms, Georg Christian 86, 105, 107,
117, 153
Leibnitz, Johann Friedrich 30
Leipzig: Bach in 6, 22–26, 35, 39–41,
46–48, 55, 56–57, 59, 61, 66, 71,
76, 83, 92, 104, 106, 107, 116, 134,
137–38, 146, 147, 184–85, 187, 212,
216, 233, 244–45, 247, 248, 251–52,
256, 265, 267, 296, 298–99, 308, 310,
313; churches and choirs in 22–25;
liturgical sources and studies 26–27
Leipzig Chorales (BWV 651–668) 40
Leipzig *Gesangbücher* 142, 315
Leipziger Kirchen-Andachten 30,
43, 52, 62
Liebfrauenkirche (Arnstadt) 129,
130, 152
Liebster Immanuel, Herzog der frommen
(BWV 123) 233
Liebster Jesu, wir sind hier (BWV 373,
633, 634, 706, 730, 731) 190
Liedpredigten 126–28
Lippius, Johannes 101
liturgical year 3–5
Lobet den Herrn, alle seine Heerscharen
(BWV Anh. 5) 105
Lobet Gott in seinen Reichen (BWV
11) 183
Löffler, Friedrich Simon 128
Löhlein, Heinz-Harald 152, 153
Lord's Prayer: in the *Hauptgottesdienst*
38–41; in the *Vespergottesdienst*
44–45; *see also* hymns, *Vater unser im
Himmelreich*
Löscher, Caspar 210
Löscher, Valentin Ernst 196–99, 200,
237–39, 245, 280, 300, 341
Lübeck, Vincent Jr. 299
Lübeckisches Gesang-Buch 125, 142
Lüneburgisches Gesangbuch
142–43

Luther, Martin: on the atonement 73–74;
books in Bach's library 11–13; *On
Christian Freedom* 225; on Confession
and Absolution 279–80; *Deutsche
Litanie* 59; *Deutsche Messe* 19, 38,
50–51, 59, 66, 76, 309; on dialectic
and rhetoric 103–4; Easter hymn
(*Christ lag in Todesbanden*) 139–41,
145; *Formula missae* 19, 232–33;
German Sanctus 41; identified with
archangel Michael 344; *Kirchen-
Postille* 232; *Large Catechism* 316–17,
325; in Leipzig 309, 311; and the
Reformation 308, 328–29; and the
Roman lectionary 5; sermons 312–13;
Small Catechism 17, 46–47, 227, 305,
316–17, 325–26; at Thomaskirche 26,
308, 312; *Tischreden* 103–4; *Von der
Freiheit eines Christenmenschen* 74;
writings of 313
Lutheran Masses (BWV 233–236) 67–82;
Christus Victor theme 73–75; *Gloria in
excelsis Deo* 75–76
Lutheran worship: Augsburg Confession
227–28, 308, 328, 331; devotional
handbooks 17, 280–82; and the
doctrine of the Trinity 314–16;
Epistles and Gospels in 5–14, 16–18;
eucharistic theology 50–53, 64, 288,
307; hymnals 17; in Leipzig 22–27,
247; and mysticism 225; and Pietism
191, 222–29; preaching in 6, 11;
theology of music 90; Vesper service
282–88; *see also Hauptgottesdienst*;
Vespergottesdienst

Magnificat: German 45–46; setting by
Bach (BWV 243a; BWV 243) 46; in
the *Vespergottesdienst* 45–46
Man singet mit Freuden vom Sieg (BWV
149) 234
Marchand, Louis 341
Marienkirche (Lübeck) 125, 246
Marienkirche (Mühlhausen) 243
Marktkirche (Halle) 122, 335–36, 337
Marperger, Bernhard Walther 244–45
Mason, Lowell 176
Matins 27
Matthäuspassion (BWV 244) 53,
61–62, 63
Mattheson, Johann 17, 94, 96–97, 98,
99–100, 102, 114–15, 182, 216, 301,
302, 349

390   *Index*

Mayer, Johann Friedrich 281
McCormick, Susan 167
mean-tone tuning 133
Mein Gott, wie lang, ach lange? (BWV 155) 153
Mein Herze schwimmt im Blut (BWV 199) 153
Mein Jesu was vor Seelenweh (BWV 487) 213
Meiningen *Gesangbuch* 205
Meissner, Christian 297
Meister, Johanna Elisabeth 275
Melanchthon, Philipp 101, 103–4
Menantes (Christian Friedrich Hunold) 105, 107, 110, 275
Mentzer, Johann 346
Messerli, Carlos 19
Meyer, Joachim 96–97
Milbradt, Jörg 226
Minear, Paul 262
Missa in A (BWV 234) 71–72, 77; compared to BWV 67 79, 81; movements adapted for 81–82; similarities to BWV 67 and BWV 158 78
Missa in F (BWV 233) 54, 59–60, 71; fugal subjects 60
Mit Fried und Freud ich fahr dahin (BWV 125) 233
Mizler, Lorenz Christoph 216
Moller, Martin 345
Moritz of Saxe-Zeitz 212
motets: in the *Hauptgottesdienst* 29–32, 40; by Italian composers 29; *Jesu, Meine Freude* 147; *stile antico* 29, 47–48; use in Leipzig churches 47; in the *Vespergottesdienst* 43
Motz, Georg 236
Mühlhausen, Bach in 6, 136, 138, 144, 148, 155, 165, 243–44, 286, 294, 333
Mühlhausen *Gesangbuch* 142
Müller, Carl Wilhelm 269, 271–72
Müller, Heinrich 13, 14, 224
Müller, Johann 338–39
musica sub communione 40, 52, 54, 60, 71, 76, 77, 200, 287
Musicalisches Gesang-Buch see Schemelli *Gesangbuch* (BWV 454)

Nach dir, Herr, verlanget mich (BWV 150) 139
Naumburg *Gesangbuch* 211, 214

Neu Leipziger Gesangbuch (Vulpius) 41–42, 61, 214
Neu vermehrtes Darmstädtisches Choral-Buch 206
Neue-Bachgesellschaft 16
Neu-eingerichtetes Hessen-Darmstädtisches Kirchen-Gesang-Buch 205–6
Neuen Kirche (Arnstadt) 121–22, 125, 129–30, 131–32, 133, 136, 149, 155, 156, 210, 243, 293
Neues vollkömliches Gesangbuch, Augspurgischer Confession 184
Neues Vollständiges Gesang-Buch 204
Neukirche (Leipzig) 22, 24, 47, 88–89, 92, 104, 272
Neumann, Werner 141
Neumeister, Erdmann 20–21, 86, 90–93, 96, 98, 102, 105–6, 107, 113, 153, 196, 240–42, 245, 274; and Bach in Hamburg 299–303; cantata libretti 276, 282–89, 290, 294–95, 296, 307; devotional handbooks 276–77, 282–84; *Geistliche Poesien* 105, 240, 296; library collection 303–5; pseudonyms 274; in Sorau and Hamburg 289–91; vehemence against Pietism 280–82; and Weissenfels 275–79
Neumeister, Johann Gottfried 176–77
Neumeister Collection 155, 176–80
Neu-Verbessertes Arnstädtisches Gesangbuch 210
Neu-vermehrtes Ratzeburgisches Gesang-Buch 209
Neuvermehrtes und verbessertes Gesang-Buch 209
Nicene Creed 59, 316; in the *Hauptgottesdienst* 34–35
Nicolai, Christian August 297
Nicolai, Philipp 62, 233, 346
Nicolaikirche (Berlin) 184
Nikolaikirche (Leipzig) 22, 24, 25, 27, 40, 47, 88, 135, 186, 214, 231, 244, 269, 270, 271; *Hauptgottesdienst* in 44; Sunday Vespers in 43
Nikolaischule (Leipzig) 250
Nun ist das Heil und die Kraft (BWV 50) 343, 345; diagrammatic representation 350; fugue subject and inversion 349–51
Nun komm, der Heiden Heiland (BWV 61/62) 29, 76, 106, 295, 200

Index 391

Nun sich der Tag geendet hat (BWV 396) 190

O! Angenehme Melodie (BWV 210a) 299
O Ewigkeit, du Donnerwort (BWV 20) 183
O Ewigkeit, du Donnerwort (BWV 60) 183, 190
O Gott, du frommer Gott (partita) (BWV 767) 131
O heiliges Geist und Wasserbad (BWV 165) 153
O Lamm Gottes, unschuldig (BWV 618) 180
O Traurigkeit, o Herzeleid (BWV Anh. I 200) 151
Olearius, Gottfried 126
Olearius, Johann Christoph 121–36, 149, 210, 243, 245, 345; in Arnstadt 156; Arnstadt chorale-based organ manual 131–34; *Arnstädtisches Verbessertes Gesangbuch* 123; on *Christ lag in Todesbanden* 144–46; as deacon in Arnstadt 122–24; *Dispositionen* 128–31; *Evangelischer Lieder-Schatz* 127–28, 130, 132, 134–35, 144, 148, 156–59; Hanseatic journeys from Arnstadt 124–25; *Hymnologia Passionalis* 130–31; influence on Bach 134–36, 156–57; and the Liedpredigten 126–28; as pioneer hymnologist 125–26
Olearius, Johann Gottfried 121–22, 243
Olearius, Johann (uncle to Johann Gottfried) 135
opera: and church music 89–98
organ chorales 311–12
organ postlude, in the *Hauptgottesdienst* 44
organ prelude: in the *Hauptgottesdienst* 38–39; in the *Vespergottesdienst* 43
organ preludes *see* chorale preludes
Orgelbüchlein (BWV 599–644) 40, 134, 150–82; chorale preambling redefined 170–76; earlier preludes that were revised and included 178; manuscript 150–53; Neumeister Collection 155, 176–80; overall plan 157–59, 164–66; Pachelbel's influence 180–82; projected contents of 160–64; question of chronology 153–57; in relation to a *Choralbuch* 166–70; source of hymns 151–53
Osanna 39

Pachelbel, Johann 170–74; chorale preludes 177; *Christ lag in Todesbanden* 139, 149; influence on *Orgelbüchlein* 180–82
Paulinerkirche (Leipzig) 23, 25, 88, 330, 337, 343
Peace of Augsburg 328, 331
Pelikan, Jaroslav 220–21
Petrikirche (Leipzig) 23, 24, 47, 313
Petzoldt, Martin 27
Pezold, Karl Friedrich 255
Pfeiffer, August 13, 14, 136, 338, 344
Picander (Christian Friedrich Henrici) 107, 111–12, 113, 117
Pietism 191–92, 196–97, 200, 219–43, 271, 282; Bach and 219–22, 225–26, 243–47; Lutheran 222–29, 242; Neumeister's objection to 280–82
Pietists: Christian Gerber 229–37; compared to Orthodox 229–43; Erdmann Neumeister 240–42; Johann Jacob Rambach 239–40; Valentin Ernst Löscher as opponent 237–39
Poelchau, Georg 172
Poetische Andachten (Scheibel) 114
post-communion collects 42
Praeludiren 182
Praetorius, Hieronymous 29
Praetorius, Michael 330; title page woodcut 347–48
Predigerkirche (Erfurt) 170–71
Printz, Wolfgang Caspar 289
Psalmlieder 163, 169, 170, 176–78, 319; *see also* chorales; hymns; psalms
psalms: cantatas based on 55, 56, 58, 66, 305–6; collections of 190, 192; in the *Gottesdienst* 42–43, 287; hymns based on 169–70, 176, 177–78, 329; at Matins 27; melodies 299; motets based on 30; in the Saxon *Agenda* 41, 53; in the *Vespergottesdienst* 43–45, 283, 284, 286, 339; *see also* Psalmlieder

Quasimodogeniti Sunday 72–73
Quehl, Hieronymus Florentinus 171–72, 181
Quintillian, Marcus Fabius 101, 258–59, 264–67

Rambach, Johann Jacob 98, 106, 205–206, 239–40
Rathey, Markus 226
Rationalism 247, 271

392 *Index*

Rauner, Narziss 192
Reformation 26, 134, 197, 212, 228, 234, 236–37, 241, 307; in Leipzig 308–12
Reformation festivals: bicentenary celebration 337–51, 351; cantatas for 328, 333–36; celebrations of 328–29; in Dresden 330–33; on the Eve of All Saints 332; first day of the bicentenary celebration 340–51; importance of 331; in Leipzig 306; in Saxony 329; Vespers on the eve of the bicentennial celebration 339
Reinken, Johann Adam 300
Rietschel, Georg 207
Rinck, Christian Heinrich 176
Rinckart, Martin 185, 224
Rist, Johann 183–87, 224, 331
Rittmeyer, Johann 281
Rosenmüller, Johann Georg 269, 271–72
Rost, Johann Christoph 26, 271
Roth, Martin 29
Rothe, Gottlob Friedrich 24–25, 268–69, 270, 272
Routley, Erik 219–20, 221
Ruetz, Caspar 246
Ruhnken, David 267

Sanctus, settings by Bach 38–39
Schade, Johann Caspar 280
Schamelius, Johann Martin 210, 215
Scheibe, Johann Adolph 107
Scheibel, Gottfried Ephraim 84, 87–90, 95–98, 102, 104, 105–6, 113, 113–15; "Ein-Affekt-Theorie" (one-affect-theory) 98–100
Scheidt, Samuel 178, 188
Schein, Johann Hermann 188–89
Schelle, Johann 30, 127, 135
Schemelli, Christian Friedrich 212
Schemelli, Georg Christian 212
Schemelli *Gesangbuch* (BWV 439–507) 187, 190, 192, 193, 194–96, 199–200, 202, 229; letter codes 211–16; texts set by Bach 196
Schieferdecker, Johann Christoph 291
Schiefferdecker, Johann David 92–93
"Schlummert ein" aria (from BWV 82) 83–87, 113
Schmieder, Wolfgang 15–16
Schmolck, Benjamin 165, 281–82
Schneegaß, Cyriakus 345
Schneider, Johann Leberecht 298
Schneiderheinze, Armin 138

Scholz, Leonard 116
Schop, Johann 183
Schrifftmässiges Gesangbuch 206–7
Schulze, Hans-Joachim 138
Schünemann, Heinrich Andreas 168–69, 180–81
Schütz, Heinrich 190, 330
Schweinitz, Johann Friedrich 254–55
Schwingt freudig euch empor (BWV 36c) 255–56
Sehet, wir gehn hinauf gen Jerusalem (BWV 159) 54
Selnecker, Nikolaus 315
sermons: in Arnstadt 128–31; based on the church year 11–13; by Bugenhagen 344; in daily home devotions 17; by Erdmann Neumeister 242; in the *Hauptgottesdienst* 37–38; hymns as (Leidpredigten) 126–28; in Leipzig 88, 231–32; by Luther 312–13; by Neumeister 277, 303–4; published anthologies of 11–14; in the *Vespergottesdienst* 45
Shantz, Douglas 228
Sicul, Christoph Ernst 26, 36
Sie werden aus Saba alle kommen (BWV 65) 233
Silberborth, Hans 207
Smend, Friedrich 93
Sondershäusisches Gesang-Buch 209
Sorge, Georg Andreas 176
Spener, Philipp Jacob 192, 226, 230, 339
Spitta, Philipp 138, 174–75, 244
Spruchmotette 19
St. George hospital/church (Leipzig) 22–23
St. John Passion (BWV 245) *see Johannespassion* (BWV 245b)
St. Nikolaus church (Leipzig) *see* Nikolaikirche (Leipzig)
St. Thomas church (Leipzig) *see* Thomaskirche (Leipzig)
Stadtkirche (Weimar) 63
Stauffer, George 150
Stein, Klaus 345
Stenger, Nicolaus 13
Stieglitz, Christian Ludwig 255–56
Stiller, Günther 27
Stinson, Russell 150, 153, 178
strophic arias 193; *see also* hymnic arias
Sursum corda 38
Sweelinck, Jan Pieterszoon 171
Symbolum Nicenum (BWV 232) 35

Tabulaturbücher 175–76, 177
Tauler, Johannes 223, 225
Te deum laudamus 329, 340, 342–43
Telemann, Georg Philipp 22, 98, 104, 289–91, 295, 299; *Ach! Wo bin ich hingeraten* (TVWV 1:42) 290; *Brockes Passion* 88; cantata libretti for 92; *Jupiter und Semele* (opera) 89; *O Seelig Vergnügen, o heilige Lust* (TVWV 1:1212) 290
Terry, Charles Sanford 27
Thomae, Johannes Gottfried 210
Thomas à Kempis 225
Thomaskirche (Leipzig) 22–23, 24, 26, 47, 88, 127, 135, 214, 231, 244, 246, 252, 255, 258, 269, 315; *Hauptgottesdienst* in 44; Luther preaching at 26, 308, 312; Sunday Vespers in 43
Thomasschule (Leipzig) 23–24, 47, 248, 249–51, 256, 272, 273
Tilgner, Gottfried 93–94
Tönet, ihr Pauken! (BWV 214) 85, 153
Tonus peregrinus 45, 46
Tovey, Donald Francis 14
Treiber, Johann Friedrich 132
Treiber, Johann Philipp 132–33, 155
Tritt auf die Glaubensbahn (BWV 152) 153
trumpet obbligato 74–75
Tue Rechnung! Donnerwort (BWV 168) 153

Ulm *Gesangbuch* 200
Ulrichskirche (Halle) 240

Verba Coena 50–51
Vespergottesdienst 43–47; Benediction and Benediction response 46; *Catechismus Examen* 46–47; collect 46; hymns 45, 46; *Magnificat* 45–46; motets 43; music for 310–11; organ prelude 43; outline 43; psalm(s), prayer, Lord's Prayer, or Cantata 44–45; sermons 45
Vetter, Daniel 186
vocal works correlated to lectionary readings 7–11
Vogler, Johann Gottfried 88, 89, 105
Vollständiges Neu aufgelegtes und vermehrtres Evangelisches Gesang-Buch 209

Vopelius, Gottfried 33, 38, 42, 61, 214, 311, 319, 325; *Gesangbüch* 325
Vorspielen 182
Vulpius, Melchior 30

Wachet! betet! betet! wachet! (BWV 70a) 153
Walter, Johann 123
Walther, Johann Gottfried 216, 270
Was Gott tut, das ist wohlgetan (BWV 98) 117
Was mir behagt, ist nur die muntre Jagd (BWV 208) 294
Weckmann, Matthias 299
Wehrmann, Johann Friedrich 275
Weimar, Bach in 6, 57, 60, 61, 63, 71, 104–6, 107, 142, 152–55, 168, 240, 244, 249, 270, 292–97, 333, 336, 341–42
Weimar *Gesangbuch* 142, 145, 165, 181
Weinen, Klagen, Sorgen, Zagen (BWV 12) 70–71
Weisenhauskirche (Georgenkirche; Leipzig) 23
Weiss, Christian 135
Weiß, Wisso 153
Weiz, Anton 27
Weldig, Adam Immanuel 295–96
Weldig, Johann Friedrich Immanuel 295–96
Welter, Kathryn 171
Wender, Johann Friedrich 121, 133, 155, 293
Wendler, Adolph Christian 269
Wer mich liebet, der wird mein Wort halten (BWV 59) 106, 296
Wer weiß wie nahe mir mein Ende? (BWV 27) 86, 113
Werckmeister, Andreas 133
Werner, Friedrich 347
Wernsdorf, Gottlieb 210
Whittaker, William Gillies 137
Widerstehe doch der Sünde (BWV 54) 105, 295
Wie schön leuchtet der Morgenstern (BWV 1) 233
Wieckowski, Alexander 279
Wilcke, Anna Katharina Georg 297
Wilcke, Dorothea Erdmunthe 297
Wilcke, Johann Caspar Jr. 297
Wilcke, Johanna Christina 297
Wilcke, Anna Magdalena *see* Bach, Anna Magdalena

394 *Index*

Wilcken, Johann Caspar 212, 297
Wir danken dir (BWV 29) 66
Wittenbergisches Gesang-Buch
   209–10
Wolff, Christoph 67, 138, 153, 292,
   312
Wolle, Christoph 269
Wustmann, Rudolf 16

Zachow, Friedrich Wilhelm 152, 171,
   333; chorale preludes 177
Zahn 166, 191
Zarlino, Gioseffo 101–2
Zehnder, Jean-Claude 153
Ziegler, Christiana Mariana von 107
Ziegler, Johann Gotthilf 240
Zwischenspielen 187

Printed in the United States
by Baker & Taylor Publisher Services